D0190173

THE *unofficial* GUIDE® TO Adventure Travel in Alaska

SECOND EDITION

THE *unofficial* GUIDE® TO Adventure Travel in Alaska

SECOND EDITION

MELISSA DEVAUGHN

WILEY

Please note that prices fluctuate in the course of time and that travel information changes under the impact of many factors that influence the travel industry. We therefore suggest that you write or call ahead for confirmation when making your travel plans. Every effort has been made to ensure the accuracy of information throughout this book, and the contents of this publication are believed to be correct at the time of printing. Nevertheless, the publishers cannot accept responsibility for errors or omissions, for changes in details given in this guide, or for the consequences of any reliance on the information provided by the same. Assessments of attractions and so forth are based upon the author's own experience; therefore, descriptions given in this guide necessarily contain an element of subjective opinion, which may not reflect the publisher's opinion or dictate a reader's own experience on another occasion. Readers are invited to write the publisher with ideas, comments, and suggestions for future editions.

Published by:
John Wiley & Sons, Inc.
111 River Street
Hoboken, NJ 07030

Produced by Menasha Ridge Press

Cover design by Michael J. Freeland

Interior design by Vertigo Design

For information on our other products and services or to obtain technical support, please contact our Customer Care Department within the United States at 800-762-2974, outside the United States at 317-572-3993, or by fax at 317-572-4002.

John Wiley & Sons, Inc. also publishes its books in a variety of electronic formats. Some content that appears in print may not be available in electronic formats.

ISBN 978-0-470-22899-9

Manufactured in the United States of America

5 4 3 2 1

CONTENTS

PART TWENTY-TWO Interior Alaska: The Heart of the State 430

PART TWENTY-THREE Bush Alaska: Solitude at Its Best 453

Index and Reader Survey 485

LIST *of* MAPS

ABOUT *the* AUTHOR

MELISSA DEVAUGHN is on the Outdoors staff at the *Anchorage Daily News,* Alaska's largest daily newspaper, and has been covering outdoors-related topics for newspapers and magazines since 1990. She has also worked at the *Roanoke Times* in Virginia; the *Peninsula Clarion,* on Alaska's Kenai Peninsula; and The Associated Press in Anchorage. Her work has also appeared in *Alaska, Backpacker, Canoe & Kayak,* and *Women's Sports & Fitness* magazines, among other publications. She hiked the Appalachian Trail in 1993 before moving to Alaska, and she continues to enjoy backpacking throughout the state. In addition, she enjoys mountain- and road-biking in the summer and in the winter spends her time dog-mushing with her team of Alaskan huskies. She lives in Chugiak, Alaska, with her husband, Andy Hall; a 7-year-old daughter, Reilly; a 10-year-old son, Roan; 11 dogs; and 1 cat.

ACKNOWLEDGMENTS

GETTING THIS BOOK FROM ITS ORIGINAL concept to reality proved to be an awesome, sometimes overwhelming task. Doing it on my own would have been impossible. Thankfully, many people helped me along the way; without them, this project could not have been completed. Your friendship, expertise, guidance, and recommendations helped shape the book, and I want to thank each of you: Charlie Sassara, one of Alaska's most accomplished mountaineers and an all-around nice guy; Tim Woody, a cycling fanatic whose attention to detail was much appreciated; Craig Medred, my colorful coworker and Outdoors editor at the *Anchorage Daily News;* Kevin Klott, whose assistance with the fishing and off-roading chapters was invaluable; and Leah Boltz, whose expertise on the state's best outfitters and guides was much appreciated. I'm also grateful to my friend Dee Ginter, who happily "adopted" my children when I got superbusy; my mother-in-law, Eileen Hall, a constant source of support; and Colleen Mueller, Liz Shen, and Kirsten Schultz, who encouraged me throughout the project. Special thank-yous go to my editors, Bob Sehlinger, Molly Merkle, and Ritchey Halphen at Menasha Ridge Press, who patiently waded through my copy and helped turn it into the book you are now holding. And most of all, I want to thank my husband, Andy Hall, and my children, Reilly and Roan, for being the best support of all. I love you.

INTRODUCTION

ALASKA: *It's a State of Mind*

ONE OF THE GREATEST THINGS ABOUT ALASKA is that it takes the term *casual* to new heights. While the state has highly cultivated enclaves, such as Anchorage, Alaska's largest city, and Juneau, the state capital (population 31,000), for the most part Alaskans are down-to-earth people. They're a friendly bunch, more comfortable in Carhartts and cutoffs than cashmere and corduroy.

Yet there is a strong sense of self among Alaskans, too. The arts thrive, not only in the larger cities but also in the small towns. In their own strong-spirited way, Alaskans embrace their independence and refuse to be stereotyped. They'll have a sold-out opera, but only half will dress up. There are ultra-fancy restaurants, but they'll entertain kids with smiles on their faces.

For visitors, this translates into a vacation completely devoid of stress. Wear your evening gown if you like—it doesn't matter if it's to the local ballgame or burger joint. Anything goes. If the cliché "Have your cake and eat it too" ever applied, it does in Alaska. It's the kind of place where you can spend your day kayaking in some beautiful cove in Prince William Sound and make it back to town in just enough time to catch the evening symphony performance. No matter if you haven't had a chance to change out of your paddling clothes: this is Alaska. We're just glad you came.

As for the landscape, it too has a bit of wildness to it. Even in the largest of Alaska's cities, you'll see this frontier quality persevering despite modern technology. You can order a tall skinny latte at a drive-through, then have to slow down for the moose crossing in front of your car. It's the type of place where old grass-roofed cabins stand next to high-rise office buildings, and where salmon fishermen in business suits cast lines at lunchtime before heading back to work.

That's what makes the Last Frontier such a great place to visit. Considered everyday moments for those of us who live here—ask any Alaskan if they've ever cursed the moose that frequent our streets and you're guaranteed a "yes"—these glimpses of wandering ungulates, calving glaciers, and spawning salmon are a real treat to visitors.

It's quite liberating to visit a place with so few pretenses, but be warned: that "anything goes" attitude can sometimes be daunting. Entrepreneurs long ago figured out that Alaska's charm sells, and many businesses out there are intent on cashing in on your inexperience. A city such as Anchorage may be easier to navigate. But go to one of the remote Bush villages, and it can be difficult to interpret the behavior of the locals. Armed with *The Unofficial Guide to Adventure Travel in Alaska,* you're assured a successful trip no matter what part of the state you want to see.

As you embark on your Alaskan adventure, we hope this *Unofficial Guide* will become your best friend, offering advice on where to stay, what to expect to pay, how to plan wisely, and, most importantly, how to plan the trip that best suits your needs.

Alaska may be big, but it needn't be intimidating. Despite the inherent romance of living in a natural paradise, the folks here are just regular people making a living and creating a space for themselves amid the beauty. No matter how daunting the landscape looks, getting around is becoming ever more convenient, and in the midst of this monumental land our communities are inviting places where smiling faces are commonplace.

Welcome to Alaska.

ABOUT *this* GUIDE

WHY "UNOFFICIAL"?

WELCOME TO *The Unofficial Guide to Adventure Travel in Alaska*. We have worked to answer all of your questions about travel and recreation in a state so remote. Like the other *Unofficial Guides,* this one attempts to target your interests and save you time, money, and effort so that nothing is wasted during your trip.

Because Alaska is so big and your options so varied, we've organized this guide so you can zero in on the activity or activities that appeal to you most. Fifteen chapters focus solely on adventure travel, each devoted to a single activity. Are you nuts for biking? Read all about it in Part Ten (page 152). Sea kayaking? Go to Part Fourteen (page 228). (For general locations, see the regional maps that begin on page 10.)

The five regional chapters that follow focus primarily on the basics in a given area of the state: getting around, shopping, lodging, dining, and entertainment. Once you've chosen the adventure of your dreams, you can go to the appropriate regional chapter to get the scoop on the best places in the vicinity to stay, eat, buy gear, rent a car, and learn about local culture and history.

We recognize that outdoor travelers also are likely independent travelers. A multitude of companies offer exciting-sounding jaunts to scenic places all over the state, but many of these outfits work only with tour providers, such as cruise-ship operators, to obtain large numbers of clients per trip—thus excluding people who wish to travel on their own. In this *Unofficial Guide*, all our listings are available to independent travelers as well as those in tour groups.

As with all the guides in this series, the objective is not to provide the most information about destinations or attractions, but, rather, the most *useful* information. We tend to be opinionated, and for good reason. Any destination or outfitter listed here has made the cut by proving itself a wonderful place to visit or a reliable company with which to do business. If, for example, you want to learn more about sea kayaking in Alaska, you will not be supplied with every operation in the business—and believe us, there are many of them competing for your dollars. What you will get is a select assortment of those we consider best, and why. After all, isn't the point of a guidebook to help you make the most informed choices?

LETTERS, COMMENTS, AND QUESTIONS FROM READERS

WHEN USING THIS GUIDE, PLEASE TAKE NOTE of what has been most helpful to you. We're especially interested in knowing what you found cumbersome and what we can do to make this book even easier to navigate. As with all publications, our guide is affected by changes in the real world after it goes to press: outfitters close, restaurants change hands, hotels go out of business, prices go up, phone numbers get disconnected—it's just the way of business. We invite, and respect, your criticism, both constructive and otherwise.

How to Write to the Author

Melissa DeVaughn
The Unofficial Guide to Adventure Travel in Alaska
P.O. Box 43673
Birmingham, AL 35243
unofficialguides@menasharidge.com (please put *Alaska* in the subject line)

When writing to us, please include a return address and give us a few weeks to respond. Because our work takes us outside most days, we often are not in the office, but we will respond to your mail as soon as possible.

Reader Survey

At the back of this guide, you will find a short questionnaire, which you can use to tell us what worked for you and what didn't. We're especially interested in any updates and corrections you may have for us. Mail the questionnaire to the address on the previous page.

UNDERSTANDING THE RATINGS

WE AT THE *UNOFFICIAL GUIDE TO OUTDOOR TRAVEL IN ALASKA* realize one very important aspect of the outdoor-travel scene: one person's idea of adventure may differ vastly from someone else's. How many times have you been in the middle of a conversation with someone over your latest camping trip only to discover that what you thought was a challenging situation—such as staying at a campground without running water and electricity—sounds luxurious compared with, say, being roped onto the side of a rock face during a weeklong climbing adventure?

Both are perfectly enjoyable ways to appreciate the natural world, but neither is for everyone. When rating our trips and travels, we let you know just how rugged *rugged* is. Not only will this give you perspective on the trips described, but it can also help you plan: Do you bring your one-man bivvy sack or the five-person, 15-pound tent? Do you rely on an inflatable mattress and down sleeping bag, or do you pack for the duration with waterproof bags and a skinny foam pad? Can you expect hordes of other travelers, or will you have the place to yourself?

Just How Rugged Do You Want to Go?

A ruggedness rating of one moose () will let you know that a given trip or destination is relatively easy and can be managed by the average outdoors lover. This may include, for example, a day hike with little elevation gain. A five-moose ruggedness rating (), on the other hand, represents a trip or destination suited to the hardiest of backpackers, boaters, or outdoors enthusiasts, likely in the most remote spots in Alaska.

We've also indicated whether or not a guide is suggested for a given trip. Our guide suggestions range from "yes," which means the trip requires a guide; to "highly recommended," which indicates a trip that can be accomplished on one's own but is probably best left to the guides; to "recommended," which describes trips in which a guide is not really needed but a nice amenity; to "no," which indicates a trip for which guides are not available or not necessary at all. We've also included general price ranges for the outfitters we recommend.

Quality and Value: We've Got You Covered

As with other *Unofficial Guides,* we tell you where to find the best lodging and dining for your travel dollar. Lodging, including bed-and-breakfasts, lodges, hotels, motels, and campgrounds, is rated from one to five stars according to overall quality, which includes service and amenities. We've also assigned star ratings for value, which is an indication of how much you will pay in relation to the quality of the accommodations. Third, we've listed a general price range for each location. Restaurants are rated on overall quality, comprising not only the tastiness of the food but also the atmosphere, the service, and the timeliness with which the food is served. We've also included ballpark price ranges for the majority of menu items.

Use these ratings as a guide in planning your trip, but also be sure to compare other amenities before making your final decision. Also be aware that prices of remote lodges often are much higher than those of your average bed-and-breakfast or hotel, because they include the costs of dining and recreation. So compare quality and value ratings among specific types of lodging to get a better idea of what you will be paying.

Are You Traveling with Kids?

If you're bringing children along, you can rest assured: we've thought of you, too. Alaska is an excellent destination for families, and kid-friendly adventures and dining options are noted in our special-interest and regional chapters. In fact, our own children have field-tested a great many of the trips we recommend, so when we say the little ones will love exploring Cove A or Hiking Trail B, we speak from experience.

When it comes to restaurants, we can honestly think of fewer than five in the entire state where children absolutely would not be welcome, but practicality dictates a larger culling method. Every parent who has taken a child into a restaurant, only to have him or her then throw a five-star temper tantrum, knows that some places are just better than others for the little ones. (Again, we speak from experience here.) As such, our evaluations are based on common sense: Is the dining area small and intimate, more suited to a dinner date or coffee with a friend than a wild rumpus? Is the menu too upscale to appeal to the chicken-fingers-and-French-fries crowd? Will the staff roll their eyes if they see you with a stroller in tow? These are the sorts of questions we ask ourselves, even regarding the most casual of restaurants.

IT'S ALL RIGHT HERE

WE'VE TRIED TO ANTICIPATE YOUR EVERY NEED when planning your Alaskan adventure, whether it's a camping trip in a motor home or a backcountry pack trip into the remotest part of the state. Our information comes not only from more than a decade of recreating in Alaska but also from interviewing people who have spent their entire lives doing the same.

Use these ratings as a guide to your overall planning. Then choose an activity or region and begin the adventure. Alaska is a magical place that will beckon you back again and again. We hope that *The Unofficial Guide to Adventure Travel in Alaska* will be with you every time.

PART ONE
UNDERSTANDING ALASKA

The LAST FRONTIER

EVERYTHING IS BIG IN ALASKA.

The fish are huge. The mountains are tall. The rivers are wide. Go fishing or hiking, and these symbols of grandness can be rationally comprehended. They can be measured and photographed and bragged about when you get back home. It's an adventure traveler's paradise.

But to fully comprehend just what *big* means in Alaska, consider this: while you can drive your car across some continental U.S. states in a few hours, here it would take you that much time in a jet to get from end to end.

What this translates to is a land that offers unlimited opportunities for the traveler who is willing to get off the beaten track and explore the nooks and crannies that make Alaska remarkable. Whether it's a deep fjord or a meandering river, a massive icefield or a steep mountain, Alaska is where the most adventurous of travelers are drawn.

The Unofficial Guide to Adventure Travel in Alaska offers you some insight into this vast land with a section-by-section outline of the state's best outdoor adventures—from rafting a Class V river and climbing a 15,000-foot mountain to hiking a scenic trail and cycling across the state. We realize that Alaska's vastness alone makes it alluring to the thousands of adventure travelers who come here each year, but we also know from experience that it can be an overwhelming place to take in all at once.

Alaska is the largest state in the union: one-fifth the size of the contiguous United States and larger than California, Montana, and Texas combined. The land is tremendous, covering some 586,000 square miles. It is home to North America's tallest mountain—Mount McKinley, also known as Denali—and many other peaks that are among the highest in the United States. Statistics are even more mind-boggling: Alaska is home to some 3,000 rivers, 10,000 glaciers, and, incredibly, more than 3 million lakes. And wildlife roams through it all: bears, moose, and, in the waters, whales and fish.

Yet Alaska is one of the least populated states in the country, with only about 680,000 residents, most of them living in the state's three largest cities and outlying areas.

These qualities combined give the outdoor traveler even more incentive to come here. Here is a place where, despite progress and all that comes with it—high-rises, cell phones, buses, cars—you can still reach the wilderness relatively easily. Think about this: it is entirely conceivable to land at one of Alaska's international airports, grab a taxi, and drive as few as five miles to the nearest state wilderness park. Pay the driver, slip on your backpack, and your adventure has begun. It really doesn't get any better than this.

Of course, there are many more-elaborate trips that can be taken in Alaska, and those are the ones of which truly memorable moments are made. But it's fun to imagine that there still exists in the United States a place where the wilderness remains so predominant.

More than a century ago, Alaska's population wasn't nearly as large as it is today, but the arrival of the gold rush brought people by the thousands, setting the foundation for today's population. When hardy miners, searching the land and water for glistening rock, hit the jackpot in the late 1800s, this harsh land suddenly had something irresistible to offer. Prospectors flocked here in search of riches beyond their wildest dreams. Some found them; others died trying.

Today, adventure travelers the world over come to Alaska with the same zeal those prospectors had, only what they seek is priceless. It is Alaska's unyielding beauty that draws visitors, who come to climb its highest peaks, travel its longest rivers, and visit its most isolated villages. They drive limited roads, photograph plentiful wildlife, and cruise glacier-studded waterways. After experiencing the Last Frontier, those visitors often become residents. And it's easy to understand why.

The landscape of Alaska was wild and awe-inspiring for millennia before the discovery of gold, and it has remained so since. Indigenous peoples were first to recognize the grandeur of this place. They worshiped the land for the riches it gave: not gold, but food and shelter. Despite the challenges of this extreme country, they survived and thrived. Today, their songs and stories tell of a time when they spoke directly to the land and the land spoke back.

Early outsiders like authors Jack London and Robert Service also appreciated the country for its rugged splendor. Their stories and poems romanticize the place, and can we argue with them? If we imagine London, cozy in his Yukon cabin, watching the aurora borealis on a frigid winter evening, it's no surprise that he was inspired to pen his classic book *The Call of the Wild*.

After all these years, the world has realized that the true wealth of Alaska remains. In contrast to our cramped and hurried lives, in

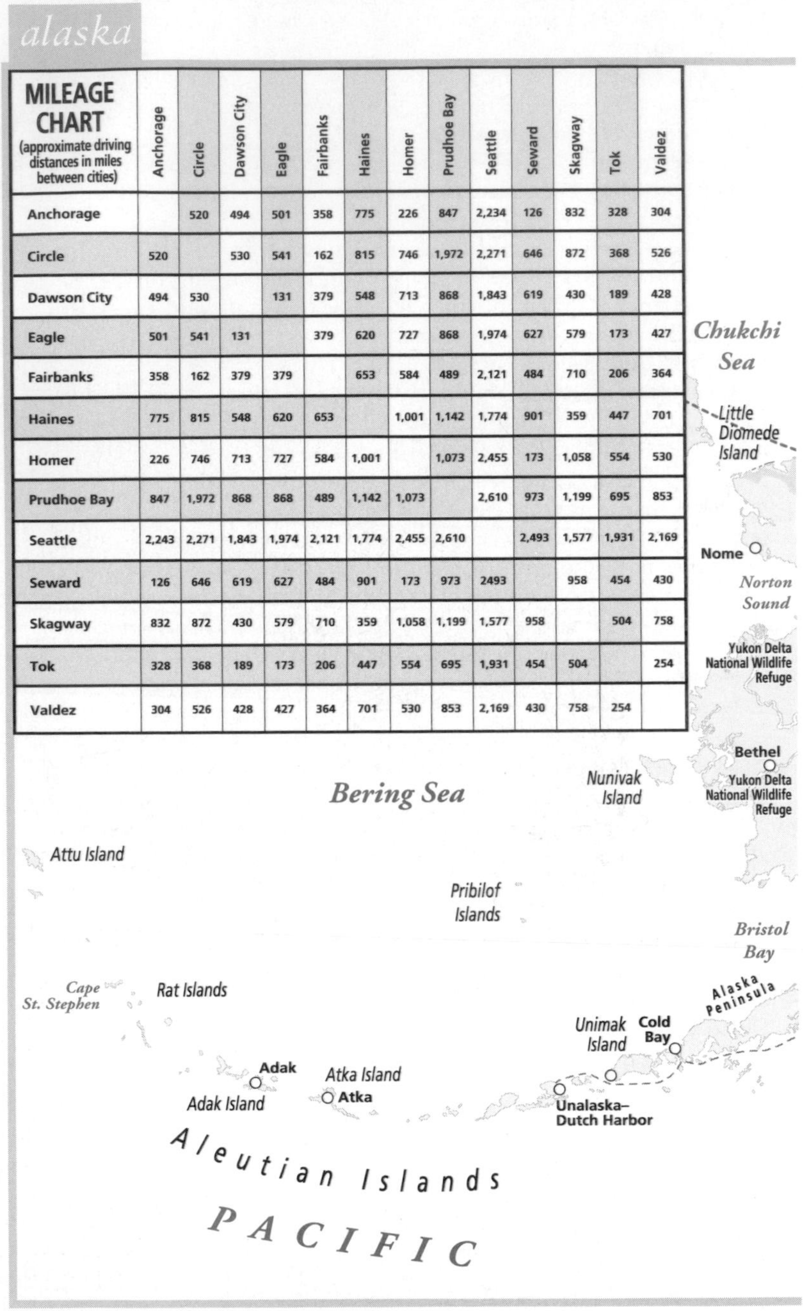

MILEAGE CHART (approximate driving distances in miles between cities)	Anchorage	Circle	Dawson City	Eagle	Fairbanks	Haines	Homer	Prudhoe Bay	Seattle	Seward	Skagway	Tok	Valdez
Anchorage		520	494	501	358	775	226	847	2,234	126	832	328	304
Circle	520		530	541	162	815	746	1,972	2,271	646	872	368	526
Dawson City	494	530		131	379	548	713	868	1,843	619	430	189	428
Eagle	501	541	131		379	620	727	868	1,974	627	579	173	427
Fairbanks	358	162	379	379		653	584	489	2,121	484	710	206	364
Haines	775	815	548	620	653		1,001	1,142	1,774	901	359	447	701
Homer	226	746	713	727	584	1,001		1,073	2,455	173	1,058	554	530
Prudhoe Bay	847	1,972	868	868	489	1,142	1,073		2,610	973	1,199	695	853
Seattle	2,243	2,271	1,843	1,974	2,121	1,774	2,455	2,610		2,493	1,577	1,931	2,169
Seward	126	646	619	627	484	901	173	973	2493		958	454	430
Skagway	832	872	430	579	710	359	1,058	1,199	1,577	958		504	758
Tok	328	368	189	173	206	447	554	695	1,931	454	504		254
Valdez	304	526	428	427	364	701	530	853	2,169	430	758	254	

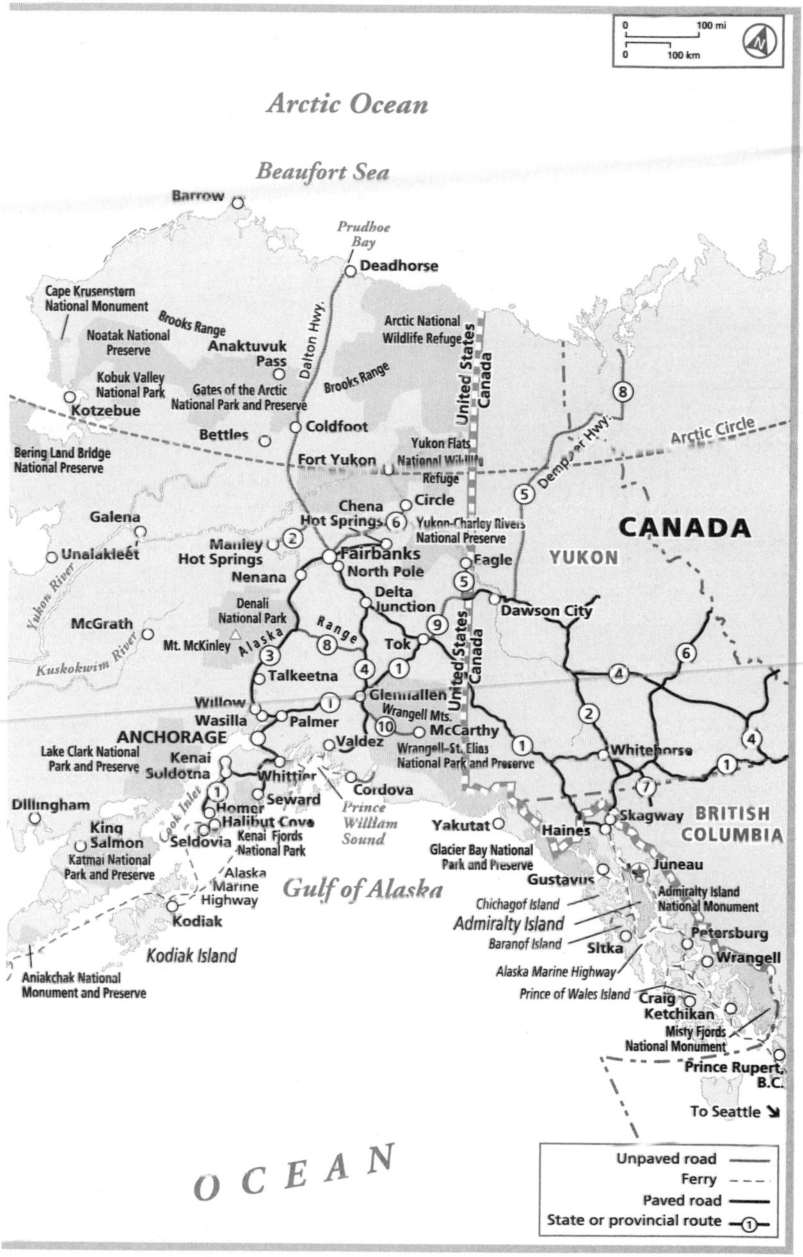

Arctic Ocean
Beaufort Sea
Barrow
Prudhoe Bay
Deadhorse
Cape Krusenstern National Monument
Brooks Range
Noatak National Preserve
Anaktuvuk Pass
Dalton Hwy.
Arctic National Wildlife Refuge
United States
Canada
Kobuk Valley National Park
Gates of the Arctic National Park and Preserve
Brooks Range
Kotzebue
Bettles
Coldfoot
Arctic Circle
Dempster Hwy.
Bering Land Bridge National Preserve
Fort Yukon
Yukon Flats National Wildlife Refuge
Circle
Chena Hot Springs
Yukon-Charley Rivers National Preserve
CANADA
Galena
Manley Hot Springs
Unalakleet
Fairbanks
North Pole
Eagle
YUKON
Nenana
Yukon River
Delta Junction
Dawson City
Denali National Park
McGrath
Mt. McKinley
Alaska Range
Tok
Kuskokwim River
Talkeetna
Glennallen
Willow
Wasilla
Palmer
Wrangell Mts.
ANCHORAGE
McCarthy
Valdez
Lake Clark National Park and Preserve
Kenai
Soldotna
Wrangell-St. Elias National Park and Preserve
Whitehorse
Whittier
Cordova
Dillingham
Homer
Seward
Prince William Sound
Skagway
BRITISH COLUMBIA
King Salmon
Cook Inlet
Halibut Cove
Seldovia
Kenai Fjords National Park
Yakutat
Haines
Katmai National Park and Preserve
Glacier Bay National Park and Preserve
Juneau
Alaska Marine Highway
Gulf of Alaska
Gustavus
Admiralty Island National Monument
Kodiak
Chichagof Island
Admiralty Island
Petersburg
Baranof Island
Sitka
Kodiak Island
Wrangell
Aniakchak National Monument and Preserve
Alaska Marine Highway
Prince of Wales Island
Craig
Ketchikan
Misty Fjords National Monument
Prince Rupert, B.C.
To Seattle
OCEAN
Unpaved road
Ferry
Paved road
State or provincial route
0 100 mi
0 100 km

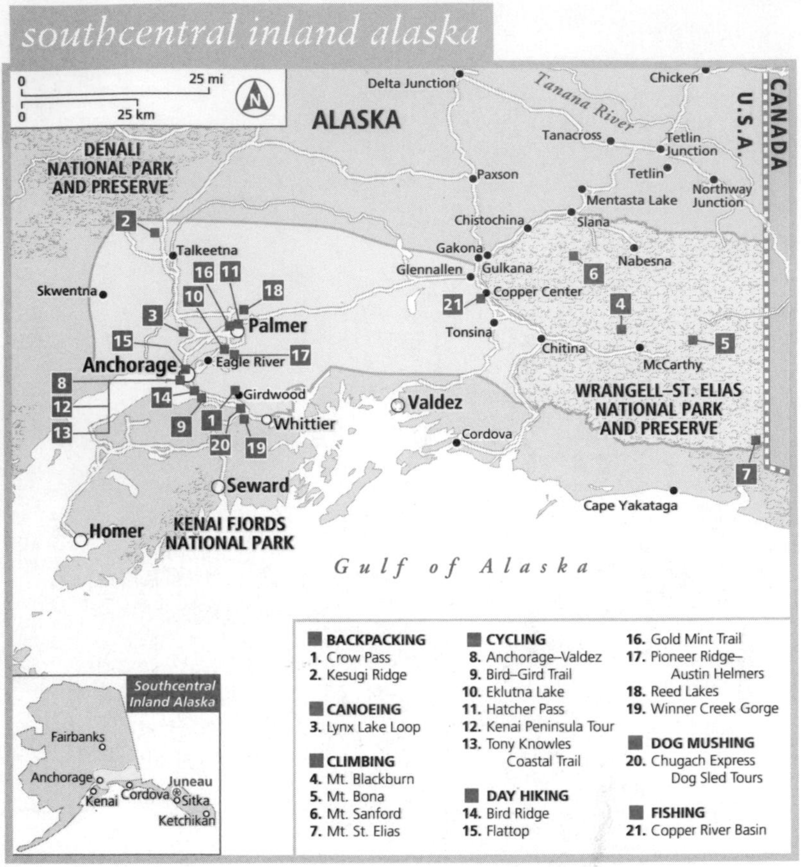
southcentral inland alaska
0 25 mi
0 25 km
N
ALASKA
DENALI NATIONAL PARK AND PRESERVE
Delta Junction
Tanana River
Chicken
U.S.A.
CANADA
Tanacross
Tetlin Junction
Paxson
Tetlin
Northway Junction
Mentasta Lake
Chistochina
Slana
Gakona
Gulkana
Glennallen
Nabesna
Talkeetna
Skwentna
Copper Center
Tonsina
Palmer
Chitina
McCarthy
Anchorage
Eagle River
Girdwood
Whittier
Valdez
WRANGELL–ST. ELIAS NATIONAL PARK AND PRESERVE
Cordova
Seward
Cape Yakataga
Homer
KENAI FJORDS NATIONAL PARK
Gulf of Alaska
Southcentral Inland Alaska
Fairbanks
Anchorage
Kenai
Cordova
Juneau
Sitka
Ketchikan
1
2
3
4
5
6
7
8
9
10
11
12
13
14
15
16
17
18
19
20
21
BACKPACKING
1. Crow Pass
2. Kesugi Ridge
CANOEING
3. Lynx Lake Loop
CLIMBING
4. Mt. Blackburn
5. Mt. Bona
6. Mt. Sanford
7. Mt. St. Elias
CYCLING
8. Anchorage–Valdez
9. Bird–Gird Trail
10. Eklutna Lake
11. Hatcher Pass
12. Kenai Peninsula Tour
13. Tony Knowles Coastal Trail
DAY HIKING
14. Bird Ridge
15. Flattop
16. Gold Mint Trail
17. Pioneer Ridge–Austin Helmers
18. Reed Lakes
19. Winner Creek Gorge
DOG MUSHING
20. Chugach Express Dog Sled Tours
FISHING
21. Copper River Basin

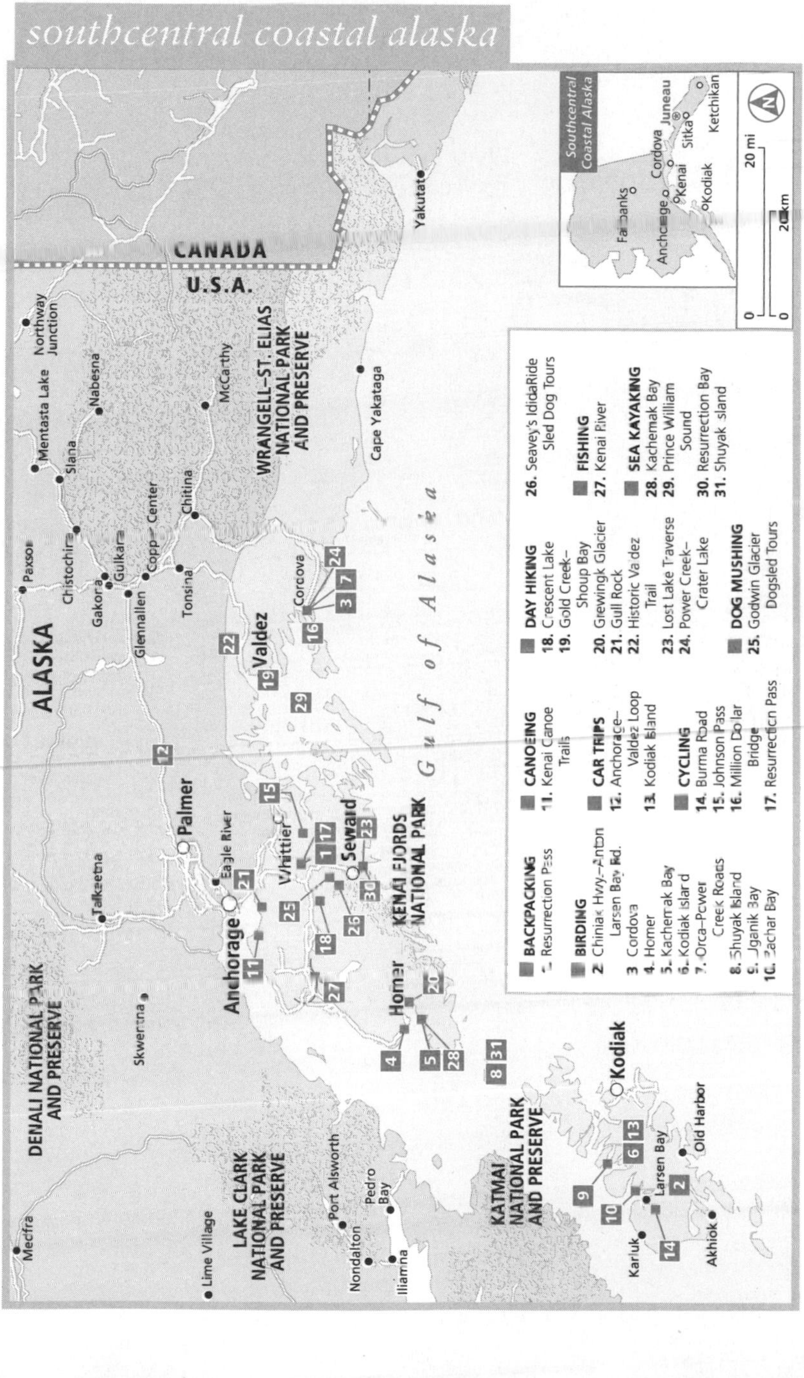
southcentral coastal alaska
CANADA
U.S.A.
ALASKA
DENALI NATIONAL PARK AND PRESERVE
LAKE CLARK NATIONAL PARK AND PRESERVE
KATMAI NATIONAL PARK AND PRESERVE
KENAI FJORDS NATIONAL PARK
WRANGELL–ST. ELIAS NATIONAL PARK AND PRESERVE
Gulf of Alaska
Medfra
Lime Village
Skwentna
Talkeetna
Palmer
Eagle River
Anchorage
Whittier
Seward
Homer
Kodiak
Old Harbor
Larsen Bay
Karluk
Akhiok
Port Alsworth
Pedro Bay
Nondalton
Iliamna
Paxson
Chistochina
Gakona
Gulkana
Glennallen
Copper Center
Tonsina
Chitina
Valdez
Cordova
Slana
Mentasta Lake
Nabesna
Northway Junction
McCarthy
Cape Yakataga
Yakutat
Southcentral Coastal Alaska
Fairbanks
Anchorage
Cordova
Kenai
Kodiak
Juneau
Sitka
Ketchikan
0 20 mi
0 20 km
BACKPACKING
1. Resurrection Pass
BIRDING
2. Chiniak Hwy.–Anton Larsen Bay Rd.
3. Cordova
4. Homer
5. Kachemak Bay
6. Kodiak Island
7. Orca–Power Creek Roads
8. Shuyak Island
9. Uganik Bay
10. Zachar Bay
CANOEING
11. Kenai Canoe Trails
CAR TRIPS
12. Anchorage–Valdez Loop
13. Kodiak Island
CYCLING
14. Burma Road
15. Johnson Pass
16. Million Dollar Bridge
17. Resurrection Pass
DAY HIKING
18. Crescent Lake
19. Gold Creek–Shoup Bay
20. Grewingk Glacier
21. Gull Rock
22. Historic Valdez Trail
23. Lost Lake Traverse
24. Power Creek–Crater Lake
DOG MUSHING
25. Godwin Glacier Dogsled Tours
26. Seavey's IdidaRide Sled Dog Tours
FISHING
27. Kenai River
SEA KAYAKING
28. Kachemak Bay
29. Prince William Sound
30. Resurrection Bay
31. Shuyak Island

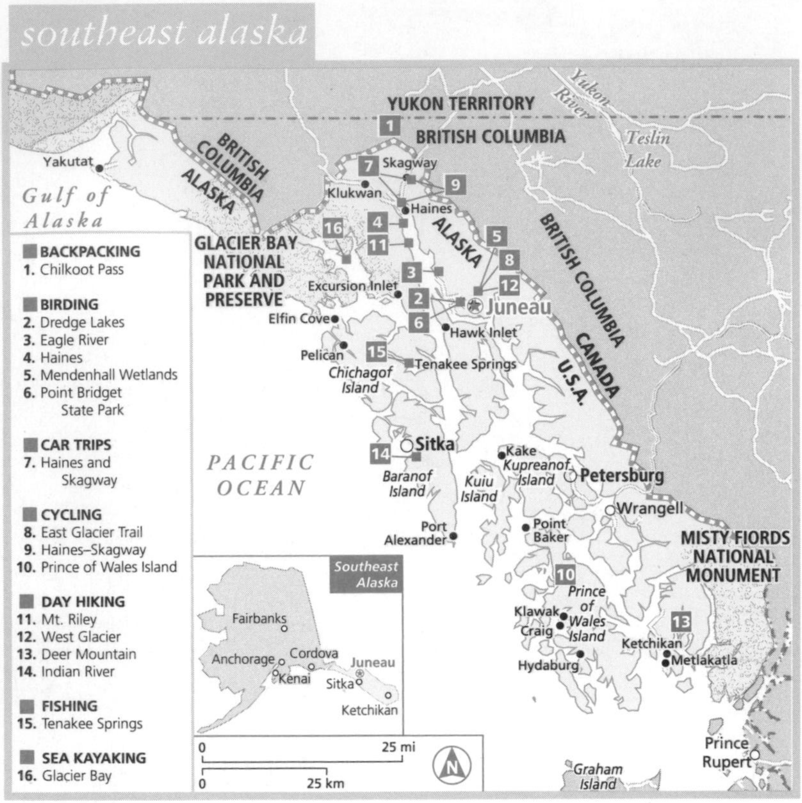

southeast alaska
YUKON TERRITORY
BRITISH COLUMBIA
Yukon River
Teslin Lake
BRITISH COLUMBIA
ALASKA
Yakutat
Gulf of Alaska
Skagway
Klukwan
Haines
ALASKA
BRITISH COLUMBIA
GLACIER BAY NATIONAL PARK AND PRESERVE
Excursion Inlet
Juneau
Elfin Cove
Hawk Inlet
Pelican
Tenakee Springs
Chichagof Island
CANADA
U.S.A.
Sitka
Baranof Island
Kuiu Island
Kake
Kupreanof Island
Petersburg
Wrangell
PACIFIC OCEAN
Port Alexander
Point Baker
MISTY FIORDS NATIONAL MONUMENT
Prince of Wales Island
Klawak
Craig
Hydaburg
Ketchikan
Metlakatla
Prince Rupert
Graham Island
Southeast Alaska
Fairbanks
Anchorage
Cordova
Kenai
Juneau
Sitka
Ketchikan
0 25 mi
0 25 km
N
BACKPACKING
1. Chilkoot Pass
BIRDING
2. Dredge Lakes
3. Eagle River
4. Haines
5. Mendenhall Wetlands
6. Point Bridget State Park
CAR TRIPS
7. Haines and Skagway
CYCLING
8. East Glacier Trail
9. Haines–Skagway
10. Prince of Wales Island
DAY HIKING
11. Mt. Riley
12. West Glacier
13. Deer Mountain
14. Indian River
FISHING
15. Tenakee Springs
SEA KAYAKING
16. Glacier Bay

interior alaska

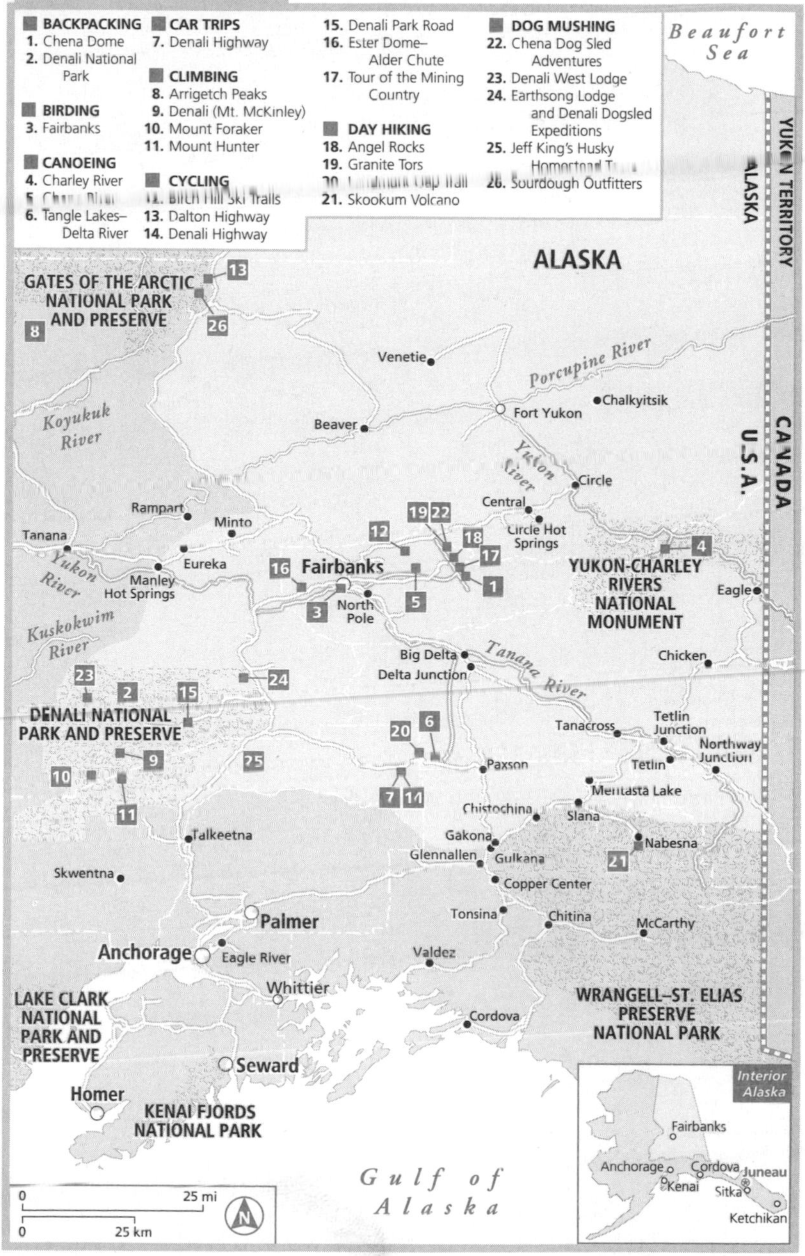
BACKPACKING
1. Chena Dome
2. Denali National Park
BIRDING
3. Fairbanks
CANOEING
4. Charley River
6. Tangle Lakes–Delta River
CAR TRIPS
7. Denali Highway
CLIMBING
8. Arrigetch Peaks
9. Denali (Mt. McKinley)
10. Mount Foraker
11. Mount Hunter
CYCLING
Birch Hill Ski Trails
13. Dalton Highway
14. Denali Highway
15. Denali Park Road
16. Ester Dome–Alder Chute
17. Tour of the Mining Country
DAY HIKING
18. Angel Rocks
19. Granite Tors
21. Skookum Volcano
DOG MUSHING
22. Chena Dog Sled Adventures
23. Denali West Lodge
24. Earthsong Lodge and Denali Dogsled Expeditions
25. Jeff King's Husky
26. Sourdough Outfitters
Beaufort Sea
ALASKA
YUKON TERRITORY
ALASKA
CANADA
U.S.A.
GATES OF THE ARCTIC NATIONAL PARK AND PRESERVE
Venetie
Porcupine River
Chalkyitsik
Fort Yukon
Beaver
Koyukuk River
Yukon River
Circle
Central
Circle Hot Springs
Rampart
Minto
Tanana
Eureka
Manley Hot Springs
Yukon River
Fairbanks
North Pole
Kuskokwim River
YUKON-CHARLEY RIVERS NATIONAL MONUMENT
Eagle
Big Delta
Delta Junction
Tanana River
Chicken
DENALI NATIONAL PARK AND PRESERVE
Tanacross
Tetlin Junction
Northway Junction
Tetlin
Paxson
Mentasta Lake
Chistochina
Slana
Gakona
Glennallen
Gulkana
Nabesna
Talkeetna
Skwentna
Copper Center
Palmer
Tonsina
Chitina
McCarthy
Anchorage
Eagle River
Valdez
Whittier
LAKE CLARK NATIONAL PARK AND PRESERVE
Cordova
WRANGELL–ST. ELIAS PRESERVE NATIONAL PARK
Seward
Homer
KENAI FJORDS NATIONAL PARK
Gulf of Alaska
0
25 mi
0
25 km
N
Interior Alaska
Fairbanks
Anchorage
Cordova
Juneau
Kenai
Sitka
Ketchikan

bush southwest alaska
RUSSIA
Nome
2
Golovin
Shaktoolik
Unalakleet
4
Stebbins
St. Michael
Kotlik
Anvik
Yukon River
Pilot Station
Bethel
Napakiak
Kuskokwim River
Tanunak
Toksook
Kipnuk
Kwigillingok
Bering Sea
St. Paul
3
St. George
BACKPACKING
1. Lake Clark National Park
BIRDING
2. Nome–Safety Sound
3. The Pribilofs
4. St. Lawrence Island–Gambell
CANOEING
5. Wood River
SEA KAYAKING
6. Katmai Coast
Cold Bay
Sand Point
King Cove
False Pass
Unalaska
Akutan
Biorka
Kashega
Nikolski
Pacific
See Inset
Atka
Bush Southwest Alaska
Fairbanks
Anchorage
Cordova
Juneau
Kenai
Sitka
Kodiak
Ketchikan
0 20 mi
0 20 km
N

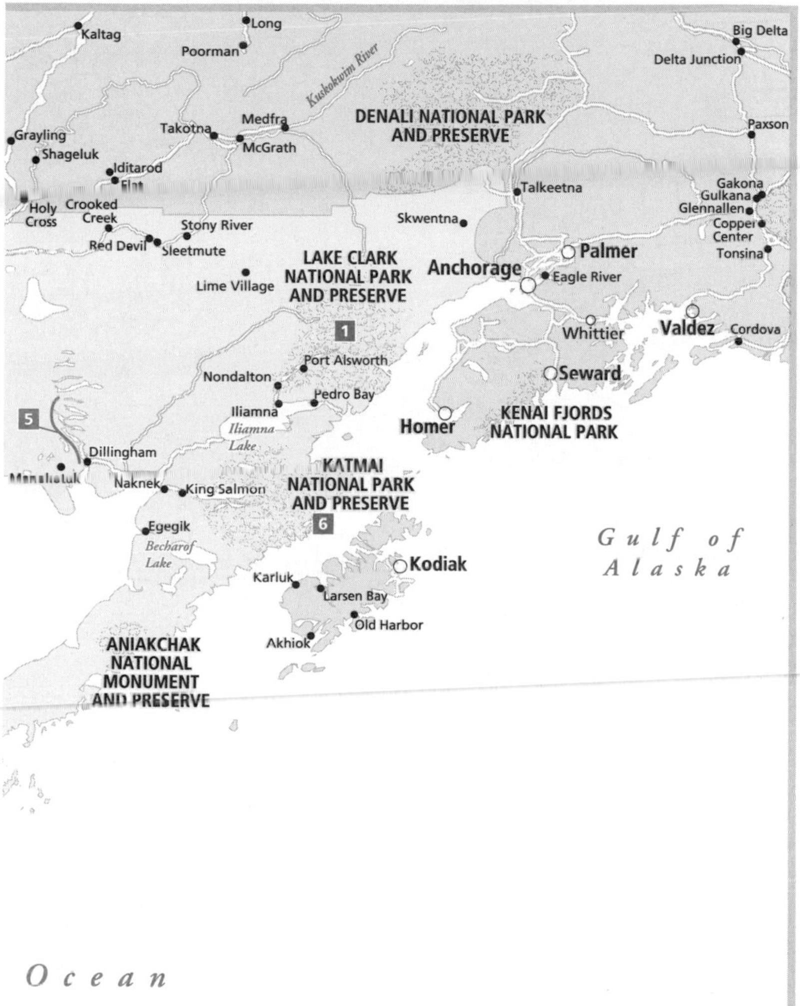
Kaltag
Long
Poorman
Kuskokwim River
Big Delta
Delta Junction
DENALI NATIONAL PARK AND PRESERVE
Medfra
Takotna
McGrath
Grayling
Shageluk
Iditarod
Paxson
Talkeetna
Gakona
Gulkana
Glennallen
Holy Cross
Crooked Creek
Stony River
Skwentna
Copper Center
Red Devil
Sleetmute
LAKE CLARK NATIONAL PARK AND PRESERVE
Anchorage
Palmer
Tonsina
Lime Village
Eagle River
1
Whittier
Valdez
Cordova
Port Alsworth
Nondalton
Seward
Pedro Bay
Iliamna
Iliamna Lake
5
Homer
KENAI FJORDS NATIONAL PARK
Dillingham
KATMAI NATIONAL PARK AND PRESERVE
Naknek
King Salmon
Egegik
6
Becharof Lake
Gulf of Alaska
Kodiak
Karluk
Larsen Bay
Old Harbor
Akhiok
ANIAKCHAK NATIONAL MONUMENT AND PRESERVE
Ocean

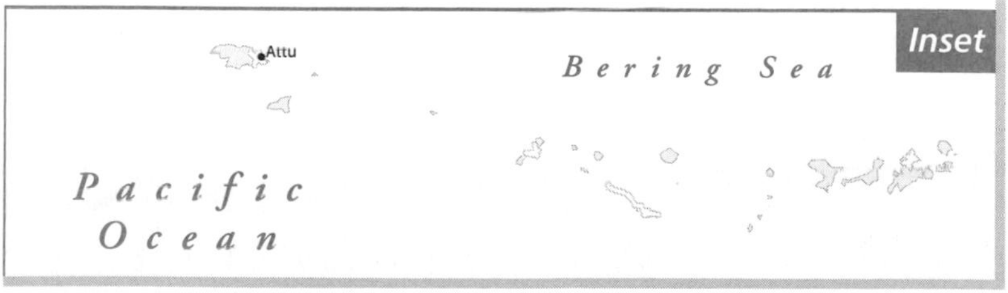
Inset
Attu
Bering Sea
Pacific Ocean

bush far north alaska
BIRDING
1. Kougarok Road
CAR TRIPS
2. Dalton Highway
CYCLING
3. Anvil Mountain
DOG MUSHING
4. Jerry Austin's Alaska Adventures
FISHING
5. Selby Lake–Kobuk River
Arctic
Wainwright
Brooks Range
Chukchi Sea
Point Hope
NOATAK NATIONAL PRESERVE
Kivalina
CAPE KRUSENSTERN NATIONAL MONUMENT
Kiana
Kotzebue
Noorvik
RUSSIA
BERING LAND BRIDGE NATIONAL PRESERVE
Buckland
Taylor
Wales
3
1
Koyuk
Elim
Golovin
Nome
Shaktoolik
Unalakleet
4
Stebbins
St. Michael
St. Lawrence Island
Kotlik
Grayling
Anvik
Bering Sea
Yukon River
Bush Far North Alaska
Fairbanks
Anchorage
Cordova
Juneau
Kenai
Sitka
Kodiak
Ketchikan
Pilot Station
Bethel
Kuskokwim River
Napakiak
Tanunak
Toksook
Nunivak Island
0
20 mi
0
20 km
N
Kipnuk
Kwigillingok

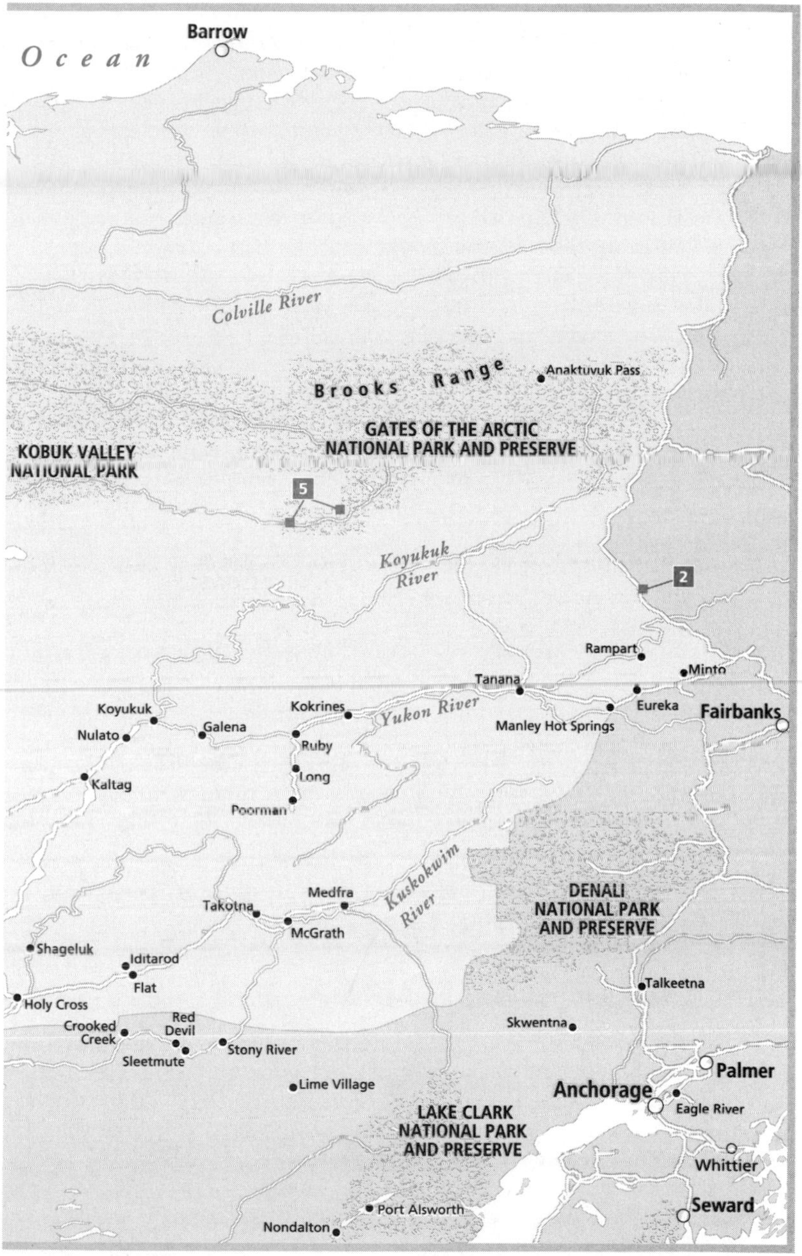
Barrow
Ocean
Colville River
Brooks Range
Anaktuvuk Pass
GATES OF THE ARCTIC NATIONAL PARK AND PRESERVE
KOBUK VALLEY NATIONAL PARK
5
Koyukuk River
2
Rampart
Minto
Tanana
Eureka
Fairbanks
Manley Hot Springs
Yukon River
Kokrines
Koyukuk
Nulato
Galena
Ruby
Long
Kaltag
Poorman
Kuskokwim River
Medfra
Takotna
McGrath
DENALI NATIONAL PARK AND PRESERVE
Shageluk
Iditarod
Flat
Holy Cross
Talkeetna
Skwentna
Crooked Creek
Red Devil
Sleetmute
Stony River
Palmer
Lime Village
Anchorage
Eagle River
LAKE CLARK NATIONAL PARK AND PRESERVE
Whittier
Seward
Port Alsworth
Nondalton

which high-rises block the skies, highways bisect the ground, and crowds fill every space, Alaska lets us breathe, slow down, and appreciate the earth. It's a good way to live.

Unfortunately, the very things that make this state so alluring—its endless possibilities and unlimited destinations—can also intimidate visitors who don't know where to begin. That's where *The Unofficial Guide to Adventure Travel in Alaska* comes to the rescue. The most-often-heard lament among travelers to this state is that they didn't get to see everything they wanted. Believe us, they're not alone. There are lifelong Alaskans who *still* have not seen the entire state, so what's the hurry for those of you seeing it for the first time?

This guide strives to narrow your focus, readjust your internal rules of measurement, and help you see that the vastness of Alaska does not have to be overwhelming. Slow down. Enjoy the special moments. Watch the sun set behind a snowcapped mountain, or peer through binoculars at a pair of bear cubs frolicking on a hillside. Sip some locally brewed beer and listen to street musicians perform. Set up camp and roast some marshmallows by the fire. Paddle to a remote cove and stop to watch sea otters play.

unofficial **TIP**
Adjust your perspective and think *s-l-o-w*.

In other words, think of Alaska as more than just a one-time vacation. This state is larger than most European countries, and there is no way you'll be able to see it all in a week, two weeks, even three.

Take time to absorb the enormousness of a place that still retains a bit of Last Frontier wildness despite the ever-quickening encroachment of progress.

No matter which part of Alaska you visit, you will experience a feeling of vastness. The distinct regions each have their own climate, culture, and geography, with unique opportunities for adventure—from rafting to backpacking to dog mushing to fishing. The one aspect they all share, however, is room to roam.

A QUICK GLIMPSE *at* OUR REGIONS

WHEN PLANNING A VISIT TO ALASKA based on outdoor adventure, the most important question to ask is, "What do I want to do?" How you get there, which region of the state you'll need to go to, and how to organize the logistics will fall into place quite easily after that first question is resolved. *The Unofficial Guide to Adventure Travel in Alaska* is set up with this premise in mind, offering a breakdown of activities and outfitters in our special-interest chapters.

However, if your trip happens to be limited to a specific region—for example, if your great-uncle on your father's side has sent you a ticket to Fairbanks, or if you have just enough frequent-flier miles to get you to Anchorage—simply start by perusing our region-by-region chapters. More details on each area are available in their respective chapters, but here's a quick overview.

SOUTHCENTRAL INLAND ALASKA

SOUTHCENTRAL INLAND ALASKA begins with the state's largest population center, the municipality of **Anchorage,** and moves inland toward **Talkeetna** to the north and the **Copper River–Glennallen** corridor to the west. At just over 280,000 people—more than 40% of the state's residents—Anchorage is the hub of Alaska's economy. With its port, train station, and international airport, it serves as a gateway for travelers from around the globe. Yet the sprawling metropolis is surrounded by wilderness: the waters of **Cook Inlet** and the dense spruce, birch, and aspen forest of **Chugach State Park.** It is entirely conceivable, then, to have an outstanding outdoor adventure without ever leaving the city limits.

Naturally, Anchorage has a cosmopolitan side. Even the most discriminating travelers will find shopping, theater, art galleries, museums, and fine dining to suit their tastes. A short drive south brings you to the world-class ski resort at **Mount Alyeska.** To the north lie such gems as the **Matanuska-Susitna Valley,** which has incredible rafting, hiking, four-wheeling, and biking options, as well as a chance for mountaineering, even in the summer.

SOUTHCENTRAL COASTAL ALASKA

THE COASTAL WATERS AND COMMUNITIES that make up **Prince William Sound,** the **Kenai Peninsula,** and **Kodiak Island** are included in the region we call Southcentral Coastal Alaska. These areas are overwhelmingly the best places for water sports such as fishing, adventure cruising, and kayaking, but don't overlook the superior hiking, biking, and wildlife viewing. The Kenai Peninsula satisfies just about any outdoor dream, which is why it is known as Alaska's playground to residents, who flock there when they have their own vacation time to spend.

SOUTHEAST ALASKA

OFTEN REFERRED TO AS "THE PANHANDLE," which reflects its status as the long, thin branch of the state holding it all together, Southeast Alaska is an especially diverse region, offering lush forests, rich native culture, and limitless coastline. It is the ideal place for adventure cruising as well as kayaking, wildlife viewing, birding, fishing, and biking. Of its communities, only **Skagway** and **Haines** connect to the road system, but it is an easy area to visit by air and water. The region's largest city in area, **Juneau,** is also the state capital. From here, day trips to outlying waterfront villages can easily be arranged. The state ferry system forms an integral part of life for those who call Southeast Alaska home.

THE INTERIOR

POINT SMACK-DAB IN THE MIDDLE of the state, and you've got the Alaska of most visitors' imaginations: the Interior. Towering mountain ranges extend forever along the Parks Highway toward **Fairbanks,** the Interior's largest city. In the north of the state looms the wild **Brooks Range,** and in the south, the **Alaska Range.** In between is land so wide open that when you pass a cabin or small business along the road, you wonder how on earth the people survive.

But survive they do. The Interior is home to hardy Alaskans who brave cold and isolation for the reward of a simple, uncluttered way of life. In summer, endless days and temperatures in the 80s Fahrenheit bring a blessed reprieve, a time to play. This is a region rich in dog-mushing expertise, remote lake and river fishing, and wilderness-hiking and backpacking opportunities galore. And if you want to see wildlife, this is the place to go.

THE BUSH

FANNING OUT FROM THE INTERIOR is land so remote, it is simply called the Bush. The majority of Alaska's native people choose to reside here, often living off the land by fishing, hunting, and gathering as their ancestors did before them. The largest communities are **Barrow, Nome, Kotzebue,** and **Bethel,** augmented by dozens of villages scattered across the country. We have included **Southwest Alaska** as part of our Bush chapter because of its remoteness and its sparse population.

The Bush's Inupiat, Yup'ik, and Aleut natives depend on boats, snowmobiles, and dog teams to get around the mostly roadless communities. In winter the rivers freeze, creating ribbon highways for snowmobile and dog-team travel; in summer, boats provide transportation. Today, most communities also have airplane service, connecting the world to these once-inaccessible places. The Bush is where some of the most adventurous of adventurers roam, rafting rivers that perhaps see fewer than a dozen people in any given year, or fishing lakes that don't know the feel of human footprints.

A BRIEF HISTORY *of a* BIG STATE

TWO CENTS AN ACRE.

That's what William H. Seward, the man responsible for purchasing Alaska from Russia in 1867, negotiated for the United States.

At the time, that rate, which totaled $7.2 million, was called outrageous. Critics said Seward was a foolish man. They called the purchase "Seward's Folly" and the land "Seward's Icebox."

But oh, what a bargain it was. Today, not only is Alaska one of the most beautiful states in the country, but it has a wealth of natural resources and a growing economy dependent on tourism. It's still lightly populated compared with other states, and it maintains a frontier attitude in many smaller communities.

The Russians were among the first to explore the area, and vestiges of their presence remain today. From their first ventures to Alaskan territory back in the 1700s, the Russians have shown that they may have sold the territory, but many of them never stopped calling it home.

Vitus Bering was the original Russian explorer. The year was 1741, and Bering and his crew reached what is now called Kayak Island. However, Bering and much of his crew perished in a shipwreck on the return trip. Those who survived the disastrous event and stayed through winter brought home luxurious sea-otter skins that spurred other Russian explorers to rush to Alaska. Grigori Shelekhov was one of those entrepreneurs; in 1784, he founded the first permanent settlement in Alaska on Kodiak Island and sent Alexander Baranov to manage his company.

Kodiak is, in fact, the first place where the Russians settled, first in secluded Three Saints Bay and later in present-day Kodiak. Their influence is evident in a modern-day walking tour of the city, including the museum, Holy Resurrection Russian Orthodox Church, and the Saint Innocent Veniaminov Research Institute Museum. There is also a yearly event celebrating the canonization of a Russian priest, Saint Herman, in an area outside of town called Monk's Lagoon.

As the Russians became involved with the sea-otter-skin industry, they inevitably clashed with Alaskan natives, who saw the foreign influx as an intrusion on their lives and livelihoods. By 1786 Russian fur traders had made their way to the Kenai Peninsula and had settled in the area by 1791. Russian Orthodox priests arrived and began introducing the natives to Christianity, and their churches grew.

But tension mounted, and in 1797 a battle for the Kenai erupted between the Dena'ina Athabascans and the Lebedev Company, the fur-trading company based on the Kenai. More than 100 Russians, Dena'ina, and other natives were killed.

Meanwhile, the majority of Russians had moved east toward Sitka and other Southeast communities, where they continued to trade furs. By 1796, they had arrived in Yakutat, later settling in Sitka, which became their capital. The Tlingit Indians living in the area knew that submitting to the Russians meant allegiance to their czar and slave labor for their fur-trade company. A battle between the Tlingits and the Russians ensued in 1802, and nearly all the Russians and their Aleut slaves were killed.

In 1804, undaunted by the battle, Baranov arrived ready to fight. For six days he fought the Tlingits, this time overpowering them. The Russians named their newly acquired land New Archangel, and the site known as Castle Hill evolved.

Sitka is one of the best places to learn about Russia's influence on Alaska. Just take a walk around the city. Enjoy lofty views of the surrounding islands and ocean from Castle Hill (where, incidentally, "Russia America" officially became Alaska, U.S.A., in 1867); see a re-created Russian blockhouse; visit the old Russian cemetery and the Lutheran cemetery, where the Russian Princess Maksoutoff lies buried; pass many historic houses; check out Saint Michael's Russian Orthodox Cathedral; and visit the Russian Bishop's House, which is part of Sitka National Historical Park.

By the time the United States took ownership of Alaska, much of the Russian conflict had subsided. The next wave of activity to reach the state had nothing to do with war and a lot to do with wealth. Gold was discovered near Sitka in 1872, prompting the beginning of a gold rush that would peak at the turn of the century. In 1897, the largest discovery was made in the Klondike, stretching from Canada's Yukon Territory into Alaska and attracting thousands of gold seekers. In 1898, prospectors found gold on the beaches in Nome, sparking another rush to the western part of the territory. The gold rush turned one-street towns into bustling cities of thousands, seemingly overnight.

By 1906, gold production was at its peak, and Alaska got its own nonvoting delegate to Congress. Gold mining was on the decline, but with the influx of so many new residents, other exciting prospects emerged. Copper mining at the Kennicott mine began, and oil production at select spots throughout the land was already under way. By 1912, Alaska was named an official U.S. territory.

Although still just a territory, Alaska played a significant role in the nation's economy, bringing in money from natural-resource development. Construction of the Alaska Railroad began in 1914, and logging in Southeast Alaska was becoming a large industry around the same time. In 1935, Depression-era farming families came to Alaska as part of the Matanuska Valley Project. The government-backed effort to create a self-sustaining farming community in Alaska gave poverty-stricken families free land in exchange for their sweat and toil in "bringing up" the wilderness into wide-open cropland and pastures. While many abandoned the project, intimidated by the harsh winters and crude living conditions the first few years, others thrived. Today, countless generations of those first families still call the Matanuska-Susitna Valley in Southcentral Alaska their home. Visitors to the area come to gawk at the giant cabbages, massive carrots, and other vegetables and fruits that grow so huge during the summer.

As those valley farmers settled into their new homes, another region of the Alaska territory came to the forefront of the public eye. Today, it's a little-known fact that the Japanese invaded American lands during World War II, but in 1942 it was headline news. On a June day on the remote archipelago that makes up the Aleutian Chain in Southwestern Alaska, just six months after the attack on Pearl Harbor in Hawaii, the Japanese came. Planes from a Japanese aircraft carrier bombed the Naval Station and Fort Mears in Dutch Harbor, then occupied nearby Attu and Kiska islands. It was the first time since the War of 1812 that foreign forces had occupied American territory.

Forty-two people from the islands were taken to Japan as hostages. Seventeen of them died in captivity. Meanwhile, the U.S. government evacuated the remaining Aleuts from their homes in the Aleutian and Pribilof islands. American troops destroyed many of the homes on the islands to prevent the Japanese from settling in too easily. Many of the natives who once called this remote region home were not able to return for years. Much of their settlement had been burned to the ground, leaving them with nothing.

Fortunately, U.S. forces did not tolerate the occupation for too long. By May 1943, the Japanese had been mostly defeated, but at a high cost to American soldiers. In the end, more than 20 U.S. pilots and 2,500 troops perished.

With the war came better access to Alaska. Recognizing the need to reach this remote territory, the government approved funds in 1942 to build the Alaska Highway. U.S. Army engineer troops designed and built the primitive 1,400-plus-mile road in a mind-boggling nine months and six days, from Dawson Creek, British Columbia, to what is now Delta Junction in Alaska. It was the first and only overland connection to the lower 48 states and still one of the primary ways of reaching Alaska today.

Alaska gained statehood in 1959, becoming the 49th state to join the nation. Over the years, defining moments put Alaska in the spotlight: On March 27, 1964, on a Good Friday afternoon, a magnitude-9.2 earthquake rattled the state, wiping out the village of Chenega in Prince William Sound and the community of Portage on Turnagain Arm. Other communities suffered millions of dollars in damage. In the end, the four-minute-long earthquake killed 131 people in Alaska, along with 14 others in Oregon and California who were swept away by tidal waves

In 1971, Congress approved the Alaska Native Claims Settlement Act, which gave 40 million acres and $900 million to Alaskan natives, officially recognizing their aboriginal ownership of the land. For years the government had been vague about its acknowledgement of natives' land ownership, but the discovery of oil brought incentive for settling the long-standing claim. The signing of the Alaska Native Claims Settlement Act then cleared the way for the construction of the Trans-Alaska Pipeline System, an 800-mile raised tube that carries oil from the North Slope oil fields to Valdez. The construction of the pipeline brought thousands of workers to the state, creating a wave of activity. A boom of construction followed, and for a time Alaskans were living large.

In 1980, the Alaska legislature, led by then-Governor Jay Hammond, recognized the value of the oil resource and created what it called the Permanent Fund, which held a quarter of all oil royalties for future generations and was paid out as a dividend to each qualified Alaskan once a year. The first checks, mailed in 1982, paid each qualified Alaskan, including babies and children, $1,000. Today, the legislature is attempting to raid the Permanent Fund to pay for government. If you're visiting Alaska and read the newspapers or watch the news, you'll likely see countless reports about the ongoing debate. So far, the voters have kept attempts to tap the fund at bay. In 2000, the dividend to each Alaskan reached a record high of $1,963.86. In 2004, it dropped to $919.84, the first time since 1995 that it was below $1,000. By 2007, it was back up to $1,654.

Through it all, Alaskans, both native to the land and those who moved north for a bit of adventure but decided it was a pretty good place to call home, have persevered. They have proved that the critics who called Alaska "Seward's Folly" or "Seward's Icebox" all those years ago were simply wrong. Seward just may have been the most brilliant man of his time, recognizing in Alaska a potential that continues to shine today. Oil production, commercial fishing, and tourism are growing industries that offer Alaskans a way to earn a living in a ridiculously beautiful setting. But above all, Alaska's biggest asset is its natural environment. It is something to be celebrated, enjoyed, and, most of all, protected for generations to come.

ALASKA'S NATIVE PEOPLES *and* CULTURES

UNLESS YOUR OUTDOOR ADVENTURE includes travel in some of the remotest sections of the state, there's a good chance you won't cross paths with that many of Alaska's native people. It's a surprisingly true and unfortunate phenomenon. Alaska natives make up only 16% of the population of today's Alaska, although there are 11 distinct cultures and 20 languages among the group as a whole.

Many natives still live in the most remote and wildest areas of the state, and that puts them off the radar for the traveler who only blows by the larger cities. Even though there are a fair number of natives in the cities, too, they share these places with tens of thousands of other people of all nationalities. In fact, Anchorage is technically the largest native village in the state, considering that nearly 29,000 American Indians and Alaska natives call it home. That's a larger population than any of the more remote, mostly native communities.

It would be a shame to come all the way to Alaska, though, and not learn more about the indigenous peoples who first called this land home. Their cultures are fascinating and impressive yet humbling and challenging. A good number of today's natives, especially those in the villages, still live entirely by the same means as their ancestors. They catch fish, harvest berries, and hunt for most of their

WHEN IN ALASKA: NATIVE ETIQUETTE

WHEN YOU VISIT AN AREA WHOSE RESIDENTS are predominantly natives, above all, be respectful. Just as you would while traveling in any other country, whether you're encountering shepherds in Ireland leading their sheep home or aborigines in Australia working on their ranches, avoid the temptation to gawk. In general, treat them as you would want to be treated.

If you are close enough and able to, ask before taking photographs.

Native cultural events are steeped in tradition. Many of them represent the living or the dead and religious in nature. The same goes for native burial sites.

You may notice that native Alaskans speak slowly and often take their time in responding to a question or comment. Do not become unnerved by this or assume they do not hear you.

Likewise, try not to interrupt when conversing with native Alaskans. It is purely a Western tendency to try finishing another person's thoughts or to jump in with your own opinions. By Alaska native standards, it is considered rude—although it would also be rude to point it out.

When traveling, especially in remote areas, be sure to secure the proper permits for visiting native owned land. With the advent of the Alaska Native Claims Settlement Act, more than 40 million acres of Alaska land is native-owned. That means it is private. Some native corporations require a fee for use of their land; others only require that visitors get permission, and a few do not allow public access at all. (For details, see "Native Lands: What You Should Know," on page 55.)

food. They go whaling and hold potlatches. Their connection to the land is as close now as it was hundreds of years ago, despite the arrival of electricity, running water, and the convenience of four-wheel-drive vehicles over dogsleds.

In general, there are three groups of Alaska natives: Indian, Eskimo, and Aleut. The terms *Inuit* and *Native American* are sometimes used in place of *Eskimo* and *Indian* in an effort to be considerate, but that doesn't always work in Alaska. It is true that in many other places, *Eskimo* is considered a derogatory word because it is said to mean "eater of raw meat"; however, using the term *Inuit* is not accurate in an Alaskan context because the Inuit language is restricted to the peoples of Arctic Canada and portions of Greenland. In Alaska and Arctic Siberia, where Inuit is not spoken, the comparable terms are *Inupiat, Yup'ik,* or one of the other cultural names within that region.

For the most part in Alaska, *Indian* and *Eskimo* are not offensive words. In fact, Eskimos pride themselves on their heritage. Still, if you feel uncomfortable using such terms, ask instead what culture a native is from. The natives of the northern reaches of Alaska will not use the word *Eskimo* when answering. Instead they likely will name a more specific culture, such as Inupiat, Yup'ik, or Cup'ik.

These three designations are further divided into five cultures, based on similarities in tradition, language, and proximity. At the **Alaska Native Heritage Center,** considered the defining authority on the subject, there are houses representing each of the five cultures, and visitors to the Anchorage-based center can learn how the varying native groups lived. They include Athabascan; Yup'ik and Cup'ik; Inupiat and St. Lawrence Island Yupik; Aleut and Alutiiq; and Eyak, Tlingit, Tsimshian, and Haida. As the state continues to grow and new residents from all over the United States and other nations arrive, Alaska's first peoples are finding it more important than ever to celebrate their heritage and educate those who want to know more about them.

ATHABASCAN

YOU'LL SEE THE WORD *Athabascan* spelled two ways, with a *c* and with a *k,* but don't be confused—they are one and the same. The geographic region for the Athabascan people traditionally begins in the Interior, just south of the Brooks Range, and follows all the way to the Kenai Peninsula, which is described in more detail in the Southcentral Coastal chapter (page 332). Before the advent of modern transportation, the Athabascans lived along five major rivers: the Copper, Yukon, Tanana, Susitna, and Kuskokwim. They were a nomadic people, often traveling hundreds of miles to follow their best sources of food, depending upon the time of year and severity of the seasons.

Today, Athabascan people live throughout the entire state, as well as in the lower 48 states. According to the Alaska Native Heritage Center, "the Athabascan people call themselves 'Dena,' or 'the people.' " They are taught a respect for all living things; hunting is for subsistence only. They also are taught to share, perhaps a throwback to a time when combining resources was the only way groups could survive. Sharing is a community-wide belief, and those who have, give.

When you see the name *Denali*—and, believe us, you will if you set foot in this state—give a nod to the Athabascan people. Denali, the native name for Mount McKinley, North America's largest peak, is an Athabascan term meaning "high one."

TLINGIT, HAIDA, EYAK, AND TSIMSHIAN

THE HAIDA ARE AN INDIAN GROUP of about 800 who emigrated from Canada and now live in Southeast Alaska, Prince of Wales Island, and surrounding areas. The Tlingit, about 11,000 strong, live mostly in the Southeast. The Tsimshian are a small group from Metlakatla living in the area on their own reservation. The Eyak are natives related to the Athabascans but influenced greatly by the Tlingits. The Eyak language became extinct in January 2008 when its last native speaker, Marie Smith Jones, died at the age of 89.

INUPIAT AND ST. LAWRENCE ISLAND YUPIK ESKIMOS

THE INUPIAQ AND THE ST. LAWRENCE ISLAND YUPIK people call themselves the "Real People," according the Alaska Native Heritage Center, and their homelands are in northern and northwestern Alaska. They depend largely on subsistence and still hunt whales, seals, walrus, and other large animals, and gather berries in season. They also hunt birds and fish when the conditions are right. These groups of natives are in the same category because of their similar subsistence patterns, the way they constructed their homes, and the tools they used to survive.

St. Lawrence Island Yupiks speak Siberian Yupik, which is different from the languages spoken by other Yup'ik Eskimos (thus the difference in the spellings *Yupik* and *Yup'ik*).

YUP'IK AND CUP'IK

THESE GROUPS OF ESKIMOS live in Southwest Alaska in such communities as Nome, Unalakleet, and Perryville. Their names come from the dialects of the languages they speak. Like the Yupiks of St. Lawrence Island and the Inupiat of north and northwestern Alaska, they depend upon a subsistence lifestyle for their livelihood, and elders tell stories of traditional ways of life to teach younger generations about their heritage.

ALEUT AND ALUTIIQ

SOUTH AND SOUTHWEST ALASKA are the original regions of the Aleut and Alutiiq peoples, although today they live all over the state and beyond. Traditionally, Aleuts and Alutiiqs depended upon the ocean for their livelihoods, living off what they could catch from the sea, creeks, rivers, or even lakes. Their territory ranged from the North Pacific and Bering Sea, from Prince William Sound to the end of the Aleutian Chain. In places such as Kodiak Island, the influence of Russians, which began in the 18th century, can still be seen today. The Orthodox Church became the focal point of every village, and the native people in these communities adopted many of the Russian traditions and the language.

WANT TO KNOW MORE? The **Alaska Native Heritage Center,** which provided the bulk of information for this section, can be contacted at 8800 Heritage Center Drive, Anchorage 99506; ☎ 800-315-6608 or 907-330-8000; **www.alaskanative.net.**

PART TWO

PLANNING *your* TRIP

IS IT COLD ALL THE TIME?

The Truth about Alaska's Seasons

YOU'VE SEEN THE PICTURES. You've heard the stories. Now that you have a copy of *The Unofficial Guide to Adventure Travel in Alaska*, you have the facts.

One key fact is that living in Alaska isn't that much different from living in any other four-season state. The winters, while very, very cold on occasion, really are not that punishing once you get used to them. The summers, while admittedly shorter than and not quite as humid as summers in the Lower 48, truly are warm enough for shorts and sandals. And the "shoulder seasons" of fall and spring are shorter,

Alaska's Climate

TAKE A LOOK AT THE CHART on the next page, based on information from the Alaska Climate Research Center and data from the National Oceanic and Atmospheric Administration, and you may conclude that Alaska is a perennially cold place—the warmest average temperature in July does not exceed 63 degrees. The truth is, these numbers can be deceiving, though they can give you an idea of which areas generally have milder climates than others.

Remember that these are averages, taken over a 24-hour period, and they reflect the day's high and low temperatures. On a sunny July day in Anchorage, for example, the temperature could easily reach the low 70s. However, it could be only 50°F in the morning or the middle of the night.

So don't be daunted by the numbers. In general, Alaska is comfortable in the summer. The winters, however, we'll let you be the judge of.

AVERAGE DAILY TEMPERATURES

City	January	April	July	October	Overall
Anchorage	14.9°F	35.8°F	58.4°F	36.6°F	35.9°F
Barrow	–13.4°F	–2.2°F	39.3°F	13.5°F	9.4°F
Fairbanks	–10.1°F	30.7°F	62.5°F	25.1°F	26.9°F
Homer	22.7°F	35.4°F	53.4°F	37.5°F	37.4°F
Juneau	24.2°F	39.7°F	56.0°F	42.2°F	40.6°F
Kodiak	29.9°F	37.5°F	54.4°F	40.7°F	40.8°F
Nome	7.0°F	17.6°F	51.5°F	28.0°F	26.2°F
Valdez	20.5°F	37.1°F	54.9°F	38.1°F	37.7°F

squeezed into just a few weeks rather than a few months. Blink and you could miss the changing colors of the leaves in the fall. In spring, it sometimes seems that there is snow on the ground one week and fully greened up trees the next.

The real difference between Alaska's climate and other places' is its variety. The coastal weather that envelops so much of the state collides with the mountainous terrain, making Alaska's weather a bit tumultuous. It may be sunny and dry at the beginning of the day but rainy by afternoon. Snowstorms in July are not unheard of. At the base of that hiking trail, the temperature might be in the high 60s, but once you get above the tree line and hit the summit, it can drop by 20 degrees or more. In more ways than one, especially when it comes to weather, Alaska is a land of extremes.

Then there is the geographic distance. The weather in Barrow, at the northern edge of Alaska, and Ketchikan, on the Southeast Panhandle, can be bizarrely different. On an average July day in Southeast Alaska, highs can reach 61°F. In Barrow, you're lucky if it rises above 45°F. That's why deciding on your destination within the state is so important.

HOW *to* STAY SAFE *in the* WILDERNESS

THE MOST IMPORTANT THING TO REMEMBER about visiting Alaska's backcountry is that it is wild. A trail that starts at the edge of the metropolitan city of Anchorage, for example, can be just as dangerous as a wilderness setting in the middle of the Bush. In fact, animal–human encounters are more likely to happen close to towns, the direct result of humans' ever-encroaching presence into the woods that bears, moose, and other wild animals call home.

However, we encourage you not to be fearful of Alaska's outdoors. Bears do not lurk around every bush; mosquitoes do not carry West Nile disease (not yet, anyway). It will not snow in the middle of a 70-degree sunny day in July, despite the temperamental weather we often experience.

To borrow a phrase from the Boy Scouts, be prepared. With a few simple precautions, you should have no problem in the woods and tundra and rivers and oceans of Alaska.

BEARS

WE COULD WRITE AN ENTIRE BOOK on the issues surrounding bears—how to avoid them, how to watch them, and how to protect yourself against them should it come to that. But let us just give you this first bit of advice: encountering a bear of any kind is very unlikely. If you go into the Alaska wilderness preoccupied with a fear of bears, it will take much of the enjoyment out of your trip. This isn't to say that bears aren't a threat at all, but if you follow these guidelines, your chance of an encounter is quite slim.

Experts agree that bear repellents are your best protective option, especially for those unaccustomed to using firearms. Repellent sprays cost anywhere from $20 to $50 and can shoot at varying distances. Do not carry a firearm unless you are skilled at using it and know that it is allowed in the particular area in which you are traveling.

Never approach bears. This seems absurd to mention, but it has happened before. Most Alaskans can tell you the story of the Australian tourist who thought Binky the polar bear at the Alaska Zoo was so cute that she decided to climb into the cage with him. Binky, needless to say, chewed on the woman for a while before she was eventually rescued. Even if bear-watching is your goal, view the beasts *from a distance.*

Keep a very clean camp, and store food, toothpaste, and anything else even slightly scented in a bearproof container at least 30 to 50 yards from your sleeping camp. Do not bury your trash, because it will attract bears and thus accustom them to humans (not to mention you'll be littering). Avoid camping near streams and other spawning areas when salmon are running—bears will be there.

unofficial **TIP**
We acknowledge that bear bells, which can be strapped onto packs to add noise, are popular, but we find them distracting to the wilderness experience and not at all necessary. The all-day jingling also diminishes your chance of seeing other wildlife that you might be seeking, such as birds, moose, or small mammals.

Make noise, sing, or clap your hands when traveling through areas that are densely populated with trees and brush and make visibility a challenge. Bears generally attack only when frightened, when protecting their food, or when you approach a sow with cubs. Making noise can give the bear a chance to run off, thus avoiding an encounter.

The chances of encountering a polar bear are close to zero unless you are wandering the

Chukchi Sea or some other Far North destination. Instead, brown or black bears are the ones to watch out for. Brown bears can range in color from honey to cinnamon and have platter-wide faces with shorter snouts; black bears, by contrast, have longer, skinnier faces and snouts and range in color from jet black to a bluish gray.

If a brown bear charges, stand your ground until the animal is approximately three feet away. If attack is imminent, drop and play dead, locking your hands behind your neck and balling up to protect your vital organs. If you are wearing a pack or riding a bicycle, try to position yourself so that the gear is between you and the animal. Do not run. You will not get away.

If a black bear charges, fight back. These animals attack to kill and are not deterred by passive behavior. We can't promise you will win the fight, but it is worth a try. The upside: black bears rarely attack.

MOOSE

ALTHOUGH MOOSE CAN SEEM AS BENIGN as cows chewing their cud in a pasture, these lanky ungulates can be quite dangerous, attacking seemingly without reason and charging or stomping pets and people. Like bears, they mainly attack when they're provoked or frightened or defending their young, but sometimes they just seem not to want people around.

You're much more likely to see a moose than a bear—moose wander the streets of Anchorage, browse in lawns, and use trails as their own personal pathways. The popular Tony Knowles Coastal Trail, which skirts the city's edge, is a veritable moose hangout.

If a moose does charge, your best bet is to try placing yourself between an obstacle such as a tree or bush, so the moose's flailing hooves cannot make contact. As with bears, do not run.

unofficial **TIP**
If you encounter a moose, give it wide berth. If the animal sets its ears back or flattens them against its head, it may be getting angry. If the hair on its back bristles, it could be about to charge. Move slowly. If you happen upon a young moose, look around for the mother. You do not want to get between her and her young. Most moose prefer to be left alone. If they are grazing on trees or shrubs and do not respond to your presence, you should be able to pass without incident.

OTHER WILDLIFE

ALASKA ALSO TEEMS WITH CREATURES such as squirrels, mice, martens, hoary marmots, beavers, and muskrats. Larger mammals such as mountain goats, caribou, wolves, and Dall sheep are usually shy but sometimes unpredictable. Among the most irksome are porcupines, which are not aggressive creatures but will chew on your gear. If you leave your sweat-soaked, salty-tasting backpack outside, chances are a porcupine will snack on it; the same goes for leather boots or rubber bike tires. And for obvious reasons, don't startle a porcupine, or you can end up with a face full of quills. As a plus, though, we have no snakes!

BUGS

ALASKANS OFTEN JOKE THAT THE STATE BIRD is not the ptarmigan but the mosquito. From the feel of their bites, these irritating insects can certainly seem as large as birds. Alaska has 25 types of mosquitoes, none of which carry disease but any of which can easily spoil your outdoor experience. They arrive each spring in the state by the millions—a cruel joke to those of us who yearn to be outdoors in short sleeves and shorts.

Mosquitoes can become overwhelming the farther away from civilization you get, and they can turn a serene camping experience into a cramped, stuck-in-your-tent nightmare. June and July are the worst months for mosquitoes, but these insects can appear as early as late April and hang around through August in some places. They can be brutal on lakes and streams as well as in wet, swampy areas and brushy areas, which you may come upon while backpacking. Pack bug spray—the most powerful kind you can stand—along with a head net and long-sleeved shirts and pants. If you don't like the chemicals in bug sprays, consider a citrus- or eucalyptus-based formula before forgoing repellent altogether.

Other bugs to look out for include biting flies and various bee species. Happily, we have no dangerous spiders or scorpions to worry about.

WEATHER

PERHAPS THE GREATEST THREAT to an outdoor vacation is the weather. If you aren't dressed properly or if you become too wet and cold, even in the summer you risk developing hypothermia, a life-threatening drop in your core body temperature. This is a very real danger in Alaska, especially in the mountains, where temperatures drop the higher you go, even in the summer. Hypothermia can also sneak up on you, making you feel as if you're just slightly cold, then rapidly developing into a disorientation that can lead to further problems.

Avoiding hypothermia is simple: don't get wet. Even a shirt damp with perspiration can be dangerous if it's all you're wearing while you stand atop a windy summit. As comfortable as cotton is, resist the temptation to wear it—the saying "cotton kills" is well known in Alaska, and most people opt for synthetics or woolen sweaters and fleece instead.

Wear polypropylene or other moisture-wicking underwear against your skin and quick-drying layers over that; add layers as the conditions warrant. Always carry a spare pair of undergarments in case you get submerged in water or otherwise wet. Bring along a hat and at least a pair of glove liners for unexpected cold weather, even in the summer. And make sure to pack a waterproof raincoat and pants as an outer shell. (See "How to Pack Smart," opposite, for additional tips.)

unofficial **TIP**
If you must pack cotton clothes, save them for town, not the wilderness.

WATER

ALASKA'S COLD WATER CAN TURN a simple slip in a stream into a potentially deadly situation. Hypothermia can set in quickly. When crossing streams and rivers, always pick the route that seems the most shallow and least swift. Cloudy water, made gray by glacial silt, can hide possible dangers such as rocks and deep spots, so if you're not sure, don't try to cross. If possible, cross streams and rivers while linking arms with a partner or partners to reduce the chance of getting swept away. If you're in a group of more than two hikers, form a triangle and pivot your way across the river, thus creating enough disturbance in the river's flow to ease walking. Walk parallel to the current, and unhook your backpack from your waist in case you slip and get pulled under—this way you can get out of it without as much of a struggle. Also, morning is the best time to cross a stream or river, when the water tends to be at its lowest. If possible, shoot for an early-morning crossing.

NAVIGATION

A MAP AND COMPASS ARE OBVIOUS NECESSITIES for anyone traveling into the backcountry, even on trails. In Alaska, many trails are quite primitive and can be crisscrossed with game trails and other unmarked paths that may create confusion when you're trying to travel a main trail. Farther out, in the roadless areas, there often are no trails at all. Acquaint yourself with how to use a topographical map and how to read a compass. The **U.S. Geological Survey** produces the most-often-used maps, but commercial maps of various regions of Alaska also can be purchased. Many outdoor travelers can read global-positioning systems (GPSs) and rely on them for backcountry travel. These can be particularly useful tools for travel in trailless areas.

ADVANCE PLANNING

DON'T LEAVE HOME WITHOUT TELLING someone where you're going and when you expect to be home. Write down your plans and leave them with someone you trust. If they change at the last minute, as can often happen if planes get delayed or the weather turns, call someone—anyone—and let him or her know your second traveling option. It's a simple thing to do, and it will make it easier for rescuers to zero in on your location if you get into trouble. Many trails and recreation areas have a sign-in sheet at the trailhead. Use it.

Alaska doesn't have the cell-phone coverage common to the Lower 48, so don't assume you'll be able to call for help in an emergency. Emergency Location Transmitters and satellite phones can be rented and are worth the peace of mind if you are going to be traveling through remote areas where you don't expect to see others.

HOW *to* PACK SMART

THE BEST WAY TO BE PREPARED for a visit to Alaska is to pack in layers, a tenet that most outdoor travelers already know well. Not only does this method make sense, but it also allows you to stay warm and dry while mixing and matching outfits to your heart's content.

The following is a suggested clothing packing list for the general outdoor traveler. Adjust your list according to the activities you plan to tackle.

UNDERWEAR Synthetic or woolen long underwear wicks moisture away from the skin and makes a good barrier against mosquitoes and sun in the summer. Because Alaska is prone to frequent rainstorms, long underwear is a must. Depending upon the length of your trip, bring one to three pairs.

SOCKS Synthetic or woolen socks work best. Bring one to three pairs.

SHIRTS Two long-sleeve shirts, preferably made of one of the new quick-drying materials available at sport shops all over, are the best choice. They double as town shirts and don't wrinkle as easily as cotton. Pack two quick-dry T-shirts, too, for the warmer days.

PANTS Fleece pants work well at night for camping; quick-drying hiking pants can be worn for all manner of outdoor adventures, from biking to backpacking.

SHORTS Despite widespread beliefs to the contrary, many days are warm enough for hiking in shorts, which are good for fording shallow streams or rivers. Pack one to two pairs. We prefer shorts with lots of pockets for keeping maps, compass, bug spray, and other necessities close at hand. Some people prefer shorts that have belt loops so they can strap on a knife, bear spray, or other safety items.

FOOTWEAR Your choice of shoes will be largely based on what type of trips you plan to take, but in general boots are best. Today's boot makers have developed boots that are light yet tough enough to handle trailless hiking and trekking. However, heavier leather boots will provide more support for longer treks when carrying more weight. Plan, too, on boots that will keep your feet warm. Bring one pair of boots and a pair of comfortable camp shoes, preferably ones that can double as town shoes. We prefer Teva river sandals because they can be used to ford streams and rivers but also dry out quickly enough to be worn in town.

FOR THE EXTREMITIES Even if you are traveling to the warmest place in Alaska at the height of summer, a knit hat and pair of glove liners are must-haves. For travel during the shoulder season, bring heavier mittens and a balaclava to cover your face.

RAIN GEAR Rain pants and an outer shell for the upper body are probably the most important pieces of gear for anyone planning to spend time outdoors. Your parka can be lightweight or beefy, depending on the trip and duration, but above all it should keep you dry.

WHEN *to* GO

SUMMER TRAVEL

SUMMER IS BY FAR THE MOST POPULAR time to visit Alaska, so be prepared to pay for the privilege. Plane tickets go up in the summer, as does lodging at hotels, bed-and-breakfasts, and restaurants. In fact, many hotels and restaurants, and most outdoor outfitters, close during the winter or switch gears to a secondary business.

Summertime trips require careful planning because you are sharing this time with tens of thousands of other travelers. The lines at the airports, especially Ted Stevens Anchorage International Airport, can be grueling. You'll have to wait for seats in the most popular restaurants, and you'll likely need advance reservations to find a place to stay. So bring patience, and lots of it.

But don't let this dissuade you from coming to Alaska in the summer. Long called the Land of the Midnight Sun for its long days and very brief sunsets, Alaska is a magical place this time of year. You can sense the energy among the residents, who, after spending a winter wrapped in a cocoon of darkness, are squeezing every possible ounce of activity out of the summer. Don't be surprised to see folks riding bikes at 11 p.m., grilling dinner at midnight, or mowing their lawns at 5 a.m. Their internal clocks are so attuned to daylight that it is nearly impossible to let a good sunshiny day go to waste.

Maximum daylight during the summer ranges from 17 hours, 28 minutes in the Southeast community of Ketchikan to 19 hours, 21 minutes in Anchorage to around the clock in far-north Barrow, which has continuous daylight from May 10 to August 2 every year. Even when the sun finally does set, it's as if someone has dimmed the lights, not completely snuffed them out.

It can be difficult to sleep in this setting if you're used to pitch darkness at night. If so, bring a sleeping mask for camping, or ask for rooms with dark curtains when you book your lodging.

WINTER TRAVEL

SURPRISINGLY, WINTER TRAVEL IS ON THE RISE in Alaska, and those adventurous enough to take advantage of an Alaska vacation this time of year are in for a real treat. As stated earlier, most of the state is not unbearably cold in the winter. Sure, the temperatures in such places as Barrow and the North Slope can stay below 0°F for weeks as a time, but in the main cities and outlying communities, it is more manageable. The average high in Anchorage in January, for example, is 21°F; in Fairbanks, it's 2°F.

Perhaps, too, Alaska is gaining more attention for its assortment of wintertime activities. With the growing popularity of the Iditarod Trail

Sled Dog Race, a 1,000-mile dog-team race across Alaska, dog mushing is becoming more and more mainstream. Visitors from around the world pay thousands of dollars to follow world-class racers from checkpoint to checkpoint by plane. Others opt to take their own dogsledding trips, and plenty of reputable guides can teach them how.

In the Interior of Alaska, a celestial pastime is now gaining momentum. Visitors flock here in the winter to watch the mystical aurora borealis, or northern lights, dance across the sky. Entire travel packages center around such viewings, complete with guided viewing, hot-springs lodging, photography lessons, and the like. Admittedly, it's a one-of-a-kind undertaking.

Of course, Alaska is prime ski country, but it still lacks the overpopulation that many ski resorts elsewhere are encountering these days. The state boasts only one world-class ski resort, although fine skiing can be found at any number of regional spots. More importantly, it offers true adventure skiing, with heli-skiing options available throughout the state, and cross-country skiing just about anywhere you go. Alaska is still a place where the activity is affordable; skiing is simply a way of life for Alaskans. Slip on some skis and head to the local bike trails, which are groomed for skiing in the winter, and there you have it: the ideal winter getaway.

When you're traveling in the winter, there are a few basic things to remember. First of all, much of the state shuts down for the season, so don't expect to see and do all of the touristy things you may have read about. Second, dress for the weather. Bring heavy winter boots, a parka, and gloves, and always wear long underwear even when walking around town. It may not be the most stylish of attire, but at least you'll be able to enjoy yourself.

Also, if traveling in a vehicle, especially on remote roads, make sure to have your cold-weather clothing items with you. Better yet, bring a sleeping bag or extra blanket just in case you break down. In most cities and towns, this could be considered overkill, but on side roads during the winter, it could be hours before a car happens by.

The bright side of winter travel in Alaska is that it is much more affordable: plane tickets plummet to half their summer rates, and hotels often offer discounted rooms and meals. You may find service a bit better, too, as overworked summer employees have a little more breathing room and time to spend with their hotel and restaurant guests. You'll also be sharing the state with the locals, so you get a true sense of what it is like to live here.

SHOULDER SEASONS

SLIP IN AN ALASKA ADVENTURE during this time of year, usually right after Labor Day and just before Memorial Day, and you just may have the best of both worlds: lower prices and summerlike weather. As we've said, Alaska weather is unpredictable.

Springtime in Alaska, unlike in many states, tends to be the drier season, while fall is when the rain comes. It is not uncommon for late April to early May to be dry and unseasonably warm, making such activities as road cycling, birding, and hiking a real treat. Even better, the mosquitoes generally haven't hatched yet, giving you one less thing to worry about.

Fall, though it can be rainy, is a gorgeous time of year to visit. It is a short season, with only about three weeks of good fall foliage to enjoy. Still, if you hit fall during its peak, when the birch trees turn bright yellow and the alpine bushes go fiery red, there is nothing quite like it.

Hotels, restaurants, and outfitters have been working overtime during the busy summer season, and fall is a reprieve. Many are eager for the smaller crowds, the breaks between bookings, the chance to slow down and relax. It's the ideal time to shop for bargains, get in on more intimate, custom-planned tours, and enjoy end-of-season outings such as backpacking and canoeing, wildlife viewing, and biking.

SHOULD I TRAVEL INDEPENDENTLY *or* *with a* GROUP?

WITH OUTDOOR RECREATION THE FOCUS of the typical adventurous traveler's destinations, we recommend that you plan your trip accordingly: choose your desired activity or activities, and then narrow your visit to the best region or regions of the state for those activities. After you've made these decisions, you'll need to make another, equally important one: do you travel independently or go with a group?

This seemingly small detail can have a lasting effect on the quality of your adventure. Whether you're backpacking to an unnamed peak in the Brooks Range, rafting across a remote river, or cycling across Southeast Alaska, get the wrong guide or the wrong group dynamic, and any adventure can turn out disastrous. But what if you rely on your own limited knowledge of Alaska and things go wrong, too?

We have experienced both. While it can be risky, traveling with a group can add a pleasurable dimension to your adventure that you never thought possible. Having a guide along can offer peace of mind; he or she knows the land well and has presumably troubleshot potential problems many times before. While you will pay slightly more for a guided trip, consider the value of having someone else organize food, gear, and logistics while you just enjoy the flight—or drive or boat trip—north.

On the other hand, traveling alone is exciting, an accomplishment of which to be proud, especially in Alaska, where everything is so big and far away and unnamed. The frugal traveler can experience thrills at a lower cost, but he or she must be savvy and quite organized.

Take a few moments to consider the scenarios below. If you answer them truthfully, they should help you determine which route to go.

What Kind of Traveler Are You?

- How do you feel when returning from a party, nightclub, or social event in which you must mingle with many people?
  - A. Exhausted
  - B. Exhilarated
- Just how organized are you?
  - A. My checkbook is always balanced.
  - B. Where *is* my checkbook?
- In my daily life . . .
  - A. I have a routine that I follow every morning before going to work.
  - B. I hit the snooze button three times and shower when I have time.
- When spending money . . .
  - A. Every penny counts, and I cut coupons daily.
  - B. I spend a few extra dollars and worry about it later.
- When taking risks . . .
  - A. I think through a situation, eliminate the risk, then move forward.
  - B. I feel hesistant and second-guess my decisions.

OK, so this is not a complete psychological evaluation, but in general, if you answered mostly A's, the chances are you should go it alone. You will prefer the control you have over your day-to-day activities by planning your own trip, and you will be careful enough to do it wisely.

Someone who answered mostly B's may be more flexible, more extroverted, and more open to the idea of traveling with people they do not know.

SPECIAL-INTEREST TRIPS

IT WAS WHEN THE BEAR CAME WITHIN THREE FEET, sniffing at us and our packs before nonchalantly wandering away, that I realized just how life-changing that nine-day backpacking trip in Denali National Park and Preserve would be. No matter how many mountains we climbed or how many rivers we forded, the "bear story" was the defining moment of that trip, more than a decade ago. That pale pink tongue sticking out to catch our scent; the small, yellowish eyes that seemed to be straining to see us; the wide, clawed feet that clicked over the gravelly riverbank—they are details held still in our memories, never to be erased by time.

This is what happens when you tighten the lens that encompasses all of Alaska and bring it into focus on one objective: "I will raft that river"; "I will climb that mountain"; "I will see those glaciers." Of course, it would be nice if you could avoid a bear encounter; even though ours turned out to be disaster-free, that isn't always the case. But the point is, every single nook and cranny in Alaska is filled with such memorable moments if only you take the time to embrace them at their own pace.

Starting on page 56, we share a collection of our favorite outdoor activities in Alaska, and where to find them. Our destinations will allow you to sample your choice of exciting aspects of Alaska and take the time to sample them well. Look them over. Think about what appeals to you. Compare the time commitment required for, say, a remote wilderness-backpacking trip versus an easily accessible river-rafting jaunt. Each has its own level of appeal, depending upon your particular needs.

GATHERING INFORMATION

IF YOU'RE STILL TRYING TO FIGURE OUT where you want to go in Alaska, these resources may be of help. Some cater to the whole state, others to just a particular region. All of the accompanying Web sites are useful. Most of the cities and towns represented will send a complimentary visitors guide if you fill in a request online. Allow a few weeks for them to actually deliver, though. Additional postage may be required for overseas requests.

STATEWIDE

***Alaska* magazine** 301 Arctic Slope Avenue, Suite 300, Anchorage 99518; ☎ 907-272-6070; **www.alaskamagazine.com.** A good place to read about the most interesting places and people in Alaska and get a feel for regional communities.

Alaska Natural History Association 750 West Second Avenue, Suite 100, Anchorage 99501; ☎ 866-257-2757 or 907-274-8440; **www.alaskanha.org.** A good source for regional publications, guidebooks, and maps of Alaska's public lands.

Alaska Travel Industry Association 2600 Cordova Street, Suite 201, Anchorage 99503; **www.travelalaska.com.** This site has some great interactive maps to explore, and travel deals often are advertised.

Alaska Wilderness Recreation and Tourism Association 2207 Spenard Road, Suite 201, Anchorage 99503; ☎ 907-258-3171; **www.awrta.org.**

Anchorage Daily News 1001 Northway Drive, Anchorage 99514; ☎ 800-478-4200 or 907-257-4200; **www.adn.com.** The state's largest daily newspaper, with more statewide coverage than any other. One of the paper's online sites, **www.alaska.com,** serves as a visitor resource, but the main news site is worth reading, too.

Fairbanks Daily News–Miner 200 North Cushman Street, Fairbanks 99701; ☎ 907-459-7566 (to order) or 907-459-7572 (newsroom); **www.news-miner.com.** The Interior's daily newspaper of choice, with an emphasis on this region and points north.

Juneau Empire 3100 Channel Drive, Juneau 99801; ☎ 907-586-3740; **www.juneauempire.com.** This longtime newspaper in the state capital, with an emphasis on Southeast Alaska issues, publishes some entertaining local-government stories.

The Milepost 301 Arctic Slope Avenue, Suite 300, Anchorage 99518; ☎ 907-272-6070 ($27.95; to order, ☎ 800-726-4707 or **www.themilepost.com**). This phone-book-sized periodical is updated every year and, true to its name, gives a good milepost-by-milepost breakdown of all roads in Alaska, including the lesser-traveled ones. It also features mini-profiles of some Bush and off-the-road-system communities.

SOUTHCENTRAL INLAND ALASKA

Anchorage

ANCHORAGE CONVENTION AND VISITORS BUREAU 524 West Fourth Avenue, Anchorage 99501-2212; ☎ 800-478-1255 or 907-276-4118; **www.anchorage.net.** Look for the sod-roofed Log Cabin and Downtown Visitor Information Center at the corner of F Street and Fourth Avenue.

Copper Valley–Glennallen

GREATER COPPER VALLEY CHAMBER OF COMMERCE P.O. Box 469, Glennallen 99588; ☎ 907-822-5558; **www.traveltoalaska.com.**

Matanuska-Susitna Valley

MAT-SU CONVENTION AND VISITORS BUREAU 7744 East Visitors View Court, Palmer 99645; ☎ 907-746-5000; **www.alaskavisit.com.** The visitor center is at Mile 35.5 Parks Highway (take the Trunk Road exit).

Talkeetna

TALKEETNA CHAMBER OF COMMERCE P.O. Box 334, Talkeetna 99676; ☎ 907-733-2330; **www.talkeetnachamber.org.**

SOUTHCENTRAL COASTAL ALASKA

Anchor Point

ANCHOR POINT CHAMBER OF COMMERCE P.O. Box 610, Anchor Point 99556, ☎ 907-235-2600; **www.anchorpointchamber.org.**

Cordova

CORDOVA CHAMBER OF COMMERCE AND VISITORS CENTER P.O. Box 99, Cordova 99574; ☎ 907-424-7260; **www.cordovachamber.com.**

Homer

HOMER CHAMBER OF COMMERCE 201 Sterling Highway, Homer 99603; ☎ 907-235-7740; **www.homeralaska.org.**

Kenai

KENAI VISITORS AND CULTURAL CENTER 11471 Kenai Spur Highway, Kenai 99611; ☎ 907-283-1991; **www.visitkenai.com.**

Kenai Peninsula

KENAI PENINSULA TOURISM MARKETING COUNCIL 35477 Kenai Spur Highway, Suite 205, Soldotna 99669; ☎ 907-262-5229; **www.kenaipeninsula.org.**

Kodiak Island

KODIAK ISLAND CONVENTION AND VISITORS BUREAU 100 Marine Way, Suite 200, Kodiak 99615; ☎ 907-486-4782 or 800-789-4782; **www.kodiak.org.**

Seldovia

SELDOVIA CHAMBER OF COMMERCE P.O. Drawer F, Seldovia 99663; ☎ 907-234-7612; **www.xyz.net/~seldovia.**

Seward

SEWARD CHAMBER OF COMMERCE P.O. Box 749, Seward 99664; ☎ 907-224-8051; **www.seward.com.**

Soldotna

GREATER SOLDOTNA CHAMBER OF COMMERCE 44790 Sterling Highway, Soldotna 99669; ☎ 907-262-9814; **www.soldotnachamber.com.**

Valdez

VALDEZ CONVENTION AND VISITORS BUREAU 200 Chenega Street, Valdez 99686; ☎ 907-835-2984; **www.valdezalaska.org.**

Whittier

GREATER WHITTIER CHAMBER OF COMMERCE P.O. Box 607, Whittier 99693; no phone; **www.whittieralaskachamber.org.**

SOUTHEAST ALASKA

Haines

HAINES CONVENTION AND VISITORS BUREAU P.O. Box 530, Haines 99827; ☎ 907-766-2234 or 800-458-3579; **www.haines.ak.us.**

Juneau

JUNEAU CONVENTION AND VISITORS BUREAU 1 Sealaska Plaza, Suite 305, Juneau 99801; ☎ 907-586-1737 or 800-587-2201; **www.traveljuneau.com.**

Ketchikan

KETCHIKAN CONVENTION AND VISITORS BUREAU 131 Front Street, Ketchikan 99901; ☎ 907-225-6166 or 800-770-3300; **www.visit-ketchikan.com.**

Prince of Wales Island

PRINCE OF WALES CHAMBER OF COMMERCE P.O. Box 490, Klawock 99925-0490; ☎ 907-755-2626; **www.princeofwalescoc.org.**

Sitka

SITKA CONVENTION AND VISITORS BUREAU P.O. Box 1226, Sitka 99835; ☎ 907-747-5940; **www.sitka.org.**

Skagway

SKAGWAY CONVENTION AND VISITORS BUREAU P.O. Box 1029, Skagway 99840; ☎ 907-983-2854; **www.skagway.com.**

THE INTERIOR

Delta Junction and Points North

DELTA JUNCTION INFORMATION CENTER Where the two highways meet; ☎ 907-895-5068.

Denali Area

DENALI CHAMBER OF COMMERCE P.O. Box 437, Healy 99743; ☎ 907-683-4636; **www.denalichamber.com.**

Denali National Park

DENALI NATIONAL PARK P.O. Box 9, Denali Park 99755-0009; ☎ 907-683-2294; **www.nps.gov/dena.**

Fairbanks

FAIRBANKS CONVENTION AND VISITORS BUREAU 550 First Avenue, Fairbanks 99701; ☎ 800-327-5774; **www.explorefairbanks.com.**

Nenana

NENANA VISITOR CENTER A Street at the Parks Highway; ☎ 907-832-5435.

Tok

TOK "MAINSTREET ALASKA" VISITORS CENTER At the junction of the Alaska Highway and Tok Cutoff; ☎ 907-883-5775; **www.tokalaska info.com.**

THE BUSH

Barrow

Visitor information is not readily available, but these agencies could be of help:

CITY OF BARROW P.O. Box 629, Barrow 99723; ☎ 907-852-5211; **www.cityofbarrow.org.**

NORTH SLOPE BARROW PUBLIC INFORMATION DIVISION P.O. Box 69, Barrow 99723; ☎ 907-852-0215.

Bethel

BETHEL CHAMBER OF COMMERCE P.O. Box 329, Bethel 99559; ☎ 907-543-2911; **www.bethelakchamber.org.**

Dillingham

DILLINGHAM CHAMBER OF COMMERCE AND VISITOR CENTER P.O. Box 348, Dillingham 99576; ☎ 907-842-5115; **www.dillinghamak.com.**

King Salmon

KING SALMON VISITORS CENTER P.O. Box 298, King Salmon 99613; ☎ 907-246-4250.

Kotzebue

KOTZEBUE VISITOR INFORMATION CENTER 154 Second Street, Kotzebue 99752; ☎ 907-442-3890.

Nome

NOME CONVENTION AND VISITORS BUREAU P.O. Box 240 H-P, Nome 99762; ☎ 907-443-6624; **www.nomealaska.org.**

Unalaska–Dutch Harbor

UNALASKA/PORT OF DUTCH HARBOR CONVENTION AND VISITORS BUREAU P.O. Box 545, Unalaska 99685; ☎ 877-581-2612 or 907-581-2612; **www.unalaska.info.**

PART THREE

GETTING AROUND

COMING *into the* STATE

THE BOTTOM LINE ON TRAVEL TO ALASKA is that it will take some time. A typical flight from the East Coast to Alaska takes at least ten hours; from Europe it will be even longer. Those coming from another country must now fly through one of the cities in the lower 48 states because the polar route from Asia is no longer a routine flight.

The other methods of travel, by land or sea, take even longer but constitute a trip in themselves, which can be filled with adventure along the way. The **Alaska Marine Highway,** which connects 30 coastal communities in Alaska, accommodates travelers with or without their own vehicles. Or take a cruise to reach the great land. Either way will be memorable.

The third option is to drive to Alaska. The **Alaska Highway** is the main artery into the state, traveling some 1,400 miles from Yukon Territory, Canada, to Alaska. Popular modes of travel to Alaska include recreational vehicle, automobile, and bus.

BY AIR

Carriers

Regardless of your ultimate destination, you'll likely pass through **Ted Stevens Anchorage International Airport,** the state's largest hub of airline activity. With connections from all over the world and more than 280 flights arriving daily, the Anchorage airport—named after longtime U.S. Senator Ted Stevens—serves as the gateway to Alaska. The Anchorage airport is served by several major carriers to the rest of the United States and sometimes flights from Japan or Korea. It's also possible to fly into Fairbanks or Southeast Alaska. Most passengers come into Anchorage through Seattle, but for a bit more money you can fly nonstop to Anchorage from various major cities. There are many more flights in the summer than in the winter.

Alaska Airlines (☎ 800-426-0333; **www.alaskaair.com**) has more flights than all other airlines combined, with as many as 20 a day to Seattle in summer and summer nonstops to various other cities, including Washington, D.C.; Chicago; Dallas–Fort Worth; Los Angeles; Minneapolis–St. Paul; Portland; Vancouver, British Columbia; and La Paz, Mexico. Alaska Airlines is the only jet carrier with more than token coverage anywhere in Alaska other than Anchorage, and it has arrangements with commuter airlines that fan out from its network to the smaller communities. Other major airlines that serve Anchorage at this writing include **Northwest** (☎ 800-225-2525; **www.nwa.com**), **Continental** (☎ 800-525-0280; **www.continental.com**), **Delta** (☎ 800-221-1212; **www.delta.com**), and **United** (☎ 800-241-6522; **www.ual.com**). Overseas airlines include **Asiana Airlines** (☎ 800-227-4262; **us.flyasiana.com**), **China Airlines** (☎ 907-248-3603; **www.china-airlines.com**), **Japan Airlines** (☎ 800-525-3663; **www.jal.com**), and **Korean Airlines** (☎ 800-438-5000; **www.koreanair.com**), as well as **Air Canada** (☎ 888-247-2262; **www.aircanada.com**) in the summer only. *Note:* Flight lineups and airlines change too fast to keep track of here, so know that all of this is subject to change.

Fares

Flying in Alaska is simply a way of life: we do it so much it comes naturally, and we've become savvy bargain-finders as a result. Fares vary wildly, so watching for sales can pay off. It's almost always cheapest to change planes in Seattle due to the competition on the Seattle–Anchorage route, and it seems the more complicated you're willing to make your route, the less you'll pay. So finding a good ticket price is a balancing act between efficiency and maintaining your sanity. If you can find a round-trip ticket for $400 or so, consider yourself lucky. Occasionally, you can nab a $300 ticket, but those are fairly restricted flights and destinations. International travelers should expect to pay a higher premium for their tickets—overseas travel runs more in the $500 to $700 range when booked far in advance, although again the occasional bargain can be found. The airlines seem to watch each other closely, and when one offers a summer sale, often in April or early May, the others usually follow suit. If you get one of these tickets, count yourself lucky, because this seems to be happening less and less.

unofficial **TIP**
If you're willing to drop everything and go, sign up for **My Alaska Air,** an online newsletter that announces fare specials weekly, with tickets sometimes less than $100 from Seattle to Anchorage (go to **www.alaskaair.com** for details).

Getting to the Bush

To fly to Alaska's most remote roadless places, collectively known as the Bush, you'll have to jump on another plane, usually a small prop-driven aircraft that can hold just a few passengers. These planes have weight limits, so the pilots and crew will ask you how much you weigh. (This is not your driver's license—resist the urge to fudge the numbers, because an overloaded plane is neither a good nor a safe thing.) Small air-taxis like this are situated all over the state; Alaska has 10,675 registered aircraft, according to Federal Aviation Administration statistics. The state has 387 public land-based airports, 33 heliports, and about 640 recorded landing areas. **Lake Hood** in Anchorage is the world's largest and busiest seaplane base. It accommodates an average of 110 takeoffs and landings daily, and more than 600 on a peak summer day. In fact, Alaska has 121 seaplane bases, more than any other state in the country.

Depending upon your destination, the plane in which you fly will be equipped with floats for landing on water, skis for landing on snow or ice, or wheels for landing on remote runways. Bush planes and their pilots can take you to isolated fishing spots, wilderness lodges, cabins, or anywhere else you might want to go. Besides the registered and known landing sites, skilled Bush pilots are able to land on unnamed gravel bars and rivers or lakes all over the state, creating a truly unique experience. Some adventurers like to be dropped off at one remote location and hike, raft, or bike to another location for pickup. Others prefer to be dropped off for an entire season, along with a summer or winter's worth of gear. Whatever it is you have in mind, there likely is an Alaskan Bush pilot willing and able to help.

Be aware that the price for these Bush adventures can rival what you paid to reach Alaska on a jet (flying from Kodiak to Homer on most small planes, for example, will cost upward of $350 round-trip). A sometimes-less-expensive way to travel is by tagging along on the numerous mail planes that fly into some of the more remote villages on a twice- or three-times-a-week basis. While it will save money, these are trips of necessity, and you will be at the whim of the mailman-cum-pilot's schedule. Check with local carriers in towns such as Kodiak, Homer, Fairbanks, Nome, and Barrow to see what the options are.

AIR-TRAVEL TIPS

- Small planes can be loud. If you're sensitive to noise, be sure to have earplugs handy. Most small-plane operators are aware of this and will provide earplugs or headphones, but be prepared with your own 50-cent pair.
- Check ahead with airline operators both big and small for the rules regarding transport of potentially hazardous materials, such as fuel for cookstoves, lighters, bear spray, or any other combustibles.
- When traveling with a backpack as your primary gear, ask for or bring a large plastic bag to wrap it in. It's not uncommon for packs to get wet, especially in floatplanes, as they land. Also, many commercial airlines require a bag to prevent backpack straps from getting caught in baggage carousels. If landing in the Bush, you can remove your plastic bag and give it to the pilot to carry back so you don't have to lug it around the wilderness.

BY SEA

WHILE IT MAY TAKE A BIT LONGER to reach Alaska via the many cruises ships that sail north, it's definitely a pleasant way to reach the Last Frontier. There are several choices and just as many destinations.

Carriers

Start searching and you'll see an abundance of cruising options, especially in Southeast and Southcentral Coastal Alaska. But to arrive in Alaska from Canada or the lower 48 states, your choices are more limited. The most affordable option is the **Alaska Marine Highway System** (☎ 800-642-0066; **www.ferryalaska.com**), a government-funded transportation system that not only offers an enjoyable way to reach Alaska but also serves as a vital link among coastal communities throughout Alaska. The Alaska Marine Highway is the only water-based transportation system recognized as a National Scenic Byway, taking passengers through the Inside Passage of Southeast Alaska, across the Gulf of Alaska, into Prince William Sound in Southcentral Coastal Alaska, and out to the Aleutians in Bush Alaska. It also brings passengers from the ports of Prince Rupert, British Columbia, and Bellingham, Washington. Passengers can come as they are or reserve a spot for their vehicles or RVs. Other choices providing transport from out-of-state include **Carnival Cruise Lines** (☎ 888-227-6482; **www.carnival.com**), which debarks from Vancouver, British Columbia; **Holland America Line** (☎ 877-724-5425; **www.hollandamerica.com**), which also leaves from Vancouver; and **Princess Cruises** (☎ 800-774-6237; **www.princesscruises.com**), which offers one-way destinations that begin in Vancouver, British Columbia, or in Alaska and sail south.

Fares

While the Alaska Marine Highway is not vastly less expensive than private cruise companies, the real value lies in the fact that travelers can bring their own vehicles, thus saving money during the duration of their stay in Alaska. It's our favorite way to see Alaska because it allows us to travel at our own pace, with no schedules to follow, and the freedom to roam once we've reached our destination. Plus, it's a great way to meet real Alaskans, who depend on the Marine Highway much like Lower 48 folks depend on interstates. The one-way fare for one person traveling with a vehicle from Bellingham, Washington, to Skagway, Alaska, for example, is $1,200 without a private cabin (add at least another $350 for that privilege, as cabins are hard to come by). Add another $400 or so for recreational vehicles, and another $250 to $350 per person, and your round-trip rate could go as high as $1,900 for a two-person getaway complete with recreational vehicle. Compare that price to the average price per person of a private cruise—$2,500—and you have quite a bargain, albeit much less lavish. You can also check the cruise-line and ferry-system Web sites for occasional specials from varying ports. Some of the deals can be up to 50% off, depending on your willingness to drop everything and go.

Getting to the Bush

Logistically, it is close to impossible to reach some of Alaska's roadless areas via cruise ship. However, small cruise-boat operators offer personalized treks into unexplored areas of Alaska aboard 5- to 15-passenger yachts and boats and even small ships. These operators work at a premium: a cruise into the remotest parts of Alaska requires extremely careful planning and specialized equipment for navigating shallow waterways. **Cruise West** (☎ 888-851-8133; **www.cruisewest.com**), a small-ship cruise company, travels to such exotic places as the Bering Sea, and **Discovery Voyages** (☎ 800-324-7602; **www.discoveryvoyages.com**) offers personalized trips in Prince William Sound. Again, the Alaska Marine Highway System is best equipped to get you to such far-flung places as Dutch Harbor and Kodiak Island. Fares for wilderness cruises vary widely depending upon your planned activities and destination. Ten days of birding in Prince William Sound will run about $3,500 per person; the two-week trip to the Bering Sea ranges from $11,000 to $19,000 per person.

(For more information on cruising as an adventure in itself rather than a means to another destination, see Part Four.)

FERRY-TRAVEL TIPS

- If traveling on the Alaska Marine Highway with a car, keep in mind that the ferry has directional loads—the heavier the load, the slower the ferry travels. In general, loads are heavier going north until about mid-July; by August, loads are heavier going south. Plan your travel accordingly.
- Walk-on reservations are almost never needed. But if you want a private cabin or want to ensure a spot for your vehicle, you should definitely call ahead of time. Cabins are comfortable but small; beds are in a bunk arrangement. If you need two beds for sleeping but neither person in your party can climb to a top bunk, get a four-berth cabin with two bunks.
- Kayaks, bicycles, and other outdoor gear are allowed, but there is a fee. Call ahead for details. Pets may travel with you but must have current health certificates (within 30 days) in order to travel through Canada or into Alaska from another state. The cost for pets is $10 to $25, depending upon your port of departure. Pets must stay in carriers or in your vehicle.

BY RAIL

ALTHOUGH THERE ARE TWO RAILWAYS IN ALASKA, the aptly named **Alaska Railroad** and the **White Pass–Yukon Route,** they can't get you to the lower 48 states. The Alaska Railroad has hubs in Anchorage, Fairbanks, and Seward, and carries passengers from the Interior through

Southcentral Inland and Coastal areas. The White Pass–Yukon Route, for visitors to Skagway who want to briefly relive the life of the gold-rush era, travels only as far as Whitehorse, Yukon Territory, Canada.

Carriers

The closest you'll get to Alaska by mainstream railway is by taking **Amtrak** (☎ 800-872-7245; **www.amtrak.com**) from the West Coast to Bellingham, Washington, and connecting with the Alaska Marine Highway System, which is quite close to the railroad depot. From the East, reserve a seat with **Via Rail** (☎ 888-842-7245; **www.viarail.ca**) out of Canada. The transcontinental route starts in Toronto and has a connection in Jasper that will take you to Prince Rupert, British Columbia, another launching point for the Alaska Marine Highway System.

Fares

The four-day journey from Toronto to Prince Rupert on Via Rail costs approximately $1,600 Canadian for a round-trip ticket, plus two stopovers at which you must pay your own lodging. On Amtrak, it's even more complicated. For example, a round-trip ticket from Albuquerque, New Mexico, to Bellingham takes three days and requires two train changes, in Los Angeles and Seattle. That trip, with a small room, is $1,500, slightly less if you travel coach. Both railway Web sites above have special online deals, so be sure to check for those. There also are discounts for booking at least five days in advance.

BY LAND

ON THE AVERAGE MAP, the distance between Alaska and the rest of the United States really doesn't look that far. Washington state, for example, appears to be quite close. But don't be fooled: Alaska is so big, it's difficult to draw it to scale on most maps. The truth is, driving to Alaska, whether in a lumbering recreational vehicle or in the speediest of sports cars, will take time. Lots of time. The distance between Seattle and Anchorage is 2,435 miles; from Chicago, it's 3,818 miles. Compare that with the distance between Miami and Los Angeles—2,720 miles—and, well, you get the picture.

Driving Your Own Car

unofficial **TIP**
We suggest that you forget all preconceived notions of interstates and high-speed travel.

If you are planning a road trip to Alaska, it will be a grand journey. Many the outdoor adventurer prefers traveling this way; the flexibility of driving on your own allows you to stay at that great campground longer, explore that wilderness area you just discovered, pull off and enjoy a sunset or watch moose browse in a kettle lake as long as you please.

While many of Alaska's main highways are paved, they also are two- and sometimes four-lane throughways that cannot accommodate high speeds. On average, you'll be traveling from 45 to 55 miles per hour, sometimes faster, sometimes slower. Be on the lookout for moose, which can destroy a vehicle when struck even at slow speeds. Also be aware that because of Alaska's arctic climate, the roads develop persistent frost heaves, which feel like giant speed bumps if you hit them too fast. Road crews spend entire summers repairing these dips and divots, so don't be surprised if you encounter frequent road construction.

The main artery into Alaska is the 1,400-mile **Alaska Highway,** which is gorgeous in some spots, boring in others. Services such as gas are adequately spaced apart, but it's a good idea to carry an extra five-gallon container of gas just in case. Auto service is harder to come by, so be sure to bring along a working spare tire and basic travel necessities such as jumper cables, flares, and flashlights. Food is also available at small cafes and convenience stores along the way, but don't count on anything very good. In fact, we prefer to pack a large cooler and carry our own hard-to-get items—fresh greens, fruits, and other snacks—and splurge on overpriced bottles of water at these stores along the way. Oddly, there is the occasional Subway sandwich shop in the remotest of towns, offering a reprieve from the fried food found at most of the local diners.

A good resource while driving any of the roads into Alaska and the Yukon is ***The Milepost*** (Morris Communications; $27.95, **www.themilepost.com**), which has good maps and mile-by-mile logs of each road. It's strictly an informational book, with basic descriptions of what you'll see along the way. It is updated yearly, too, so it often includes anticipated construction projects to give you an idea of the day's driving ahead of you.

Renting a Vehicle

Of course, you can accomplish the same goal of reaching Alaska by renting a vehicle instead of putting wear and tear on your own. Be sure to check with the company from which you plan to rent to make sure crossing state lines and entering Canada is permitted.

If you reach Alaska by plane or ship and want to get around while here, you can also rent cars locally in just about any community. All the major national car-rental companies are represented in Anchorage and Fairbanks, and there are a few local dealers as well. Sometimes the latter are a bit more expensive, but they also allow driving on gravel roads, which you will soon see is quite common in Alaska. This is an important item to notice on your rental contract: many of Alaska's most scenic roads, such as the Denali Highway, are mostly gravel. If you plan to drive roads such as these, check the rental company's fine print before signing. Rates vary depending on the vehicle you want and the company you use, but on average, prices start at $45 a day. Renting a vehicle by the week also cuts the price. Or check **Travelocity** (**www.travelocity.com**) to get a comparison of prices. This site has begun to outperform other competitors such as **Priceline** (**www.priceline.com**), particularly when it comes to Alaska flights and rentals. Another source for good car-rental comparisons is **Orbitz** (**www.orbitz.com**), which will call up all available car rentals in a given location in an easy-to-read layout. Once you research the rate online, though, call the company to see if it will honor the rate, thus saving you a surcharge to Orbitz.

Word of warning: we once, out of necessity, rented a vehicle in Homer and drove it one-way to Anchorage. The distance: 226 miles. The rental period: 24 hours. The price: $170. Renting vehicles for one-way travel tends to be too expensive to make much sense. Instead, plan your road trip from Anchorage or Fairbanks or wherever you happen to fly or sail in from, and return the car to its home location. There are some fine mini–driving adventures that launch from these destinations covered in Part Five, Adventure Trips by Car (page 65).

CAR-RENTAL COMPANIES

There are more than a dozen rental options for the Anchorage area, but we have found **Budget** (☎ 800-527-0700; **www.budgetrentacar.com**), **Denali Car** (☎ 907-276-1230; **www.denalicarrentalak.com**), **Enterprise** (☎ 800-261-7331; **www.enterprise.com**), and **Hertz** (☎ 800-654-3131; **www.hertz.com**) among the best. In Fairbanks, try **Affordable New Car Rental** (☎ 907-452-7341), **Arctic Rent-A-Car** (☎ 907-479-8044; **www.arcticrentacar.com**), Budget, **Dollar Rent A Car** (☎ 800-800-4000 or 907-451-4360), or **Heindl's Car & Truck Leasing** (☎ 907-451-0004), which offers truck and van rentals and camper packages. In Juneau, **Evergreen Motors** (☎ 907-789-9300; **www.evergreenfordjuneau.com**), **Hertz** (☎ 907-789-9494; **www.hertz.com**), **National Car Rental** (☎ 800-CAR-RENT or 907-789-9814; **www.nationalcar.com**), and **Rent A Wreck** (☎ 800-535-1391 or 907-789-4111; **www.rentawreck.com**) can provide a good price comparison. If Skagway is your first stop, there's **Sourdough Car Rentals** (☎ 907-983-2523). If you're stopping in Haines first, try **Eagle's Nest Car Rentals** (☎ 907-766-2891; **www.alaskaeagletours.com**); if you're arriving by cruise ship in Ketchikan, there's **Southeast Auto Rental** (☎ 907-225-8778).

By RV

Whether you are in your own RV or a rental, you'll soon figure out why so many people travel this way: it just makes sense.

unofficial **TIP**
RV travel lets you see some of the harder-to-reach places in Alaska.

You can be as close to nature as possible yet still have the comfort of a dry bed if the weather should turn. You can change your itinerary at a moment's notice. For the outdoors traveler, an RV can be a good base of operations, a traveling home that can store your climbing gear, mountain bike, kayak, and everything else you need for your more off-the-beaten-path destinations.

The key, though, is figuring out if it makes financial sense. RVs rent for about $250 per day—about the same price as a room at one

RV-RENTAL TIPS

- Consider your goals before costs. Rent an RV for the additional experience it will give you, serving as a house on wheels and allowing for access to some far-off places. RV rental rates and the current price of gasoline combined can rival the cost of staying in hotels and eating out every night.
- If you're willing to travel last-minute during the shoulder seasons of spring and fall, RV companies sometimes look for drivers to deliver their vehicles to their home locations.
- Most RV rentals come with additional items such as bed linens, cooking utensils, and pots and pans, as well as unlimited mileage. Make sure these items are included before reserving your RV. Some rental companies still have cleaning charges, but as the companies compete for business, they have begun waiving that fee.
- If you're a nonsmoker, make sure you get a nonsmoking vehicle. Some companies claim their RVs are smoke-free but will not guarantee it. Ask ahead of time to avoid having to return your vehicle.

of the better hotels during the height of summer. Considering a budget of $5,000, a family of four could rent a spacious RV for two weeks (the rates drop with longer-term rentals), buy all their groceries and gas, and still have money left over for a few guided activities such as day cruises, rafting, biking, or kayaking. A mega-cruise-ship excursion for a family of four, however, would be in the $10,000 range. Staying at that fine hotel in the city, dining out every night, and renting a car for day trips would be about $7,000.

While active, outdoors-oriented families will most definitely benefit from the $250-per-day RV rental, we think it is overkill for solo travelers and couples. But there is another option. Finally, the travel industry has discovered that not all RV travelers want to sit in a generator-equipped campground every night grilling hot dogs. Some of us want to get *way* out there. A few companies, such as **ABC Motor Home Rentals** in Anchorage (☎ 800-421-7456; ☎907-279-2000; **www.abcmotorhome.com**), rent pickup trucks with camper shells to help adventurers reach even farther into the backcountry. The rates range from $190 per day for high-season travel to $90 per day for winter use.

Yet another option is to sample just a bit of Alaska by RV. **Alaska Travel Adventures** (☎ 800-323-5757; **www.alaskarv.com**), one of the state's longest-running outdoors tour companies, offers a package it calls the Alaska Highway Cruise. In these trips you take a one-way cruise to Alaska, then hop into a reserved RV for a drive along some of Alaska's more scenic routes. The trips range from $2,200 to $3,300 per person, from 11 to 22 days. It's a great way to experience the luxury of a cruise ship yet still have some private "real Alaska" time on the road. We jokingly refer to it as the "marriage-saver tour," as it is a great, and surprisingly affordable, compromise in all Alaska has to offer.

As with car rentals, one-way RV rentals are more expensive yet still available. **Cruise America** (☎ 800-671-8042 or 907-349-0499; **www.cruiseamerica.com**) offers one-way rentals between Anchorage and rental centers around the country.

unofficial **TIP**
The law in Alaska is that if five or more vehicles are trailing behind you, you must pull over.

RV ROAD ETIQUETTE Being behind the wheel of a 21-foot recreational vehicle, especially if you're used to sports cars or pickups, can be daunting at first. It is only natural, and safe, to want to slow down a bit. However, drive according to the speed limit.

Because Alaska is such a popular travel destination, the roads during the summer can become clogged with recreational vehicles and visitors who slow to a snail's pace to take in the mountains, oceans, and wildlife that seem to be around every bend. Not only can this be dangerous but it can also lead to short tempers. Locals use the roads to get to and from work and other destinations. Most of the scenic roads have overlooks spaced along the road for slower vehicles to pull into. It takes only a moment, and allows you all the time you need to shoot that great photo or take a break from driving.

RV-RENTAL COMPANIES IN ANCHORAGE ABC Motor Home and Car Rentals (☎ 800-421-7456 or 907-279-2000; **www.abcmotorhome.com**) has a range of RVs as well as a luxury van for large groups and camper rentals for smaller parties. No smoking or pets allowed.

Alaska Affordable Motor Home Rental (☎ 907-349-4878 or 360-624-6507; **www.alaska-rv-rental.com**) is much less expensive than its competitors, with rates at $165 per day with free, unlimited miles in Alaska. Vehicles are not as fancy but are quite functional. No smoking or pets allowed. **Alaska Best RV Rentals** (☎ 866-544-4981 or 907-344-4981; **www.alaskabestrvrentals.com**) offers rates of $155 to $185—lower than the large-company averages. No smoking or pets allowed.

WHERE *to* STAY

IN EACH OF OUR REGIONAL CHAPTERS, we go into more detail on the best camping and lodging opportunities for that particular area. In roadless areas such as the Bush, lodging opportunities can be scarce, but you'll still be able to find a place to sleep in most any town or village you come to. Charts within each chapter provide an alphabetical listing of the campgrounds, lodges, bed-and-breakfasts, and hotel accommodations, with rankings for quality, value, and price.

VISITING *the* PARKS *and* REFUGES

ONE OF THE THINGS YOU'LL NOTICE about Alaska is that the land seems to go on forever. It would seem easy to just step out into it and go for an adventure. The truth is, though, nearly three-quarters of Alaska is protected as public land through the passage of the Alaska National Interest Lands Conservation Act. Tribal corporations own another large chunk, the result of the passage of the Alaska Native Claims Settlement Act. Because these lands are protected, there are limitations on their use, and restrictions are set by the various owners. One of the most important planning aspects of your trip should be investigating the land-use regulations. Some agencies allow online reservations or phone reservations up to six months in advance. Others work on a first-come, first-served basis. Still others require you to show up in person to register or pay for access.

State Lands: Getting More Information

ALASKA STATE PARKS For information on all of Alaska's state parks, including the popular **Chugach State Park,** contact 550 West Seventh Avenue, Suite 1260, Anchorage 99501-3557; ☎ 907-269-8400; or 3700 Airport Way, Fairbanks 99709-4699; ☎ 907-451-2705. The Web site is **www.alaskastateparks.org.**

Federal Lands: Getting More Information

NATIONAL PARK SERVICE Four **Alaska Public Lands Information Centers** in the state have details on all 19 of Alaska's nationally managed areas (as well as state-park, refuge, and national-forest information). Access them online at **www.nps.gov/aplic/center,** or visit any of the following locations: **Anchorage** (605 West Fourth Avenue, Suite 105, Anchorage 99501; ☎ 907-271-2737); **Fairbanks** (250 Cushman Street, Suite 1A, Fairbanks 99701; ☎ 907-456-0527); **Ketchikan** (Southeast Alaska Discovery Center, 50 Main Street, Ketchikan 99901; ☎ 907-228-6234); or **Tok** (P.O. Box 359, Tok 99780; ☎ 907-883-5667).

NATIONAL REFUGES These vast public lands are managed by the U.S. Fish and Wildlife Service, which can be reached at 1011 East Tudor Road, Anchorage 99503; ☎ 907-786-3309; **www.r7.fws.gov.**

U.S. BUREAU OF LAND MANAGEMENT For Fairbanks-area information, which is regulated by the BLM, contact 1150 University Avenue, Fairbanks 99709; ☎ 907-474-2200; **www.blm.gov/ak/st/en.html.** The Alaska state offices are at 222 West Seventh Avenue, Suite 13, Anchorage 99513; ☎ 907-271-5960.

U.S. FOREST SERVICE There are two national forests in Alaska: **Tongass** and **Chugach.** Information on the Tongass can be accessed at the Tongass National Forest office, 648 Mission Street, Ketchikan,

99901; ☎ 907-225-3101; **www.fs.fed.us/r10/tongass.** Chugach National Forest information is available at 3301 C Street, Anchorage 99503; ☎ 907-743-9500; **www.fs.fed.us/r10/chugach.**

Native Lands: What You Should Know

There are 13 regional native corporations, all of which own certain lands throughout Alaska. Many of these corporations allow public use of their lands, but it is always prudent to check ahead of time if you know your trip will pass private property. Contact the **Alaska Native Heritage Center** (☎ 907-330-8000; **www.alaskanative.net**) in Anchorage to learn more about the area in which you plan to travel, or contact the corporations directly. Most of the following Web sites have maps that illustrate the land and region owned by a particular corporation.

- **AHTNA, Inc.:** Based in Glennallen (Southcentral Inland). ☎ 907-822-3476; **www.ahtna-inc.com.**
- **Aleut Corporation:** Based in Western Alaska and the Aleutians (Bush). ☎ 907-561-4300; **www.aleutcorp.com.**
- **Arctic Slope Regional Corporation:** Based in Barrow (Bush). ☎ 907-339-6000; **www.asrc.com.**
- **Bering Straits Native Corporation:** Based in Nome (Bush). ☎ 907-443-2985; **www.beringstraits.com.**
- **Bristol Bay Native Corporation:** Based in Bristol Bay (Bush). ☎ 907-278-3602; **www.bbnc.net.**
- **Calista Corporation:** Based in Southwest Alaska (Bush). ☎ 907-279-5516; **www.calistacorp.com.**
- **Chugach Alaska Corporation:** Based in Copper River Delta (Southcentral Coastal, Southcentral Inland). ☎ 907-563-8866; **www.chugach-ak.com.**
- **Cook Inlet Region, Inc.:** Based in Southcentral Inland and Coastal Alaska. ☎ 907-274-8638; **www.ciri.com.**
- **Doyon, Ltd.:** Based in Yukon Interior region. ☎ 888-478-4755 or 907-459-2000; **www.doyon.com.**
- **Koniag, Inc.:** Based in Kodiak (Southcentral Coastal). ☎ 800-658-3818 or 907-486-2530; **www.koniag.com.**
- **NANA Regional Corporation:** Based in Kotzebue (Bush). ☎ 907-442-3301; **www.nana.com.**
- **Sealaska Corporation:** Based in Southeast Alaska (Southeast). ☎ 907-586-1512; **www.sealaska.com.**
- **Thirteenth Regional Corporation:** Based in Seattle, this corporation represents out-of-state Alaskans. You'll likely not need to contact them, but here's the information just in case: ☎ 206-575-6229; **www.the13thregion.com.**

PART FOUR

ADVENTURE CRUISING

THINK OF CRUISING, AND YOU MIGHT IMAGINE one of those behemoths lumbering across the ocean carrying thousands of people in crate-sized "staterooms." You might also think of all-night gambling, Vegas-style entertainment, and dinner buffets that are nothing short of an over-the-top smorgasbord.

If you're an independent outdoor traveler, this might not sound like much fun.

The truth is, cruising on giant luxury ships such as those run by Holland America, Princess Cruises, and Carnival Cruise Lines is not what it used to be. Sure, you can have the glitz and glamour of those fancy packages, but you can also enjoy your own mini-adventures, leaving the ships at their ports of call and embarking on land adventures that range from four-wheeling across an old logging road to dog mushing on a glacier. The larger cruise-ship companies are realizing that today's travelers are more active, more adventurous, and more willing to create their own entertainment.

This chapter strives to introduce you to a different type of cruising, though. Sure, those large cruise ships can sometimes seem a bargain, and there is plenty onboard to keep you busy. But we think the true adventure traveler is looking for something a bit more "out there."

The trips listed in this chapter run the gamut. The vessels are small and their destinations sometimes quite remote. You don't need to pack a tux or an evening gown, but don't forget your hiking boots. This is a different mode of cruising, a true outdoor traveler's vacation. We call it adventure cruising.

The two most popular places to find an adventure cruise are the coastal waters of **Prince William Sound** in Southcentral Coastal Alaska and the island-studded waters of the **Southeast Panhandle.** Southeast Alaska is one of the best places to watch whales breech and glaciers calve; however, its popularity draws the larger ships, too. Prince William Sound also gets big-cruise-ship traffic, but not as much. The city of **Seward,** at the tip of the Kenai Peninsula in Southcentral Coastal Alaska, is also a hot spot for cruisers.

ADVENTURE-CRUISING TIPS *and* RESOURCES

Ten Tips for a Great Cruise

To get the most for your money, consider the following advice:

1. **Go off the beaten path.** Don't make this an ordinary trip; instead, do something new and adventurous. It is, after all, an adventure, so make it a memorable one.
2. **Check out the crew,** the boat, and the company's credentials and testimonials. Make sure you know what you're getting and that you'll get what you pay for.
3. **Look for Web specials** throughout the year. Also ask about specials and current discounts when you call to make reservations. There may be unlisted deals, and it never hurts to ask.
4. **Consider traveling during shoulder seasons,** when tickets can be bought at reduced rates. You may also get unique opportunities to see and do things not offered during peak seasons.
5. **Look for specialized tours** or companies that will build a tour to fit your travel needs and desires.
6. **Shop judiciously.** Cruise-ship shops have you as their captive audience. Resist buying from them. If you must shop, wait until the last day to buy, when items usually go on sale.
7. **Make it a family trip.** You may get a group discount, and your adventure will be more memorable if you share it with your friends and family.
8. **Find out exactly what is** and what isn't included in the cost of the cruise. Add-ons can multiply rapidly.
9. **Book early in the season.** Smaller ships have very limited space and are often booked a year or more in advance. You might also get early-booking discounts.
10. **Find out ahead of time** if your ship's room has outlets for plugging in electrical items such as hair dryers, irons, computers, etc. Many staterooms have only one outlet, so if having access to several electrical items at once will be an issue, bring your own power strip.

Add-on trips

While some of the land-based tour companies in Alaska team up with the larger cruise ships to offer special add-on trips not available to other travelers, be aware that you'll pay a premium for these trips. Most are offered at a discounted group rate to the cruise companies, but the savings aren't always passed on to the traveler.

unofficial **TIP**
On the smaller ships and yachts that offer a custom experience, add-ons are not usually offered, and they're not usually necessary, as your hosts will often cater to your group's desires.

WHAT TO BRING

ONE OF THE JOYS OF CRUISING is that while you are undoubtedly venturing into Alaska's wilderness, you can still go inside your heated cabin if its gets too cold. On adventure cruises, though, you should be prepared for whatever activities are included in the trip. Some companies will provide cold-weather gear or other equipment necessary for the trip, but most do not. Check with the cruise company, asking what they provide and what you'll need to bring for each activity. For example, on some cruises, you may need to bring a sleeping bag for overnight camping trips onshore.

Also remember that you may be out at sea for a few days or even a couple of weeks. These are wilderness adventures, and there are no stores, so be prepared with everything you'll need for the break from civilization.

Most of these ships are smaller than the luxury liners, too, so you'll probably need to pack lighter than you normally would.

The following items are essentials:

- All necessary prescriptions
- Binoculars
- Brimmed hat
- Camera with extra batteries and film or digital storage cards for filming and photography
- Good tennis shoes for walking or lightweight hiking boots
- Insect repellent
- A journal and a pen to document your experiences
- Layered clothing
- Polarized sunglasses (polarized lenses are better for seeing into water)
- Sunscreen
- Waterproof, windproof rain gear
- Lightweight winter hat and gloves (yes, even in the summer)

RESOURCES

FOR THE BEST IN-DEPTH INFORMATION about travel and activities, visit or call the local visitors bureaus and chambers of commerce for the closest communities at which you will be stopping. Here's a sampling.

STATEWIDE Anchorage Convention and Visitors Bureau, 524 West Fourth Avenue, Anchorage 99501-2212; ☎ 800-478-1255 or 907-276-4118; **www.anchorage.net.**

SOUTHCENTRAL COASTAL ALASKA Greater Whittier Chamber of Commerce, P.O. Box 607, Whittier 99693; **www.whittieralaska chamber.org; Kodiak Island Convention and Visitors Bureau,** 100 Marine Way, Suite 200, Kodiak 99615; ☎ 800-789-4782 or 907-486-4782; **www.kodiak.org; Seward Chamber of Commerce,** P.O. Box 749, Seward 99664; ☎ 907-224-8051; **www.seward.com.**

SOUTHEAST ALASKA Juneau Convention and Visitors Bureau, 1 Sealaska Plaza, Suite 305, Juneau 99801-1245; ☎ 907-586-1737 or 800-587-2201; **www.traveljuneau.com; Ketchikan Convention and Visitors Bureau,** 131 Front Street, Ketchikan 99901; ☎ 907-225-6166 or 800-770-3300; **www.visit-ketchikan.com; Sitka Convention and Visitors Bureau,** P.O. Box 1226, Sitka 99835; ☎ 907-747-5940; **www.sitka.org; Skagway Convention and Visitors Bureau,** P.O. Box 1029, Skagway 99840; ☎ 907-983-2854; **www.skagway.com.**

Web Sites

Several useful sites can offer insight on cruising in Alaska, whether you decide to travel with a large cruise ship or select a smaller, adventure-based excursion.

- **www.adn.com:** This Web site is the *Anchorage Daily News*'s daily online edition. Three-month subscriptions are an option for those who want to bone up on local happenings before visiting their area of choice.
- **www.alaska.com:** Hosted by the state's largest newspaper, the *Anchorage Daily News,* this site offers travel tips, special booking savings, and other links of interest for potential visitors to the state.
- **www.alaskamagazine.com:** Like its print counterpart, the Web site of *Alaska* magazine covers life on the Last Frontier through travel features, personality profiles, community issues, and other bits and pieces of interest to both local and outside readers.
- **www.alaskatia.org:** The Alaska Travel Industry Association's Web site lists member groups that offer cruising options throughout the state. The organization's visitor-targeted site, **www.travelalaska.com,** offers maps, resources, and stories about traveling in Alaska, either on a cruise or on your own.
- **www.cruisecritic.com:** This cool site allows you to get the down and dirty on cruise ships. Which ones really are the best? Let those who have been cruising themselves tell you. CruiseCritic.com also can help you find cruises that cater to specific demographics, such as senior trips, family-oriented trips, or trips for gays and lesbians. The Independent Traveler sponsors the site.
- **www.cruise411.com:** Here you'll find unbiased reviews on ships and cruises across the world, including Alaska. The site also offers Web

specials and last-minute travel specials for those ready to toss a few items in a bag and go.

- **www.juneauempire.com:** For those traveling to Southeast Alaska, the *Juneau Empire* is the newspaper of choice. Online subscriptions are available.
- **www.themilepost.com:** This periodical is one of the most accurate Alaska travel resources because it is updated annually, unlike many guidebooks that are updated only every two to three years. *The Milepost* covers the road systems of Alaska in mile-by-mile increments and contains special features on such off-the-road communities as Cordova, Nome, and Unalaska.
- **www.weather.com:** This Web site will give you an idea of what sort of weather to expect in the communities through which you will be traveling. However, we can give you a general idea: rain. It rains often in the coastal areas, so come prepared for that. When you get the occasional sunny day—and you will—it makes your trip even more glorious.

Booking Companies

- **Alaska Cruises:** ☎ 800-201-6937; **www.alaskacruises.com.** The site alone is worth checking out—it's a visitors' brochure packed with information on all the things to do and see in Alaska. Another good thing about this site is that the selection of cruises is larger than that of other booking companies.
- **Alaska Visitors Center–Alaska Statewide Marketing:** ☎ 888-655-4020 (reservations) or 907-929-2822 (other questions); **www.alaskavisitorscenter.com.** This independent company books trips and lodging and rentals for more than 150 businesses and outfitters throughout the state. A good resource for finding out more about local attractions in any given town or city you plan to visit.
- **All Alaska Tours:** ☎ 907-277-3000; **www.alaskatours.com.** Based in Anchorage, this company offers a handful of cruises, with early-booking discounts.

Books and Magazines

- ***Arthur Frommer's Budget Travel:*** $4.50 on newsstands, $12 for ten issues if you subscribe online; **www.budgettravelonline.com.** This magazine offers affordable ideas for getting the most out of your trip.
- ***Frommer's Alaska Cruises and Ports of Call 2007:*** $18.99 at **www.frommers.com** and other retailers. Thorough, timely, and objective. The 2006 guide gives the real details on the actual boats that are featured on various cruises, as well as what to expect in the way of on-board entertainment. Readers appreciate its honest evaluations.
- ***The Milepost:*** $27.95 at **www.themilepost.com.** A mile-by-mile guide to Alaska and western Canada; publishes up-to-date information on cruise-ship travel to and in Alaska.
- ***The Unofficial Guide to Cruises, Tenth Edition:*** $22.99 at

www.frommers.com and other retailers. Has an excellent planning section for cruises both large and small.

ADVENTURE-CRUISE OUTFITTERS

- **Alaska Passages Adventure Cruises:** Petersburg; ☎ 888-434-3766; **www.alaskapassages.com.** Alaska Passages provides the ideal trip for small groups of six or fewer cruisers. The intimate and family-oriented atmosphere aboard the M/V *Heron* makes for a unique experience, and the adventures and activities are customized for you and your companions. This private charter yacht offers sea kayaking, glacier cruises, wildlife viewing, fishing, hiking, whale-watching, and more. Hosts Scott and Julie Hursey are Alaska naturalists, ex–commercial fishermen, and longtime residents of Petersburg. Tours range from five to ten days, and rates are $2,895 to $4,750 per person.
- **American Safari Cruises:** Lynnwood, Washington–Inside Passage; ☎ 888-862-8881 or 206-284-0300; **www.amsafari.com.** Luxury and hospitality are the themes of these yacht-based adventures, as guests are greeted at the dock with Champagne, hors d'oeuvres, and warm smiles. Alaska tours range from four to eight days and start at around $4,400 per person; activities include kayaking, heli-hiking, air tours, and exploration. The truly rich and famous can even rent the entire yacht for a mere $189,995 and entertain up to 38 other guests. Uniquely northern-inspired gourmet meals and comfortable staterooms round out the experience. American Safari also focuses on education, as the company's expedition leaders offer lectures and tour narratives for each location.
- **Anadyr Adventures:** Valdez; ☎ 800-TO-KAYAK or 907-835-2814; **www.anadyradventures.com.** Anadyr offers two- to five-day trips around Prince William Sound out of Valdez from its yacht-based vessel. Kayak or hike by day, and sleep in comfort each night. Trips cost $1,080 per person for the two-day adventure or $3,600 for six days and include gourmet meals and a casual atmosphere amid the spectacular scenery and wildlife of the sound. Adventures center around sea kayaking; however, hiking, berry picking, wildlife viewing, beachcombing, fishing, and glacier exploration also fill your days on these excursions.
- **The Boat Company:** Poulsbo, Washington–Inside Passage; ☎ 360-697-4242; **www.theboatcompany.com.** This outfitter takes visitors on eight-day journeys up the Inside Passage, doing it in style aboard the 157-foot M/V *Mist Cove* and the 145-foot M/V *Liseron.* The ships offer spacious and luxurious accommodations; Alaska naturalists and a crew of 10 to 12 take care of your every need. Fishing, hiking, birding, nature walks, naturalist tours, kayaking, wildlife viewing, beachcombing, and a variety of other leisure activities are led by experienced Alaska guides. Unique to

Adventure-cruise Outfitters at a Glance

Alaska Passages Adventure Cruises
☎ 888-434-3766
www.alaskapassages.com

REGIONAL LOCATION	SOUTHEAST
COST	$$
SUITABLE FOR KIDS?	YES
ACTIVITY LEVEL	MODERATE
TRIP LENGTH	5–10 DAYS

American Safari Cruises
☎ 888-862-8881 or 206-284-0300
www.amsafari.com

REGIONAL LOCATION	SOUTHEAST
COST	$$$
SUITABLE FOR KIDS?	YES
ACTIVITY LEVEL	LIGHT
TRIP LENGTH	4–8 DAYS

Anadyr Adventures
☎ 800-TO-KAYAK or 907-835-2814
www.anadyradventures.com

REGIONAL LOCATION	SOUTHCENTRAL COASTAL
COST	$$$
SUITABLE FOR KIDS?	OLDER KIDS
ACTIVITY LEVEL	MODERATE
TRIP LENGTH	2–5+ DAYS

The Boat Company
☎ 360-697-4242
www.theboatcompany.com

REGIONAL LOCATION	SOUTHEAST
COST	$$$$
SUITABLE FOR KIDS?	NO
ACTIVITY LEVEL	LIGHT
TRIP LENGTH	8 DAYS

Discovery Voyages
☎ 800-324-7602
www.discoveryvoyages.com

REGIONAL LOCATION	SOUTHCENTRAL COASTAL
COST	$$$
SUITABLE FOR KIDS?	YES
ACTIVITY LEVEL	LIGHT
TRIP LENGTH	4–6 DAYS

Pangaea Adventures
☎ 800-660-9637 or 907-835-8442
www.alaskasummer.com

REGIONAL LOCATION	SOUTHCENTRAL COASTAL
COST	$$
SUITABLE FOR KIDS?	OLDER KIDS
ACTIVITY LEVEL	HIGH
TRIP LENGTH	4–8 DAYS

Sea Wolf Adventures
☎ 907-957-1438
www.seawolf-adventures.com

REGIONAL LOCATION	SOUTHEAST
COST	$$$
SUITABLE FOR KIDS?	OLDER KIDS
ACTIVITY LEVEL	MODERATE
TRIP LENGTH	6 DAYS

Sikumi Custom Alaska Cruises
☎ 425-806-2083
www.sikumi.com

REGIONAL LOCATION	SOUTHEAST
COST	$$$$
SUITABLE FOR KIDS?	NO
ACTIVITY LEVEL	LIGHT
TRIP LENGTH	4–8 DAYS

Walrus Islands Expeditions
☎ 907-235-9349
www.alaskawalrusisland.com

REGIONAL LOCATION	THE BUSH
COST	$
SUITABLE FOR KIDS?	NO
ACTIVITY LEVEL	HIGH
TRIP LENGTH	3 DAYS

The World Outdoors
☎ 800-488-8483 or 303-413-0938
www.theworldoutdoors.com

REGIONAL LOCATION	SOUTHEAST
COST	$$$
SUITABLE FOR KIDS?	YES
ACTIVITY LEVEL	MODERATE
TRIP LENGTH	7 DAYS

this company are its early-morning kayaking, hiking, and fishing trips, which allow guests to greet the beauty and tranquility of an Alaska sunrise. Prices range from $4,995 to $6,395, double occupancy.

- **Discovery Voyages:** Whittier; ☎ 800-324-7602; **www.discoveryvoyages.com.** Offers a great selection of tours that range from 7 to 13 days. Itineraries vary, and activities change with the seasons, encompassing seasonal wildlife viewing, photography, kayaking, hiking, birding, and even a sea-life-centered natural-history tour. The spring birding tour, guided by a local naturalist, is one of the company's finest. You won't go hungry on these adventures either, with their emphasis on fresh Alaska seafood and delicious desserts. Custom tours are also available, with prices starting at $3,750 per person.

- **Pangaea Adventures:** Valdez; ☎ 800-660-9637 or 907-835-8442; **www.alaskasummer.com.** Pangaea offers unique adventures aboard a four-person sailboat or a powerboat. These relaxing trips are like no others in the area, as guests explore Prince William Sound at their own pace, stopping to hike, comb the beaches, kayak, and enjoy the wildlife, glaciers, and world-famous scenery of the area. With your crew of three, you will also be very well taken care of and very well fed. The vessels range from the near-luxurious M/V *Raven* to the more functional *Tempest,* a working boat that is ideal for hardened adventurers who just want a dry, comfortable place to sleep after a day's outing. Pangaea Adventures are entirely customized—dates, activities, and all—to your party's desires. Trips range from four to eight days and start at $487 per person per day.
- **Sea Wolf Adventures:** Elfin Cove; ☎ 907-957-1438; **www.seawolfadventures.com.** This company provides accessible adventures for people of all ages, interests, and abilities aboard the M/V *Sea Wolf.* With several guides on board to cater to your every whim, and with a chef who also leads the kayak excursions, your six-day adventure is sure to be memorable. At around $3,180 per person for all activities, rooms, and meals, it's also a pretty good bargain. This is a good choice for those adventurers confined to wheelchairs—one of the vessel's staff is a paraplegic adventurer and has tested its comforts himself.
- **Sikumi Custom Alaska Cruises:** Girdwood–Prince William Sound, Inside Passage; ☎ 425-806-2083; **www.sikumi.com.** This is truly an intimate luxury cruise aboard the 67-foot M/V *Sikumi,* which sleeps 12 and includes private staterooms (each with its own bathroom, which is a plus), spacious decks, and a richly appointed salon and dining room. If you can pull yourself away from the relaxing atmosphere of the boat, the company's guides offer a multitude of only-in-Alaska adventures throughout the Inside Passage and Prince William Sound. Kayaking, hiking, beachcombing, birding, and fishing are just a few of the activities offered. One trip even features a soak in a natural hot spring. Sikumi's cruises range from four to eight days and cost about $4,750 per person, double occupancy. Book early, as cruise dates sell out quickly. Deals often are available for May and June cruises.
- **Walrus Islands Expeditions:** Homer–Togiak–Round Island; ☎ 907-235-9349; **www.alaskawalrusisland.com.** It doesn't get much more adventurous than a small inflatable boat on the Bering Sea and getting up close and personal with a sea of 2,000-pound walruses. And that's just what Walrus Islands Expeditions provides—via a 40-foot enclosed motorboat, that is. This company offers three-day cruises to Round

Island, one of the most rugged, wildlife-rich areas in the country, with exploration by day, and meals and sleeping (in snug but comfortable quarters) on board the boat. In addition to observing the walruses and cruising through this vast wild land, tundra hiking, beachcombing, birding, and other wildlife viewing on Round and other islands are on the itinerary. Trip cost is $1,495 per person.

- **The World Outdoors:** Boulder, Colorado–Inside Passage; ☎ 800-488-8483 or 303-413-0938; **www.theworldoutdoors.com.** Hiking, sea kayaking, and zodiac excursions are the highlights of these adventure cruises through the Last Frontier. This company explores the vast wilderness of the Inside Passage, which includes forays off-board to hike, pick berries, go beachcombing, kayaking, or tide-pooling. Rates start at $4,990. The ship holds up to 62 guests, larger than some of the previous options, but also includes a library and lecture/slide-show room for the naturalist in all of us.

PART FIVE

ADVENTURE TRIPS *by* CAR

SEEING WHAT ALASKA HAS TO OFFER from behind the wheel of an automobile is an unforgettable experience. It's a huge state, so driving offers a chance to see more in less time, and in relative comfort. If you have several trips in mind, driving makes perfect sense because surprisingly, much of remote Alaska is accessible by car. And while you will save time, it doesn't mean you'll be cruising along at a steady 65 miles per hour. On the contrary, Alaska's roads, like the state itself, are rustic and require thoughtful, planned travel. Some roads are little more than gravel paths over mountain passes. A few are wide four-lane affairs with lots of amenities along the way. And most are something in between, well tended but modest, with a few restaurants, roadhouses, or gas stations that make for convenient rest stops.

ALASKA'S ROAD SYSTEM

MOST OF THE STATE'S ROAD SYSTEM lies within the Interior and Southcentral regions of the state, connecting with the Alaska Highway through Canada. Southeast Alaska also has an extensive system of highways and logging roads, but most do not connect with one another, and only two highways—the **Haines and South Klondike highways**—connect with the mainland highway system in Canada.

The main highway system within Alaska includes 200 miles of the **Alaska Highway** between the Canadian border and Delta Junction; the **Parks Highway,** connecting Anchorage and Fairbanks; the **Steese Highway,** from Fairbanks to Circle; the **Elliott Highway,** from Fox to Manley Hot Springs; the **Taylor Highway** to Eagle; the **Glenn Highway–Tok Cutoff,** between Tok and Anchorage; the **Denali Highway,** between Paxson and Cantwell; the **Richardson Highway,** from Valdez to Fairbanks; the **Edgerton Highway–McCarthy Road** to Chitina and the McCarthy-Kennicott area; the **Seward Highway,** from Anchorage to Seward on the Kenai Peninsula; the **Sterling Highway,** which connects the Seward Highway with Homer;

Alaska Road Trips at a Glance

Anchorage–Valdez Loop

REGIONAL LOCATION	SOUTHCENTRAL COASTAL/INLAND
DISTANCE	367 MILES
TRAFFIC	MODERATE
DIFFICULTY	🫎🫎
TRIP LENGTH	3–5 DAYS
SUITABLE FOR KIDS?	YES
GUIDE SUGGESTED?	NO

Dalton Highway

REGIONAL LOCATION	THE BUSH/ THE INTERIOR
DISTANCE	414–498 MILES
TRAFFIC	LIGHT/MODERATE
DIFFICULTY	🫎🫎🫎🫎
TRIP LENGTH	2–6 DAYS
SUITABLE FOR KIDS?	YES
GUIDE SUGGESTED?	NO

Denali Highway

REGIONAL LOCATION	THE INTERIOR
DISTANCE	134 MILES
TRAFFIC	LIGHT
DIFFICULTY	🫎🫎🫎
TRIP LENGTH	1–4 DAYS
SUITABLE FOR KIDS?	YES
GUIDE SUGGESTED?	NO

Haines and Skagway

REGIONAL LOCATION	SOUTHEAST
DISTANCE	355 MILES
TRAFFIC	LIGHT/MODERATE
DIFFICULTY	🫎🫎
TRIP LENGTH	3–5 DAYS
SUITABLE FOR KIDS?	YES
GUIDE SUGGESTED?	NO

Kodiak Island

REGIONAL LOCATION	SOUTHCENTRAL COASTAL
DISTANCE	100 MILES
TRAFFIC	LIGHT
DIFFICULTY	🫎🫎
TRIP LENGTH	2 DAYS
SUITABLE FOR KIDS?	YES
GUIDE SUGGESTED?	NO

unofficial **TIP**
Gas prices vary widely between communities but tend to be less expensive the closer you are to Fairbanks and Anchorage. Don't be surprised to pay $5 a gallon in very remote areas; in cities, the average is about $3.05.

and the **Dalton Highway** to Deadhorse–Prudhoe Bay on the Arctic coast. Not connected to the main highway system is the **Copper River Highway** from Cordova.

THE ALASKA HIGHWAY

THIS IS THE MAIN CONNECTION BETWEEN the lower 48 states and the Last Frontier. Most of the road's 1,390 miles are actually in Canada, beginning in Dawson Creek, British Columbia, and ending in Delta Junction, Alaska.

Gas, food, and lodging can be found along the highway every 20 to 50 miles or so, but in at least one section the distance between services is 100 miles. There are nearly 100 private campgrounds, which tend to have more amenities but also cost more than the approximately 30 government-run campgrounds, which are rustic, without RV hookups. If you're traveling in the summer, it's a good idea to have reservations. In winter the road will be mostly deserted, and many of the campgrounds shut down, too, so make sure to check availability ahead of time.

unofficial **TIP**
The shoulder seasons are the best time for the spur-of-the-moment traveler because reservations are rarely needed, and you can adjust your travel plans at whim.

The Alaska Highway, or "Alcan" as it is more commonly known, celebrated its 60th anniversary in 2002. It has come a long way from the dirt path it once was. Today the road is paved, but it's not uncommon for improvement projects to slow you down. Take the time to look for wildlife, including bears, moose, caribou, and even the occasional wolf if you're really lucky.

As on any Alaska road trip, you should carry plenty of extra food, repair equipment (including a spare tire or two), and some way to keep comfortable if you end up stranded or sleeping in your vehicle. It is rare, but it can happen, and even though you're on the road system, wilderness is all around.

THE DALTON HIGHWAY

THIS IS THE ROAD TO TAKE if you simply want to drive as far north as possible. From its starting point at the Elliott Highway, about 85 miles north of Fairbanks, it continues for more than 400 miles until it nearly reaches the shores of the Arctic Ocean in Deadhorse. The town isn't much to write home about as far as visitor amenities go: there are only a couple of hotels, a store, and a gas station, and the majority of people you'll see live there only a few weeks at a time for their jobs in the oil fields. But the community is a superlative of sorts—as far north as you can go on Alaska's primary road system. And it is worth exploring, especially if your goal is to dip your toes into the Arctic Ocean.

The Dalton is perhaps one of the roughest roads in Alaska, and although it was constructed in the mid-1970s to haul freight to and from the oil fields, it offers relatively little in the way of modern conveniences. The washboards are many, the grades can be steep (as much as 10% or 12% in some places), and the trucks delivering products to and from Prudhoe Bay can be dangerous and numerous. In fact, it is still known locally as the "Haul Road."

Be prepared for this road trip. Carry two spare tires, a jack, a tool kit, emergency flares, extra gasoline, oil, wiper fluid, and a first-aid kit. Also bring drinking water, plenty of ready-to-eat-food, and all of your camping gear. A CB radio isn't a bad idea, either (monitor channel 19).

unofficial **TIP**
Travel services are limited—north of Coldfoot is the longest service-free stretch of highway in North America: 244 miles.

The drive is worth the effort, though. Consider the scenery, which includes views of the mighty **Yukon River,** the **Arctic Circle** (just past Mile 115), **Atigun Pass** (at the crest of the Continental Divide), the caribou of the **North Slope** plains, 375-million-year-old limestone-filled **Sukakpak Mountain** (elevation 4,459 feet at Mile 203.5), and any number of sweeping mountain vistas opening into the **Brooks Range, Gates of the Arctic National Park,** or **Arctic National Wildlife Refuge.**

THE RICHARDSON HIGHWAY

THE 366-MILE RICHARDSON runs from Valdez to Fairbanks and can be an incredibly scenic road trip for those willing to take it slow. The **Chugach Mountains** and the **Alaska Range** will keep you company along the way, as well as parts of the **Trans-Alaska Pipeline System,** for those interested in Alaska's more commercial side.

The Richardson is Alaska's oldest road, having begun as a sled-dog trail in 1898 from Valdez to Eagle. By 1902 it led to Fairbanks, and in 1910 it was upgraded to a bona fide wagon trail by Brig. Gen. Wilds P. Richardson of the U.S. Army.

Thompson Pass, just outside of Valdez, is a breathtaking spot, with open mountain vistas at an elevation of 2,678 feet. You'll be passing a landmark here, because Thompson Pass is the site of some of the deepest snowfalls Alaska has ever encountered. In 1952 and 1953, for example, the area experienced an unprecedented 81-plus feet of snow during the season.

The **Klutina and Gulkana rivers** are also popular roadside locations, and during the summer are rich with wild Alaskan salmon. Fishing guides and charter-boat operators can help arrange a fishing expedition. Check at the **Delta Junction Visitor Center** (☎ 907-895-5068) for more information.

MAIN ROADS

THE **Glenn, Parks, and Seward highways** are three of Alaska's most-traveled roads because they connect the majority of communities to each other. All these roads have plenty of services, but that does not detract from the wild scenery. Driving the Seward Highway from Anchorage to Seward affords spectacular views of the coastal waters of **Turnagain Arm,** then climbs to **Turnagain Pass,** which is a winter playland for skiers and snowmobilers.

Likewise, the Glenn and the Parks travel through some of the interior portions of the state, offering mountain views and stops at quaint communities along the way. While all of these roads serve as main arteries through Alaska, they have a charm of their own.

SIDE HIGHWAYS

FOR THOSE SEEKING A SHORTER DRIVE, there are several one- or two-day jaunts to enjoy along some of the lesser-traveled roads. The **Elliott Highway** covers 152 miles from just north of Fairbanks to Manley Hot Springs in the state's interior. Look for such attractions as **Minto Lakes** and **Manley Hot Springs,** which draws locals seeking pure solitude (there is also no better place for viewing the northern lights). You'll find several campgrounds and a few places to restock on supplies along the way, but in general expect the mostly gravel road to be lightly traveled.

Another northern road worthy of exploration is the **Steese Highway,** a 162-mile-long road heading from Fairbanks to Circle. Most of the highway is gravel, and conditions can vary with the weather. But the road's unobstructed views and access to summer and winter play areas make driving it worth the effort. The **Chena River and Chatanika River recreation areas** offer summertime amusement for visitors and locals alike, and in the winter there is access to the **White Mountains National Recreation Area,** which offers miles and miles of groomed snow surface for skiers, snowmobilers, and dog mushers.

Farther south is the equally stunning but sometimes less-maintained **Denali Highway,** which connects the communities of Cantwell, on the

Parks Highway, and Paxson, on the Richardson Highway. All but 24 miles of the 134-mile road are gravel (21 miles at one end and 3 miles at the other), and depending upon the weather the highway can become washed out, carved with washboards, and slick.

Tangle Lakes is a particularly popular area, with grayling fishing, canoeing, and outstanding birding.

CHECKLIST *for* SUCCESS

NO MATTER YOUR LEVEL OF EXPERIENCE, one of the first items you should purchase when planning a road trip in Alaska is ***The Milepost,*** a phone-book-size guide that offers mile-by-mile descriptions of the roadways in Alaska and parts of Canada ($27.95; visit **www.themilepost.com** to order). Even the advertisements are helpful, alerting you to upcoming restaurants, gas stations, or campgrounds along the way. Each of Alaska's main roads is covered in the book, and by reading the basic descriptions you'll see why any one of them will make a nice driving destination.

Here's some additional advice to take into account before heading on your trip.

- **Bring a spare tire,** and have emergency supplies on hand for flat tires. Auto service is hard to come by on many Alaska roads.
- **Stock up on gas—and not just in your tank.** On very remote roads, such as the Dalton Highway, bring an extra five-gallon container or two. They can be attached to the outside of your vehicle, but don't store them in the trunk.
- **Read up on your rental car.** Check your contract to make sure traveling on gravel roads is allowed.
- **Grab extra gear.** If you're camping, you'll likely already have appropriate overnight supplies such as sleeping bags, extra food, and clothing. But even if you're planning to stay in motels or bed-and-breakfasts, it's still a good idea to have emergency blankets and other gear to keep you warm in case you get stranded. Even on Alaska's more remote roads, there is usually enough summer tourist traffic to ensure that help is not far away if you break down. But during shoulder seasons and winter, many of Alaska's roads are rarely traveled. Take note of the time of year in which you are traveling, and prepare accordingly. For example, May can be a good time for travel, but there are fewer people on the roads. In June and July, there are more vehicles about and lots of sunlight, as much as 20 hours a day, making travel less solitary. In August and September, the fall colors emerge and the scenery is astounding, but there will be fewer people on the road.
- **Be ready for emergencies.** Carry flares, tire jack, jumper cables, and other gear, including a small first-aid kit that can be purchased at any sporting-goods shop. There are very few medical facilities, especially on the more remote roads.

- **Get picture-perfect.** Bring plenty of film, or have a digital camera that is capable of taking hundreds of photos.

OTHER ROAD-TRIP TIPS

TO MAKE THE DRIVING EXPERIENCE more enjoyable, here are a few rules of the road to keep in mind while exploring Alaska:

- **Drive at the posted speed limit** or at a safe speed for road conditions, and check your rearview mirror often. On most main roads in Alaska, you must pull off to let five or more vehicles behind you pass. If you want to be really nice, pull off when you see three or more.
- **Always drive with your headlights on.** Even in the summer, when the sun stays above the horizon to all hours, those headlights can be helpful. Oncoming traffic is more likely to see you, especially in rainy weather.
- **Park only at waysides or other designated parking areas.** Don't assume a pull-off is a good place to camp; you may just be blocking someone's access road to his or her remote cabin.
- **Keep Alaska beautiful.** Save RV waste for dumping stations and trash for your stops in town. Not only is litter unsightly, but it can be dangerous to animals that might happen to munch on it.

OUR FAVORITE ROAD TRIPS

THE INDEPENDENT TRAVELER RECOGNIZES and appreciates a flexible schedule. When you're traveling in your own car, you can change plans whenever you wish. Like that camping spot you found last night? Then go ahead, stay another day. This is a luxury that those traveling in their own vehicles have.

We have a few favorite road trips, each with its own advantages. Read on to see which one suits you best.

The Anchorage–Valdez Loop

Distance 367 miles, not counting nautical miles on the ferry. **Regional location** Southcentral Coastal and Inland Alaska. **Road configuration** A loop drive that includes a ferry ride. **Difficulty** Easy, with many options for side trips; . **Suitable for kids?** Yes. **Time to drive** 3–5 days. **Scenery** The coastal waters of Prince William Sound are the highlight, but you'll also pass through a long train-and-vehicle tunnel, climb the steep and snow-prone Thompson Pass, and see great views of the Wrangell–St. Elias mountains. **Traffic level** Moderate, depending on the time of year. Expect RV traffic. **Facilities** All amenities are available at various spots along the road.

ROAD SUMMARY Driving the Anchorage–Valdez Loop requires travel on several roads, starting with the **Seward Highway,** then the **Whittier Access Road** (which includes a fun drive through the Anton Anderson Memorial Tunnel, at 2.5 miles the longest highway tunnel in North America), then the

Richardson Highway, and finally the **Glenn Highway.** Not to be forgotten, though, is the **Alaska Marine Highway,** which you will travel via the new high-speed ferry *Chenega* or the slower, traditional ferry, the M/V *Kennicott,* across Prince William Sound to Valdez (or Whittier if you're reversing your trip). All these roads are paved and well marked.

DIRECTIONS The best way to begin this trip is to start in Anchorage and drive south on the Seward Highway to the turnoff for Portage and the Whittier Access Road, at Mile 48. Drive the Whittier Road for 11 miles; on the way you'll pass through the Anton Anderson Memorial tunnel, which requires a toll and leads into the Prince William Sound community of Whittier. From there, travel is via Alaska State Ferry, which departs daily. Board the ferry for the 2-hour-and-45-minute trip on the fast ferry (6 hours on the *Kennicott*) to Valdez, at the other end of the sound. From Valdez, drive north on the Richardson Highway to the community of Glennallen, 119 miles away. At Glennallen, head west on the Glenn Highway, which will take you back to Anchorage in 189 miles. The trip can be reversed just as easily. Or you can opt to go the length of the Richardson Highway all the way to Fairbanks and return to Anchorage via the Parks and Glenn Highways (about 790 miles total).

ROAD DESCRIPTION Although traveling this loop takes a bit more scheduling, it too is its own vacation. Most drivers will start in Anchorage and drive south to Whittier, where they will catch the ferry to Valdez. Enjoy a relaxing ride across **Prince William Sound,** complete with naturalist narration along the way. Watch for sea lions, otters, whales, and other marine mammals. In **Valdez** you'll find plenty of camping and lodging alternatives. Spend a day or two hiking, cycling, kayaking, rafting, or fishing here; then move up the Richardson Highway back toward Glennallen and the Glenn Highway and Anchorage. Anchorage is the ideal location from which to start—car-rental agencies are plentiful, and it's the least expensive place to stock up on food, fuel, and other supplies. This trip tickles the edge of the Southcentral Coastal region of Prince William Sound but also takes in some of Southcentral Inland Alaska. For details on other aspects of these regions, see their respective chapters (pages 332 and 283).

ANCHORAGE–VALDEZ LOOP RESOURCES

NO OUTFITTERS OFFER TOURS of this route, but you'll find the following information helpful.

- **Anton Anderson Memorial Tunnel information:** ☎ 877-611-2586; **dot.alaska.gov/creg/whittiertunnel/index.shtml.**
- **Alaska Marine Highway information:** ☎ 907-835-4436 (Valdez terminal); **www.ferryalaska.com.**

The Dalton Highway

Distance 414 miles one-way (from Fairbanks, 498 miles). **Regional location** Interior Alaska. **Road configuration** Out-and-back, identified as Alaska State Route 11; 75% gravel, 25% paved. **Difficulty** For the confident or experienced car traveler who knows how to handle his or her own repairs; 🫎🫎🫎🫎. **Suitable for kids?**

Yes. **Time to drive** 2–6 days. **Scenery** Vast river and valley views, with above-tree-line vistas throughout most of the journey. You will cross the Continental Divide on this road trip. **Traffic level** Limited to the occasional vehicle, but beware of fast-moving semis and tractor-trailers. **Facilities** Gas, food, and lodging are available at **Yukon River Camp** (Mile 56; ☎ 907-474-3557; **www.yukonrivercamp.com**); at **Coldfoot Camp** (Mile 175; ☎ 866-474-3400; **www.coldfootcamp.com**); and in Deadhorse, at the northern end of the road. There are 2 lodging and food options in Wiseman, just a few miles north of Coldfoot Camp: **Arctic Getaway Cabin and Breakfast** (☎ 907-678-4456; **www.arcticgetaway.com**), which is rustic but authentic, and **Boreal Lodging** (☎ 907-678-4566; **www.boreallodge.com**), which is scenic and well kept; otherwise, services are not available. The **Bureau of Land Management** (☎ 907-474-2200 or 907-678-5209; **www.blm.gov/ak/dalton**), which manages much of the land along the road, has 4 campgrounds, 3 of which are primitive camping areas. There is a private campground in Coldfoot. In Deadhorse, your options are the **Arctic Caribou Inn** (☎ 877-659-2368; **www.arcticcaribouinn.com**); the **Prudhoe Bay Hotel** (☎ 907-659-2449; **www.prudhoebayhotel.com**); and the **Arctic Oilfield Inn** (☎ 907-659-2614).

ROAD SUMMARY The road begins just north of Fairbanks and ends at Deadhorse, a community supported by the oil-field industry. Driving the Dalton is one of the best ways for road-trippers to appreciate the vastness of the state by vehicle. The Web site **www.alaskaroads.com,** designed by Oscar Voss, a traveler to Alaska in the mid-1990s and early 2000s, offers a nice, albeit dated, photo tour of the highway. The photos, taken by Voss when he drove the road in 2001, give you an idea of its remoteness; we like the site because it takes some of the mystery out of what lies ahead.

unofficial **TIP**
The Dalton is the only highway in the United States and one of only two in North America that cross the Arctic Circle. Some people like to stop at the **Arctic Circle Trading Post** (☎ 907-474-3507; **www.arcticcircletradingpost.com**) at Mile 49 on the Elliott Highway to officially record their passage across the Arctic Circle (the sign might still say Wildwood General Store, but it's Arctic Circle you've reached). The shop offers an official Arctic Circle registry, upon which you can list your name and receive a souvenir certificate of arrival to the Far North.

DIRECTIONS From Fairbanks, travel approximately 85 miles north on the Elliott Highway (Alaska State Route 2) until you reach the turnoff for the Dalton Highway. The road is mostly gravel and is washboarded in places, so be prepared to drive slowly and enjoy the scenery. There is some chip sealing happening, which is an improvement, but otherwise the road is very basic.

ROAD DESCRIPTION The Dalton is, as mentioned, a mostly gravel road with intermittent washboards and no painted lanes, so be ready to drive at a slow pace, which is part of the charm of such a trip. From the Elliott Highway, the road travels north near the community of Livengood. The **Trans-Alaska Pipeline System** parallels the road for quite a while, zigzagging with the contours of the hills and valleys. The road crosses the Yukon River at Mile 56 and passes through **Gates of the Arctic National Park** and the **Arctic National Wildlife Refuge.** Look for caribou, moose, and bear throughout this area. The road passes the Arctic Circle at Mile 115.

The next place to restock your supplies is **Coldfoot,** 175 miles into the drive. There is an RV campground with hookup, food, and lodging. Just up the road is **Wiseman,** which also has a couple of lodging options.

DALTON HIGHWAY OUTFITTERS

For the Less-experienced Traveler

- The **Northern Alaska Tour Co.** (☎ 907-474-8600 or 800-474-1986; **www.northernalaska.com**) can show you around if you want to see more of the oil field at Deadhorse or walk on the shores of the Arctic Ocean.
- **Trans Arctic Circle Treks, Ltd.** (☎ 800-336-8735; **www.arctictreks.com**), a small-tour operator, does the driving during its High-Arctic Three Day Tour, featuring smaller passenger vans for a more personalized tour. Optional "flightseeing" jaunts can also be arranged. A great tour, but more tourist-oriented.

For the More-experienced Traveler

- **Arctic Outfitters–Dalton Highway Auto Rentals** (☎ 907-474-3530; **www.arctic-outfitters.com**) is one of the few companies that rent vehicles you can use on the Haul Road, including all the necessary gear to help you along if you break down. The vehicles even come equipped with CB radios in case of problems. The rates are $149 per day for a Jeep Cherokee and $129 per day for a Ford Taurus, if you rent for four or more days. The company also can arrange shuttles and lodging.
- We like **Dalton Highway Express** (☎ 907-474-3555; **www.daltonhighwayexpress.com**) because it caters to independent travelers who may be carrying backpacks. This small company will take you anywhere along the Dalton Highway from Fairbanks and drop you off wherever you want to be left; they'll pick you up at a later, prearranged time as well. It's an extremely affordable way to reach such places as Gates of the Arctic and the Arctic National Wildlife Refuge—it's $196 to get to Deadhorse, $88 to Coldfoot. (Bicycles and canoes cost extra to transport.)

The Denali Highway

Distance 134 miles one-way. **Regional location** Interior Alaska. **Road configuration** Out-and-back, or loop if connected with the Richardson and Parks highways. Identified as Alaska State Route 8; 85% gravel, 15% paved. **Difficulty** Moderate because of the frequent washboards; 🫎🫎🫎. **Suitable for kids?** Yes. **Time to drive** 1–4 days. **Scenery** Sweeping views of surrounding mountains, above tree line much of the way. **Traffic level** Light; this is a good road for bringing along a mountain bike and doing some exploring. **Facilities** Gas, food, and lodging are available intermittently along the road. For those not interested in camping, we like the lodging options at **Tangle River Inn** (☎ 907-822-3970 or 907-895-4022; **www.tangleriverinn.com**), on the Paxson end of the highway; **Maclaren**

River Lodge (at Mile 42; ☎ 907-822-5444; **www.maclarenlodge.com**); and **Gracious House Lodge** (at Mile 82; ☎ 907-333-3148 or 907-259-1111; **www.alaskaone.com/gracious**). Tangle River is a great place for birders, and canoes are available to rent if you want to explore the nearby Tangle Lakes. **Camp Maclaren,** one of the newer lodging options on the road, is close to fishing and dog mushing—be sure to check out the nearby **Crazy Dog Kennels,** in which you can learn about this state sport from one of Alaska's best mushers, John Schandelmeier (pets are welcome here, by the way), and his significant other, Zoya DeNure (☎ 907-822-5424; **www.dogsleddenali.com**). At Gracious House, on the Cantwell end of the highway, you'll like the pies served at Butch and Carol Gratias's place, as well as the simple but tidy accommodations, which include private bathrooms with showers. The Gratiases also have a bar, meals, tent sites, and RV parking. Butch will even take you flightseeing in one of his planes or get his mechanics to fix your flat tire. Nice places to camp in the area include **Tangle Lakes Campground** at Mile 22, which offers 25 tent and RV sites with bathroom facilities, water, picnic tables, and fire rings; and **Brushkana Creek Campground** at Mile 105, with 12 sites, bathroom facilities, water, picnic tables, garbage barrels, and fire rings. The campgrounds conveniently occupy either end of the highway (for more information on both, visit **www.ak.blm.gov/gdo/denali.html**).

ROAD SUMMARY This 134-mile road trip is on mostly gravel roads. There are cavernous potholes. The washboards are relentless. And the services—a couple of lodges here and a campground or two there—are few and far between. But those who do venture onto this frontier highway are blessed with a rolling self-guided tour of Alaska that bisects some of the state's most spectacular mountain ranges. The area, with its open tundra and countless kettle lakes (scattered lakes that are remnants of a once-glacier-covered land), attracts thousands of birds, including the rare arctic warbler and Smith's longspur. Anglers are drawn to the tranquil fishing; grayling and trout are abundant at the height of summer. Mountain bikers love the congestion-free travel.

When it first opened in 1957, the Denali was the only road link to Denali National Park, replacing the Alaska Railroad as the source of primary access. When the Parks Highway opened in 1971, the Denali Highway became obsolete. Today the road is still used as a summertime link for those who choose to drive it. It closes in mid-fall, when the snow gets too deep, and doesn't reopen until spring, usually in mid-May. It's a piece of history that hasn't changed much since the day it was first carved across Alaska.

DIRECTIONS From Fairbanks, drive south on the Richardson Highway until you reach Paxson. The Denali Highway connects to the right and is well marked. From Anchorage, drive north on the Glenn Highway to the Parks Highway. Travel north on the Parks Highway until you reach Cantwell. The turnoff for the Denali Highway is on the right. Or take the Glenn Highway all the way to the Richardson; turn left (north), and at Paxson turn left (west) on the Denali.

ROAD DESCRIPTION The Denali Highway is a mostly gravel road—only the first 20 miles on the eastern end and 3 miles on the western end are paved.

Maclaren Summit is the highest point to the highway—4,086 feet at about Mile 40 from the eastern end. From there the road gets narrower and windier, and potholes and washboards can be numerous. The recommended travel speed is 30 miles per hour when it's rough. The road also gets dry and dusty when there is a season with little rain, so we like to keep our headlights on at all times just in case. Also, be on the lookout for mountain bikers, who appreciate the road's deserted feel and often can be found riding the length.

Much of the land surrounding the Denali Highway is managed by the **Bureau of Land Management,** which allows camping all along the road. There are a few campgrounds and three lodging options (see page 73 and left), but pulling off to find a spot makes for a remote-feeling experience.

DENALI HIGHWAY OUTFITTERS

For the Less-experienced Traveler

- The **Copper River Princess Wilderness Lodge** (☎ 800-426-0500; **www.princesslodges.com**), at the edge of Wrangell–St. Elias National Park, at the junction of the Klutina and Copper rivers, sometimes arranges drives of the Denali Highway, but you have to call ahead to make sure, and usually this is only done for guests. It is the only operation around, though, that travels the road with any regularity. The lodge is quite luxurious, with rates beginning at $179.

For the More-experienced Traveler

- The best way to see the Denali Highway is to drive it yourself and camp along the way.

Haines and Skagway Road Trip

Distance 355 miles, connecting 3 roads (Haines, Alaska, and South Klondike highways). **Regional location** Southeast Alaska. **Road configuration** Out-and-back. **Difficulty** Easy, but services are few; . **Suitable for kids?** Yes. **Time to drive** 3–5 days. **Scenery** High mountain vistas, riverside driving, and the wide-open Chilkat Valley give the drive nice variety. Bald eagles are seen often, as well as black bears. **Traffic level** Moderate at the height of the summer travel season. **Facilities** Most amenities available along the way, including lodging, food, and gas.

ROAD SUMMARY Also known as the Golden Circle Route, this beautiful road trip takes in some of the most scenic areas of Southeast Alaska and affords the leisurely traveler a chance to add a ferry trip–Inside Passage cruise to the itinerary. *Note:* Those choosing to make a loop trip with the ferry must research vehicle requirements well in advance. Vehicle transport between Haines and Skagway is limited. A good option is to rent a vehicle one-way, for drop-off in Haines (or vice versa).

DIRECTIONS These Southeast communities are accessible via daily jet service from Anchorage (☎ 800-252-7522; **www.alaskaair.com**) or the **Alaska Marine Highway** ferry system (☎ 800-642-0066; **www.ferryalaska.com**), which can transport you and your vehicle from the lower 48 states.

ROAD DESCRIPTION When you see **Haines** and **Skagway,** don't be surprised if the word *quaint* just pops out of your mouth. Both towns are quintessentially Alaskan and have not lost their historic charm. Haines is a mix of art, culture, and history, and Skagway is caught in the gold-rush era, with clapboard-fronted houses, saloons, and all manner of turn-of-the-20th-century trappings still to be found. A drive along the 146-mile **Haines Highway,** via the Alaska Highway, is scenic in itself.

Then you have two other highways to touch upon before making perhaps the best connection of all on a ferry between Skagway and Haines. That is the direction from which this road trip description embarks. However, a reverse trip, starting in Skagway and ending in Haines, also is possible.

As you leave Haines, the first one-third of the driving on the Haines Highway is relatively flat and easygoing, traveling alongside the river and passing through the **Chilkat Valley Bald Eagle Preserve.** The spectacular peaks of the Chilkat Range define the boundary between Haines and the heart of **Glacier Bay National Park,** and they are stunning to see behind the wheel of a vehicle.

unofficial **TIP**
You cannot travel past Canadian Customs between the hours of 11 p.m. and 7 a.m. If coming from the reverse direction, this is not an issue because U.S. Customs is open 24 hours a day. Also, the time is one hour earlier in Alaska than in Canada, so reset your watch.

You'll cross the Canadian border just past Mile 40. Canadian Customs will likely stop you and ask questions; occasionally they will even search a vehicle.

Three Guardsmen Lake, at about Mile 50, is a good place for a picnic. The slight breeze here keeps the bugs at bay, and the view is amazing. Three Guardsmen Mountain rises like a volcano from the surrounding landscape and makes an unforgettable photo opportunity in good weather.

Chilkat Pass (elevation 3,510 feet), at Mile 59, climbs dramatically in a short period of time. It's another windy location, and also a good option for stopping and grabbing something to eat.

A good place to camp on your first night out is **Million Dollar Falls Campground,** about 93 miles from Haines (see details in Resources, page 78).

At **Haines Junction,** about 150 miles into the trip, you can stop for lodging, food, and other necessities. Haines Junction is home to some 800 residents, many of whom cater to visitors just like you. There are tours and guides available, as well as other in-town activities. It's a small place, but you'll see it has everything you could need, and if it doesn't, well, you can likely live without it for a few days anyway.

The Haines Highway ends at Haines Junction and connects with the Alaska Highway, on which you will travel east for the next 100 miles. This is perhaps the least scenic of the three roads, although that's relative when you consider that all of them are amazingly breathtaking. It's just that the Alaska Highway serves as a main artery to and from Alaska, and there are more cafes, gas stations, and mom-and-pop operations alongside the road, breaking up the wilderness feel compared with some other sections of this drive.

Whitehorse will be a culture shock after your day or two on the road. About 28,000 people live here, and in the summer tourists swell the population by the hundreds. There are gift shops galore, no shortage of bed-and-breakfasts and hotels, and plenty of other tourist attractions for the driver ready to get out from behind the wheel of his or her vehicle. (The ***S/S Klondike,*** a giant riverboat that plied the Yukon until 1955, is just such an attraction.)

If you've planned an extra day of relaxation into your itinerary, we suggest you take it here. On any given night, you'll find live music, from country to blues, or you can take in the cheesy-but-entertaining gold-rush-themed vaudeville performances at the infamous **Frantic Follies.** Or brush up on territorial history at the **MacBride Museum,** which covers everything from the cultural heritage of the Yukon First Nations to wildlife to the Klondike. Still, we like Whitehorse for its lesser-known opportunities just outside of town. Plenty of outfitters are eager to take you rafting, kayaking, hiking, or fishing. Check at the **Whitehorse Tourism Centre** for details (see Resources, page 79).

Leaving Whitehorse for the final leg of your journey requires hopping onto the southbound Alaska Highway for a few miles before turning south onto the South Klondike Highway. This road will amaze you. Some of the hills are of mammoth proportions, the climbs stupendous and beautiful. Just make sure your car is up to the task.

But before you even think about this drive ahead, you've got to take a short side trip to **Takhini Hot Springs,** less than ten miles to the north. Leave Whitehorse going north onto the Alaska Highway, and turn onto the North Klondike Highway. Look for the turnoff on the left, about 3.5 miles in, for the Takhini Hot Springs Road. Drive another six miles on this road to reach the springs, which are naturally occurring and just hot enough to make you wince a little the farther you sink into them. Once you're in, though, it's hard to get out.

The springs also have a small cafe and campground for those who want to stay longer. Guided horseback rides are available, as well as hiking trails and an outdoor climbing wall that you can descend via zip line.

OK, now back to the main trip. Once, you've pulled yourself away from the springs, head south again, back onto the Alaska Highway, and keep going south until you connect to the South Klondike Highway, which will take you to Skagway.

Camping along the road is sparse—the last established campground is in **Carcross,** at about Mile 33. **Tutshi Lake,** at Mile 70, is a good option for those willing to pull over and wing it.

White Pass is the large climb of this drive, but you'll be rewarded with great views as you come into Skagway.

Entering Skagway is like taking a step back in time, with people in period costumes, building facades that look as if they came straight out of a Western movie set, and even music from the turn of the century playing on speakers in many shops and storefronts. It's a bit over the top, but fun if you just let yourself enjoy the moment.

Most of the town's historic buildings have been restored to their gold-rush glory. The **White Pass & Yukon Route Railroad** is based here, as well as the beginning of the **Chilkoot Pass Trail,** which follows the steps of gold-rush stampeders more than 100 years ago.

To complete the road trip, reserve a spot on one of the ferries available back to Haines.

HAINES AND SKAGWAY ROAD TRIP RESOURCES

NO OUTFITTERS OFFER TOURS OF THIS ROUTE, but you'll find the following information helpful.

- For ferry service on the **Alaska Marine Highway** between Haines and Skagway, you must book a complicated ticket. Call an agent to arrange this plan rather than booking online (☎ 800-642-0066). The Haines ferry service can help locally if the 800-folks don't seem to understand what you're trying to arrange (☎ 907-766-2111).
- **Carcross Territorial Campground** (☎ 877-737-3783; **www.pccamping.ca**), in the village of Carcross, on the South Klondike highway, features 12 campsites, firewood, and outhouses. Camping is $12.
- The **Haines Convention and Visitors Bureau** (☎ 800-458-3579 or 907-766-2234; **www.haines.ak.us**) can give you plenty of options for lodging and eating and can mail its annual Travel Planner, including a special brochure on driving the Golden Circle Route.
- The **Haines–Skagway Fast Ferry** (☎ 888-766-2103 or 907-766-2100; **www.chilkatcruises.com**) offers multiple trips daily, sometimes as many as 26. It's rarely a problem to walk on. No vehicles are accepted, though.
- Informative, affordable tours of Whitehorse's ***S/S Klondike*** (☎ 800-661-0486; ☎ 867-667-3910; **www.pc.gc.ca**), a retired riverboat, are available daily.
- Located in Haines Junction, the **Kluane National Park Visitor Center** (☎ 867-634-7207) can give you an idea of what this Canadian park is all about. If you plan a hike within the park, register ahead of time.
- The **MacBride Museum** (1124 First Avenue in downtown Whitehorse; ☎ 867-667-2709; **www.macbridemuseum.com**) is another worthwhile stop; a high point to this visit is a look at Sam McGee's cabin. Other area museums include the **Old Log Church** (Third Avenue and Elliott Street; ☎ 867-668-2555); the **Yukon Transportation Museum** (by the airport off the Alaska Highway; ☎ 867-668-4792); and the **Yukon Beringia Interpretive Centre** (at the airport on the Alaska Highway; ☎ 867-667-8855; **www.beringia.com**).
- We love the local and Alaska sections at **Mac's Fireweed Books** (203 Main Street in Whitehorse; ☎ 800-661-0508, **www.yukonbooks.com**).
- As always, ***The Milepost*** ($27.95; **www.themilepost.com**) is a good reference for your road trips.
- The **Million Dollar Falls Campground,** located at Mile 93.5 on the Haines Highway, features 33 campsites and kitchen shelters. Camping is $12 per night. There are hiking trails and a boardwalk trail at the edge of the campground, and the grayling and salmon fishing is great.

- **Raven Hotel and Gourmet Dining** in Haines Junction (☎ 867-634-2500; **www.yukonweb.com/tourism/raven**) offers delicious meals and excellent lodging.
- **Silver Eagle Transport** (☎ 907-766-2418 or 888-766-2594; **alaskaferry@hotmail.com**) can handle a few vehicles at a time and is a much easier bet than the ferry system.

unofficial **TIP**
Beware of grizzlies near the Million Dollar Falls Campground; they flock to the area during salmon spawning season in the summer.

- The **Skagway Convention and Visitors Bureau** (☎ 907-983-2854; **www.skagway.com**) has information on car rentals, lodging, and other practicalities in the area.
- **Takhini Hot Springs** (off Mile 3.5 of the Klondike Highway; ☎ 867-633-2706; **www.takhinihotsprings.yk.ca**) is a must-stop destination, with naturally occurring hot springs for communal soaking, camping, hiking, horseback riding, and more.
- The **Whitehorse Tourism Centre** (2121 Second Avenue in downtown Whitehorse; ☎ 867-668-8687; **www.visitwhitehorse.com**) can offer suggestions on lodging, dining, entertainment such as the Frantic Follies, and outdoor-recreation opportunities.
- The **Yukon Adventure Company** in Whitehorse (☎ 866-417-7365; **www.yukonadventures.com**) offers fly-fishing, canoeing, rafting, and hiking tours at rates from $99 to $325 Canadian, depending on the adventure.

Kodiak Island Odyssey

Distance Less than 100 miles, spread over 4 separate drives. **Regional location** Southcentral Coastal Alaska. **Road configuration** Out-and-back. **Difficulty** Easy, but services are few and access requires ferry or flight; . **Suitable for kids?** Yes. **Time to drive** 2 days. **Scenery** A range of lush coastal mountains and ocean views, above tree line and amid thick forests. **Traffic level** Light; mostly local traffic. **Facilities** A few stores closer to the community of Kodiak; a few campgrounds.

ROAD SUMMARY There aren't that many roads on Kodiak Island, but the ones that do exist will take the outdoor traveler to spectacularly beautiful destinations. You'll cross over countless bridges spanning rivers teeming with salmon. You'll access remote beaches where surfers brave the cold while riding waves. You'll reach recreation areas where camping and hiking options are endless. The four main roads worth driving in Kodiak are **Chiniak Highway,** a 42-mile route that takes you along the coast; **Pasagshak Bay Road,** a 17-mile spur road that crosses the island to its southern end; **Anton Larsen Bay Road,** a 12-mile stretch that heads north around the mountains; and **Monashka Bay Road,** another 12-miler that ends at one of the island's prettiest public recreation areas, Fort Abercrombie State Historic Park. While much of the land along the road system is privately owned, you can obtain free permits to gain access.

DIRECTIONS Kodiak Island is accessible via daily jet service from Anchorage (☎ 800-252-7522; **www.alaskaair.com**) and the **Alaska Marine Highway**

ferry system (☎ 800-642-0066; **www.ferryalaska.com**), which can transport you and your vehicle from the mainland in Homer, on the Kenai Peninsula. Once in Kodiak, check at the **Kodiak Island Convention and Visitors Bureau** (see Resources section following) for a driving map of Kodiak Island. It's virtually impossible to get lost.

ROAD DESCRIPTION The heart of Kodiak Island, where the town center is situated, begins with pavement, but before long all roads become gravelly and washboarded in places. They are all slated to be paved by 2008, but that goal is far from being complete. The Chiniak Highway is the main road leading south out of town. At about Mile 4, enjoy views of **Barometer and Pyramid mountains,** two of the more noticeable bumps on the island. Near Mile 5, you'll come to the right-hand turnoff for **Anton Larsen Bay Road,** which we particularly like because it ends at a peaceful dead-end overlooking Anton Larsen Bay. There is a boat launch at the end of the 12-mile Anton Larsen Bay Road, as well as access to hiking and good berry picking from the end of the road.

unofficial **TIP**
Go a short way up the unmarked trail at the end of Anton Larsen Bay Road to enjoy a hidden waterfall just off the trail.

Back on the Chiniak Highway, the road continues over numerous salmon-fishing streams and provides access to off-road freshwater-fishing lakes that can be reached by foot or all-terrain vehicle. Mile 10 is the place to stop if you need any services. Groceries, tire repairs, food, and gas are available, but after this there are no more services.

The roadside activities are endless along this section of road. Access the trailhead to **Heitman Lake** at Mile 14. At around Mile 20, stop at the **American River** for some great salmon fishing in season.

The **Olds River,** at about Mile 29, is another good fishing spot. At Mile 30, where the pavement ends, you'll turn left to continue along the Chiniak Highway and veer right to access Pasagshak Bay Road, which turns inland, cutting across the southern tip of the island to access **Pasagshak State Recreation Site.**

Pasagshak Bay Road is another 17 miles and takes in sweeping views of the ocean as well as a unique look at Alaska farming. Out in the middle of nowhere are ranches with cows and crops and farming equipment, and you wonder how people can survive. It's incredibly scenic, and a popular place for residents to visit. **Pasagshak State Recreation Site** is at Mile 8.9, but the road continues to an even more impressive treat just a mile or two farther down the road: Mile 10 is the location of a popular surfing beach where Alaskans brave the freezing waters in dry suits to catch the Pacific waves that crash on the shore.

unofficial **TIP**
At Mile 24 of the Chiniak Highway is **Mayflower Beach,** a spot the locals like for beachcombing. We like it because it's rarely crowded and the tide-pooling opportunities are amazing.

Curious science-oriented travelers can continue along the road to Mile 15 and the **U.S. Coast Guard Kodiak Launch Complex,** a training area for missile launching. It's heavily guarded, so just keep driving. The road ends in another mile or two, and you'll have to backtrack to return to the Chiniak Highway.

Once back on the Chiniak Highway, you'll stay along the edge of **Chiniak Bay;** on a sunny day, the view from here is so outstanding it's virtually impossible to think of anyplace more beautiful. The sleepy community of **Chiniak** is around Mile 34, and you'll find several places to stop and reach the beach. World War II buffs will enjoy the end of the road, at Mile 42, where there is access to period bunkers and gun sites. The road is unmaintained, so be careful.

The last road worth checking out on Kodiak Island is Monashka Bay Road, on the northern end of town, beginning in downtown Kodiak and traveling nearly 12 miles to the **Termination Point** trailhead. (*Note:* You need permission from Leisnoi Village landowners to hike the trail, but it's worth the effort—☎ 907-486-7004). We like this day hike because it is a wonderful example of all of Kodiak's beauty in one spot. You'll hike through the dense spruce rain forest and walk along a sandy beach. You'll also be high above the oceans at the cliff's edge and walk through brushy forest.

Also along Monashka Bay Road are **Mill Bay Beach Park** at Mile 3.6, with picnicking and beachcombing, and **Fort Abercrombie State Historic Park** less than a mile away, with great hiking trails and chances to see lots of wildlife, including bears. The pavement ends at about Mile 6.5, but keep going to reach a truly secluded beach. At Mile 8 is **Pillar Creek Beach,** a peaceful place to while away a sunny afternoon.

KODIAK ISLAND ODYSSEY RESOURCES

NO OUTFITTERS OFFER TOURS OF THIS ROUTE, but you'll find the following information helpful.

- If you want to take your own car on this drive, you'll have to arrange for ferry service from Homer, on the Kenai Peninsula (☎ 800-642-0066; **www.ferryalaska.com**), or fly in from Anchorage and rent a car. The options are few, so call ahead if you're coming during the peak season. We like **Budget Rent-a-Car** at the airport (☎ 907-487-2220) and **Rent-A-Heap** in downtown Kodiak (☎ 907-487-4001), a less-expensive option. (The same people operate both.)
- **Kodiak Island Convention and Visitors Bureau:** 100 Marine Way, Suite 200, Kodiak 99615; ☎ 800-789-4782 or 907-486-4782; **www.kodiak.org.**

PART SIX

BACKPACKING

IT'S NO EXAGGERATION TO SAY THAT BACKPACKING in Alaska will be unlike any other backpacking experience you've ever had. In most backpacking excursions, hikers follow a marked trail to an ultimate destination—a mountaintop, remote lake, or ocean view. Think of the East Coast's Appalachian Trail, which stretches from Georgia to Maine, or the West Coast's Pacific Crest Trail, from Mexico to Canada. These are clearly marked, well traveled, and designed to meet the needs of hikers.

This type of backpacking experience does exist in Alaska, and this section will highlight some of the finest marked-trail options in the state. But Alaska is not called the Last Frontier without reason: it's a place where there is land so remote, nary a clue of human interference exists. The majority of Alaska's backcountry is trailless and accessible only by plane or boat—no roads, no trailheads, no signs to mark the trail. Backpackers in Alaska must rely on their own outdoors skills, their ability to read maps, compasses, and GPS units to make their way across the wilderness.

In this chapter we have focused on the mostly marked trails throughout the state, ranging from overnight destinations to trips that will take several days to complete. They will serve as a guide for planning your adventure. We have rated them from easy, meaning the trails are well marked and maintained with bridges, bog barriers, and other means of navigational assistance, to difficult, meaning you'll have to do some bushwhacking and follow ridgelines to travel from end to end.

But don't limit your exploration of the Last Frontier to these suggestions. Backpacking in country that is truly wide open and without trails is exhilarating and exciting, challenging and rewarding. We could never lay one of these trips out for you, because each one is unique. We have, however, included a section on trailless backpacking and how to go about planning your own excursion. It is located just before the individual trail descriptions.

CHECKLIST *for* SUCCESS

- **Be weight-conscious.** We're not talking about cutting the handle off your toothbrush or tearing chapters out of your reading book (although these techniques really do shave off ounces!), but traveling in backcountry Alaska is hard work. You're often bushwhacking and navigating among thick brambles and brush, crossing rivers and scaling bumpy alpine slopes. Bringing along too much gear can turn one of these adventures into a slow, painful slog. A pack that snags on branches and other brush can also be cumbersome.
- **Dress appropriately.** We acknowledge the need for weight-conscious backpacking, but also respect the necessity of having enough clothing for the duration. Do not travel into the backcountry ill-prepared. Wear polypropylene or other moisture-wicking underwear against your skin and quick-dry layers over the top. Add layers as conditions warrant. Always carry a spare pair of undergarments in case you get wet. Bring a hat and at least a pair of glove liners for unexpected cold weather, even in the summer. And make sure to have a waterproof raincoat and pants. But resist the urge to overpack–if you have the proper waterproof shell, you can get by with the same basic outer layer for an entire week or more. Another tip: long-sleeve shirts and long pants are great for keeping mosquitoes at bay.
- **Know how to navigate.** A map and compass are obvious necessities for anyone traveling into the backcountry, even on trails. In Alaska, many trails are quite primitive and can be crisscrossed with game trails and other unmarked paths that are potentially confusing when trying to travel a main trail. Farther out, in the roadless areas, there often are no trails at all. Acquaint yourself with a topographical map and compass. The **U.S. Geological Survey** has the most-often-used maps, but commercial maps of various regions of Alaska also can be purchased. Many outdoor travelers can read global-positioning systems and rely on them for backcountry travel. These can be particularly useful tools for travel in trailless areas.
- **Be bear-aware.** See "How to Stay Safe in the Wilderness" (page 29) for our tips on avoiding the beasts and maximizing your safety in case of an encounter.
- **Use care in crossing streams and rivers.** Alaska's cold water can turn a simple slip in a stream into a life-threatening situation. Hypothermia (see page 85) can set in quickly. When crossing water, always pick the route that seems the most shallow and least swift. Cloudy water, made gray by glacial silt, can hide possible dangers such as rocks and deep spots, so if you're not sure, don't chance it. If possible, link arms with a partner or partners while crossing to reduce the risk of getting swept away. If there are more than two hikers, form a triangle and pivot your way across the river, thus creating enough disturbance in the river's flow to ease movement. Walk parallel to

unofficial **TIP**
Morning is the best time to cross a stream or river, because the water tends to be at its lowest. If possible, shoot for an early-morning crossing.

Alaska Backpacking at a Glance

Brooks Range

REGIONAL LOCATION	THE BUSH
DISTANCE	VARIES
TRAIL/TRAILLESS?	TRAILLESS
DIFFICULTY	(symbols)
TIME TO HIKE	VARIES
CONFIGURATION	VARIES
SUITABLE FOR KIDS?	NO
GUIDE SUGGESTED?	HIGHLY RECOMMENDED

Chena Dome

REGIONAL LOCATION	THE INTERIOR
DISTANCE	30 MILES
TRAIL/TRAILLESS?	TRAIL
DIFFICULTY	(symbols)
TIME TO HIKE	2–4 DAYS
CONFIGURATION	LOOP
SUITABLE FOR KIDS?	TEENS
GUIDE SUGGESTED?	NO

Chilkoot Pass

REGIONAL LOCATION	SOUTHEAST
DISTANCE	33 MILES
TRAIL/TRAILLESS?	TRAIL
DIFFICULTY	(symbols)
TIME TO HIKE	3–5 DAYS
CONFIGURATION	OUT AND-BACK/END-TO-END
SUITABLE FOR KIDS?	TEENS
GUIDE SUGGESTED?	NO

Crow Pass

REGIONAL LOCATION	SOUTHCENTRAL INLAND
DISTANCE	26 MILES
TRAIL/TRAILLESS?	TRAIL
DIFFICULTY	(symbols)
TIME TO HIKE	2–3 DAYS
CONFIGURATION	END-TO-END
SUITABLE FOR KIDS?	TEENS
GUIDE SUGGESTED?	NO

Denali National Park

REGIONAL LOCATION	THE INTERIOR
DISTANCE	VARIES
TRAIL/TRAILLESS?	TRAILLESS
DIFFICULTY	(symbols)
TIME TO HIKE	VARIES
CONFIGURATION	VARIES
SUITABLE FOR KIDS?	NO
GUIDE SUGGESTED?	NO

Kesugi Ridge

REGIONAL LOCATION	SOUTHCENTRAL INLAND
DISTANCE	27.4 MILES
TRAIL/TRAILLESS?	TRAIL
DIFFICULTY	(symbols)
TIME TO HIKE	2–4 DAYS
CONFIGURATION	OUT-AND-BACK/END-TO-END
SUITABLE FOR KIDS?	9 AND OLDER
GUIDE SUGGESTED?	NO

Lake Clark National Park

REGIONAL LOCATION	THE BUSH
DISTANCE	VARIES
TRAIL/TRAILLESS?	TRAILLESS
DIFFICULTY	(symbols)
TIME TO HIKE	VARIES
CONFIGURATION	VARIES
SUITABLE FOR KIDS?	NO
GUIDE SUGGESTED?	RECOMMENDED

Resurrection Pass

REGIONAL LOCATION	SOUTHCENTRAL COASTAL
DISTANCE	39 MILES
TRAIL/TRAILLESS?	TRAIL
DIFFICULTY	(symbols)
TIME TO HIKE	2–5 DAYS
CONFIGURATION	OUT-AND-BACK/END-TO-END
SUITABLE FOR KIDS?	9 AND OLDER
GUIDE SUGGESTED?	NO

the current. We always unhook our backpacks from our waists in case we slip and are pulled under; if packs are unhooked and loosened we can get out of them without as much of a struggle.

- **Avoid giardiasis.** The intestinal parasite *Giardia lamblia* occurs in Alaska lakes and streams despite our remoteness. You can get it from drinking untreated water in areas of beaver and other water-mammal activity. It's not fun: symptoms are diarrhea and severe cramping, and they may appear up to two weeks after exposure. Treat water by boiling or using chemical tablets or a portable water filter.

unofficial **TIP**
June and July are the worst times of year for mosquitoes and biting flies, but the pests can appear as early as late April and continue through August in some places.

- **Guard against mosquitoes.** You won't necessarily get sick from too many mosquito bites, but they sure can ruin an otherwise unforgettable outdoor adventure.

The general rule of thumb is that the farther out you travel into the backcountry, the more mosquitoes you're likely to encounter. On lakes and streams, they can be brutal, as well as in wet, swampy areas and brushy spots. Pack bug spray—

the most powerful kind you can withstand—along with a head net, long-sleeve shirts, and pants.

- **Beware of hypothermia.** When the body gets so cold that its core temperature drops, this is called hypothermia, and it can kill. It is a very real danger in Alaska, especially in the mountains, where temperatures drop the higher you go, even in the summer. Hypothermia can also sneak up on you, rapidly developing into a disorientation that can lead to further problems. Avoiding hypothermia is simple: do not get wet. Even a shirt damp from perspiration can be dangerous if it's all you're wearing while standing atop a windy summit.
- **Carry the essentials.** We've mentioned clothing. We've stressed the importance of having the proper guidance equipment. Here are a few more items to pack:

1. ***A first-aid kit*** that can patch up minor cuts and bruises, as well as any specific medications that may be needed for anyone in your traveling party. The longer the trip, the more equipped this kit should be.
2. ***A camp stove*** that is light and can heat water quickly. This is a better choice than building fires, which can be hard to do in treeless areas and is more damaging to the landscape. In some places, fires are prohibited.
3. ***Matches or a lighter*** that will work even in extreme cold and/or wind. When camping in winter, you're better off with matches, as lighters can become temperamental.
4. ***Headlamps*** (unless you're traveling in the far, far north at the height of summer) are useful tools to have and can also double as SOS devices. Other signaling devices you may consider carrying include flares, whistles, and guns.
5. ***A tent.*** Sleeping under the stars may sound romantic, but as soon as the mosquitoes start biting, you'll be dreaming of shelter. Tents also keep you warm and dry, thus protecting against hypothermia. Bring a tent that is easy to pitch, because staking one down in the tundra can be tricky. Make sure the fly is completely waterproof. If you truly want to sleep outside, we prefer the milder nights of winter, when gazing up at the northern lights sans mosquitoes is a wondrous experience.

TRAILLESS HIKING

MORE THAN 75% OF ALASKA'S land belongs to the public—in the form of national parks or preserves, wildlife refuges, state parks, even city-owned park land. This opens up backcountry travel like no other place on earth, but it also can be a bit overwhelming. Do you need permits? How do you gain access? When do you travel? All these questions have different answers, too, depending upon which public agency's land you plan to travel.

To get started, get in touch with one of the four **Alaska Public Lands Information Centers** throughout the state (for contact information, see

unofficial **TIP**
The Alaska Public Lands Information Centers are responsible for circulating information about all of the publicly owned land in the state and directing you more specifically to the particular agencies that handle permits, reservations, and other trip-planning details within their land ownership.

"Federal Lands: Getting More Information" in Part Three, page 54).

The centers are a great source for maps and other details of the areas in which you will be traveling, or for getting information on which maps you will need. *Note*: Although topographical maps can sometimes be purchased at such places as sporting-goods stores and map shops, the best sources for detailed maps of trailless areas in Alaska are the **Geophysical Institute at the University of Alaska Fairbanks,** 930 Koyukuk Drive, Fairbanks 99775; ☎ 907-474-7558; **www.gi.alaska.edu;** and the **ESIC Map Office,** U.S. Geological Survey, on the Alaska Pacific University Campus, 4230 University Drive, Room 101, Anchorage 99508; ☎ 907-786-7011.

As mentioned in Part Three, five main agencies control public land in Alaska:

ALASKA STATE PARKS The Alaska Department of Natural Resources' Division of Parks and Outdoor Recreation protects and interprets areas of natural and cultural significance and supports the state's tourism industry in park units as small as a half acre and as large as 1.6 million acres. One of the most popular facilities is **Chugach State Park** (Potter Section House, Mile 115 Seward Highway, Anchorage; ☎ 907-345-5014), covering 495,000 acres just outside of Anchorage and offering some excellent marked-trail backpacking. Other state parks, such as **Wood-Tikchik** outside of Dillingham, are a bit harder to reach. One of our favorites is **Kachemak Bay State Park** (Mile 168.5 Sterling Highway, Homer 99603; ☎ 907-235-7024), located on the Kenai Peninsula in Southcentral Coastal Alaska. Here you can combine the best of land and sea, with snowcapped mountains being the setting for one day's adventures while gentle ocean waves provide the next day's. To get general contacts for all of Alaska's state parks, see "State Lands: Getting More Information" in Part Three (page 54).

NATIONAL PARK SERVICE National parks comprise more than 45 million acres of public land in Alaska—an astonishing number if you stop to think about it. **Denali National Park** alone, for instance, is 6 million acres, about the size of Massachusetts. Alaska has 17 national-park sites, most of which contain very few maintained trails. Access is quite remote, and travelers here must be very well equipped to handle backcountry travel on their own: in emergencies it can be days before help arrives. Some Alaska national parks allow firearms, others don't. Some require backcountry travel permits, others don't. Be sure to check with each park individually when planning your trip. For more information on Alaska National Parks, visit **www.nps.gov** and link to the "Alaska" section.

Backpacking Outfitters at a Glance

ABEC's Alaska Adventures
☎ 877-424-8907 or
907-457-8907
www.abecalaska.com

REGIONAL LOCATION	THE INTERIOR/ THE BUSH
COST	$$$
SUITABLE FOR KIDS?	NO
ACTIVITY LEVEL	HIGH
TRIP LENGTH	8–19 DAYS

Alaska Alpine Adventures
☎ 877-525-2577 or
907-781-2253
www.alaskaalpineadventures.com

REGIONAL LOCATION	STATEWIDE
COST	$$
SUITABLE FOR KIDS?	VARIES
[illegible]	[illegible]
TRIP LENGTH	VARIES

Alaska Mountain Guides and Climbing School
☎ 800-766-3396 or
907-766-3366
www.alaskamountainguides.com

REGIONAL LOCATION	SOUTHEAST
COST	$
[illegible]	[illegible]
ACTIVITY LEVEL	MODERATE–HIGH
TRIP LENGTH	4–5 DAYS

Alaska Wildland Adventures
☎ 800-334-8730 or
907-783-2928
www.alaskawildland.com

REGIONAL LOCATION	STATEWIDE
COST	$$$
SUITABLE FOR KIDS?	VARIES
ACTIVITY LEVEL	LIGHT–MODERATE
TRIP LENGTH	CUSTOM

Arctic Wild
☎ 907-479-8203 or
888-577-8203
www.arcticwild.com

REGIONAL LOCATION	STATEWIDE
COST	$$$
SUITABLE FOR KIDS?	NO
ACTIVITY LEVEL	MODERATE–HIGH
TRIP LENGTH	10+ DAYS

1st Alaska Outdoor School
☎ 907-590-5900
www.1stalaskaoutdoorschool.com

REGIONAL LOCATION	THE INTERIOR
COST	$
SUITABLE FOR KIDS?	VARIES
ACTIVITY LEVEL	MODERATE
TRIP LENGTH	2+ DAYS/CUSTOM

Sea to Sky Expeditions
☎ 800-990-8735 or
604-594-7701
www.canadianexpeditions.com

REGIONAL LOCATION	SOUTHEAST
COST	$$
SUITABLE FOR KIDS?	YES
ACTIVITY LEVEL	MODERATE
TRIP LENGTH	7 DAYS

Vision Quest Adventures
☎ 907-258-7238 or
866-529-2525
www.alaskavisionquest.com

REGIONAL LOCATION	STATEWIDE
COST	$$$
SUITABLE FOR KIDS?	YES
ACTIVITY LEVEL	MODERATE–HIGH
TRIP LENGTH	6–10 DAYS/CUSTOM

Wilderness Birding Adventures
☎ 907-694-7442
www.wildernessbirding.com

REGIONAL LOCATION	THE BUSH
COST	$$
SUITABLE FOR KIDS?	VARIES
ACTIVITY LEVEL	MODERATE
TRIP LENGTH	5+ DAYS

U.S. BUREAU OF LAND MANAGEMENT This federal agency oversees approximately 85 million acres. These lands offer many opportunities for remote recreation and solitude. Millions of acres are found away from the primary highway system, but some, such as the **Steese National Conservation Area,** the **White Mountains National Recreation Area,** the **Brooks Range,** historic **Fort Egbert** in Eagle, and the **Forty Mile Wild and Scenic River,** can be accessed by road. For information on the Bureau of Land Management in Alaska, contact the **Alaska State Office** (222 West Seventh Avenue, Suite 13, Anchorage 99513; ☎ 907-271-5960); the **Anchorage Field Office** (6881 Abbott Loop Road, Anchorage 99507-2599; ☎ 907-267-1246); the **Glennallen Field Office** (at Mile 186.5 on the Glenn Highway; ☎ 907-822-3217); or the **Fairbanks District Office** (1150 University Avenue, Fairbanks 99709; ☎ 907-474-2200). Or visit **www.blm.gov.**

U.S. FISH AND WILDLIFE SERVICE–NATIONAL WILDLIFE REFUGES There are 16 National Wildlife Refuges in Alaska totaling nearly 77 million acres, the most well known of which is the **Arctic National Wildlife Refuge,** which sits at the center of an oil-drilling debate that has been going on in Washington, D.C., for decades. In general, these lands are less developed (and in most cases not developed at all) than their national-park counterparts. Our favorites are the **Alaska Maritime National Wildlife Refuge** (95 Sterling Highway, Suite 1, Homer 99603; ☎ 907-235-6546; **alaska.fws.gov/nwr/akmar/index.htm**) for its kayak-paddling opportunities; the **Kenai National Wildlife Refuge** (P.O. Box 2139, Soldotna 99669; ☎ 907-262-7021; **alaska.fws.gov/nwr/kenai**) for its wildlife viewing, canoeing, and backpacking; and the Arctic National Wildlife Refuge (101 12th Avenue, Room 236, Box 20, Fairbanks 99701; ☎ 800-362-4546 or 907-456-0250; **alaska.fws.gov/nwr/arctic**) for its rafting and backpacking. To see an overview of all the national refuges in Alaska, visit **alaska.fws.gov/nwr/nwr.htm.**

U.S. FOREST SERVICE Alaska is home to only two national forests, but combined they are vast—the largest in the nation. **Chugach National Forest** surrounds Prince William Sound and is close to Anchorage, while **Tongass National Forest** includes the islands of Southeast Alaska and surrounds the cities of Ketchikan, Sitka, and Juneau. To get contact information for both parks, see "Federal Lands: Getting More Information" in Part Three (page 54).

The BEST TRAILLESS HIKING *in* ALASKA

SURE, YOU CAN STEP OFF INTO THE WOODS for a great trailless-backpacking experience, but we have a few favorites we'd like to share. These are places of unparalleled beauty that offer a little bit of the best of Alaska. Our listings include contact information so you can tailor your trip to your needs—how far you want to travel, which route you want to take, etc. First, here's a little advice to help get you started.

Travel with a Guide?

If ever there's a time to consider paying a guide to lead a backpacking trip, it's when traveling in remote backcountry. Even the most seasoned backpacker can benefit from traveling with a guide, and for several reasons.

First, guides know the area like most folks know their backyards. When venturing into the wilderness for the first time, backpackers must carry maps, compasses, GPS units, and maps. While guides will do the same, they often don't need to, instead relying on their own years of experience and knowledge of the area to lead them. Having a guide can take a lot of pressure off you and let you enjoy the trek rather than, say, fretting over whether you crossed the correct mountain pass.

Second, there is safety in numbers. While you probably want to maintain a sense of peace and solitude on a backcountry excursion, it also is wise to have at least a few companions in case of emergency. In the Alaska backcountry, you could go months without encountering another human. And the more people there are in your group, the smaller your chances of having dangerous encounters with wildlife such as bears.

unofficial **TIP**
Having more than two people in your group—but no more than seven for the sake of the fragile ecosystems—can be a lifesaver if something goes wrong.

Third, it can be cost-effective. You do the math. We'll use a trip to the Brooks Range as an example. An eight-day backpacking trip in the Arctic National Wildlife Refuge ranges from $2,300 to $3,695 depending on the guide you choose. Those trips include ground transportation and use of gear and guiding skills, as well as Bush plane airfare and food. Flying in the Bush on your own can cost hundreds of dollars, and food can be equally expensive: rates vary by the type of plane used and the number of passengers, as well as the distance between points. As for food, expect to pay at least 25% more for perishables such as produce and milk than you would in, say, Anchorage or Fairbanks.

BROOKS RANGE

NINE MOUNTAIN SYSTEMS make up the whole of the Brooks Range, which passes through the **Arctic National Wildlife Refuge** and **Gates of the Arctic National Park,** two masses of federally protected land the size of South Carolina and West Virginia, respectively. There are so many incredible places to see here that it may be difficult to decide in which direction to go. The **Romanzof Mountains,** where Dall sheep graze peacefully, is one choice. Or go to the rugged mountains of the **Arrigetch Peaks.** Gates of the Arctic is a mind-blowing option as well. The Brooks Range extends east to west from one end of Interior Alaska to the next, and separates the far-north Arctic land from Interior Alaska, which is more centrally located and not quite as extreme in its climate.

Traveling in either the Arctic National Wildlife Refuge or Gates of the Arctic requires great skill and knowledge of backcountry travel and navigation. Access is via plane or off the Dalton Highway. Refuge managers encourage small groups—no more than seven backpackers at a time—to minimize impact on the fragile Arctic terrain. When hiking in groups, travel in a fan pattern to avoid creating long-lasting trails. Fires are discouraged because there is little to no wood in the Arctic, but if you do choose to build a fire, remove all evidence of it upon leaving.

Permits are not required for travel in the Brooks Range, with the exception of Gates of the Arctic National Park and Preserve, in which travelers are required to attend a backcountry orientation at the Anaktuvuk, Bettles, or Coldfoot ranger stations (see Resources on the next page). But even if you're traveling in another part of the range, always file a trip plan with someone who knows when you are due to return.

Resources

- For more details on travel in the Brooks Range within Gates of the Arctic National Park, contact one of the park offices. They are open year-round, but hours vary, so call ahead of time to make sure someone is around. The **Anaktuvuk Pass Ranger Station** (☎ 907-661-3520; **www.nps.gov/gaar/index.htm**) has a year-round outside visitor display, but the ranger-station hours vary, so call ahead. The **Bettles Ranger Station/Visitor Center** (☎ 907-692-5494) is open daily from mid-June to Labor Day but sometimes closes for lunch; it's open 8 a.m. to 5 p.m. the rest of the year except holidays. The **Coldfoot Visitor Center** (☎ 907-678-5209) is open Memorial Day to Labor Day, 10 a.m. to 10 p.m. The **Fairbanks Headquarters** (☎ 907-457-5752) is open weekdays 8 a.m. to 4:30 p.m. and closed holidays.
- For further information on travel in the Brooks Range within the Arctic National Wildlife Refuge, contact 101 12th Avenue, Room 236, Box 20, Fairbanks 99701; ☎ 800-362-4546 or 907-456-0250; **alaska.fws.gov/nwr/arctic**
- **U.S. Geological Survey (USGS) maps** can be used for travel in the Brooks Range (check with one of the **Alaska Public Lands Information Centers** listed in Part Three, page 54, or go to **www.usgs.gov** and click on "Maps, Products & Publications"). Shaded relief maps are available at the **Arctic National Wildlife Refuge** Web site (**alaska.fws.gov/nwr/arctic/index.htm**). A single all-inclusive map of the refuge is not available because the area is too vast; instead, figure out which section you plan to travel in and order those indexed maps accordingly.

Brooks Range Backpacking Outfitters

- **ABEC's Alaska Adventures:** ☎ 877-424-8907 or 907-457-8907; **www.abecalaska.com.** This Fairbanks-based guide company has been in business since 1980, offering some ultra-remote backpacking trips in the area. The outfitter also offers paddling trips. Best suited for active travelers. Trips range from 8 to 19 days, $2,350 to $4,350.
- **Vision Quest Adventures:** ☎ 907-258-7238 or 866-529-2525; **www.alaskavisionquest.com.** A trained biologist who works in the Arctic National Wildlife Refuge runs this outfit, and trips are custom-designed around the numbers of people in your party. Owner-operator Wade Willis also can accommodate children for those with active and fit families. Trips start at $3,699 per person for ten days, but call for shorter treks.
- **Arctic Wild:** ☎ 907-479-8203 or 888-577-8203; **www.arcticwild.com.** The company has been around for nearly ten years, but its guides have 30-plus years of experience in the far north of Alaska. This environmentally conscious guide outfit is highly recommended for the most adventurous of travelers with trip offerings as long as 20 days and most in the category of "challenging" (think "real adventure"). Options include base camp, backpack, rafting, or canoeing. Prices, per person, range from $2,750 to $4,300.

- **Wilderness Birding Adventures:** ☎ 907-694-7442; **www.wildernessbirding.com.** One of the best outfitters in the state. Although its trips are focused on birding, you will enjoy the guides and their expertise in the area. The company offers a gray-headed-chickadee trip in the Arctic National Wildlife Refuge as well as a base-camp birding trip, also in the refuge. Trips start at $2,400 for three days and longer.

DENALI NATIONAL PARK AND PRESERVE

THIS PARK'S 6 MILLION ACRES beckon travelers. You need a permit to travel within the park, which is divided into 87 numbered units. A limited number of campers are allowed in nearly half of those units at a time in an effort to maintain a wilderness environment for the wildlife that frequents this world-class park.

unofficial **TIP**
You must apply in person for permits no sooner than one day before you plan to leave; no phone reservations are accepted.

Self-reliance is absolutely necessary. You must be prepared to travel cross-country through remote terrain in harsh weather, and to rescue yourself if there are emergencies. You must also travel responsibly, leaving no fire rings, trash, human waste, or other traces of your presence. This protects the habitat for wildlife as well as other backpackers out to enjoy a wilderness experience.

Obtaining a permit requires first planning your trip. A backcountry unit map is necessary to do this, so you can travel from one unit to the next without interruption. At the height of the backpacking season many units fill up, so plan several itineraries before obtaining your permit.

Resources

- The **Alaska Natural History Association (ANHA)** sells two books that are useful to backcountry hikers: ***The Backcountry Companion*** by Jon Nierenberg and ***Backcountry Bear Basics*** by Dave Smith. Both are available through ANHA (☎ 907-274-8440; **www.alaskanha.org**).
- For general information, call **Denali Backcountry Operations** at ☎ 907-683-2294, or visit **www.nps.gov/dena** and go to the page on backpacking. There is a free, downloadable "Backcountry Camping Guide," too.
- **USGS maps** can be used for travel within the park.

Denali National Park Backpacking Outfitters

- **Alaska Alpine Adventures:** ☎ 877-525-2577 or 907-781-2253; **www.alaskaalpineadventures.com.** The company doesn't lead exclusive trips through Denali (although custom trips are available), but it does offer a three-park tour that includes Denali on its itinerary. The cost is $2,600 for 12 days. The company also offers a great tour of Denali State Park to the south. That seven-day trip starts at $1,800—a better option in our view, because there are no flying costs and the scenery is just as spectacular.

LAKE CLARK NATIONAL PARK AND PRESERVE

LAKE CLARK OFFERS AN IMPRESSIVE cross-section of Alaska. Here, you can walk along the shores of **Cook Inlet,** hike close to volcanoes, and see impressive lakes and rivers all in one trip. Backcountry permits are not required here; however, there are generally accepted rules of travel for the area. Leave no trace when camping—this includes removing all signs of fires and carrying out trash to avoid attracting wildlife.

The park's western end offers the easiest hiking, because the drier tundra enables hikers to travel without getting as wet or tangled in bushes. Farther south, where there is more timber and brush, count on more bushwhacking but also more-remote hiking, where you'll be less likely to encounter other people.

Twin Lakes is one of the more popular places to hike and fish. The park service has a backcountry patrol cabin on the lower lake that is usually staffed all summer. **Turquoise Lake** is higher in elevation, with tundra vegetation and generally less wildlife, but it has great scenery and hiking in all directions. For hard-core hikers, there is the multiday option of accessing **Telaquana Lake.** This will require serious knowledge of backcountry travel but can be an epic adventure for the truly rugged traveler.

Access to Lake Clark National Park can be expensive because of air-taxi costs, which range from $300 to $400, depending on where you land. Unlike road-accessible Denali National Park, Lake Clark is truly remote but, as a reward, far less frequented by travelers.

Resources

- For more details on Lake Clark, call headquarters at ☎ 907-644-3626 or 907-781-2218, or visit **www.nps.gov/lacl** and go to the page on backpacking.
- **USGS maps** can be used for travel in Lake Clark.

Lake Clark Backpacking Outfitters

- **Alaska Alpine Adventures:** ☎ 877-525-2577 or 907-781-2253; **www.alaskaalpineadventures.com.** The company has been around since 1998, which isn't that long in the guide business, but we like them because they have incredible experience overall, first as mountaineers and now as guides for recreational backpacking, rafting, and other wilderness adventures. Their Lake Clark trips are some of the best options available, and they put together custom trips. Prices start at $2,600.

The BEST HIKING TRAILS *in* ALASKA

IF HIKING OFF-TRAIL INTO THE BACKCOUNTRY makes you just a little too uncomfortable, don't worry. There are some world-class trails in Alaska that are well marked (at least by Alaskan standards!) and well established, making for an excellent Alaska vacation for those who love to travel on foot. There are dozens of such trails throughout the state, but many of them are best suited as day hikes because they are not long enough to constitute a multiday trip (for more on day hiking, see Part Eleven). We are sharing our favorite five trips, which are long enough to include at least one night's camping and usually more. For experienced hikers, a 35-mile trail will seem like a simple overnighter, but if we can convince you of anything, it is to slow down and really enjoy these trails. If you must make miles, set up camp early and explore the region around you. All of the trips we suggest afford you this opportunity.

Travel with a Guide?

Guided trips are excellent when traveling into the trailless backcountry where intimate knowledge of the area and excellent orienteering skills are absolutely necessary. But, honestly, anyone with previous backpacking experience will be able to handle the marked trails in Alaska we suggest. If you follow leave-no-trace practices and are careful to protect yourself against dangerous wildlife, traveling Alaska's marked trails can be a grand adventure.

Still, if you feel the need to travel with a guide, we've included a few suggestions at the end of each trail description. Not that many wilderness guides cater to marked-trail hiking, so the choices are few. The ones we have suggested are the best you'll find.

Chena Dome Trail

Regional location The Interior. **Distance** 30 miles. **Trail configuration** Loop. **Difficulty**. **Suitable for kids?** Teens. **Time to hike** 2–4 days. **Best time of year to hike** Mid-June–early September. **Traffic level** Light–moderate. **Facilities** Marked trailheads within a mile and a half of each other; one trail shelter located within Chena River State Recreation Area.

TRAIL SUMMARY This loop hike offers great alpine hiking and views, with great berry-picking late in the summer. The longest hike in the **Chena River State Recreation Area,** it's best suited to conditioned hikers. It has a total 8,500-foot elevation gain, one of the highest of any trail in Alaska. It's well marked in most places until it reaches the open treeless areas, and then is designated by mileposts and cairns. It can get dry late in the season, so carry plenty of additional water if traveling in late summer. Fires are prohibited; wildlife is plentiful.

DIRECTIONS TO TRAILHEAD The trailheads are only 1.5 miles away from each other, one at Mile 49 and the other at Mile 50.5 of Chena Hot Springs Road, 55 miles east of Fairbanks. Take the Steese Highway north five miles to Chena Hot Springs Road, and turn east. The trailheads are on the west side of the road, just beyond the trailhead for **Angel Rocks,** another day-hike option at about two miles one-way on a steep out-and-back trail.

TRAIL DESCRIPTION The Chena Dome Trail is one of those treks that will be imprinted in your mind. The views are so expansive, it feels as if you are perched on top of the highest ridgeline in Alaska. The trail circumnavigates the Angel Creek watershed but can be dry at times because of its elevation. Resupply your water at every opportunity. Most people start from the north-end trailhead at Mile 50.5 because the climbing is spread out. But traveling this way also means you'll end up doing most of your climbing later in the trip. You decide. If you want to get the worst over, start on the south end. However, if you like to climb hills with a lighter pack, save it for the end.

The trail is well marked in some places, not so much in others, so be prepared with backup navigational tools. A compass and map are musts. In poor weather, be prepared to travel by compass or GPS, or set up camp and wait for conditions to clear. After the first mile of climbing, a view of the **Angel Creek Valley** opens up; by Mile 3, you're about at tree line. The ridgeline is at 3,700 feet and follows dips and climbs until you reach **Chena Dome,** the high point, at 4,421 feet. The only trail shelter is at Mile 17, and there are no reservations required–it's first-come, first-served, although if you have already set up camp here, by all means welcome newcomers or those in distress. After the shelter, the trail dips and climbs like a yo-yo, offering some steep and challenging hiking, but still with open views. Sometimes this section of trail can be hard to follow, but on clear days it should be pretty self-explanatory. The descent to the south-end trailhead begins about three miles out and is pretty quick traveling.

Resources

- The Chena Dome Trail is located in the **Chena River State Recreation Area,** which is part of Alaska State Parks. For details on specific regulations within the area, visit **www.dnr.state.ak.us/parks/units/chena.** The **Alaska Public Lands Information Center** in Fairbanks can also help (250 Cushman Street, Number 1A, Fairbanks 99701; ☎ 907-456-0527; **www.nps.gov/aplic**).
- **USGS topographic maps**–in particular Circle A-5 and A-6, and Big Delta D-5–will come in handy on this route, especially in poor weather. Check with one of the **Alaska Public Lands Information Centers** listed in Part Three (see page 54), or go to **www.usgs.gov** and click on "Maps, Products & Publications." Alaska State Parks also publishes a hiking pamphlet, "Chena Dome Trail," available at Alaska Public Lands Information Centers.

Chena Dome Outfitters

- **1st Alaska Outdoor School:** ☎ 907-590-5900; **www.1stalaskaoutdoor school.com.** This adult-education-oriented guide service can get you started on your own adventure or guide you along the way. Owner Ralf Dobrovolny was born in Germany and has experienced extreme northern adventures throughout Canada and Alaska. The rates are extremely affordable–$100 per day per person, to just about any Interior location you want, including Chena Dome.

Chilkoot Pass Trail

Regional location Southeast Alaska. **Distance** 33 miles. **Trail configuration** End-to-end. **Difficulty**. **Suitable for kids?** Teens. **Time to hike** 3–5 days. **Best time of year to hike** June–September. **Traffic level** Moderate–heavy. **Facilities** Marked trailheads and designated campsites with toilets, cooking shelters, and caches to keep food safe from bears. Fees and permits are required to hike on the Canada side but not on the U.S. side. A permit is required for all overnight backpackers regardless of where you're hiking.

TRAIL SUMMARY The trail is historic as well as scenic, following the route of gold seekers during the gold rush of 1898–1900. It begins at the Taiya River bridge, near the community of **Dyea,** and travels over the Chilkoot Pass to **Lake Bennett** in Canada. The route passes through forests, past streams and lakes, and opens into high alpine country.

DIRECTIONS TO TRAILHEAD From downtown Skagway, drive two miles north on the Klondike Highway to the Dyea Road. Turn left and drive seven miles to the trailhead, which is marked and has a ranger station nearby. Reaching Lake Bennett is more complicated, as there is no road access. Drive north on the Klondike Highway 27 miles to a parking area on the left side of the road for Log Cabin. You can follow the railroad tracks to a spur trail to Chilkoot Pass, or walk along the tracks all the way to Lake Bennett to start the hike from the north. When the White Pass and Yukon Route train is running, it is a better and safer option.

TRAIL DESCRIPTION Because the Chilkoot Pass Trail is such an important historic asset to Southeast Alaska and Canada, a permit is needed to hike it, and everyone is asked not to remove artifacts they may come across: old rusting cook pans, wagon wheels, mining equipment, and the like. These are all evidence of one of the grandest rushes for gold in North America, when in 1898 gold was discovered and tens of thousands of prospectors flocked to the area, intent on claiming their share of the riches. The trail was the shortest and best-known route to the Klondike gold fields, and these hardscrabble prospectors traveled the route year-round in winds, rain, and snow.

unofficial **TIP**
The Chilkoot Pass Trail is one of the best examples of Alaska's varied climates.

While hiking the Chilkoot Pass Trail from end to end, you'll experience everything from lush rain forests to rocky, craggy cliff sides and alpine valleys. There are lakes and streams, and snow is in the pass year-round. For these reasons, it can become a popular place at the height of the hiking season, and it will be quite unlike Alaska's more-remote hikes. Still, it is a mind-blowing experience, imagining what it must have been like for the thousands of souls who lugged their belongings over it in search of riches.

If you want to trace the steps of the 30,000 gold miners of 1898, you'll want to travel from Dyea to Lake Bennett, although either direction is OK. We prefer traveling from the Dyea side because it is actually easier climbing up the steepest section of the trail known as the Scales than it is to climb down. The first five miles of the Chilkoot Trail travel along a creek, with some climbing to reach **Finnegan's Point**, which is the first place to camp. The next uphill section travels through an area known as **Canyon City,** which was the base for hauling supplies over the pass during the gold rush. The old town site is practically gone now, and if you continue another two miles or so you will reach **Pleasant Camp,** at Mile 10.5, which tends to be less crowded than other camps.

Sheep Camp is at Mile 13, and most people overnight here before climbing **The Scales,** which tops out at about Mile 18. Between these miles, expect steep climbing and boulder-hopping. Take breaks often to look over your shoulder and enjoy the view. On clear days, it is breathtaking. On foul-weather days, though, the hike can be almost scary. Watch your footing, and dress in plenty of layers. Despite the high traffic level here, the route can still be quite dangerous if you take a fall. The distance from Sheep Camp to the Pass is only 3.5 miles, but it sometimes feels practically vertical.

The Scales is so named because it's where miners would stop and reweigh their gear for the climb upward (miners called the slope the Golden Stairs for its sharp 45-degree grade). These days, no one will weigh your pack, but try to keep it as light as possible while still carrying the appropriate gear. Your lungs will thank you. When you reach the pass, at 3,535 feet, you've also reached the border between the United States and Canada. During the gold rush, the Royal Canadian Mounted Police stationed themselves at this point, checking to be sure each person who passed the area had enough supplies to last them for the year. If they did, they were allowed through. If not, they had to turn around and go back down.

unofficial **TIP**
We like Happy Camp because it tends to be less crowded than Deep Lake, three miles farther down the trail, where the majority of hikers stay.

The next best camping location from the pass is four miles north of the summit at **Happy Camp,** but there is an emergency shelter at **Stone Crib,** just a few hundred feet below the pass, for those caught in bad weather atop the pass. The area used to be an anchor for the aerial tramway.

Reaching Happy Camp is a nice walk, marked by cairns and temporary poles that the National Park Service and Parks Canada remove each winter. There is snow in the region year-round, often even in July, so be aware of the weather. You'll be in open country and pass a few streams, including Morrow Lake and a small waterfall at Mile 20. Staying at Happy Camp can be a fun experience, with campers celebrating their accomplishments and relating stories of survival.

The last ten miles are your reward for all your hard work in reaching this area. The trail follows a gradual descent along **Deep Lake** and the canyon that drops into **Lindeman City.** Today, the area is a campground and Canadian ranger station, but during the Klondike gold rush more than 10,000 people at a time set up tents and lived here while building the boats they would use to take them to the gold fields. On the way to Lake Bennett are a couple of campgrounds, and you hike through a forested area that drops in elevation until you reach the end of the trail.

Resources

- The U.S. portion of the trail is part of **Klondike Gold Rush National Historical Park.** For general information, contact the National Park Service at Box 517, Skagway 99840; ☎ 907-983-2921; **www.nps.gov/klgo/chilkoot.htm.** The **Southeast Alaska Discovery Center** in Ketchikan can also help (50 Main Street, Ketchikan 99901; ☎ 907-228-6220; **www.nps.gov/aplic**). The Canadian leg is part of the **Chilkoot Trail National Historic Site.** For general information, contact **Parks Canada** (205-300 Main Street, Whitehorse, YT Y1A2B5; ☎ 800-661-0486 or 867-667-3910; **www.pc.gc.ca/lhn-nhs/yt/chilkoot/index_e.asp**). (*Note:* When crossing the border into Canada, adults must present a passport and another form of picture ID; children must show a birth certificate, plus a letter of authorization if one or both parents are absent.)
- Every person camping on the Chilkoot Pass Trail must have a permit, and it's best to get one in advance because this hike is so popular. Only eight permits a day are held for hikers without reservations. Day users in Canada must also have a permit (day hikers in the United States do not need one). All fees are payable at the time of reservation, or at the time permits are obtained if no reservation is made. Permit fees are refundable up to a month before your planned departure; reservation fees are nonrefundable. Rates are $52.50 for adults, $26.25 for children 6 to 16 years old. The reservation fee is an additional $10 per hiker. Those hiking in the United States pay only $20 per adult and $10 per youth (in Canada, the rate is $34.65 for adults and $17.30 for youth). Canadian day-use permits are $9.90. Pick up a permit at the **International Trail Center** in Skagway (at Second and Broadway; ☎ 907-983-9234). You are required to present the permit upon request by rangers and wardens. The center also offers a useful 12-minute video on hiking the Chilkoot Pass Trail.
- **USGS topographic maps** for the area are Skagway C-1 (SW, NW) and Canadian topo maps White Pass (104 M/11); Homan Lake (104 M/14); and Tushi Lake (104 M/15). **"A Hiker's Guide to the Chilkoot Trail,"** an illustrated guide that includes everything backpackers need to know before heading onto the trail, is more convenient than the full topo maps. A USGS topo map with side scale shows the trail's elevation gain to help hikers plan their days. It also includes detailed historical descriptions of major points along the way and basics such as customs, permits, and weather info, along with an equipment checklist. The guide is available for $3.95 at **www.alaskanha.org** or at the National Park Service Visitor Center information desk in Skagway (291 Second Avenue; ☎ 907-983-9200 or 907-983-2921; **www.nps.gov/klgo**).
- The **White Pass and Yukon Route** (☎ 800-343-7373 or 907-983-2214; **www.whitepassrailroad.com**) offers rail transportation from the end of the trail at Lake Bennett to Skagway, Alaska, or Fraser, British Columbia.

Chilkoot Pass Trail Outfitters

- **Alaska Mountain Guides and Climbing School:** ☎ 800-766-3396 or 907-766-3366; **www.alaskamountainguides.com.** This Haines-based outfit can do it all, and hiking the Chilkoot Trail is offered as a four-day ($790) or five-day ($940) trek with as many as eight participants at a time and is scheduled on arrangement only. The price is reasonable, covering everything from gear rentals to permit fees to transportation and lodging in Whitehorse, Yukon Territory, on the way back.
- **Sea to Sky Expeditions:** ☎ 800-990-8735 or 604-594-7701; **www.canadianexpeditions.com.** Another excellent choice, organized by a company that offers a slightly longer itinerary for those who want to see Skagway in a little more depth. A seven-day trip ($1,325) includes stays in Whitehorse and Skagway.

Crow Pass–Historic Iditarod Trail

Regional location Southcentral Inland Alaska. **Distance** 26 miles. **Trail configuration** End-to-end. **Difficulty** . **Suitable for kids?** Teens. **Time to hike** 2–3 days. **Best time of year to hike** June–late September. **Traffic level** Light. **Facilities** Marked trailheads and one cabin on the south end.

TRAIL SUMMARY This hike connects the **Eagle River Valley** to **Girdwood,** on the other end of the municipality of Anchorage, and passes through some of the most scenic land in **Chugach State Park** and **Chugach National Forest.** The route loosely follows the old Iditarod mail route, a dogsled path and footpath traveled by those going from Seward northward at the turn of the 20th century. While many Alaskans step up to the challenge of covering the Crow Pass Trail in one day, it is best enjoyed as an overnight trip, or even as a two-night trip if you really want to take in the scenery.

DIRECTIONS TO TRAILHEAD From Anchorage, reach the south-end trailhead by driving south on the Seward Highway and turning left on the Alyeska Highway, at Mile 90 of the Seward Highway. Drive two miles and turn left onto Crow Creek Road. Drive five miles and turn right at the fork in the road. The trailhead and parking area are about a mile up the road. To reach the north-end trailhead, drive north on the Glenn Highway out of Anchorage until you reach the Hiland Road–Eagle River Loop exit just before Eagle River. Take that exit, staying to the right, and follow Eagle River Loop to the intersection of Eagle River Road (there is an oddly placed Wal-Mart at this intersection). Follow Eagle River Road all the way to the end, about ten more miles, and park at the Eagle River Nature Center. The trail is behind the center. Parking at the center is $5.

TRAIL DESCRIPTION Most people choose to travel the Crow Pass Trail from south to north, so our descriptions will also follow this route. The climb out of Crow Creek Road is steep, reaching 2,500 feet to the pass and offering great views of **Raven Glacier.** About two miles in, you'll see the remains of an old gold mine that operated from the early 1900s to 1948. Feel free to explore the area, but be careful because the buildings are in rough shape. At 3,550 feet is the sole Forest Service cabin, which is available on a fee basis, so don't assume it is OK to stay there. The cabin sleeps up to six,; a loft upstairs can squeeze in additional people.

After the cabin, you'll be following rock cairns that mark the trail to the pass. One of the most popular places to camp is right at the pass, and at Raven Glacier, although it can get windy and foul weather can blow in quickly. But the views rival any in the state, and the mountains and glacier provide great contrast to the greens of the summer foliage.

From the pass, the trail continues along the edge of Raven Glacier, eventually reaching **Clear Creek** at Mile 8. You'll have to ford this creek, but in less than a mile you'll pass over Raven Creek via bridge. The next creek crossing is at Mile 9.5. The trail will then begin a climb, opening to a view of **Eagle Glacier,** before descending again toward the biggest water crossing of the trip, Eagle River.

Fording Eagle River can be very easy if the water is low or challenging if it is roaring fast and deep. The ford, at Mile 13 and halfway through the trip, requires sure footing and more than one person. Most times, it is about knee-deep and not very difficult, so if you reach it after heavy rains or the spring thaw, consider camping overnight and crossing in the morning, when it tends to be lower. **Thunder Gorge,** at Mile 14, is a good place for camping and even has a metal ring for contained fires.

Mile 16.5 brings you to Twin Falls, another camping option. Beyond this you'll travel on fairly benign terrain, with a slight decline and a few small stream crossings. At Mile 23 is the **Echo Bend** campsite, a popular spot in winter for ice climbers. From there the hike continues through a pretty birch-and-aspen forest dotted with old cottonwoods. You'll arrive at the **Eagle River Nature Center,** a nonprofit organization that offers interpretive and educational programs for budding naturalists, and helps maintain the trails in the area.

Resources

- The Crow Pass Trail passes through **Chugach State Park** and **Chugach National Forest** lands. For details on specific regulations within the state-park area, visit **www.dnr.state.ak.us/parks/units/chugach.** For details on the **Chugach National Forest** end to the south, visit **www.fs.fed.us/r10/chugach** and click on the Glacier Ranger District link. National-forest employees cannot make reservations for the cabin (see below) but can answer questions better than reservation agents; call ☎ 907-783-3242.
- Chugach National Forest manages the **Crow Pass Cabin,** which rents for $35 per night by permit only. Reservations may be made up to 180 days in advance (☎ 877-444-6777; **www.recreation.gov**). The **Alaska Public Lands Information Center** in Anchorage can also help (see Resources for Resurrection Pass Trail, page 102).
- **Eagle River Shuttle** (☎ 907-338-8888 or 907-694-8888; **www.akshuttle.com**) will take you pretty much anywhere you want to go; the newest van accommodates up to nine people at a time. Rate for passage to the south trailhead of Crow Creek Trail is $175 for up to four people; with larger groups, the rate per person goes down.

- **USGS topographic maps** for the area are Anchorage A-6 and A-7 (NE). The **Glacier Ranger District** (☎ 907-783-3242) also has information.

Crow Pass Outfitters

- **Alaska Alpine Adventures:** ☎ 877-525-2577 or 907-781-2253; **www.alaskaalpineadventures.com.** A seven-day traverse of the Crow Pass Trail, from Girdwood to Eagle River, costs $1,700 per person.

Kesugi Ridge Trail

Regional location Southcentral Inland. **Distance** 27.4 miles. **Trail configuration** Out-and-back or end-to-end. **Difficulty**. **Suitable for kids?** 10 and older. **Time to hike** 2–4 days. **Best time of year to hike** Mid-June–late September. **Traffic level** Light–moderate. **Facilities** Marked trailheads on either end and a campground at the south-end trailhead.

TRAIL SUMMARY The majority of this hike lies amid alpine meadows offering open vistas and stunning views of **Mount McKinley** and the **Alaska Range.** Accessing the high ridges is a strenuous climb but well worth the effort, and once you're above tree line, the ridges climb and drop frequently. Although the trail is marked, foul weather can sock the entire alpine trail in a shroud of fog and mist.

DIRECTIONS TO TRAILHEAD The south-end trailhead is at **Byers Lake Campground,** off the Parks Highway, Mile 147. Turn east into the campground and park near the boat launch. Be sure to check for closures, as the trail is sometimes closed due to bear activity. The north-end trailhead is at **Little Coal Creek,** at Mile 164 of the Parks Highway. A sign on the east side of the road directs you to the trailhead.

TRAIL DESCRIPTION Kesugi Ridge is located in **Denali State Park,** between the Talkeetna Mountains and Alaska Range, an hour and a half south of its national-park big sister. The state park was established in 1970 and expanded to its present size (comparable to Rhode Island) in 1976; its western boundary meets the boundary of Denali National Park and Preserve. Denali State Park is less traveled but offers great ridgeline hiking, fishing, and other activities. Wildlife is plentiful here, including black and grizzly bears, moose, lynx, coyotes, fox, and even wolves. *Kesugi* is a Tanaina Indian word meaning "the ancient one," and getting to this place may make you feel ancient—the climb to the tree line is steep and hard, but well worth it.

The high point is also at the north end, about four miles in and at 3,500 feet. The trails are well used as they approach tree line and, once you're in the alpine areas, are marked only by a well-worn path or an occasional cairn. In poor weather, be prepared to travel by compass or GPS, or set up camp and wait for things to clear up.

unofficial **TIP**
The gentler approach to the tree line is from the north end at Little Coal Creek, but we prefer the Byers Lake route because of its base-camp options at the campground.

Resources

- **Alaska Backpacker Shuttle** (☎ 800-266-8625 or 907-344-8775) provides a van shuttle between Seward and Anchorage and Anchorage and Denali.

- For fishing regulations in the waters along the trail—Skinny Lake, Byers Lake, Byers Creek, and Little Coal Creek—contact the **Alaska Department of Fish and Game** or the **Alaska Public Lands Information Center** in Anchorage (see Resources for Resurrection Pass Trail, page 102).
- In case of an emergency, contact the **Alaska State Troopers** at the Talkeetna Post, Mile 12.5, Talkeetna Road (☎ 911 or 907-733-2256), or in Cantwell, Mile 209.6, Parks Highway (☎ 907-768-2202).
- **Denali State Park** is part of the Alaska State Parks system, managed by the Department of Natural Resources. More information about the area is available at **www.dnr.state.ak.us/parks/units/denali1.htm.** The Denali Ranger, through the **Mat-Su/CB Area Headquarters,** can answer specific questions (☎ 907-745-3975).
- **USGS topographic maps** include Talkeetna C-1, C-2, and D-1, and Talkeetna Mountains C-6 and D-6. For Kesugi Ridge only, you will need Talkeetna C-1 and Talkeetna Mountains C-6 and D-6. Maps are also available at the Visitor Contact Station at the Alaska Veterans Memorial, Mile 147.1, Parks Highway (☎ 907-745-3975).

Kesugi Ridge Outfitters

- **Alaska Alpine Adventures:** ☎ 877-525-2577 or 907-781-2253; **www.alaskaalpineadventures.com.** These guides do it all, including their seven-day traverse of Kesugi Ridge, which includes six nights for $1,800.

Resurrection Pass Trail

Regional location Southcentral Coastal. **Distance** 39 miles. **Trail configuration** Out-and-back or end-to-end. **Difficulty** 🫎🫎🫎. **Suitable for kids?** 10 and older. **Time to hike** 2–5 days. **Best time of year to hike** Mid-June–September. **Traffic level** Moderate–heavy. **Facilities** Established tent sites, U.S. Forest Service cabins, and marked trailheads with parking and outhouses.

TRAIL SUMMARY Resurrection Pass, a national recreation trail, is one of the most popular road-accessible hikes on the Kenai Peninsula. Its scenery ranges from forested, riverside habitat to high alpine meadows. The highest elevation is at the pass itself, at about 2,600 feet. Good lake fishing for rainbow and lake trout, Dolly Varden, and some burbot.

DIRECTIONS TO TRAILHEAD From Anchorage, take the Seward Highway south to reach either end of the trail. The north-end trailhead is in the community of **Hope,** 70 miles from Anchorage. Look for the Hope turnoff; turn right onto the Hope Highway, and travel about 16 miles to a left-hand turn onto Palmer Creek Road. Follow this gravel road until it branches to the right onto Resurrection Creek Road. The trailhead is on the right, with plenty of parking. The south end of the trail is in **Cooper Landing,** off the Sterling Highway. From Anchorage, follow the Seward Highway south to Mile 90, at its junction to the Sterling Highway. Follow the Sterling Highway about 15 miles to Mile 52, and turn right (north) into the marked trailhead parking area.

TRAIL DESCRIPTION From the north end of the trail, near the community of Hope, the path climbs continuously along **Resurrection Creek,** where gold-seekers once panned for gold. There is a cabin at Mile 7, but we like **Fox Creek Cabin,** about 12 miles in, which offers a reprieve to an even-steeper climb out of the woods to Resurrection Pass. The **Devil's Pass Trail** connects to the Resurrection Pass Trail at the pass. The **Devil's Pass Cabin** here is an excellent base for a few days of exploring. The southern end of the hike is a more gradual downhill route through lakes and the **Juneau Creek** basin. Look for wildlife including bears, moose, and porcupines in this section. The prettiest part of the hike, in our opinion, occurs from **Swan Lake,** at about Mile 26 from the Hope direction, to the trailhead in Cooper Landing. Through this area, you will pass Juneau Lake and its two lakeside Forest Service cabins, and **Juneau Falls,** four miles from the southern terminus of the trail. The falls are a great place for tent camping but can get busy on weekends.

Resources

- For fishing regulations in the waters along the trail–Trout, Juneau, and Swan lakes, as well as Resurrection and Juneau creeks–contact the **Alaska Department of Fish and Game** (☎ 907-262-9368; **www.sf.adfg.state.ak.us**).
- Cabins in **Chugach National Forest** cost $25 to $45 per night and must be reserved in advance either online or over the phone. Reservations can be made up to 180 days (six months) in advance of the first night's stay; ☎ 877-444-6777; **www.recreation.gov.** For details about the cabins, in the Seward Ranger District, call ☎ 907-271-2500 or visit **www.fs.fed.us/r10/chugach/cabin_web_page/cabin_files.** Check this site before making reservations online or over the phone, because the agents at **www.recreation.gov** are located somewhere in the lower 48 states and don't know much about the cabins. The **Alaska Public Lands Information Center** in Anchorage can also help (605 West Fourth Avenue, Suite 105, Anchorage 99501; ☎ 907-271-2737; **www.nps.gov/aplic**).
- **USGS maps** for the area are Seward B-8, C-8, and D-8. Kenai National Wildlife Refuge maps can be downloaded online at **kenai.fws.gov/maps.htm** or purchased through the **Alaska Natural History Association** ($9.95; ☎ 907-274-8440; **www.alaskanha.org**).

Resurrection Pass Trail Outfitters

- **Alaska Wildland Adventures:** ☎ 800-334-8730 or 907-783-2928; **www.alaskawildland.com.** This company, based in Girdwood and Cooper Landing, can arrange custom tours within Chugach National Forest. We like them because the owner is a longtime Alaskan with good judgment in the guides he hires, and a winner of the Green Star recycling-practices award. We've never been disappointed by Alaska Wildland's services.

PART SEVEN

BIRDING

VISITORS TO ALASKA WHO ALSO HAPPEN TO COUNT BIRDING as their favorite pastime can be wowed by the opportunities here. The Alaska Department of Fish and Game has recorded 471 species of birds identified in the state. Its program, **Wings over Alaska,** encourages birders to seek out as many species as possible. The program, which launched in March 2003, includes four levels of certificates that birders can earn by keeping track of the species they identify. Alaska's governor will sign the highest-level certificate, which can be earned after identifying at least 275 avian species.

Because of its plentiful lakes, rivers, streams, and coastline, Alaska offers many places to spot birds in their habitats, no matter which region you happen to be visiting.

CHECKLIST *for* SUCCESS

- **Bring along a good pair of binoculars.** Alaskan birders recommend binoculars with power levels of at least 7 or 8, and an objective lens that is at least five times the size of the power level. That means they need to be better than your basic $100 pair from a discount store, but they don't have to cost $1,500. In general, expect to pay $300 to $500 for a good midrange pair. Local birders frequent **www.binoculars.com, birds.cornell.edu,** and **www.eagleoptics.com** to get the best deals on binoculars. The sites also offer advice on which features to look for in good binoculars and spotting scopes.
- **Get the scoop online.** Before going to Alaska, check out the **American Birding Association**'s Web site (**www.americanbirding.org/resources/index.html**), which discusses the basics of birding and what to expect when visiting a particular area. It also has a page listing the general etiquette and accepted practices of responsible birding. Visit **AK Birding,** an online discussion group (**groups.yahoo.com/group/akbirding**), to

find out what the locals are seeing. Enthusiasts share their sightings and favorite places to search for birds.

- **Be book-savvy.** Although it is tempting to go for color photos, expert birders use guidebooks with illustrations rather than photos. Your best bet, though, is to invest in several guides, because not all photos or illustrations will always exactly match the birds you see in the field. Also, get your hands on a copy of the American Birding Association's ***Birder's Guide to Alaska*** by George C. West ($26.95; ☎ 800-634-7736; **www.americanbirding.org;** available in most Alaska bookstores). It is the book of choice for serious birders in the state.
- **Earn your wings.** Contact **Wings over Alaska,** a program organized by the Alaska Department of Fish and Game and sponsored by Alaska Airlines, for a birding checklist to use once you arrive in Alaska. Earn recognition by keeping track of bird sightings all over the state. For details and to get a copy of the quarterly newsletter, call ☎ 907-465-5157, or visit **birding.alaska.gov.**
- **Always dress in layers, and be prepared for foul weather**. Even in the summer, the weather can get cold, wet, and uncomfortable, and the patient birder wants to be comfortable. Rainproof gear is a must.
- **Keep on top of the tide schedule.** The tidal range in many places in Alaska can be quite wide, so stay informed to make sure you don't get stranded. Free tide-table booklets are available at just about every grocery store, gas station, and bank in Alaska.
- **Watch your step.** Many of Alaska's mudflats may look like inviting sandy beaches, but they are deceiving: the silty glacial residue in the waters creates beaches that are more like quicksand. Avoid walking on any mudflats unless you can confirm that it is safe to do so.
- **Go to the source.** Consider a trip to the **Alaska Bird Observatory** in Fairbanks (☎ 907-451-7159) if you plan to be anywhere in the general vicinity, but even if you are heading to another part of the state, the Web site (**www.alaskabird.org**) is worth a visit. The observatory, a statewide bird-education and learning center, is a great resource for those wanting to find the best birding in the state.

ALASKA'S BEST BIRDING

Copper River Delta–Cordova

Suitable for All levels of birders. **Regional location** Southcentral Coastal Alaska. **Bird species** Alaska's largest gathering of spring migrant shorebirds—as many as 5 million, particularly western sandpipers and dunlins. **Ruggedness level** Comfortable–rustic; . **Time commitment** 3–5 days. **Road access?** Yes. **Suitable for kids?** Yes. **Best time of year to visit** Late April–early May, during the annual Cordova Shorebird Festival. **Scenery** A rain-forest environment is the background to this community, situated on Orca Inlet, on the east side of Prince William Sound. We think it is one of Alaska's prettiest towns. **Traffic level**

Alaska Birding at a Glance

	Copper River–Cordova	Fairbanks	Haines	Homer–Kachemak Bay	Kodiak Island	Mendenhall Wetlands	The Pribilofs	St. Lawrence Island–Gambell
REGIONAL LOCATION	SOUTHCENTRAL COASTAL	THE INTERIOR	SOUTHEAST	SOUTHCENTRAL COASTAL	SOUTHCENTRAL COASTAL	SOUTHEAST	THE BUSH	THE BUSH
EXPERIENCE LEVEL	ALL LEVELS	ALL LEVELS	ALL LEVELS	ALL LEVELS	ALL LEVELS	ALL LEVELS	MID–HIGH	MID–HIGH
RUGGEDNESS LEVEL	🫎🫎	🫎🫎	🫎🫎	🫎🫎–🫎🫎🫎🫎	🫎🫎	🫎🫎	🫎🫎🫎🫎	🫎🫎🫎🫎
ROAD ACCESS?	YES	YES	YES	ONLY IN HOMER	YES	YES	NO	NO
SUITABLE FOR KIDS?	YES	YES	YES	YES	YES	YES	NO	NO
GUIDE SUGGESTED?	RECOMMENDED	NO	NO	YES	NO	NO	HIGHLY RECOMMENDED	HIGHLY RECOMMENDED

Moderate–heavy, due to its attractiveness to serious birders. **Facilities** Indoor lodging, camping, and plenty of resupply available.

LOCATION SUMMARY The Copper River Delta is the largest contiguous wetlands on the Pacific Coast. The delta is shallow, and the tidal range is quite wide, making it the perfect feeding and stopover grounds for migrating birds. The views are expansive, and the sheer numbers of birds will boggle your mind.

DIRECTIONS Access is by **Alaska Marine Highway** ferry (☎ 800-642-0066; **www.ferryalaska.com**) or air (☎ 800-252-7522; **www.alaskaair.com**). You can drive to Valdez and take the **M/V *Bartlett*** or the speedier **M/V *Chenega*** to Cordova, with or without your vehicle, or take a commuter plane from Anchorage and rent a car while in town. The ferry system carries passengers and vehicles between Cordova, Valdez, Seward, and Whittier on a year-round basis. Experienced birders will definitely want a vehicle, though, because some of the best birding is located on the road system.

DESCRIPTION Today Cordova is mostly a fishing and fish-processing town of about 2,200 residents, but it began as a port for shipping copper brought from the mines outside of Kennicott. It has the best of both worlds—all the supplies you need in a small, friendly place where the locals are more than happy to share their hospitality. As for birding, **Hartney Bay** and **Alagnik Slough** are the hot spots for major activity during the spring migration, but you can spend days exploring any number of other locations, too. Expect to find as many as 45 different species of birds, including common loon; black oystercatcher; tree swallow; yellow-billed, Pacific, and arctic loons; semipalmated plover; killdeer; purple martin; grebes; godwits; swallows; and all species of ducks.

To get to Hartney Bay, drive Whitshed Road for 5.5 miles to its end. In front of you will be the 300,000-acre Copper River Delta mudflats and an excellent shorebird- and waterfowl-viewing area. High tides are the best time to go birding here, as the birds are pushed up a bit closer. Because the area is so vast, most birders bring powerful scopes with which to see the farther-off species.

There is a **U.S. Forest Service** recreation area at Alagnik Slough, which is 20 miles outside of town. Look for trumpeter swans along the boardwalk and viewing blind at the slough.

Other Local Options for the More-experienced Birder

- Bring your spotting scope to **Orca Inlet** to view yellow-billed loons that can be seen several hundred yards off shore beginning in the fall. On the way there, stop at **Fleming Spit,** which is a good place to see bald eagles, ravens, gulls, and crows feeding on spawned-out salmon beginning in the spring and continuing through the fall. Other possibilities along this road include horned and red-necked grebes, murres, harlequin and long-tailed ducks, scoters (even black scoters, although they are considered rare), Barrow's goldeneyes, and cormorants.
- From Second Avenue downtown, take Lake Avenue, which becomes **Power Creek Road,** for a winding, sometimes slippery (be prepared for winter driving), but quite scenic birding foray to the eastern end of town. Birds to look for include Barrow's goldeneyes and common mergansers, winter wrens, thrushes, Townsend's warbler, and a variety of owls. A trailhead for the **Ridge Trail** lies at the end of the road. Look for harlequin ducks, spotted sandpiper, American dippers, and greater and lesser yellowlegs.
- The **Crater Lake Trail** is another good spot, located just past the small-plane airport across from Skater's Cabin (parking is on the cabin side of the road). Spruce grouses can be found squatting along this trail and are always a pleasure to watch. Willow and rock ptarmigan also frequent the area.

Resources

- **Chinook Auto Rentals:** ☎ 877-424-5279; **www.chinookauto rentals.com.**
- **Chugach National Forest:** ☎ 907-424-7661; **www.fs.fed.us/r10/ chugach/cordova.** For information on trails, public-use cabins, and other uses of national-forest land. Cabins can be reserved at ☎ 877-444-6777; **www.recreation.gov.**
- **Cordova Auto Rentals:** ☎ 907-424-5982; **cars@ctcak.net.**
- **Cordova Chamber of Commerce:** ☎ 907-424-7260; **www.cordova chamber.com.**

Birding Outfitters at a Glance

Bay Excursions Water Taxi & Tours
☎ 907-235-7525
www.bayexcursions.com

REGIONAL LOCATION	SOUTHCENTRAL COASTAL
COST	$
SUITABLE FOR KIDS?	YES
ACTIVITY LEVEL	LIGHT
TRIP LENGTH	DAY TRIP

Cordova Rose Lodge
☎ 907-424-7673
www.cordovarose.com

REGIONAL LOCATION	SOUTHCENTRAL COASTAL
COST	$$
SUITABLE FOR KIDS?	YES
ACTIVITY LEVEL	LIGHT–MODERATE
TRIP LENGTH	6 DAYS

Hallo Bay Bear Camp
☎ 907-235-2237
www.hallobay.com

REGIONAL LOCATION	SOUTHCENTRAL COASTAL
COST	$$$
SUITABLE FOR KIDS?	NO
ACTIVITY LEVEL	MODERATE–HIGH
TRIP LENGTH	2–7 DAYS

High Lonesome Eco Tours
☎ 800-743-2668
www.hilonesome.com

REGIONAL LOCATION	THE BUSH
COST	$$
SUITABLE FOR KIDS?	YES
ACTIVITY LEVEL	LIGHT
TRIP LENGTH	5 DAYS

Mako's Water Taxi
☎ 907-235-9055
www.makoswatertaxi.com

REGIONAL LOCATION	SOUTHCENTRAL COASTAL
COST	$
SUITABLE FOR KIDS?	YES
ACTIVITY LEVEL	LIGHT
TRIP LENGTH	DAY TRIP

Quartz Creek Lodge
☎ 011-8816-3144-4939 (satellite phone)
www.quartzcreeklodge.com

REGIONAL LOCATION	SOUTHCENTRAL COASTAL
COST	$$$
SUITABLE FOR KIDS?	YES
ACTIVITY LEVEL	LIGHT–MODERATE
TRIP LENGTH	CUSTOM

St. George Island Tours
☎ 907-272-9886
www.stgeorgetanaq.com

REGIONAL LOCATION	THE BUSH
COST	NEGOTIABLE
SUITABLE FOR KIDS?	NO
ACTIVITY LEVEL	LIGHT–MODERATE
TRIP LENGTH	CUSTOM

St. Paul Island Tours
☎ 877-424-5637
www.alaskabirding.com

REGIONAL LOCATION	THE BUSH
COST	$$$
SUITABLE FOR KIDS?	NO
ACTIVITY LEVEL	LIGHT–MODERATE
TRIP LENGTH	3–8 DAYS

Wilderness Birding Adventures
☎ 907-694-7442
www.wildernessbirding.com

REGIONAL LOCATION	STATEWIDE
COST	$$
SUITABLE FOR KIDS?	SOME
ACTIVITY LEVEL	MODERATE
TRIP LENGTH	3–7 DAYS

Zachar Bay Lodge
☎ 800-693-2333 or 907-486-4120
www.zacharbay.com

REGIONAL LOCATION	SOUTHCENTRAL COASTAL
COST	$$$
SUITABLE FOR KIDS?	YES
ACTIVITY LEVEL	LIGHT–MODERATE
TRIP LENGTH	CUSTOM

- **Out the Road RV Rentals:** ☎ 907-424-7279; **ecolano@gci.net.**
- **Prince William Sound Audubon Society:** P.O. Box 2511, Cordova 99574; contact: Milo Burcham, president, **milosphotos@yahoo.com.**

Cordova-area Birding Outfitters

- **Cordova Rose Lodge:** ☎ 907-424-7673; **www.cordovarose.com.** We like this locally owned outfit, with its lodge beautifully located on the water, because the guide is a longtime Cordovan who knows the area probably better than anyone else. Prices are extremely reasonable:

$795 for six nights and five days, including breakfasts, lodging, and car rental. You pay airfare or ferry costs. The rooms are not luxurious but are quite comfortable nonetheless—and the trip is only available in May, during the annual shorebird festival there.

Fairbanks

Suitable for All levels of birders. **Regional location** The Interior. **Bird species** Bank swallows, belted kingfishers, Townsend's warblers, white-winged crossbills, and a host of cranes, ducks, and geese. **Ruggedness level** Comfortable–rustic; . **Road access?** Yes. **Suitable for kids?** Yes. **Time commitment** 1–3 days. **Best time of year to visit** August, to view the annual migration of sandhill cranes. **Scenery** Rolling hills of the Yukon-Tanana uplands to one side and the open views of the Tanana and Chena rivers surrounding it; spruce and birch uplands and alpine tundra highest up. **Traffic level** Moderate to heavy. **Facilities** Indoor lodging, camping, and resupply plentiful.

LOCATION SUMMARY Fairbanks is Alaska's second-largest city center, with a population of about 31,000. (U.S. Census statistics officially rank Juneau second after Anchorage in its latest statistics, but Fairbanks, with its outlying communities, still draws a larger population overall at close to 97,000.) The **University of Alaska Fairbanks** maintains a large presence here, giving the city a college-town feel, with many enjoyable activities available besides birding. The primary birding center here is **Creamer's Field Migratory Waterfowl Refuge,** a former dairy farm.

DIRECTIONS Reach Fairbanks by heading north on the Richardson or Parks highways, or by flying into the Fairbanks International Airport via daily jet service from Seattle or Anchorage, as well as other cities. **Alaska Airlines** is the primary service provider (☎ 800-252-7522; **www.alaskaair.com**). Reach Creamer's Field by taking College Road and turning north on Danby Street. Go north on the frontage road in front of the Alaska Department of Fish and Game offices, and follow the signs to Creamer's Field.

DESCRIPTION The primary draw for birders seeking specific species in Alaska is the annual **Sandhill Crane Festival,** held each August. The weekend-long event is held at Creamer's Field, one of the best birding locations in Fairbanks proper. The event includes bird-watching, presentations, nature walks, and many other related activities, along with ample time for observing cranes and other fall migrants. Friends of Creamer's Field, the Arctic Audubon Society, and the Alaska Bird Observatory jointly sponsor it.

Creamer's Field was a dairy farm from the 1920s until 1966, when bird enthusiasts convinced the state to help them purchase the 250-acre property. Since then another 1,500 acres have been added to the area, making it a waterfowl refuge. There is a series of trails in the refuge, including the Boreal Forest Trail, where you can spot boreal chickadees, Swainson's thrush, blackpoll warbler, and Northern waterthrush; the Seasonal Wetland Trail, which is home to horned and red-necked grebes, blue-winged teal, Barrow's goldeneyes, and solitary sandpipers; and Farm Road Trail, home to various shorebirds and waterfowl.

While in Fairbanks, you can also check out the ponds around the airport and close to the airport terminal, as well as **12-Mile Summit** and **Eagle Summit,** where you can spot such rarities as wheatear.

Resources

- **Alaska Bird Observatory:** 418 Wedgewood Drive, Fairbanks 99701; ☎ 907-451-7159; **www.alaskabird.org.** A must-see destination for serious birders; staff there can direct you to other good area birding locations.
- **Alaska Public Lands Information Center:** 250 Cushman Street (at Third Avenue), Fairbanks 99701; ☎ 907-456-0527; **www.nps.gov/aplic.** The staff here will advise you on outings, outfitters, and where to find rental equipment.
- **Arctic Audubon Society:** ☎ 907-451-9213; **www.arcticaudubon.org.** Occasional tours can be arranged on request.
- **Creamer's Field Migratory Waterfowl Refuge:** ☎ 907-452-5162; **www.creamersfield.org.** Located in Fairbanks, with a visitor center.
- **Sandhill Crane Festival:** ☎ 907-452-5162. Sponsored by Friends of Creamer's Field and held each August.
- **University of Alaska Museum:** ☎ 907-474-7505; **www.uaf.edu/museum.** Located on the University of Alaska Fairbanks campus, this museum has an ornithology collection.

Haines

Suitable for All levels of birders. **Regional location** Southeast Alaska. **Bird species** Bald eagles. **Ruggedness level** Comfortable–rustic; . **Road access?** Yes. **Suitable for kids?** Yes. **Time commitment** 2–5 days. **Best time of year to visit** November. **Scenery** A diverse ecosystem of coastal habitat and lush forests of Western hemlock and Sitka spruce, surrounded by tidal flats and high alpine meadows. **Traffic level** Moderate during the fall arrival. **Facilities** Indoor lodging, camping, and resupply available.

LOCATION SUMMARY Haines is on the Chilkat Peninsula, surrounded by Lynn Canal and the Chilkat Inlet. It has never been a major general birding destination, but each fall it attracts serious birders by the hundreds with the arrival of the bald eagles.

DIRECTIONS Haines is located 80 air miles northwest of Juneau. You get there by a circuitous road route, ferry, or plane. Access is via state ferry (☎ 800-642-0066; **www.ferryalaska.com**) or air (**L. A. B. Flying Service,** ☎ 907-766-2222; **www.labflying.com;** or **Skagway Air,** ☎ 907-766-3233; **www.skagwayair.com**). You can drive to Haines via the 145-mile Haines Highway, off the Alaska Highway. There also are several fast ferry shuttles between some of the coastal communities near and around the town.

> *unofficial* **TIP**
> The Haines area is home to the largest gathering of eagles in the world, and as such 48,000 acres of prime bald-eagle territory were designated in 1982 as the Alaska Chilkat Bald Eagle Preserve.

DESCRIPTION In the fall and winter, Haines is transformed into a temporary home to thousands of bald eagles, who flock to the Chilkat Valley late in the year to search for late-running salmon in the still-open waters of the Chilkat, Tsirku, and Klehini rivers and nearby streams. Several hundred bald eagles live in Haines year-round, but come fall, that number rises to more than 3,500. It is not uncommon to see more than 30 bald eagles perched on a single tree. So inspiring is the sight that nature lovers and wildlife photographers from all over the world come to view these birds.

Bald eagles are fascinating creatures to watch. They grow up to 12 pounds and can have a wingspan of seven feet, so to see them up close and in motion is almost intimidating. They can fly nearly 30 miles per hour, and they can dive for salmon at speeds up to 100 miles per hour, which is a sight to behold.

The best time to visit is during the annual **Alaska Bald Eagle Festival,** usually held the first or second week of November, although the eagles stick around from October to January for those whose schedules can't accommodate a November arrival. At Miles 18 through 21.5 in the preserve are four off-road parking areas, two with interpretive displays and one with restroom facilities. Also, a total of two miles of surfaced off-road trails and 4,000 square feet of elevated boardwalk have been designed and constructed to make the viewing even better. During the weeklong festival, there are tours, family-oriented outings, and educational seminars. Usually, there is at least one release of a rehabilitated bald eagle, as well as photo workshops and other events of interest to birders.

Resources

- **Alaska Bald Eagle Festival:** ☎ 907-766-3094; **www.baldeaglefestival.org.** Brings in avid birders by the hundreds.
- **America Bald Eagle Foundation:** ☎ 907-766-3094; **www.baldeagles.org.** On the Haines Highway, this organization offers a wealth of information on bald eagles, their preservation, and their future.
- **Haines Convention and Visitors Bureau:** ☎ 800-458-3579 or 907-766-2234; **www.haines.ak.us.** Can help plan a trip during this popular time of year.

Homer–Kachemak Bay

Suitable for All levels of birders. **Regional location** Southcentral Coastal Alaska. **Bird species** Western sandpipers, dunlins, short-billed dowitchers, plovers, whimbrels, bald eagles, puffins, and many species of gulls. **Ruggedness level** Comfortable–rustic; –. **Road access?** Only in Homer. **Suitable for kids?** Yes. **Time commitment** 3 days. **Best time of year to visit** May. **Scenery** Dramatic mountain views across the waters of Kachemak Bay, with rolling mountains of the Caribou Hills behind town. **Traffic level** Moderate–heavy. **Facilities** Indoor lodging, camping, and plenty of resupply available.

LOCATION SUMMARY Kachemak Bay, on the southwestern shore of the Kenai Peninsula, is one of our favorite places in Alaska, if not our absolute favorite. Perched between boreal forest, alpine tundra, temperate rain forest, and a productive marine environment, the area accommodates a rich diversity of birdlife in all seasons and spectacular abundance at particular times. The town of **Homer** (population 9,000 including the surrounding towns) is funky and offbeat, combining artistic personalities with salty fishermen and Russian Orthodox old-believers, giving the community a diverse, accepting feel. There is plenty of lodging and good food available, but those who want a more rustic camping experience can find it easily without straying far from town. Birding in Homer is a great pastime any time of year, but it peaks in early May, with the very popular **Kachemak Bay Shorebird Festival.**

DIRECTIONS You can drive to Homer from Anchorage by heading south on the Seward Highway, then turning off on the Sterling Highway as you approach the town of Cooper Landing. The trip takes about four hours in good conditions. Homer is often called "The End of the Road," and for good reason. Follow the Sterling Highway to its end, and you are here. Access is also available by daily commuter plane from Anchorage; **Era Aviation** (☎ 800-478-1947; **www.flyera.com**) is the primary carrier. Round-trip airfare from Anchorage is about $250 to $300, depending upon the deal you can find. Web specials can drop the rate considerably.

DESCRIPTION Birding in the Homer area is a dual treat: you will see not only countless shorebirds, waterfowl, and gulls but also scenery unlike any place in Alaska. Homer has wide tidal ranges, giving it safe-to-walk-on mudflats that can increase birding possibilities exponentially. The tidal fluctuations in Kachemak Bay are some of the largest in the world. During new and full moons the high and low tides may vary by almost 30 feet in just six hours. Because of this fluctuation, you must be aware of which way the tide is going when you walk the beaches. Don't get caught by incoming tides—they can creep up surprisingly fast.

One of the best places to spot the most species of birds is along the **Homer Spit,** a narrow stretch of land that juts into Kachemak Bay for some 4.5 miles. To reach the Spit, follow the Sterling Highway, bypassing the Homer business district, then veer to the right across Beluga Lake and Slough. The road will turn to the left and again to the right, and then head straight along the Spit. In the summer the road can get clogged with sightseers, so drive slowly because pedestrians frequent the adjoining pathways.

Or better yet, join the walkers and do your birding from the roadside. Just down Kachemak Drive from the Spit Road there is a parking lot across from the airport with a gravel road that leads down to the beach. There is access to a small sand spit that juts out into **Mud Bay,** making an excellent spot to watch shorebirds, waterfowl, cranes, and gulls, especially during a receding tide. Look for Western sandpipers, dunlins, short-billed dowitchers, plovers, whimbrels, and godwits, among others. The pathway, on the east side of the Spit Road, has two viewing platforms and free spotting scopes, so it's well suited to birders. The path continues to what locals call "The Fishing Hole," about four miles out. From there, the road is lined with touristy shops and the boat harbor, so the best birding is had within its limits.

Also at the beginning of the Spit Road, on the west, or right-hand side of the road, is the **Lighthouse Village** viewing platform, which looks into Mariner Park Lagoon. This is a good place to view birds during the spring and fall migrations. The public **Mariner Park** just down the road, which offers camping sites right on the beach, is a good place to see loons, sea ducks, eiders, black turnstones, surfbirds, and harlequin ducks. The best time to visit is at high tide.

Along the Spit Road pathway, be on the lookout for sparrows, which flit about among the shorebirds. If you're driving, there are several parking areas in which you can pull off. Be sure to do this if your birdwatching is causing you to drive too slowly. Traffic can get heavy on the Spit Road at the height of the summer season.

At low tides, the Fishing Hole is a good place to watch gulls seeking out scraps of fish and other beach life. Look, too, for kittiwakes and black brant. About 200 yards from the end of the road is the **Homer Spit Campground,** where one of the locals feeds the bald eagles. We don't recommend it, but it attracts the birds by the dozens and makes for some excellent photo opportunities.

At the very end of the road is one of the more popular hotels, appropriately named **Land's End,** where the viewing of seabirds is quite enjoyable along the beaches. Or sit out on the hotel's deck and watch from there.

Other Area Options for All Levels of Birders

- **Beluga Lake and Slough** compose a diverse birding area located just before you reach the Homer Spit Road. Waterfowl, nesting red-necked grebes, gulls, shorebirds, hunting raptors, cranes, and lots of songbirds frequent the area. There are several viewing options. Just behind the McDonald's restaurant, off Ben Walters Lane, is a short trail on the north side of the lake that leads to the dock at **Ben Walters Park.** It's a good place to go in the evening. Look for mallards, American widgeon, northern pintail, green-winged teal, bufflehead, and the occasional trumpeter swan. From the dock, take the path leading east to look for land birds. Short-eared owls are fun to catch a glimpse of, as well as Steller's and gray jays, magpies, and black-capped chickadees. Townsend's warblers also are a nice sound to hear when walking along this area. It is possible to check out the birds in the mornings by visiting the other side of the lake, but you'll be entering a residential area, so take care to stay off of private property. Drive across Beluga Lake to Ocean Drive and turn left on Douglas Street, then right on Lakeshore Drive. At the end of the road is a set of condominiums and a road called Landings Street. You can turn here and park in the lot, affording a nice view of the center of the lake.

  Viewing birds from the comfort of a boat is always an option in Homer, which offers several ways to get on the water. One choice is to board a ferry operated by the **Alaska Marine Highway** (☎ 800-642-0066; **www.alaskaferry.com**). The **M/V *Tustumena*** is not a tour boat but can provide excellent birding, with trips to Seldovia, Kodiak, the Alaska Peninsula, and Dutch Harbor. We like the ferry trip to Seldovia because it can be done in one day, and the Alaska Maritime National

Wildlife Refuge employs a naturalist to accompany the ferry on Sundays and Mondays during the summer. Other boating options include tour boats and water-taxi services, which are available at all times of the day. While many of the operators are knowledgeable birders by virtue of being on the water so often, do not assume they are experts. Waters are usually calmest in the morning, and breezes pick up in the evening around 7, although that can vary. Temperatures on the water will feel colder, so wear layers and bring hats and gloves, even in the summer. **Gull Island** is one of the birding locations of choice for boaters. Only a few miles from the end of the Spit, it is an easily accessible seabird colony with nonstop activity and the raucous sound of birds as a constant background noise. More than 15,000 birds and at least nine species nest here, including red-faced cormorant, tufted and horned puffin, common murre, and pigeon guillemot.

Resources

- **Alaska Islands and Ocean Visitor Center:** 95 Sterling Highway, Homer 99603; ☎ 907-235-6961; **www.islandsandocean.org.** Has an impressive surround sound birding display that lets you glimpse Homer's birds in action. Also offers plenty of bird-oriented walks, programs, and informational meetings.
- **Alaska Maritime National Wildlife Refuge:** ☎ 907-235-6546; **alaska maritime.fws.gov/index.htm.** The refuge, comprising 4.9 million acres of spectacular wilderness, was created to protect marine mammals, seabirds, migratory birds, and the habitat they depend upon. The refuge provides sanctuary for more than 30 species and 40 million birds.
- The Web site **A Birder's Guide to Kachemak Bay** (**www.birdinghomer alaska.org**) is sponsored by the Kachemak Bay Shorebird Festival steering committee and is an excellent introduction to birding around Kachemak Bay.
- **Carl E. Wynn Nature Center:** ☎ 907-235-5266; **www.alaskacoastal studies.org/wynn.htm.** A good source for birding from the trails and hillsides behind the town of Homer. Bird walks are often held there.
- **Center for Alaskan Coastal Studies:** ☎ 907-235-6667; **www.akcoastalstudies.org.** This longtime learning center offers educational and experiential opportunities on marine life, birds, and other coastal areas of the Alaska Maritime National Wildlife Refuge.
- **Central Peninsula Birding Hotline:** ☎ 907-262-2300. Maintained by the Kenai National Wildlife Refuge for those who will be birding on the drive down to Homer.
- **Kachemak Bay Birding Hotline:** ☎ 907-235-7337. Provides the latest sightings of birds in the region. Callers also can leave their own sighting information. The Alaska Maritime National Wildlife Refuge maintains the hotline.
- The annual **Kachemak Bay Shorebird Festival** (☎ 907-235-7740; **www.homeralaska.org**), sponsored by the Homer Chamber of Commerce and the U.S. Fish and Wildlife Service, is held every May, early in the month. It is a great event to attend because the Kachemak Bay

Wooden Boat Festival, another fun weekend-long event for boat aficionados, accompanies it. More than 100,000 shorebirds pass through this region, and great viewing opportunities exist on the Homer Spit.

- **Kachemak Bay State Park:** ☎ 907-235-6999 (Halibut Cove Ranger Station) or 907-262-5581 (state-park headquarters in Soldotna); **www.dnr.state.ak.us/parks/units/kbay/kbay.htm.** Across the bay you'll find great birding, but trips to this side of the water require careful planning. There are a few state park cabins for rent, as well as plenty of camping. Kachemak Bay ranks as our favorite camping area in Alaska.
- Noted ornithologist and former Homer resident **George C. West,** author of ***A Birder's Guide to Alaska,*** also offers some great birding publications for Kachemak Bay, including ***Checklist of Birds of Kachemak Bay, Alaska; Shorebird Guide for Kachemak Bay and Homer, Alaska;*** and ***Discovery Guide to Birds on the Marine Waters of Southcoastal Alaska.*** The **Pratt Museum** in Homer (☎ 907-235-8635; **www.prattmuseum.org**) has these books and also is a good place to learn more about birding in the area.

Kachemak Bay and Homer-area Birding Outfitters

- **Bay Excursions Water Taxi and Tours:** ☎ 907-235-7525; **www.bayexcursions.com.** Birding is Bay Excursions owner Karl Stoltzfus's specialty, and he has a nice boat to get you to some great viewing locations. Bay Excursions provides birding and wildlife tours, plus water-taxi service to the trailheads and cabins in Kachemak Bay State Park on the south side. We like their flexible schedule and affordable rates. A three-hour guided tour is $60, with lower rates for children under age 12. Possible bird sightings include red-faced cormorant, Kittlitz's murrelets, and Aleutian terns. The Web site includes a bird list for those seeking new species.
- **Hallo Bay Bear Camp:** ☎ 907-235-2237; **www.hallobay.com.** This outfit specializes in bear viewing, but productive birding can also be found at Hallo Bay, in Katmai National Park, thanks to guides who know what they're doing. We also like the camp because it is eco-friendly and blends in well with the environment. The trips range from $1,400 for a basic three-day trip to $3,900 for a full week. Possible birds to see: common and thick-billed murres; pigeon and spectacled guillemots; boreal, snowy, Northern hawk, and short-eared owls; horned and red-necked grebes; and countless loons. Check the Web site for the complete bird list for the Hallo Bay area.
- **Mako's Water Taxi:** ☎ 907-235-9055; **www.makoswatertaxi.com.** For a very affordable glimpse of the popular Gull Island, take this guide's $50 Bay Wildlife Tour. The boat circles Gull Island, a protected marine-bird rookery with a population of about 15,000 puffins, murres, and kittiwakes. You may see eagles, sea otters, or even whales. Bring good binoculars and/or telescopic lenses.

Kodiak Island

Suitable for All levels of birders. **Regional location** Southcentral Coastal Alaska. **Bird species** Loons, grebes, cormorants, sea ducks, Steller's eider, emperor goose, tufted puffins, tundra swans, terns, passerines. Other common species include fox sparrows, golden-crowned sparrows, Wilson's warblers, golden-crowned kinglets, winter wrens, pine siskins, water pipits, and rock and willow ptarmigan. Also, large numbers of eagles–more than 200 nesting pairs–have been recorded in the Kodiak National Wildlife Refuge. **Ruggedness level** Comfortable–rustic; . **Road access?** Yes. **Suitable for kids?** Yes. **Time commitment** 1–5 days. **Best time of year to visit** Winter and spring, through April. **Scenery** The Kodiak Archipelago has a 100-mile road system that allows for several day trips from the town center. **Scenery** Ranges from coastal cliffsides to towering rain forests and above-tree-line mountainsides. **Traffic level** Light. **Facilities** Indoor lodging, camping, and (except where noted) easy resupply available.

LOCATION SUMMARY The Kodiak Archipelago is roughly 90 miles southwest of the Kenai Peninsula and accessible by jet service or state ferry. It extends more than 150 miles into the Gulf of Alaska and is separated from **Katmai National Park and Preserve,** on the Alaska Peninsula, by the 30-mile-wide **Shelikof Strait.** Kodiak is the second largest island in the United States.

DIRECTIONS Kodiak Island is accessible via daily jet service from Anchorage (☎ 800-252-7522; **www.alaskaair.com**) and the **Alaska Marine Highway** ferry system (☎ 800-642-0066; **www.ferryalaska.com**), which can transport you and your vehicle from the mainland in Homer, on the Kenai Peninsula. Once in Kodiak, check at the **Kodiak Island Convention and Visitors Bureau** (see Resources section following) for a driving map of Kodiak Island. It's virtually impossible to get lost.

DESCRIPTION Kodiak Island is one of the easiest-to-reach of the remote places in Alaska, which is why we like it so much. Traveling here is doubly rewarding without the weather concerns and costs associated with some of the more far-flung bird-rich communities in Alaska (although Kodiak does have its fair share of rainy days, it doesn't seem to get as weathered in as the southwestern communities on the Alaska Peninsula). Yet birders can still enjoy the feel of a remote experience, because Kodiak is truly off the beaten path. You'll still have to fly or take the state ferry from the mainland to get to Kodiak, but once here you'll be rewarded with some of the best birding in the state. Kodiak offers great winter bird-watching and usually outnumbers the statewide **Christmas Bird Count,** which is held around Christmastime each year in communities throughout the state (local birders spend the day counting the species they spot and record their findings in a communal register). Tundra swans, shorebirds, and bald eagles are abundant. Emperor geese, Steller's eiders, and a variety of ducks mark the arrival of winter as well. Because of its relatively mild climate and plentiful food, Kodiak Island is home to more than 200 species of birds and offers excellent bird viewing year-round.

For a road-accessible birding experience, it's easiest to start downtown, where from right on the waterfront, a bevy of seagulls gather regularly. The city's **Pier 2** is a good place to stop, but if you don't see anything, try **Near Island** or any of the pull-offs and parking lots around town. Look for glaucous-winged and mew gulls, black-legged kittiwakes, slaty-backed gulls, and herring and Thayer's gulls, depending upon the time of year.

If you want to see what is up high, take a drive up **Pillar Mountain,** heading north from town on Lower Mill Bay Road. Turn left onto Birch and right onto Thorsheim Street, and then left again on Maple Avenue. The road will take you up steeply, but keep going. It is an impressive 1,400-foot climb even on the numerous cloudy, rainy days, but on a sunny day the view will blow you away.

Walk the tundra up here, which often is windy and much cooler than down below, and look for American pipit, bald eagle, northern goshawk, and merlin species, as well as a variety of plovers.

There are four main roads, called highways but not at all what comes to mind, being mostly gravel two-way affairs with no shoulders. Of these roads, the **Chiniak Highway** and **Anton Larsen Bay Road** offer probably the best birding opportunities. Chiniak Highway follows more than 40 miles mostly along the coastline, so expect to find shorebirds and other waterfowl there. **Women's Bay,** one of three of the larger bays you'll pass, is a good birding location. Look for emperor geese and other shorebirds, waterfowl, and gulls. Common eiders also can be seen in this region, although you may have to walk a ways off the road to spot them. Terns, among the favorites of birders in the area, can also be spotted here, including arctic and Aleutian species.

Another gull- and waterfowl-spotting location is at **Middle Bay,** at about Mile 17 through 20. Gulls and kittiwakes can be spotted along the mudflats in the area. Or stop right before the bridge to the **American River,** a popular fishing spot but also a good place to get out and walk far from the road.

Beyond the American River, you'll travel through forests for a while, but for the most parts, views are expansive with many forays along the coastline. Terns, yellowlegs, loons, grebes, cormorants, and a bevy of other birds can be seen or heard along this section.

At Mile 30, the road diverges. Veer left to continue on Chiniak Highway, or right to take the **Pasagshak Bay Road.** We like both roads, and plenty of birds can be spotted on both. But local birders prefer the Chiniak Highway, so that's where this route will follow.

About a quarter-mile down the road, on the left-hand side, is **Kalsin Pond,** which enthusiasts from the local birding group in Kodiak say is perhaps the best birding location on the road system. The highly recommended guidebook ***A Birder's Guide to Alaska*** (see page 104) also touts the location. Tundra swans, black brand, and ducks stop here, as well as all four of the world's species of godwits, according to West's book. It's also a good spot for shorebirds.

Fossil Beach is another good place to stop, about 16 miles from the intersection of Chiniak Highway and Pasagshak Bay Road. Or travel all the way to the end of the road, and walk along **Cape Chiniak** to search for birds from the observations posts of World War II bunkers.

Anton Larsen Bay Road, only 12 miles long and an easy afternoon outing not far from town, will take you through more-forested areas before reaching the mouth of Anton Larsen Bay, a peaceful, flat-water enclave on the north end of the island. Along this road, keep an eye out for cormorants, ducks, scaups, and mergansers. From the island's sole golf course, you can hike up into the hills, searching for a variety of ptarmigan and other alpine species.

Other Area Options for the More-experienced Birder

- **Shuyak Island,** a 47,000-acre island on the northernmost end of the Kodiak Archipelago, is one of the best places for an adventurous birder to combine other outdoor activities with bird-watching. **Shuyak Island State Park,** which covers most of the island, is surrounded by rugged coastline, beaches, and calm waterways that encourage all levels of sea kayaking (for more on that, see Part Fourteen) as well as offer great bird viewing. To get here, you'll have to fly in a small prop plane or take a water taxi: the 12-mile-long island is 54 air miles from Kodiak. The birding list is endless; look for puffins, black oystercatchers, cormorants, common and red-throated loons, mergansers, harlequin ducks, and bald eagles, among many others. Migrant birds also begin showing up in mid-May to June. The seabird viewing is particularly rich here, as is the chance to see other marine wildlife, including otters, whales, harbor seals, sea lions, and Dall porpoises. The state park offers four public-use cabins that we really like because they are well equipped and provide dry lodging if you happen to visit during a rainy spell. Camping is nice, too, because you can access some of the more-remote aspects of the island and conceivably never see another person during your entire stay. *Note:* There are no facilities for resupply, so all gear and food must be packed in and out.
- **Uganik Bay,** on the west side of Kodiak Island in the heart of Kodiak National Wildlife Refuge, is another great choice for birders who want a remote experience with a variety of species. Even though it's part of Kodiak's mainland, it is still best to access the coastal area via small plane or water taxi; hiking in isn't feasible. Many of the pelagics, seabirds, and waterfowl that people travel to Alaska to see can be spotted in this one location. Look for gulls, terns, and seabirds along the coastal areas, as well as red-breasted mergansers, common eiders, harlequin ducks, Barrow's goldeneyes, and American dippers. On the cliffs you'll find literally thousands of mews and glaucous-winged gulls, black-legged kittiwakes, double-crested and red-faced cormorants, tufted and horned puffins, pigeon guillemots, commons murres, marbled murrelets, and surfbirds. In the refuge look for golden-crowned, fox, and Savannah sparrows; hermit thrushes; winter wrens; black-billed magpies; belted kingfishers; common ravens; violet, green, and bank swallows; and eagles, which appear to be everywhere. There are seven public-use cabins, each available on a reservation basis by a lottery held four times a year. *Note:* No facilities for resupply; all gear and food must be packed in and out.
- **Zachar Bay,** about 50 miles southwest of the city of Kodiak, is another special place for bird-watching because of its remote location and protected bay. It is also is in the middle of the **Kodiak National Wildlife**

Refuge, with camping and public-use-cabin availability. Look for species similar to those found in Uganik Bay, including horned and tufted puffins, black oystercatchers, cormorants, arctic terns, kittiwakes, many gull species and sea ducks, and, as always, the bald eagle. In the trees farther inland, look for the black-capped chickadee, varied thrush, yellow-crowned sparrow, and belted kingfisher. Harlequin, mallards, and common mergansers can be sighted on the river as well. *Note:* No facilities for resupply; all gear and food must be packed in and out.

Resources

- **Kodiak Audubon Society:** ☎ 907-486-6498; **www.kodiak audubon.org.** Trail guides can be obtained at the visitor center (100 Marine Way). The Web site also includes a local-area bird list.
- **Kodiak Island Convention and Visitors Bureau:** 100 Marine Way, Suite 200, Kodiak 99615; ☎ 800-789-4782 or 907-486-4782; **www.kodiak.org.**
- For details on visiting the **Kodiak National Wildlife Refuge,** call ☎ 888-408-3514 or 907-487-2600, or go to **kodiak.fws.gov.**
- For details on visiting **Shuyak Island,** call ☎ 907-486-6339 or go to **www.dnr.state.ak.us/parks/units/kodiak/shuyak.htm.**
- To get a bird list for the Kodiak area, visit the **U.S. Geological Survey** Web site (**www.npwrc.usgs.gov/resource/othrdata/chekbird/r7/kodiak.htm**) or the Kodiak Audubon Society Web site, listed above.

Kodiak-area Birding Outfitters

- **Quartz Creek Lodge:** ☎ 011-8816-3144-4939 (satellite phone); **www.quartzcreeklodge.com.** Owners David and Pam Pingree and their family offer birding on the water and around the land of their remote and bird-rich lodge on Uganik Bay. David, an experienced and avid birder, is an excellent guide. Possible birds to see: red-breasted mergansers, common eiders, harlequins, Barrow's goldeneyes, American dippers, mews, glaucous-winged gulls, black-legged kittiwakes, double-crested and red-faced cormorants, tufted and horned puffins, pigeon guillemots, commons murres, marbled murrelets, and surfbirds.
- **Wilderness Birding Adventures:** ☎ 907-694-7442; **www.wilderness birding.com.** One of the best outfitters in the state, and the only one offering kayaking and birding opportunities in Shuyak Island State Park. Possible birds to see: northern fulmars, fork-tailed storm petrels, cormorants, common eiders, harlequin ducks, Barrow's goldeneyes, bald eagles, northern goshawks, peregrine falcons, wandering tattlers, Aleutian terns, murrelets, puffins, and more. $2,600 for a seven days, all-inclusive.
- **Zachar Bay Lodge:** ☎ 800-693-2333 or 907-486-4120; **www.zachar bay.com.** This family-owned business has an impeccable reputation and offers guided birding, fishing, hiking, and sightseeing in Zachar Bay. Operated by Marty and Linda Eaton and their sons, the lodge is a renovated cannery right on the waterfront, affording spectacular views and peaceful evenings. Possible birds to see: nesting puffins,

black oystercatchers, cormorants, arctic terns, bald eagles, kittiwakes, numerous gull species and sea ducks, black-capped chickadees, varied thrushes, yellow-crowned sparrows, and belted kingfishers.

Mendenhall Wetlands State Game Refuge, Juneau

Suitable for All levels of birders. **Regional location** Southeast Alaska. **Bird species** Bald eagles, harlequin ducks, red-breasted sapsucker, ruby-crowned kinglets, brown creeper, and winter wren in old-growth forests; Vancouver and Canada geese, and mallards year-round. A rare viewing of the Steller's sea eagle is still a possibility, although sightings of the bird have diminished since the late 1990s. Other rare but possible sightings include dusky thrush, Eastern kingbirds, and swamp sparrows. **Ruggedness level** Comfortable–moderate; . **Road access?** Yes. **Suitable for kids?** Yes. **Time commitment** A series of day trips, 1–5 days. **Best time of year to visit** During the spring migration in May, during nesting in June, and during the fall migration. **Scenery** Lots of open, expansive viewing areas surrounded by mountains and glaciers in the background. **Traffic level** Moderate; expect cruise-ship crowds in summer, light traffic in fall and winter. **Facilities** All amenities are close by, ranging from comfortable campgrounds to rated hotels.

LOCATION SUMMARY A combination of mountains, forest, wetlands, intertidal, and marine habitats, all accessible from the Juneau road and trail system, and all offering good visibility.

DIRECTIONS No roads lead to Juneau, but there is daily jet service (☎ 800-252-7522; **www.alaskaair.com**), or you can travel on the **Alaska Marine Highway** ferry system (☎ 800-642-0066; **www.ferryalaska.com**). To reach the Mendenhall Wetlands, go north on Egan Drive from downtown Juneau. At the light past the Nugget Mall (about seven miles from downtown), turn left onto Glacier Highway, past McDonald's and Shell Simmons Drive, which is where the airport is. Turn left on Berner's Avenue and left onto Radcliffe Road. Park at the end of the street.

DESCRIPTION One of the most productive places to go birding in Alaska because it is road-accessible and thousands of birds pass through every spring and summer. There are nearly 300 bird species in the Juneau area, almost half of which nest there, so the possibilities are endless. The walk along the pathway to the refuge winds into the intertidal wetlands and heads to the mouth of the Mendenhall River.

The airport is nearby, so expect jet noises, although the birds seem used to it. Along the way, birds can be spotted along the river, which is right by the runway. There is a grassy area between the end of the runway and the fence that also is home to such birds as pectoral sandpipers and buff-breasted sandpipers, according to the local birding society.

At the end of the runway are two trail options—the **Wetlands Trail** goes down toward the Mendenhall River and is slightly more difficult to walk, requiring mud boots. We like to take this trail about an hour or two before low tide so that by the time we reach the mudflats they are the most exposed, thus offering more birding options. Plan to spend at least two hours there, but time your return so the tides don't strand you. Birds to look for in this section of the refuge include nearly a dozen duck species (including the rare gadwall, blue-winged, and cinnamon teal), horned grebe, Pacific and common loons, and marbled murrelet. Bonaparte's gulls and arctic terns can be spotted, as well as the always-enjoyable black-legged kittiwake.

The second option is the **Dike Trail,** which continues for more than a mile along the dike by the airport and is relatively easy hiking. There are marshes on one side and marine sloughs on the other; it takes about two hours for the thorough birder to travel. Sightings include the commonly spotted bald eagles, magpies, ravens, Steller's jays and chickadees, but also be on the lookout for such species as the hermit and varied thrushes, Lincoln's sparrows, Oregon junco, and pine siskin. Warblers include the orange-crowned, Audubon's, Townsend's, and Wilson's varieties.

Other Area Options for the More-experienced Birder

- A day trip out of town to **Point Bridget State Park** (☎ 907-465-4563; **www.dnr.state.ak.us/parks/units/ptbridg1.htm**) and **Cowee Creek** will reward you with birding that ranges from woodland to coastal. The park is 41 miles north of Juneau and near the end of the road system, with forest, meadow, river, and marine habitats. Follow the state trail into the forest along the edge of the Cowee Meadow; then head toward an excellent view of Berners Bay. Species you might see include Townsend's solitaire, Northern goshawk, warbling vireo, three-toed woodpecker, and maybe even the rare red-eyed vireo. This is a buggy area, so wear mosquito nets and/or repellent. Also, salmon spawn in Cowee Creek, attracting black and brown bears, so be on the lookout, and make plenty of noise to let them know you are coming.
- There are a few places to spot shorebirds, gulls, waterfowl, and seabirds near and on the **Eagle River.** For example, **Eagle Beach,** at the mouth of the Eagle-Herbert River Drainage, is 29 miles north of Juneau off the Glacier Highway. Walk along the eastern shore of Lynn Canal for the best bird-watching. Adjoining the Eagle River is the **Amalga Marsh,** an inland wetland that is accessible from Mile 28 of the Glacier Highway, off the Eagle River Trail. The best time to visit this area is late May through the end of summer. You'll pass through old-growth forests before reaching the marsh area, so look for a variety of species along the way. In the forest, look for the Pacific-sloped flycatcher, Townsend's warbler, and brown creeper, among other species. In the marsh, look for red-winged blackbirds, common yellowthroat, and red-breasted sapsuckers. The local birding society suggests this location as a place to hear the sora, or Virginia rail, although these are rarities.
- Part of the Mendenhall Glacier Recreation Area, **Dredge Lakes** is made up of seven small freshwater lakes that create a diverse habitat for birds in the area. Wood ducks, blackpoll, and the warbling vireo are a few of the treats for local birders. From downtown, drive eight miles on Egan Drive and turn right on Mendenhall Loop Road. Turn onto Dredge Lake Avenue; at the Mendenhall Bridge, stop and park on the right side of the road, and follow a trail to the lakes. (Locals sometimes

refer to the Mendenhall Loop Bridge Road as the Back Loop Road, so if you get lost and have to ask for directions, you might mention this.) On the trails, it is also important to keep your bearings because there are many interconnecting trails that can turn you around easily. Dress for buggy conditions, and travel with more than one person. This is a destination for the experienced outdoorsperson who can navigate with a compass or GPS.

Resources

- ***Finding Birds in Juneau:*** This booklet, written by Robert Armstrong and Richard Gordon and illustrated by Richard Carstensen, is available from the U.S. Forest Service in Juneau (☎ 907-586-8800). You can also download a Juneau bird list from **www.npwrc.usgs.gov/resource/birds/chekbird/r7/juneau.htm.**
- **Juneau Audubon Society:** P.O. Box 21725, Juneau 99802-1725; ☎ 907-586-6678; **www.juneau-audubon-society.org.**
- **Juneau Raptor Raptor Center:** ☎ 907-586-8393; **www.juneau raptorcenter.org.** Features live eagles and other birds of prey, as well as educational exhibits and experts to answer your questions.

The Pribilofs

Suitable for The more-experienced birder. **Regional location** The Bush. **Bird species** More than 240 species identified, including murres, auklets, gulls, kittiwakes, cormorants, and puffins, among other species. Occasionally a rare Asian species may blow in—a wood sandpiper is among the best possibilities. **Ruggedness level** Moderate–rustic; ★★★★. Come with a flexible schedule, as flights are sometimes postponed due to poor weather. **Road access?** No. **Suitable for kids?** No. **Time commitment** 3–8 days. **Best time of year to visit** Mid-May–mid-June for migrant birding, late June for breeding seabirds. **Scenery** Open vistas with gently sloping mountains, craggy sea cliffs, and sandy beaches. Also home to more than a million fur seals, which haul out here for breeding and birthing. **Traffic level** Light, very remote. **Facilities** Indoor lodging, camping, and limited resupply available, although most supplies should be flown in with you.

LOCATION SUMMARY The Pribilofs are a lonesome place comprising five islands, only two of which are inhabited. There are about 900 residents total, but many more birds, fur seals, and other marine mammals to enjoy. Craggy sea cliffs and beaches surround the islands, and impressive volcanoes loom in the horizon. The cluster of homes that makes up the communities of **St. Paul** (population 700) and **St. George** (population 160) is rich in native Aleut history, with more-recent signs of the Russian Orthodox Church's influence. Birders often compare the Pribilofs to their counterpart in the Southern Hemisphere, the Galápagos Islands.

DIRECTIONS The Pribilofs are accessible by plane, although the occasional cruise ship does dock there. Located about 800 air miles west-southwest of Anchorage and more than 200 miles north of the Aleutian Islands, the Pribilofs are most commonly accessed through direct service from Anchorage aboard **PenAir,** a local airline. St. Paul is the more-often-visited island, although St. George also offers excellent birding and has the largest seabird colony in the Northern Hemisphere.

DESCRIPTION World-class birding can be found on St. Paul and St. George islands. The Pribilofs support the largest populations of nesting alcids and seabirds in the world, and their sheer numbers make birding a real treat for the aficionado. But in both locations, be prepared for unpredictable weather that can cause travel delays. Also, amenities are few, and although independent birding expeditions can be arranged, it is often worth the cost to go with a tour that can arrange the logistics. St. Paul is 14 miles long and nearly 8 miles wide, and its 45 miles of shoreline are rich with birding opportunities. St. George is a smaller island with craggier cliffs and an even more remote feel, if that is possible, and the birding options are even more diverse. There are actually more birds on St. George than on St. Paul, but the species are the same.

The **St. George Hotel,** recently designated a National Historic Landmark, sits on a sloped road in the cluster of houses that make up the community. The ten-room hotel, built by the federal government to house visiting officials, can serve up to 18 visitors. You can see birds from the windows and hear the bellows of the fur seals, too. In St. Paul, a new hotel, constructed out of converted trailer homes, was added near the airport in 2006, after closing the old one, which was situated above a bar and could get loud. The new King Eider Hotel offers simple lodging, with twin and double beds and bath facilities down the hall.

unofficial **TIP**
Although it costs a couple hundred extra dollars, we like the birding at St. George for the off-chance of spotting a very rare species, but it is quite remote.

As with any way-off-the-beaten-path location, you'll be rewarded with some of the most unique birding experiences possible, but you'll also pay for it. Prices are high, and if the weather turns and you get stuck a few extra days, you have to pay the bill for lodging. It can add up. Be sure to dress warmly and in layers because even in the summer it can get cold, damp, and windy.

Resources

- **King Eider Hotel:** ☎ 907-546-2477. Known as the POSS Camp by locals, this new addition in St. Paul is clean and very functional. But don't think "luxury," rather, "Alaska Bush." It has one or two twin beds, or a few doubles, a nightstand, lamp, and "a window overlooking a literal junkyard outside," according to one of our sources. Bath facilities are down the hall. Rates are $125 in summer, $95 in the off-season.
- **PenAir:** ☎ 800-448-4226; **www.penair.com.** Operates between the communities of St. George and St. Paul for $120 round-trip and to and from Anchorage for $850.
- The **St. George, Alaska, Web site** (**www.stgeorgealaska.com**), run by the Aleutian Pribilof Islands Association, provides details on where to stay and how to get around. The Native Association is trying to make it easier for the independent traveler to visit here, but we still recommend going with a guide.

- **St. George Hotel:** ☎ 907-859-2255 or 907-272-9886. The only indoor lodging option on St. George Island, with room for 18 guests at a time. No food is available, but you can use the kitchen to cook what you bring with you. It's not fancy at all, but in poor weather, which is common in the Pribilofs, the shelter is nice to have. Rates are $169 per person.

Pribilof-area Birding Outfitters

- **St. George Island Tours:** ☎ 907-272-9886; **www.stgeorgetanaq.com.** Arrange for a guide to show you the bird and seal rookeries and other points of interest, or explore the island on your own. The St. George community is welcoming of visitors. Prices are negotiable.
- **St. Paul Island Tours:** ☎ 877-424-5637; **www.alaskabirding.com.** This company offers three- to eight-day excursions that include round-trip airfare from Anchorage, accommodations at the new King Eider Hotel, and daily forays to beaches and cliffs for bird viewing. Prices range from $1,406 to $2,420, with buffet-style meals that are an additional $10 to $19 each.
- **Wilderness Birding Adventures:** ☎ 907-694-7442; **www.wildernessbirding.com.** Operated by experienced birders Lisa Moorehead and Bob Dittrick, this first-class outfit is one of the best in the state, and one of the few that travel to the Pribilofs. They offer three-day trips to St. Paul, leaving from Anchorage. Possible birds to see: red-legged kittiwakes; red-faced cormorants; common and thick-billed murres; parakeets; least and crested auklets; horned and tufted puffins; all types of eiders; and many Asiatic shorebirds, waders, waterfowl, passerines, and raptors. The price for a three-day trip is $1,950, which includes airfare, lodging, meals, and guiding.

St. Lawrence Island–Gambell

Suitable for The more-advanced birder. **Regional location** The Bush. **Bird species** Shorebirds include western and rock sandpiper and Pacific golden plovers. Also look for rarities such as long-billed dowitchers, common-ringed plovers, black-tailed godwits, and common greenshanks, among others. **Ruggedness level** Moderate–rustic; . **Road access?** No. **Suitable for kids?** No. **Time commitment** At least 3 days. **Best time of year to visit** Mid–late May and June, and the end of August through the first week of September. **Scenery** St. Lawrence is a rather barren place, with open vistas and, on the occasional clear day, a nice view of the surrounding Bering Sea. It's home to Yup'ik Eskimos, whose subsistence lifestyle continues despite modern technology. It can be cold here, even in the summer, and you should be prepared for rainy weather. **Traffic level** Light, very remote. **Facilities** Indoor lodging, camping, and resupply available. The main town of St. Lawrence (population 700) has a post office, groceries, and lodging.

LOCATION SUMMARY The best thing about birding on St. Lawrence Island is that you are bound to find one or two rare birds to add to your life list, which for any birder is a true treat. The village of Gambell is on the northwest tip of the island, about 190 miles southwest of Nome. The community is composed mostly of Siberian Yup'ik people, and although some 700 souls call this place home, it is still a community that feels—and *is*—out in the middle of nowhere.

DIRECTIONS The best way to reach Gambell is through **Bering Air** (☎ 907-443-5464; **www.beringair.com**), which flies from Nome, where jet service is also available through **Alaska Airlines** (☎ 800-252-7522; **www.alaskaair.com**). Round-trip rates from Nome to Gambell are in the $300 price range.

DESCRIPTION There are several birding hot spots in Gambell, but the truth is, you really won't have much trouble at all spotting rare and numerous species of birds in this lonely corner of the world.

One of the most popular birding spots in springtime is **The Point,** where alcids and other seabirds come by in the hundreds during the spring migration. Crested and least auklets can be seen all over the place, as well as murres, guillemots, parakeet auklets, and puffins both horned and tufted. There's also a rarely seen bird called the dovekie, which can be spotted from The Point. To get there, go beyond the school and the old town center to the area beyond the airstrip and to the west of what is called North Beach.

Another popular spot to sit and watch or listen for birds is **The Cliffs,** a mile east of The Point. Here, nesting alcids can be spotted on most spring and summer days.

A road along the mountainside leads to a place called **Troutman's Lake,** which has good fishing and great birding opportunities. Take the dirt road out of town by the lake's edge to find snow buntings, McKay's bunting, Lapland longspurs, and the occasional red-throated pipit. The lake will likely still be frozen in May, but when it opens, even such species as gulls and puffins will hang out there.

Other Area Options for the More-experienced Birder

If your budget won't allow the extra leg of travel to Gambell, **Nome** is quite a nice place to bird-watch, bounded by treeless tundra on three sides and the Bering Sea coast on the other. As the winter sea-ice retreats and migration begins, usually in early June, waterfowl birding opens wide. Nome has a developed but limited road system, so you can explore the area on your own. There are about 300 miles of roads, three of which extend 70 to 75 miles one-way into the surrounding wilderness (there are few services along the way, so stock up before leaving town). Plan for cool, wet weather and quickly changing conditions, which bring in the migrant species that settle in to wait for better weather. Birding also is good into mid-August, when migration is in full swing. Here are two of our favorite self-guided options.

- **Safety Sound,** less than 20 miles from Nome on the 72-mile Nome–Council Road, is a great place to spot migrating birds before the ice breaks up. Look for Emperor geese, Steller's eiders, scoters, eiders, harlequin ducks, old squaws, arctic and Pacific loons and, occasionally, yellow-billed loons. Tufted and horned puffins, common murres, and cormorants all are possibilities as well. The **Safety Roadhouse** (☎ 907-

443-3060) is a nice place to stop for refreshments after a day of birding, and many like to continue to **Council,** a small community of mostly native residents. The road follows the Bering Sea coast for another ten miles or so, then turns inland toward Council. At the end of the road there is a river that you have to cross to get to Council, but don't try to cross it. The locals do, but they know exactly which way to go.

- Drive along the 85-mile **Kougarok Road** to look for the nesting habitats of gyr and peregrine falcons and golden eagles. High cliffs and rocky ledges line the road, creating a wonderful place for wheatears, bluethroats, wandering tattlers, and bristle-thighed curlews. The road leads north past many of the old mining claims of the gold rush, and signs of mining can be spotted in the surrounding hillsides with stretches of earth scraped away and left in straight, not-so-pretty horizontal lines across the landscape. About ten miles from Nome is the **Dexter Roadhouse** (no phone), which some say was once owned by Wyatt Earp. It's a good place to stop for a cup of coffee or a cold drink. For more birding, stop at the **Penny River** and look for such species as the arctic warbler. The road ends at the Kougarok River Bridge, and you can't go into Taylor. Turn around here for the drive back.

Resources

- **Nome Convention and Visitors Bureau:** ☎ 907-443-6624; **www.nomealaska.org.** Keeps a "birding board" that enthusiasts update and check daily. This is a popular display, and helpful to those looking for specific species.
- **Stampede Rent-A-Car Ventures:** ☎ 907-443-3838. For car rentals in the Nome area.

Gambell/Nome area Birding Outfitters

- **High Lonesome Eco Tours:** ☎ 800-743-2668; **www.hilonesome.com.** This outfit does a good job with their tours, and its prices are reasonable. The cost for five days in Nome, with all meals and transportation provided, is $2,525. The group also goes to the Pribilofs and Gambell, but no word on the quality of its trips there.
- **Wilderness Birding Adventures:** ☎ 907-694-7442; **www.wildernessbirding.com.** Our birding company of choice, it offers three-day trips to Nome along with combined Nome and Gambell trips. The price for the Nome trip is $1,550. For the combined trip, which is nine days, you pay $3,700, meals included. Possible birds to see: red-legged kittiwakes; red-faced cormorants; common and thick-billed murres; parakeets; least and crested auklets; horned and tufted puffins; all of the eiders; and many Asiatic shorebirds, waders, waterfowl, passerines, and raptors.

PART EIGHT

CANOEING

MOST VISITORS TO ALASKA WILL NOT VENTURE BEYOND the fringes of development. Planes can carry you to isolated lodges, parks, and communities, but even when setting out from a remote airstrip, there often are established routes and trails that one must follow. Stay on these and you'll most likely share your wilderness experience with others. It's easy to leave the tour-package travelers behind, but you'll have to work a little harder to shake the backcountry hikers and campers. Rather than paring your supplies to the bare minimum and trying to get farther off the beaten path, why not leave the path behind altogether?

Alaska has far more river than road or trail and, with more than a million, lakes outnumber people at least two to one. Put a canoe in the water and a few paddle strokes will pull you into the solitude many seek and few find without tremendous effort.

Take, for example, a family weekend trip we spent exploring the **Kenai Canoe Trails** near Sterling on the tourist-heavy Kenai Peninsula. While the main roads, campgrounds, and popular fishing holes were packed with people, the entrance to the canoe system held just a few vehicles. We passed several canoeists on the first two lakes but soon found ourselves alone. We camped that night on an island and enjoyed a spectacular sunset accompanied only by the crackle of the campfire and the haunting call of a loon. While other Kenai Peninsula visitors likely were stacked camper to camper in the surrounding campgrounds, we had the place to ourselves. Over the course of the entire weekend, we spotted only a half-dozen other people.

This chapter explores some of the canoeing options in Alaska, focusing on a few of our favorite trips. In some cases, you'll be able to go with a guide; in many cases, you'll have to organize the expedition yourself. But we are confident you can do it. Canoeing in Alaska is a great way to explore regions of the land not easily seen from the road, and, luckily, many of our best canoeing destinations are road-accessible.

The Alaska boating season generally extends from June through August since many lakes do not become ice-free until June. Water levels are unpredictable, so paddlers are encouraged to get information on levels from local residents, the district office of the land-managing agency for that river, air-taxi operators, or the **Alaska River Forecast Center** in Anchorage (☎ 907-266-5160).

CHECKLIST *for* SUCCESS

WHEN IT COMES TO ALASKA WEATHER, you can count on one thing: it will change. We've seen wind-driven rain arrive even before clouds had a chance to obscure the sun and awakened to snow early on a June morning. Combine the unpredictable weather with the inherent risks that come with canoeing in colder waters, and the need for solid preparation becomes clear.

Here is a checklist of must-haves when it comes to canoeing Alaska waters, whether you're setting off down the Yukon or exploring a small lake you've discovered along the highway.

What to Bring

- **Personal flotation device (PFD).** There are more ways to tip a canoe than can be listed here. Canoe long enough and it will happen, usually with no warning, so wear your PFD whenever you're in the boat. Take the time to get a jacket that fits, and you'll be more likely to wear it.
- **Paddle.** It might seem obvious, but you'll move more efficiently with a paddle that is fitted to you. Height and arm length are just part of the equation. Whether you sit or kneel, the height of the canoe seat and the style of paddle all come into play. So take your time when buying or renting, and make sure the fit is right for you and the canoe you will be using.
- **Canoe.** Few visitors to Alaska will bring their own canoe, so you'll have to make the best of it once you're here. You'll be faced with aluminum versus fiberglass or Kevlar, wider lake vessels versus narrower riverboats. Choose based on the type of trip you'll be making and your skill level. If you're going to make a lot of portages, be sure the canoe has a comfortable yoke. If you have one you like, bring it along. Packing a yoke is a lot easier than bringing the whole canoe, and you can always pack it away or mail it home if it doesn't fit.

  Many of the guides, outfitters, and charter companies licensed to do business on public lands also rent boats. Listings of these companies are available from the **Alaska Public Lands Information Center** (605 West Fourth Avenue, Suite 105, Anchorage 99501; **www.nps.gov/aplic/center;** ☎ 907-271-2737).
- **Rain gear.** Rain is inevitable, so be prepared for it. Because you'll be sitting with your legs exposed to the rain and the runoff from your rain jacket, don't skimp on rain pants. Breathable fabrics help battle sweat

Alaska Canoeing at a Glance

Charley River

REGIONAL LOCATION	THE INTERIOR
DISTANCE	88–175 MILES
TRAFFIC LEVEL	LIGHT
DIFFICULTY	CLASS II–V
CONFIGURATION	ONE-WAY
SUITABLE FOR KIDS?	NO
GUIDE SUGGESTED?	RECOMMENDED

Chena River

REGIONAL LOCATION	THE INTERIOR
DISTANCE	100 MILES
TRAFFIC LEVEL	MODERATE
DIFFICULTY	CLASS I
CONFIGURATION	ONE-WAY
SUITABLE FOR KIDS?	NO
GUIDE SUGGESTED?	NO

Kenai Canoe Trails

REGIONAL LOCATION	SOUTHCENTRAL COASTAL
DISTANCE	64 MILES
TRAFFIC LEVEL	LIGHT
DIFFICULTY	CLASS I
CONFIGURATION	OUT-AND-BACK
SUITABLE FOR KIDS?	YES
GUIDE SUGGESTED?	NO

Lynx Lake Loop

REGIONAL LOCATION	SOUTHCENTRAL INLAND
DISTANCE	8 MILES
TRAFFIC LEVEL	MOD–HEAVY
DIFFICULTY	CLASS I
CONFIGURATION	LAKE
SUITABLE FOR KIDS?	YES
GUIDE SUGGESTED?	NO

Tangle Lakes–Delta River

REGIONAL LOCATION	THE INTERIOR
DISTANCE	29–114 MILES
TRAFFIC LEVEL	LIGHT
DIFFICULTY	CLASS I–III
CONFIGURATION	LAKES/RIVER
SUITABLE FOR KIDS?	YES
GUIDE SUGGESTED?	NO

Wood River

REGIONAL LOCATION	THE BUSH
DISTANCE	115 MILES
TRAFFIC LEVEL	LIGHT
DIFFICULTY	CLASS I–II
CONFIGURATION	LAKE/RIVER
SUITABLE FOR KIDS?	YES
GUIDE SUGGESTED?	NO

buildup while deflecting rain, so look for fabrics like Gore-Tex and Sympatex when shopping for gear. A raincoat also will double as a windbreaker, so make sure it's comfortable enough to spend a lot of time in.

- **Footwear.** Touting one type of footwear over another is a good way to start a fight between canoeists. Hip boots that can be rolled down are versatile but can be tough to walk in while portaging, and they're dangerous if you fall into deep water while wearing them. Knee boots probably do the job most efficiently. Many Alaskans swear by XtraTuf brand neoprene boots. They're expensive but comfortable, and they last.
- **Bug repellent.** Unless you're canoeing in early May or September, you'll probably be greeted at every portage and campsite by hundreds of bloodthirsty insects, notably mosquitoes, white socks, and no-see-ums. Bring a head net and plenty of bug spray. Repellents containing DEET are the most effective, but some people are wary of the health risks that can come with its use. Consider a citrus- or eucalyptus-based product before forgoing repellent altogether. Halfway down a wilderness river is no place to discover the bugs are unbearable.
- **Sleeping bag.** Summer temperatures can dip below freezing, so use that as your guide when choosing a bag. Synthetic material might be more bulky than down, but it has the advantage of maintaining its insulating ability when wet. It's too easy to get wet traveling over water in rainy country, so leave the down bag at home and make more room for the synthetic. You won't regret it.
- **Stove.** Bring a light, portable stove. Campfires are one of the pleasures of wilderness travel where they're allowed, but weather and the availability of wood can make a fire more work than it's worth. And when the weather is at its worst, a warm drink and a hot meal are most enjoyable. If you're going to be flown out to a remote launching point,

Canoeing Outfitters at a Glance

Alaska Outdoor Rental and Guides
☎ 907-457-2453
www.2paddle1.com

REGIONAL LOCATION	THE INTERIOR
COST	$
SUITABLE FOR KIDS?	YES
ACTIVITY LEVEL	[illegible]
TRIP LENGTH	CUSTOM

Arctic Wild
☎ 907-479-8203; 888-577-8203
www.arcticwild.com

REGIONAL LOCATION	THE INTERIOR
COST	$$
SUITABLE FOR KIDS?	NO
ACTIVITY LEVEL	MODERATE–DIFFICULT
TRIP LENGTH	8 DAYS

Canoe Alaska
☎ 907-883-2628
www.canoealaska.net

REGIONAL LOCATION	THE INTERIOR
COST	$$
SUITABLE FOR KIDS?	YES
ACTIVITY LEVEL	LIGHT–MODERATE
TRIP LENGTH	CUSTOM

Fresh Water Adventures
☎ 907-842-5060
www.freshwateradventure.com

REGIONAL LOCATION	THE BUSH
COST	$$
SUITABLE FOR KIDS?	YES
ACTIVITY LEVEL	MODERATE
TRIP LENGTH	CUSTOM

Great Alaska Fish Camp Safaris and Adventures
☎ 800-544-2261; 907-262-4515

REGIONAL LOCATION	SOUTHCENTRAL COASTAL
COST	$$
SUITABLE FOR KIDS?	YES
ACTIVITY LEVEL	MODERATE
TRIP LENGTH	CUSTOM

Weigner's Backcountry Guiding ☎ 907-262-7840
www.alaska.net/~weigner

REGIONAL LOCATION	SOUTHCENTRAL COASTAL
COST	$$
SUITABLE FOR KIDS?	YES
ACTIVITY LEVEL	MODERATE
TRIP LENGTH	DAY TRIPS–3+ DAYS

be sure to discuss any rules regarding transport of flammable liquids well before you leave.

- **Fire starter.** Waterproof, strike-anywhere matches ought to be in every backcountry traveling kit. They're light, easy to pack, and they don't run out of fuel. Bring a butane lighter, too, but the matches are a sure thing, so don't forget them.
- **Layered clothing.** Temperatures can fluctuate dramatically in a matter of hours, so dressing in layers is the best way to cope with the changing weather. Polypropylene, fleece, and other synthetics don't absorb water, and they provide good insulation, but do not block the wind. Wool is bulkier but has many of the same qualities and provides some water repellency. However, if wool gets wet, it takes forever to dry. A knitted wool sweater or thick fleece sweater combined with a wind-blocking jacket or vest will get you through all but the most extreme conditions. Long pants will help keep the bugs off and keep you warm.
- **Tent.** Make sure it's large enough to accommodate your party and that its rain fly has been waterproofed recently.

What to Do

- **Share your destination.** Don't leave home without telling someone where you're going and when you expect to be home. Write it down and leave it with someone you trust. It's an easy thing to do, and it will help rescuers to zero in on your location if you get into trouble. Many canoe areas have a sign-in sheet at the trailhead. Use it.

  Alaska doesn't have the cell-phone coverage common to the Lower 48, although it is getting better each year. Don't expect to call for help in an emergency. Emergency location transmitters and satellite phones can be rented and are worth the peace of mind if you are going to be traveling through remote areas.

- **Set realistic travel goals.** Give yourself enough time to make the trip. A good rule of thumb is 10 to 15 miles per day. That'll give you enough time to cover the distance while indulging in sportfishing, photography, and the many other enjoyable activities one might encounter along the way. And with the long days of the Alaska summer, you'll have plenty of daylight, even if you get a late start.
- **Filter your water.** Giardia is ubiquitous in Alaska, so don't take any chances. Water filters are light and compact, and using one is easier than boiling water and produces better-tasting results than iodine pills. Treating water might seem like an inconvenience, but one bout of gut-wrenching giardia will convince you otherwise.
- **Pack efficiently.** Canoe travel allows you the option of bringing a few more conveniences along than you would on a backpacking trip. Just remember that you'll probably have to portage your gear at some point, so don't overdo it—for example, coolers may sound great, but on a three-day canoe trip with multiple portages, it will get old quickly. Most canoeing experts agree that packing all of your gear in one canoe backpack (watertight stuff-sacks that come with shoulder straps) makes for the easiest portaging.
- **Carry waterproof maps.** You'd be surprised how easy it is to miss a portage, even on a well-marked canoe system. A map will keep you oriented on even the most convoluted river or lake system. Modern GPS units have maps built in, but a paper map won't run out of batteries or quit working if it's dropped in the water. Carry your map in a Ziploc bag with the day's route showing, or treat it with waterproofing chemicals available at most sporting-goods stores.

  Find maps for the region you'll be visiting at **www.nps.gov/aplic.** There you'll be able to click the region you're planning to visit. Trip-planning pages for specific public lands usually identify the maps needed for specific rivers.
- **Get a fishing license.** If you're traveling over water anywhere in Alaska, the fishing is probably exceptional, but sportfishermen tend to focus on a handful of rivers. Fishing licenses are required. You can pick one up at local fishing and game offices and most sporting-goods stores throughout Alaska. While you're there, pick up a regulation book since many lakes and rivers are designated for catch and release only.
- **Secure all permits, and pay all fees.** Alaska has some of the most progressive water-rights laws in the country, ensuring public access to virtually all navigable water in the state. But camping regulations change as rivers pass through various public and private lands. Research your route and check with the government agencies that control the lands through which you will pass. Native corporations own large swaths of lands in remote Alaska and often require permits for camping, so be sure you've got permission before setting up camp.

Travel with a Guide?

The following trips can be made by those with moderate canoeing skills. Guide services are available, but whether or not you need them is up to you. For some, venturing into the wilds of Alaska without a guide is unthinkable. However, if you're going to hire a guide, do your homework. When investigating a guide service, here are a few tips.

- **Ask for references.** You'll get an unvarnished evaluation from past clients. Don't go by testimonials on an outfitter's Web site, because those are only the best of the best.
- **Make sure your guide has experience** on the river or lake system you'll be traveling. There's nothing worse than discovering that you're paying a guide who has less experience than you have.
- **Listen to word-of-mouth referrals.** Call sporting-goods shops in the areas in which you want to travel. They know the lakes, rivers, and people who travel them as well as past customers.
- **Look for federal certification.** Guides licensed to operate in National Parks and Refuges must prove they are capable. If you choose a guide off these listings, you can be reasonably sure they know what they are doing.

ALASKA'S BEST CANOEING

Charley River

Regional location The Interior. **Distance** 88 miles to confluence with the Yukon River, additional 63 miles to the town of Circle. **Trail configuration** One-way. **Difficulty** Class II–IV. **Suitable for kids?** No. **Best time of year to go** June–September. **Traffic level** Light. **Facilities** None.

DESTINATION SUMMARY For the advanced paddler, the Charley River offers many challenges over the 88-mile run from put-in until it joins the Yukon River. The river descends through rock gardens at an average of 31 feet per mile at a speed of four to six miles per hour.

DIRECTIONS TO TRAILHEAD There is no direct road access into the Charley River basin. The region surrounding the basin is accessible by the Taylor and Steese highways, which terminate at Eagle and Circle, respectively. Access to the river is by fixed-wing aircraft with short takeoff and landing. The most popular airstrip is **Gelvin's** (☎ 907-443-3879), an unmaintained gravel landing area located in the upper portion of the Charley, just above Copper Creek. Take out at the Yukon, or paddle to Circle 63 miles downriver.

DESCRIPTION The Charley is a National Wild and Scenic River flowing through the **Yukon-Charley Rivers Preserve.** Snowmelt usually keeps the river high during May and June, making the upper river a challenging passage. In late summer and fall, low water exposes boulders and gravel bars, so paddlers must be vigilant and willing to scout before running some stretches of white water.

The river originates in the Yukon-Tanana uplands and flows northward about 108 miles to the **Yukon River.** The river passes through three distinct environments—open alpine valleys, entrenched river, and open floodplain—offering spectacular scenery as well as unspoiled wilderness. The upland valleys drain a rugged mountain area where peaks taller than 6,000 feet are common.

Average float time to the Yukon River is six days. An additional two to three days are needed to float the Yukon River to Circle. There are no rapids on this section of the Yukon.

The river passes through rolling alpine tundra, mountainous terrain, and high, river-carved bluffs. Rustic cabins and historic sites from the 1898 gold rush are preserved along its path. Paleontological and archaeological sites are also plentiful. Peregrine falcons nest in the high bluffs that overlook the river, while the rolling hills that make up the preserve are home to a vast array of wildlife. The Charley descends from 4,000 feet above sea level to 700 at the Yukon River. It is considered by many to be the most spectacular river in Alaska.

Resources

- **Alaska Outdoor Rentals & Guides:** ☎ 907-457-2453; **www.2paddle1.com.** This outfit gets our highest recommendation for shuttle support and canoe rentals. Can also provide some guide service.
- The **Alaska Public Lands Information Center** (250 Cushman Street, Fairbanks 99701; ☎ 907-456-0527; **www.nps.gov/aplic**) can advise you on good local trails and places to find rental equipment.
- **Go North Alaska Travel Center** in Fairbanks (☎ 866-236-7272 or 907-479-7272; **www.paratours.net**) rents RVs and camper trucks if you want a SAG vehicle for road support. Their rates are affordable, too, ranging from $125 to $219 per day, depending on the vehicle you choose.
- **U.S. Geological Survey (USGS) maps** include Charley River A-4, A-5, B-4, B-5, B-6, Circle D-1, Eagle C-6, D-5, and D-6. Check with one of the **Alaska Public Lands Information Centers** listed in Part Three, or go to **www.usgs.gov** and click on "Maps, Products & Publications."

Charley River Outfitters

- **Arctic Wild:** ☎ 907-479-8203; 888-577-8203; **www.arcticwild.com.** This Fairbanks-based outfitter leads multiday trips on the Charley River starting at the headwaters of the river, and through Class II and III rapids for 108 miles of extraordinary scenery. The cost is $2,700 per person.

Chena River

Regional location The Interior. **Distance** 100 miles. **Trail configuration** One-way, downriver. **Difficulty** Class I. **Suitable for kids?** No. **Best time of year to go** June–September. **Traffic level** Moderate–heavy. **Facilities** None; camp on your own.

DESTINATION SUMMARY This clear-water river runs west from Chena Hot

Springs and flows into the Tanana River near Fairbanks. It's a Class I stream, but sweepers and logjams can upset the unwary canoeist.

DIRECTIONS TO TRAILHEAD From Fairbanks, drive ten miles out Chena Hot Springs Road. Turn right on Nordale and leave one car at the Chena River Bridge. Continue on down Chena Hot Springs Road for 48 miles and put in at the Angel Rocks trailhead. If you prefer a shorter trip, start at several spots between Mile 30 and Angel Rocks.

DESCRIPTION The Chena's braided headwaters join to form a narrow, moderately difficult river that cuts through forested mountains and hills and muskeg lowlands, meandering close to the road for much of its length. This westerly flowing river drains 2,000 square miles and draws moderate-to-high amounts of recreational use due to its proximity to Fairbanks. There's no white water, but be alert for logjams and sweepers that can span the narrow channel. Even though you see and hear automobile traffic on parts of the river, don't forget this is wild country. Use of bear-proof containers is recommended for food. Campsites are plentiful along the banks and on gravel bars. Expect high, fast-moving water during May and early June due to snowmelt. August rains can also raise water levels, so watch the weather and choose your campsite carefully. A floodwater abatement dam spans the upper river. Call the **Army Corps of Engineers** (☎ 907-488-2748) to see if the floodgates are open.

Resources

- The **Alaska Public Lands Information Center** (250 Cushman Street, Fairbanks 99701; ☎ 907-456-0527; **www.nps.gov/aplic**) can advise you on good local trails and places to find rental equipment.
- Canoe rentals are available at **Alaska Outdoor Rentals and Guides** (☎ 907-457-2453; **www.2paddle1.com**). They offer foldable and lightweight vessels, as well as river-worthy boats.
- The **Fairbanks Convention and Visitors Bureau** (550 First Avenue, Fairbanks 99701; ☎ 800-327-5774; **www.explorefairbanks.com**) can help book lodging and rentals.
- **USGS maps** for the area are Circle A-5, Big Delta D-5, D-6 and Fairbanks D-1 and D-2.

Chena River Outfitters

- **Alaska Outdoor Rentals and Guides:** ☎ 907-457-2453; **www.2paddle1.com.** Guided floats on the Chena as well as other locations.

Kenai Canoe Trails

Regional location Southcentral Coastal Alaska. **Distance** 64 miles. **Trail configuration** Out-and-back and end-to-end. **Difficulty** Class I. **Suitable for kids?** Yes. **Best time of year to go** Mid-May–September. **Traffic level** Light. **Facilities** Unimproved campsites; fires are allowed within fire rings, marked portages with some boardwalks.

DESTINATION SUMMARY Located on the Kenai Peninsula between Sterling and the Cook Inlet shoreline, the Kenai Canoe Trails consist of two canoe routes: **Swan Lake Trail,** which winds 60 miles through spruce and birch forest, connecting 30 lakes and three forks of the Moose River; and the **Swanson River Trail,** an 80-mile-long route that connects more than 40 lakes with 46 miles of the Swanson River. Both trail systems offer multiple route options, so canoeists can make excursions of various lengths, from overnights to weeklong meanders through the lakes and lowland forest. Portages vary in length from a couple of hundred yards to three-quarters of a mile.

DIRECTIONS TO TRAILHEAD From Anchorage, take the Seward Highway South to Mile 90, where it joins the Sterling Highway. Follow the Sterling Highway to Mile 80.3 and turn right on Swanson River Road. Follow Swanson River Road to Swan Lake Road at Mile 17. The Swan Lake system has two entrances, the first at Mile 3 and the second at Mile 9.5. Farther on, at Mile 17.5, you'll find the entrance to the Swanson River system at Paddle Lake.

DESCRIPTION Start at the west (Mile 3) entrance on Canoe 1 Lake. The portage between Canoe 1 and Canoe 2 is a wet one. We wouldn't call it a water portage because you can't exactly paddle it, and walking is difficult since water levels vary from ankle- to hip-deep. Hip boots are valuable here, allowing one person to drag the canoe while the other paddles. The passage between **Spruce and Marten lakes** is a true water portage, a beautiful channel through a marshy landscape, wide enough for a canoe and not much more. The lakes are surrounded by low, birch-covered hills and lowlands thick with black spruce. Glacial erratics stand out of the water in several lakes throughout the system.

Portages are clearly marked, wide, and well maintained, with boardwalks spanning the wettest portions of the trail. Watch for roots that can trip up the unwary canoe carrier.

The biggest danger for canoeists on this system is wind. Some of the larger lakes, such as **Gavia** and **Swan,** can get pretty choppy when the wind blows, so head for the shoreline if the wind starts to build. It's better to paddle the long way around than to swim.

In addition to fine canoeing, the area is rich in wildlife; moose are common, as are black and grizzly bears, wolves, ptarmigan, grouse, beaver, mink, and numerous waterfowl.

Resources

- The Kenai Trails lie within the **Kenai National Wildlife Refuge.** For more information, visit **kenai.fws.gov/VisitorsEducators/visiting/canoe/canoeing.htm.**
- For fishing regulations, contact the **Alaska Department of Fish and Game;** ☎ 907-262-9368; **www.sf.adfg.state.ak.us** (click on "sportfishing").The page offers maps of area lakes, fishing regulations, and dates of open fisheries. Or call ☎ 907-262-9368. The **Alaska Public Lands Information Center** in Anchorage can also help (605 West Fourth Avenue, Suite 105, Anchorage 99501; ☎ 907-271-2737; **www.nps.gov/aplic**).

- **Alaska Canoe and Campground** (☎ 907-262-2331; **www.alaska canoetrips.com**) and **Weigner's Backcountry Guiding** (☎ 907-262-7840; **www.alaska.net/~weigner**) rents canoes in the area. Weigner's also provides shuttles between put-ins.
- The most comprehensive guide to the trails is ***The Kenai Canoe Trails,*** by Daniel Quick, published by Northlite Publishing Company. The 168-page book sports a water-resistant cover and provides a tremendous amount of practical information gathered by Quick over 20 years of paddling the trail system. Inside you'll find detailed maps and descriptions of every lake and trail, campsite locations, fishing information, what to wear, how to choose a canoe, and more. To order ($15.95 plus $3.85 shipping and handling), call ☎ 907-262-5997 or visit **www.northlite.biz/canoe.**
- **USGS maps** for the area are Kenai C-2 and C-3. Kenai National Wildlife Refuge maps can be downloaded online at **kenai.fws.gov/maps.htm** or purchased through the **Alaska Natural History Association** ($9.95; ☎ 907-274-8440; **www.alaskanha.org**).

Kenai Canoe Trails Outfitters

- **Great Alaska Fish Camp Safaris & Adventures:** ☎ 800-544-2261 or 907-262-4515. Sterling-based operator with a solid reputation.
- **Weigner's Backcountry Guiding:** ☎ 907-262-7840; **www.alaska.net/~weigner.** This longtime guide knows the area extensively and is recommended by locals. Weigner also rents Old Town canoes and provides a shuttle service for those on independent trips. Cost is $165 per day for day trips and $195 per day for multiday trips.

Lynx Lake Loop

Regional location Southcentral Inland Alaska. **Distance** 8 miles. **Trail configuration** Lake. **Difficulty** Class I. **Suitable for kids?** Yes. **Best time of year to go** June–September. **Traffic level** Moderate–heavy. **Facilities** Designated campsites and public-use cabins.

DESTINATION SUMMARY The Lynx Lake Loop is an easy paddle through a chain of small, undeveloped lakes. It's a good place for novice paddlers to test their skills. More-experienced boaters will also enjoy the scenery and peacefulness of the lake-speckled region. It's an ideal weekend trip, although it can be paddled in a full day.

DIRECTIONS TO TRAILHEAD The turnoff for Nancy Lake State Recreation Area is located at Mile 66.5 of the Parks Highway. From Anchorage, take the Glenn Highway north toward Wasilla, and turn on the Parks Highway interchange.

DESCRIPTION The **Nancy Lake State Recreation Area** contains an eight-mile chain of lakes called the Lynx Lake Loop, in the Matanuska-Susitna Valley region of Southcentral Inland Alaska. The canoe trail consists of easy lake paddling through small, wild lakes; well-marked portages; and designated campsites. Public-use cabins are also available for rent. A longer trip can be made by continuing south from **Lynx Lake** to **Butterfly** and **Skeenta lakes** before returning on the same route to rejoin the loop. Cabins are located on **Red Shirt, Lynx, Nancy, James, and Bald lakes.**

Ten thousand years ago, this area, like much of Alaska, was covered with ice. Though the ice has retreated, it still bears the marks of the recent glaciation. As the glaciers melted, they left an impermeable layer of glacial silt and clay that underlies the region. Water trapped above that layer saturates the landscape, creating the many lakes that cover the region.

For those who prefer river canoeing, there is a put-in via the **Little Susitna River,** at Mile 57, Parks Highway, in Houston. The river is mostly easy traveling but some canoeing experience is advisable since sweepers and powerboat traffic are common. Travel time on the river is four to five hours.

Resources

- **Alaska State Parks Public Information Center:** 550 West Seventh Avenue, Suite 1260, Anchorage 99501; ☎ 907-269-8400; **www.alaskastateparks.org.**
- Canoe rentals are available through **Tippecanoe Rentals** (☎ 907-495-6688; **www.paddlealaska.com**).
- **USGS maps** for the area are Tyonek C-1 and Anchorage C-8.

Lynx Lake Outfitters

- There are no guides available for this area, but the paddling is reasonably easy and a good place for beginners.

Tangle Lakes–Delta River

Regional location The Interior. **Trail configuration** Lake crossings and river passage. **Distance** 29–114 miles. **Difficulty** Class I–III. **Suitable for kids?** Yes. **Best time of year to go** May–September. **Traffic level** Light. **Facilities** None.

DESTINATION SUMMARY Designated as a Wild and Scenic River, the Delta begins at Lower Tangle Lake and flows north through the Amphitheater Mountains to the foothills of the Alaska Range. The trip length can vary from 29 to 114 miles depending on the takeout.

DIRECTIONS TO TRAILHEAD From the Richardson Highway, turn west onto the Denali Highway. Follow the Denali 21 miles to the put-in at the Tangle Lakes Campground, on the right. Take out along the Richardson Highway at either Mile 212.5 or Mile 229 across from Ann Creek (see Resources, opposite, for shuttle information). Take out at Big Delta if you choose to make the longer float.

DESCRIPTION The float begins with a 16-mile-long chain of lakes that requires no portages. Watch for wind on the lake crossings. The first mile of river is shallow and rocky. At Mile 2, the river enters a half-mile-long canyon with an impassable waterfall. Watch for the portage on the right. The half-mile trail is interrupted by a small pond, so gear must be reloaded in the boat, ferried across, and then carried to the put-in point below the canyon. Below the falls, Class III rapids stretch on for a couple of miles before smoothing out into Class I for the remaining 12 miles. Camp spots are easy to find along the bank and on gravel bars. Six miles prior to the takeout at Mile 212.5, the river becomes braided. Look for the takeout on the right bank below the confluence of **Phelan Creek.** The Class IV, 20-mile stretch of river between Ann and One Mile creeks is known as **Black Rapids,** and portaging around it by car is recommended. Put in again around Mile 230, and float Class III water through braided channels for about 30 miles before the waters calm to Class I. Take out at Big Delta.

Resources

- From Fairbanks, vehicle rentals are available through **Alaska Outdoor Rentals & Guides** (☎ 907-457-2453; **www.2paddle1.com**) and **Go North Alaska Travel Center** (☎ 866-236-7272 or 907-479-7272; **www.paratours.net**). Rates start at $108 per day, depending on the vehicle.
- The **Alaska Public Lands Information Center** in Anchorage can help with details on the best places to camp or stay along the road (605 West Fourth Avenue, Anchorage 99501; ☎ 907-271-2737; **www.nps.gov/aplic**), as can the Fairbanks location (250 Cushman Street, Fairbanks 99701; ☎ 907-456-0527).
- The **Fairbanks Convention and Visitors Bureau** (550 First Avenue, Fairbanks 99701; ☎ 800-327-5774; **www.explorefairbanks.com**) can help you plan lodging and transportation. The **Anchorage Convention and Visitors Bureau** (☎ 907-276-4118 or 907-274-3531; **www.anchorage.net**) is a good option if your trip is starting from the south.
- Canoe rental and shuttle service available at **Tangle Lakes Lodge** (☎ 907-688-9173).
- **USGS maps** for the area include Mount Hayes A-4, A-5, B-4, C-4, D-4, and Big Delta A-4.

Tangle Lakes Canoe Outfitters

- **Canoe Alaska** (☎ 907-883-2628; **www.canoealaska.net**), based in Tok, offers guided trips in the Interior. The family-owned business has been operating since 1980.

Wood River

Regional location The Bush. **Distance** 115 miles. **Trail configuration** Lake/river. **Difficulty** Class I–II. **Suitable for kids?** Yes. **Best time of year to go** June–September. **Traffic level** Light–moderate. **Facilities** None.

DESTINATION SUMMARY A classic lake-and-river journey through pristine, fjordlike lakes teeming with world-class fishing.

DIRECTIONS TO TRAILHEAD Commercial air to Dillingham Airport; air charter from Dillingham Airport to trailhead. The area is operated by Alaska State Parks.

DESCRIPTION Part of **Wood-Tikchik State Park,** the route descends the Wood River Lake system, five lakes varying from 20 to 45 miles long and interconnected by short, rocky, and swift rivers. The state park allows powerboats and contains several fishing lodges, but the wild nature of the region is largely preserved.

The surrounding terrain includes spired peaks, rolling mixed upland forest, and large, open tundra fields. Bounded on one side by the spruce-, birch-, and alder-covered **Wood River Mountains** and on the other by the muskeg-covered **Nushagak Lowlands,** the variety and beauty of the terrain is remarkable.

From **Lake Kulik,** follow the **Wind River** to **Mikchalk Lake.** From Mikchalk, follow the **Peace River** to **Lake Beverly.** From Beverly, follow the **Agulukpak River** to **Nerka Lake,** which flows into the **Agulowak River** and finally to **Aleknagik Lake.** Short stretches of Class II white water can be found on several of the interconnecting rivers. The trail terminates at the community of **Aleknagik.**

Open fires are permitted only on gravel beaches and bars. Use dead and down wood only. Extinguish fully and bury completely before leaving the site. The use of portable camp stoves is permitted throughout the park and is encouraged. Live-tree cutting is not permitted.

All five species of Pacific salmon—king, red, pink, silver, and chum—spawn in the Wood River and Tikchik systems. Rainbow trout, grayling, lake trout, arctic char, Dolly varden, and northern pike also are present and bring many sportfishermen to the region.

Moose, caribou, and brown bears can be seen throughout the park. Birds nesting in the area include a wide variety of waterfowl, gulls, bald eagles, golden eagles, arctic tern, various loons, spotted and least sandpipers, semipalmated plover, willow ptarmigan, and spruce grouse.

Resources

- **Alaska State Parks, Wood-Tikchik District,** can supply information on conditions and places to camp. The main office is open year-round (550 West Seventh Avenue, Suite 1390, Anchorage 99501; ☎ 907-269-8698; **www.dnr.state.ak.us/parks/units/woodtik**); the ranger station is open seasonally, late May through late September (P.O. Box 3022, Dillingham 99576; ☎ 907-842-2375).
- Visitor information is available at **Dillingham Chamber of Commerce and Visitor Center** (P.O. Box 348, Dillingham 99576; ☎ 907-842-5115; **www.dillinghamak.com**).
- **USGS maps** for this area are Dillingham C-8, C-7, and D-8; one-inch-to-the-mile scale (1:63,360) recommended.

Wood-Tikchik Outfitters

- **Fresh Water Adventures:** ☎ 907-842-5060; **www.freshwateradventure.com.** A longtime operator in the area that can fly you in and guide you.
- The **Wood-Tikchik Ranger Station** (see Resources, above) has information on other guides licensed to lead trips into the area.

PART NINE

CLIMBING *and* MOUNTAINEERING

WITH THREE OF THE TEN HIGHEST PEAKS in North America and 20 peaks over 14,000 feet within our borders, it's no wonder Alaska is a Mecca for mountaineers the world over. Each year more than 1,000 people attempt to summit **Denali,** and, on average, two die trying. Others head for lesser-known peaks like **Hunter** or **St. Elias** because the climbs are more challenging and provide more solitude.

Whether you're joining the crowds on Denali or you've set your sights on a lesser-known peak in the high north **Arrigetch Peaks** or one tucked away in the coastal range of the Southeast, there are enough mountains here for a lifetime of climbing.

If you prefer smaller climbs, there are even more options. For a day of bouldering while visiting the Interior town of Fairbanks, head for the unearthly landscape of the **Granite Tors,** a short hike from Chena Hot Springs Road, northeast of the city. Looking for something with a shorter approach? Try the single-pitch routes along the **Seward Highway** that begin just a few feet from the blacktop.

Come winter, the rock-climbing options turn to ice. The high mountains are forbidding to all but the most hard-bitten adventurers, but closer to sea level, an altogether different type of climbing presents itself as waterfalls solidify into fantastic cascades of ice. From **Bridal Veil Falls** on the Richardson Highway to **Ripple** and **Boone's Farm** deep in the Eklutna Gorge, there is plenty of ice for climbing. Glacier climbing is another popular way to explore the landscape, whether it's in the winter or summer. Some of it doesn't require the technical skills of climbing vertical ice, but you shouldn't venture out alone, either.

Unlike other special-interest chapters in this book, this chapter will not outline do-it-yourself trips and related information. Mountaineering and climbing is a specialized sport that requires experience and thorough knowledge of the conditions before you head out. All mountaineers should understand the science behind the behavior of snow—how it lies, when it falls, and under what conditions it is most likely to

Alaska Climbing and Mountaineering at a Glance

	Regional Location	Elevation	Difficulty	Time Needed	Suitable for Kids?	Guide Suggested?
Arrigetch Peaks	THE BUSH/ THE INTERIOR	VARIES	🫎🫎–🫎🫎🫎🫎🫎	VARIES	NO	RECOMMENDED
Denali (Mount McKinley)	THE INTERIOR	20,320 FEET	🫎🫎🫎🫎🫎	20–30 DAYS	NO	HIGHLY RECOMMENDED
Mount Blackburn	SOUTHCENTRAL INLAND	16,390 FEET	🫎🫎🫎🫎	12–20 DAYS	NO	HIGHLY RECOMMENDED
Mount Bona	SOUTHCENTRAL INLAND	16,550 FEET	🫎🫎🫎🫎	9–15 DAYS	NO	HIGHLY RECOMMENDED
Mount Foraker	THE INTERIOR	17,400 FEET	🫎🫎🫎🫎🫎	10–15 DAYS	NO	HIGHLY RECOMMENDED
Mount Hunter	THE INTERIOR	14,573 FEET	🫎🫎🫎🫎🫎	12–18 DAYS	NO	HIGHLY RECOMMENDED
Mount Sanford	SOUTHCENTRAL INLAND	16,237 FEET	🫎🫎🫎🫎🫎	9–15 DAYS	NO	HIGHLY RECOMMENDED
Mount St. Elias	SOUTHCENTRAL INLAND	18,008 FEET	🫎🫎🫎🫎🫎	15–30 DAYS	NO	HIGHLY RECOMMENDED

cause an avalanche. Even if you are a novice, it is important to go with someone who has experience and can show you the ropes—literally.

The sport also requires specific tools such as ropes, axes, crampons, and hardware, all of which are not cheap. While this gear is readily available, it helps to get on the ice a few times before going out and purchasing the gear on the spot.

We will, however, whet your appetite to learn more. Several regions of the state are popular for climbing, and there are many resources to help you plan your adventure. This chapter offers a description of the best climbing locations, a list of resources for planning, and outfitters that lead guided trips up big mountains.

If big-mountain climbing is something you are considering for the future, we also suggest a few outfitters and locations that offer day trips at area ice-climbing and trekking locales. Think of these outfitters' trips as samplings of what could be. While trekking along Matanuska Glacier with a guide, you can get a small idea of what it would be like to do the same thing for weeks on a remote peak in Alaska. The major difference: you get to sleep in a warm bed come nighttime!

Check out our brief chapter on mountaineering and see if climbing is right for you. If you decide it is, we agree that Alaska is one of the best places to perfect the sport.

GENERAL CLIMBING RESOURCES

NO MATTER WHICH ALASKA PEAK you decide to pursue, these resources can help prepare you for the journey and give you an idea of what resources are available once you land in Alaska. These are general tips; resources for specific climbing areas—such as area air taxis, books on the mountains themselves, or rental companies that cater to just one area—are listed later in this chapter.

International Climbers

Go to **www.cbp.gov/xp/cgov/travel/id_visa** for details on getting through U.S. Customs with the equipment you need. Keep required traveling documents in a safe place during your expedition. Several years ago, an Italian climber cached his paperwork on Denali and a snowstorm buried his marker. It was not a wise move. The site outlines visa and passport requirements; another option is to contact your nation's embassy or consulate.

Reading

These references can help you learn about important safety issues such as wilderness first aid and avalanche dangers.

- ***Alaska: A Climbing Guide,*** by Mike Wood and Colby Coombs.
- ***American Alpine Journal,*** various issues. Go to the library or do an Internet search for journal issues that have information on climbing Denali. An excellent resource, and the accepted journal of choice for serious climbers. The journal is a publication of the **American Alpine Club** (**www.americanalpineclub.org**), which has an Alaska section based in Anchorage (visit **www.mcak.org/aac**).
- ***The Illustrated Guide to Glacier Travel and Crevasse Rescue,*** by Andy Tyson and Mike Clelland.
- ***Medicine for Mountaineering,*** edited by James A. Wilkerson, MD. A reality in climbing is the possibility of everything from altitude sickness to high-altitude pulmonary edema.
- ***Snow Sense: A Guide to Evaluating Snow Avalanche Hazard,*** by Jill Fredston and Doug Fesler. These Alaska residents are experts worldwide in avalanche safety. A must-read for mountaineers.

Gear, Etc.

- Some rental gear is available in Anchorage at **Alaska Mountaineering and Hiking** (2633 Spenard Road, Anchorage 99503; ☎ 907-272-1811;

Climbing Outfitters at a Glance

Alaska Mountain Guides and Climbing School
☎ 800-766-3396
www.alaskamountainguides.com

REGIONAL LOCATION	STATEWIDE
COST	$$$
SUITABLE FOR KIDS?	NO
ACTIVITY LEVEL	HIGH
TRIP LENGTH	VARIES

Alaska Mountaineering School–Alaska Denali Guiding
☎ 907-733-1016
www.climbalaska.org

REGIONAL LOCATION	THE INTERIOR
COST	$$$$
SUITABLE FOR KIDS?	NO
ACTIVITY LEVEL	HIGH
TRIP LENGTH	10–24 DAYS

Alaska Rock Gym
☎ 907-562-7265
www.alaskarockgym.com

REGIONAL LOCATION	SOUTHCENTRAL INLAND
COST	$$
SUITABLE FOR KIDS?	6 AND UP
ACTIVITY LEVEL	LIGHT–MODERATE
TRIP LENGTH	DAY TRIP

Alpine Ascents International
☎ 206-378-1927
www.alpineascents.com

REGIONAL LOCATION	THE INTERIOR
COST	$$$$
SUITABLE FOR KIDS?	NO
ACTIVITY LEVEL	HIGH
TRIP LENGTH	6–21 DAYS

Alpine Guides Alaska
☎ 907-373-3051
www.alaska.net/~alpineak

REGIONAL LOCATION	SOUTHCENTRAL INLAND
COST	$$
SUITABLE FOR KIDS?	NO
ACTIVITY LEVEL	HIGH
TRIP LENGTH	4–14 DAYS

The Ascending Path
☎ 877-783-0505 or 907-783-0505
www.theascendingpath.com

REGIONAL LOCATION	SOUTHCENTRAL INLAND
COST	$$
SUITABLE FOR KIDS?	VARIES
ACTIVITY LEVEL	MODERATE–HIGH
TRIP LENGTH	DAY TRIP

Exposure Alaska
☎ 907-761-3761
www.exposurealaska.com

REGIONAL LOCATION	SOUTHCENTRAL INLAND
COST	$$
SUITABLE FOR KIDS?	NO
ACTIVITY LEVEL	MODERATE–HIGH
TRIP LENGTH	DAY TRIPS–EXPEDITIONS

MICA Guides
☎ 800-956-6422
www.micaguides.com

REGIONAL LOCATION	SOUTHCENTRAL INLAND
COST	$
SUITABLE FOR KIDS?	6 AND UP
ACTIVITY LEVEL	MODERATE
TRIP LENGTH	DAY TRIP

Mountain Trip International
☎ 866-886-8747 or 970-369-1153
www.mountaintrip.com

REGIONAL LOCATION	THE INTERIOR
COST	$$$
SUITABLE FOR KIDS?	NO
ACTIVITY LEVEL	HIGH
TRIP LENGTH	16–26 DAYS

North Star Trekking
☎ 866-590-4530 or 907-790-4530
www.northstartrekking.com

REGIONAL LOCATION	SOUTHEAST
COST	$$
SUITABLE FOR KIDS?	SOME TRIPS
ACTIVITY LEVEL	MODERATE
TRIP LENGTH	DAY TRIP

NOVA River Runners
☎ 800-746-5753
www.novalaska.com

REGIONAL LOCATION	SOUTHCENTRAL INLAND
COST	$
SUITABLE FOR KIDS?	TEENS
ACTIVITY LEVEL	MODERATE
TRIP LENGTH	DAY TRIP

St. Elias Alpine Guides
☎ 888-933-5427 or 907-554-4445
www.steliasguides.com

REGIONAL LOCATION	SOUTHCENTRAL INLAND
COST	$$$
SUITABLE FOR KIDS?	NO
ACTIVITY LEVEL	HIGH
TRIP LENGTH	8–16 DAYS

www.alaskamountaineering.com) and **REI** (1200 West Northern Lights Boulevard, Anchorage 99503; ☎ 907-272-4565; **www.rei.com**).

- **Exposure Alaska** (☎ 907-761-3761; **www.exposurealaska.com**), an Anchorage-based outfit, provides support for climbing ascents, including van support and food. The company also offers a seven-night fly-in trip to Wrangell–St. Elias National Park for ice climbing, backpacking, and remote camping. Prices range from $425 for support packages to $2,790 for fly-in expeditions.

DENALI NATIONAL PARK *and* PRESERVE

THE GRANDDADDY OF ALL MOUNTAINS lies in the midst of Denali National Park and Preserve, the tallest peak in all of North America: **Denali,** or as it is known to many, **Mount McKinley.** Denali is 20,320 feet high, and on a clear day it looms so high over the horizon it does not look real.

The mountain lures climbers by the hundreds, sometimes as many as 1,000 attempting to reach its summit per season. Equally as alluring is neighboring Mount Foraker, which, because of its technical aspects, is considered just as challenging and sometimes more enjoyable because of the smaller crowds.

By nature of its largest-mountain status, Denali is the most popular mountain scale attempted each year, and as a result can get crowded at the base camp. Where Wrangell–St. Elias is practically deserted, Denali National Park is a veritable party. Both have their advantages; it is up to you as the climber to decide which appeals to you more.

All climbers attempting Mounts Denali and Foraker must register with Denali National Park and Preserve (**www.nps.gov/dena/planyourvisit/mountaineering.htm**) and pay a special-use charge of $200 per climber, in addition to the park-entrance fee of $10 per person or $20 per family. The fee helps pay for the high-altitude base camp at **Kahiltna Glacier,** which has a manned ranger station and rescue team available. Each year, injured climbers are hoisted off the mountain, at a great expense and often risking the lives of the rescuers. Climbers die on the mountain regularly.

In addition to the special use fee, a 60-day preregistration regulation allows mountaineering rangers to contact climbers before they arrive in Talkeetna, which is the launching point for most expeditions. Rangers are able to evaluate the would-be climbers and suggest appropriate routes for different levels of expertise.

The **Talkeetna Ranger Station** (P.O. Box 588, Talkeetna 99676; ☎ 907-733-2231) the contact point for climbers, will send its informative mountaineering booklet (written in eight languages) for review ahead of time. Its stark introduction, written by South District Ranger Daryl Miller, sets forth the life-or-death realities of climbing in Alaska, without any sugarcoating or romanticizing things. It is a must-have for anyone considering climbing the "High One." The booklet can be ordered or downloaded at no charge at **www.nps.gov/archive/dena/home/mountaineering/booklet.htm.** See our listings on the next page for other climbing resources in Denali.

Denali (Mount McKinley)

Regional location The Interior. **Type of climbing** Mountaineering. **Elevation** 20,320 feet. **Difficulty** . **Suitable for kids?** No. **Best time of year to**

go May–July. **Time commitment** 20–30 days. **Best suited for** Experienced mountaineers; West Buttress is Grade II. **Maps** U.S. Geological Survey (USGS) Mount McKinley A-1 and A-3 (1-inch/mile scale recommended); 24 maps within this region; to order or download, visit **www.usgs.gov.**

DESTINATION SUMMARY Even the easiest of the 30-plus routes to reach Denali's summit, the West Buttress route, is not easy. No matter how you approach it, Denali is a challenging climb, as much for the extreme weather as anything else. There are only a handful of licensed guides with whom to travel, and we suggest three in our outfitters section on the facing page. Be prepared for a logjam of travelers at the Kahiltna Base Camp. This is far from a wilderness experience.

Mount Foraker

Regional location The Interior. **Type of climbing** Mountaineering. **Elevation** 17,400 feet. **Difficulty**. **Suitable for kids?** No. **Best time of year to go** May–July. **Time commitment** 10–15 days. **Best suited for** Experienced mountaineers. **Maps** USGS Talkeetna D-3 Quad.

DESTINATION SUMMARY The less-traveled Mount Foraker is a challenging hike from whichever direction you choose to approach it. Many accomplished Denali climbers also attempt this peak. The mountain's current name is English, but its native names were *Sultana* and *Menlale,* meaning "Denali's wife."

Mount Hunter

Regional location The Interior. **Type of climbing** Mountaineering. **Elevation** 14,573 feet. **Difficulty**. **Suitable for kids?** No. **Best time of year to go** May–July. **Time commitment** 12–18 days. **Best suited for** Experienced mountaineers; Grade III. **Maps** Visit **www.topographicalmaps.com.**

DESTINATION SUMMARY Athabascans called Hunter *Begguya,* which means "Denali's child." It is the steepest and most technical of the three great peaks in Denali National Park. It has a north and south summit, and is considered the hardest-to-climb 14,000-foot mountain in North America. Those who climb all these peaks will round out the entire Denali family.

Resources

- **"Mountaineering in Denali National Park and Preserve"** is required reading (see the Denali National Park and Preserve introduction for details on ordering). But there are many other excellent books on climbing Denali and other peaks. For example, ***Denali's West Buttress: A Climber's Guide to Mount McKinley's Classic Route*** by Colby Coombs outlines the most popular route taken by climbers and will help prepare you mentally. And ***The Ascent of Denali*** by Hudson Stuck is a classic story of climbing the mountain.
- Several air-taxi operators in Talkeetna can get climbers to the base camp at Kahiltna Glacier. We know and recommend **K-2 Aviation**

(☎ 800-764-2291 or 907-733-2291; **www.flyk2.com**), but climbers also use **Fly Denali** (☎ 866-733-7768 or 907-733-7768; **www.flydenali.com**); **Hudson Air Service** (☎ 800-478-2321 or 907-733-2321; **www.hudsonair.com**); **Talkeetna Aero Services** (☎ 888-733-2899 or 907-733-2899; **www.talkeetnaaero.com**); and **Talkeetna Air Taxi** (☎ 800-533-2219 or 907-733-2218; **www.talkeetnaair.com**). These companies also can take you sightseeing at the glacier to see the climbers in action, if they have space and time during the climbing season. It's a great way to get a feel for the real thing.

- **The Park Connection** (☎ 800-266-8625; **www.alaskacoach.com**) and **Talkeetna Shuttle Service** (☎ 888-288-6008 or 907-733-1725) can get you from Anchorage to Talkeetna and back if you don't have your own transportation. Most climbers use **Denali Overland Transportation** (☎ 800-651-5221 or 907-733-2384; **www.denalioverland.com**).

Denali National Park Outfitters

- **Alaska Mountaineering School–Alaska Denali Guiding:** ☎ 907-733-1016; **www.climbalaska.org;** Talkeetna–Mount McKinley. This goal-oriented educational institution and guiding service is dedicated to providing safe and successful Denali ascents while also focusing on improving your mountaineering skills. They've led more than 100 expeditions around the world, most within the Alaska Range. AMS provides instruction in general mountaineering, wilderness expeditions, and medicine and other custom courses. Expeditions include the West Buttress ($5,300) and West Rib ($6,700). Climbing expeditions to Mount Hunter are $4,000; Mount Foraker, $5,100.
- **Alpine Ascents International:** ☎ 206-378-1927; **www.alpineascents.com;** Seattle–Mount McKinley. Alpine Ascents begins its ascents with a six-day Denali Prep Course designed to give all climbers the tools necessary for a safe and rewarding expedition. Climbers are carefully screened to ensure the enjoyment and safety of the entire group. With a maximum of six climbers, the guides offer an intimate mountain experience on a 20-day climb up McKinley's West Buttress. The $5,400 fee includes an air taxi to the base camp on Kahiltna Glacier, group gear, guide fees, and meals during the expedition. The company also offers private climbs in Alaska and around the globe.
- **Mountain Trip International:** ☎ 866-886-8747 or 970-369-1153; **www.mountaintrip.com;** Ophir, Colorado–Mount McKinley. This company, which has been guiding in Denali since 1976, leads trips up the West Buttress and the West Rib. Its experience and summit success rate are its claims to fame; mountain experiences are available for a variety of ability levels and interests. Trips range from 21 to 26 days and start at $4,850, including air taxi and group gear. Mountain Trip also offers private climbs, ski mountaineering, rock climbing, and other climbing and mountaineering seminars.

GATES *of the* ARCTIC NATIONAL PARK *and* PRESERVE

ABOUT 8.2 MILLION ACRES make up the vast lands of Gates of the Arctic National Park, but it is the Arrigetch Peaks, within the Brooks Range, that attract the most climbers. The National Park Service does not maintain information on specific routes within the park, nor does it keep track of climbs there. Here, as in any other wilderness location in Alaska, it is imperative that climbers have emergency medical skills and a keen knowledge of wilderness survival.

The Arrigetch Peaks are an interesting collection of geologic formations, made up of granite horns, cirques, and arêtes carved by centuries of glaciation. The area was first mapped in 1911, and while it has been explored numerous times, accounts of those expeditions have rarely been recorded. In the early 1960s, modern-day climbers began to arrive in the area, yet still very few trips launch from here today. The park sees only 1,000 to 1,500 visitors a year who backpack, raft, and canoe through the land, and only a handful of those are mountain climbers.

Climbing routes in the Arrigetch vary from nontechnical hikes to routes that require ropes and other aid. The *American Alpine Journal* entries list 41 different routes in the Arrigetch, but even that number is vague because so much is not recorded. Part of this is due to the remoteness of the peaks and part because the park service encourages minimal impact and small parties. The park is considered an Area of Wilderness Concern, meaning that in the past it was heavily used and camping should now be kept to a minimum.

unofficial **TIP**
The Arrigetch Peaks offer something different from the two larger and more-often-climbed parks of Denali and Wrangell–St. Elias: total anonymity. If you seek a truly unique climbing experience, it can be found here.

For more information on climbing the Arrigetch Peaks or anything else in Gates of the Arctic National Park and Preserve, contact Bettles Ranger Station (P.O. Box 26030, Bettles 99726; ☎ 907-692-5494) or the National Park Service (201 First Avenue, Fairbanks 99701; ☎ 907-457-5752; **www.nps.gov/gaar**).

Resources

- ***Alaska's Brooks Range: The Ultimate Mountains,*** by John Kauffman. This book explores the beauty and importance of the northernmost mountain range in the world, from its first human inhabitants to military exploration to protection of its critical habitat.
- ***This Last Treasure,*** adapted by William E. Brown, encapsulates the ideals behind National Park Service leader John Kauffman when talking about Gates of the Arctic National Park and Preserve.

Gates of the Arctic–Arrigetch Outfitters

- **Alpine Guides Alaska:** ☎ 907-373-3051; **www.alaska.net/~alpineak;** Wasilla/Wrangell–St. Elias. Alpine Guides Alaska takes climbers on expeditions of some of the most spectacular and well-known peaks in the park and preserve, too, but unique to this company are its ascents of more-remote peaks near the Canadian border. Mounts Drum, Bona, Blackburn, Naslund, Marcus Baker, Sanford, and Bear are included in Alpine Guides's repertoire, and they also offer climbers the opportunity to "challenge the unknown" on first ascents and first routes. Guiding fees for a 4- to 14-day adventure (airfare, gear, and food not included) are around $290 per person per day for a summit ascent.

WRANGELL–ST. ELIAS NATIONAL PARK *and* PRESERVE

THIS REMOTE PARK SHARES BORDERS with Canada's **Kluane National Park** and features some of the most remote and least-climbed mountains in the world, all part of the Chugach and St. Elias mountain ranges. Many of them are higher than 15,000 feet. There are so many mountains here, in fact, that often they don't even have names.

Because the park is so remote and the climbing community so small and elite, there is no high-altitude rescue team here such as you will find at Denali National Park and Preserve. Climbers should know how to navigate not only with GPS units, but also with topographical map and compass.

Extreme physical fitness is a must here, as are knowledge of avalanche dangers, glacier travel, and self-arrest techniques, as well as the ability to read the ice for crevasse dangers.

Access to the most remote and highest mountains is usually by chartered plane from Yakutat or other points within the park. Because the park borders Canada, all climbing expeditions that enter Kluane National Park must secure a permit before heading out (contact Superintendent, Kluane National Park, P.O. Box 5495, Haines Junction, YT Y0B 1L0; ☎ 867-634-7208). On the American side, climbers are encouraged to fill out a trip itinerary at park headquarters or one of the outlying ranger stations. Contact Wrangell–St. Elias National Park and Preserve, 106.8 Richardson Highway, P.O. Box 439, Copper Center 99573; ☎ 907-822-5234; or the Yakutat District Ranger, P.O. Box 137, Yakutat 99689; ☎ 907-784-3295; **www.nps.gov/wrst.**

Mount Blackburn

Regional location Southcentral Inland Alaska. **Type of climbing** Mountaineering. **Elevation** 16,390 feet. **Difficulty** 🫎🫎🫎🫎. **Suitable for kids?** No. **Best time of**

year to go April–July. **Time commitment** 12–20 days. **Best suited for** Experienced mountaineers. **Maps** USGS McCarthy Quad C-7 and D-7 (1:63,360 scale), McCarthy (1:250,000 scale).

DESTINATION SUMMARY Four potential routes along the North, East, Southeast, and South/Southwest ridges. The South/Southwest ridge has been attempted numerous times without success. Avalanche danger is high throughout.

Mount Bona

Regional location Southcentral Inland Alaska. **Type of climbing** Mountaineering. **Elevation** 16,550 feet. **Difficulty** . **Suitable for kids?** No. **Best time of year to go** April–June. **Time commitment** 9–15 days. **Best suited for** Experienced mountaineers. **Maps** USGS McCarthy B-2 Quad.

DESTINATION SUMMARY Located in the Wrangell Mountains, this challenging peak also is one of the more doable treks within the park. It gets less traffic, too. It is the 4th-highest peak in Alaska and the 11th-highest peak in North America.

Mount St. Elias

Regional location Southcentral Inland Alaska. **Type of climbing** Mountaineering. **Elevation** 18,008 feet. **Difficulty** . **Suitable for kids?** No. **Best time of year to go** April–June. **Time commitment** 15–30 days. **Best suited for** Experienced mountaineers. **Maps** Purchase the 1:250K USGS map of Mount St. Elias, or zoom in on the 11 15-minute Alaska maps, depending on the route.

DESTINATION SUMMARY Stormy weather patterns and a lack of high-altitude rescue teams in Wrangell–St. Elias make this a trek for only the most advanced of mountaineers. St. Elias and the other many unnamed peaks in the park are rarely traveled, providing amazing solitude but requiring advanced outdoor-survival skills. Mount St. Elias was the first of the Alaska mountains to be discovered and the first to be climbed. It long was thought to be the highest peak in North America but ranks at number three.

Mount Sanford

Regional location Southcentral Inland Alaska. **Type of climbing** Mountaineering. **Elevation** 16,237 feet. **Difficulty** . **Suitable for kids?** No. **Best time of year to go** April–July. **Time commitment** 9–15 days. **Best suited for** Experienced mountaineers. **Maps** USGS Gulkana Quad, A-1 (1:63,360 scale), Gulkana, B-1 (1:250,000 scale).

DESTINATION SUMMARY This trip requires travel across tundra and along Sheep Glacier to reach the summit. Riddled with crevasses and buffeted by excessively strong winds, it is not the romanticized trip it has been made out to be in written accounts.

Resources

- ***A Most Hostile Mountain*** by Jonathan Waterman. This engaging tale deals in part with Waterman's time in Wrangell–St. Elias while also re-creating the steps of the Italian explorer who first discovered the mountain.

- ***Hiking in Wrangell–St. Elias National Park*** by Danny Kost. This is a hiking guidebook, but Kost, also an accomplished climber, knows the area better than most.
- ***Mountain Wilderness: An Illustrated History of the Wrangell–St. Elias National Park and Preserve*** by William R. Hunt. A good overview of the Wrangell–St. Elias region.
- ***National Geographic–Trails Illustrated*** has produced a 1:375,000-scale map of Wrangell–St. Elias that is good for pretrip planning. It covers the entire park, including detailed inserts of the Nabesna Road and McCarthy-Kennicott areas. It is available at the ranger stations or online through the Alaska Natural History Association ($9.95; **www.anha.org**).
- Air taxis serving the area include **Alsek Air Service** (☎ 907-784-3231; **www.alsekair.com**) out of Yakutat; **McCarthy Air** (☎ 907-554-4440; **www.mccarthyair.com**) in McCarthy; **Ultima Thule Outfitters and Lodge** (☎ 907-688-1200; **www.ultimathulelodge.com**) out of Chitina; and **Wrangell Mountain Air** (☎ 800-478-1160; **www.wrangellmountainair.com**) in Glennallen.

Wrangell–St. Elias Outfitters

- **Alaska Mountain Guides and Climbing School:** ☎ 800-766-3396; **www.alaskamountainguides.com;** Haines. Leads several expeditions around the state, mostly in Denali and Wrangell–St. Elias National Park. Mountaineering, expedition, and rock- and ice-climbing classes are also offered through the climbing school. The company also guides skiing, hiking, sea-kayaking, rafting, and multisport adventures around the state and the country. Prices range from $160 for a one-day rock-climbing course to $4,800 for a 22-day Denali ascent.
- **Alpine Guides Alaska:** ☎ 907-373-3051; **www.alaska.net/~alpineak;** Wasilla/Wrangell–St. Elias. Takes climbers on expeditions of some of the most spectacular and well-known peaks in the park and preserve, too, but unique to this company are its ascents of more-remote peaks near the Canada border. Mounts Drum, Bona, Blackburn, Naslund, Marcus Baker, Sanford, and Bear are included in Alpine Guides' repertoire, and they also offer climbers the opportunity to "challenge the unknown" on first ascents and first routes. Guiding fees for a 4- to 14-day adventure (airfare, gear, and food not included) are around $290 per person per day for a summit ascent.
- **St. Elias Alpine Guides LLC:** ☎ 888-933-5427 or 907-554-4445; **www.steliasguides.com;** Anchorage/Wrangell–St. Elias. One of Alaska's most experienced and trusted guiding services, St. Elias offers expeditions to Mounts Bona, Blackburn, St. Elias, and Drum and other well-known peaks. Trips range from 8 to 16 days and from $1,000 for a glacier- and ice-climbing excursion to $3,500 for mountaineering expeditions, including transportation to remote areas. Also offers ski mountaineering and other adventure trips in Alaska's wild country.

DAY TRIPS

AFTER SCANNING THE PREVIOUS LISTINGS, you may be encouraged to see what all this talk of climbing is really about. The following trips are offered by experienced guide companies that can give you a sampling of ice and glacier climbing. No experience is necessary, although it helps to be in good shape.

Alaska Rock Gym

Regional location Southcentral Inland Alaska. **Type of climbing** Indoor. **Cost** $$. **Activity level** Light–moderate. **Suitable for kids?** 6 and up. **Best time of year to go** Year-round. **Traffic level** Moderate–heavy. **Contact information** 4840 Fairbanks Street, Anchorage 99503; ☎ 907-562-7265; **www.alaskarockgym.com.**

DESTINATION SUMMARY This 6,000-square-foot facility is an excellent way to practice skills if you're in town and rained out. The gym features bouldering and climbing walls and experts who can help belay or teach, either in classes or individually. Day passes are $6 for kids 13 and younger, $14 for adults and kids age 14 and up (gear and instruction cost $13 and $20 for these respective age groups). There are Thursday classes and special events.

The Ascending Path

Regional location Southcentral Inland Alaska. **Type of climbing** Glacier trekking, ice climbing, rock climbing. **Cost** $$. **Activity level** Moderate–high. **Suitable for kids?** Some trips. **Best time of year to go** Mid-June–September. **Traffic level** Moderate. **Contact information** At the yurt at Alyeska Resort Hotel; ☎ 877-783-0505 or 907-783-0505; **www.theascendingpath.com.**

DESTINATION SUMMARY This experienced guide company can introduce the budding climber to ice or rock climbing and glacier trekking in summer. The three-hour $139 glacier trek includes interpretive glaciology discussions, great views of the seven glaciers in the Girdwood bowl, a round-trip ticket up the mountain on the Tramway, trekking poles, and overboot rentals. Learn about moats; lateral, medial, and terminal moraine; firn line; and nunataks, among other topics. The three-hour rock-climbing and five-hour ice-climbing programs are $129 and $189, respectively. A women's yoga–rock-climbing course is offered occasionally for $100.

MICA Guides

Regional location Southcentral Inland Alaska. **Type of climbing** Glacier trekking, ice climbing. **Cost** $. **Activity level** Moderate. **Suitable for kids?** 6 and up. **Best time of year to go** Mid-June–September. **Traffic level** Light. **Contact information** Based in Chickaloon, north of Palmer; ☎ 800-956-6422; **www.micaguides.com.**

DESTINATION SUMMARY MICA stands for Matanuska Ice Climbing Adventures, and that is what you get with this family-friendly outfit. It offers 1½-hour glacier treks on Matanuska Glacier for an extremely affordable

$35 per person. The 1½-hour trek isn't as educational as the three-hour trek, which takes in natural ice formations and costs $70 per person. MICA's six-hour ice-climbing course is another bargain at $130 per person. At the same Matanuska Glacier location, participants can learn about the technical aspects of climbing and hit the ice themselves. MICA allows younger kids on the glacier, while their ice-climbing trips are for folks 12 and older.

North Star Trekking

Regional location Southeast Alaska. **Type of climbing** Glacier trekking, ice climbing. **Cost** $$. **Activity level** Moderate. **Suitable for kids?** Some trips. **Best time of year to go** June–September. **Traffic level** Moderate. **Contact information** Based in Juneau; ☎ 866-590-4530 or 907-790-4530; **www.northstartrekking.com.**

DESTINATION SUMMARY These glacier treks are combined with a helicopter ride to reach Mendenhall Glacier, so the price is a bit higher than the walk-to locations in Southcentral Inland. Still, the helicopter flight is an adventure in itself. The Level 1 Walkabout ($295) is the cheapest, but it's sort of boring. The two-hour Level 2 Glacier Trek ($359) emphasizes proper use of gear and learning glacier features. The Level 3 X-Trek ($459) is an extended outing that includes four hours of trekking, ice climbing, and learning how to use ropes. We recommend getting the most for your helicopter-riding hours by tackling this one. The price is only $100 more for twice as much learning.

NOVA River Runners

Regional location Southcentral Inland Alaska. **Type of climbing** Glacier trekking. **Cost** $. **Activity level** Moderate. **Suitable for kids?** Preteens and up. **Best time of year to go** Mid-June–September. **Traffic level** Light. **Contact information** Based in Chickaloon, north of Palmer; ☎ 800-746-5753; **www.novalaska.com.**

DESTINATION SUMMARY NOVA is a longtime outdoor-adventure company, and as its name implies, rivers are what it does. However, the Chickaloon-based outfitter also offers an exciting 2½-hour Matanuska Glacier trek in which guests can walk on the glacier and experience the ice up close while wearing crampons. View crevasses, caves, and surface ponds, among other naturally occurring formations. The hike is $80 per person, unless you choose the $149 raft trip to Lion Head, a local point of interest (hike included in price).

PART TEN

CYCLING

YOU MIGHT NOT BE ABLE TO CLIMB Mount McKinley on a bike in Alaska, but there is no shortage of other scenic places to check out by means of pedal power. Ride from the coastal communities of the Kenai Peninsula clear to the Interior. Pedal mountain passes and wide-open valleys. Or get really adventurous and wait until wintertime, when a few studs in your tires will give you plenty of traction for riding on ice and snow.

Cycling in Alaska requires preparation and good conditioning. This is not Kansas, and by that we mean that just about any road, trail, or path you choose to follow will eventually climb a hill. Some mountains, so small as to not even be named, can challenge even the fittest of cyclists. Still, the reward is justified when you've climbed a long stretch of road or trail and are greeted by a view that will knock your cycling socks off.

This chapter will share with you some of our favorite cycling destinations and give you some tips on how best to prepare for the trip. We have focused one section on road riding, which includes touring with panniers or trailers. The next section covers routes that are best traveled on mountain bikes, which include overnight camping on single-track trails while hauling gear to roadways that are mostly gravel and best suited for beefier bikes. We have also included a section on our favorite day rides for those of you who prefer to keep your bike as light as possible and sleep in comfort at night.

We've rated our rides from easy to difficult, but the truth is just about all of them will be challenging. For example, we list a day jaunt on a paved bike path skirting Anchorage as easy, but that's just because it is paved and well traveled, and it requires very little planning to experience. Still, there are some hilly climbs and windy sections that will take at least average biking skills to navigate. At the other end of the spectrum, we rate a mountain-biking camp trip on the Resurrection Pass as moderate to difficult because you'll be carrying all of your gear and experiencing roots, rocks, mud, and overgrown single-track quite often. Still, it is a very manageable ride for a mountain biker with off-road-cycling skills.

All that said, don't let yourself become too intimidated by the ratings, and consider instead the type of cycling experience you want. Look at the mileage of the trip, its level of technical challenges (for the mountain-bike section), and its accessibility and affordability. Some trips, such as a tour of the Nome Road System, offer quite pleasant riding but require an out-and-back ride, which some cyclists don't like. It gets expensive to reach Nome, too, so keep your budget in mind.

CHECKLIST *for* SUCCESS

- **Plan ahead.** Even if your cycling adventure will keep you on the road system, where there is easy access to telecommunications, it is still a good idea to let someone you trust know where you are going, when you are coming back, and how often you plan to make contact. On some of the more-deserted sections of road in Alaska, you could crash off the side of the road and not be discovered for days. When traveling the backcountry by mountain bike, it's even more important to file a trip plan with someone you know, as well as with the managing agency on whose land you will be traveling: national forests, state parks, etc.
- **Know your equipment, and how to make repairs if necessary.** Know how to change or patch tires, fix broken chains, and adjust brakes and other movable parts.
- **Always wear a helmet and appropriate safety gear.** That means reflective gear for road trips and knee or elbow pads if traveling in extreme downhill-mountain-bike areas.
- **Keep a light load.** There's nothing like an extra five or ten pounds of unnecessary gear to really bog down what could otherwise be an enjoyable ride. Resist the urge to load your panniers or bike trailer down with every imaginable amenity. Also, load up with the gear you will be bringing before you even leave for your trip, and ride around with it to get a feel for how it will affect your maneuverability.

unofficial **TIP**
It is important, especially with panniers, to distribute weight evenly. This lessens the chance of losing control or braking too much on either the rear or front brakes.

- **Dress appropriately.** The most important piece of gear you'll need for any cycling trip is a wind- and waterproof rain jacket and pants. We prefer pants that zip open at the ankles so you can get them on and off without having to remove your shoes. We also like arm and leg warmers, which are good options in the flaky Alaska weather we encounter.
- **Know how to navigate.** When traveling in the backcountry, carry a map of the trails you are riding. If you're in trailless areas, bring along a compass as well, or a GPS unit. On road rides, a road map, available at any convenience store, should suffice. We are in the middle of

nowhere, but it's pretty hard to get lost because there aren't that many roads in Alaska.

- **Guard against mosquitoes.** Even cyclists riding at 20 miles per hour will want to be prepared for mosquitoes because the minute you stop, they will be on you. This is even more apparent when mountain biking. The same precautions in Part Six (see page 84) apply here.
- **Bring along first aid.** Carry basic emergency-care items, including bandages, antibiotic ointment, self-stick bandages, and a space blanket for warmth. We have been known to dissolve ibuprofen in our water bottles, which really helps for those next-day aches and pains, too.
- **Carry basic bike-repair equipment.** This includes:
  1. ***A park tool*** with Phillips and flathead screwdriver attached.
  2. ***A patch kit.***
  3. ***At least one spare tube.*** (We recommend one spare for each week of planned riding. If you're traveling for six weeks at a time, consider mailing tubes to yourself at post offices in towns along the way.)
  4. ***A chain tool and/or missing-link adapter*** that can be used in place of a broken chain.
  5. ***Extra lubricant*** for long rides to keep the chain working smoothly and quietly.
  6. ***A tire wrench or wrenches*** to help remove tires from rims in case of a flat.
  7. ***An old sock or bandanna*** to use as a cleaning rag during repairs.
  8. ***A small pump*** that can fit in an under-the-seat bag or day pack.
  9. ***A Swiss Army knife.***

Travel with a Guide?

Whether you travel with a guide will depend upon two things: how much experience you have and how much planning you are willing to do.

FOR MOUNTAIN BIKING If you've ridden backcountry single-track trails many times and can handle the technical difficulties that come with them, then by no means should you be intimidated by Alaska's trails. They are a challenge, to be sure, but anyone who has ridden in Utah, Colorado, or any of the other popular off-road-riding spots in the country will be able to handle Alaska trails just fine.

So far, so good? Now ask yourself these questions:

1. Can I confidently navigate in places where the trails may disappear—where I may be traveling across trailless high-country tundra or the banks of dried-out riverbeds?
2. Am I comfortable with the fact that I could very well run into a bear or moose that is not too happy to see me? Do I know how to defend myself properly and reduce the chances of such an encounter?
3. Do I recognize other trail hazards specific to Alaska, such as devil's club, a prickly plant that is hell to land on, or cow parsnip, which if rubbed against the skin can cause a red, itchy burn that can last for months?

Alaska Cycling at a Glance

Anchorage–Valdez Loop

REGIONAL LOCATION	SOUTHCENTRAL INLAND/COASTAL
DISTANCE	360 MILES
MOUNTAIN/ROAD?	ROAD
DIFFICULTY	🫎🫎🫎🫎
CONFIGURATION	LOOP
TIME TO RIDE	6–8 DAYS
SUITABLE FOR KIDS?	NO
GUIDE SUGGESTED?	NO

Anvil Mountain

REGIONAL LOCATION	THE BUSH
DISTANCE	9 MILES ROUND-TRIP
MOUNTAIN/ROAD?	MOUNTAIN
DIFFICULTY	🫎🫎🫎
CONFIGURATION	OUT-AND-BACK
TIME TO RIDE	DAY TRIP
SUITABLE FOR KIDS?	YES
GUIDE SUGGESTED?	NO

Birch Hill Ski Trails

REGIONAL LOCATION	THE INTERIOR
DISTANCE	VARIES
MOUNTAIN/ROAD?	MOUNTAIN
DIFFICULTY	🫎🫎🫎
CONFIGURATION	LOOP/ OUT-AND-BACK
TIME TO RIDE	DAY TRIP
SUITABLE FOR KIDS?	VARIES
GUIDE SUGGESTED?	NO

Bird–Gird Trail

REGIONAL LOCATION	SOUTHCENTRAL INLAND
DISTANCE	12 MILES ONE-WAY
MOUNTAIN/ROAD?	MOUNTAIN/ROAD
DIFFICULTY	🫎🫎
CONFIGURATION	OUT-AND-BACK
TIME TO RIDE	DAY TRIP
SUITABLE FOR KIDS?	YES
GUIDE SUGGESTED?	NO

Burma Road

REGIONAL LOCATION	SOUTHCENTRAL COASTAL
DISTANCE	12 MILES ONE-WAY
MOUNTAIN/ROAD?	MOUNTAIN
DIFFICULTY	🫎🫎🫎🫎🫎
CONFIGURATION	LOOP
TIME TO RIDE	DAY TRIP
SUITABLE FOR KIDS?	NO
GUIDE SUGGESTED?	RECOMMENDED

Dalton Highway

REGIONAL LOCATION	THE INTERIOR
DISTANCE	414 MILES ONE-WAY
MOUNTAIN/ROAD?	MOUNTAIN
DIFFICULTY	🫎🫎🫎🫎🫎
CONFIGURATION	END-TO-END
TIME TO RIDE	8–12 DAYS
SUITABLE FOR KIDS?	NO
GUIDE SUGGESTED?	NO

Denali Highway

REGIONAL LOCATION	THE INTERIOR
DISTANCE	134 MILES ONE-WAY
MOUNTAIN/ROAD?	MOUNTAIN
DIFFICULTY	🫎🫎🫎
CONFIGURATION	END-TO-END
TIME TO RIDE	2–4 DAYS
SUITABLE FOR KIDS?	TEENS
GUIDE SUGGESTED?	NO

Denali Park Road

REGIONAL LOCATION	THE INTERIOR
DISTANCE	85 MILES ONE-WAY
MOUNTAIN/ROAD?	MOUNTAIN
DIFFICULTY	🫎🫎🫎🫎
CONFIGURATION	OUT-AND-BACK
TIME TO RIDE	2–4 DAYS
SUITABLE FOR KIDS?	NO
GUIDE SUGGESTED?	NO

East Glacier Trail

REGIONAL LOCATION	SOUTHEAST
DISTANCE	4.5 MILES
MOUNTAIN/ROAD?	MOUNTAIN
DIFFICULTY	🫎🫎🫎
CONFIGURATION	LOOP
TIME TO RIDE	DAY TRIP
SUITABLE FOR KIDS?	NO
GUIDE SUGGESTED?	NO

Eklutna Lake

REGIONAL LOCATION	SOUTHCENTRAL INLAND
DISTANCE	16 MILES ONE-WAY
MOUNTAIN/ROAD?	MOUNTAIN
DIFFICULTY	🫎🫎🫎
CONFIGURATION	OUT-AND-BACK
TIME TO RIDE	DAY TRIP
SUITABLE FOR KIDS?	YES
GUIDE SUGGESTED?	NO

Ester Dome–Alder Chute

REGIONAL LOCATION	THE INTERIOR
DISTANCE	9.3 MILES ROUND-TRIP
MOUNTAIN/ROAD?	MOUNTAIN
DIFFICULTY	🫎🫎🫎
CONFIGURATION	LOOP
TIME TO RIDE	DAY TRIP
SUITABLE FOR KIDS?	NO
GUIDE SUGGESTED?	NO

Haines–Skagway

REGIONAL LOCATION	SOUTHEAST
DISTANCE	355 MILES
MOUNTAIN/ROAD?	ROAD
DIFFICULTY	🫎🫎🫎
CONFIGURATION	LOOP OPTION
TIME TO RIDE	5–9 DAYS
SUITABLE FOR KIDS?	NO
GUIDE SUGGESTED?	RECOMMENDED

Hatcher Pass

REGIONAL LOCATION	SOUTHCENTRAL INLAND
DISTANCE	9 MILES ONE-WAY
MOUNTAIN/ROAD?	MOUNTAIN
DIFFICULTY	🫎🫎🫎🫎
CONFIGURATION	OUT-AND-BACK
TIME TO RIDE	DAY TRIP
SUITABLE FOR KIDS?	NO
GUIDE SUGGESTED?	NO

Johnson Pass

REGIONAL LOCATION	SOUTHCENTRAL COASTAL
DISTANCE	20 MILES
MOUNTAIN/ROAD?	MOUNTAIN
DIFFICULTY	🫎🫎🫎🫎
CONFIGURATION	OUT-AND-BACK
TIME TO RIDE	DAY TRIP
SUITABLE FOR KIDS?	NO
GUIDE SUGGESTED?	RECOMMENDED

Kenai Peninsula Tour

REGIONAL LOCATION	SOUTHCENTRAL INLAND/COASTAL
DISTANCE	302 MILES
MOUNTAIN/ROAD?	ROAD
DIFFICULTY	🫎🫎🫎
CONFIGURATION	Y-SHAPED
TIME TO RIDE	4–8 DAYS
SUITABLE FOR KIDS?	NO
GUIDE SUGGESTED?	NO

Alaska Cycling at a Glance (continued)

Million Dollar Bridge

REGIONAL LOCATION	SOUTHCENTRAL COASTAL
DISTANCE	48 MILES
MOUNTAIN/ROAD?	MOUNTAIN
DIFFICULTY	🫎🫎
CONFIGURATION	OUT-AND-BACK
TIME TO RIDE	DAY TRIP
SUITABLE FOR KIDS?	YES
GUIDE SUGGESTED?	NO

Prince of Wales Island

REGIONAL LOCATION	SOUTHEAST
DISTANCE	60–300 MILES
MOUNTAIN/ROAD?	MOUNTAIN
DIFFICULTY	🫎🫎🫎
CONFIGURATION	VARIES
TIME TO RIDE	3–6 DAYS
SUITABLE FOR KIDS?	NO
GUIDE SUGGESTED?	NO

Resurrection Pass

REGIONAL LOCATION	SOUTHCENTRAL COASTAL
DISTANCE	39 MILES
MOUNTAIN/ROAD?	MOUNTAIN
DIFFICULTY	🫎🫎🫎
CONFIGURATION	END-TO-END
TIME TO RIDE	1–3 DAYS
SUITABLE FOR KIDS?	TEENS
GUIDE SUGGESTED?	NO

Tony Knowles Coastal Trail

REGIONAL LOCATION	SOUTHCENTRAL INLAND
DISTANCE	10 MILES ONE-WAY
MOUNTAIN/ROAD?	MOUNTAIN/ROAD
DIFFICULTY	🫎🫎
CONFIGURATION	OUT-AND-BACK
TIME TO RIDE	DAY TRIP
SUITABLE FOR KIDS?	YES
GUIDE SUGGESTED?	NO

Tour of the Mining Country

REGIONAL LOCATION	THE INTERIOR
DISTANCE	46 MILES
MOUNTAIN/ROAD?	MOUNTAIN
DIFFICULTY	🫎🫎🫎🫎
CONFIGURATION	OUT-AND-BACK
TIME TO RIDE	DAY TRIP
SUITABLE FOR KIDS?	NO
GUIDE SUGGESTED?	YES

Still feeling good? Then go it alone. We say you'll be fine on Alaska's mountain-biking trails.

FOR ROAD BIKING Experienced road cyclists needn't use a guide unless they desire the camaraderie of numbers and the ease of not carrying their own gear.

Now, on to the next question: how much work are you willing to invest to plan your trip? There aren't that many cycling guides in Alaska, and those who do exist do a superb job of working out all the details so all you have to do is show up and hop on your bike or one they provide for you. Many cyclists like this option because it eliminates the unknown: how much food you should pack, what type of camping gear works best, and the like. Also, traveling with a guide provides safety in numbers. For some, this is reassuring; for others it feels invasive. This is a question only you can answer because your cycling experience will be vastly different traveling with a group than if you are traveling alone.

Traveling with a guide also eliminates the need to carry your own gear. Road cyclists might be particularly happy with this option, because it allows them to see more of the state traveling more miles per day than if they were hauling their gear in panniers or a trailer.

ROAD BIKING

TRUE, IT'S THE LARGEST STATE IN THE COUNTRY, but Alaska is noticeably lacking in roads. There are only a few main paved ones, and some of our so-called highways are still gravel in some places.

Cycling Outfitters at a Glance

Alaska Backcountry Bike Tours
☎ 866-354-2453 or 907-746-5018
www.mountainbikealaska.com

REGIONAL LOCATION	SOUTHCENTRAL COASTAL/INLAND, INTERIOR
COST	$$
SUITABLE FOR KIDS?	TEENS
ACTIVITY LEVEL	MODERATE–HIGH
TRIP LENGTH	1–7 DAYS

Alaska Outdoor Rentals and Guides
☎ 907-457-2453
www.akbike.com

REGIONAL LOCATION	THE INTERIOR
COST	$$
SUITABLE FOR KIDS?	TEENS
ACTIVITY LEVEL	MODERATE
TRIP LENGTH	CUSTOM

Alaskan Bicycle Adventures
☎ 907-245-2175
www.alaskabike.com

REGIONAL LOCATION	SOUTHCENTRAL COASTAL/INLAND
COST	$$$
SUITABLE FOR KIDS?	TEENS
ACTIVITY LEVEL	ALL LEVELS
TRIP LENGTH	7–8 DAYS

Alaska Ultra Sport
☎ 907-745-6680
www.alaskaultrasport.com

REGIONAL LOCATION	SOUTHCENTRAL COASTAL/INLAND
COST	$$$
SUITABLE FOR KIDS?	TEENS
ACTIVITY LEVEL	LIGHT/ MODERATE/HIGH
TRIP LENGTH	CUSTOM

Denali Outdoor Center
☎ 888-303-1925 or 907-683-1925
www.denalioutdoorcenter.com

REGIONAL LOCATION	THE INTERIOR
COST	$
SUITABLE FOR KIDS?	TEENS
ACTIVITY LEVEL	MODERATE
TRIP LENGTH	DAY TRIPS

Ride the Circle
☎ 262-736-BIKE (2453)
www.pactour.com

REGIONAL LOCATION	STATEWIDE
COST	$$$
SUITABLE FOR KIDS?	TEENS
ACTIVITY LEVEL	MODERATE–HIGH
TRIP LENGTH	13 DAYS

Sockeye Cycle Co.
☎ 877-292-4154
www.cyclealaska.com

REGIONAL LOCATION	SOUTHEAST
COST	$$
SUITABLE FOR KIDS?	TEENS
ACTIVITY LEVEL	MODERATE
TRIP LENGTH	2–9 DAYS

For Alaskans, this is a good thing—it keeps the state rugged and natural, and lessens the tendency for traffic to fill up every lane. We pride ourselve on our remoteness.

For cyclists, this can create a road-touring challenge. The ability to travel on skinny tires is limited to just a few places in the state. But they are beautiful places. The travel options we suggest here will allow you to stay on your road bike, although you may want to upgrade to 25-millimeter tires to navigate the sometimes-gravelly sections of road that constantly seem to be under construction in Alaska. You will notice two of the three routes we suggest begin in Anchorage, the state's most-populated city and thus the one with the most developed road system. Other "highway" riding options are listed in the more extensive mountain-biking section because they will require mountain bikes to navigate.

The Anchorage–Valdez Loop

Regional location Southcentral Coastal and Southcentral Inland Alaska. **Distance** 360 miles, connecting 3 roads (Seward Highway, Richardson Highway, and Glenn

Highway). **Route configuration** This loop ride is made possible by a pleasant ferry passage between the communities of Whittier and Valdez, putting the cyclist back in Anchorage at the end. **Difficulty** . **Suitable for kids?** No. **Time to ride** 6–9 days. **Best time of year to ride** Early June–late-August. **Traffic level** Moderate–heavy in summer; lightest in early June. **Facilities** Most amenities available along the way, although they are spread out in some places.

ROUTE SUMMARY The Anchorage–Valdez Loop offers it all—a train ride, a ferry trip, and some of the most awesome road-climbing challenges in the state. The loop also offers relatively well-shouldered roads and all-pavement riding.

DIRECTIONS TO ANCHORAGE The Anchorage–Valdez Loop starts in Anchorage. For particulars on how to get here, see our profile for the Kenai Peninsula Tour (page 163).

DESCRIPTION There are two ways to do the Anchorage–Valdez Loop. We prefer the first option, although it requires a bit of hitchhiking, and that is a personal choice.

This option involves riding the Seward Highway from Anchorage to the turnoff for the Whittier–Portage Glacier Access Road, at Mile 48. Turn here and ride another 12 miles to the entrance to the **Anton Anderson Memorial Tunnel,** which will take you to Whittier. The catch here is that due to safety concerns, cyclists are not allowed to ride through the tunnel. The trick is to find someone with a pickup or fifth wheel that will allow you to ride through the tunnel with them. Offer to share or even pay the $12 toll. There is no shortage of pickups, and plenty of people line up for the every-half-hour departures.

The second option, and the only other way through the tunnel with a bike, is to take the regularly scheduled train trips through the tunnel. You can board the train at the **Alaska Railroad** depot in downtown Anchorage (but you will miss some of the most scenic riding of the entire trip) or take the Seward Highway from Anchorage to Mile 46 and the Alaska Railroad parking area. The rate for passage from here is $20 one-way, plus a $20 fee for carrying bikes. (For more information on the Seward Highway section of the road, see the relevant part of the Kenai Peninsula Tour route, on page 165.)

unofficial **TIP**
Now, once you have arrived in Whittier, it will be time to board the **Alaska State Ferry** for passage across Prince William Sound to Valdez. Enjoy a relaxing seven-hour ride across the sound (or three and a half hours if you are lucky enough to be on the fast ferry M/V *Chenega*), complete with naturalist narration along the way. Watch for sea lions, otters, whales, and other marine mammals.

In Valdez, there are many places to camp, lodge, or resupply (see the Southcentral Coastal chapter, page 332, for our suggestions). The bike ride out of Valdez begins relatively flat on the Richardson Highway, but soon climbs the spectacular 2,678-foot **Thompson Pass,** at about Mile 26, which is one of the highest mountain climbs on the road system in Alaska, as well as one of the snowiest road-accessible areas in the state. After the pass you'll enjoy a steep 7.5-mile descent, but beware of trucks and other fast-driving vehicles. This section of road has incredible views, including glimpses of **Worthington Glacier,** which is accessible by road.

Squirrel Creek State Recreation Site, at Mile 80, is a good place to stop for the night if you're camping, with campsites right by the creek. Just across the road is a place to buy some snacks.

The ride from Squirrel Creek to Glennallen is wide open, with rolling hills and some large climbs, but nothing as challenging as Thompson Pass. **Glennallen,** at Mile 119, is a good resupply point, but if you continue past the town, there are some beautiful camping options farther south. One such choice is the **Tolsona Wilderness Campground,** about 20 miles from Glennallen and right by the creek. Lake Louise Road is another ten miles away and an excellent option if you're up to riding your bike another 20 miles to **Lake Louise State Recreation Area.** The camping is wonderfully peaceful, with loons and other birds keeping you constant company.

unofficial **TIP**
Intermittently throughout the Richardson Highway ride, you'll notice the **Trans-Alaska Pipeline System,** which pumps crude oil from the North Slope to Valdez, where it is transported throughout the United States. It's an engineering wonder, and interesting to look at. At Mile 65 is a pullout and interpretive site for Pump Station Number 12, which offers some of the history of the pipeline.

From Lake Louise Road, you'll still have 150 miles left to reach Anchorage, and the last 75 miles are some of the most harrowing as traffic picks up and the road narrows in places. **Eureka Summit,** 20 miles from Lake Louise Road and the highest point on the Glenn Highway at 3,322 feet, will be a challenge, especially if you experience the infamous head- and side winds that seem to prevail in the area. Just after the summit, you'll descend to **Sheep Mountain.** Be sure to stop at **Sheep Mountain Lodge** (☎ 877-645-5121) for some of their baked goods to keep you going. Owner Zack Steer is familiar with the cycling scene, hosting the annual Fireweed 400 bike race from the lodge each year. The lodge has great little cabins (and a welcome hot tub for those sore legs) if you want to take another day off and enjoy the view.

From Sheep Mountain Lodge, the road narrows, and recent construction has the road torn up in many places, so cycle with care. Even after you've reached Palmer, you will still be 45 miles from Anchorage. Some cyclists like to end their trip here and schedule a ride into Anchorage. For those who prefer to pedal all the way back to the state's largest city, just keep heading south on the Glenn until it ends in downtown Anchorage.

Resources

- The ***Alaska Bicycle Touring Guide,*** by Pete Praetorius and Alys Culhane, is available through various outlets if you do a Google search. But it is more than 15 years old, so many of the businesses in the more populated areas will no longer be around. We like it for its elevation-profile information, though.

- The **Alaska Marine Highway** (☎ 800-642-0066; **www.ferryalaska.com**) offers ferry service from Whittier to Valdez, and vice versa. Fare is $85 one-way for adults; $12 extra for bicycles.
- To book yourself and your bike on the **Alaska Railroad,** call ☎ 800-544-0552 or visit **www.alaskarailroad.com.** Rates are $20 from Portage to Whittier; bikes cost an extra $20.
- The **Anchorage Convention and Visitors Bureau** (☎ 907-276-4118 or 907-274-3531; **www.anchorage.net**) has plenty of brochures for places to stay and things to do while in the state's largest city. The nearby **Alaska Public Lands Information Center** (605 West Fourth Avenue, Suite 105, Anchorage 99501; ☎ 907-271-2737; **www.nps.gov/aplic**) can help with details on the best places to camp or stay along the road.
- Anchorage's **Arctic Bicycle Club** supports the annual **Fireweed 400,** a road race that begins at Sheep Mountain Lodge on the Glenn Highway and travels to Valdez (visit **www.fireweed400.com** for details). Teams and individuals can sign up for distances of 50, 100, 200, or 400 miles, testing their grit against Alaska's toughest section of road riding. The race attracts participants from around the world and is a qualifying event for the grueling Race Across America ultra-endurance-cycling challenge.
- For detailed mile-by-mile information on the roads and amenities along the way, a great resource for all the trips in this chapter (but not one you want to take with you on your bike, because it's as big as a phone book) is ***The Milepost,*** published by Morris Communications ($27.95; **www.themilepost.com**). We suggest photocopying the pages that cover a particular trip and bringing them with you as a reference. If you're camping along the way, they can be burned as you go.
- Anchorage has many bike shops from which to choose if you need last-minute supplies or repairs. We like **Chain Reaction Cycles** (12201 Industry Way, Unit 2 Anchorage, 99515 ☎ 907-336-0383; **www.chainreactioncycles.us**); **The Bicycle Shop** (1035 West Northern Lights Boulevard, Anchorage 99503; ☎ 907-272-5219); and **Paramount Cycles** (1320 Huffman Park Drive, Anchorage 99515; ☎ 907-336-2453). Chain Reaction accepts your bike shipment and will put your bike back together for you if you're flying in from out of state. You can pick it up once you arrive. This is a safer option than shipping your bike via the airlines. Just call the shop ahead of time to arrange. **Downtown Bicycle Rental** in Anchorage (333 West Fourth Avenue, Suite 206, Anchorage 99501; ☎ 907-279-5293; **www.alaska-bike-rentals.com**) is the only place that rents road bikes (dated but functional), along with clipless pedals and shoes. Rates are $43 for 24 hours, but ask about discounts for rentals by the week.

Anchorage–Valdez Loop Cycling Outfitters

- The **Alaska Ride the Circle Tour** (visit **www.pactour.com** for details) is a 1,283-mile expedition that takes in the Anchorage–Valdez Loop and more. For the cyclist who wants the ultimate adventure ride and is up to the challenge of high-mileage days. The rate is $3,500 per person.

Haines–Skagway (Golden Circle) Route

Regional location Southeast Alaska. **Distance** 355 miles, connecting 3 roads (Haines, Alaska, and South Klondike highways). **Route configuration** Can be made into a loop by taking a fast ferry between communities of Skagway and Haines. **Difficulty** 🫎🫎🫎. **Suitable for kids?** No. **Time to ride** 5–8 days. **Best time of year to ride** Early June–October. **Traffic level** Moderate in summer; light in June, September, and October. **Facilities** Most amenities available along the way, including lodging, food, and camping.

ROUTE SUMMARY Also known as the Golden Circle Route, this cycling trip takes in some of the most scenic areas of Southeast Alaska and affords the vacationing cyclist a chance to take the ferry and see parts of the Inside Passage.

DIRECTIONS TO HAINES You can reach Haines from the lower 48 states via the **Haines Highway,** which connects to the **Alaska Highway.** The **Alaska Marine Highway** ferry also travels to Haines regularly, offering access from the Lower 48 and other Alaska communities. Three regional airlines serve Haines, each with several scheduled flights daily throughout the year, which can connect you to Juneau. From there, you're linked through **Alaska Airlines** to Canada and the rest of the United States.

DESCRIPTION From Haines, the cyclist riding the Golden Circle Route will travel three highways: 146 miles on the Haines Highway to Haines Junction, 100 miles on the Alaska Highway to Whitehorse, and 109 miles to Skagway on the South Klondike Highway. The first 20 miles out of Haines will ease you into the cycling rhythm. The road is flat and well paved, and follows the river for an added bit of scenery. For the next 10 to 15 miles, the road rises slightly, but passes through the **Chilkat Valley Bald Eagle Preserve,** which is home to thousands of bald eagles, and even more during the fall salmon-spawning season. There is a roadhouse at about Mile 33 that is a good stopping spot.

From the aptly but not-so-creatively named **Mile 33 Roadhouse** (☎ 907-767-5510), the road gets a bit more challenging, and there is some climbing all the way to the Canada border, at Mile 40.5.

From the customs station, the route climbs gently for about ten more miles, to tree line (be aware that measurements will be in kilometers while in Canada, but we'll stick to miles for sanity's sake). At about Mile 50, you'll begin climbing steeply to **Three Guardsmen Lake,** a beautiful spot with dramatic views, followed by a short descent and a final climb to **Chilkat Pass.**

The pass is 59 miles into the trip and, at 3,510 feet, an impressive place to stop and take in the view. One of the few access points from the Pacific for explorers, gold miners, and adventurers, Chilkat today is appreciated for its beauty and ruggedness. It is windy here almost constantly, and snow remains in the pass longer than in other areas, as late as early June.

The ride from the summit begins to descend, with wondrous views of the St. Elias Mountains beginning to dominate the background over the next 15 to 20 miles. You'll also be at the **Tatshenshini-Alsek Wilderness Provincial Park (www.env.gov.bc.ca/bcparks)**, which is one of the most popular places for rafting and kayaking.

At Mile 85, you'll pass from British Columbia into the Yukon Territory. **Million Dollar Falls,** at Mile 93.5, boasts more than 30 campsites, water spots, a kitchen shelter, and fishing opportunities in the nearby rivers.

unofficial **TIP**
Canada customs will likely stop you at the border and quiz you carefully—at least that's what's happened to everyone we know who's cycled it. This is mostly to find out how well prepared you are. It is not uncommon to see bears, overestimate your cycling abilities in the conditions, or underestimate the availability of supplies along the way. Be patient, answer their questions, and you will soon be on your way.

From Million Dollar Falls, it's a 55-mile ride to **Haines Junction** and the Alaska Highway. Haines Junction also is the first town of mention since leaving Haines, and a good place to resupply (unless you can hold off one more day and get your supplies in Whitehorse, which has even more services). The **Kluane Range** dominates the background for this section of ride.

The ride from Haines Junction to Whitehorse is 100 miles—a good place to attempt a century ride if that's part of your goal. The route is flat and mostly smooth, with only an occasional steep but short hill. The shoulder is narrow for the first half of the ride, so be careful when being approached by RVs and vehicles hauling trailers. The route follows through forest and is a good place for spotting bears, which with any luck will run away if they see you.

Whitehorse offers every amenity imaginable, plus some interesting visitor attractions. The ***S/S Klondike,*** a giant boat that plied the Yukon River until 1955, is a nice stop, with tours daily. The visitor center has many suggestions for things to do and places to see. If you've planned a recovery day in your trip, this is the place to stop.

From Whitehorse you will begin traveling the last 109 miles of your route, first getting back onto the Alaska Highway to connect with the **South Klondike Highway,** south of Whitehorse. The last established campground is at Carcross, but that is only 33 miles into the trip (a better option exists at scenic **Tutshi Lake,** at about Mile 60). At Mile 48, you'll cross back into British Columbia, headed for Alaska.

The last 50 miles into Skagway begin to climb up and over **White Pass,** but you'll be rewarded by some nice downhills, too. Six miles outside of Skagway is the U.S. border station, where you will have to stop and present identification.

Skagway, you'll immediately notice, is tourist-oriented, with lots of shops selling trinkets and catering to the 7,000-plus cruise-ship passengers that disembark almost daily. But on your bike you'll be able to uncover some of its charm, too. Drive the back streets and get outside the visitor-center area, and you can get a glimpse of the town it once was.

Resources

- The **Alaska Marine Highway** (☎ 800-642-0066; **www.ferryalaska.com**) offers ferry service from the lower 48 states to Haines and/or Skagway. From Bellingham, Washington, to Haines, a two-day trip, expect to pay about $350 one-way (Haines Ferry Terminal: ☎ 907-766-2111) plus an extra $60 for your bike. For fast-ferry service between Haines and Skagway, choose one of the following, both of which can accommodate bicycles: the **Haines–Skagway Fast Ferry** offers up to 20 crossings per day for $30 one-way or $54 for a round-trip (☎ 888-766-2103 or 907-766-2100; **www.chilkatcruises.com**), while the **Silver Eagle Transport** can also transport a few vehicles at a time (☎ 907-766-2418; **alaskaferry@hotmail.com**).
- The **Haines Convention and Visitors Bureau** (☎ 800-458-3579 or 907-766-2234; **www.haines.ak.us**) offers options aplenty for lodging and eating, and can mail its annual travel planner.
- The **Kluane Chilkat International Bike Relay** is an option for those who want to turn their cycling trip into a 150-mile competition or fun run (**www.kcibr.org**). It's also the largest cycling event in the state, attracting more than 1,200 riders of all ages and abilities.
- **L. A. B. Flying Service** (Fourth and Main streets, downtown Haines; ☎ 907-766-2222; **www.labflying.com**) has $200 round-trip flights from Juneau to Haines. Carrying your bike (which must be stowed in a bike box) costs $40.
- The **Southeast Alaska Discovery Center** in Ketchikan (50 Main Street, Ketchikan 99901; ☎ 907-228-6220; **www.nps.gov/aplic**) can help with details on the best places to camp or stay along the road.
- **Wings of Alaska** (Haines Airport Terminal; ☎ 907-766-2030; **www.wingsofalaska.com**) has $195 round-trip flights from Juneau to Haines; no extra charge for carrying bikes.

Haines–Skagway Cycling Outfitters

- **Sockeye Cycle Co.:** ☎ 877-292-4154; **www.cyclealaska.com.** This longtime Southeast company has a reputation for hosting some of the most fun trips in Alaska. They offer guided tours in locations throughout Southeast, including an overnight mountain-bike trek to Chilkat Pass that we love. But its Golden Circle Tour is the best: at ten days and $2,243 from Haines to Skagway, you'll travel 360 miles through this very route. The company also is the only one around that offers bike service if you're traveling independently and have mechanical problems.

The Kenai Peninsula Tour

Regional location Southcentral Coastal–Southcentral Inland Alaska. **Distance** 302 miles, connecting 2 road systems, the Seward and Sterling highways; 127 miles to Seward, 37 back to cutoff, 138 to Homer on Sterling. **Difficulty** . **Suitable for kids?** No. **Time to ride** 4–8 days. **Best time of year to ride** Late May–late September. **Traffic level** Heavy in summer, moderate in May and

unofficial **TIP**
Mileposts on the Seward Highway start at 0 in Seward and work upward to Anchorage. Our mileage reflects, roughly, what your bike computer will be telling you when riding in the Anchorage-to-Seward direction.

September. **Facilities** Most amenities available along the way, including lodging, food, and camping.

ROUTE SUMMARY The Kenai Peninsula Tour skirts one of the most breathtaking scenic routes in Alaska, following the waters of **Turnagain Arm** and climbing into the **Chugach National Forest** to Seward. The **Seward Highway** is designated a National Scenic Byway. The Sterling Highway section, connecting to Homer, also has expansive views of **Cook Inlet** and the volcanoes that make up the Alaska Peninsula.

DIRECTIONS TO ANCHORAGE The Kenai Peninsula Tour starts in **Anchorage,** the state's largest city, in Southcentral Inland Alaska (for more on Anchorage amenities, go to the Southcentral Inland Alaska chapter, page 283). It's accessible via daily jet service to Anchorage's **Ted Stevens International Airport** from any number of carriers, including **Alaska Airlines** (☎ 800-426-0333; **www.alaskaair.com**), **Northwest** (☎ 800-225-2525; **www.nwa.com**), **Continental** (☎ 800-525-0280; **www.continental.com**), **United** (☎ 800-241-6522; **www.ual.com**), and **Delta** (☎ 800-221-1212; **www.delta.com**). Overseas airlines include **Korean Airlines** (☎ 800-438-5000; **www.koreanair.com**), **China Airlines** (☎ 907-248-3603; **www.china-airlines.com**), and **Asiana Airlines** (☎ 800-227-4262; **us.flyasiana.com**), as well as **Air Canada** (☎ 888-247-2262; **www.aircanada.com**) in the summer only. The flight lineups change constantly, so be sure to check ahead of time to make sure a specific carrier is still serving the state.

Access to Anchorage from the lower 48 states also is via road. Travel into the state on the **Alaska Highway,** which connects to the **Richardson Highway,** and then the **Glenn Highway,** which travels directly into Anchorage.

DESCRIPTION Traveling the Kenai Peninsula affords an all-encompassing sample of what Alaska is about. This section of the state ranges from coastal tidewater habitat to snow-covered glaciers and mountains. You'll travel through forests and along open valleys above the tree line.

Our route will take you first to Seward, minus the 37-mile backtrack to the turnoff for the Sterling Highway and Homer. Some cyclists like to get a ride back to this cutoff, while others prefer to depend on their own pedaling power the whole way. We suggest getting a ride for this section, however, because there is a 5- to 10-mile section of road that is probably the most hazardous along the entire Kenai Peninsula route. The road is windy and the shoulders nonexistent. Travelers in the summer tend to drive too fast, making for some scary riding during that particular section. The Department of Transportation is constantly upgrading this section of road, and in some places the shoulder is wide and inviting. But until the entire 37 miles from the Sterling Highway cutoff to Seward is upgraded, we suggest hitching a ride back to the turnoff. In the Resources section, we have suggested a few outfits that will get you back to the cutoff safely.

The Seward Highway Now, on to the road: you will start by riding south out of Anchorage on the Seward Highway, named an All-American Road in 2000 and a National Scenic Byway in 1998. The first third of the road travels along the base of the **Chugach Mountains.** The shoulders are wide and the cycling but can be enjoyable, despite the numerous recreational vehicles, fifth-wheels, and trucks that whiz by. Look for Dall sheep to the left and beluga whales in the water to the right. This section also can get vicious headwinds, so prepare to be blasted by the wind. (*Hint:* Start your travel in the morning, when the winds tend to be gentler.)

About 24 miles into the ride, you'll cross a bridge over **Indian Creek** and notice a parking and rest area adjacent to the Indian Creek ball fields. We suggest you get off the road here and begin following the bike path that is right next to the highway. This newly constructed trail travels 12 miles to the intersection of the Alyeska Highway and Seward Highway. Most of the trail is alongside the highway, but some of it dips into the woods and climbs the surrounding mountains, giving cyclists an incredibly scenic diversion from their road ride while still on pavement.

At the Alyeska Highway cutoff, there is a gas station and cafe with coffee, fresh baked goods, and other goodies. It's a great place for a power snack. Get back onto the Seward Highway, heading south. Beware this area: it is often crowded with traffic and pedestrians, and can get a bit hectic.

The Seward Highway continues on a relatively flat (and often windblown) stretch but climbs await past the 50-mile mark. Leaving Turnagain Arm behind, the road winds up and over **Turnagain Pass,** reaching an elevation that takes you from sea level to 988 feet in a matter of six miles. It doesn't sound like much, but it's a long, slow climb. Beware, too, of fast drivers on this straightaway.

The junction with the Hope Highway is the next major intersection at about 70 miles, and you'll enjoy a high-rise ride over a new bridge that spans **Canyon Creek,** a natural wonder carved deep into the mountains and rushing swiftly from the surrounding glacier-fed creeks and rivers. This is another good place to take a break, enjoy the views, and use the restroom facilities.

After an extended climb to **Summit Lake,** you will begin a well-earned descent—and then another short but steep climb—that will bring you to **Summit Lake Lodge** (☎ 907-244-2031; **www.summitlakelodge.com**), at Mile 80.5 in bike miles. This is a good place to camp and eat—the Chugach National Forest Tenderfoot Creek Campground ($11) is adjacent to the lodge, and the lodge offers reasonable cabin rentals for $90 per night.

In less than ten miles, you will reach a Y-intersection that branches off toward Homer and the Sterling Highway or stays straight and continues south on the Seward Highway to Seward. Stay straight and begin riding defensively, because two-thirds of the way into this section of road is narrow and winding, and cars drive too fast.

You'll soon come to the roadside town of **Moose Pass,** which will make its existence known with obvious signs warning drivers to slow down, at about Mile 97. Moose Pass residents like peace and quiet, and the hustle and bustle of summertime activity can be overwhelming at times. The town is surprisingly well stocked with a general store, lodging, food, and a hotel. There's even a campground and a few nicely appointed artists' studios.

Beyond Moose Pass, the road alternately widens and narrows, and it won't be until you reach Mile 110 that the shoulders will become broad enough to comfortably accommodate your bike and let other drivers pass without feeling the force of their speed as they go by. Road improvements have made the last 20 miles into town an enjoyable ride, with awesome views.

At Mile 110 is the quaint **Primrose Campground,** off Primrose Road. We like it for its smallness—only ten sites with pit toilets at either end—and its scenery, from its perch right on the side of the lake. It's a quiet place to camp (for only $11) and maintains the Alaska wilderness feel that you won't get in the town-centered campgrounds in Seward.

Still, most people will opt to continue on to Seward, which is a few hill climbs away but nothing too challenging. Be on the lookout for moose or bears along the roadsides and by the **Snow River,** which you'll ride alongside for a while. The road takes you straight into town, and the **Seward Chamber of Commerce** visitor center is on the right-hand side of the road, not to be missed. If you have any questions on camping, they can surely help. There is almost always an open site, and plenty of bed-and-breakfasts and hotels from which to choose.

The Sterling Highway This road travels nearly 143 miles to what we consider the prettiest town in all of Alaska: **Homer,** a seaside community that is as eclectic in its personality as it is in its inhabitants. Here, farmers, artists, fishermen, and people from all political, personal, and religious backgrounds live harmoniously (at least most of the time). This is a place where the mountains meet the ocean, where the best of Alaska comes together to be explored in one compact location. We could easily spend an entire summer in Homer and never run out of things to do.

unofficial **TIP**
If you're traveling to Seward in mid-August, you may be competing with Silver Salmon Derby fishermen for the best lodging spots.

Cycling to Homer will be an adventure. The route passes first through the scenic lakeside community of **Cooper Landing,** tucked into the mountains and quickly becoming a tourist destination itself. Just ten years ago, this sleepy little town hosted a few river-rafting companies and a bed-and-breakfast or two. Today it bustles with visitors, there for the famed Kenai River king salmon. Anglers, rafters, and nature lovers come here during the summer, so when you cycle through the first 15 miles of the Sterling Highway, don't be surprised by the crowds. The aquamarine water of **Kenai Lake,** around which Cooper Landing is based, is breathtaking. It almost doesn't look real, but it certainly is. There are plenty of places to stop for a bite to eat or fill up water bottles, and the 350 or so year-round residents are superfriendly. A visitor-information center operates during the summer right off the Kenai River bridge.

The **Cooper Creek Campground,** 14 miles into the Sterling, is a good place to camp ($11).

Beyond Cooper Landing, things get a little quieter, and the route follows gentle hills that gain and lose elevation, but not at the alarming rates of Turnagain Pass. The **Russian River Campground** is two miles out of town, but it often is full during the summer due to the rush of king-salmon fishermen. Bears are seen often, so be on the lookout. The trailhead to the **Resurrection Pass Trail,** a mile beyond the campground, is a good option for mountain bikers (see page 179 of the "Mountain Biking" section for details).

The road is relatively flat for the next five miles, leading into the **Kenai National Wildlife Refuge,** the most visited of the 16 National Wildlife Refuges in Alaska. The shoulder is not bad in this section, but because it is straight, drivers are eager to make up time and often speed. Ride defensively.

Sterling, the community for which the highway was named, is surprisingly small, given the signs you'll notice of its impending arrival. The road widens at about Mile 43, and lampposts line the street, giving one the impression that the town is somehow metropolitan. That is far from the reality of Sterling, a community of about 4,900 people, most of them living on side streets and off in the woods, not along the well-lit and lightly traveled road.

Sterling is another good place to stop for a snack. The cinnamon buns at **Cook's Corner** (☎ 907-260-1950) are locally famous and will jump-start your engine if you're beginning to tire from the miles.

Another 15 miles of riding will bring you to the city of **Soldotna,** a tourist destination centered on fishing the Kenai River, but also offering some wonderful jaunts into the Kenai National Wildlife Refuge. Here, you can get anything you need—groceries, camping supplies, even a charter flight the rest of the way to Homer if you're ready to stop cycling. There is no real charm to the place, but it is functional, with the grocery stores and fast-food restaurants that so many travelers seem to want. Soldotna has a visitor center with a database of places to stay and things to do. If you're going to stop and sample some of life on the Kenai, this is a good place to call it a day. The ride from Soldotna to Homer has some decent hills and outstanding views to enjoy, and it's best to start off early in the morning, when the traffic is not so heavy.

Leaving Soldotna, you will continue along the Sterling Highway, although another option is to take **Kalifornsky Beach Road** on the south end of town toward Homer. It reconnects with the Sterling Highway at the town of Kasilof and is slightly less traveled and less hilly. Still, neither road offers much in the way of wide shoulders, so take your pick. They are both beautiful (we prefer Kalifornsky Beach, or K-Beach as it is called locally).

Kasilof (Kuh-**SEE**-lof), located at about Mile 72 and reached from either road, is another funky little community, although you can't appreciate its character from the main road. It's home to nearly 600 year-round residents, most of whom depend on fishing for their living.

The road continues with slight ups and downs and passes several points of interest, including campgrounds and recreation sites that draw visitors all summer. **Clam Gulch State Recreation Site,** at Mile 81, is very popular. Time your ride with the tides, and you can stop, camp on the beach, and dig for wrist-thick clams to cook over a fire and eat fresh.

Farther down the road, at about Mile 99, is **Ninilchik Village,** at the mouth of the Ninilchik River. The **Holy Transfiguration of Our Lord Russian Orthodox Church** sits atop a hill overlooking Cook Inlet and the river, dominating the landscape. Images of this ornate green-and-white church show up in books and magazines all over the world.

From Ninilchik, there are more than 40 miles of up-and-down cycling ahead of you, and it seems to go on forever. To the left are the **Caribou Hills,** mountains that become snow covered early in the season and remain that way until late in the spring. It is a winter-sports lover's destination—dog mushers, snowmobile riders, and skiers flock there in winter.

To the right of the road, you'll enjoy views of several volcanoes that all have been active at one time or another. There's **Mount Augustine,** far to the south and sometimes hidden from view, this one has been spewing ash off and on since 2006; **Iliamna; Redoubt;** and **Spurr.** Mount Redoubt is the most impressive of the four, and on a sunny day it appears to loom almost directly in front of you. While the riding itself might begin to feel monotonous, the views will never get old.

Ten miles outside of Homer, you'll pass through **Anchor Point,** which has a few amenities, but we don't quite consider a destination. If you do decide to stop here, it's worth the extra two miles of riding to reach the **Halibut Campground,** at the end of Anchor River Road. The state recreation area is right at the water and has 20 camp spots, toilets, water, and other facilities. Camping is $10.

Prepare for your arrival in Homer as you climb the last hill that offers a pullout to the west overlooking **Kachemak Bay.** You'll still have another nine miles or so before you reach the very end of the road, at the **Homer Spit,** which literally peters out into the sea. But at the overlook, you have officially greeted Homer.

Riding down the hill into Homer will be a well-earned achievement. Reward yourself by staying here as many days as possible. The recreation opportunities are vast—hiking, birding, beachcombing, fishing, kayaking, and more. There are museums, restaurants, and gift shops, too. You won't find a bicycle shop in town, but basic repair supplies can be purchased at the local hardware stores.

Resources

- The **Homer Chamber of Commerce** (☎ 907-235-7740; **www.homeralaska.org**) can help you find food and lodging, and can mail its annual visitor guide if you sign up online.

- **Seward Bike Shop** (☎ 907-224-2448) services bikes, and sells Kona, KHS, and Specialized products. They rent mountain bikes, comfort bikes, and cruisers as well, with half-day and daily rates.
- The **Seward Chamber of Commerce** (☎ 907-224-8051; **www.seward.com**) can give you plenty of options for lodging and eating.
- The **Tenderfoot Creek Campground** at Summit Lake, **Bertha Creek Campground** at Mile 61.5; **Granite Creek Campground** at Mile 64; and **Primrose Campground** at Mile 110 are all managed by **Chugach National Forest** (☎ 907-743-9500; **www.fs.fed.us/r10/chugach**). Camping is $11 per night. **Chugach State Park** (☎ 907-345-5014; **www.dnr.state.ak.us**) is in charge of the **Bird Creek Campground,** just outside of Anchorage. Some cyclists like to stay here before heading into Anchorage on the last day of their ride; sites are $15. The **Alaska Public Lands Information Center** in Anchorage (605 West Fourth Avenue, Suite 105, Anchorage 99501; ☎ 907-271-2737; **www.nps.gov/aplic**) can help with details on the best places to camp or stay along the road.

Kenai Peninsula Route Outfitters

- While a few companies out there offer day trips and overnighters on the Kenai Peninsula, they are strictly mountain-biking adventures. Those who opt for this trip must go it alone.

MOUNTAIN BIKING

unofficial **TIP**
We suggest bringing your own bike with you for long trips, as it's better to ride a bike with which you are familiar.

RIDING OFF-TRAIL OR ON THE GRAVEL ROADS of Alaska can be one of the best ways to see the state. On these treks, you get a good dose of the outdoors with the efficiency of following a path that covers more ground than walking. While road-bike trips are few and limited to city centers, where pavement is more commonplace, mountain bikes open up a whole new world of cycling. There are great roads and trails for cycling from as far south as Prince of Wales Island to as far north as Nome, in western Alaska.

This section outlines a few of our favorite cycling destinations, ranging from camping trips on remote trails to vehicle-supported road rides along scenic gravel "highways." We think of Alaska as a mountain biker's paradise. There is no shortage of places in which to ride and explore, from day trips just outside the city centers to weeklong treks into the wilderness.

There is, however, a shortage of experienced mountain-bike outfitters to guide you on your journey. We have listed the few that we know to be reputable and have excellent outdoors skills. You will find them at the end of the mountain-biking trip suggestions (see "mountain-bike Outfitters," page 184).

The Dalton Highway

Regional location The Interior. **Distance** 414 miles one-way. **Route configuration** Bike out and arrange a ride back, or go out-and-back. **Difficulty** . **Suitable for kids?** No. **Time to ride** 8–12 days. **Best time of year to ride** June–August. **Traffic level** Steady tourist traffic as well as heavy trucks. **Facilities** Very few; food and lodging are available at the **Yukon River Camp** (Mile 56; ☎ 907-474-3557), in **Coldfoot** (Mile 175; ☎ 866-474-3400; 907-474-3500; **www.coldfootcamp.com**), and in **Deadhorse,** at the northern end of the road. There are 2 lodging and food options in **Wiseman,** just a few miles north of Coldfoot Camp: **Arctic Getaway Cabin and Breakfast** (☎ 907-678-4456; **www.arcticgetaway.com**), which is rustic but authentic; and **Boreal Lodging** (☎ 907-678-4566; **www.boreallodge.com**), which is scenic and well kept. Otherwise, services are not available. The **Bureau of Land Management** (☎ 907-474-2200; **www.blm.gov/ak/dalton**), which manages much of the land along the road, has 4 campgrounds, 3 of which are primitive camping areas. Download its 35-page Dalton Highway guide online. There is a private campground in Coldfoot. In Deadhorse, your options are the **Arctic Caribou Inn** (☎ 877-659-2368; **www.arcticcaribouinn.com**) or the **Arctic Oilfield Inn** (☎ 907-659-2614). Camping options include **Finger Mountain** (Mile 98), **Arctic Circle** (Mile 115), **Gobblers Knob** (Mile 131), **Grayling Lake** (Mile 150), **South Koyukuk River** (Mile 156), **Marion Creek** (Mile 179), **Middle Fork Koyukuk River** (Mile 204), **Last Spruce Tree** (Mile 235), **Galbraith Camp** (Mile 274), and **Last Chance** (Mile 355). Some have pit toilets and other amenities.

ROUTE SUMMARY The Dalton Highway, built in 154 days in 1974 to provide access to the oilfields of the North Slope, is a rugged 414-mile road that begins 84 miles north of Fairbanks and crosses the **Brooks Range** to **Prudhoe Bay.** The first 100 miles of the road are paved, but from there it is rough gravel. Views are outstanding. The Dalton Highway is known locally as the "Haul Road" because it is used to convey supplies to and from the North Slope oilfields.

DIRECTIONS TO FAIRBANKS Reach Fairbanks by driving north on the Richardson or Parks highways, or by flying in to the Fairbanks International Airport via daily jet service from Seattle or Anchorage, as well as other cities. **Alaska Airlines** is the primary service provider (☎ 800-252-7522; **www.alaskaair.com**). Reach the Dalton Highway by taking the Elliott Highway 84 miles north out of downtown Fairbanks.

DESCRIPTION The Dalton Highway, or State Route 11, was for decades—and still is today—used as a supply route for oilfield work. However, in 1995, the state opened the once-closed road to tourist traffic as well, and travelers will notice the constant truck and tourist traffic. Note that the term "constant" in Alaska is relative. This means that perhaps one truck and a half-dozen cars will pass by every half hour or so. And that's on busy days.

Cycling the Haul Road, as it is known locally, is an epic ride involving steep climbs (as much as 10% to 12% in some places), rough gravel, and, in the summer, some of the state's fiercest mosquitoes. But don't let that description deter you from riding this road, because it also offers an awesome glimpse of Alaska, as you travel through the Brooks Range and past the Arctic Circle to reach the farthest-north point in Alaska. It's a superlative-filled journey. The scenery includes views of the mighty **Yukon River,** the **Arctic Circle** (just past Mile 115), **Atigun Pass** (at the crest of the Continental Divide), the caribou of the **North Slope** plains, 375-million-year-old limestone-filled **Sukakpak Mountain** (elevation 4,459 feet at Mile 203.5), and any number of sweeping mountain vistas opening into the **Brooks Range, Gates of the Arctic National Park,** or **Arctic National Wildlife Refuge.**

From the Elliott Highway, the road travels north near the community of Livengood. The **Trans-Alaska Pipeline System** parallels the road along the way, rising and falling with the contours of the hills and valleys. The road crosses the Yukon River at Mile 56, and passes through **Gates of the Arctic National Park** and the **Arctic National Wildlife Refuge,** the same refuge at the heart of controversy among conservationists who want to protect it and big-oil interests who want to develop it. Look for caribou, moose, and bears throughout this area. The road passes the Arctic Circle at Mile 115. (Incidentally, the Dalton is the only highway in the United States and one of only two in North America that crosses the Arctic Circle.) The next place to resupply is Coldfoot, 175 miles into the drive. There is an RV campground with hookup, food, and lodging. Just up the road is Wiseman, which also has a couple of lodging options. Travel services are limited—north of Coldfoot is the longest service-free stretch of highway in North America: 244 miles.

A good camping option is **Galbraith Lake,** at Mile 274. The terrain gets a little rough here, as the road changes course and begins crossing drainages. There will be occasional slow climbs and a few good descents before you reach pavement again at Mile 334. The pavement continues until you're about 50 miles outside of Deadhorse, where it again turns to gravel. This section also gets muddy from the heavy traffic coming in and out, so be prepared for a bumpy last 50 miles.

Deadhorse is on the shores of the Arctic Ocean. It's not much to write home about as far as visitor amenities go: there are only a couple of hotels, a store, and gas station, and the majority of people you'll see live there only a few weeks at a time for their jobs in the oilfields. But the community is as far north as you can go on Alaska's primary road system. And it is worth exploring, especially if your goal is to dip a toe into the Arctic Ocean.

Resources

- **Alaska Outdoor Rentals and Guides** (☎ 907-457-2453; **www.akbike.com**) gets our highest recommendation for shuttle support and rentals. The outfitter rents bicycles and gear for all your Interior adventures. They also can provide "SAG" (support and gear) and/or deliver you wherever you want to go with your bike or one of theirs.
- The **Alaska Public Lands Information Center** (250 Cushman Street, Fairbanks 99701; ☎ 907-456-0527; **www.nps.gov/aplic**) can advise you on good local rides and places to find rental equipment.

unofficial **TIP**
No matter the road or trail you travel, it's a good idea to have tires beefy enough to withstand gravel, dirt, roots, and rocks. On roads such as the Dalton Highway, 700-by-35 tires are a good choice.

- **Arctic Outfitters–Dalton Highway Auto Rentals** (☎ 907-747-3555; **www.daltonhighway.com**) is one of the few companies that rent vehicles that can be used on the Haul Road, including all the necessary gear to help you along if you break down. The vehicles even come equipped with CB radios in case of problems. The rates are $149 per day for a Jeep Cherokee and $99 per day for a Ford Taurus, if you rent for four or more days. The company also can arrange shuttles and lodging.
- We like **Dalton Highway Express** (☎ 907-474-3555; **www.daltonhighwayexpress.com**) because it caters to independent travelers with their own equipment. This small company will take you anywhere along the Dalton Highway from Fairbanks and drop you off wherever you want to be left. They will pick you up at a later, prearranged time, as well. It's $196 to get to Deadhorse, $88 to Coldfoot; bicycles cost extra.
- The **Fairbanks Convention and Visitors Bureau** (550 First Avenue, Fairbanks 99701; ☎ 800-327-5774; **www.explorefairbanks.com**) can help you plan lodging and transportation.
- **Go North Alaska Travel Center in Fairbanks** (☎ 866-236-7272 or 907-479-7272; **www.paratours.net**) rents RVs and camper trucks if you want a SAG vehicle for road support. Their rates are affordable, too, starting at $125, depending on the vehicle you rent. There is a gravel dent fee for RVs, though, so be prepared to be "dinged," so to speak, an extra $200 for that.
- Access to the Arctic Ocean is limited due to ongoing oilfield work, but many cyclists like the idea of dipping their tires into the northernmost ocean. Contact the **Northern Alaska Tour Co.** (☎ 907-474-1986) to make it happen. Its guides also can show you around if you want to see more of the oilfield at Deadhorse.

The Denali Highway

Regional location The Interior. **Distance** 134 miles one-way. **Route configuration** Out-and-back, or loop if connected with the Richardson and Parks highways. Identified as Alaska State Route 8; 85% gravel, 15% paved. **Difficulty** 🫎🫎🫎. **Suitable for kids?** Preteens and up. **Time to ride** 2–4 days. **Best time of year to ride** Late June–August. **Traffic level** Light. **Facilities** Food and lodging are available intermittently throughout the road. Much of the land surrounding the Denali Highway is managed by the **Bureau of Land Management** (☎ 907-822-3217), which allows camping all along the road. There are a few campgrounds and 3 lodging options, but pulling off to find your own spot makes for a more-remote-feeling experience. Some nice campgrounds in the area include the **BLM Tangle Lakes Campground** at Mile 21.5, which offers 25 tent and RV sites with toilet facilities, water, picnic tables, and fire rings; and the **BLM Brushkana Creek Campground** at Mile 105, which has 12 sites, toilet facilities, water, picnic tables, garbage barrels, and fire rings. Located on either end of the highway, the camps make good places to stop on each end of the ride. For those not interested in camping, we like the lodging options at **Tangle River Inn** (☎ 907-822-3970 or 907-259-3970; **www.tangleriverinn.com**) on the Paxson end of the highway; **Maclaren River Lodge** (at Mile 42; ☎ 907-822-5444; **www.maclarenlodge.com**), and **Gracious House Lodge** (at Mile 82; ☎ 907-333-3148 or 907-259-1111; **www.alaskaone.com/gracious**).

ROUTE SUMMARY The Denali Highway, Alaska State Route 8, is an mostly gravel roads but takes in some of the most scenic country in the state. There are cavernous potholes. The washboards are relentless. And the services—a couple of lodges here and a campground or two there—are few. But those who do venture onto this frontier highway are blessed with a rolling self-guided tour of Alaska bisecting some of the state's most spectacular mountain ranges. The area, with its open tundra and countless kettle lakes, attracts thousands of birds, including the rare arctic warbler and Smith's longspur. Anglers are drawn to the tranquil fishing, where grayling and trout are abundant at the height of summer.

DIRECTIONS TO DENALI HIGHWAY From Fairbanks, drive south on the Richardson Highway until you reach Paxson. The Denali Highway connects to the right, and is well marked. From Anchorage, drive north on the Glenn Highway to the Parks Highway. Travel north on the Parks Highway until you reach Cantwell. The turnoff for the Denali Highway is on the right and well marked.

unofficial **TIP**
The Denali Highway can get dry and dusty, so carry good riding glasses with changeable lenses for the conditions.

DESCRIPTION When it first opened in 1957, the Denali Highway was the only road link to Denali National Park, replacing the Alaska Railroad as primary access. Then the Parks Highway opened in 1971, and the Denali Highway became obsolete. Today the road is still used as a summertime link for those who choose to drive it. It closes in mid-fall, when the snow gets too deep, and doesn't reopen until spring, usually in mid-May. It's a piece of history that hasn't changed much since the day it was first carved across Alaska.

The highway is a mostly gravel road—only the first 20 miles on the eastern end and three miles on the western end are paved. **Maclaren Summit** is the highest point of the highway—4,086 feet at about Mile 40 from the eastern end. From there the road gets narrower and windier, and potholes and washboards can be numerous. Mountain bikers can make good time on the road, although we recommend the three-night, four-day option. Cycling at this pace allows you to stop at some of the better camping and lodging locations, and gives you driving time on either end to travel to Fairbanks or Anchorage, depending upon your ultimate destination.

From Paxson, the road starts out on pavement, but within 20 miles gives way to gravel. The **BLM Tangle Lakes Campground,** at Mile 21.5, is a good place to camp if you've gotten a late start. There is no fee for the 23 established campsites with picnic tables.

Once the gravel begins, you will slow down a bit, but the scenery is stunning. The Denali Highway is popular with off-road vehicles, so you may see four-wheeler trails going off into the woods. Those routes are open to mountain bikes, too, and many cyclists like to explore off-road. If you do go, take a GPS, compass, and map, because it can get confusing once you get back in the mountains.

Maclaren Summit is the highest climb of the trip, at Mile 40. The 4,086-foot pass is the second highest on the road system (**Atigun Pass,** on the Dalton Highway, is the highest). Look for a pullout here with views of the **Susitna River Valley, Mount Hayes,** and the rest of the **Alaska Range.** It can be windy and cold, though—not conducive to camping.

At Mile 43.5, a side road called the **Maclaren River Road** leads to **Maclaren Glacier.** Mountain bikers like this road, too. The glacier is 12 miles in, and you have to cross the **Maclaren River.** This is for very experienced cyclists only.

The next 20 miles follow winding road with numerous kettle lakes and creek crossings. You'll find plenty of pullouts for taking breaks or camping. The **Susitna River Bridge** is at Mile 79, and is impressive to look at with its multiple trusses and 1,036-foot length. The bridge can get extra slippery when wet, so slow down and ride carefully here. There's just one lane, so be on the lookout for oncoming traffic.

Camping or lodging is available at Mile 82 at the **Gracious House Lodge.** From there, expect relatively gradual climbs until Mile 94, which begins a steep, well-deserved descent.

After crossing the Brushkana Creek Bridge, near Mile 105, you'll see the entrance to the **BLM Brushkana Campground.** Camping is $6, and there are a few trails around the campground to explore. Store your food well. Bears and curious squirrels can be eager to raid your stash.

Leaving Brushkana Creek will lead to a nice climb that begins a steep descent at Mile 110. From there the riding is relatively easy, although washboards can get rough in this section due to frequent flooding. The pavement picks up again at Mile 131 and is smooth riding all the way into **Cantwell,** a small community at the intersection of the Denali and Parks highways. Lodging, food, gas, and other amenities are available here.

Resources

- Vehicle rentals are available through **Alaska Outdoor Rentals and Guides** (☎ 907-457-2453; **www.akbike.com**) and **Go North Alaska Travel Center** (☎ 866-236-7272 or 907-479-7272; **www.paratours.net**). Rates start at $125 per day, depending on the vehicle. Alaska Outdoor Rentals is our choice because they provide custom support packages; just call and ask.
- The **Alaska Public Lands Information Center** in Anchorage can help with details on the best places to camp or stay along the road (605 West Fourth Avenue, Anchorage 99501; ☎ 907-271-2737; **www.nps.gov/aplic**), as can the Fairbanks location (250 Cushman Street, Fairbanks 99701; ☎ 907-456-0527).

- The **Fairbanks Convention and Visitors Bureau** (550 First Avenue, Fairbanks 99701; ☎ 800-327-5774; **www.explorefairbanks.com**) can help you plan in-town lodging and transportation. The **Anchorage Convention and Visitors Bureau** (☎ 907-276-4118 or 907-274-3531; **www.anchorage.net**) is a good option if your trip is starting from the south.
- ***Mountain Bike Alaska*** by Richard Larson features a one-page chapter on riding the Denali Highway. Although more than ten years old, the guide will provide some additional details on the road. It's available at Amazon.com or any local Alaska bookstore for around $15.

Denali National Park and Preserve Road

Regional location The Interior. **Distance** 85 miles one-way to Wonder Lake; 91 miles to Kantishna. **Route configuration** Out-and-back. **Difficulty** 🫎🫎🫎🫎. **Suitable for kids?** No. **Time to ride** 2–4 days. **Best time of year to ride** June–August. **Traffic level** Moderate–heavy; mostly tour buses. **Facilities** 6 primitive campgrounds, most of which require advance registration.

ROUTE SUMMARY The Denali National Park and Preserve Road is a narrow, sometimes-one-lane dirt-and-gravel road that meanders through the **Alaska Range** in some of the most pristine land in the world. Vehicle traffic is limited to permitted tour buses and those traveling to and from the mining community of **Kantishna,** at the far end of the road. The scenery is simply stunning, providing the cyclist a glimpse of wild Alaska from the chirping of ground squirrels to the purposeful lumbering of grizzly bears.

DIRECTIONS TO DENALI NATIONAL PARK AND PRESERVE From Fairbanks, drive 124 miles south on the Parks Highway until you reach the entrance to the park, at Mile 237. From Anchorage, take the Glenn Highway north to the intersection of the Parks Highway, and drive north on the Parks until you reach the park entrance. Charter flights are available from Anchorage, Talkeetna, or Fairbanks. Visit the **National Park Service** Web site (**www.nps.gov/archive/dena/home/visitorinfo**) for details on qualified air-taxi services. The **Alaska Railroad** also offers daily summer service into the park, either from Fairbanks or Anchorage (☎ 800-544-0552; **www.alaskarailroad.com**). For more rail details, go to the Resources section.

DESCRIPTION Riding the Denali Park Road is an adventure suited for cyclists who are more concerned about enjoying the scenery than getting in a lot of miles. The road is only 91 miles long, but it is challenging. It is narrow, winding, and steep in many places, and the gravel is better in some spots than in others. In the summer, it can also get dry, and passing tour buses create a lot of dust that you have to drive through.

There are a few rules of the road. First, if you plan to camp along the way, you must have a campground reservation or a backcountry permit. You cannot simply pull over and camp where you wish. The backcountry buses that take passengers into the park for sightseeing can also transport cyclists and their bikes on a first-come, first-served basis.

Bikes are allowed only on the roads. They cannot be taken onto trails, riverbeds, etc. If you have a backcountry permit to camp, you must park

unofficial **TIP**
Cyclists on the Denali Park Road are asked to stop whenever a bus passes, which can be every five to ten minutes at the height of the summer travel season. So don't be intent on making miles. Instead, soak in the scenery of the most-visited national park in Alaska, and see if you can spot any wildlife along the way.

your bikes at established bike racks, at any campground, the Toklat Rest Stop or the Wonder Lake Ranger Station. Park officials recommend cyclists reserve campsites well ahead to ensure they can be at least close to their bicycles. Because of the dust, you should carry good riding glasses with changeable lenses for the conditions.

Now, for the road. Travel begins at the intersection of the Parks Highway and the entrance to the park. The first 15 miles are paved to the Savage River Campground. All vehicles are allowed on this section, so traffic may be heavier until you reach the gravel part of the road. From there, traffic is limited to the park-service backcountry shuttle buses, which take passengers into the park. A fair number of private tour buses also travel the road.

Across the **Savage River,** the road follows the base of **Primrose Ridge,** staying mostly above tree line until it reaches the **Sanctuary River** at Mile 23. The road climbs briefly, then turns along the **Teklanika River.** This is a good spot for viewing grizzly bears, which often forage along the braided riverbed. The **Teklanika Campground** is a popular stopping point for cyclists because it is a third of the way into the trip. However, as of this printing, it was closed due to wildlife activity in the area. Check before you go to see if it has reopened. **Igloo Campground,** four miles farther along the road, is another option, but check to see if it is open. It too has been closed in recent seasons because of wildlife activity (visit **www.nps.gov/archive/dena/home/visitorinfo/camping/index.html** for the latest information).

The next ten miles are some of the most scenic along the entire road. First is **Sable Pass,** at Mile 40, 3,900 feet in elevation. It doesn't sound high, but when you're riding it, you'll appreciate the views. At Mile 43, you'll go over the **Toklat River.** This portion of road is known for its prime bear viewing. The Toklat River bears of the park are somehow more impressive than any you'll see along the route. From the bridge you will begin a steep climb up **Polychrome Pass,** at Mile 46 and 3,700 feet high. A rest stop here provides a good place to hook up your bike and take a hike in the open tundra. In the early fall, the pass lives up to its name, coming alive in vibrant colors of orange, red, and yellow. Even in the summer and winter, the terrain has a multicolored appearance. Dall sheep are common along this section of road. We once spotted seven just off the road and spent a half hour watching them graze on the rugged slopes.

Highway Pass, at Mile 58 and 3,980 feet in elevation, is the highest point along the road. From there it is a gentle ride to Mile 66 and the **Eielson Visitor Center,** which is in the process of being rebuilt and will likely be closed in 2008. From the visitor center, the summit of **Mount McKinley,** aka **Denali**—North America's tallest peak, at 20,320 feet—is just 33 miles away, according to the *Denali Road Guide.* On a clear day, it will feel even closer. The mountain dominates the landscape and from this close, feels as if it is literally towering over you.

Beyond Eielson, the terrain changes dramatically, opening up to a tundra plain that seems to go on forever. **Wonder Lake Campground,** at Mile 85, is a picturesque place to pitch a tent. For those who want to add a few more days of adventure to their trip and cycle back out, the **North Face Lodge–Camp Denali** and **Denali Backcountry Lodge** are good places to rest and explore the interior of the park through hiking or other activities.

Resources

- The **Alaska Public Lands Information Center** (250 Cushman Street, Fairbanks 99701; ☎ 907-456-0527; **www.nps.gov/aplic**) can advise you on good local rides and places to find rental equipment. The **Fairbanks Convention and Visitors Bureau** (550 First Avenue, Fairbanks 99701; ☎ 800-327-5774; **www.explorefairbanks.com**) can help you plan your trip.
- The **Alaska Railroad** offers daily summer service into the park, from either Fairbanks or Anchorage (☎ 800-544-0552; **www.alaskarailroad.com**). From Anchorage, the train ride is about 7½ hours. From Fairbanks, it will take 3½ hours. Rates are $135 from Anchorage and $59 from Fairbanks; bikes are $20 extra.
- The **Denali Chamber of Commerce** (☎ 907-683-4636; **www.denalichamber.com**) can provide you with information on local sights and happenings.
- The Denali National Park and Preserve Web site offers some more details on biking. Go to **www.nps.gov/dena** and click on "Plan Your Visit" and "Things to Do."
- The ***Denali Road Guide,*** published by the Alaska Natural History Association (ANHA), is a great companion to take along on your ride. Light and informative, it offers insight into the flora and fauna that you see along the way. It also helps let you know what is coming ahead with each mile. It's available in the park visitor headquarters or through ANHA ($6; ☎ 866-257-2757 or **www.alaskanha.org**). You can also order a ***Trails Illustrated*** map of the park through ANHA ($9.95)—good to have on hand if you plan to go off road at all.

Prince of Wales Island

Regional location Southeast Alaska. **Distance** Varies from 60 to 300 miles round-trip or more. **Route configuration** Out-and-back, with numerous side-trip options. **Difficulty** 🚴🚴🚴. **Suitable for kids?** No. **Time to ride** 3–6 days. **Best time of year to ride** Early June–late September. **Traffic level** Light. **Facilities** Campgrounds, bed-and-breakfasts, and resupply points are all available. Remote routes have fewer amenities.

ROUTE SUMMARY Prince of Wales Island is part of the 16.9-million acre **Tongass National Forest** and for years has been central to the logging

unofficial **TIP**
We especially like this trip because the people on Prince of Wales are exceedingly nice, giving the place a small-town friendliness that is often hard to find.

industry in Southeast Alaska. As a result, there are thousands of miles of logging roads, both paved and gravel, on which to cycle. Views, while often scarred by clear cuts, also are breathtaking.

There is no specific route to follow, although the most common would be to travel from **Hollis** to **Coffman Cove** and back for a 150-mile round-trip. However, the adventure is yours to create. You can even travel as far north as **Labouchere Bay** and **Port Protection** at the northwest tip of Prince of Wales Island, essentially adding another 100 miles your overall mileage.

DIRECTIONS TO PRINCE OF WALES ISLAND The easiest way to get to the island with bikes is to fly to Ketchikan and then take the **Inter-Island Ferry** (☎ 866-308-4848 or 907-826-4848; **www.interislandferry.com**) to Hollis. Be clear about your plans to include a bicycle. The folks in this small town don't get many cyclists, so be sure they don't charge you the same rate that they would a car. Access to Ketchikan is through **Alaska Airlines** (☎ 800-426-0333; **www.alaskaair.com**).

DESCRIPTION Prince of Wales Island is the third-largest island in the United States after the Big Island of Hawaii and Kodiak Island in Southcentral Coastal Alaska. It has a wet maritime climate and affords travels through some of the largest forests you will see in Alaska, despite the years of logging it has undergone. It boasts more roads than anywhere else in Southeast Alaska, with 105 miles of paved road, 155 miles of improved gravel, and more than 2,000 miles of rough-cut logging roads, most of which experienced mountain bikers can easily handle.

Starting from the ferry terminal at Hollis, you'll first ride the paved and aptly named **Craig-Klawock-Hollis Highway,** 23 miles west to Klawock, then turn south for the remaining eight miles into Craig. Craig has most amenities, including a bank, a post office, restaurants, a laundromat, and a supermarket.

To head north on the island to the North Prince of Wales Road (the main connector of all the main roads), backtrack on the Craig-Klawock-Hollis Highway to the intersection of Boundary Road, which becomes Big Salt Lake Road. That road travels 16 miles to a T-intersection that will take you north up the island, or east on the paved Thorne Bay Road. We recommend checking out **Thorne Bay.** It's an easy 17 miles of low grades and gentle curves. Plus, it's right on the water and has several nice lodging and camping options, a few restaurants, and a post office.

You'll backtrack again to reach **North Prince of Wales Road,** also known as the "island highway" by locals. The 78-mile-long road is well maintained but narrow in places with no shoulders. There are some challenging climbs that are rewarded with winding downhills, and several spots where you can branch off and explore the local communities, including **Coffman Cove, Tuxekan,** and **Naukati.**

If you opt to ride all the way to **Labouchere Bay,** be prepared for a less-than-exciting end to your trip. There's not much there other than a sign and a rocky, sandy beach. No one lives there.

Resources

- The easiest way to get to the island with bikes is to fly to Ketchikan and then take the **Inter-Island Ferry** (☎ 866-308-4848 or 907-826-4848; **www.interislandferry.com**) to Hollis. Bikes are free. Adult passage is $35.
- The **JT Brown General Store** in Craig (☎ 907-826-3290) is the local Trek dealer and might have a couple of spare parts such as tires or brake pads. They likely won't have disc-brake parts or anything else fancy, though, so be prepared to do your own repairs.
- The **Prince of Wales Chamber of Commerce** (☎ 907-755-2626; **www.princeofwalescoc.org**) in Klawock can help you set up lodging—if they're open, that is. We suggest trying to reserve your spots ahead of time, because in the summer you can never count on people being around. The Web site also has a helpful printable map that is good to take with you.
- For details on **Thorne Bay,** visit the great Web site **www.thornebay alaska.net**. You can see photos and check out local businesses for reservations.
- Cabins in **Tongass National Forest** cost $25 to $45 per night and must be reserved in advance either over the phone or online (☎ 877-444-6777; **www.recreation.gov**). Reservations can be made up to 180 days (six months) in advance of the first night's stay. For details about the 19 cabins in the Craig and Thorne Bay ranger districts, call ☎ 907-826-3271 (Craig) or 907-828-3304 (Thorne Bay), or visit **www.fs.fed.us/r10/tongass/cabins/cabins.shtml.** Check this site before making reservations online or over the phone, because the agents at **www.recreation.gov** are located somewhere in the lower 48 states and don't know much about the cabins. The **Alaska Public Lands Information Center** in Anchorage can also help (605 West Fourth Avenue, Suite 105, Anchorage 99501; ☎ 907-271-2737; **www.nps.gov/aplic**).
- Camping also is available through the Tongass National Forest, and private campgrounds are scattered across the island. Of the five U.S. Forest Service campgrounds on Prince of Wales, only two have running water. Rates are $8 per night at **Harris River Campground** in Craig and $8 per night at **Eagle's Nest Campground** in Thorne Bay. The other three, all in Thorne Bay, are free. Call ☎ 907-826-3271 in Craig or 907-828-3304 in Thorne Bay, or visit **www.fs.fed.us/r10/tongass/recreation/rec_facilities/campground_info.html.** The **Southeast Alaska Discovery Center** in Ketchikan can also help (50 Main Street, Ketchikan 99901; ☎ 907-228-6220; **www.nps.gov/aplic**).

Resurrection Pass Trail

Regional location Southcentral Coastal Alaska. **Distance** 39 miles. **Route configuration** Out-and-back or end-to-end. **Difficulty** ★★★. **Suitable for kids?** Preteens and up. **Time to ride** 1–3 days. **Best time of year to ride** Mid-June–September. **Traffic level** Moderate–heavy. **Facilities** Established tent sites, U.S. Forest Service cabins, and marked trailheads with parking and outhouses.

ROUTE SUMMARY The Resurrection Pass Trail is a National Recreation Trail that is one of the most popular routes on the Kenai Peninsula, attracting hikers, mountain bikers, equestrians, and hunters. Its scenery ranges from forested, riverside habitat to high alpine meadows. The highest elevation is at the pass itself, at about 2,600 feet and in an open alpine valley. Good lake fishing for rainbow and lake trout, Dolly Varden, and some burbot.

DIRECTIONS TO RESURRECTION PASS From Anchorage, take the Seward Highway south to reach either end of the trail. The north-end trailhead is in the community of **Hope,** 70 miles from Anchorage. Look for the Hope turnoff. Turn right onto the Hope Highway and travel about 16 miles to a left-hand turn onto Palmer Creek Road. Follow this gravel road until it branches to the right onto Resurrection Creek Road. The trailhead is on the right, with plenty of parking. The south end of the trail is in **Cooper Landing,** off the Sterling Highway. From Anchorage, follow the Seward Highway south to Mile 90, at its junction to the Sterling Highway. Follow the Sterling Highway about 15 miles to Mile 53, and turn right (north) into the marked trailhead parking area.

DESCRIPTION From the north end of the route, near the community of Hope, the dirt single-track trail climbs continuously along **Resurrection Creek,** where gold-seekers once panned for gold (people still try it today). About 12 miles in is **Fox Creek Cabin,** which offers a reprieve to an even-steeper climb out of the woods to Resurrection Pass (this section is one of the best for blueberry picking in late summer). The **Devil's Pass Trail** connects to this trail at Resurrection Pass. The nearby **Devil's Pass Cabin** is an excellent place to spend a few days exploring through day hikes. The southern end of the ride is a more gradual downhill through lakes and the Juneau Creek basin. Look for wildlife including bears, moose, and porcupine in this section. The prettiest section of the ride, in our opinion, occurs from **Swan Lake,** at about Mile 26 from the Hope direction, to the trailhead in Cooper Landing. Through this area you will pass **Juneau Lake** and its two lakeside Forest Service cabins, along with **Juneau Falls,** four miles from the southern terminus of the trail. The falls are a great place for tent camping but can get busy on the weekends with large groups.

Resources

- Before gearing up, head to one of the many bike shops in Anchorage (see our picks in the Kenai Peninsula Tour), and drop by the **Anchorage Convention and Visitors Bureau** (☎ 907-276-4118 or 907-274-3531; **www.anchorage.net** to find out what's going on in the city.
- Cabins in **Chugach National Forest** cost $25 to $45 per night and must be reserved in advance either over the phone or online (☎ 877-444-6777; **www.recreation.gov**). Reservations can be made up to 180 days (six months) in advance of the first night's stay. For details about the cabins in the Seward Ranger District, call ☎ 907-271-2500 or visit **www.fs.fed.us/r10/chugach/cabin_web_page/cabin_files.** Check this site before making reservations online or over the phone, because the agents at **www.recreation.gov** are located somewhere in the lower 48

states and don't know much about the cabins. The **Alaska Public Lands Information Center** in Anchorage can also help (605 West Fourth Avenue, Suite 105, Anchorage 99501; ☎ 907-271-2737; **www.nps.gov/aplic**).

- ***Mountain Bike Alaska*** by Richard Larson features a one-page chapter on riding the Resurrection Pass Trail. Although more than ten years old, it will provide some additional details on the trail. It's available at Amazon.com or any local Alaska bookstore for around $15.
- One option to lengthen your journey is to connect with the **Resurrection River–Russian Lakes Trail System,** which travels another 32 miles and comes out on Exit Glacier Road off the Seward Highway, outside of Seward. This trip is for experienced mountain bikers only: bears, rough terrain, and frequent blowdowns are common, but the trip is unforgettable. The best source on details for the ride are available in the book ***55 Ways to the Wilderness in Southcentral Alaska*** by Helen Nienhueser and John Wolfe Jr., available at Amazon.com or through local bookstores for around $17.
- **U.S. Geological Survey maps** for the area are Seward B-8, C-8, and D-8 (visit **www.usgs.gov**). **Kenai National Wildlife Refuge maps** can be downloaded online at **kenai.fws.gov/maps.htm** or purchased through the **Alaska Natural History Association** ($9.95; ☎ 907-274-8440; **www.alaskanha.org**).

OUR FAVORITE DAY TRIPS

IF YOU DON'T HAVE ENOUGH TIME for a multiday adventure, you still have several other great options for biking in Alaska. Here is just a sampling. Our best advice is to stop in the local bike shops and ask for current recommendations, because trail conditions vary with the weather.

SOUTHCENTRAL COASTAL ALASKA

Burma Road with Optional Old Women's Mountain Return

Closest town Kodiak. **Configuration** Loop, old road, and some gnarly single-track. **Distance** 12 miles one-way. **Difficulty** Moderate on Burma Road; difficult for Old Women's Mountain return. ✱✱✱✱✱. **Suitable for kids?** No. **Riding time** 2–3 hours.

DIRECTIONS Take Rezanof Drive West out of town to Anton Larsen Bay Road, on the right. Ride until you cross Buskin Bridge Number 6. Burma Road is on the far side. *Note:* Part of this route is on U.S. Coast Guard property, so you'll need to get advance permission to ride (☎ 907-487-5372). The ***Kodiak Island Mountain Bike Guide,*** available at 58 Degrees North Bike Shop in Kodiak, has a complete log of the ride (☎ 907-486-6249).

Johnson Pass Trail

Closest town Seward. **Configuration** Out-and-back, narrow single-track. **Distance** Up to 20 miles. **Difficulty** . **Suitable for kids?** Teens and older. **Riding time** 3–5 hours.

DIRECTIONS From Anchorage, take the Seward Highway south to Mile 63.8, the Granite Creek trailhead, or drive to the Upper Trail Lake trailhead, at Mile 32.7. Both trailheads are on the left side of the road. **Chugach National Forest** (☎ 907-271-2500) has more information.

Million Dollar Bridge to Child's Glacier

Closest town Cordova. **Configuration** Out-and-back, gravel road. **Distance** 48 miles. **Difficulty** . **Suitable for kids?** Yes. **Riding time** 4 hours.

DIRECTIONS The only access to Cordova is via air or ferry; once you're in town, take Whitshed Road, which turns into the Copper River Highway. The **Cordova Chamber of Commerce** (☎ 907-424-7260) has more information.

SOUTHCENTRAL INLAND ALASKA

Bird–Gird Trail

Closest town Anchorage. **Configuration** Out-and-back, paved pathway. **Distance** 12 miles one-way. **Difficulty** . **Suitable for kids?** Yes. **Riding time** 2 hours. This trail is a misnomer because the newly improved and repaved bike path actually spans 12 miles from the community of Indian to Girdwood, rather than Bird Creek to Girdwood, where it used to begin.

DIRECTIONS Mile 103 of the Seward Highway. Cross a bridge over Indian Creek, and park in the parking and rest area adjacent to the Indian Creek ball fields immediately on your right. (Parking is $5.) Most of the trail is alongside the highway, but some of it dips into the woods and climbs the surrounding mountains, giving cyclists an incredibly scenic road ride. **Chugach State Park** (☎ 907-345-5014) has more information.

Eklutna Lake

Closest town Eagle River. **Configuration** Out-and-back, dirt-and-gravel nontechnical trail. **Distance** 13 miles one-way. **Difficulty** . **Suitable for kids?** Yes. **Riding time** 3–4 hours.

DIRECTIONS Take the Glenn Highway north through Eagle River to about Mile 25, the Thunderbird Falls exit. Take this exit and follow the road about a half mile to the Eklutna Lake Road. Follow Eklutna Lake Road to its end. Parking at Chugach State Park (☎ 907-345-5014) is $5.

unofficial **TIP**
A great logbook for Anchorage trails is ***Mountain Bike Anchorage*** by Rosemary Austin ($17.95; available at local bookstores and bike shops or online at **www.nearpointpress.com**), which gives detailed descriptions of these and other popular Anchorage-area rides. We highly recommend it.

Hatcher Pass–Gold Mint Trail

Closest town Palmer. **Configuration** Out-and-back, technical single-track. **Distance** 9 miles one-way, but gets pretty brushy after 5 miles. **Difficulty** . **Suitable for kids?** No. **Riding time** 2 hours.

DIRECTIONS Take the Glenn Highway north through Palmer to about Mile 49, and then turn left on Hatcher Pass Road (Fishhook–Willow). The Gold Mint trailhead is 13 miles up the road, just past the Motherlode Lodge. **Mat-Su State Parks** (☎ 907-745-3975) has more information.

Tony Knowles Coastal Trail

Closest town Anchorage. **Configuration** Out-and-back, paved pathway. **Distance** 10 miles one-way. **Difficulty** . **Suitable for kids?** Yes. **Riding time** 1½ hours.

DIRECTIONS From downtown Anchorage, head north at the intersection of Fifth Avenue and H Street. At Third Avenue, H Street becomes Christensen Drive. Follow it down the hill, and turn left onto Second Avenue. The trailhead is not large, but there is a sign and parking is alongside the road. The **Anchorage Convention and Visitors Bureau** (☎ 907-276-4118 or 907-274-3531) has more information.

SOUTHEAST ALASKA

East Glacier Trail

Closest town Juneau. **Configuration** Loop. **Distance** 4.5 miles. **Difficulty** . **Suitable for kids?** No. **Riding time** 1 hour.

DIRECTIONS The trail leaves from behind the visitor center at Mendenhall Glacier. *Warning:* There are many hikers on it during the peak tourist season, so be considerate of those users. **Mountain Gears Bike Shop** (☎ 907-780-6002) has more information.

THE INTERIOR

Birch Hill Ski Trails

Closest town Fairbanks. **Configuration** Loops, out-and-back, a variety of single-track and dual-track riding choices. **Distances** Vary depending on the loops and routes you take. **Difficulty** (an average; some choices are more difficult than others). **Suitable for kids?** Depends on the trail. **Riding time** 1–4 hours will pretty much cover the whole area.

DIRECTIONS Drive north on the Steese Highway to Fairhill Road. From Fairhill, turn left on Birch Hill Road to the sign for the cross-country-skiing trails. **Alaska Outdoor Rentals and Guides** (☎ 907-457-2453, **www.akbike.com**) has more information.

Ester Dome and Alder Chute

Closest town Fairbanks. **Configuration** Loop. **Distance** 9.5 miles on single-track and old fire roads. **Difficulty** . **Suitable for kids?** No. **Riding time** 1 hour.

DIRECTIONS From Fairbanks, drive south to the little community of Ester and turn right. Park at the Ester Community Park, near the firehouse. Bike back up the highway about 100 yards to the entrance to the mining area. There is an old dirt road that heads up the hill. This road winds up Ester Dome about four miles. The Alder Chute follows a power line for 2.5 miles downhill and is very steep. **Alaska Outdoor Rentals and Guides** (☎ 907-457-2453) has more information.

Tour of the Mining Country

Closest town Fairbanks. **Configuration** Out-and-back, single-track and fire roads. **Distance** 46 miles. **Difficulty** . **Suitable for kids?** No. **Riding time** 3½–6 hours.

DIRECTIONS Take Chena Hot Springs Road; when it meets up with Steele Creek Road, park and start the ride from the bike path there. The route is complicated, so ask at local bike shops for details. **Alaska Outdoor Rentals and Guides** (☎ 907-457-2453; **www.akbike.com**) has more information.

THE BUSH

Anvil Mountain

Closest town Nome. **Configuration** Out-and-back, gravel road that goes from sea level to 1,062 feet. **Distance** 9 miles round-trip. **Difficulty** . **Suitable for kids?** Yes. **Riding time** 1 hour.

DIRECTIONS From downtown Nome, drive north onto the Teller Road. After the road curves west, about 3.5 miles from town, watch for a turn to the right for Glacier Creek Road. Follow Glacier Creek Road directly up Anvil Mountain. On a clear day you will have an expansive view of the city of Nome, the Bering Sea, Sledge Island, and the surrounding tundra. The **Nome Convention and Visitors Bureau** (☎ 907-443-6624) has more information.

MOUNTAIN-BIKE OUTFITTERS

- **Alaska Backcountry Bike Tours** (serving Kenai Peninsula, Denali National Park Road, and other statewide locations): ☎ 866-354-2453 or 907-746-5018; **www.mountainbikealaska.com.** This Palmer-based company is one of our favorites for any biking adventure from Denali National Park south to the Kenai Peninsula. They offer a seven-day Denali Park Road Riding tour that includes transfers, park fees, and admissions, bike rental, road trips through other national parks, and all meals except one dinner. The cost is $2,595 per person. They also offer 100%-single-track trips that range from two to eight days and cost $445 to $2,195. Day trips to such locations as Eklutna Lake and the Tony Knowles Coastal Trail (see pages 182 and 183) begin at $69.

- **Alaska Outdoor Rentals and Guides** (serving Dalton Highway, Denali Highway, and Denali National Park Road): ☎ 907-457-2453; **www.akbike.com.** They can guide you on whichever route you choose to ride, including single-track trips in the Interior. The outfitter also can provide SAG support and/or deliver you wherever you want to go, with your bike or one of theirs on the Dalton or Denali highways (there is no vehicle support on the Denali Park Road, however).
- **Alaska Ultra Sport** (serving Denali Highway, Nome, Kenai Peninsula, Prince of Wales Island, and other locations): ☎ 907-745-6680; **www.alaskaultrasport.com.** Longtime adventurers Bill and Kathi Merchant guide mountain bikers in the summer and winter to locations throughout Alaska. Recognized as among the most accomplished cyclists in the state, the Merchants also organize the annual Iditarod Trail Invitational, a winter mountain-bike race that travels 1,100 miles from Southcentral Alaska to Nome, in the Bush, using mountain bikes designed for riding on the snow and ice. Custom trips are available; most range from one to nine days, and average about $250 per day. Our top pick for guided tours.
- **Alaskan Bicycle Adventures** (serving Kenai Peninsula, Denali Highway, and other state locations): ☎ 907-245-2175; **www.alaskabike.com.** The outfitter offers a Bicycle Alaska trip for serious cyclists. The eight-day tour costs $2,995; cyclists average 65 miles a day, with an opportunity to skip portions if they like. The less-strenuous Alaskan Adventure is seven days, costs $2,995, and averages 30 miles of riding per day, plus some kayaking to mix things up.
- **BicyclingWorld.com:** ☎ 610-683-5000; **www.bicyclingworld.com.** This Web site won't guide a trip for you, but you can often book discounted trips through its Web specials.
- **Denali Outdoor Center** (serving Denali National Park Road): ☎ 888-303-1925 or 907-683-1925; **www.denalioutdoorcenter.com.** The center rents bikes on a multiday basis and offers guided day trips into the park for $55.

PART ELEVEN

DAY HIKING

WHETHER YOU'RE WARMING UP FOR A WILDERNESS HIKE or just looking to stretch your legs after a long drive, a day hike is great way to leave the crowds behind and get a feel for the region you're visiting.

Many good trails can be found close to Alaska's population centers, so don't assume that one won't be interesting or challenging because of its proximity to town. **Indian River,** for instance, starts within walking distance of downtown Sitka and quickly delivers the willing hiker into the heart of the rain forest, where black bears, deer, and eagles are commonly spotted. In Anchorage, trail-laced **Chugach State Park** offers many trails that will take you into truly wild country and lead you back to town in time for dinner at one of the city's fine restaurants.

Other great trails begin with little fanfare along remote highways with nothing more than a trail marker to indicate what wonders lie down the path.

Turn to our Backpacking chapter, which begins on page 82, if you are intent on a remote wilderness expedition or a multinight hike. In this chapter, we stick to short hikes that can be done in a day or less. We'll tell you how to find a few of our favorites and give you the resources to find others in the regions you'll be visiting. Remember, these are just a sampling. Entire guidebooks can be—and have been—written about the hiking in various regions of the state. These represent our favorites, some very popular, a few not quite as well known.

Late spring or early summer is the best time for hiking in most parts of Alaska. The weather tends to be drier, and the vegetation isn't high enough to obscure the scenic views and the less-than-pleasant surprises that might be lurking along the path. Most animals will avoid humans at all costs, but it's easy to surprise an animal in heavy brush, and inadvertently stepping between a mama and baby, whether it's a bear or a moose, can be life-threatening.

Spring hiking also means that you're more likely to encounter snow in higher elevations, so plan your hike based on the time of year in which you are visiting. Late April may be perfect for a lower-elevation hike, while trails up high might keep snow until June.

That said, don't be intimidated if you're hiking later in the season, either. In Part Two, Planning Your Trip (page 28), we provide a few specifics to help you avoid an unpleasant wildlife encounter, so be sure to read it before you head down the trail.

CHECKLIST *for* SUCCESS

- **Let others know your whereabouts.** Tell someone where you're going and when you plan to return. If the trailhead doesn't have a sign-in sheet, leave a note in your car.
- **Be bear-aware.** See "How to Stay Safe in the Wilderness" (Part Two, page 29) for our tips on avoiding the beasts and maximizing your safety in case of an encounter.
- **Don't count on your cell phone for emergency communication.** While cell-phone coverage is getting better in Alaska all the time, it is still spotty in many parts of the state, particularly the backcountry.
- **Carry emergency food and water.** You never know when you might need it.
- **Bring along a good rain jacket.** It will keep you dry and provide wind (and bug) protection.
- **Allow about one hour for every 2.5 miles of hiking.** Some people hike faster than that, others slower, but on average this will give you an idea of how long a hike on established trails should take you.

Travel with a Guide?

If you are an experienced backpacker who has hiked extensively in the Lower 48, you pretty much know what to expect from a hike. But if you're relatively new to the pursuit or you're just not sure, there's no shame in hiring a guide to help you get the lay of the land. Besides, most guides have local knowledge about the flora, fauna, geography, and geology of the area. We offer a few suggestions for guides in our recommended areas. Not all of them cover all of our suggested hikes, but there are plenty of trails from which to choose. Most Alaska guides will arrange custom hikes, too, so if you have a particular hike in mind, don't hesitate to ask. Most likely, they can accommodate you.

SOUTHCENTRAL INLAND DAY HIKES

Bird Ridge

Location South of Anchorage. **Distance** 4–12 miles round-trip. **Trail configuration** Out-and-back. **Difficulty** (4 moose). **Suitable for kids?** Yes, but not

Alaska Day Hiking at a Glance

Angel Rocks

REGIONAL LOCATION	THE INTERIOR
DISTANCE	3.5–8 MILES
TIME TO HIKE	6–9 HOURS
DIFFICULTY	
CONFIGURATION	END-TO-END
SUITABLE FOR KIDS?	NO
GUIDE SUGGESTED?	NO

Bird Ridge

REGIONAL LOCATION	SOUTHCENTRAL INLAND
DISTANCE	4–12 MILES ROUND-TRIP
TIME TO HIKE	2–5 HOURS
DIFFICULTY	
CONFIGURATION	OUT-AND-BACK
SUITABLE FOR KIDS?	OLDER KIDS OK
GUIDE SUGGESTED?	NO

Crescent Lake

REGIONAL LOCATION	SOUTHCENTRAL COASTAL
DISTANCE	6 MILES ONE-WAY
TIME TO HIKE	4–6 HOURS
DIFFICULTY	
CONFIGURATION	OUT-AND-BACK
SUITABLE FOR KIDS?	YES
GUIDE SUGGESTED?	NO

Gold Mint Trail

REGIONAL LOCATION	SOUTHCENTRAL NLAND
DISTANCE	18 MILES ROUND-TRIP
TIME TO HIKE	6 HOURS
DIFFICULTY	
CONFIGURATION	OUT-AND-BACK
SUITABLE FOR KIDS?	YES
GUIDE SUGGESTED?	NO

Granite Tors

REGIONAL LOCATION	THE INTERIOR
DISTANCE	15 MILES
TIME TO HIKE	6–8 HOURS
DIFFICULTY	
CONFIGURATION	LOOP
SUITABLE FOR KIDS?	NO
GUIDE SUGGESTED?	NO

Grewingk Glacier Lake

REGIONAL LOCATION	SOUTHCENTRAL COASTAL
DISTANCE	6.5 MILES ROUND-TRIP
TIME TO HIKE	4 HOURS
DIFFICULTY	
CONFIGURATION	OUT-AND-BACK
SUITABLE FOR KIDS?	YES
GUIDE SUGGESTED?	NO

Landmark Gap Trail

REGIONAL LOCATION	THE INTERIOR
DISTANCE	5 MILES ROUND-TRIP
TIME TO HIKE	3 HOURS
DIFFICULTY	
CONFIGURATION	OUT-AND-BACK
SUITABLE FOR KIDS?	YES
GUIDE SUGGESTED?	NO

Lost Lake Traverse

REGIONAL LOCATION	SOUTHCENTRAL COASTAL
DISTANCE	15 MILES
TIME TO HIKE	6–9 HOURS
DIFFICULTY	
CONFIGURATION	END-TO-END
SUITABLE FOR KIDS?	NO
GUIDE SUGGESTED?	NO

Mount Riley

REGIONAL LOCATION	SOUTHEAST
DISTANCE	8 MILES ROUND-TRIP
TIME TO HIKE	2–5 HOURS
DIFFICULTY	
CONFIGURATION	OUT-AND-BACK
SUITABLE FOR KIDS?	YES
GUIDE SUGGESTED?	NO

Skookum Volcano

REGIONAL LOCATION	THE INTERIOR
DISTANCE	3–7.4 MILES ROUND-TRIP
TIME TO HIKE	2–3 HOURS
DIFFICULTY	
CONFIGURATION	OUT-AND-BACK/ LOOP
SUITABLE FOR KIDS?	YES
GUIDE SUGGESTED?	NO

West Glacier

REGIONAL LOCATION	SOUTHEAST
DISTANCE	6.5 MILES ROUND-TRIP
TIME TO HIKE	4 HOURS
DIFFICULTY	
CONFIGURATION	OUT-AND-BACK
SUITABLE FOR KIDS?	YES
GUIDE SUGGESTED?	NO

Winner Creek Gorge

REGIONAL LOCATION	SOUTHCENTRAL INLAND
DISTANCE	6 MILES ROUND-TRIP
TIME TO HIKE	2–3 HOURS
DIFFICULTY	
CONFIGURATION	OUT-AND-BACK/ LOOP
SUITABLE FOR KIDS?	YES
GUIDE SUGGESTED?	NO

young ones. **Time to hike** 2–5 hours. **Best time of year to hike** Mid-May–September. **Traffic level** Moderate at lower levels, light up top. **Facilities** Large parking lot; Alaska State Parks $5 parking fee required. **Maps** U.S. Geological Survey (USGS) Quads Seward D-7 (NW) and Anchorage A-7.

unofficial **TIP**
The Bird Ridge Trail is snow-free earlier than others in the area, especially in the lower elevations.

TRAIL SUMMARY The hike climbs gently and then emerges from the trees after a mile. It has a steep uphill and offers fine alpine hiking views of **Turnagain Arm** and **Bird Creek Valley** as it ascends

Deer Mountain

REGIONAL LOCATION	SOUTHEAST
DISTANCE	6 MILES ROUND-TRIP
TIME TO HIKE	3 HOURS
DIFFICULTY	
CONFIGURATION	OUT-AND-BACK
SUITABLE FOR KIDS?	YES
GUIDE SUGGESTED?	NO

Flattop

REGIONAL LOCATION	SOUTHCENTRAL INLAND
DISTANCE	3 MILES ROUND-TRIP
TIME TO HIKE	3 HOURS
DIFFICULTY	
CONFIGURATION	OUT-AND-BACK
SUITABLE FOR KIDS?	YES
GUIDE SUGGESTED?	NO

Gold Creek–Shoup Bay

REGIONAL LOCATION	SOUTHCENTRAL COASTAL
DISTANCE	7–22 MILES ROUND-TRIP
TIME TO HIKE	3–14 HOURS
DIFFICULTY	
CONFIGURATION	OUT-AND-BACK
SUITABLE FOR KIDS?	FIRST HALF OK
GUIDE SUGGESTED?	NO

Gull Rock

REGIONAL LOCATION	SOUTHCENTRAL COASTAL
DISTANCE	11 MILES ROUND-TRIP
TIME TO HIKE	3 HOURS
DIFFICULTY	
CONFIGURATION	OUT-AND-BACK
SUITABLE FOR KIDS?	YES
GUIDE SUGGESTED?	NO

Historic Valdez Trail

REGIONAL LOCATION	SOUTHCENTRAL COASTAL
DISTANCE	8 MILES
TIME TO HIKE	4–5 HOURS
DIFFICULTY	
CONFIGURATION	END-TO-END
SUITABLE FOR KIDS?	YES
GUIDE SUGGESTED?	NO

Indian River Trail

REGIONAL LOCATION	SOUTHEAST
DISTANCE	8 MILES ROUND-TRIP
TIME TO HIKE	2–5 HOURS
DIFFICULTY	
CONFIGURATION	OUT-AND-BACK
SUITABLE FOR KIDS?	YES
GUIDE SUGGESTED?	NO

Pioneer Ridge–Austin Helmers

REGIONAL LOCATION	SOUTHCENTRAL INLAND
DISTANCE	9 MILES ROUND-TRIP
TIME TO HIKE	5–7 HOURS
DIFFICULTY	
CONFIGURATION	OUT-AND-BACK
SUITABLE FOR KIDS?	NO
GUIDE SUGGESTED?	NO

Power Creek–Crater Lake

REGIONAL LOCATION	SOUTHCENTRAL COASTAL
DISTANCE	12.5 MILES
TIME TO HIKE	4–6 HOURS
DIFFICULTY	
CONFIGURATION	END-TO-END
SUITABLE FOR KIDS?	NO
GUIDE SUGGESTED?	NO

Reed Lakes

REGIONAL LOCATION	SOUTHCENTRAL INLAND
DISTANCE	9 MILES ROUND-TRIP
TIME TO HIKE	5–7 HOURS
DIFFICULTY	
CONFIGURATION	OUT-AND-BACK
SUITABLE FOR KIDS?	YES
GUIDE SUGGESTED?	NO

to **Bird Peak** (elevation 3,505 feet). At this point, you've traveled about two miles and can turn around, or you can keep going another four miles or so along the ridgeline.

DIRECTIONS TO TRAILHEAD From Anchorage, take the Seward Highway South 25 miles to Mile 102. Look for the large parking lot and trailhead on the inland side of the highway.

Flattop

Location Anchorage. **Distance** 3 miles round-trip. **Trail configuration** Out-and-back. **Difficulty** . **Suitable for kids?** Yes. **Time to hike** 2–3 hours. **Best time of year to hike** Mid-June–September. **Traffic level** Heavy. **Facilities** Well-maintained trail, man-made stairsteps on the lower mountain, parking area; Alaska State Parks $5 parking fee. **Maps** USGS Quad Anchorage A-8.

TRAIL SUMMARY Flattop is the most-climbed mountain in Alaska due to its proximity to Anchorage and spectacular views of **Cook Inlet,** downtown Anchorage, the **Chugach Mountains** to the east, and, on a clear day, **Denali (Mount McKinley)** to the north. The trail climbs gradually at first, then ascends steeply via man-made steps. A few hundred feet below the summit, the path gives way to a boulder scramble marked sparsely with orange paint. If you can't find the paint, don't worry; there are usually plenty of people up there whom you can follow. It's an overused trail, but one you'll be glad you hiked.

DIRECTIONS TO TRAILHEAD From downtown Anchorage head south six miles on the Seward Highway. Take the O'Malley Road exit. Turn left, following O'Malley for four miles to Hillside Drive. Turn right on Hillside, drive one mile, and turn left on Upper Huffman. Then turn right on Toilsome Hill Road to the Glen Alps parking lot at Mile 2. A shuttle is available from downtown (for details, see Southcentral Inland Resources at the bottom of the next page).

Gold Mint Trail

Location Matanuska-Susitna Valley. **Distance** 18 miles round-trip. **Trail configuration** Out-and-back. **Difficulty** . **Suitable for kids?** Yes. **Time to hike** 6 hours. **Best time of year to hike** Mid-June–September. **Traffic level** Moderate. **Facilities** Parking lot. **Maps** USGS Quad Anchorage D-7.

TRAIL SUMMARY Level but rocky trail can be wet early in the year and after heavy rains, although trail work has been done in some of the more wet sections recently. The trail climbs alongside the **Little Susitna River** through a beautiful mountain valley to the river's source at **Mint Glacier.** Mountain bikers as well as hikers use it.

DIRECTIONS TO TRAILHEAD From Anchorage, take the Glenn Highway north through Palmer. Turn left on Fishhook Road and drive 13.8 miles toward Hatcher Pass. The Gold Mint Trailhead parking lot is directly across from the Motherlode Lodge.

Pioneer Ridge–Austin Helmers Trail

Location Matanuska-Susitna Valley. **Distance** 9 miles round-trip. **Trail configuration** Out-and-back. **Difficulty** . **Suitable for kids?** No. **Time to hike** 6–7 hours. **Best time of year to hike** Mid-June–September. **Traffic level** Moderate–light. **Facilities** Well-maintained trail with benches. **Maps** USGS Quads Anchorage B-5, B-6.

TRAIL SUMMARY Named after a Mat-Su Valley visionary trail builder, this challenging route accesses the main ridge that connects with **Pioneer Peak.** Starting about 300 feet above sea level, the trail ascends to 5,330 feet over its 4.5-mile length. Spectacular views make it worth the effort.

DIRECTIONS TO TRAILHEAD Head north from Anchorage on the Glenn Highway. At Mile 30, take the Old Glenn Highway exit and drive 8.5 miles to the intersection of Knik River Road. Stay straight on Knik River Road; the trailhead is at Mile 3.9 on the right. An Austin Helmers trailhead sign, added in 2004, adorns the parking lot.

Reed Lakes

Location Matanuska-Susitna Valley. **Distance** 9 miles round-trip. **Trail configuration** Out-and-back. **Difficulty** . **Suitable for kids?** Yes. **Time to hike**

5–7 hours. **Best time of year to hike** Mid-June–September. **Traffic level** Moderate. **Facilities** Marked trailhead. **Maps** USGS Quad Anchorage D-7.

TRAIL SUMMARY The trail begins with a 1.5-mile hike on an old mining road. At the old **Snowbird Mine** village you'll pass a decrepit cabin. Cross **Glacier Creek** and then **Reed Creek** before ascending via well-made switchbacks; then rock-hop through a boulder field. Follow Reed Creek through meadows to **Lower Reed Lake.** Visit the waterfall on the way to **Upper Reed Lake.**

DIRECTIONS TO TRAILHEAD From Anchorage, take the Glenn Highway north through Palmer. Turn left on Fishhook Road and drive 14.5 miles toward Hatcher Pass. About a half mile past the switchback at the Motherlode Lodge, you'll see Archangel Road on the right. Follow it for 2.3 miles. Look for the pullout and trailhead marker on the right.

Winner Creek Gorge

Location Girdwood. **Distance** 6 miles round-trip. **Trail configuration** Out-and-back (see loop option in summary). **Difficulty** . **Suitable for kids?** Yes. **Time to hike** 2–3 hours. **Best time of year to hike** June–October. **Traffic level** Moderate. **Facilities** Trailhead; hand-pull tram over Winner Creek Gorge. **Maps** USGS Quad Seward D-6 (NW).

TRAIL SUMMARY This easy hike winds through the northernmost rain forest in Alaska, composed of big spruce and hemlocks.

At Mile 1.5, the trail splits at a bluff above **Winner Creek.** Go left to see the crashing water of the gorge. A right turn takes you upstream past the remains of an old miner's cabin to a pretty alpine basin. You can create an eight-mile loop connecting to the historic **Iditarod Trail** by using the hand tram at the gorge and crossing to the trail. It comes out at **Crow Creek Mine Road** and follows a bike path and road back into Girdwood. Local guide service is available for this hike (for details, see Southcentral Inland Resources below).

unofficial **TIP**
The trees you'll see along the Winner Creek Gorge Trail are huge compared with others in the Southcentral Inland region, which is why we like this hike so much.

DIRECTIONS TO TRAILHEAD From Anchorage, take the Seward Highway south 35 miles to Mile 90. Turn inland onto the Alyeska Highway. At Mile 3 the highway ends at an intersection with Arlberg Road. Go left on Arlberg, past the Alyeska Prince Hotel, and park in the area across from the shuttle-bus stop. Cross the road; there is a bike path with a sign for the trail. Or park at the hotel and walk around either side of the building beneath the tram. Follow the access road to the edge of the forest where the trail begins.

Southcentral Inland Resources

- The **Alaska Public Lands Information Center** (605 West Fourth Avenue, Anchorage 99501; ☎ 907-271-2737; **www.nps.gov/aplic**) can offer advice on dozens of area hikes ranging from 1-mile beginner walks to 15-mile all-day treks.

Day-hiking Outfitters at a Glance

Alaska Nature Tours
☎ 907-766-2876
www.alaskanaturetours.net

REGIONAL LOCATION	SOUTHEAST
COST	$$
SUITABLE FOR KIDS?	YES
ACTIVITY LEVEL	ALL LEVELS
TRIP LENGTH	DAY TRIP

The Ascending Path
☎ 907-783-0505
www.theascendingpath.com

REGIONAL LOCATION	SOUTHCENTRAL INLAND
COST	$
SUITABLE FOR KIDS?	YES
ACTIVITY LEVEL	LIGHT–MODERATE
TRIP LENGTH	DAY TRIP

1st Alaska Outdoor School
☎ 907-590-5900
www.1stalaskaoutdoorschool.com

REGIONAL LOCATION	THE INTERIOR
COST	$
SUITABLE FOR KIDS?	YES
ACTIVITY LEVEL	LIGHT–MODERATE
TRIP LENGTH	DAY TRIP

Gastineau Guiding
☎ 907-586-8231
www.stepintoalaska.com

REGIONAL LOCATION	SOUTHEAST
COST	$$
SUITABLE FOR KIDS?	YES
ACTIVITY LEVEL	LIGHT–MODERATE
TRIP LENGTH	DAY TRIP

Kodiak Treks
☎ 907-487-2122
www.kodiaktreks.com

REGIONAL LOCATION	SOUTHCENTRAL COASTAL
COST	$$$
SUITABLE FOR KIDS?	YES
ACTIVITY LEVEL	LIGHT–MODERATE
TRIP LENGTH	DAY TRIP

Pangaea Adventures
☎ 800-660-9637 or
907-835-8442
www.alaskasummer.com

REGIONAL LOCATION	SOUTHCENTRAL COASTAL
COST	$$
SUITABLE FOR KIDS?	YES
ACTIVITY LEVEL	LIGHT–MODERATE
TRIP LENGTH	DAY TRIP

Xtremely Alaska
☎ 877-914-2735 or
907-868-4098
www.xtremelyalaska.com

REGIONAL LOCATION	SOUTHCENTRAL INLAND
COST	$$
SUITABLE FOR KIDS?	YES
ACTIVITY LEVEL	LIGHT–MODERATE
TRIP LENGTH	DAY TRIP

- **Alaska's Flattop Mountain Shuttle** (West 333 Fourth Avenue, Suite 206; ☎ 907-279-3334; **www.alaska-bike-rentals.com**), a service of the Downtown Bicycle Rental Shop, carries hikers from downtown and Midtown to Flattop and back for $22 per adult, $15 for kids ages 6 to 12 and free for those younger. We think it's sort of a steep price to pay—taking a taxi might be cheaper, but the rate is round-trip and scheduled, taking the guesswork out of your transportation.
- The **Chugach National Forest** (3301 C Street, Suite 300, Anchorage 99503; ☎ 907-271-2500) includes many great trails for hiking, most of which are located in Southcentral Coastal Alaska. The Winner Creek Gorge Trail, however, is partly on Chugach land.
- Without **Chugach State Park** (Potter Section House, Mile 115, Seward Highway; ☎ 907-345-5014; **www.dnr.state.ak.us/parks/units/chugach**), there would not be the incredible trail system surrounding the municipality that we have today. The Bird Ridge, Flattop, and Pioneer Ridge–Austin Helmers trails are part of this great swath of land.
- The **Division of Natural Resources Public Information Center** (550 West Seventh Avenue, Suite 1260, Anchorage 99501; ☎ 907-269-8400;

www.dnr.state.ak.us) can answer questions about Alaska State Parks lands, which include all of Chugach State Park and state recreation areas such as Hatcher Pass.

- The **Finger Lake State Recreation Site** (☎ 907-745-3975 or 907-269-8400; **www.alaskastateparks.org**), in our opinion, contains some of the most underused and underappreciated lands in the state—for example, the **Hatcher Pass** area, where the Reed Lakes and Gold Mint trails, among many others, are located. The hiking and views are outstanding, and access is easy.

Southcentral Inland Outfitters

- **The Ascending Path:** At the yurt at Alyeska Prince Hotel; ☎ 907-783-0505; **www.theascendingpath.com.** This experienced guide company specializes in ice climbing and glacier trekking, but they also take time out to lead day hikes on the popular Winner Creek Trail. It's a good family destination. The hike takes four hours and is $59 for adults, $49 for kids 17 and younger. The outfit can arrange guided hikes to other Southcentral Inland areas as well. Just ask
- **Xtremely Alaska:** In Anchorage; ☎ 877-914-2735 or 907-868-4098; **www.xtremelyalaska.com.** Xtremely Alaska allows travelers to explore the expansive backcountry that is Anchorage's backyard. The company offers various day trips on Chugach State Park's numerous scenic trails. Trips and trails vary in length and difficulty, so there's something for everyone. At $121 to $136 per person, most of the trips also include lunch. Custom trips are also available. Unique to this company are its $86 evening hikes in the midnight sun and its evening birding trips to a few of Southcentral's prime birding areas.

SOUTHCENTRAL COASTAL DAY HIKES

Crescent Lake

Location Cooper Landing. **Distance** 12.5 miles round-trip (see end-to-end option in summary). **Trail configuration** Out-and-back. **Difficulty** 🫎🫎🫎. **Suitable for kids?** Yes. **Time to hike** 4–6 hours. **Best time of year to hike** June–September. **Traffic level** Moderate–heavy. **Facilities** U.S. Forest Service cabins and marked trailhead with parking. **Maps** USGS Seward Quads B-7, C-7, and C-8.

TRAIL SUMMARY The trail makes a long, gradual climb through spruce and hemlock forest to **Crescent Lake,** which sits right at tree line. From the lake the country is wide open for exploring above tree line, and some like to continue on around Crescent Lake to the **Crescent Saddle Cabin,** past the lake, and on to **Carter Lake,** which spits you out on the Seward Highway, Mile 33. That makes for a 19-mile end-to-end trek. The trail gets heavy use in the summer, so it's not uncommon to cross paths with

unofficial **TIP**
Crescent Lake is a great place to stop and fish. Grayling is the resident species.

mountain bikers and horseback riders. A local guide leads horsepacking trips out here often.

DIRECTIONS TO TRAILHEAD From Anchorage, take the Seward Highway south to the cutoff for the Sterling Highway. Follow the Sterling Highway to Mile 44.9. Turn left onto Quartz Creek Road (just past the **Sunrise Inn,** ☎ 907-595-1222; **www.alaskasunriseinn.com**) and drive a little more than three miles to the trailhead. It is well marked.

Gold Creek–Shoup Bay

Location Valdez. **Distance** 7–22 miles round-trip. **Trail configuration** Out-and-back. **Difficulty** 🫎🫎🫎. **Suitable for kids?** First half OK. **Time to hike** 3–14 hours. **Best time of year to hike** May–September. **Traffic level** Light. **Facilities** Marked trailheads with outhouses and sign-in kiosk, two public-use cabins and campgrounds. **Maps** USGS Valdez A-7.

TRAIL SUMMARY The trail can be muddy, but spectacular views of **Valdez, Shoup Glacier,** and **Shoup Bay** make any mess worthwhile. A campsite, latrine, and food-storage locker can be found at **Gold Creek,** which is a wonderful place to camp among the giant spruce and hemlock trees. The trail becomes more rugged beyond Gold Creek; for day hikers this is a good place to turn around, a seven-mile round-trip. For endurance hikers, the trip is just beginning and starts to climb and turn, eventually offering spectacular views of Shoup Glacier. Two public-use cabins and a camping area are at the end of the trail. Flood damage to the trail in 2006 created some particularly challenging areas, so this hike is not for the faint of heart.

DIRECTIONS TO TRAILHEAD Follow Egan Drive west through Valdez. The road dead-ends just past Mineral Creek. Look for a small parking lot with outhouses and a trail marker.

Grewingk Glacier Lake

Location Homer. **Distance** 6.5 miles round-trip. **Trail configuration** Out-and-back. **Difficulty** 🫎🫎🫎. **Suitable for kids?** Yes. **Time to hike** 4 hours. **Best time of year to hike** June–September. **Traffic level** Light. **Facilities** Marked trailhead and an outhouse on Glacier Spit.

TRAIL SUMMARY Start at the **Glacier Spit** trailhead north of **Halibut Cove.** Pass through stands of cottonwood and spruce to an area of low vegetation. About 1.5 miles into the hike, the trail veers to the left for the more challenging 13-mile **Grewingk Glacier Trail,** in which you have to use a hand tram to cross Grewingk Creek. Stay on the main trail to get to the lake, veering left at the next turnoff for an alpine ridge hike. The trail to the lake is marked with cairns.

DIRECTIONS TO TRAILHEAD **Homer** lies at the end of the Kenai Peninsula, 226 miles south of Anchorage. The Grewingk Glacier Lake Trail is across Kachemak Bay from Homer. Note that this trip takes extra planning to arrange water transportation. Water taxis are available from the Homer Spit for as little as $50 (see our Resources listing on page 196).

Gull Rock

Location Hope. **Distance** 11 miles round-trip. **Trail configuration** Out-and-back. **Difficulty** . **Suitable for kids?** Yes. **Time to hike** 4–6 hours. **Best time of year to hike** June–September. **Traffic level** Light. **Facilities** Starts at the Porcupine Campground area, and is signed. **Maps** USGS Quad Seward D-8.

unofficial **TIP**
The Gull Rock Trail is a great place to spot sea mammals in the water (beluga whales most often) and land mammals on the trail (moose more often than not).

TRAIL SUMMARY The route is an old wagon trail along **Turnagain Arm** providing occasional ocean views. The remains of an old cabin, stable, and bridge can still be seen at **Johnson Creek.** The trail stays well above the tide line, climbing to 620 feet before dropping down **Gull Rock.** It's rooty and rocky in places, so wear good boots.

DIRECTIONS TO TRAILHEAD From Anchorage, take the Seward Highway South 70 miles to Mile 56.7. Follow the 18-mile-long Hope Highway to Porcupine Campground, where you'll find the trailhead.

Historic Valdez Trail

Location Valdez. **Distance** 8 miles. **Trail configuration** End-to-end. **Difficulty** . **Suitable for kids?** Yes. **Time to hike** 4–5 hours. **Best time of year to hike** May–September. **Traffic level** Moderate. **Facilities** Marked trailheads with parking, outhouses, and several entry points. Interpretive signs along the way point out the history of the trail. **Maps** USGS Valdez Quads A-5, A-6 (SE).

TRAIL SUMMARY After a steep climb, the trail follows a level, easy path locally known as the **Pack Trail** and **Goat Trail,** established by gold seekers who first passed through Keystone Canyon a century ago. Visitors like the hike because of its fantastic views of big waterfalls, tall spruce and hemlock, and great gorges carved over centuries. You will traverse the **Lowe River,** a popular rafting destination, and sometimes will see the boats splashing through the rapids. **Snowslide Gulch** is about two-thirds of the way through the trail (for those headed north); sometimes snow from earlier avalanches can be found in the chutes as late as July.

DIRECTIONS TO TRAILHEAD From Valdez, drive to Mile 11.8 of the Richardson Highway. Turn left on the Old Richardson Highway Loop. Look for the trailhead on the left at Mile 0.3. The park is in a clearing on the other side of the road. Another access point, if you want a short hike, is at the pull-off for the Bridal Veil Falls overlook, at Mile 13.8.

Lost Lake Traverse

Location Seward. **Distance** 15 miles. **Trail configuration** End-to-end. **Difficulty** . **Suitable for kids?** Veteran kid hikers can handle it. **Time to hike** 6–9 hours. **Best time of year to hike** June–September. **Traffic level** Light–moderate. **Facilities** U.S. Forest Service cabin; Primrose Campground on the north end. **Maps** USGS Quads Seward B-7, A-7.

unofficial **TIP**
The Lost Lake Traverse is the site of an annual mountain race in August to raise money for the Cystic Fibrosis Foundation—don't hike it on that day, or you'll be trampled.

TRAIL SUMMARY Considered by many to be the most beautiful trail on the Kenai Peninsula, the trail quickly rises above tree line into alpine meadows. The glacier-sculpted landscape is dotted with lakes. Surrounding peaks remain snow-covered year-round.

DIRECTIONS TO TRAILHEAD From Anchorage, take the Seward Highway south 110 miles to Primrose Landing Campground at Mile 17.1. Turn right on Primrose Road, and drive to the end of the road. Parking is in front of the campground at the lake, by the boat ramp. The trailhead is at the back of the campground near the rear outhouses. There is a sign-in kiosk and trailhead marker. To get to the southern trailhead, drive to Mile 5.3 of the Seward Highway. Turn west on Scott Way, left on Heather Lee Lane, and right on Hayden Berlin Road to the end of the road. This trailhead is not as easily recognized.

Power Creek–Crater Lake

Location Cordova. **Distance** 12.5 miles. **Trail configuration** End-to-end. **Difficulty** . **Suitable for kids?** No. **Time to hike** 4–6 hours. **Best time of year to hike** June–September. **Traffic level** Light. **Facilities** Established campsites, public-use cabin, and a marked trailhead with parking. **Maps** USGS Quad Cordova C-5.

TRAIL SUMMARY **Crater Lake** is the high point to this scenic hike outside of Cordova. The **Power Creek** side has numerous switchbacks, and the **Crater Lake Trail** is steep at the beginning as well. From either direction, you'll be doing a lot of climbing. But the reward is the scenery.

DIRECTIONS TO TRAILHEAD From downtown Cordova, take Second Avenue to Lake Avenue and turn right. Follow Lake Avenue about two miles, past the airport and floatplane base to the trailhead at Crater Lake, which is on the left side of the road. You'll probably have to park on the other side of the road. To reach the Power Creek trailhead, keep driving to the end of the road, another 5.5 miles.

Southcentral Coastal Resources

- **Central Charters** (☎ 800-478-7847 or 907-235-7847; **www.centralcharter.com**) can arrange a water taxi across Kachemak Bay. Prices start at $50.
- Lands of the **Chugach National Forest** (3301 C Street, Suite 300, Anchorage 99503; ☎ 907-271-2500; **www.fs.fed.us/r10/chugach**) include many great hiking trails, most of which are located in Southcentral Coastal Alaska. The Glacier District can be reached at ☎ 907-783-3242, the Seward District at ☎ 907-224-3374, and the Cordova District at ☎ 907-424-7661.
- **Cordova Coastal Outfitters** (☎ 800-357-5145 or 907-424-7424; **www.cdvcoastal.com**), located at the harbor in the brightly colored boathouse, will rent you everything you need for an impromptu day hike. Rates start at $5.
- **Kachemak Bay State Park:** More information is available through Alaska State Parks, Kenai Area Office, P.O. Box 1247, Soldotna 99669; ☎ 907-262-5581; **www.dnr.state.ak.us/parks/units/kbay/kbay.htm.**

The **Halibut Cove Ranger Station** (☎ 907-235-6999) can answer questions in the summer.

- **Kenai National Wildlife Refuge** (Ski Hill Road, P.O. Box 2139, Soldotna 99669; ☎ 907-262-7021; **kenai.fws.gov**) affords many hiking opportunities. Check out the Web site, or stop by the visitor center in Soldotna, where a few trails leave right from the center.
- ***Trails Illustrated*** makes a Kenai Fjords National Park Map (Map 760) that outlines hikes such as Lost Lake, mentioned in this chapter, along with many other hikes worth exploring. Available at **www.rei.com**; **www.alaskanha.org;** and the company Web site, **www.trails illustrated.com.**
- **U.S. Geological Survey (USGS) maps** are available at most sporting-goods stores, although you'll have better luck finding the ones you need in Anchorage. Or check **www.usgs.gov.**

Southcentral Coastal Outfitters

- **Kodiak Treks:** ☎ 907-487-2122; **www.kodiaktreks.com.** The company offers guided day hikes in one of the world's most renowned bear-viewing areas. Guide Harry Dodge has more than 30 years' experience and provides a wealth of information on the bears and their life cycles and habitat. This eco-friendly guide service offers small group tours with minimal impact on the animals, while offering an up close experience you'll never forget. Prices start at $300 per person, per night, and include cabin lodging and bear viewing. Other activities are also offered.
- **Pangaea Adventures:** ☎ 800-660-9637 or 907-835-8442; **www.alaskasummer.com;** Valdez. Pangaea offers day hikes on Valdez and Worthington glaciers. Prices range from $65 to $129 per person for four to five hours, with hikes accommodating various ability levels. For the novice, the Valdez Glacier hike offers easy hiking and climbing, while the trip atop Worthington Glacier is more challenging, allowing hikers to try out glacier ice climbing (with excellent instruction, of course). Crampons and ice-climbing gear are provided.

SOUTHEAST DAY HIKES

Deer Mountain

Location Ketchikan. **Distance** 6 miles round-trip. **Trail configuration** Out-and-back. **Difficulty** . **Suitable for kids?** Yes. **Time to hike** 3 hours. **Best time of year to hike** May–September. **Traffic level** Heavy when cruise ships are in; moderate otherwise. **Facilities** A U.S. Forest Service shelter and marked trail. **Maps** USGS Ketchikan B-5.

TRAIL SUMMARY The trail begins with a muskeg-spanning boardwalk and quickly ascends toward the peak. Stay to the right when the trail forks and you'll reach the summit, which on clear days offers great views of the **Tongass Narrows** and **Prince of Wales Island.** You can keep going for a traverse to Silvis Lakes and beyond, but there are no markers and it takes more planning than a simple day hike. Deer Mountain is the most popular trail in Ketchikan, but we still recommend it because it leads to the summit of the distinctive peak that dominates the town.

DIRECTIONS TO TRAILHEAD Take Stedman Street south through town to Deermount. Turn east and continue 0.3 miles to Fair Street. Turn right on Fair, and follow to the top of the hill. Cross Nordstrom Drive, and turn right into the parking lot at the trailhead, which is marked.

Indian River Trail

Location Sitka. **Distance** 8 miles round-trip. **Trail configuration** Out-and-back. **Difficulty** . **Suitable for kids?** Yes. **Time to hike** 2–5 hours. **Best time of year to hike** May–September. **Traffic level** Moderate. **Facilities** Marked trail. **Maps** USGS Sitka A-4.

TRAIL SUMMARY This trail is easily accessed from downtown Sitka and has a rewarding waterfall view at the end. The path follows the **Indian River,** a popular salmon stream, to the 80-foot waterfall at the base of **Three Sisters Mountain.** Black bears, deer, and eagles are often seen along the trail, and the forested hike affords a nice contrast to all the other popular mountain climbs in Southeast Alaska.

DIRECTIONS TO TRAILHEAD From downtown, follow Sawmill Creek Road to the intersection with Indian River Road near the State Trooper Training Academy. Follow Indian River Road to the gate. Park there and walk to the trailhead near the abandoned city water plant.

Mount Riley

Location Haines. **Distance** 8 miles round-trip. **Trail configuration** Out-and-back. **Difficulty** . **Suitable for kids?** Yes. **Time to hike** 2–5 hours. **Best time of year to hike** May–September. **Traffic level** Moderate. **Facilities** A marked trail with 3 access points. **Maps** USGS Quads Skagway A-2 (NE) and A-1 (NW).

TRAIL SUMMARY At 1,760 feet, **Mount Riley** is the highest point on the Chilkat Peninsula. There are three ways to access the trail, and you can connect those access points to make longer hikes. But we like the Beach Road access point because in its eight-mile round-trip you get a sampling of everything that makes the area so pretty. It is north-facing, though, so hike it when you know the sun will be shining, or later in the season when all the snow has melted. The trail climbs gradually, going through coastal forest that at some points overlooks **Chilkat Inlet.** The side trail to **Kelgaya Point** is also nice.

DIRECTIONS TO TRAILHEAD Drive along the waterfront, following Haines Highway east until it becomes Beach Road. Follow Beach Road past Portage Cove Campground and up a hill to the road's end and the trailhead. You will be on the Battery Point Trail until it forks off for the Mount Riley hike.

West Glacier

Location Juneau. **Distance** 6.5 miles round-trip. **Trail configuration** Out-and-back. **Difficulty** . **Suitable for kids?** Yes. **Time to hike** 4 hours. **Best time of year to hike** May–September. **Traffic level** Moderate–high. **Facilities** Marked trail and established overlook. **Maps** USGS Quad Juneau B-2 (NW).

TRAIL SUMMARY This scenic hike along the west side of **Mendenhall Lake** and the **Mendenhall Glacier** leads to a spectacular view of the glacier.

DIRECTIONS TO TRAILHEAD Drive 9 miles north on the Glacier Highway to the junction with Mendenhall Loop Road. Drive 3.7 miles and turn right on Montana Creek Road. Go right on Mendenhall Lake Road past the campground; the trailhead is at the end of the road.

unofficial **TIP**
The West Glacier Trail, though scenic, is far from a wilderness experience—be prepared for helicopter noise, as the glacier is a popular destination for cruise-ship passengers on day excursions.

Southeast Resources

- The **Division of Natural Resources Public Information Center** (400 Willoughby Avenue, Fourth Floor, Juneau; ☎ 907-465-3400; **www.dnr.state.ak.us**) can answer questions about Alaska State Parks lands, including the Mount Riley Trail, which is part of Chilkat State Park.
- The **Southeast Alaska Discovery Center** (50 Main Street, Ketchikan 99901; ☎ 907-228-6214; **www.nps.gov/aplic/center**) offers information on trails across Southeast Alaska, including Deer Mountain.
- The **Southeast Alaska Trail System,** a nonprofit organization also known as SEAtrails (in Douglas, across the bridge in Juneau; ☎ 907-364-2427; **www.seatrails.org**), uses grant and donor money to upgrade and maintain the wealth of trails throughout Southeast Alaska.
- The **Tongass National Forest** (☎ 907-225-3101; **www.fs.fed.us/r10/tongass**) manages the Deer Mountain Trail in Ketchikan, the Indian River Trail in Sitka, and the West Glacier Trail in Juneau.
- **USGS maps** are available at the public-information centers in Southeast Alaska and online at **www.usgs.gov.**

Southeast Coastal Outfitters

- **Alaska Nature Tours:** ☎ 907-766-2876; **www.alaskanaturetours.net;** Haines. Enjoy nature hikes through the rain forests of the Chilkat Valley or more-strenuous, vista-oriented treks high atop the mountain peaks that tower over Haines. Hikes are four to eight hours and vary in difficulty; prices range from $75 to $110 per person, with lunch included on some trips.
- **Gastineau Guiding:** ☎ 907-586-8231; **www.stepintoalaska.com;** Juneau. Gastineau offers options for the independent traveler as well as for cruise-ship passengers. You can take seaside or rain-forest hikes—or combine the two into one trip—but our favorite is the guide's choice, which is suited to fit hikers who want less of a tour and more of an outdoor adventure. Rates are $69 to $79, which is a bargain.

INTERIOR DAY HIKES

Angel Rocks–Chena Hot Springs Traverse

Location The Interior. **Distance** 3.5 miles, 8 miles with traverse. **Trail configuration** End-to-end. **Difficulty** 🫎🫎🫎🫎. **Suitable for kids?** No. **Time to hike**

6–9 hours. **Best time of year to hike** June–September. **Traffic level** Moderate on Angel Rocks; light on traverse. **Facilities** Trail shelter; marked trailheads. **Maps** USGS Circle A-5.

TRAIL SUMMARY The steep and rocky trail accesses the granite outcrop known as **Angel Rocks.** An alpine ridge traverse marked by rock cairns links up with the **Chena Hot Springs Trail,** which leads to the popular resort. The traverse is particularly nice, although challenging, passing through the saddle before turning east. Eventually it connects with the **Overlook Trail,** which leads to **Chena Hot Springs Resort** and eventually the **Hillside Cutoff.** When the trail dead-ends at a dirt road, turn right and follow it to the resort.

DIRECTIONS TO TRAILHEAD Drive five miles north on the Steese Highway to Chena Hot Springs Road. The trailhead is on the right side of the road at Mile 49. If you do the traverse, you will come off the trail at Mile 56.5, 7.5 miles down the road.

Granite Tors

Location Outside Fairbanks. **Distance** 15 miles. **Trail configuration** Loop. **Difficulty** . **Suitable for kids?** No. **Time to hike** 6–8 hours. **Best time of year to hike** June–September. **Traffic level** Moderate–heavy. **Facilities** A trail shelter, campground at trailhead, and marked trailhead. **Maps** USGS Big Delta D-5.

unofficial **TIP**
The Granite Tors Trail is one of the few loops that start and stop in the same place, which is one of the reasons we like it.

TRAIL SUMMARY The trail circles the **Rock Creek** drainage accessing the **Plain of Monuments,** also known as Alaska's natural Stonehenge for its otherworldly rock-outcropping arrangement. Five miles of the trail are marked by stone cairns. It is a challenging hike, and those who want a similar yet shorter hike can tackle the **Angel Rocks** trail (see previous profile).

DIRECTIONS TO TRAILHEAD Drive north on the Steese Highway to Chena Hot Springs Road. Drive east 40 miles to the Tors Trail Campground. The trailhead is at the campground.

Landmark Gap Trail

Location The Interior–Denali Highway. **Distance** 5 miles round-trip. **Trail configuration** Out-and-back. **Difficulty** . **Suitable for kids?** Yes. **Time to hike** 3 hours. **Best time of year to hike** Mid-June–September. **Traffic level** Low but can include ATVs during hunting season. **Facilities** Well-developed trail. **Maps** USGS Mount Hayes A-5.

TRAIL SUMMARY The trail is a crude dirt road that accesses its namesake lake, which fills a glacier-carved gap in the **Amphitheater Mountains.** The glaciated **Alaska Range** is visible beyond.

DIRECTIONS TO TRAILHEAD From Paxson, off the Richardson Highway, turn west on the Denali Highway. Drive approximately 25 miles; the trailhead is on the north side, about 12 miles east of Maclaren Summit.

Skookum Volcano

Location Nabesna. **Distance** 3 miles round-trip (7.4 miles on loop option). **Trail configuration** Out-and-back. **Difficulty** ✱✱✱. **Suitable for kids?** Yes. **Time to hike** 2–3 hours. **Best time of year to hike** Mid-June–September. **Traffic level** Low. **Facilities** None. **Maps** USGS Nabesna G-5.

TRAIL SUMMARY Explore the unique environment of an extinct, eroded 7,125-foot volcano, including cinder cones and ancient lava flows. We like this hike because you'll likely have the area to yourself. The **Nabesna Road** is rarely traveled. At first you'll follow along an unnamed creek to the open valley at tree line. The trail markers end at this point, and some may opt to turn around for a three-mile round-trip. To keep going for a loop hike, follow the pass to the south on a trail that is somewhat obvious under normal weather conditions. Because the trail is unmarked in this area, it is imperative that you bring a map and compass.

DIRECTIONS TO TRAILHEAD The trail is off the Nabesna Road, which is accessed via the Tok Cutoff Highway, Mile 59.8. The 42-mile-long dirt road requires several stream crossings, so a four-wheel-drive vehicle is necessary. The trailhead is in a pullout at about Mile 37.

Interior Resources

- The **Alaska Public Lands Information Center** (250 Cushman Street, Suite 1A, Fairbanks 99701; ☎ 907-456-0527; **www.nps.gov/aplic/center**) can provide information on day hikes in the Fairbanks and surrounding areas, including the Granite Tors and Angel Rocks hikes.
- **Department of Natural Resources Public Information Center:** 3700 Airport Way, Fairbanks 99709, ☎ 907-451-2705; **www.dnr.state.ak.us.** This office can answer questions about Alaska State Parks lands, which include the Granite Tors and Angel Rocks trails.
- ***Trails Illustrated*** makes a map of Wrangell–St. Elias National Park and Preserve (Map 249) that outlines hikes in the McCarthy area, as well as the Nabesna Road hike. Available at **www.rei.com; ww.alaskanha.org;** or the company Web site, **www.trailsillustrated.com.**
- The **U.S. Bureau of Land Management**'s Northern District office (1150 University Avenue, Fairbanks 99709; ☎ 907-474-2250; **www.ak.blm.gov**) can point you toward hikes in the White Mountain National Recreation Area. The Glennallen District office (☎ 907-822-3217) can provide more details on the Landmark Gap Trail.
- **USGS maps** are available at sporting-goods stores and **www.usgs.gov.**

Interior Outfitters

- **1st Alaska Outdoor School:** ☎ 907-590-5900; **www.1stalaskaoutdoorschool.com.** Whether it's a berry-picking trek or a wildlife-watching expedition, these guys can guide you. The rates start at $100, but less-costly day trips can be arranged. The owners offer classes in everything from canning and preserving to remote-traveling skills.

PART TWELVE

DOG MUSHING

DOGSLEDDING IS TO ALASKA WHAT SURFING IS TO HAWAII or rodeo is to Wyoming: it is a way of being for the many, many dog lovers here who also happen to enjoy spending time outdoors. In fact, dog mushing is considered the state sport, and every March spectators locally and from the world over arrive in Alaska by the thousands to watch the start of the **Iditarod Trail Sled Dog Race,** in which teams and their drivers run 1,000 miles from Anchorage to Nome, in western Alaska.

The Iditarod commemorates the feats of sled dogs in 1925, when an outbreak of diphtheria struck the town of Nome and poor weather prevented the delivery of the life-saving serum needed to treat those afflicted. Quick-thinking mushers suggested a relay in which they could bring the medicine to Nome by dogsled. (The train carrying the serum made it to Nenana, a small Interior village, before getting stuck, so the actual relay began there. Today's race covers the entire route, however.) Twenty-one teams took part in the relay, traveling as fast as they could go. The trip that the Nome doctor thought would take 15 days took fewer than 6, amazing not only the doctor, but the mushers and townspeople as well. The dogs' bravery saved the town from the deadly epidemic and gave Alaskans a renewed appreciation for the working canines of Alaska.

Today, the Iditarod attracts racers from all over the world, and the prize is hefty—usually more than $50,000 in cash and a brand-new pickup truck. Critics of the race claim the dogs are asked to go beyond their abilities, pushed for the prize, and treated as objects to help their owners win that ultimate reward. Supporters say the dogs are born to run, happiest when in harness leading a team through a wilderness path, and healthiest by staying so active.

Whatever your opinion, we say come to Alaska and find out for yourself. The sport of dog mushing extends far beyond the high profile of the Iditarod. There are hundreds of recreational dog mushers throughout the state—ordinary people who enjoy working with dogs and getting into the backcountry during winter. Some take part in local sprint or distance races, or they meet on weekends to run their teams together.

The center of dog mushing is, without a doubt, the Fairbanks area, especially the outlying communities of **Two Rivers** and **Chena Hot Springs**. Here the land is vast, the trail system endless, and the snow season longer than anywhere else in the state. In Southcentral Inland Alaska, **Chugiak** and the **Matanuska-Susitna Valley** are dog-mushing hot spots. In Southcentral Coastal Alaska, the **Caribou Hills** of the Kenai Peninsula draw mushers from such communities as Kasilof, Clam Gulch, and Ninilchik, among other locales. Southeast Alaska has a few mushers, but the snow season is short and inconsistent. In the Bush, dog mushing is still an accepted mode of transportation, and dog teams are as common as snowmobiles and pickup trucks.

unofficial **TIP**
Many mushers make a living sharing their sport with those who don't know much about it. They teach people how to harness a dog to a team and how to drive a sled; many also let their clients share in chores such as feeding and cleaning up after the animals.

This short chapter spotlights a handful of outfitters that can guide you on a backcountry dog-mushing expedition. This is a sport for which we can say, definitively, that you must travel with a guide. Mushers understand and recognize safety issues that can affect their dogs—tangled lines, wildlife encounters, overflow, and other concerns. They understand their dogs well enough to know if one of the pack is getting tired or is not running quite right due to an injury or fatigue. These skills are the mushers' responsibility, so they will not and should not let inexperienced people loose with their dogs without first knowing for sure that they can handle it. But while dog mushing requires specialized gear and some dog-handling knowledge, even someone who has never driven a sled can become a musher for a day or a week or even two weeks with a little guidance.

Dog-mushing trips can range from an hour to two weeks, from a kennel tour to an interpretive program on the history of sled dogs in Alaska. We offer all of this to you and encourage you to get a little education while you're here in Alaska. Learn about our state sport and gain a better understanding of these amazing animals we call sled dogs.

GENERAL DOG-MUSHING RESOURCES

WANT TO LEARN A LITTLE more about dog mushing ahead of time? Here are a few resources that you can look up before landing in Alaska.

- Most Alaska communities that have concentrations of dog mushers also have local clubs that help support the sport. The **Alaska Dog**

Dog-mushing Outfitters at a Glance

Chena Dog Sled Adventures
☎ 907-488-5845
www.ptialaska.net/~sleddogs

REGIONAL LOCATION	THE INTERIOR
COST	$$
SUITABLE FOR KIDS?	YES
ACTIVITY LEVEL	LIGHT–MODERATE
TRIP LENGTH	1–2 DAYS

Chugach Express Dog Sled Tours
☎ 907-783-2266
home.gci.net/~alaskasnowdogs

REGIONAL LOCATION	SOUTHCENTRAL INLAND
COST	$
SUITABLE FOR KIDS?	YES
ACTIVITY LEVEL	LIGHT
TRIP LENGTH	DAY TRIP

Earthsong Lodge and Denali Dogsled Expeditions
☎ 907-683-2863
www.earthsonglodge.com

REGIONAL LOCATION	THE INTERIOR
COST	$$$
SUITABLE FOR KIDS?	TEENS
ACTIVITY LEVEL	MODERATE
TRIP LENGTH	1–10 DAYS

1st Alaska Outdoor School
☎ 907-590-5900
www.1stalaskaoutdoorschool.com

REGIONAL LOCATION	THE INTERIOR
COST	$
SUITABLE FOR KIDS?	SOME
ACTIVITY LEVEL	MODERATE–HIGH
TRIP LENGTH	1–11 DAYS

Godwin Glacier Dogsled Tours
☎ 888-989-8239 or 907-224-8239
www.alaskadogsled.com

REGIONAL LOCATION	SOUTHCENTRAL COASTAL
COST	$$$
SUITABLE FOR KIDS?	YES
ACTIVITY LEVEL	LIGHT
TRIP LENGTH	1–2 DAYS

Jeff King's Husky Homestead Tours
☎ 907-683-2904
www.huskyhomestead.com

REGIONAL LOCATION	THE INTERIOR
COST	$
SUITABLE FOR KIDS?	OLDER THAN 7
ACTIVITY LEVEL	LIGHT
TRIP LENGTH	DAY TRIP

Jerry Austin's Alaska Adventures
☎ 877-923-2419
www.alaskadogsledding.com or www.alaskaadventures.net

REGIONAL LOCATION	THE BUSH
COST	$$$
SUITABLE FOR KIDS?	TEENS
ACTIVITY LEVEL	MODERATE–HIGH
TRIP LENGTH	6 DAYS

Seavey's IdidaRide Sled Dog Tours
☎ 800-478-3139, 888-221-6874 or 907-224-8607
www.ididaride.com

REGIONAL LOCATION	SOUTHCENTRAL COASTAL
COST	$
SUITABLE FOR KIDS?	YES
ACTIVITY LEVEL	LIGHT
TRIP LENGTH	DAY TRIP/CUSTOM

Sky Trekking Alaska
☎ 907-357-3153
www.skytrekkingalaska.com

REGIONAL LOCATION	STATEWIDE
COST	$$$$
SUITABLE FOR KIDS?	NO
ACTIVITY LEVEL	LIGHT
TRIP LENGTH	4–12 DAYS

Mushers Association in Fairbanks (☎ 907-457-6874; **www.sleddog.org**) and the **Chugiak Dog Mushers Association** in Chugiak (☎ 907-689-7899; **www.chugiakdogmushers.com**) are two. For statewide information, contact Fairbanks-based **Mush with PRIDE** (Providing Responsible Information on a Dog's Environment; P.O. Box 84915, Fairbanks 99708; ☎ 800-507-7433 or 907-490-6874; **www.mushwithpride.org**), which promotes responsible care and humane treatment of all dogs. The **Alaskan Sled Dog and Racing Association** in Anchorage (**www.asdra.org**) concentrates on sprint racing and racing regulations.

- The annual **Iditarod Trail Sled Dog Race** (visit **www.iditarod.com** for details) takes place the first weekend in March. Watch as up to 80 teams take off from downtown Anchorage, then restart the next day in the Matanuska-Susitna Valley. Iditarod Headquarters, at Mile 2.2 Knik Goose Bay Road in Wasilla, has an office and gift shop that are open weekdays 8 a.m. to 5 p.m. Some outfitters allow armchair mushers to follow the race via small plane; see listings following for details.

- ***Mushing*** magazine (P.O. Box 246/3875 Geist Road, Suite E, Fairbanks 99709; ☎ 917-929-6118; **www.mushing.com**) has been published in Interior Alaska for nearly 20 years. Back issues are available for a fee. Another resource is ***Sled Dog Sports*** magazine (online at the same address). The Web site features a listing of sled-dog tours.

DOG-MUSHING OUTFITTERS

BETTLES

1st Alaska Outdoor School

Regional location The Interior. **Type of mushing** Day or multiday. **Cost** $. **Activity level** Moderate–high. **Suitable for kids?** Sometimes. **Best time of year to go** January–March. **Summer activities** Hiking, canoeing, backpacking, remote lodging, camping, and other educational programs. **Contact** ☎ 907-590-5900; **www.1stalaskaoutdoorschool.com.**

OUTFITTER SUMMARY 1st Alaska Outdoor School not only can teach you how to run dogs in a day program, but it also helps coordinate and guide multiday treks in the Interior backcountry by dogsled.

These trips explore some of the most serene, untraveled country in the world. They are designed for those who want to be part of the team, helping with the dogs and camp chores at the end of the day and enjoying the ride during the day. Some winter trips require you to wear a headlamp, as sunlight is scarce, but the northern lights and an immense blanket of stars are your reward. Prices are dependent on the length of trip, but we have found this outfit to be one of the most reasonably and inexpensively priced offerings in the market—and they're friendly to boot.

DENALI

Jeff King's Husky Homestead Tours

Regional location The Interior. **Type of mushing** Day tours. **Cost** $. **Activity level** Light. **Suitable for kids?** Older than 7. **Best time of year to go** June–August. **Summer activities** Summer-only kennel tours. Contact ☎ 907-683-2904; **www.huskyhomestead.com.**

OUTFITTER SUMMARY Jeff King, a four-time Iditarod champion and longtime Denali Park musher, offers 1½-hour kennel tours during which guests are shuttled to his scenic log home at Goose Lake and immediately greeted with tiny puppies to pet and hold. Learn about the training, equipment, and tenacity needed to become a successful competitive dog musher. Tours are $45 for adults.

GIRDWOOD

Chugach Express Dog Sled Tours

Regional location Southcentral Inland. **Type of mushing** Hourly and day trips. **Cost** $. **Activity level** Light. **Suitable for kids?** Yes. **Best time of year to go**

January–March. **Summer activities** Camp tour in summer via helicopter flight to glacier. **Contact** ☎ 907-783-2266; **home.gci.net/~alaskasnowdogs.**

OUTFITTER SUMMARY For the sampler in you, this outfitter offers short dogsled rides in the winter at the base of Mount Alyeska in Girdwood. In the summer, however, you can take part in dogsledding tours atop a glacier. Your guide, a longtime Alaska musher, handles both. His summer tour costs $395 and comprises a 1½-hour Iditarod training camp, including a scenic helicopter flight to the site. During the fall season, you can take a wheeled cart ride behind the dogs for $55. A one-hour training and educational program is offered at Alyeska Resort for $149; a half-day program on a nearby snowfield costs $395 and includes instruction, lunch, gear, and the opportunity to drive your own dog team on a guided run. Make sure to call and confirm ahead of time, because business is come-and-go depending on how busy the guide is. If you can catch him, it's well worth the trip.

HEALY

Earthsong Lodge and Denali Dogsled Expeditions

Regional location The Interior. **Type of mushing** Day trips, overnighters, expeditions, interpretive programs. **Cost** $$$. **Activity level** Moderate. **Suitable for kids?** Preteens and older. **Best time of year to go** November–January. **Summer activities** Dogsled training via cart; kennel tours. **Contact** ☎ 907-683-2863; **www.earthsonglodge.com.**

OUTFITTER SUMMARY The lodge owners are Denali National Park concessionaires who can get you closer to Denali (Mount McKinley) than any other guides around. The retreat is open all winter, providing dogsled adventures ranging from lodge-based to weeklong expeditions in the park. Very small groups (no more than four people) make this an exceptionally enjoyable trip. Prices start at $125 for day trips and go up to $6,200 for ten-day expeditions. This is our highest-recommended location for accessible dog mushing. Owner Jon Nierenberg is a former Denali park ranger and an experienced musher; the lodge is an exceptionally nice spot to relax pre- and post-mush.

IDITAROD TRAIL

Sky Trekking Alaska

Regional location Along the trail. **Type of mushing** Armchair mushing. **Cost** $$$$. **Activity level** Light. **Suitable for kids?** No. **Best time of year to go** March. **Summer activities** Other non-dog-related tours available. **Contact** ☎ 907-357-3153; **www.skytrekkingalaska.com.**

OUTFITTER SUMMARY This Wasilla-based outfit offers three itineraries for 4 to 12 days. All trips are centered on the Iditarod; you'll see the sights, hear the sounds, and experience the exhilaration of the race as you follow the trail from start to finish via small plane. Sky Trekking caters to those who prefer a restaurant-style meal and a warm cabin to camping food and a trailside tent. Prices range from $3,360 to $9,350 per person.

NOME–ST. MICHAEL

Jerry Austin's Alaska Adventures

Regional location The Bush. **Type of mushing** Overnighters and expeditions. **Cost** $$$. **Activity level** Moderate–high. **Suitable for kids?** Teens. **Best time of year to go** January–March. **Summer activities** Fishing lodge, fishing packages available. **Contact** ☎ 877-923-2419; **www.alaskadogsledding.com** or **www.alaskaadventures.net.**

OUTFITTER SUMMARY Iditarod Hall of Fame inductee Jerry Austin (he has run the race an incredible 18 times) and his friendly wife, Clara, a Yup'ik Eskimo from St. Michael, have been leading small groups on dogsled eco-tours since 1976. Not only does Jerry cater to the average outdoors enthusiast, but he also offers corporate retreats, women-only trips, even family-reunion packages. You'll travel on frozen tundra and can even time your trip during the Iditarod to meet the mushers as they cross the finish line in Nome. Prices range from $2,350 to $3,500 per person for a six-day trip, which includes lodging, home-cooked meals, and winter gear.

SEWARD

Godwin Glacier Dogsled Tours

Regional location Southcentral Coastal. **Type of mushing** Day and overnight trips. **Cost** $$$. **Activity level** Light. **Suitable for kids?** Yes. **Best time of year to go** Summer. **Summer activities** This is a summer-only operation. **Contact** ☎ 888-989-8239 or 907-224-8239; **www.alaskadogsled.com.**

OUTFITTER SUMMARY Godwin Glacier bills itself as "the oldest glacier dog-mushing operation and only helicopter dog-mushing operator in Seward, Alaska, on USFS land." Your tour begins as a helicopter ride high above the glaciers and mountains surrounding Resurrection Bay. After landing, enjoy a day tour or an overnight camping trip with guides who can tell Alaska tales and answer all your Iditarod-related questions. Rates range from about $430 to $520 per person and include winter gear.

Seavey's IdidaRide Sled Dog Tours

Regional location Southcentral Coastal. **Type of mushing** Day tours. **Cost** $. **Activity level** Light. **Suitable for kids?** Yes. **Best time of year to go** Summer for short tours; winter for extended tours. **Summer activities** Cart rides, kennel tours. **Contact** ☎ 800-478-3139, 888-221-6874 (Wild Ride Show) or 907-224-8607; **www.ididaride.com.**

OUTFITTER SUMMARY Three generations of Seaveys have run the Iditarod—most recently, in 2004, second-generation musher Mitch Seavey won the race. The tour includes a summer cart ride (two-mile and 1½-hour options) and kennel visit, plus a full-day tour including Exit Glacier, or a Sterling-based presentation. The Seaveys also have begun offering winter tours in which you can join the family during their training and preparation for the Iditarod. Summer tours range from $59 to $130 per adult; winter tours vary due to their custom-designed nature. A recent addition in 2007 is the Anchorage-based Wild Ride Sled Dog Show, in which Seavey's dogs perform and educate visitors in an entertaining and sometimes hilarious manner. That tour is daily in the summer and costs $19.

TWO RIVERS

Chena Dog Sled Adventures

Regional location The Interior. **Type of mushing** Day, overnight, and multiday expeditions. **Cost** $$. **Activity level** Light–moderate. **Suitable for kids?** Yes. **Best time of year to go** December–April. **Summer activities** Kennel tours, dogsled demonstrations, fishing, canoeing, hiking. **Contact** ☎ 907-488-5845; **www.ptialaska.net/~sleddogs.**

OUTFITTER SUMMARY This outfitter offers trips ranging from an hour to two days in Chena River State Recreation Area. Trips include a dog-handler training course, short dog-team rides, multisport adventures, and overnight mushing expeditions. In addition, you'll have the choice to visit Chena Hot Springs and try your hand at ice fishing or snowshoeing. Prices range from $35 for a two-mile dogsled ride to $500 for a one-and-a-half-day mushing expedition.

PART THIRTEEN

FISHING

ALASKA'S NUMBER-ONE OUTDOOR-RECREATION and summer activity is sportfishing. Locals say that if you're not using the summer to fish, you don't have a pulse. And the majority of Alaska's tourists spend their vacations with rods in their hands, mostly because there's no place like it on the planet. In the peak of summer, Alaska is a place where you can enjoy around-the-clock fishing under the midnight sun.

Preparing for your Alaska visit can easily make you feel like you're heading for a foreign country. The culture is slightly different, and compared with the rest of the United States, the place is huge. Think of Alaska's fishing the same way. Once you reach the Great North, you'll discover that it's a land of numerous fishing opportunities and wonderful adventures.

Catching fish is a matter of preparation—of aligning the timing of your trip with when the fish are running. And when you time your Alaska trip right, you'll come away with the trophy you've always dreamed about. But even if you don't come home with a freezer full, the purpose of fishing trips are to have fun and learn about new places.

Glaciers cover about 5% of Alaska, or 29,000 square miles. These massive blocks of moving ice feed thousands of freshwater streams, rivers, and lakes, and eventually flow into oceans. What's more, each water source serves as a fishing-information highway from mid-March to early October. Most people, especially those who are fishing in the Last Frontier for the first time, start their trip preparation by researching information on charters, lodges, and off-the-grid fishing holes. But gathering pamphlets, brochures, and maps can clutter your kitchen table.

In this chapter we won't make you a better angler, but we will unclutter your table and give you a better understanding of when and where to visit. You can troll for king salmon on the **Kenai Peninsula,** spin-fish for silver salmon in **Prince William Sound,** bob bait on the bottom for halibut off the coast of Ketchikan, or fly-fish for rainbow

Alaska Fishing at a Glance

Copper River Basin

REGIONAL LOCATION	SC INLAND
TYPE OF WATER	RIVER
TYPE OF GEAR USED	6- TO 8-WEIGHT FLY ROD, SPINNING ROD
ROAD ACCESS?	YES
SUITABLE FOR KIDS?	NO
GUIDE SUGGESTED?	HIGHLY RECOMMENDED

Kenai River

REGIONAL LOCATION	SC COASTAL
TYPE OF WATER	RIVER
TYPE OF GEAR USED	6- TO 8-WEIGHT FLY ROD, SPINNING ROD
ROAD ACCESS?	YES
SUITABLE FOR KIDS?	YES
GUIDE SUGGESTED?	RECOMMENDED

Selby Lake–Kobuk River

REGIONAL LOCATION	THE BUSH
TYPE OF WATER	LAKE, RIVER
TYPE OF GEAR USED	6- TO 8-WEIGHT FLY ROD, FLOAT TUBE
ROAD ACCESS?	NO
SUITABLE FOR KIDS?	NO
GUIDE SUGGESTED?	YES

Tenakee Springs

REGIONAL LOCATION	SOUTHEAST
TYPE OF WATER	RIVER, OCEAN
TYPE OF GEAR USED	8- TO 12-WEIGHT FLY ROD
ROAD ACCESS?	NO
SUITABLE FOR KIDS?	YES
GUIDE SUGGESTED?	NO

trout in **Chugach State Park.** Whatever you choose, the clear, concise information we provide will lead you to the best spots. But know that it's only a fraction of what's out there.

At the end of this chapter are our favorite outfitters, their locations, and the types of fishing you can find in their regions, because, really, narrowing down a best-of-the-best list for fishing is quite difficult! Even if you decide not to use a guide or outfitter, you can use these locations as a reference for finding the particular fish you are looking for.

The majority of Alaska is remote, which equals expensive adventures. Numerous fishing lodges are accessible only by plane or boat. And if you're fishing for saltwater species like halibut, rockfish, and lingcod, your best bet for success is taking a chartered boat. But sportfishing doesn't always have to break the bank. Fishing for trout or salmon in freshwater streams, rivers, and lakes along the roadside is inexpensive, with the exception of the necessary few gallons of gasoline. And it can often be very successful. Fishing in Alaska is about *when,* not *where.*

CHECKLIST *for* SUCCESS

- **Dress appropriately.** Hypothermia is possible even if temperatures are above freezing. We realize it's difficult for anglers to avoid getting wet, especially if a mammoth king salmon is running you downstream. Of course, we don't want you to lose your trophy, and you don't want to find yourself in water that's too deep (falling in always ends up being a fishing tale that lasts forever!). That's why we recommend wearing polypropylene or other moisture-wicking underwear against your skin. As stated earlier, cotton can kill: it sucks in water and takes hours to dry.

- **Get your bearings.** Visiting Alaska is accomplished in one of three ways: flying commercial airlines, riding the state ferry, or driving the Alaska Highway. Most of the fishing trips we recommend are accessed by roads, so once you reach Alaska, knowing the highway systems is helpful in finding your destination. But remember, this is the state with the fewest roads in the United States, which means there are two places to drive if you're leaving a town: one end of the road and the other end of the road.

unofficial **TIP**
Rivers and streams are rarely warm, but in late June through mid-August, temperatures can be very warm by Alaska standards. We suggest wearing neoprene waders just to be safe. But if you want something more breathable for those "hot" Alaska afternoons, bring a pair made from Gore-Tex.

- **Be watchful around wildlife.** Be aware that spawning salmon attract bears as well as people. When fishing in the woods, pack bear spray, otherwise known as pepper spray. It's not guaranteed to stop a charging bear, but it's better than having nothing at all. Make noise if you're traveling through thick brush, and always pay attention to your surroundings. If a bear takes your fishing spot, let him have it and move on. Carry a gun only if you're comfortable with handling firearms and are properly trained, and only use it when absolutely necessary.
- **Block those bugs.** Alaska's biggest nuisance is the mosquito. June and July are the worst months for mosquitoes and biting flies. None of them carry diseases, but they can easily spoil your fishing experience. Alaska has 25 types of mosquitoes, which, as we've noted, hatch as early as late April and last until August in some spots. Generally, the farther you travel in Alaska's backcountry, the worse the insects become. Lakes and streams can be awful, as can wet, marshy areas that fishermen trudge through to reach their fishing destinations. Bring bug repellent—a dab of 100% DEET works best, but go with whatever feels most comfortable on your skin. Wearing a long-sleeve shirt and a hat helps, too. Mosquito head-nets are a must in some places.
- **Don't forget your fishing license.** Anybody 16 years or older needs one to fish in Alaska. Licenses and king salmon stamps are available at any tackle shop and at most grocery stores; you can also obtain a license by contacting the **Alaska Department of Fish and Game** (apply online at **www.admin.adfg.state.ak.us/license**). Be aware that out-of-staters pay more to fish than Alaska residents.
- **Think ahead.** Most of Alaska is untouched wilderness, which makes a fishing adventure full of excitement. Sometimes it just takes a short drive from town to reach locations that are remote and wild. Don't assume your cell phone will work. Be aware of your physical limitations, and carry essential items in case of an emergency: extra food, extra water, map, multitool kit, wet-weather gear, first-aid kit, waterproof matches, and compass. Note that Alaska has a variety of poisonous plants, so identify any berry or mushroom before you eat it. Cow parsnip, a uniquely Alaskan botanical bummer, isn't poisonous,

unofficial **TIP**
Children get bored easily, and fishing takes patience and coordination. Let them know they can still have fun even if they don't catch a fish. Look at fishing from a kid's point of view. Exposing children to Alaska fishing could turn them into lifelong anglers (and possibly future Alaskans!). However, it's important to recognize their limitations, like trying to catch a 100-pound halibut or fishing for the entire day.

but it is abundant and can cause allergic reactions that look like blisters. Wearing long-sleeve shirts will prevent a breakout.

- **Be wary of water.** Another form of misery particular to our state is giardia, an intestinal parasite found in Alaska lakes, rivers, and streams. It's carried by beavers, not humans, and is present in their feces, so it's likely to lurk in water sources near beaver ponds or swampy rivers. And if you drink from such sources without boiling or treating the water first, you could be in for a world of hurt, as we explained in Part Six (see page 84).
- **Pack smart.** We recommend always traveling light. On floatplanes, for example, baggage space is limited, and you often are charged by the amount of weight you carry. Avoid hard-shell suitcases, instead taking only waterproof duffel bags or dry bags. In the summer, weather changes from cool to warm and sunny to cloudy very fast, so be prepared to dress in layers. Also bring polarized sunglasses, fleece gloves, and a fleece hat. Extra tennis shoes or camp shoes are a must, as well as long underwear and a lightweight down vest or jacket. Of course, bring a camera with extra batteries to back up your big-fish tale.

ALASKA'S FISH

ALASKA IS POPULAR FOR ITS FIVE SPECIES of Pacific salmon: chum, king, pink, silver, and sockeye. Availability of each species depends on the month, week, or even day. Locals aren't kidding when they say, "You should have been fishing here yesterday." A day can indeed make all the difference in what was an awesome run of salmon.

Current sportfishing regulations and availability vary. We suggest checking with the **Alaska Department of Fish and Game** (**www.adfg.state.ak.us**) for rules of open seasons, specific fishing waters, and bag limits before you fish.

CHUM (DOG SALMON) are the most abundant of all Pacific salmon species. They are a metallic greenish blue with tiny black specks, and are often confused with sockeyes and silvers when they are fresh. They run from June to October and weigh 7 to 18 pounds. Alaskans often call them "dog salmon" because mushers use them to feed teams of sled dogs.

KING (CHINOOK) SALMON is Alaska's state fish. It is best when caught from May to early August and generally weighs 15 to 20 pounds. Kings are the most prized species of salmon because of their power and size. The state's largest sport-caught king was a 97-pounder taken from the Kenai River in 1986.

PINK (HUMPY) SALMON are the smallest of the Pacific salmon species. They are available between late June and mid-October and weigh three to five pounds. Pinks are often called "humpy" because the backs of males have pronounced, flattened humps. These are good species for children to fish because they are easy to catch.

SILVER (COHO) SALMON are highly adaptable and swim in just about every freshwater source in Alaska, ranging from small tributaries to large watersheds. They run from late July to September, and adults weigh 8 to 12 pounds. They are bright silver with small black spots.

SOCKEYE (RED) SALMON is a primary food source for Alaskans with subsistence lifestyles because it tastes delicious and runs in large schools, generally in waves from June to late August. Sockeyes are metallic green and blue, silver on the sides and belly, and they weigh six to ten pounds. They lack the large black spots that most other salmon have.

Alaska's fishing scene has more to offer than just salmon, though. Freshwater species like arctic grayling, arctic char, Northern pike, Dolly Varden, rainbow trout, steelhead, and lake trout give anglers plenty of options. And saltwater fish like rockfish, halibut, Pacific cod, and lingcod make for great ocean-vessel adventures.

ARCTIC CHAR are closely related to Dolly Varden (see below) but are generally larger and have darker bodies with fluorescent orange-and-white markings. They have excellent pink meat and weigh one to six pounds.

DOLLY VARDEN are classified as char fish (which means they have light spots on their sides) instead of salmon or trout (which are black-speckled or spotted). Their pink meat tastes wonderful, much like that of arctic char, and they weigh one to six pounds.

GRAYLING, cousins of the trout, are some of the most beautiful, delicate fish in Alaska. They have vibrant colors, sport a large dorsal fin, and live in clear, cold streams. We think they're great to catch on fly rods.

HALIBUT are bottom-dwelling fish known for their barn-door dimensions. Catching one usually requires bait-fishing from a boat and using a wooden club to kill it before hauling it onboard. They weigh 15 to 150 pounds, and the body width is one-third of its length.

KOKANEE is another name for sockeye. The difference is that kokanees are freshwater only and rarely grow more than 14 inches (sockeyes are ocean-reared and can be much bigger).

LINGCOD are bottom dwellers that are wonderful for sportfishing. They put up a great fight, and we prefer catching them to halibut because of their succulent white meat. They are found at depths of up to 1,000 feet and weigh 20 to 60 pounds.

Fishing Outfitters at a Glance

Alaska Good Time Charters
☎ 907-373-7447
www.alaskagoodtimecharters.com

REGIONAL LOCATION	SOUTHCENTRAL INLAND
COST	$$$
SUITABLE FOR KIDS?	OLDER KIDS
ACTIVITY LEVEL	LIGHT–MODERATE
TRIP LENGTH	3–6 DAYS

Alaska Rivers Company
☎ 888-595-1226
www.alaskariverscompany.com

REGIONAL LOCATION	SOUTHCENTRAL COASTAL
COST	$$
SUITABLE FOR KIDS?	OLDER KIDS
ACTIVITY LEVEL	LIGHT–MODERATE
TRIP LENGTH	DAY TRIP

Alaska Trout Fitters
☎ 907-595-1212
www.aktroutfitters.com

REGIONAL LOCATION	SOUTHCENTRAL COASTAL
COST	$$
SUITABLE FOR KIDS?	YES
ACTIVITY LEVEL	LIGHT–MODERATE
TRIP LENGTH	1–2 DAYS

Grayling on a Fly
☎ 907-522-6663
www.grayling-on-a-fly.com

REGIONAL LOCATION	THE BUSH
COST	$$$
SUITABLE FOR KIDS?	YES
ACTIVITY LEVEL	ALL LEVELS
TRIP LENGTH	3 DAYS

Great Alaska Safaris
☎ 907-262-4515
www.greatalaska.com

REGIONAL LOCATION	SOUTHCENTRAL COASTAL
COST	$$$
SUITABLE FOR KIDS?	YES
ACTIVITY LEVEL	LIGHT–MODERATE
TRIP LENGTH	5–10 DAYS

Liquid Adventures
☎ 888-325-2925
www.liquid-adventures.com

REGIONAL LOCATION	SOUTHCENTRAL COASTAL
COST	$$
SUITABLE FOR KIDS?	OLDER KIDS
ACTIVITY LEVEL	ALL LEVELS
TRIP LENGTH	1–12 DAYS

Puffin Fishing Charters
☎ 800-978-3346 or
907-278-3346
www.puffincharters.com

REGIONAL LOCATION	SOUTHCENTRAL COASTAL
COST	$$
SUITABLE FOR KIDS?	OLDER KIDS
ACTIVITY LEVEL	LIGHT–MODERATE
TRIP LENGTH	DAY TRIP

Rainbow River Lodge
☎ 907-571-1210 or
503-429-0511
www.alaskarainbowriverlodge.com

REGIONAL LOCATION	THE BUSH
COST	$$$$
SUITABLE FOR KIDS?	OLDER KIDS
ACTIVITY LEVEL	ALL LEVELS
TRIP LENGTH	6 DAYS

Waterfall Resort
☎ 800-544-5125
www.waterfallresort.com

REGIONAL LOCATION	SOUTHEAST
COST	$$$$
SUITABLE FOR KIDS?	YES
ACTIVITY LEVEL	LIGHT–MODERATE
TRIP LENGTH	4–6 DAYS

NORTHERN PIKE are Alaska's most ferocious predatory fish, eating ducks, muskrats, and other creatures that swim their way. They are the same sharp-toothed species found in Midwest regions and have recently become established in Susitna River drainages and on the Kenai Peninsula. They don't taste nearly as good as salmon or trout.

PACIFIC COD have been commercially fished in Alaska since 1882 and in 2004 made up 12.5% of the ground-fish catch. They are fast-growing, short-lived fish that prefer soft-bottom habitats such as clay, sand, or mud.

RAINBOW TROUT are popular for their powerful fight and giant leaps when hooked. They are named for their colorful sides of reddish pink and silver. They weigh three to ten pounds, depending on population and habitat.

ROCKFISH are the only fish in Alaska with venomous fins. They are mildly toxic to the touch, but we think their delicious white meat is worth the catch. They vary in color; some are black while others are florescent orange.

Alaska Wilderness Guides
☎ 907-345-4470
www.akwild.com

REGIONAL LOCATION	SOUTHCENTRAL INLAND
COST	$$
SUITABLE FOR KIDS?	NO
ACTIVITY LEVEL	ALL LEVELS
TRIP LENGTH	6 DAYS

Daniel's Custom Charters
☎ 800-230-3843 or 907-235-3843
www.homerfishing.com

REGIONAL LOCATION	SOUTHCENTRAL COASTAL
COST	$$
SUITABLE FOR KIDS?	OLDER KIDS
ACTIVITY LEVEL	LIGHT–MODERATE
TRIP LENGTH	DAY TRIP

Deep Creek Fishing Club
☎ 907-567-7373
www.alaskafishinglodge.com

REGIONAL LOCATION	SOUTHCENTRAL COASTAL
COST	$$$
SUITABLE FOR KIDS?	NO
ACTIVITY LEVEL	LIGHT–MODERATE
TRIP LENGTH	CUSTOM

The Lodge at Hidden Basin
☎ 907-345-7017
www.hiddenbasinalaska.com

REGIONAL LOCATION	SOUTHCENTRAL COASTAL
COST	$$$
SUITABLE FOR KIDS?	YES
ACTIVITY LEVEL	ALL LEVELS
TRIP LENGTH	5 DAYS

McFarland's Floatel
☎ 888-828-3335 or
☎ 907-828-3335
www.geocities.com/mcfarlands floatel

REGIONAL LOCATION	SOUTHEAST
COST	$$
SUITABLE FOR KIDS?	YES
ACTIVITY LEVEL	LIGHT–MODERATE
TRIP LENGTH	CUSTOM

Peace of Selby Wilderness Lodge
☎ 907-672-3206
www.alaskawilderness.net

REGIONAL LOCATION	THE BUSH
COST	$–$$$$
SUITABLE FOR KIDS?	NO
ACTIVITY LEVEL	ALL LEVELS
TRIP LENGTH	CUSTOM

SHEEFISH are known as the "Tarpon of the North" because of their resemblance. The subarctic species is a member of the whitefish family and is found along the western Brooks Range in northern Alaska. Their white meat rivals halibut's, and they average 30 to 40 pounds.

STEELHEADS are actually rainbow trout that have spent parts of their life in salt water. They display an acrobatic fight similar to that of rainbow trout. Their pale, reddish meat tastes like trout and is best served panfried or baked.

BAIT *or* FLY?

WHETHER YOU'RE USING BAIT, artificial flies, or spinners, all three angling experiences in Alaska will surely challenge your fishing knowledge. This opens up diverse vacation choices.

To get started, we suggest inquiring with local experts at tackle stores, fishing outfitters, lodges, or even gas stations that sell bait, flies, spoons, and licenses. Locals will give you inside information on

unofficial **TIP**
Effective lures for catching Southcentral Alaskan trout (rainbow, brook, steelhead, grayling, and cutthroat) and char (Dolly Varden, arctic) include spoons, spinners, flies, streamers, muddlers, and egg patterns. We've had the most success using egg-sucking leeches, woolly buggers, and glo-bugs on rainbows.

what fishing holes are hot and what fly- or bait fish are biting.

Also check with the **Alaska Department of Fish and Game** (P.O. Box 25526, Juneau 99802; ☎ 907-465-4100) to obtain important up-to-date information. The agency provides current fish counts, fishing regulations, enhanced maps, and more to improve fishing experiences. Visit its Web site at **www.adfg.state.ak.us,** and link to the sportfishing section.

Alaska's fishing options depend on the month and type of species, which we have split into five regions: the Interior, Southcentral Coastal, Southcentral Inland, Southeast, and the Bush.

For instance, on a trip to the Yentna River in Southcentral Inland Alaska, anglers can catch all five sea-run salmon species (kings, chums, sockeyes, pinks, and silvers) with a variety of large trolling lures, oakie drifters, and egg clusters from early June to mid-October. We've had the most success using Pixies when fishing for sockeyes and pinks.

Travel with a Guide?

Landing a job as a fishing guide in Alaska is considered a prestigious accomplishment in the outdoor world. Alaska lodges and charters often hire guides with previous experience and general fishing knowledge. If you are a beginner, novice, or even veteran angler, paying a guide to lead your annual fishing trip or family vacation to Alaska would be worth the money. Here are a few reasons why.

First, guides will know the good fishing spots, because their paychecks, tips, and companies' reputation depend on the quality of their work (and because they're fishing freaks!). Even if it's their first season in Alaska, we've encountered guides who rely on their own years of experience to find fish and make the customer happy. Sometimes, where allowed, they fish with you. They provide good company and ease the "What am I doing wrong?" pressure.

Have you heard the phrase "If it flies or floats, rent it or lease it?" Well, it applies with guides, too. Hiring one might be expensive, but why fish blindly when an extra hand could give you an extra set of eyes? Guides will tie your flies, untangle your lines from snags, and show you places you wouldn't visit otherwise. Plus, they have access to boats and pose as your personal fishing chauffeur (except they wear waders and hip boots, not suits and ties).

Third, even if you're a veteran angler looking to mount five fish on your wall, a guide can bring you to an area that holds big fish. You might know how to fish, but not where or when. This can be cost-effective. We'll use the guided trip on the Yentna River as an example. A one-day trip will cost you between $350 and $400, including boat transportation, use of gear, and guiding skills, as well as Bush airfare and food. In contrast, if you plan your own trip, Bush plane tickets alone can range from $150 to $700 depending on the plane's size, the number of occupants, and the distance to your destination. Plus, it's always nice to let someone else do the cooking.

FABULOUS FISHING TRIPS

GOOD FISHING CAN BE FOUND in just about any corner of Alaska, but we have a few favorite places to share. Some are easily accessible; others require planning and initiative. Our listings include contact information, so you can sculpt your trip as you wish—which fish you want to catch, what rod you want to use, what region to visit, and so on. This will help you get started.

Copper River Basin–Chugach National Forest

Regional location Southcentral Inland Alaska. **Type of water** River. **Species to be caught** Kings, sockeyes, silvers, pinks, chums. **Best gear to use** 6- to 8-weight fly rod, spinning rod. **Suitable for kids?** No. **Best time of year to go** Late June–September. **Traffic level** Light–moderate. **Facilities** Established tent sites, U.S. Forest Service cabin, parking, and outhouses.

DESTINATION SUMMARY Locals have been fishing the **Copper River Basin,** which includes the **Klutina and Gulkana rivers,** for decades. It has managed to maintain its peaceful surroundings yet thrive as a sportfishing paradise.

DIRECTIONS **Klutina River:** From Anchorage, take Glenn Highway–Alaska Route 1 north to Glennallen. Turn right at the Glennallen junction. The Klutina River Trail is approximately 14 miles from the junction in Copper Center (Mile 100). From Valdez, drive 100 miles north on Richardson Highway–Alaska Route 4 to Copper Center. **Gulkana River:** From Anchorage, take the Glenn Highway north to Glennallen. Turn left at the Glennallen junction and drive north to Gulkana. The Gulkana River crosses the Richardson and follows it north toward Delta Junction.

DESTINATION DESCRIPTION All five salmon species can be caught in the **Copper River Valley,** particularly in the Klutina and Gulkana rivers, both of which feed off the powerful Copper River. The Copper River Valley is located east of Southcentral Alaska by about 150 miles, and while the Copper River itself is a bit too muddied by glacier runoff to be good for fishing, the Klutina and Gulkana are ideal. The 300-mile Gulkana is a nationally designated Wild and Scenic River, and it offers some excellent king salmon fishing. It is fly-fishing only below the highway bridge near the community of **Gulkana,** and bright lures are recommended above the bridge. Salmon eggs

unofficial **TIP**
The Copper River Basin is perhaps Alaska's newest hot spot for salmon fishing. For many years, it was the Kenai River that anglers gravitated toward, but for anglers who want for peaceful fishing, the basin is gaining appeal.

also are permissible above the bridge. The Klutina has swifter, cloudier waters and is accessible through permission only from the local native corporation, **AHTNA.** King salmon fishing peaks in midsummer, followed by the red run into the end of the season. For those who like other types of fishing, there are grayling, rainbow trout, steelhead, and Dolly Varden prowling the waters, too. Locals say the best way to fish the Klutina is to hire **Klutina River Association** guides because they have blanket permission to use the river, and it saves the hassle of obtaining permission on your own. The rest of the Copper River Valley is rich in wildlife, snow-capped mountains, and endless forests of spruce and birch trees.

Resources

- **AHTNA Native Corporation:** Call the Glennallen office at ☎ 907-822-3476 or visit **www.ahtna-inc.com** for permit information.
- The **Alaska Department of Fish and Game** in Anchorage (☎ 907-267-2415) or Glennallen (☎ 907-822-3461) can answer questions on fishing regulations and provide a list of registered guides, including those affiliated with the Klutina River Association. Licenses are available at most Alaska sporting-goods stores.
- **Copper Valley Chamber of Commerce:** P.O. Box 469, Glennallen 99588; ☎ 907-822-5558; **www.traveltoalaska.com.**
- **Delta Junction Visitors Center:** At the junction of the Alaska and Richardson highways; ☎ 877-895-5068 or 907-895-9941.

Kenai River–Lower and Upper Russian Rivers

Regional location Southcentral Coastal Alaska. **Type of water** River. **Species to be caught** Kings, silvers, Dolly Varden, sockeyes, rainbows. **Best gear to use** 6- to 8-weight fly rod, spinning rod. **Suitable for kids?** Yes. **Best time of year to go** Late May–September. **Traffic level** Moderate–heavy. **Facilities** Established tent sites, U.S. Forest Service cabin, parking, and outhouses.

DESTINATION SUMMARY The Kenai Peninsula's Lower and Upper Russian rivers are clear streams that flow into the emerald-green Kenai River. Access to all three rivers is relatively easy. **Lower Russian:** Take a short trip on a privately operated ferry, which is a bargelike boat tethered to a cable stretched across the Kenai River just downstream from its mouth. **Upper Russian:** Take an easy hike up the Russian Lakes Trail. **Kenai:** Take a very short hike off the Sterling Highway.

DIRECTIONS From Anchorage, drive south on the Seward Highway to the Sterling Highway toward Kenai. **Ferry crossing:** At Mile 55, Sterling Highway, turn into the ferry-crossing parking lot on the Kenai River side. **North trailhead end:** At Mile 52 of the Sterling Highway, turn onto Russian River Campground Road. Trailhead parking is one mile farther. **East trailhead end:** At Mile 48, Sterling Highway, turn onto Snug Harbor Road and travel nine miles to Cooper Lake Road, three miles to parking.

unofficial **TIP**
If you want salmon and trout, the Kenai River–Russian River area is the place for you: it's home to the biggest salmon and trout in the world.

DESTINATION DESCRIPTION The confluence of the Russian and Kenai rivers is perhaps the most crowded sportfishing area in Alaska because of its reputation for big and plentiful fish. We would be remiss to leave it out of our best-of, though, because the fishing is quite good. What's more, crowds are easily avoidable if you don't mind hiking. The farther you venture upstream of the Russian River toward the Upper Russian, the fewer people you will encounter. The Kenai River is home to eight world-record kings, including the largest sport-caught, weighing 97 pounds, 4 ounces. A Kenai king averages 35 to 40 pounds and will undoubtedly challenge even the most knowledgeable and accomplished fisherman. Both the Kenai and Russian rivers yield two distinct king runs each summer: mid-May to mid-June and July 1 to July 31. There are two sockeye runs as well. The early run arrives June 15, with an average return of about 70,000 fish, half of which are caught by sport fishermen. The second run arrives in mid-July and consists of smaller fish, about five to six pounds on average. The Russian River offers the largest sport fishery in Alaska for sockeyes. But certain areas of the Upper and Lower Russian rivers are fly-fishing only. Catching salmon is prohibited upstream of the **Russian River Falls,** which includes the area around the U.S. Forest Service cabin, located on **Upper Russian Lake** in the Kenai Mountains. The cabin is used year-round and is located 12 miles from the Russian River Campground. It's 12 by 14 feet, sleeps up to six people, and has a woodstove, wood-splitting maul and crosscut saw, boat with oars, and an outhouse. Wildlife includes brown bears, black bears, moose, and wolves.

Resources

- For fishing regulations in the waters along the trail—the Kenai, Lower Russian, and Upper Russian rivers as well as Upper and Lower Russian lakes—contact the **Alaska Department of Fish and Game;** ☎ 907-260-2920; **www.sf.adfg.state.ak.us** (click on the "Southcentral" section of the Alaska map). The Web site offers maps of area lakes, fishing regulations, and dates of open fisheries.
- Cabins in **Kenai National Wildlife Refuge** cost $35 to $45 per night and most must be reserved in advance either online or over the phone (☎ 877-444-6777; **www.recreation.gov**). Reservations can be made up to 180 days (six months) in advance of the first night's stay. For details about the cabins, call ☎ 907-262-7021 or visit **kenai.fws.gov/cabin.htm.** Check this site before making reservations online or over the phone, because the agents at **www.recreation.gov** are located somewhere in the lower 48 states and don't know much about the cabins.
- **U.S. Geological Survey (USGS) maps** for the area are Seward B-8, C-8, and D-8 (check with one of the **Alaska Public Lands Information Centers** listed in Part Three [see page 54], or go to **www.usgs.gov** and click on "Maps, Products & Publications"). Kenai National Wildlife Refuge maps can be downloaded online at **kenai.fws.gov/maps.htm** or purchased through the **Alaska Natural History Association** ($9.95; ☎ 907-274-8440; **www.alaskanha.org**).

Selby Lake–Kobuk River–Gates of the Arctic National Park

Regional location The Bush. **Type of water** Lake, river. **Species to be caught** Sheefish, lake trout, arctic grayling, pike, arctic char. **Best gear to use** 6- to 8-weight fly rod, float tube. **Suitable for kids?** No. **Best time of year to go** July–August. **Traffic level** Light. **Facilities** Privately owned lodge.

DESTINATION SUMMARY Twenty miles north of the Arctic Circle lies a pristine, little-known body of water called **Selby Lake.** Located in the southern **Brooks Range** and **Gates of the Arctic National Park,** Selby dumps into the Kobuk River, which is known for its exceptional sheefishing and float trips. Lakes at this latitude are ice-free for roughly eight weeks in the summer. But during this time the sun never sets, which makes fishing this land a true Far North experience.

DIRECTIONS Driving to Selby Lake, Kobuk River, or even Gates of the Arctic National Park is not possible. The only transportation option in the summer is floatplane. Fly from Fairbanks 200 miles north, across the Yukon River to the settlement of **Bettles.** From here transfer to a smaller plane, and fly west another 100 miles along the southern hills of the Brooks Range to Selby Lake.

DESTINATION DESCRIPTION If there are any truly good fishing lakes or rivers in the Brooks Range, Selby and the Kobuk are among them. They are home to arctic grayling, edacious northern pike, and the world-famous Kobuk River sheefish. Most of these fish have never seen a fly and will bite just about anything. Some sheefish have weighed in at 60 pounds, but they average 30 to 40 pounds. Sheefish are best caught in August. The Kobuk flows more than 300 miles along the southern edge of the Brooks Range through forest and tundra country and dumps into the **Chukchi Sea.** Along the way, you should see moose, beavers, red fox, black bears, and brown bears. It's not unusual to hear wolves howling or to see lynx and wolverines—and these are all rare treats elsewhere in the state. Gates of the Arctic National Park is four times the size of Yellowstone National Park. It includes the Brooks Range, which is the northernmost extension of the Rocky Mountains. The park encourages catching and releasing fish properly to preserve the number of species, and also using barbless hooks. Short growing seasons and long winters results in slow growth for fish found in the Brooks Range.

Resources

- For fishing regulations in **Gates of the Arctic National Park,** contact the **Alaska Department of Fish and Game** ☎ 907-459-7229; **www.sf.adfg.state.ak.us** (click on the "Interior" section of the Alaska map). The Web site offers maps of area lakes, fishing regulations, and dates of open fisheries. You can also call ☎ 907-692-5494 or e-mail **gaar_visitor_information@nps.gov.**
- For more details on travel in the **Brooks Range** within **Gates of the Arctic National Park,** contact one of the park offices. They are open year-round, but call ahead to make sure someone is available, because

hours vary. **Fairbanks Headquarters:** Open weekdays, 8 a.m. to 4:30 p.m.; closed on holidays (☎ 907-457-5752); **Bettles Ranger Station/Visitor Center:** Open daily from mid-June to Labor Day, although sometimes closed for lunch, and 1 p.m. to 5 p.m. the rest of the year, except holidays (☎ 907-692-5494); **Coldfoot Visitor Center:** Open Memorial Day to Labor Day, 10 a.m. to 10 p.m. (☎ 907-678-5209); **Anaktuvuk Pass Ranger Station:** There's a year-round outside visitor display, but the ranger station hours vary, so call ahead (☎ 907-661-3520). The park Web site is **www.nps.gov/gaar.** For more details on travel in the Brooks Range within the **Arctic National Wildlife Refuge,** contact the park office at 101 12th Avenue, Room 236, Box 20, Fairbanks 99701; ☎ 907-456-0250 or 800-362-4546; **alaska.fws.gov/nwr/arctic.**

- **USGS maps** can be used for travel in the Brooks Range. Shaded relief maps are available at the Arctic National Wildlife Refuge Web site (see above). A single all-inclusive map of the refuge is not available because the area is too vast. Instead, figure out which section you plan to travel in, and order those indexed maps accordingly.

Tenakee Springs–Tongass National Forest

Regional location Southeast Alaska. **Type of water** River, ocean. **Species to be caught** Halibut, kings, chums, pinks, steelhead, Dolly Varden. **Best gear to use** 8- to 12-weight fly rod. **Suitable for kids?** Yes. **Best time of year to go** Early May–September. **Traffic level** Light. **Facilities** Privately owned cabins, hot-springs bathhouse, post office, small grocery store, liquor store. No established tent sites.

DESTINATION SUMMARY This fascinating Alaska Marine Highway trip starts in Juneau and ends in **Tenakee Springs,** a town on the Tenakee Inlet with a population around 100. Tenakee Springs may be small, but it's big for fly-fishing opportunities and other outdoor recreational activities, such as sea kayaking, hiking, soaking in the hot springs, or watching a plethora of wildlife.

DIRECTIONS From Juneau, which is only accessible by plane or boat, board the ferry ***Le Conte,*** which travels 45 miles to Tenakee Springs two to three times a week (☎ 800-642-0066; **www.ferryalaska.com**). The ferry holds cars, but there are no off-loading areas in Tenakee. In fact, there are no cars or true roads in town. Though taking the **Alaska Marine Highway** from Juneau is the best route, Tenakee can also be reached from **Sitka,** a town located directly south as the crow flies, or by floatplane.

DESTINATION DESCRIPTION Once you spend time in Tenakee Springs, it will be difficult to depart. This adventure is located in protected solitude in **Tongass National Forest,** the largest unit in the national-forest system (approximately 17 million acres, or the

unofficial **TIP**
The crown jewel of Tenakee Springs is the bathhouse, built in 1895. After a long day of fishing, you can bathe free. The bathhouse is open 24 hours a day, with designated hours for men and women. Times are posted on the door, and contributions to cleaning and maintenance can be handed over to Snyder Mercantile Company across the street.

size of West Virginia). This is an opportunity to catch halibut on fly rods, as well as three species of salmon, steelhead, and Dolly Varden. Watching wildlife and picking wild berries will keep you entertained, too. There are opportunities to see brown bears, deer, river otters, mink, humpback and killer whales, porpoises, seals, and sea lions. Tenakee Springs is stocked with salmonberries, blueberries, and red huckleberries in July and August. The 40-mile-long **Tenakee Inlet** is protected, which means the water isn't rough. Fourteen rivers flow into **Tenakee Inlet,** where approximately 750,000 salmon migrate to spawn. A forest road parallels the **Indian River,** which flows into the inlet. Brown bears are abundant along this road.

From May to June, you can catch steelhead and Dolly Varden. From July to August, catch pinks and chums. Silvers run in September. There are plenty of places to camp along its shore. And in Tenakee, anywhere north of the harbor is acceptable for pitching a tent. Sometimes bears stroll down the main street during berry time.

Resources

- For fishing regulations in the waters that flow into the Tenakee Inlet and around Tenakee Springs, contact the **Alaska Department of Fish and Game;** ☎ 907-747-5355; **www.sf.adfg.state.ak.us** (click on the "Southeast" section of the Alaska map). The Web site offers maps of area lakes, fishing regulations, and dates of open fisheries.
- The **Alaska Marine Highway** (☎ 800-642-0066; **www.ferry alaska.com**) provides shuttles between Juneau and Tenakee Springs. Fares and schedules vary during these two seasons: May 1 to September 30 and October 1 to April 30.
- For more information on **Tenakee Springs,** including demographics, businesses, and tourist information, visit **www.epodunk.com** (click on "Alaska" and go to "Alaska communities").
- More than 150 rustic cabins are scattered throughout **Tongass National Forest.** They provide wooden bunks, tables, benches, and warming stoves and cost between $25 and $45. Learn more about the locations and regulations by visiting **www.fs.fed.us/r10/tongass/ recreation/recreation.shtml.** For general information about the forest, call ☎ 907-225-3101 or visit **www.fs.fed.us/r10/tongass.**

FISHING OUTFITTERS

Alaska Good Time Charters

Based in Wasilla, Southcentral Inland Alaska. **Areas visited** Whittier, Prince William Sound. **Fishing offered** Salmon, trout, halibut, and other species on streams and in waters few others have fished; saltwater fishing excursions. **Cost** $$$. **Activity level** Light–moderate. **Suitable for kids?** Older ones. **Contact** ☎ 907-373-7447; **www.alaskagoodtimecharters.com.**

OUTFITTER SUMMARY In addition to its hunting and cruising adventures, Alaska Good Time provides guests with some of the state's best and most scenic fishing out of Whittier and Prince William Sound. You will fish for more than ten species of Alaskan saltwater fish on a three- to six-day voyage around the sound. The company even offers salmon shark fishing for those who are really looking for a challenge. This guide has been fishing Alaska waters for 40 years. Rates range from $1,350 (three days) to $3,275 (one week) per person.

Alaska Rivers Company

Based in Cooper Landing, Southcentral Coastal Alaska. **Areas visited** Kenai River. **Fishing offered** Sockeye, coho, Dolly Varden, rainbow trout. **Cost** $$. **Activity level** Light–moderate. **Suitable for kids?** Older ones. **Contact** ☎ 888-595-1226; **www.alaskariverscompany.com.**

OUTFITTER SUMMARY Longtime Alaskan and river fanatic Gary Galbraith provides a relaxing and family-oriented experience on the Kenai River and at his cabins and lodge on the river in Cooper Landing. Gary's guides offer half- to full-day fishing excursions in drift boats and rafts on the Upper Kenai and in the canyon. Sockeye and coho salmon, Dolly Varden, and trophy rainbow trout are Alaska Rivers' fortes, and you will catch plenty as you glide along the stunning waters of the Kenai. Alaska Rivers also offers scenic floats, guided hiking, and cabin rentals. Prices range from $99 to $245 for fishing trips.

Alaska Trout Fitters

Based in Cooper Landing, Southcentral Coastal Alaska. **Areas visited** Kenai River and surrounding area. **Fishing offered** Salmon, trout. **Cost** $$. **Activity level** Light–moderate. **Suitable for kids?** Yes. **Contact** ☎ 907-595-1212; **www.aktroutfitters.com.**

OUTFITTER SUMMARY Alaska fly-fishing pioneer Curt Trout—we're not kidding; that's his name—has been fishing the Kenai River and perfecting his specialized techniques for more than 20 years. He and his guides will share this experience in a two-day fly-fishing class and drift-boat trip or on a variety of daylong trips around the Kenai River area. Though trout is the company's specialty, the Kenai wouldn't be the Kenai without salmon fishing, too. You'll fish for some of the biggest trout and salmon you've ever seen, and there is even a hike-in option to get at some of the more-remote streams. The fly-fishing class is $550 per person, including a night's lodging; day trips ranging from four to nine hours are around $150 to $250. We like the $175 hike-in fly-fishing option, which gets you away from the crowds.

Alaska Wilderness Guides

Based in Anchorage, Southcentral Inland Alaska. **Areas visited** Lake Creek, Alaska Range. **Fishing offered** Salmon, rainbow trout. **Cost** $$. **Activity level** All levels. **Suitable for kids?** No. **Contact** ☎ 907-345-4470; **www.akwild.com.**

OUTFITTER SUMMARY Alaska Wilderness Guides offers a great remote fishing experience with a fly-in trip to Lake Creek, where guests can take in the serenity of the wilderness and enjoy views of Mount McKinley and the rest of the Alaska Range. This guide's favorite season is silver salmon season, but they'll also cater to whatever you're interested in, be it tackle-breaking kings or vibrant rainbow trout. This can be a camping trip and/or a trip to a remote lodge on Lake Creek; the rate is $2,800 per person for six days in the summer.

Daniel's Custom Charters

Based in Homer, Southcentral Coastal Alaska. **Areas visited** Kachemak Bay. **Fishing offered** Saltwater fishing for halibut and salmon; crabbing and clamming. **Cost** $$. **Activity level** Light–moderate. **Suitable for kids?** Older ones. **Contact** ☎ 800-230-3843 or 907-235-3843; **www.homerfishing.com.**

OUTFITTER SUMMARY This experienced charter service offers halibut and salmon charters for all ages and abilities. Unique to this company are its crabbing and clamming trips in addition to fishing for other exotic Alaska fish. Daniel's also offers The Nest or The Raven, breathtaking rental guesthouses high atop the bluff overlooking Kachemak Bay and Cook Inlet. This year-round charter operation's rates are around $215 per person for a full day of fishing. Lodging at the guesthouses starts at $310 per night.

Deep Creek Fishing Club

Based in Ninilchik, Southcentral Coastal Alaska. **Areas visited** Kenai Fjords National Park, Resurrection Bay. **Fishing offered** Salmon, trout, halibut, and other species on streams and in waters few others have fished; saltwater fishing excursions. **Cost** $$$$. **Activity level** Light–moderate. **Suitable for kids?** No. **Contact** ☎ 800-770-7373; **www.alaskafishinglodge.com.**

OUTFITTER SUMMARY "Grand Lodge" is an understatement at this decadent 14,000-square-foot log and river-rock palace that's more luxury than rustic fishing lodge. And it doesn't end with the amazing accommodations. There are also private cabins that mimic the cozy Alaska elegance of the lodge and gourmet meals of fresh crab and other delicacies. If you can bring yourself to leave the lodge, the freshwater- and saltwater-fishing excursions are also quite lavish. If a giant Cook Inlet halibut isn't enough, hop aboard the club's helicopter for a day of epic fly-fishing on a remote stream. Call for package pricing and special offers.

Grayling on a Fly

Based in Council (outside of Nome), the Bush. **Areas visited** Niukluk River. **Fishing offered** Arctic char, grayling, salmon. **Cost** $$$. **Activity level** All levels. **Suitable for kids?** Yes. **Contact** ☎ 907-522-6663 (October–May only); **www.grayling-on-a-fly.com.**

OUTFITTER SUMMARY From June to September, John Elmore, a guide with more than 30 years' experience, offers remote angling on the Niukluk River, 75 miles northeast of Nome. Rates are $2,310 per person for three days and nights of guided fishing and $770 per additional day; for those who want to go it alone, unguided trips are available for $1,680 per person for three days and $560 per additional day. There are two guest cabins; families traveling with children under 12 receive half-price rates for the young ones. When you're not pulling in the fish, John, a former Alaska state trooper, can regale you with stories of patrolling the Kobuk River by dog team. His wife, Fran, the state's first female state trooper, does the cooking.

Great Alaska Safaris

Based in Sterling, Southcentral Coastal Alaska. **Areas visited** Kenai, Kasilof rivers; Cook Inlet, Kenai National Wildlife Refuge. **Fishing offered** Sockeye, coho, halibut, Dolly Varden, rainbow trout, arctic char. **Cost** $$$. **Activity level** Light–moderate. **Suitable for kids?** Yes. **Contact** ☎ 907-262-4515; 800-544-2261; **www.greatalaska.com.**

OUTFITTER SUMMARY Catch some of the biggest, most beautiful fish in the world in one of the biggest, most beautiful settings in the world. Great Alaska Safaris takes clients to the Kenai and Kasilof rivers, in Cook Inlet and the Kenai National Wildlife Refuge, and on remote streams accessible only by plane. Whether you've never fished before or you're a seasoned angler, this company can provide you with the experience you seek, from fly-in trips to fishing from the private beach. Stay in the gorgeous lodge for $1,095 to $5,300 per person for one to ten days.

Liquid Adventures

Based in Seward, Southcentral Coastal Alaska. **Areas visited** Kenai Fjords National Park, Resurrection Bay. **Fishing offered** Saltwater halibut, rockfish, salmon, lingcod. **Cost** $$. **Activity level** All levels. **Suitable for kids?** Older ones. **Contact** ☎ 888-325-2925; **www.liquid-adventures.com.**

OUTFITTER SUMMARY Trends, you will soon notice if you spend enough time in Alaska, are slow to reach the Last Frontier. Maybe it's because we are so far away. Liquid Adventures, for instance, is one of just two outfitters in the state that we know of that offers kayak fishing, using specially designed kayaks made for fishing from the ocean. (The other one, incidentally, is in Ketchikan, in Southeast Alaska.) Anglers across the country are enjoying this newly growing sport, combining sea kayaking with fishing for a truly unique adventure. Pull in a giant halibut from your tiny boat–it can be done. Liquid Adventures offers combination fishing-kayaking trips out of Seward using the craft, providing peaceful paddling . . . until you land the big one. Imagine hauling in a 50-pound halibut from a kayak. A bit more adventurous now, isn't it? Prices start at $165 for the half-day trip and $399 for the remote trip. We recommend the latter. You will catch more fish.

The Lodge at Hidden Basin

Based in Kodiak Island, Southcentral Coastal Alaska. **Areas visited** Local streams and waters of Kodiak Island. **Fishing offered** Sea bass, red snapper, lingcod, halibut, rainbow trout, steelhead, Dolly Varden, salmon. **Cost** $$$. **Activity level**

All levels. **Suitable for kids?** Yes. **Contact** ☎ 907-345-7017; **www.hiddenbasinalaska.com.**

OUTFITTER SUMMARY Billed as a genuine wilderness experience, The Lodge at Hidden Basin offers a six-day trip for $3,995. Trips include superb Kodiak Island fishing, meals, lodging, guided fishing, equipment, and other summer activities including beachcombing, wildlife viewing of all kinds, and simple relaxation at the lodge. It's not the fanciest lodge out there, but it definitely has some of the friendliest people. Rates start at $795 per person per day.

McFarland's Floatel

Based in Thorne Bay, Prince of Wales, Southeast Alaska. **Areas visited** Southeast waters. **Fishing offered** Halibut, rockfish, lingcod, salmon, trout, Dolly Varden. **Cost** $$. **Activity level** Light–moderate. **Suitable for kids?** Yes. **Contact** ☎ 888-828-3335 or 907-828-3335; **www.mcfarlandsfloatel.com.**

DESTINATION SUMMARY The Floatel serves as a floating town center for an array of cozy wilderness cabins set against the lush forest of Thorne Bay. McFarland's offers freshwater- and saltwater-fishing experiences: halibut, rockfish, lingcod, salmon, trout, Dolly Varden, and others. Prices vary depending on lodging and activity preferences. Beachfront log cabins in Thorne Bay that can sleep up to four people rent for $295 a night. An added bonus for you e-mail/BlackBerry addicts: free wireless Internet in the middle of nowhere.

Peace of Selby Wilderness Lodge

Based in Brooks Range of Arctic National Wildlife Refuge, the Bush. **Areas visited** Kobuk River. **Fishing offered** Grayling, northern pike, lake trout, arctic char, sheefish. **Cost** $–$$$$. **Activity level** All levels. **Suitable for kids?** No. **Contact** ☎ 907-672-3206; **www.alaskawilderness.net.**

OUTFITTER SUMMARY This comfortable, fully furnished lodge comes with all the meals and activities you can fit in a day, although you may be tempted to just sit back and enjoy the view. Situated in the Brooks Range, on Narvak Lake, this idyllic area is known for its excellent fishing. Lodging begins at $500 per night, so it's for those who have money to spend; but oh, what a trip it could be. For $9,000 per week, the owners will create your own unique adventure. Another option for the more independent, adventurous soul is the $300-per-night self-serve cabins, which sleep one to four people, are furnished, and come with canoes, paddles, and life vests. You bring your food and sleeping bag.

Puffin Fishing Charters

Based in Seward, Southcentral Coastal Alaska. **Areas visited** Resurrection Bay, Prince William Sound, Montague Island, Nuka Bay, and Kenai Fjords National Park. **Fishing offered** Salmon, halibut, rockfish, and lingcod. **Cost** $$. **Activity level** Light–moderate. **Suitable for kids?** Older ones. **Contact** ☎ 800-978-3346 or 907-278-3346; **www.puffincharters.com.**

OUTFITTER SUMMARY This experienced guiding service specializes in fun and efficient fishing. The guides advertise faster boats and more fishing than other local outfits, and they pride themselves on getting you to the fish faster so you can make the most of your time. Prices start at $175 per person for a full day of halibut fishing and go up to $250 per person for a combination halibut-and-salmon trip.

Rainbow River Lodge

Based in Iliamna, beyond Lake Clark National Park, the Bush. **Areas visited** The Copper River (not of Southcentral Inland status; rather, a local river of the same name, named one of the 50 best trout streams in the world by *Trout Unlimited*). **Fishing offered** Rainbow trout, arctic grayling, arctic char, pike, lake trout, and all five species of salmon. **Cost** $$$$. **Activity level** All levels. **Suitable for kids?** Older ones. **Contact** ☎ 907-571-1210 or 503-429-0511; **www.alaskarainbow riverlodge.com.**

OUTFITTER SUMMARY A favorite of former President Jimmy Carter, the Rainbow River Lodge is located on the Copper River. Anglers will fish for ten species of fish, in addition to enjoying Alaskan hospitality, incredible gourmet meals, and comfortable surroundings. Six days of fishing at the lodge costs $6,700 and includes meals, guiding, accommodations, and more. It's a top-end lodge, and for good reason.

Waterfall Resort

Based in Prince of Wales, Southeast Alaska. **Areas visited** Southeast waters. **Fishing offered** Saltwater fishing for several types of salmon, halibut, rockfish, lingcod, and a variety of other ocean fish. **Cost** $$$$. **Activity level** Light–moderate. **Suitable for kids?** Yes. **Contact** ☎ 800-544-5125; **www.waterfall resort.com.**

OUTFITTER SUMMARY Renowned for its prime location on the edge of the annual salmon-run grounds and productive ocean surges, Waterfall offers phenomenal fishing, no matter the species. The lodge itself is a restored 1900s-era salmon cannery, a perfect setting for comfortable accommodations and family-oriented hospitality in this unbeatable fishing haven. Packages range from $3,795 for four days to $5,495 for six days.

PART FOURTEEN

SEA KAYAKING

KAYAKS—or *bidarkas* or *umiaks,* as you also will hear them called in Alaska—are among the oldest modes of transportation in the far north, used for hundreds of years by Eskimos and Aleuts to hunt seals and whales. Back then the boats were constructed of wooden frames covered by the dried skins of sea mammals such as walrus and seal. They were light and quiet on the water, and they moved swiftly, making them the perfect hunting vessel. One or two men could carry them, and maintenance involved little more than letting them dry out between uses to keep the skins from rotting. *Bidarkas,* the Aleut versions, carried one man; the *umiaks* used in the Chukchi and Bering seas were sometimes as long as 40 feet. Today, the kayaking tradition continues, and some native whale hunters still use their skin boats. Recreationists also enjoy the ease of kayaks, paddling into remote channels and bays to explore parts of Alaska that really aren't accessible any other way.

This chapter explores the myriad places to which a sea kayaker can travel. With more than 6,600 miles of coastline, the destinations are endless. Creating a best-of-the-best list for this sport was particularly difficult, because we have a bias. We love sea kayaking: the smell of the ocean, the sounds of the birds, the occasional sea otter playfully following alongside.

If you're here to experience the wonders of Alaska, it easy to appreciate while paddling along at a comfortable pace and taking in the whales and glaciers and other assorted Alaska scenery.

The best places to go sea kayaking in Alaska are, predictably, the coastal regions, including Southcentral Coastal and Southeast Alaska. The communities of **Homer, Seward, Whittier, Valdez, Juneau, Ketchikan,** and **Gustavus** are particularly promising places from which to embark.

We offer a few of our favorite trips, which take in some of the most dramatic coastal landscapes in the state.

CHECKLIST *for* SUCCESS

- **Kayak with at least one other person,** and stay within shouting or whistling distance. A two-person rescue is much easier than a self-rescue.
- **Rethink your packing strategies.** The nice thing about sea kayaking is that you can pack more luxuries than you can on canoe trips, when portages are necessary, or on backpacking trips, when the weight is on your back. So let up a little and bring that bigger tent, that thicker book, that bottle of wine. Carry everything in waterproof stuff-sacks with double seals. Using small stuff-sacks allows you to pack into smaller compartments of the kayak's holds, and to better distribute weight.
- **Dress appropriately.** It rains a lot on the coast, so you'll be battling the wet from the sea and the rain. Wear layers and a paddling jacket that seals tightly at the wrists. On those glorious clear, sunny days, stuff extra clothes in your hold and let the summer sun bathe you in its warmth (while properly covered in sunscreen, of course). Need we mention the necessity of life jackets?

unofficial **TIP**
Knee-high or calf-length rubber boots are a must in Alaska waters. Neoprene white-water booties usually aren't enough to keep you comfortably dry. We can't stress this enough. If you want to fit in with the locals, **XtraTufs** are a brand that most Alaskans prefer.

- **Know how to navigate.** Topographic maps and marine charts are your best mapping sources, especially on longer trips in which you are traveling from point to point. **U.S. Geological Survey (USGS)** and **National Oceanic and Atmospheric Administration (NOAA)** maps are the most accurate for the conditions. Many outdoor travelers can read global-positioning systems (GPS) and rely on them for backcountry travel. These can be particularly useful tools for travel in areas with multiple channels and bays, but if they drop into the water (it's happened to us!), they're done for. Always have hard-copy maps on hand.
- **Avoid giardia.** If you plan on drinking water from a natural source, boil or treat it first to avoid catching this nasty intestinal bug.
- **Protect against hypothermia.** If you roll your kayak, an enjoyable trip can quickly turn dangerous. Get to land and find a way to get warm, whether by building a fire or by changing into dry clothes or huddling with a dry partner.
- **Carry basic first-aid items,** including bandages to patch up minor cuts as well as any specific medications that may be needed for anyone in your traveling party.
- **Bring along a camp stove that can heat water quickly.** This is a better choice than building fires, which can be hard to do in treeless areas and is more damaging to the landscape. In some places, fires are even prohibited. Also, carry waterproof matches as well as a lighter.
- **Pack a whistle, flares,** or something else to use as an SOS device in case of an emergency.

Alaska Sea Kayaking at a Glance

	Glacier Bay	Kachemak Bay	Katmai Coast	Prince William Sound	Resurrection Bay	Shuyak Island
REGIONAL LOCATION	SOUTHEAST	SOUTHCENTRAL COASTAL	THE BUSH	SOUTHCENTRAL COASTAL	SOUTHCENTRAL COASTAL	SOUTHCENTRAL COASTAL
DISTANCE	VARIES	VARIES	30–50 MILES	VARIES	VARIES	35–40 MILES
TRAFFIC	MODERATE	MODERATE–HEAVY	LIGHT	MODERATE	LIGHT–MODERATE	LIGHT
DIFFICULTY						
TRIP LENGTH	3–10 DAYS	3–5 DAYS	6–10 DAYS	3–15 DAYS	3–7 DAYS	3–5 DAYS
SUITABLE FOR KIDS?	YES	YES	NO	VARIES	VARIES	YES
GUIDE SUGGESTED?	NO	NO	HIGHLY RECOMMENDED	RECOMMENDED	NO	NO

- **Clam with caution.** If you plan to harvest shellfish such as clams or mussels, make sure the area in which you will be paddling is open to gathering and that what you take is safe to eat. The big risk is paralytic shellfish poisoning, or PSP, which can cause numbness, paralysis, disorientation, even death. Microscopic algae called dinoflagellates, which some shellfish feed on, produce the toxins that cause the disorder. The state tests for the presence of these organisms often and issues warnings when dinoflagellates are detected. The **Marine Advisory Program**'s main office (1007 West Third Avenue, Suite 100, Anchorage 99501; ☎ 907-274-9691; **www.uaf.edu/map**) can offer more information. Also be aware that a fishing license is required to harvest shellfish; you can buy one at most sporting-goods stores and grocery stores; fees range from $10 to $50 for nonresidents, depending upon how long you plan to fish. You'll also need a Household Shellfish Permit (if you're searching for littleneck or butter clams), which is free but requires registration.
- **Check marine conditions** for your area from a marine-radio forecast, by calling the local marine weather office, or by checking online with the Alaska Marine Weather Forecast (**pafc.arh.noaa.gov/marfcst.php**).
- **Know the tides.** Tides may determine your launch site and destination. Tides also cause currents, so know the rise and ebb for the area where you are planning on paddling. In general, if the tide and wind are traveling the same direction, water conditions will be somewhat calm. Wind traveling against the tidal current creates waves. Attach your paddle to the kayak with a paddle leash to avoid losing it in these conditions.

> *unofficial* **TIP**
> Free tide-table booklets are available at most grocery stores and banks and some gas stations.

- **Always carry fresh water for drinking.** It is surprisingly easy to get dehydrated while paddling. We like to attach a looped-lidded Nalgene bottle to the top front of our kayak for easy reach. We also store easily accessible snacks in an inflatable snap-on pouch.

Travel with a Guide?

Traveling with a guide is a personal choice that should reflect exactly what you are looking for in a kayaking trip. Even seasoned paddlers sometimes choose to travel with a guide if they are visiting areas with which they are not familiar, so the decision is not solely based on experience level.

Using a guide is an excellent way to eliminate the guesswork from any trip. Guides know the areas well, and can predict which type of gear will work best, what the weather will be like, and how far you will be able to paddle in reality versus what you may think you can paddle by looking at a map. These are invaluable perks, but they will cost you extra.

unofficial **TIP**
If you choose to travel with a guide, be sure to research his or her travel habits well. Some guides do almost all the work, and your paddling days end in a fully set-up camp with food and hot beverages waiting. Others take a more primitive approach, and you may carry your own gear and help set up camp each evening. You may even help prepare meals.

Another reason you might choose is a guide is logistics. Unless you have a folding kayak, traveling with a kayak is extremely cumbersome, and renting one can quickly get expensive. Most rental companies charge at least $45 per day for a single kayak, usually more.

Whether you choose a leisurely approach to kayaking or want to make the experience as close to your own camping trip as possible is up to you. Neither choice is right or wrong.

Another consideration particular to water sports is the necessity of traveling in groups. Because a simple tip into the water can turn life-threatening in minutes (Alaska's water in July, for instance, averages 48°F to 58°F, depending on the location. By comparison, the water temperature in Baja at that time of year is 80°F to 86°F). If you are a solo kayaker, you may consider traveling with a guide if for no other reason than the safety in numbers.

That said, we believe a kayaker with reasonably good skills can easily arrange his or her own trip in Alaska. Many kayaking locations here cater to these independent travelers and can offer advice on specific routes and locations that allow for the most enjoyment with the least amount of risk. The trips we suggest in this chapter, with the exception of the Katmai Coast trip, are all easily arranged on your own.

ALASKA'S BEST KAYAKING

Glacier Bay

Regional location Southeast Alaska. **Distance** Infinite options. **Difficulty** 🫎🫎🫎. **Suitable for kids?** Yes. **Time to paddle** 3–10 days is ideal. **Best time of year to**

Sea-kayaking Outfitters at a Glance

Alaska Alpine Adventures
☎ 877-525-2577 or 907-781-2253
www.alaskaalpineadventures.com

REGIONAL LOCATION	THE BUSH
COST	$$$
SUITABLE FOR KIDS?	NO
ACTIVITY LEVEL	MODERATE–HIGH
TRIP LENGTH	12 DAYS

Alaska Discovery
☎ 800-586-1911
www.akdiscovery.com

REGIONAL LOCATION	SOUTHEAST
COST	$$$
SUITABLE FOR KIDS?	SOME TRIPS
ACTIVITY LEVEL	ALL LEVELS
TRIP LENGTH	3–9 DAYS

Alaska Kayak School
☎ 907-235-2090
www.alaskakayakschool.com

REGIONAL LOCATION	SOUTHCENTRAL COASTAL
COST	$$
SUITABLE FOR KIDS?	YES
ACTIVITY LEVEL	ALL LEVELS
TRIP LENGTH	DAY TRIP

Anadyr Adventures
☎ 800-TO-KAYAK or 907-835-2814
www.anadyradventures.com

REGIONAL LOCATION	SOUTHCENTRAL COASTAL
COST	$$$
SUITABLE FOR KIDS?	YES
ACTIVITY LEVEL	LIGHT–MODERATE
TRIP LENGTH	1–7 DAYS

Cordova Coastal Outfitters
☎ 907-424-7424
www.cdvcoastal.com

REGIONAL LOCATION	SOUTHCENTRAL COASTAL
COST	$
SUITABLE FOR KIDS?	YES
ACTIVITY LEVEL	MODERATE
TRIP LENGTH	½ DAY/CUSTOM

Exposure Alaska
☎ 907-761-3761 or 800-956-6422
www.exposurealaska.com

REGIONAL LOCATION	SOUTHCENTRAL COASTAL
COST	$$$
SUITABLE FOR KIDS?	YES
ACTIVITY LEVEL	MODERATE
TRIP LENGTH	7 DAYS

Pangaea Adventures
☎ 800-660-9637 or 907-835-8442
www.alaskasummer.com

REGIONAL LOCATION	SOUTHCENTRAL COASTAL
COST	$$$
SUITABLE FOR KIDS?	SOME TRIPS
ACTIVITY LEVEL	ALL LEVELS
TRIP LENGTH	1–8 DAYS

Prince William Sound Kayak Center
☎ 877-472-2452, 907-276-7235, or 907-742-2452
www.pwskayakcenter.com

REGIONAL LOCATION	SOUTHCENTRAL COASTAL
COST	$$
SUITABLE FOR KIDS?	YES
ACTIVITY LEVEL	LIGHT–MODERATE
TRIP LENGTH	DAY TRIP

Southeast Exposure Alaska Sea Kayaking Adventures
☎ 907-225-8829
www.southeastexposure.com

REGIONAL LOCATION	SOUTHEAST
COST	$
SUITABLE FOR KIDS?	SOME TRIPS
ACTIVITY LEVEL	LIGHT–MODERATE
TRIP LENGTH	1–6 DAYS

Wilderness Birding Adventures
☎ 907-694-7442
www.wildernessbirding.com

REGIONAL LOCATION	SOUTHCENTRAL COASTAL
COST	$$$
SUITABLE FOR KIDS?	TEENS AND OLDER
ACTIVITY LEVEL	MODERATE
TRIP LENGTH	7 DAYS

go June–September. **Traffic level** Moderate. **Facilities** Required camper orientation, visitor station with nautical charts, and other limited book supplies.

PADDLING SUMMARY Some of the best protected-waterway paddling in the state, with great lush forests, deep fjords, and open beaches for camping. There are also paddling opportunities among the icebergs, with proper precautions, of course. Routes can be easily accessed just a few miles from the park visitor center or as far away as 50 or 60 miles.

DIRECTIONS Access to Glacier Bay is by small plane, usually from Ketchikan or Juneau. **Alaska Airlines** (☎ 800-426-0333; **www.alaskaair.com**)

Alaska Mountain Guides and Climbing School
☎ 800-766-3396
www.alaskamountainguides.com

REGIONAL LOCATION	SOUTHEAST
COST	$$
SUITABLE FOR KIDS?	YES
ACTIVITY LEVEL	LIGHT–MODERATE
TRIP LENGTH	1–7 DAYS

Alaska on the Home Shore Coastal Wilderness Adventures
☎ 800-287-7063 or 360-738-2239
www.homeshore.com

REGIONAL LOCATION	SOUTHEAST
COST	$$$$
SUITABLE FOR KIDS?	NO
ACTIVITY LEVEL	LIGHT–MODERATE
TRIP LENGTH	8 DAYS

Alaska Sea Kayakers
☎ 877-472-2534 or 907-472-2534
www.alaskaseakayakers.com

REGIONAL LOCATION	SOUTHCENTRAL COASTAL
COST	$$$
SUITABLE FOR KIDS?	SOME
ACTIVITY LEVEL	MODERATE
TRIP LENGTH	1–5 DAYS

Lifetime Adventures
☎ 907-952-8624
www.lifetimeadventures.net

REGIONAL LOCATION	SOUTHCENTRAL COASTAL
COST	$$$
SUITABLE FOR KIDS?	NO
ACTIVITY LEVEL	MODERATE
TRIP LENGTH	7 DAYS

Liquid Adventures
☎ 888-325-2925
www.liquid-adventures.com

REGIONAL LOCATION	SOUTHCENTRAL COASTAL
COST	$$
SUITABLE FOR KIDS?	SOME TRIPS
ACTIVITY LEVEL	MODERATE–HIGH
TRIP LENGTH	1–5 DAYS

Miller's Landing
☎ 866-541-5739 or 907-224-5739
www.millerslandingak.com

REGIONAL LOCATION	SOUTHCENTRAL COASTAL
COST	$$
SUITABLE FOR KIDS?	SOME TRIPS
ACTIVITY LEVEL	MODERATE
TRIP LENGTH	DAY TRIP/CUSTOM

Southeast Sea Kayaks
☎ 800-287-1607 or 907-225-1258
www.kayakketchikan.com

REGIONAL LOCATION	SOUTHEAST
COST	$$
SUITABLE FOR KIDS?	YES
ACTIVITY LEVEL	LIGHT–MODERATE
TRIP LENGTH	1–5 DAYS

Sunny Cove Sea Kayaking Co.
☎ 907-224-8810 or 800-770-9119
www.sunnycove.com

REGIONAL LOCATION	SOUTHCENTRAL COASTAL
COST	$$
SUITABLE FOR KIDS?	SOME TRIPS
ACTIVITY LEVEL	MODERATE–HIGH
TRIP LENGTH	1–10 DAYS

True North Adventures
☎ 907-235-0708
www.truenorthkayak.com

REGIONAL LOCATION	SOUTHCENTRAL COASTAL
COST	$$
SUITABLE FOR KIDS?	YES
ACTIVITY LEVEL	MODERATE
TRIP LENGTH	1–3 DAYS

provides daily jet service from Seattle via Juneau to Gustavus during the summer visitor season. The Gustavus airport is ten miles by road from park headquarters at Bartlett Cove. Shuttles usually are available. **Glacier Bay Lodge and Tours** (☎ 888-229-8687; **www.visitglacierbay.com**) began offering a ferry between Bartlett Cove and Auk Bay, outside of Juneau. The fare is $75 one-way, and no vehicles are allowed. Check in future years to see if the service is still available, and be sure to give advance warning if you are loading a kayak.

PADDLING DESCRIPTION Glacier Bay is perhaps one of the best places for kayaking in Alaska, which also means you will be sharing the land with many other kayakers enjoying this wonderful Southeast Alaska park. However, remember that Alaska is a *huge* place, and here the term *crowded* often can be translated into "We saw ten people during our week on the water."

Actually, it's quite possible you will encounter more than ten people at the height of the kayaking season in Glacier Bay, but you can still have a wonderfully blissful experience. The infrastructure in Glacier Bay is such that planning your own trip is quite simple. A concessionaire within the

unofficial **TIP**
Experienced Glacier Bay paddlers can handle the open water alone if they understand the conditions, but the real risk is the constant flow of cruise ships and pleasure boats. The largest ships can barely make out a kayak, so always paddle on the defensive, assuming they do not see you. We prefer taking the water taxi across because it eliminates the open-water paddle, which is just a lot of work, really!

park helps plan trips, offers shuttles, and rents kayaks (see Resources below). With their help, your trip will be relatively hassle-free.

Be prepared for wilderness camping conditions, wildlife encounters, and finicky weather. Southeast Alaska can be rainy and foggy, making for cold, wet conditions even in summer. Temperatures in the summer range from a dry, warm 70°F to cool, wet, and windy weather in the 50s.

The park is gorgeous, with snowcapped mountain ranges rising 15,000 feet and higher, and coastal beaches that offer some of the most protected kayaking in the state. There are receding glaciers, complex tide pools, deep fjords, and long valleys.

The four most popular areas for kayaking are **Bartlett Cove** and the **Beardslee Islands,** which make for great two- to three-day adventures, and the **West Arm** and **Muir Inlet,** which are farther out and offer a glimpse of tidewater glaciers. These trips are in the five- to ten-day range.

Resources

- All of Glacier Bay is included in **NOAA Nautical Chart 17318** (available at **nauticalcharts.noaa.gov/mcd/ccatalogs.htm**). **U.S. Geological Survey (USGS)** maps also are helpful (check with one of the **Alaska Public Lands Information Centers** listed in Part Three, or go to **www.usgs.gov** and click on "Maps, Products & Publications"). Tide tables are provided at no charge at the **Bartlett Cove Visitor Information Station** (☎ 907-697-2627) during the required camper orientation.
- The **Alaska Natural History Association** offers several books that focus solely on Glacier Bay National Park and Preserve. ***Adventure Kayaking: Trips in Glacier Bay*** by Don Skillman is worth checking out if you want to read about your route in great detail ($12.95; ☎ 866-257-2757 or **www.alaskanha.org**). Limited copies are available at the Bartlett Cove Information Station. The book is available locally at the **Glacier Bay Alaska Natural History Association** (P.O. Box 140, Gustavus 99826-0140; ☎ 907-697-2635).
- **Glacier Bay Sea Kayaks** (☎ 907-697-2257; **www.glacierbaysea kayaks.com**) is the kayak-rental concessionaire in the park. They also lead the required backcountry camper orientations and can help arrange water taxis for drop-offs and pickups. Kayak rentals range from $35 for a single for a half day to $45 per day for an expedition-sized double kayak being used for ten days or more. A double kayak for the average three-day trip is $40 per day. Rental and transportation outfits in Gustavus include **Sea Otter Kayaks Glacier Bay** (☎ 907-697-3007; **www.he.net/~seaotter,** which although very friendly and capable is a bit overpriced) and the **M/V *Taz* Cross Sound Express** (☎ 888-698-2726 or 907-766-3000; **www.gustavus.com/taz/tours.html**).

- Visitor information is available at the **Gustavus Visitors Association** (☎ 907-697-2454; **www.gustavusak.com** or **www.gustavus.com**).
- The **Southeast Alaska Discovery Center** in Ketchikan (50 Main Street, Ketchikan 99901; ☎ 907-228-6220; **www.nps.gov/aplic**) can help with trip planning in other regions of Southeast Alaska.
- Taxi service in and around Gustavus is available through **TLC Taxi** (☎ 907-697-2239). They can accommodate kayaks.
- ***Trails Illustrated*** has a map of Glacier Bay National Park, Number 255 ($9.95; available through the Alaska Natural History Association (☎ 866-257-2757; **www.alaskanha.org**) or at the Bartlett Cove Visitor Information Station).

Glacier Bay–Southeast-area Outfitters

- **Alaska Discovery:** ☎ 800-586-1911; **www.akdiscovery.com;** Juneau. With nine adventures, Alaska Discovery is perhaps one of the most versatile kayaking companies in Southeast, and one of the most experienced, even though they are now owned by an Outside company. Trips range from whale-watching at Point Adolphus to exploring Glacier Bay. Choose trips from three to nine days long. Prices range from $1,155 for three days of coastal paddling to $3,715 for the nine-day Ultimate sea-kayaking adventure.
- **Alaska Mountain Guides and Climbing School:** ☎ 800-766-3396; **www.alaskamountainguides.com;** Haines. Offers the ultimate in versatile sporting adventures. The company's experienced guides offer sea-kayaking trips up the Inside Passage, in Lynn Canal out of Haines, and in Glacier Bay. No experience is necessary for these half-day to seven-day trips; prices range from $85 to $2,200.
- **Alaska on the Home Shore Coastal Wilderness Adventures:** ☎ 800-287-7063, 360-738-2239; **www.homeshore.com;** Deming, Washington, and Glacier Bay. Home Shore offers three memorable kayaking adventure routes in the Sitka and Petersburg areas and up the Inside Passage, giving you alternative destinations to Glacier Bay. Focusing on wildlife, especially whale-watching, guides will take you gliding past lush Admiralty Island, historic Baranof Island, and scenic Chichagof Island. This option is nice because it includes lodging in a cozy stateroom aboard Home Shore's adventure ship. The eight-day trip starts at $3,200 per person for groups of four or more.
- **Southeast Exposure Alaska Sea Kayaking Adventures:** ☎ 907-225-8829; **www.southeastexposure.com;** Ketchikan. Since 1986, Southeast Exposure has been taking guests on some great trips in the area, from scenic no-experience-necessary trips through Clover Passage out of Ketchikan to expeditions in Misty Fjords National Monument, another kayaking jewel in Southeast Alaska. They also offer tours through the rain-forest trees via zip lines and ropes, but they're mostly geared to cruise-ship passengers. Trips range from six hours to six days and from $125 to $950.
- **Southeast Sea Kayaks:** ☎ 800-287-1607 or 907-225-1258; **www.kayakketchikan.com;** Ketchikan. Takes guests on half-day, full-day,

and overnight kayak excursions in and around Misty Fjords National Monument. Overnight trips give you a weekend or five days to explore Misty Fjords in depth. These trips are designed for novice and experienced paddlers and focus on the scenery and abundant wildlife of the area. The weekend trip is $899, and the five-day Misty Fjords trip costs $1,399.

Kachemak Bay

Regional location Southcentral Coastal Alaska. **Distance** You choose. **Difficulty** 🫎🫎. **Suitable for kids?** Yes. **Time to paddle** 3–5 days. **Best time of year to go** June–September. **Traffic level** Moderate–heavy. **Facilities** Established campsites, private lodge options, public-use cabins, marked trailheads.

PADDLING SUMMARY **Kachemak Bay State Park** is one of the jewels of the Kenai Peninsula, with glaciers and snowcapped mountains dipping dramatically to coastal waters that creep into protected inlets, shaded coves, and wide bays. It's a great place for wildlife-watching and exploring in protected waters.

DIRECTIONS Kachemak Bay is off the coast of **Homer,** a seaside community at the tip of the Kenai Peninsula at the end of the Sterling Highway. From Anchorage, drive approximately 225 miles south on the Seward Highway, then the Sterling Highway. Park at the Homer Spit long-term parking area, which we have found to be relatively safe. You can also get there by air from Anchorage aboard **Alaska Airlines** commuter flights (☎ 800-426-0333; **www.alaskaair.com**).

PADDLING DESCRIPTION Many exciting coves and bays make great kayaking destinations in Homer, including **Sadie Cove, Otter Cove,** and **Tutka Bay.** We are going to describe Tutka Bay, but pull out a map and take a look yourself; there are myriad options.

unofficial **TIP**
Camping in Tutka Bay is generally wherever you can find a clear spot, but be sure to avoid any beaches that are near homes, as you could be trespassing.

Tutka Bay is nine miles across Kachemak Bay to the south of Homer and has only about 30 year-round residents; you will spot homes and cabins tucked in the woods as you paddle along the coves and lagoons in this bay. The area looks dramatic, with virgin forests and cascading waterfalls visible from a distance. The tide pooling is terrific, and we have enjoyed many a clam plucked from the beaches at low tide. Although people live here, there are no stores or facilities in the area.

For a nice four-day paddle, get dropped off at the head of the bay, at a protected beach just across from **Tutka Bay Wilderness Lodge.** You can set up camp in the woods and spend the day paddling around the mouth of the bay and peeking into **Little Tutka Bay** when the tide is right.

On day two, you can paddle deeper into the bay, stopping at the defunct Tutka fish hatchery at **Tutka Lagoon.** The best time to go into the area is at high tide, when the water is deep—get caught there at mid- to low tide when the shoals are exposed and you'll have to wait a while to get out. The Tutka hatchery, once managed by the Cook Inlet

Aquaculture Association, produced pink salmon, which returned to Tutka Creek at spawning time. Tutka Bay is still the most consistent producer of pink salmon in the area, so if you want to fish on light tackle, this will be a fun endeavor. The first two weeks of July are the peak.

There is one established public camping area in Tutka Bay, past the hatchery on a spit of land jutting into the water, but it has seen heavy use. If you choose to camp here, beware of bold squirrels that will filch your food, and avoid building campfires unless you can use driftwood. The trees have been scavenged.

In 2007, Alaska State Parks, through an agreement with Nomad Yurts, allowed the addition of six yurts for rent at various locations in Kachemak State Park, all within 100 yards of the coastline. Each yurt has bunks, woodstove, table and chairs, and sleeps a maximum of five people. Wood for the stove is provided. (☎ 907-235-0132; **www.nomadshelter.com**). Rentals are $65 per day.

On day three, leave your tent (or yurt) site intact and take a basecamp paddle to the mouth of the bay. Hop out for a walk in the woods or paddle the opposite side of the bay for a different perspective. Camp in the same spot.

On day four, return to your original location for a prearranged meeting with your water taxi. You will probably have time to explore Sadie Cove, to the north, by popping out into Eldred Passage and swinging into the next bay. Only attempt this in good weather and if you are confident in your paddling abilities.

Communications, if you are traveling with a marine radio, are by VHF Channel 16, CB Channel 13. There also is a telephone at **Tutka Bay Wilderness Lodge** (see Resources below), although it should only be used in emergencies. Overall, the paddling in Tutka Bay and the vicinity is easy, assuming the weather is good. Even if there are high seas, the coves and lagoons stay protected and offer paddling close to shore, but use good judgment: one flip and you can be in danger quickly.

Resources

- **Homer Ocean Charters** (☎ 800-426-6212 or 907-235-6212; **www.homerocean.com**) can get you safely across the bay, which we recommend. Even in good water, there is a lot of boat traffic, both commercial fishing and recreational, and you can get swamped easily. A round-trip is $65, with discounts for larger groups and children.
- Call the **Marine Advisory Program** (☎ 907-269-7640) to check on shellfish-harvesting conditions, or ask at local charter offices. Only clams on the south side of Kachemak Bay are tested for paralytic shellfish poisoning (discussed in the beginning of this chapter). Clamming in all other locations is at your own risk. Kachemak Bay is generally safe.
- **NOAA Nautical Chart 16645** for Tutka Bay and Tutka Bay Lagoon is available at **nauticalcharts.noaa.gov/mcd/ccatalogs.htm.** Use the Seldovia Tide Tables for Tutka Bay.
- To insert some luxury into your Tutka Bay adventure, book a few nights at the posh **Tutka Bay Wilderness Lodge** (☎ 800-606-3909 or

907-235-3905; **www.tutkabaylodge.com**), a remote four-star retreat that offers the finest in rooms, food, amenities, and overall spoiling. Rates are steep, beginning at $790 per person for a two-night package, but this is a place you won't forget.

Kachemak Bay Outfitters

- **Alaska Kayak School:** ☎ 907-235-2090; **www.alaskakayakschool.com.** This outfit not only serves as an educational center but also offers adventures to locals and visitors alike. It can provide great advice on the proper gear to use when in Alaska, and might even have it for sale in its used-items collection. Schedules vary according to the teaching schedule.
- **True North Adventures:** ☎ 907-235-0708; **www.truenorthkayak.com.** This outfit will take you to Eldred Passage near Tutka Bay for guided kayaking. Half-day trips start at $90. All-day trips are $139. Overnighters also are available for $350 or $480 for three days. This outfit is one of the most experienced in Homer, and the guides are friendly and knowledgeable about the area. They also rent kayaks for do-it-yourselfers; $45 for singles, $65 for doubles.

Katmai Coast

Regional location The Bush. **Distance** 30–50 miles. **Difficulty**. **Suitable for kids?** No. **Time to paddle** 6–10 days. **Best time of year to go** June–September. **Traffic level** Light. **Facilities** None; camping on beaches, islands.

PADDLING SUMMARY **Katmai National Park** comprises 4.7 million acres and hundreds of miles of coastline for exploration, with chances to view the more than 2,000 brown bears that frequent the area. This is one of the most unobtrusive ways to watch these creatures in their natural habitat.

DIRECTIONS Access is by small plane from Kodiak, Homer, or King Salmon, where park headquarters is located. **Alaska Airlines** provides daily flights into these towns (☎ 800-426-0333; **www.alaskaair.com**). Driving to Homer and flying from there is the cheapest option because it eliminates the flight to King Salmon or Kodiak.

PADDLING DESCRIPTION The coast of Katmai National Park is one of the most ecologically diverse areas in Alaska, and it is an especially nice place to kayak because the chances are good that you will see more bears than humans on this adventure. The beaches along Katmai are home to some of the largest concentrations of brown bears in the world, and viewing them from the comfort of a kayak that is safely out of their way is a truly unforgettable experience. Katmai also is home to hundreds of species of migratory birds such as puffins, cormorants, kittiwakes, and murres. Whales and porpoises are common, too.

unofficial **TIP**
The Katmai Coast also has active volcanoes and wonderful hiking.

The mountains of Katmai provide a dramatic backdrop, with 15 active volcanoes sprouting up here and there. This is why the park also is home to a region known as the **Valley of 10,000 Smokes.** While

Prince William Sound and Southeast Alaska are certainly gorgeous, the privacy that one feels in Katmai is simply unsurpassed, and that is why this trip is high in our best-of selection. Even in Alaska, it sometimes can be hard to find total solitude. Not many people come here to kayak; but a lot of them come to see bears—about 900 applied for permits to the nearby McNeil River Bear Viewing Area in 2006, but only 183 permits were issued. We say you can do both and get away from those crowds.

Katmai is a 4.7-million-acre national park and preserve, home to more than 2,000 brown bears, which congregate by the dozens during salmon-spawning season to feed on the carcasses of the nutrient-rich fish. They usually congregate in **Brooks Camp** along the Brooks River and the **Naknek Lake** and **Brooks Lake** shorelines. However, the bears' range goes beyond this region, and they can be found all along the 480-mile Katmai Coast feeding on clams, crabs, and an occasional whale carcass.

The paddling is excellent from **Kukak Bay** to **Geographic Harbor** and beyond. Plenty of camping is available along the beaches and islands on this stretch of coast. There are countless fjords, islands, bays, and rocky headlands to explore, and all along the way are views of the volcanoes.

Resources

- For more information on **Katmai National Park,** contact Field Headquarters (P.O. Box 7, 1 King Salmon Mall, King Salmon 99613; ☎ 907-246-3305) or Administrative Headquarters (4230 University Drive, Suite 311, Anchorage 99508-4626). The Web site is **www.nps.gov/katm.**
- **NOAA Nautical Chart 16603** covers Kukak Bay and Kukak Point; 16576 and 16580 cover Geographic Bay. Available at **nauticalcharts.noaa.gov/mcd/ccatalogs.htm.**

Katmai Coast Outfitters

- **Alaska Alpine Adventures:** ☎ 877-525-2577 or 907-781-2253; **www.alaskaalpineadventures.com.** The company specializes in this awesome Katmai Coast paddle, which is truly a once-in-a-lifetime opportunity. Their 12-day trip includes 9 days of paddling in the remote national park. The cost is $3,300.
- **Lifetime Adventures:** ☎ 800-952-8624; **www.lifetimeadventures.net.** This company offers a guided seven-day trip kayaking the Savonoski Loop, a high-level kayak trip that will allow you to glimpse all manner of wildlife. The rate is $1,700 per person, which is a steal, but that doesn't include food, so be sure to factor in that added cost.

Prince William Sound

Regional location Southcentral Coastal Alaska. **Distance** Infinite options. **Difficulty**. **Suitable for kids?** In some places. **Time to paddle** 3–15 days is ideal; good location for expeditions. **Best time of year to go** June–September. **Traffic level** Moderate close to towns. **Facilities** Some public-use cabins and camping areas; some marked trailheads onshore.

PADDLING SUMMARY One of the largest areas for kayak exploration, this region of the state is a paddler's paradise. Glaciers, forested islands on inland hiking trails, excellent fishing, and flat-calm protected waterways are just some of the highlights. A particularly active place for wildlife.

DIRECTIONS There are several ways to access Prince William Sound. By vehicle, drive from Anchorage east on the Glenn Highway and south on the Richardson Highway until you reach the town of Valdez, at the head of Prince William Sound. Or drive south from Anchorage on the Seward Highway to the Portage Valley Road through the Anton Anderson Memorial Tunnel, which spits you out at the sound in the tiny town of Whittier. You can also fly into Valdez or Cordova on **Alaska Airlines** (☎ 800-426-0333; **www.alaskaair.com**) or take the **Alaska Marine Highway** ferry system from points south (☎ 800-642-0066; **www.ferryalaska.com**).

PADDLING DESCRIPTION If anything is synonymous with Prince William Sound, it is kayaking, and for good reason. From Valdez to Cordova to Whittier, this vast body of water at the northern tip of the Gulf of Alaska offers some of the most protected waterways in Southcentral Coastal Alaska.

Surrounded to the west by the **Kenai Mountains** and the east by the **Chugach Mountains,** the area is literally bounded by peaks. Its 15,000 square miles are all open to exploration. There are whales, sea otters, seals, sea lions, and more seabirds than you can imagine. On land, there are Dall sheep, fox, mountain goats, deer, and plenty of bears (mostly black bears).

Prince William Sound lends itself to longer kayaking expeditions, although overnight and day trips are easily accomplished as well. It's just that there is so much to see, it is hard to resist the "just around the next corner" mentality. You could do that for days and still only scrape the surface of what this area has to offer.

unofficial **TIP**
Camping in Prince William Sound is relatively easy, although you may have to search for good sites in some locations. It's a good idea to get maps ahead of time and estimate your route before leaving. Even if you plan to travel alone, contact local outfitters for their advice.

The best places from which to launch a Prince William Sound trip are **Whittier** and **Valdez** because the easy road access eliminates part of the expense. However, don't overlook trips that leave from **Cordova,** the other primary Prince William Sound community, accessible only by ferry or airplane. If privacy and solitude are your goals, you might consider a Cordova-based trip.

Columbia Glacier is the most impressive of Prince William Sound's many glaciers, but paddling among the bergs near any of the glaciers is an awe-inspiring feat. (Never approach too closely, though—calving ice can flip a kayak before you can blink.)

Resources

- Kayak rentals are available in **Cordova, Valdez,** and **Whittier** (see Outfitters listing opposite).
- ***Kayaking and Camping in Prince William Sound,*** by Paul Twardock, features maps and sketches of many of the trips outlined in the book.

Twardock is a well-respected paddler in Alaska with more than 20 years of guiding and kayaking experience. The book is $18.95, available through the **Alaska Natural History Association,** along with other books and maps on the region (☎ 907-274-8440; **www.alaskanha.org**).

- There are a half-dozen public-use cabins throughout Prince William Sound, managed by **Chugach National Forest,** Glacier Ranger District (☎ 907-783-3242). They cost $25 to $45 per night and must be reserved in advance either over the phone or online (☎ 877-444-6777 or **www.recreation.gov**). Reservations can be made up to 180 days (six months) in advance of the first night's stay. For details about the cabins, visit **www.fs.fed.us/r10/chugach/cabins/index.html.** Visit this site before making your reservations online or over the phone, because the agents at **www.recreation.gov** are located somewhere in the lower 48 states and don't know much about the cabins. The **Alaska Public Lands Information Center** in Anchorage can also help (605 West Fourth Avenue, Suite 105, Anchorage 99501; ☎ 907-271-2737; **www.nps.gov/aplic**).
- More information on the Prince William Sound communities is available through the **Cordova Chamber of Commerce** (☎ 907-424-7260; **www.cordovachamber.com**); the **Valdez Convention and Visitors Bureau** (☎ 800-770-5954; **www.valdezalaska.org**); and the **Greater Whittier Chamber of Commerce** (**www.whittieralaskachamber.org**). Or read up on Prince William Sound in Part 20 (see page 346).

Prince William Sound Outfitters

- **Alaska Sea Kayakers:** ☎ 877-472-2534 or 907-472-2534; **www.alaskaseakayakers.com;** Whittier. Offers day and multiday trips in addition to kayaking, rentals, and kayaking classes. We like this outfit because the guides take you to areas of the sound not explored by most other companies. For a group of four on a "mother ship" tour, the price is $3,000 per day for up to four people. Alaska Sea Kayakers also is one of the few companies that rent fiberglass doubles, if that is your preference ($130 for two days).
- **Anadyr Adventures:** ☎ 800-TO-KAYAK or 907-835-2814; **www.anadyradventures.com;** Valdez. Anadyr has something for everyone. This Prince William Sound company offers mother-ship adventures, lodge-based trips, multiday paddles, and day trips in some of the most spectacular water in Alaska. Also offered are custom trips, youth eco-tours, and theme trips focusing on natural history, ecology, and other fascinating topics. Guides will take you to a variety of bays, glaciers, islands, and waterways within Prince William Sound. Other activities are also available, and we like the company's family-friendly environment. Tours range from three hours to seven days. The popular mother-ship tours start at $425 per person per day.
- **Cordova Coastal Outfitters:** ☎ 907-424-7424; **www.cdvcoastal.com;** Cordova (at the harbor, in the brightly colored boathouse). The company rents kayaks and offers guided half-day, day, and custom

kayak tours to Orca Cove and beyond. Kayaks are $35 per day for singles, $50 for doubles. Guided trips start at $75.

- **Exposure Alaska:** ☎ 907-761-3761 or 800-956-6422; **www.exposurealaska.com;** Anchorage–Prince William Sound. A Prince William Sound trip is among this company's many excursions. No paddling experience is necessary for this seven-day camping adventure, but some moderate hiking is included in the trip. Cost is $1,950 per person and includes amenities designed to make the trip comfortable and enjoyable for each paddler.
- **Pangaea Adventures:** ☎ 800-660-9637 or 907-835-8442; **www.alaskasummer.com;** Valdez. Pangaea takes paddlers on day trips and kayaking-camping trips out of Prince William Sound. A three-hour tour costs $55 and takes in Duck Flats, one of the most calm and unspoiled spots in the area. Wildlife viewing and scenery are phenomenal, and guides will even give you a natural-history lesson. The company's eight-day Whales and Ice Kayak Camp is $1,895 per person and includes trips to Icy Bay and Knight Island, two great areas for paddling among the whales. Pangaea also offers a plethora of other adventures, including numerous multisport trips.
- **Prince William Sound Kayak Center:** ☎ 877-472-2452, 907-276-7235, or 907-742-2452; **www.pwskayakcenter.com;** Whittier. This longtime outfit will teach classes, rent boats, and escort you on your first kayaking outing without adding guide charges—just to make sure you are comfortable. They are one of the most highly respected companies in the field, so you can't go wrong with their trips. Rentals start at $80 per day for doubles and $50 for singles, but the price goes down for added days. Day tours start at $160 and get cheaper the more people you have in your party (as low as $70 per person if six people sign up).

Resurrection Bay

Regional location Southcentral Coastal Alaska. **Distance** Infinite options. **Difficulty** 🛶🛶🛶. **Suitable for kids?** Some areas. **Time to paddle** 3–7 days is ideal. **Best time of year to go** June–September. **Traffic level** Light–moderate. **Facilities** Some public-use cabins, private cabins, and camping areas; some marked trailheads onshore.

PADDLING SUMMARY Resurrection Bay surrounds the coastal community of **Seward,** on the Kenai Peninsula, and is part of **Kenai Fjords National Park,** one of the most visited parks in the state, as well as **Caines Head State Recreation Area.** This glacier-studded waterway is also home to some of the best whale-watching in Alaska.

DIRECTIONS From Anchorage, drive south on the Seward Highway approximately 127 miles until the road ends in Seward. Long-term parking is available by the boat harbor, and water taxis are easily available to take you across to the more-protected waters. Or launch from **Lowell Point,** 3.5 miles south of town, where all the kayaking outfits are located. Regular flights don't go to Seward, but there is a landing strip in town for charter flights. The **Alaska Railroad** travels to Seward from Anchorage

(☎ 800-544-0552 or 907-265-2494; **www.alaska railroad.com**). Rates are $109 round-trip for adults; kayaks cost extra, but we recommend getting your kayak in Seward to save the hassle of loading a boat in Anchorage. The **Alaska Marine Highway** ferry system travels from points south (☎ 800-642-0066; **www.ferryalaska.com**).

unofficial **TIP**
If kayaking with whales is one of your goals, Resurrection Bay is the place to go. It is also one of the least-expensive trips on our list because of its proximity to Anchorage. Be forewarned, though. The Bay can get ultra-windy, so this is an area best suited for very experienced paddlers. If you take a water taxi to more-secluded areas within the bay, the paddling will be easier.

PADDLING DESCRIPTION The options for paddling in Resurrection Bay are about as endless as the sea feels once you are out there. Resurrection Bay—which includes **Kenai Fjords National Park, Caines Head State Recreation Area,** and **Resurrection Bay State Marine Parks**—lies on the southeast coast of Alaska's Kenai Peninsula, capped by the **Harding Ice Field,** the largest ice field within U.S. borders. Otters, puffins, bears, moose, and mountain goats are just a few of the creatures that can be spotted here. Glaciers are everywhere, and whales breach often. This is one of the best places to spot the gray whale on its annual migration from Baja California in Mexico.

You can choose protected bays and inlets or venture to the outer coast for some high seas—this is one of the best places for seasoned kayakers to visit.

Popular destinations include **Fox Island, Thumb Cove, Sunny Cove, Humpy Cove, Kayaker's Cove,** and Kenai Fjords National Park. State-park cabin rentals are available at **Thumb Cove State Marine Park** and Caines Head State Recreation Area. U.S. Forest Service cabin rentals are available in the **Aialik Bay** area of Kenai Fjords National Park.

The climate of the park is maritime, meaning it rains often and is windy most of the time. Dress in layers in gear that can protect you in ultra-wet conditions.

Resources

- Camping is allowed in most areas of **Kenai Fjords National Park.** Three public-use cabins at Aialik, Holgate, and Northarm, along the Kenai Fjords coast, are available on a reservation basis and accessible by boat or floatplane; kayaking trips can be launched from the cabins. For reservations, contact the **Alaska Public Lands Information Center** in Anchorage (☎ 907-271-2737). For more information on Kenai Fjords, contact the **Seward Information Center** (1212 Fourth Avenue; ☎ 907-224-2132 or 907-224-7500; **www.nps.gov/kefj**), which offers maps, publications, videos, interpretive displays, and other helpful resources.
- Caines Head State Recreation Area and **Resurrection Bay State Marine Parks** information: ☎ 907-262-5581; **www.dnr.state.ak.us/parks/units/caineshd.htm.** Cabin rentals can be arranged online at **www.dnr.state.ak.us/parks/cabins/onlineres.htm,** or in person or by mail at the **DNR Public Information Center** (550 West Seventh Avenue, Suite 1260, Anchorage 99501-3557; ☎ 907-269-8400).

- NOAA Nautical Chart 16682 for Resurrection Bay is available at **nauticalcharts.noaa.gov/mcd/ccatalogs.htm.**
- For kayak rentals, see the outfitters listed below.
- For more details on Seward, see page 343 of Part 20, Southcentral Coastal Alaska.

Resurrection Bay Outfitters

- **Liquid Adventures:** ☎ 888-325-2925; **www.liquid-adventures.com;** at Lowell Point, 3.5 miles south of Seward. Explores the waters around Seward, including Holgate Arm, Kenai Fjords, and Northwestern Lagoon. This is our first choice in guides for its laid-back demeanor and years of experience. The main guide is an expert fisherman and can help you land that fish, big or small. From three hours to five days, Liquid Adventures teaches paddlers about the area's landscape, wildlife, and history. The company even offers customized trips upon request. Prices range from $60 to $1,349 per person.
- **Miller's Landing:** ☎ 866-541-5739 or 907-224-5739; **www.millerslandingak.com;** Lowell Point. Kayak rentals are $45 per day for singles, $50 for doubles. An overnight trip to Thumb Cove is $315 per person. An overnight to Kayaker's Cove (one of our favorite Resurrection Bay areas) is $335. Longer tours also are available.
- **Sunny Cove Sea Kayaking Co.:** ☎ 907-224-4426 or 800-770-9119; **www.sunnycove.com;** Lowell Point. Sunny Cove takes you to Lowell Point, Fox Island, and Kenai Fjords National Park on day trips or overnight and multiday kayaking adventures. Prices range from $65 to $1,399 per person.

Shuyak Island

Regional location Southcentral Coastal Alaska. **Distance** 35–40 miles. **Difficulty** . **Suitable for kids?** Yes. **Time to paddle** 3–5 days. **Best time of year to go** June–September. **Traffic level** Very light. **Facilities** 4 public-use cabins, ranger station; kayak-rental facility.

PADDLING SUMMARY Shuyak Island has the most extensive protected-waterway kayaking on all the Kodiak Archipelago. Access to the outer coast provides more-challenging kayaking for experienced paddlers and offers stunning scenery of the forested island and the Katmai Coast, across Shelikof Strait.

DIRECTIONS Shuyak is 40 minutes north of Kodiak, accessible by boat or plane. There is also access via Homer, a 50-minute flight from the north. Access by water taxi is available from Kodiak, but not from Homer.

PADDLING DESCRIPTION Kayakers the world over recognize **Shuyak Island State Park** as one of the best kayaking destinations in Alaska. It is the northernmost of the islands that make up the Kodiak Archipelago, with the state park comprising most of the island's 47,000 acres. The park provides access to an intricate maze of sheltered bays, channels, and inlets and has a limited but impressive trail system for hiking, as well as fishing opportunities in just about every lake, stream, or saltwater location (especially in

August and September, when the silver salmon are spawning). There is an infinite variety of seabirds, otters, whales, harbor seals, sea lions, and Dall porpoises. Even some of Kodiak's famed brown bears wander the island.

Visitors can tent-camp nearly anywhere on the island or rent one of four $60-to-$75-per-night public-use cabins. There is a ranger station at one end of the park and a place to pick up your rented kayak (rental must be arranged in advance), but other than that there are no facilities, and groceries and other supplies must be purchased in Kodiak or Homer.

Resources

- For more information about **Shuyak Island State Park,** contact the Kodiak District Office (1400 Abercrombie Drive, Kodiak 99615; ☎ 907-486-6339; **www.dnr.state.ak.us/parks/units/kodiak/shuyak.htm**). You must reserve cabins in advance. *Important:* Because Kodiak's weather is notorious for changing quickly, work a few extra days into your itinerary in case your plane cannot pick you up as planned.
- **Mythos Expeditions** (☎ 907-486 5536; **www.thewildcoast.com**) is the only outfitter with a permit to lease kayaks out of Shuyak Island State Park. If you don't have your own kayak or don't want to pay to have it shipped to the island, this is the only other option. The rate is $171 (three-day minimum) for doubles, $141 for singles.
- **NOAA Nautical Chart 16604** for Shuyak and Afognak islands is available at **nauticalcharts.noaa.gov/mcd/ccatalogs.htm.**
- The best places to get supplies in Kodiak before leaving are **Safeway** (2685 Mill Bay Road; ☎ 907-486-6811) and **Alaska Commercial Co.** (111 West Rezanof Drive, ☎ 907-486-5761). In Homer, get supplies at **Safeway** (90 Sterling Highway, ☎ 907-235-2408) or **Smoky Bay Natural Foods** (248 West Pioneer Avenue; ☎ 907-235-7252, **www.smokybaynaturalfoods.com**).
- Our number-one choice for an air charter from Kodiak is **SeaHawk Air** (☎ 800-770-4295 or 907-486-8282; **www.seahawkair.com**). From Homer, we recommend **Bald Mountain Air** (☎ 800-470-7969 or 907-235-7969; **www.baldmountainair.com**).
- For more details on planning your trip from Kodiak or Homer, see Part 20, Southcentral Coastal Alaska (page 332).

Shuyak Island Sea-kayaking Outfitters

- **Wilderness Birding Adventures:** ☎ 907-694-7442; **www.wildernessbirding.com.** This is the only outfit that consistently offers trips to Shuyak Island, and they combine birding with kayaking for a well-rounded adventure. Check with them first to see if Shuyak is on their current year's itinerary. The rate is $2,600 for seven days and includes local air and ground transportation (you get to Alaska on your own), kayaks, food, cooking gear, and guide service. The trip combines cabin and tent camping.

PART FIFTEEN

MULTISPORT ADVENTURES

MORE AND MORE IN ALASKA, outdoor travelers are realizing that there are many ways to enjoy the state. A kayaking trip might be perfect for Prince William Sound, but what about all that lovely wooded forest that you paddle by? It just begs to be explored. The rivers and creeks are filled with fish for anglers. The towns are great places to rent a bike and pedal along back roads and trails.

To a certain extent, any experienced outdoor traveler can accomplish a multiadventure trip on his or her own. While kayaking, for instance, you can simply set up a base camp and spend the day hiking. Maybe the next day, you will decide to go fishing. Day three might even include some cycling back in town.

unofficial **TIP**
Outfitters often offer trips that take in more than one region of the state, giving you a sampling of places to explore. They arrange transportation, take care of gear rentals, and book lodging (and, most of the time, meals as well). Sure, you can cobble together your own trip, but handling logistics such as this can be complicated and overwhelming.

This section helps you come up with a few ways to enjoy the state while sampling some of your favorite outdoor recreational activities. But, really, the opportunities are endless. We can't predict what your favorite pastimes are, but we have several favorite outfitters who offer itineraries that cover the gamut.

In this short chapter you'll find details on multisport adventures offered by ten guides and outfitters throughout the state. These trips represent some of our favorite parts of the state, the most esteemed outfitters, and the best variety of adventures within one package.

Use this information in two ways. If you prefer the ease of traveling with a guide (with some added expense), choose a multiple-adventure trip and contact the outfitter. Or use its itineraries as a guide to your own adventure. If, for example, a weeklong hiking-biking-rafting trip sounds to your liking but the price of a guide seems too steep, see what you can come up with on your own.

Go to the special-interest chapters that cover day hikes, cycling, and river running, and find trips that correspond to your needs. Then go to the chapter representing the region (or regions) in which you'll be traveling, and arrange your lodging and dining from there.

Many trips you can probably arrange on your own, but most of them require planning on several levels, which makes using an outfitter more cost-efficient for this type of travel.

For each listing that follows, we indicate whether the outfitter offers custom trips. However, even companies that don't can sometimes be persuaded to accommodate your needs. Therefore, if you see an outfitter listed that piques your interest but doesn't offer the type of trip you're seeking, don't hesitate to ask. In general, we believe using outfitters for multiadventure trips is the best way to go for this type of travel, but we also do not underestimate the ability of any traveler to pull it off on his or her own.

OUR OUTFITTER PICKS

Alaska Alpine Adventures

Based in Port Alsworth, the Bush. **Activities offered** Rafting, backpacking. **Regions visited** Lake Clark National Park and Preserve, Gates of the Arctic National Park. **Cost** $$$. **Activity level** Moderate–high. **Suitable for kids?** No. **Custom trips available?** No. **Contact** ☎ 877-525-2577; **www.alaskaalpineadventures.com.**

OUTFITTER SUMMARY Alaska Alpine is a hard-core outfitter that knows how to create adventure. They've been featured in *Canoe and Kayak, National Geographic,* and *Outside* magazines, among other publications. Their trips generally go where no others do, giving you a truly unique experience. We love places like Denali National Park and Preserve, but, really, there is a lot more to Alaska than that. The outfitter's two coolest trips (among other mountaineering, day-hiking, and rafting-kayaking adventures) include the ten-day Kontrashibuna Lake–Gladiator Basin trip, which includes kayaking on the giant lake in Lake Clark National Park and Preserve, then putting on backpacks and heading to Gladiator Basin. You should be in good shape and able to carry at least 40 pounds. The price: $2,550. For those in even better shape (that is, able to carry at least 60 pounds), there's the Gates of the Arctic National Park expedition, a 12-day trip that takes you backpacking in the Arrigetch range and rafting down the Alatna River. The Alatna's clear water, good fishing, and moderate white water (mostly Class I and II) make it the perfect river for a novice floater and a great complement to strenuous backpacking. The price is $3,895.

Alaska Backcountry Bike Tours

Based in Palmer, Southcentral Inland Alaska. **Activities offered** Mountain biking, fly-fishing, rafting, sea kayaking, ice climbing. **Regions visited** Chugach

Multisport Outfitters at a Glance

Alaska Alpine Adventures
☎ 877-525-2577
www.alaskaalpineadventures.com

REGIONS VISITED	THE BUSH
COST	$$$
SUITABLE FOR KIDS?	NO
ACTIVITY LEVEL	MODERATE–HIGH
TRIP LENGTH	10–12 DAYS

Alaska Backcountry Bike Tours
☎ 866-354-2453
www.mountainbikealaska.com

REGIONS VISITED	SC COASTAL/ INLAND
COST	$
SUITABLE FOR KIDS?	TEENS
ACTIVITY LEVEL	MODERATE–HIGH
TRIP LENGTH	6 DAYS OR LONGER

Alaska Discovery
☎ 800-586-1911
www.akdiscovery.com

REGIONS VISITED	STATEWIDE
COST	$$$$
SUITABLE FOR KIDS?	TEENS
ACTIVITY LEVEL	MODERATE–HIGH
TRIP LENGTH	9 DAYS

Alaska Wildland Adventures
☎ 800-334-8730 or 907-783-2928
www.alaskawildland.com

REGIONS VISITED	STATEWIDE
COST	$$$$
SUITABLE FOR KIDS?	YES
ACTIVITY LEVEL	ALL LEVELS
TRIP LENGTH	5–10 DAYS

Arctic Wild
☎ 877-577-8203
www.arcticwild.com

REGIONS VISITED	INTERIOR, THE BUSH
COST	$$
SUITABLE FOR KIDS?	NO
ACTIVITY LEVEL	MODERATE–HIGH
TRIP LENGTH	7–14 DAYS

Camp Alaska Tours
☎ 907-376-9438; 800-376-9438
www.campalaska.com

REGIONS VISITED	SC COASTAL/ SC INLAND/ THE INTERIOR
COST	$$$
SUITABLE FOR KIDS?	YES
ACTIVITY LEVEL	MODERATE–HIGH
TRIP LENGTH	7–9 DAYS

Center for Alaskan Coastal Studies
☎ 907-235-6667
www.akcoastalstudies.org

REGIONS VISITED	SOUTHCENTRAL COASTAL
COST	$
SUITABLE FOR KIDS?	TEENS
ACTIVITY LEVEL	LIGHT–MODERATE
TRIP LENGTH	1–2 DAYS

Chugach Powder Guides
☎ 907-783-4354
www.chugachpowderguides.com

REGIONS VISITED	SC INLAND
COST	$$$$
SUITABLE FOR KIDS?	NO
ACTIVITY LEVEL	MODERATE–HIGH
TRIP LENGTH	7 DAYS

Get Up and Go! Alaska Tours
☎ 888-868-4147 or 907-245-0795
www.getupandgotours.com

REGIONS VISITED	STATEWIDE
COST	$$
SUITABLE FOR KIDS?	YES
ACTIVITY LEVEL	ALL LEVELS
TRIP LENGTH	1–10 DAYS

Liquid Adventures
☎ 888-325-2925
www.liquid-adventures.com

REGIONS VISITED	SOUTHCENTRAL COASTAL
COST	$$
SUITABLE FOR KIDS?	TEENS
ACTIVITY LEVEL	MODERATE–HIGH
TRIP LENGTH	1–12 DAYS

National Forest; Chugach State Park; and Kenai Peninsula, Seward. **Cost** $. **Activity level** Moderate–high. **Suitable for kids?** Teens. **Custom trips available?** Yes. **Contact** ☎ 866-354-2453; **www.mountainbikealaska.com.**

OUTFITTER SUMMARY Alaska Backcountry specializes in mountain-biking adventures throughout Southcentral Alaska. This outfit is one of our favorites because it is one of the few companies out there that understand the meaning of "single-track," and they make sure that mountain bikers get to experience it. Unique to this company is its combination mountain-bike and sea-kayak trip (it also includes white-water rafting and hiking). Some experience is recommended for this six-day single-track ride. You'll cover more than 65 miles on three favorite Kenai Peninsula trails, but you'll also have time to raft the white-knuckle Sixmile

Creek, go sea kayaking in Kenai Fjords National Park, and hike the locally popular Lost Lake Trail (also a good mountain-biking destination). This tour can also be customized to your interests—just ask Tony! Trip price is $1,795 for camping or $2,195 with five nights' lodging, per person.

Alaska Discovery

Based in Juneau, Southeast Alaska. **Activities offered** Rafting, backpacking, sea kayaking, mountain biking, ice climbing, and more. **Regions visited** Statewide. **Cost** $$$$. **Activity level** Moderate–high. **Suitable for kids?** Teens. **Custom trips available?** No. **Contact** ☎ 800-586-1911; **www.akdiscovery.com.**

OUTFITTER SUMMARY For those who want to fit it all in on their trip to the Great Land, Alaska Discovery offers multisport adventures that cover all quintessential Alaska activities. The eight-day Alaska Gold trip ($3,090 per person) combines glacier trekking, camping, white-water rafting, sea kayaking, whale-watching, mountain biking, and ice climbing in some of the most spectacular areas Southeast Alaska has to offer. The Ultimate adventure ($3,715 with six to ten guests; $3,915 with three to five guests), also nine days, is the company's most popular trip and adds bear viewing at Pack Creek to the Alaska Gold package. Alaska Discovery is likely the longest-running and oldest guiding company in the state, so its trips can seem a bit more polished than those of the family-run businesses. This appeals to some but may feel too slick to others. It's your choice.

Alaska Wildland Adventures

Based in Girdwood, Southcentral Inland Alaska; Cooper Landing, Southcentral Coastal Alaska. **Activities offered** Rafting, kayaking, fishing, canoeing, hiking, camping, gold panning. **Regions visited** Denali National Park and Preserve, Kenai Fjords National Park, Kenai Peninsula. **Cost** $$$$. **Activity level** All levels. **Suitable for kids?** Yes. **Custom trips available?** No. **Contact** ☎ 800-334-8730 or 907-783-2928; **www.alaskawildland.com.**

OUTFITTER SUMMARY Alaska Wildland specializes in multisport, multiactivity adventures for all travelers. We are particularly fond of them for their environmentally responsible way of doing business. In fact, they recently were named one of the best eco-tour operators in the world by *Condé Nast Traveler*. Combined with tourist attractions, including bus and train rides through Denali and wildlife cruises in Kenai Fjords, the company provides opportunities that run the gamut of outdoor activities, generally of a lower adrenaline level, to accommodate all levels of outdoors enthusiasts. They also offer an Alaska photo safari. Trips include a bit of luxury, as you will be based out of the company's well-appointed lodges and cabins. Prices range from $2,500 to $5,000 per person for a week-long adventure.

Arctic Wild

Based in Fairbanks, the Interior. **Activities offered** Hiking, yoga, rafting, backpacking, canoeing. **Regions visited** The Bush, Arctic National Wildlife

Refuge, other Interior locations. **Cost** $$. **Activity level** Moderate–high. **Suitable for kids?** No. **Custom trips available?** Yes. **Contact** ☎ 877-577-8203; **www.arcticwild.com.**

OUTFITTER SUMMARY Arctic Wild offers some of the most interesting boating and backpacking combinations out there, including a 19-day backpack and canoe of the Kokolik River In the western Arctic for $6,100. Other trips include rafting and hiking excursions and wildlife-viewing and backpacking trips with Alaska biologists and naturalists. Canoeing trips and base-camp adventures are also on the menu. Prices start at about $2,300 for four days; nine-day trips average about $2,700.

Camp Alaska Tours

Based in Wasilla, Southcentral Inland Alaska. **Activities offered** Hiking, canoeing, sea kayaking, mountain biking, rafting, glacier trekking. **Regions visited** Interior, Southcentral Inland, Southcentral Coastal. **Cost** $$$. **Activity level** Moderate–high. **Suitable for kids?** Yes. **Custom trips available?** Yes. **Contact** ☎ 800-376-9438 or 907-376-9438; **www.campalaska.com.**

OUTFITTER SUMMARY Camp Alaska Tours specializes in camping tours around the state, but the company also offers a couple of options for multi-adventure trips. The Trailblazer Tour ($1,650 per person) takes you to Interior Alaska and Denali National Park for nine days of hiking, canoeing, kayaking, mountain biking, and rafting. The Pathfinder Trip ($1,850 per person) explores Wrangell–St. Elias National Park, the Chugach Mountains, and Prince William Sound, and includes hiking, rafting, glacier trekking, and kayaking. Camp Alaska even offers tours specially designed for families or women's groups.

Center for Alaskan Coastal Studies–St. Augustine's Kayak and Tours

Based in Homer, Southcentral Coastal Alaska. **Activities offered** Educational eco-tours, sea kayaking, hiking. **Regions visited** Kachemak Bay. **Cost** $. **Activity level** Light–moderate. **Suitable for kids?** Teens. **Custom trips available?** No. **Contact** ☎ 907-235-6667 or 907-299-1894; **www.akcoastalstudies.org.**

OUTFITTER SUMMARY The Center for Alaskan Coastal Studies combines wildlife and ecosystem research with adventure sports for a unique Alaska eco-tour. The center gives guests a special opportunity to experience Alaska's marine life up close. These eco-tours include sea-kayaking, hiking, and natural-history tours, in addition to an overnight stay in one of the yurts at the Peterson Bay Coastal Science Field Station. These unique tours start at $100 for the natural-history tour and $150 for the kayaking-hiking tour. Yurt rentals are $25 to $80 per night.

Chugach Powder Guides

Based in Girdwood, Southcentral Inland Alaska. **Activities offered** Heli-skiing, rafting, king salmon fishing. **Regions visited** Tordrillo Mountains of the Alaska

Range, Southcentral Inland. **Cost** $$$$. **Activity level** Moderate–high. **Suitable for kids?** No. **Custom trips available?** No. **Contact** ☎ 907-783-4354; **www.chugachpowderguides.com.**

OUTFITTER SUMMARY Chugach Powder Guides offers the ultimate Alaska adventure, combining outstanding corn-snow heli-skiing, white-water rafting, and king salmon fishing. You may even get a chance to ski and fish in the same day. Based out of the Tordrillo Mountain Lodge, this adventure provides rough and rugged Alaska sports with all the luxuries of a grand wilderness lodge. This weeklong trip runs $7,900 per person.

Get Up and Go! Alaska Tours

Based in Anchorage, Southcentral Inland Alaska. **Activities offered** Sea kayaking, rafting, hiking, glacier trekking, ice climbing, fishing, canoeing, horseback riding. **Regions visited** Denali Highway, Wrangell–St. Elias National Park, Prince William Sound, Matanuska-Susitna Valley, Denali National Park. **Cost** $$. **Activity level** All levels. **Suitable for kids?** Yes. **Custom trips available?** Yes. **Contact** ☎ 888-868-4147 or 907-245-0795; **www.getupandgotours.com.**

OUTFITTER SUMMARY Get Up and Go! covers the range of multisport adventures. No experience is necessary for any of the company's trips. Guests have the option of tent camping or basing their adventures out of a lodge or cabins. Trips start at around $1,200 per person and range from six to ten days. This is a good option for those traveling with children.

Liquid Adventures

Based in Seward, Southcentral Coastal Alaska. **Activities offered** Sea kayaking, fishing, hiking. **Regions visited** Kenai Fjords National Park, Resurrection Bay. **Cost** $$. **Activity level** Moderate–high. **Suitable for kids?** Teens. **Custom trips available?** Yes. **Contact** ☎ 888-325-2925; **www.liquid-adventures.com.**

OUTFITTER SUMMARY Trends, you will soon notice if you spend enough time in Alaska, are slow to reach the Last Frontier. Maybe it's because we are so far away. Liquid Adventures, for instance, is quite possibly the only outfitter in the state that offers kayak fishing, using specially designed kayaks made for fishing from the ocean. Anglers across the country are enjoying this newly growing sport, combining sea kayaking with fishing for a truly unique adventure. Pull in a giant halibut from your tiny boat—it can be done. Liquid Adventures offers combination fishing-kayaking trips out of Seward using the craft, providing peaceful paddling . . . until you land the big one. Imagine hauling in a 50-pound halibut from a kayak. A bit more adventurous now, isn't it? Prices start at $135 for the half-day trip and $399 for the remote trip. We recommend the latter. You will catch more fish.

PART SIXTEEN

OFF-ROAD ADVENTURES

ALASKA IS PART OF A VAST, UNTAMED LAND in the Northern Hemisphere that attracts visitors seeking solitude and primeval landscapes. It possesses one-fifth the land mass of the Lower 48 and, according to the Alaska Department of Transportation, has only 5,603 miles of connecting highways—some paved, some gravel. More than 90% of America's roads are paved, with the exception of Alaska, which has less than 20% paved. The result: 100%-guaranteed off-roading paradise.

Alaskans use a variety of transportation to get around the Last Frontier—ferries, Bush planes, cars, snowmobiles, four-wheelers, bikes, dogsleds, horses—for recreation and everyday purposes.

In this chapter, we focus on motor vehicles and the thousands of miles you can discover on roads and trails that the Department of Transportation doesn't take into account. We're talking gravelly, muddy, snowy, and sometimes rocky roads that require four-wheel-drive vehicles, all-terrain vehicles, or snowmobiles. Off-roading is a popular yet specialized sport that requires experience and thorough knowledge of the rules and terrain conditions before heading out. Whether you're driving a snowmobile to watch the Iditarod Trail Sled Dog Race near Knik or taking a four-wheeler on a hunt for caribou off the Denali Highway, you must plan ahead, be prepared, and, most of all, love to get dirty (or snowy!).

unofficial **TIP**
Off-roading requires specific tools such as towropes, assorted crescent wrenches, bottle jacks, air pumps, and other automotive hardware, all of which should be provided by guides. Because this gear is readily available, you should familiarize yourself with it before your trip so you won't have to learn to use it on the spot if a mishap does occur.

Unless a vehicle is operating on private property, it must be registered and titled with the state's **Division of Motor Vehicles** (**www.state.ak.us**). But we understand that the majority of visitors won't bring their own off-roading toys to Alaska and likely will be renting or traveling with a guide.

Even if you're not an off-roading novice, it's important to travel with someone who has experience and can show you the terrain. For example, when traveling by snowmobile, it's important to know the science behind the behavior of snow and ice—how they lie, when they fall, under what conditions they are most likely to cause an avalanche, or when ice is too thin to travel across. Traveling with an experienced guide will safely take you places in Alaska that most blacktop dwellers only dream about.

Several regions of the state are popular for off-roading, and many guides are available to help you experience the land responsibly without tearing it to shreds. While other special-interest chapters in *The Unofficial Guide to Adventure Travel in Alaska* show you how to plan a trip on your own, this chapter will not do that. Instead, it presents a listing of the best off-roading locations and outfitters that offer guided trips along tundra, through valleys and forests, and over massive mountain ranges.

OFF-ROADING *in* SOUTHCENTRAL INLAND ALASKA

THE GLENN HIGHWAY AND PART OF THE Richardson Highway are the two major arteries in Southcentral Inland. From these road systems, visitors can exit pavement and enter off-road adventures while remaining close to **Anchorage** or **Glennallen** in Southcentral Inland Alaska, or **Valdez** in Southcentral Coastal Alaska.

Perhaps the most popular off-road destination closest to Anchorage is the **Eklutna Lakeside Trail.** The Eklutna exit is at Mile 26 on the Glenn Highway and follows the Chugach State Park signs. It leads to the gray-blue **Eklutna Lake** and a 13-mile lakeside trail that's surrounded by the jagged peaks of the **Chugach Mountains.** The scenic year-round-four-wheeling and winter-snowmobiling trail gains only 300 feet in elevation. Visitors enjoy its public-use cabins; campsites; glacier views; and wildlife such as black bears, brown bears, sheep, moose, and an occasional wolverine.

As you travel farther north along the Glenn Highway (past the Eklutna exit), the road crosses the silty channels of the **Knik River.** Taking the Old Glenn Highway (an exit before you cross the Knik) can grant visitors access to the river's miles upon miles of dry beds, gradual hills, river crossings, mud holes, and water holes that eventually lead to the **Knik Glacier.**

> *unofficial* **TIP**
> Besides deep river crossings, be aware of Knik Glacier's quicksand. It looks like moist, hard-packed sand, and it can unexpectedly sink your vehicle.

Looking for something a little tamer? Try the **McCarthy Road,** which begins 35 miles south of

Off-road Outfitters at a Glance

Alaska All-Terrain Tours–Alaska Snow Safaris
☎ 888-414-7669 or 907-868-7669
www.atv-alaska.com or www.snowmobile-alaska.com

REGIONAL LOCATION	SOUTHCENTRAL INLAND
COST	$$
SUITABLE FOR KIDS?	VARIES
ACTIVITY LEVEL	ALL LEVELS
TRIP LENGTH	1–7 DAYS

Alaska ATV Adventures
☎ 907-694-4294
www.alaskaatvadventures.com

REGIONAL LOCATION	SOUTHCENTRAL INLAND
COST	$$
SUITABLE FOR KIDS?	VARIES
ACTIVITY LEVEL	LIGHT–MODERATE
TRIP LENGTH	DAY TRIP

Alaska Backcountry Adventure Tours
☎ 800-478-2506 or 907-745-2505
www.youralaskavacation.com

REGIONAL LOCATION	SOUTHCENTRAL INLAND
COST	$$$
SUITABLE FOR KIDS?	SOME
ACTIVITY LEVEL	ALL LEVELS
TRIP LENGTH	1–7 DAYS

Alaska Travel Adventures
☎ 800-323-5757 or 907-789-0052
www.alaskaadventures.com

REGIONAL LOCATION	SOUTHEAST, THE INTERIOR
COST	$$
SUITABLE FOR KIDS?	YES
ACTIVITY LEVEL	LIGHT–MODERATE
TRIP LENGTH	DAY TRIP

Black Diamond Resort Company
☎ 907-683-4653
www.blackdiamondgolf.com

REGIONAL LOCATION	THE INTERIOR
COST	$
SUITABLE FOR KIDS?	YES
ACTIVITY LEVEL	LIGHT
TRIP LENGTH	DAY TRIP

Copper River Adventures and Tours
☎ 907-868-8243
www.alaskaatv.com/info/home.htm

REGIONAL LOCATION	SOUTHCENTRAL INLAND
COST	$
SUITABLE FOR KIDS?	VARIES
ACTIVITY LEVEL	LIGHT–MODERATE
TRIP LENGTH	DAY TRIP

Denali Sightseeing Safaris
☎ 907-240-0357
www.denalisights.com

REGIONAL LOCATION	THE INTERIOR
COST	$$
SUITABLE FOR KIDS?	YES
ACTIVITY LEVEL	LIGHT–MODERATE
TRIP LENGTH	DAY TRIP

Frontier Excursions
☎ 877-983-2512 or 907-983-2512
www.frontierexcursions.com

REGIONAL LOCATION	SOUTHEAST
COST	$$
SUITABLE FOR KIDS?	YES
ACTIVITY LEVEL	LIGHT
TRIP LENGTH	DAY TRIP

the Richardson Highway. This 61-mile dirt road leads to the town of **McCarthy,** the ghost town of **Kennicott,** and into **Wrangell–St. Elias National Park**—the largest park in the United States (six times the size of Yellowstone National Park). It follows the **Copper River** and abandoned **Northwest Railway** and dead-ends on the banks of the **Kennicott River.** Along the way, spur roads lead to primitive campgrounds and remarkable views of the **Wrangell Mountains.**

The following outfitters can lead you to these places and more.

Alaska All-Terrain Tours–Alaska Snow Safaris

Location Anchorage. **Trip length** Hourly–weekly. **Activities offered** Four-wheeling, snowmobiling, dog mushing. **Cost** $$. **Activity level** All levels. **Suitable for kids?** Varies depending on trip. **Best time of year to go** Year-round. **Traffic level** Light. **Contact** ☎ 888-414-7669 or 907-868-7669; **www.atv-alaska.com** or **www.snowmobile-alaska.com.**

OUTFITTER SUMMARY Alaska All-Terrain Tours–Alaska Snow Safaris offers four- and six-hour day tours and overnight trips starting at $189 to $500 per person. Riders explore open meadows, old mining routes, and mountain trails around Southcentral Alaska and the Matanuska-Susitna area. Experienced guides take you past waterfalls and mountain streams right up to the spectacular Knik Glacier. The company that is Alaska All-Terrain Tours in the summer becomes Alaska Snow Safaris in the winter, which offers snow-machine safaris, dog mushing, and other winter activities.

Alaska ATV Adventures

Location Eagle River. **Trip length** Hourly. **Activities offered** Four-wheeling, kayaking. **Cost** $$. **Activity level** Light–moderate. **Suitable for kids?** Varies depending on trip. **Best time of year to go** Late June–early October. **Traffic level** Light–moderate. **Contact** ☎ 907-694-4294; **www.alaskaatvadventures.com.**

OUTFITTER SUMMARY Alaska ATV is good for a day trip or if you just have a few hours to get out and get dirty in Southcentral Alaska. This company guides visitors around the wilderness of Chugach State Park and Chugach National Forest. Take a custom tour, combination ATV and kayak trips at Eklutna Lake, or unique team-building exercises for corporate retreats or family fun. Gold panning, fishing, mountain biking, trap shooting, and other team-oriented activities are combined with group four-wheeler tours to offer an exciting day for everyone. Tours start at $145 per person and include destinations around Eagle River, Eklutna, and Girdwood. Two twists for Alaska ATV Adventures are their other trip offerings: the High Arctic and Polar Bear tours out of Alaska's Arctic and Interior Native villages (visit **www.alaskapolarbeartours.com** for more information).

Alaska Backcountry Adventure Tours

Location Palmer. **Trip length** Hourly–weekly. **Activities offered** Vary. **Cost** $$$. **Activity level** All levels. **Suitable for kids?** Some. **Best time of year to go** Year-round. **Traffic level** Varies. **Contact** ☎ 800-478-2506 or 907-745-2505; **www.youralaskavacation.com.**

OUTFITTER SUMMARY For this trip, four-wheeling isn't just a summer activity. Alaska Backcountry Adventure Tours offers year-round ATV expeditions around Southcentral and Interior Alaska. The emphasis is sightseeing and wildlife viewing—especially caribou—and the tours include three- to seven-hour day tours throughout the year (with meals provided for the longer tour) or overnight camping trips in summer. ATV trips range from $179 to $795 per person. Snowmobiling, hiking, fishing, flightseeing, and rafting are also available. The company operates a bed-and-breakfast, too, with sweeping views of Pioneer Peak in the Matanuska Valley.

Copper River Adventures and Tours

Location Kenny Lake–Copper Center. **Trip length** Hourly. **Activity offered** Four-wheeling. **Cost** $. **Activity level** Light–moderate. **Suitable for kids?** Varies depending on trip. **Best time of year to go** Mid-June–September. **Traffic level** Light. **Contact** ☎ 907-868-8243; **www.alaskaatv.com/info/home.htm.**

OUTFITTER SUMMARY Formerly known as Scotty's ATV Adventures, this outfit gears toward novice riders. It's located on the Copper River and offers visitors of all ages a chance to travel deep into the heart of the Copper River Basin and surrounding mountains. Ride atop scenic bluffs, through diamond willow forests, and along the 1,000-mile Trans-Alaska Pipeline System on this guided tour. Riders can take the two-hour tour for around $75 per person; half-day rentals and specialized tours are available as well.

OFF-ROADING *in* SOUTHEAST ALASKA

ALASKA'S INSIDE PASSAGE is simply known as Southeast. The region is 60% covered by dense forested islands of spruce, hemlock, and cedar. It measures about 125 by 400 miles, and commercial fishing boats practically outnumber automobiles.

unofficial **TIP**
In 2006, the Federal Highway Administration and the U.S. Forest Service were seeking to authorize a Public Forest Service Road program in Alaska, but so far funding has been denied. For off-roading fans, that's a good thing: the 3,600 or so miles of gravel roads are open for fun. Such roads often are rough and poorly marked, though, which is why we recommend guided adventures.

So where are all the roads? Many are old logging routes located throughout the **Tongass National Forest,** the largest national forest in the United States. **Ketchikan,** a quaint town on the western edge of Revillagigedo Island, and **Prince Wales Island,** to the west of Revillagigedo with many abandoned villages, have rugged roads that were built to reach valuable timber.

At Tongass National Forest's northern edge lies the charming town of **Carcross.** It's just outside the more populated Skagway, which is at the end of the **Klondike Highway.** Tour guides will bring you back to the gold-rush era with trips near the famous **Chilkoot Trail** and along **Dead Horse Gulch, Moore Bridge,** and the **Bracket Wagon Trail** aboard sport-utility vehicles.

The following outfitters can lead you to these places and more.

Alaska Travel Adventures

Location Juneau. **Trip length** Hourly. **Activity offered** Jeep safaris. **Cost** $$. **Activity level** Light–moderate. **Suitable for kids?** Yes. **Best time of year to go** June–mid-September. **Traffic level** Light–moderate. **Contact** ☎ 800-323-5757 or 907-789-0052; **www.alaskaadventures.com.**

OUTFITTER SUMMARY Alaska Travel Adventures offers Jeep-safari day trips from Skagway and Ketchikan. The trips are four to five and a half hours long and range from $129 to $139 for adults (children are allowed, too, at lower rates). In Ketchikan, you'll explore the mountainous roads of Tongass National Forest, which take you through lush rain forests and beautiful scenery. The Jeeps are equipped with two-way radios so that your guide can provide you with information on natural history and the timber industry's reforestation methods. Enjoy an Alaskan snack of chowder and smoked salmon at a remote camp before heading back to downtown Ketchikan.

Frontier Excursions

Location Skagway. **Trip length** Hourly. **Activities offered** Four-wheeling, off-road vehicles. **Cost** $$. **Activity level** Light. **Suitable for kids?** Yes. **Best time of year to go** All year. **Traffic level** Light. **Contact** ☎ 877-983-2512 or 907-983-2512; **www.frontierexcursions.com.**

OUTFITTER SUMMARY Offers in-town, off-road, and four-wheel explorations for those who want to get a little closer to the land and its gold-rush history. And while the majority of their tours are via ATV and ORV, those who wish to be pampered a bit can still explore the famous Chilkoot Trail area in the style and comfort of a luxury SUV. Tours are from one and a half to six hours and cost from around $75 to around $200 per person.

OFF-ROADING *in the* INTERIOR

WHEN PEOPLE THINK OF ALASKA'S INTERIOR REGION, visions of rugged gravel highways often come to mind—for good reason. Whether it's off-roading the high tundra along the Alaska Range, snowmobiling across dogsled trails, or kicking up dust on old mining roads, visiting the beautiful Interior usually leaves visitors speechless.

Let's begin with our favorite—the 136-mile **Denali Highway** (110 miles of which are gravel), which stretches from Cantwell to Paxson. From October to mid-May, snow closes the highway and turns the area into a snowmobiling haven. During the tourist season, this can be a dusty drive—especially for four-wheelers—in dry weather. At Mile 37 (if you're driving from Paxson), **Maclaren Summit** marks the highway's highest elevation. Pull out and enjoy gorgeous views of the **Susitna River Valley, Mount Hayes** (13,382 feet), and the **Alaska Range.** Keep your eyes peeled for clear-water streams filled with good fishing, caribou herds roaming across the tundra, and spur roads that seemingly lead to nowhere (and free camping!).

In Healy, visitors find themselves on the edge of **Denali National Park and Preserve**—home to **Denali** (20,320 feet), also known as Mount McKinley, the highest mountain in North America. Only one road (**Denali Park Road**) takes you into the 6-million-acre park, which is bigger than Massachusetts. Off-roading opportunities in certain parts of the park are popular in the summer; in the winter, snowmobiling and dogsleds take over this pristine terrain.

South of Denali National Park and Preserve, about 125 miles, lies **Trapper Creek** and the beginning of the historic **Petersville Road,** which leads to the Petersville Recreation Area. Catch some great views of Denali (weather permitting) and guided history lessons of **Petersville,** a booming mining community in the early 1900s, on a four-wheeler (or a snowmobile in the winter). There are no established campsites or facilities in the recreation area, but several remote lodges lie along the trail system. Low-impact camping is encouraged.

The following outfitters can lead you to these places and more.

Alaska Travel Adventures

Based in Juneau; trips in Denali, Petersville. **Trip length** Hourly. **Activity offered** Jeep safaris. **Cost** $$. **Activity level** Light–moderate. **Suitable for kids?** Yes. **Best time of year to go** Late May–mid-September. **Traffic level** Light. **Contact** ☎ 907-789-0052 or 800-323-5757; **www.alaskaadventures.com.**

OUTFITTER SUMMARY This outfitter offers off-road adventures in Southeast but also goes to the Petersville Road in the Matanuska-Susitna Valley, just north of Talkeetna, and Stampede Road, just north of Denali National Park. The trips are three to five hours long and range from $119 to $145 for adults (children are allowed, too, at lower rates). Petersville Road is mostly unpaved and becomes more rugged and primitive the farther out you drive; Stampede Road was carved out by gold miners years ago. Both trips include a hearty Alaskan snack and keep-what-you-find gold panning.

Black Diamond Resort Company

Location Healy. **Trip length** Hourly. **Activities offered** Variety. **Cost** $. **Activity level** Light. **Suitable for kids?** Yes. **Best time of year to go** Mid-June–early September. **Traffic level** Light–moderate. **Contact** ☎ 907-683-4653; **www.blackdiamondgolf.com.**

OUTFITTER SUMMARY Offers a fantastic full-service restaurant, a nine-hole golf course, ATV adventures, covered-wagon tours, a gift shop, and tundra mini-golf. ATV trips ($85 per person) are two to three hours long and offer great photo ops along the back roads, old coal-mining trails, and historic Athabascan sites just outside Denali National Park.

Denali Sightseeing Safaris

Location South of Cantwell. **Trip length** Hourly. **Activity offered** 4 x 4 monster trucking. **Cost** $$. **Activity level** Light–moderate. **Suitable for kids?** Yes. **Best time of year to go** Mid-June–early September. **Traffic level** Light. **Contact** ☎ 907-240-0357; **www.denalisights.com.**

OUTFITTER SUMMARY If over the river and through the woods is closer to your style than a crowded tour bus, Denali Sightseeing Safaris has the tour for you. Climb aboard one of their three beefy monster trucks (yes, you read right), and enjoy the ride of your life through some of the most spectacular wilderness on the planet. Its trucks weigh 9,000 to 12,000 pounds and have 64-inch tires. These customized tours last six to seven and a half hours (depending on your desires) and cost $140 per person. Be prepared with food and cold-weather clothing.

PART SEVENTEEN

RIVER RUNNING

ALASKA BOASTS MORE THAN 3,000 RIVERS, many of which are suitable for running in canoes, kayaks, or, most popularly, rafts. These adventures range from leisurely float trips to white-water adrenaline rushes. It doesn't matter where you go in the state—from Southeast Alaska to the Far North—there are rivers to be explored.

We think all of Alaska's rivers are beautiful, but 25 are considered so spectacular that they have been named National Wild and Scenic Rivers; only Oregon has more such designated.

This chapter introduces you to just a small sampling—the best of the best—of Alaska's rivers. We have provided two sections, one for splashy day trips that can be enjoyed in a few hours or a full day, and multiday float trips that can take as long as ten days. Our river descriptions are brief and designed to pique your interest in one or the other based on a given overview. As any river runner knows, once you've selected your river of choice, it helps immensely to get detailed descriptions, topographic maps, hints from local experts, and up-to-date weather conditions so you can accurately assess the river's safety.

To that end, we offer additional resources that can help make your river-running trip a success. The more information you have before your trip, the better prepared you will be for any possible surprises.

CHECKLIST *for* SUCCESS

- **Obtain current information on the river you plan to paddle.** Water levels can change drastically, even with small amounts of rainfall or snowmelt. Bush pilots, park rangers, and local outfitters are the best sources of information because they are on the rivers regularly. Another good information source is the Anchorage-based group **Knik Canoers and Kayakers** (**www.kck.org**).
- **Protect against hypothermia.** Many of Alaska's rivers are glacially fed. (Need we mention they are cold?) Always wear a wet or dry suit and

Alaska River Running at a Glance

	American Creek	Canning River	Chilkat River
REGIONAL LOCATION	THE BUSH	THE BUSH	SOUTHEAST
DISTANCE	50 MILES	125 MILES	20 MILES
TRAFFIC	LIGHT	LIGHT	LIGHT–MODERATE
DIFFICULTY	CLASS I–III	CLASS II–III	CLASS I
TRIP LENGTH	4–9 DAYS	7–12 DAYS	DAY TRIP
SUITABLE FOR KIDS?	YES	NO	YES
GUIDE SUGGESTED?	HIGHLY RECOMMENDED	HIGHLY RECOMMENDED	RECOMMENDED

	Lowe River	Matanuska River–Lion Head	Nenana River
REGIONAL LOCATION	SOUTHCENTRAL COASTAL	SOUTHCENTRAL INLAND	THE INTERIOR
DISTANCE	5–25.5 MILES	5.3 MILES	8–38 MILES
TRAFFIC	LIGHT–MODERATE	LIGHT–MODERATE	LIGHT
DIFFICULTY	CLASS III	CLASS III–IV	CLASS II–IV
TRIP LENGTH	DAY TRIP	DAY TRIP	DAY TRIP
SUITABLE FOR KIDS?	NO	YES	SOME PARTS
GUIDE SUGGESTED?	HIGHLY RECOMMENDED	HIGHLY RECOMMENDED	RECOMMENDED

appropriate footwear on rivers with Class III rapids or above. Your chances of falling in are higher on some rivers than others, so it's best to play it safe. Ask at your local kayak or raft-rental facility for water-wear rentals.

- **Always wear a helmet and life vest** that are beefy enough to hold you up under the pressure of river water. (Lighter personal flotation devices are OK for lakes and other calm waters.)
- **Carry basic first-aid items,** including bandages to patch up minor cuts as well as any specific medications that may be needed for anyone in your traveling party.
- **Pack a whistle, flares,** or something else that can be used as an SOS device in an emergency.
- **Don't go alone.** Always run rivers with at least one other person, and stay within shouting or whistling distance. A two-person rescue is much easier than a self-rescue.

GENERAL RIVER-RUNNING RESOURCES

- The **Alaska Kayak School** in Homer (☎ 907-235-2090; **www.alaskakayakschool.com**) can offer advice on white-water and sea kayaking.
- The **Alaska Natural History Association** (☎ 866-257-2757; **www.alaskanha.org**) carries many Alaska-themed books, including volumes on river travel and rivers in general.
- The **Alaska River Forecast Center** in Anchorage (6930 Sand Lake Road; ☎ 907-266-5160; **aprfc.arh.noaa.gov/data**) tracks water levels and dangers. Check with the center before departing on a trip on your own.

Copper River		Eagle River		Kenai River	
REGIONAL LOCATION	SC COASTAL/ INLAND	REGIONAL LOCATION	SOUTHCENTRAL INLAND	REGIONAL LOCATION	SOUTHCENTRAL COASTAL
DISTANCE	100 MILES	DISTANCE	8–21 MILES	DISTANCE	18 MILES
TRAFFIC	LIGHT	TRAFFIC	MODERATE	TRAFFIC	MODERATE–HEAVY
DIFFICULTY	CLASS I	DIFFICULTY	CLASS II–IV	DIFFICULTY	CLASS II–III
TRIP LENGTH	6 DAYS	TRIP LENGTH	DAY TRIP	TRIP LENGTH	DAY TRIP
SUITABLE FOR KIDS?	YES	SUITABLE FOR KIDS?	SOME PARTS	SUITABLE FOR KIDS?	YES
GUIDE SUGGESTED?	RECOMMENDED	GUIDE SUGGESTED?	RECOMMENDED	GUIDE SUGGESTED?	RECOMMENDED

Nizina River		Sixmile Creek		Tatshenshini-Alsek Rivers	
REGIONAL LOCATION	SOUTHCENTRAL INLAND	REGIONAL LOCATION	SOUTHCENTRAL COASTAL	REGIONAL LOCATION	SOUTHEAST
DISTANCE	45 MILES	DISTANCE	9 MILES	DISTANCE	129 MILES
TRAFFIC	LIGHT	TRAFFIC	MODERATE	TRAFFIC	LIGHT
DIFFICULTY	CLASS II–III	DIFFICULTY	CLASS III–V	DIFFICULTY	CLASS I–IV
TRIP LENGTH	2–3 DAYS	TRIP LENGTH	DAY TRIP	TRIP LENGTH	9–12 DAYS
SUITABLE FOR KIDS?	YES	SUITABLE FOR KIDS?	NO	SUITABLE FOR KIDS?	SOME PARTS
GUIDE SUGGESTED?	RECOMMENDED	GUIDE SUGGESTED?	YES	GUIDE SUGGESTED?	YES

- *The Alaska River Guide* by Karen Jettmar outlines 85 waterways worth exploring throughout the state. Updated in 2008, her book is well regarded by locals and is a must-have for any in-depth river trip in Alaska. $17.95; available at Amazon.com and **www.menasharidge.com.**
- *Fast and Cold: A Guide to Alaska Whitewater* by Andrew Embick is a great resource for any paddler intent on sampling Alaska's rivers. Embick was a well-known expert in Alaska on the most challenging white water in Southcentral and beyond, completing trips so difficult that some have never been duplicated. The book provides in-depth details of each of the 79 trips outlined. $27.50; available at bookstores in Alaska and Amazon.com.
- The Web sites **www.riverfacts.com** and **www.americanwhitewater.org** are helpful for getting details on the rivers of your choice.

There are some sports that, because of their inherent risks, are best left to the experts to lead. We believe that river running is one of them. If, however, you are intent on traveling alone, do not use this chapter as your sole source of information during planning: it is meant mainly to discuss our favorite trips based on years of living and playing in Alaska, and these are samplings that just scratch the surface of what is out there. Entire books have been written about running rivers in Alaska—for starters, we suggest reading the ones above before you leave.

unofficial **TIP**
Even if you're an experienced paddler, it can be difficult to read Alaska's often-silty water, and immersion in the colder-than-normal waters can lead to problems much sooner than it would in locations in the Lower 48.

River-running Outfitters at a Glance

Alaska Discovery
☎ 800-586-1911
www.akdiscovery.com

REGIONAL LOCATION	SOUTHEAST
COST	$$$
SUITABLE FOR KIDS?	TEENS
ACTIVITY LEVEL	MODERATE–HIGH
TRIP LENGTH	9–12 DAYS

Alaska Outdoors
☎ 800-320-2494
www.alaskaoutdoorstours.com

REGIONAL LOCATION	SOUTHCENTRAL INLAND
COST	$$$
SUITABLE FOR KIDS?	TEENS
ACTIVITY LEVEL	MODERATE–HIGH
TRIP LENGTH	6 DAYS

Alaska Rivers Company
☎ 888-595-1226
www.alaskariverscompany.com

REGIONAL LOCATION	SOUTHCENTRAL COASTAL
COST	$$
SUITABLE FOR KIDS?	YES
ACTIVITY LEVEL	LIGHT–MODERATE
TRIP LENGTH	DAY TRIP

Alaska Wildland Adventures
☎ 800-334-8730 or 907-783-2928
www.alaskawildland.com

REGIONAL LOCATION	SOUTHCENTRAL COASTAL
COST	$$
SUITABLE FOR KIDS?	MOST TRIPS
ACTIVITY LEVEL	LIGHT–MODERATE
TRIP LENGTH	DAY TRIP

Arctic Treks
☎ 907-455-6502
www.arctictreksadventures.com

REGIONAL LOCATION	THE INTERIOR/ THE BUSH
COST	$$$$
SUITABLE FOR KIDS?	TEENS
ACTIVITY LEVEL	MODERATE–HIGH
TRIP LENGTH	10 DAYS

Chilkat Guides
☎ 888-292-7789
www.raftalaska.com

REGIONAL LOCATION	SOUTHEAST
COST	$–$$$$
SUITABLE FOR KIDS?	VARIES
ACTIVITY LEVEL	ALL LEVELS
TRIP LENGTH	1–12 DAYS

Keystone Raft and Kayak Adventures
☎ 907-835-2606
www.alaskawhitewater.com

REGIONAL LOCATION	SOUTHCENTRAL COASTAL
COST	$–$$$$
SUITABLE FOR KIDS?	VARIES
ACTIVITY LEVEL	ALL LEVELS
TRIP LENGTH	1–7 DAYS

NOVA River Runners
☎ 800-746-5753
www.novalaska.com

REGIONAL LOCATION	SOUTHCENTRAL INLAND
COST	$$
SUITABLE FOR KIDS?	VARIES
ACTIVITY LEVEL	LIGHT–MODERATE
TRIP LENGTH	1–6 DAYS

Wilderness Birding Adventures
☎ 907-694-7442
www.wildernessbirding.com

REGIONAL LOCATION	THE INTERIOR/ THE BUSH
COST	$$$$
SUITABLE FOR KIDS?	TEENS
ACTIVITY LEVEL	MODERATE–HIGH
TRIP LENGTH	12 DAYS

DAY TRIPS

Chilkat River

Regional location Haines, Southeast Alaska. **Distance** 20 miles. **Difficulty** Class I. **Experience level** Beginner. **Time to paddle** 1 day. **Suitable for kids?** Yes. **Best time of year to go** June–September. **Traffic level** Light–moderate. **Facilities** Established put-ins and takeouts.

PADDLING SUMMARY An enjoyable float with little in the way of danger and a lot in the way of scenery. The river flows through the **Chilkat Bald Eagle Preserve,** and wildlife in the area is abundant. Most of the time, it is silty and runs gray; it is also quite cold.

DIRECTIONS The put-in for this float actually begins on the **Klehini River,** off Mile 26.3 of the Haines Highway in Southeast Alaska. Travel the first few miles on the Klehini, which eventually feeds into the Chilkat. Follow the Chilkat back toward Haines, about a mile outside of town. For a shorter version, drive to Mile 19 of the Haines Highway and put in at the Chilkat.

Alaska Trophy Adventures
☎ 877-801-2289
www.alaskatrophyadventures.com

REGIONAL LOCATION	THE BUSH
COST	$$$
SUITABLE FOR KIDS?	NO
ACTIVITY LEVEL	MODERATE–HIGH
TRIP LENGTH	7 DAYS

Alaska Vistas
☎ 866-874-3006 or 907-874-3006
www.alaskavistas.com

REGIONAL LOCATION	SOUTHEAST
COST	$$$
SUITABLE FOR KIDS?	VARIES
ACTIVITY LEVEL	LIGHT–MODERATE
TRIP LENGTH	1–9 DAYS

Alaska Wilderness Guides
☎ 907-345-4470
www.akwild.com

REGIONAL LOCATION	STATEWIDE
COST	$$$
SUITABLE FOR KIDS?	NO
ACTIVITY LEVEL	MODERATE–HIGH
TRIP LENGTH	7 DAYS

Chugach Outdoor Center
☎ 866-277-RAFT or 907-277-RAFT
www.chugachoutdoorcenter.com

REGIONAL LOCATION	STATEWIDE
COST	$$
SUITABLE FOR KIDS?	SOME TRIPS
ACTIVITY LEVEL	MODERATE–HIGH
TRIP LENGTH	1–7 DAYS

Copper Oar Alaska Adventure Travel
☎ 800-523-4453 or 907-554-4453
www.copperoar.com

REGIONAL LOCATION	SOUTHCENTRAL INLAND
COST	$$$
SUITABLE FOR KIDS?	YES
ACTIVITY LEVEL	LIGHT–MODERATE
TRIP LENGTH	6 DAYS

Cordova Coastal Outfitters
☎ 800-357-5145 or 907-424-7424
www.cdvcoastal.com

REGIONAL LOCATION	SOUTHCENTRAL COASTAL
COST	$
SUITABLE FOR KIDS?	YES
ACTIVITY LEVEL	ALL LEVELS
TRIP LENGTH	DAY TRIP

Wilderness River Outfitters
☎ 800-252-6581
www.wildernessriver.com

REGIONAL LOCATION	SOUTHEAST
COST	$$$
SUITABLE FOR KIDS?	TEENS
ACTIVITY LEVEL	MODERATE–HIGH
TRIP LENGTH	11 DAYS

PADDLING DESCRIPTION Two rivers, the **Tsirksu** and **Klehini,** drain into the Chilkat, and both are floatable if you want to extend your trip. Many people like to put in on the Klehini River, farther up the Haines Highway, to extend the trip a few more miles, which is what we suggest. For most of the way, the river skirts alongside the highway, so you will not have a total wilderness experience. However, your possibility of viewing wildlife is just as high.

> *unofficial* **TIP**
> **The Chilkat River is an ideal destination for families. Swift but stable, this river takes you through pristine country, home to thousands of bald eagles, as well as moose, brown bears, and other wildlife. There are plenty of places to pull over to take a break, enjoy some lunch, and learn about the country.**

Eagle River

Regional location Eagle River, Southcentral Inland Alaska. **Distance** Up to 21 miles, 8 miles of good paddling. **Difficulty** Class II–IV. **Experience level** Beginner–advanced, depending on the section. **Time to paddle** 1 day. **Suitable for kids?** Some parts. **Best time of year to go** June–September. **Traffic level** Moderate. **Facilities** Public boat launches and parking; some signage.

PADDLING SUMMARY Silty and cold, this river has several hazards, including sweepers and boulders; the Eagle is popular with kayakers and rafters but not recommended for canoeists.

DIRECTIONS From Anchorage, drive north on the Glenn Highway to the Hiland Road exit. Veer right off the exit and follow Eagle River Loop Road to Eagle River Road (there is a stoplight and an oddly out-of-place Wal-Mart here). Turn right and follow to Mile 7.4 of Eagle River Road. The most-often-used put-in is located here.

unofficial **TIP**
Don't let Eagle River's somewhat-urban location fool you. There are some snarly sweepers and tricky boulder fields that make running the river a thrill for the experienced kayaker.

PADDLING DESCRIPTION This river is popular because of its proximity to Anchorage. On many a summer day you can spot rafters and kayaks on the river, usually locals looking for a quick paddle before heading back to their homes in Anchorage. The first 11 miles are the most benign, with Class I and II rapids and sweepers for which to be on the lookout, although you will miss the first three miles because there is no put-in. Once you reach the area around **Briggs Bridge,** however, the water gets trickier. The rapids become Class II and III, and steep banks provide challenges for pulling out if you want to scout the exposed boulders along the river. This section lasts for about 3.5 miles, and there is a place to take out just above the **Eagle River Campground.** There will be large signs pointing this out, and we hope you see them. Unless you are extremely experienced, it is very wise to stop here and scout the rapids below. If you go forward, the last six miles get even more hairy, passing underneath the **Glenn Highway–Eagle River Bridge** and going onto military land owned by **Fort Richardson Army Base.** The rapids become Class III and IV at this section, and it's nearly impossible to take out. It leads to the **Route Bravo Bridge,** then to the **Knik Arm** mudflats, which have dangerous bore tides and quicksand. We do not recommend this section.

The best and most convenient place to take out is at the **Eagle River Day Use Area,** adjacent to the Eagle River campground, 5.8 miles shy of the 21-mile length of the river.

Kenai River

Regional location Cooper Landing, Southcentral Coastal Alaska. **Distance** 18 miles. **Difficulty** Class II–III. **Experience level** Beginner–intermediate depending on the section. **Time to paddle** Half day–full day. **Suitable for kids?** Yes. **Best time of year to go** May–September, peak flow in mid-June–July. **Traffic level** Heavy during tourist season. **Facilities** Established put-ins and takeouts; outhouses; some signage.

PADDLING SUMMARY The scenic aquamarine waters of the Kenai are a pleasant float from one big lake (**Kenai**) to the next (**Skilak**). Relatively easy paddling with a high probability of spotting wildlife.

DIRECTIONS From Anchorage, take the Seward Highway south to the turnoff for the Sterling Highway. Follow the Sterling Highway into Cooper Landing, about eight miles. The rafting companies are located right on the river, past the Kenai Lake bridge, on the right. The best takeout, if you go all the way to Skilak Lake, is **Jim's Landing,** on Skilak Lake Road.

PADDLING DESCRIPTION The famed Kenai River is known for its great angling, but it is also a wonderfully relaxing place to explore in a raft. You can choose a shorter float with easy waves and only a few Class II rapids. Or continue on for the 18-mile trip to **Skilak Lake,** through the **Kenai National Wildlife Refuge.** Look for moose, river otters, bears, and eagles. With a guide, the shorter trip is appropriate for families.

Lowe River

Regional location Valdez, Southcentral Coastal Alaska. **Distance** 25.5 miles (5 miles for the Keystone Canyon section). **Difficulty** Class III. **Experience level** Beginner–advanced. **Time to paddle** 1 hour or longer depending on distance. **Suitable for kids?** No. **Best time of year to go** May–September, peak flow in mid-June. **Traffic level** Moderate during tourist season. **Facilities** Established put-ins and takeouts; some signage.

PADDLING SUMMARY A scenic, steep-walled river near Valdez that offers spectacular views of waterfalls and spruce-covered forests. The most popular section, **Keystone Canyon,** is Class III, but Class II and Class V segments also exist.

DIRECTIONS Most people come to the Lowe River from the Prince William Sound community of Valdez, at the beginning of the Richardson Highway. The Lowe River is half an hour north of Valdez, along the Richardson Highway.

PADDLING DESCRIPTION The Lowe River through Keystone Canyon gives you a brief (one-hour) but splashy introduction to white-water rafting. The canyon itself is stunning, and because the rapids are not too challenging you can actually look around to enjoy the surroundings. You can stop at **Bridal Veil Falls** to view the 900-foot-tall waterfalls right off the road. The vertical rock walls and thickly forested mountain slopes make you feel like you're at the center of the earth.

The river can be made much more challenging and exciting in other parts. The 7.5-mile **Heiden Canyon** upstream of Keystone Canyon is Class V and should not be attempted without local experts. Downstream from Keystone Canyon is easy Class II water.

Matanuska River–Lion Head

Regional location Palmer, Southcentral Inland Alaska. **Distance** 5.3 miles. **Difficulty** Class III–IV. **Experience level** Intermediate–advanced. **Time to paddle** Half day. **Suitable for kids?** Yes, in rafts. **Best time of year to go** Late May–August; best run between 5 feet and 12 feet. **Traffic level** Light–moderate. **Facilities** Pull-offs for put-ins and takeouts.

PADDLING SUMMARY A challenging, wide, glacially fed river that is silty, making it difficult to detect hidden obstacles. Very experienced paddlers can manage it; paddlers with some experience should do well, too, if accompanied by those who have run the river before.

DIRECTIONS From Anchorage, drive northeast on the Glenn Highway through the town of Palmer to the Caribou Creek bridge at Mile 107. Look just past the bridge to the left—you should find the put-in access from there, although the Caribou Creek bridge has undergone reconstruction the past two years. The takeout is off the Glenn Highway, at Mile 102. Follow the dirt road with steep switchbacks (a four-wheel-drive vehicle is recommended). Parking is at a clearing just before the Glacier Park Resort bridge. The resort is private property, but it is generally accepted that you can park there.

PADDLING DESCRIPTION The Matanuska River is wide, with impressive waves and open vistas for viewing the surroundings (during the rare moments when you can relax, that is).

The **Lion Head** portion of the Matanuska is some of the most scenic on this 77-plus-mile stretch of runnable river. The rapids are formed where the Matanuska Glacier pinches the Matanuska against a rock outcropping known as Lion Head. The massive stone feature stands like a gatekeeper to the upper Matanuska-Susitna Valley, and when viewed from a right angle does indeed look like a lion. The rapids are big-water style, with dramatic waves and more-technical challenges at low water levels.

unofficial **TIP**
The Matanuska River is frigid. Wet or dry suits, neoprene foot covers, and a warm head covering (and helmet) are strongly advised.

Both kayakers and rafters tackle this section of river. From the put-in at **Caribou Creek,** beware the braids that are just enough to get rafts stuck and push kayakers to the bank where sweepers hang low. You'll reach the **East Fork** of the Matanuska in less than half an hour, and the river forms a more manageable single channel. The steep rock bank that forms Lion Head will be the first major rapid, and it is a splashy one. When the water is high, you can go for almost four miles from rapid to rapid, wave after wave, with little stopping. It makes for an exhilarating but slightly white-knuckle experience. At low water, things get tricky with rock outcroppings, and you'll be slowed down considerably.

Nenana River

Regional location The Interior. **Distance** 38 miles (8 miles for the mellowest part of the river). **Difficulty** Class II–IV. **Experience level** Beginner–advanced depending on the section. **Time to paddle** Half day–full day. **Suitable for kids?** Some parts. **Best time of year to go** May–September, peak flow in mid-June. **Traffic level** Moderate–heavy during tourist season. **Facilities** Established put-ins and takeouts; some signage.

PADDLING SUMMARY A scenic, steep-walled river near **Denali National Park** that can be split into four segments, depending upon the challenges you seek. The first section provides opportunities for mild, Class II trips. As you travel downstream, you encounter more-challenging Class IV rapids near Nenana Canyon.

DIRECTIONS From Anchorage, take the Parks Highway north approximately 210 miles. At Cantwell, you can turn off onto the Denali Highway for a longer trip, but we are concentrating on the day trips. Keep driving to Carlo Creek.

PADDLING DESCRIPTION The **Carlo Creek–McKinley Village** section of the Nenana River is eight miles long and includes Class II and III rapids that are manageable by most people with intermediate to advanced skills. The challenge with the Nenana, as with many of Alaska's rivers, is its silty gray color, which makes it difficult to see obstacles under water. **McKinley Village** to **Riley Creek** provides a mostly Class III 10.5-mile section of water and is suitable for rafts and kayaks. The intriguingly named **Terror Corner** is a particularly challenging spot in this section of river.

The 9.5-mile segment from **Twin Rocks** to **Nenana Canyon** is the most challenging, with easy access off the Parks Highway, just outside the park. This section is perhaps Alaska's most popular white-water trip, and an annual competition draws kayakers from all over for slalom and wild-water races. Several outfitters offer trips on this stretch of river, as well as milder versions upstream.

Sixmile Creek

Regional location Hope, Southcentral Coastal Alaska. **Distance** 9 miles. **Difficulty** Class III–V. **Experience level** Advanced paddlers only. **Time to paddle** 1 day. **Suitable for kids?** No. **Best time of year to go** June–August. **Traffic level** Moderate. **Facilities** Alaska River Forecast Center gauge; public boat launch and parking; some signage.

PADDLING SUMMARY A challenging, mostly clear-water creek that slices through some of the most dramatic landscape of the **Kenai Peninsula**, and at some points can be seen right off the Seward Highway. There are three canyons, each getting progressively harder as you travel downstream. An ideal kayaker's river, although rafters now use it regularly as well.

DIRECTIONS From Anchorage, drive south on the Seward Highway to mile 59, just a few miles before the turnoff to Hope. There is a paved parking lot on the right side of the road. There are three takeouts, all along the Hope Road. The first is at about Mile 1 of the Hope Road, below the first canyon. There is a small road on the right leading to the Hope Road, and it can be easy to miss. The second takeout is at Mile 4.5, past the second canyon and also on the right and leading up a hill. The third takeout is at Mile 7. There is a driveway on the right that leads to the main road.

PADDLING DESCRIPTION Sixmile is one of the best-known waters for kayaking because it is technical and gets more difficult as it flows downstream, giving kayakers an ever-increasing challenge as they travel along. It wasn't until 10 to 15 years ago that commercial operators started using rafts to float the river, and today it is a popular day trip for those coming from Anchorage or the Kenai Peninsula.

The creek has some great sections, including **Seventeen Ender, The Slot, Predator, Waterfall,** and **Pearly Gates** (the last one makes us nervous!).

unofficial **TIP**
Sixmile Creek can be run at high and low levels, but it becomes more technical with less water. Many river runners also don't go out when it's at 11 feet or more, feeling it is too dangerous.

You can scout the river ahead of time by driving along the **Hope Highway** and going along the road for glimpses of certain canyons. Debris and logs often get moved into the water—we recommend scouting for such dangers.

Day-trip Resources

- **Alaska Raft and Kayak** (401 West Tudor Road, Anchorage 99503; ☎ 800-606-5950 or 907-561-7238; **www.alaskaraftandkayak.com**) rents rafts ($60 per day) and catamarans, which are used on the Sixmile.
- The **Chilkat River** is managed by the Chilkat Bald Eagle Preserve and the Juneau office of the **Alaska Division of State Parks** (☎ 907-465-4563; **www.dnr.state.ak.us/parks/units/eagleprv.htm**).
- Sixmile Creek and all its takeouts are on **Chugach National Forest** property. For more information, contact the administrative offices in Anchorage (3301 C Street, Anchorage 99503; ☎ 907-743-9500; **www.fs.fed.us/r10/chugach**).
- **Chugach State Park** manages the Eagle River and surrounding land (☎ 907-345-5014; **www.dnr.state.ak.us/parks/units/chugach**). The **Division of Natural Resources Public Information Center** can provide details on the Eagle River as well (550 West Seventh Avenue, Suite 1260; Anchorage 99501-3557; ☎ 907-269-8400; **www.dnr.state.ak.us/pic/index.htm**).
- **Denali National Park** and the **U.S. Bureau of Land Management** manage most of the Nenana River. For more information on Denali National Park, call ☎ 907-683-2294 or visit **www.nps.gov/dena;** to get in touch with the Bureau of Land Management, call the Glennallen District office (☎ 907-822-3217) or visit **www.blm.gov/ak.** (Incidentally, the Glennallen office can also give you information on the Delta National Wild and Scenic River, and the Gulkana National Wild River as well.)
- **Denali Outdoor Center** (☎ 888-303-1925 or 907-683-1925; **www.denaliparkrafting.com**) can provide information on Nenana River conditions; it also offers rentals and guided trips.
- **Fort Richardson Army Base** requires a paddler's permit to enter the six-mile section of Eagle River on its property. Permits are $50; call ☎ 907-384-1476 for details.
- The Anchorage-based paddling club **Knik Canoers and Kayakers** has a great Sixmile Creek mile-by-mile guide written by one of its members that is an entertaining must-read for do-it-yourselfers. Access it online at **www.kck.org.** The club also covers other rafting and kayaking locales.
- For more information on the Matanuska River, contact **Matanuska-Susitna Borough** (**www.matsugov.us**).
- **U.S. Geological Survey maps,** available locally or through **www.usgs.gov,** include: *Chilkat*—Skagway A-2, B-2, B-3, B-4; *Eagle River*—Anchorage A-7, B-6, and B-7; *Kenai River*—Seward B-8, and Kenai B-1; *Matanuska*—Anchorage D-2, D-3; *Nenana*—Fairbanks A-5, B-5, C-5; Healy B-3, B-4, C-4, D-4, D-5; *Sixmile*—Anchorage B-8.
- There are no nearby kayak- or raft-rental outfits in Valdez for the Lowe River. Check at the **Valdez Visitors and Convention Bureau** (off

Fairbanks Street, between Chenega and Fidalgo: ☎ 907-835-2984; **www.valdezalaska.org**).

Day-trip Outfitters

- **Alaska Rivers Company:** ☎ 888-595-1226; **www.alaskarivers company.com;** Cooper Landing. Along with phenomenal fishing and other Alaska adventures, Alaska Rivers Company offers two options for scenic floating on the Kenai River. The three-hour trip is suitable for all ages and takes guests on a relaxing float on the Upper Kenai. The seven-hour float explores Kenai Canyon and includes a guided nature hike. These day trips range from three to seven hours and include a knowledgeable guide, a gourmet lunch, and gear. Trips are $49 to $122 per person.
- **Alaska Vistas:** ☎ 866-874-3006 or 907-874-3006; **www.alaskavistas .com;** Wrangell. Alaska Vistas provides custom adventures for almost any skill level and desire. Pick a trip based on your interests and where you'd like to go, and Alaska Vistas will arrange for guided or independent trips as well as equipment rentals. The company is known for its Stikine River trips and also provides a jet-boat tour and other activities on the river. Other destinations include Anan Wildlife Observatory, Telegraph Creek, and numerous scenic areas in the Tongass National Forest and Stikine-LeConte Wilderness. A one-day guided trip to Anan is $191, and a nine-day guided trip on the Stikine is $2,400 per person.
- **Alaska Wildland Adventures:** ☎ 800-334-8730 or 907-783-2928; **www.alaskawildland.com;** Cooper Landing and Girdwood. The longest-running float-trip outfitter on the river, Alaska Wildland offers a half-day Kenai River float ($49) and the more exhilarating seven-hour Kenai Canyon Tour ($135). Both offer some nice waves, but nothing too technical.
- **Chilkat Guides:** ☎ 888-292-7789; **www.raftalaska.com;** Haines. Founded in 1978, Chilkat Guides offers day and multiday trips on the Chilkat, Kongakut, and Tatshenshini-Alsek rivers. The half-day scenic float on the Chilkat offers a chance to see the world's largest concentration of bald eagles up close at the Chilkat Bald Eagle Preserve. A 12-day trip on the Alsek offers serene floating and rugged white water against a backdrop of dramatic glacier and mountain scenery. More-remote trips include an eight-day excursion on the Kongakut, which cuts through Arctic National Wildlife Refuge. Trips start at $79 for the Chilkat River float and can be up to $4,495 for the Kongakut River trip.
- **Chugach Outdoor Center:** ☎ 866-277-RAFT or 907-277-RAFT; **www.chugachoutdoorcenter.com;** Hope. Leads trips on Sixmile Creek and on the Talkeetna and Tana rivers. Denali National Park trips via the Nenana River are also offered. Denali raft trips range from a couple of hours to multiple days requiring helicopter support. Whether on short day trips or weeklong camping excursions, guides lead guests through exhilarating white water and dramatic Alaska scenery. Rates range from $69 to $2,400 per person.

- **Keystone Raft and Kayak Adventures:** ☎ 907-835-2606; **www.alaskawhitewater.com;** Valdez. From 1½ hours on the Lowe River to multiple days on the Tazlina, Tana, Copper, Chitina, and Talkeetna rivers, Keystone Raft and Kayak offers the opportunity to float in a variety of regions and terrains. The company also provides half- and full-day trips on the Tonsina and Tsaina rivers. These trips are for more-adventurous types, as white water is Keystone's specialty. Rates start at $50 for the 1½-hour trip; call for multiday rates.
- **NOVA River Runners:** ☎ 800-746-5753; **www.novalaska.com;** Chickaloon. NOVA has been guiding Alaskans and visitors on rafting and other adventures through the wilderness since 1975. The company offers four- to five-hour day trips on Sixmile Creek and the Matanuska River. A favorite of NOVA's guides is the remote Kings River trip, a five-hour tour that includes a helicopter or mountain-bike ride to the put-in. Multiday adventures are available on the Matanuska, Tana, Talkeetna, and Copper rivers and on Lake Creek. Flightseeing, fishing, and other activities are also part of the adventure. Rates start at $90 for day trips to $1,950 for six-day trips.

MULTIDAY TRIPS

HERE'S WHERE THE PICKINGS GET EVEN more difficult to pare down. There are so many wilderness rivers in Alaska from which to choose, and all have something special to offer the person who chooses to explore them. We have selected five such rivers, and the guides we trust who can get you there.

We recommend traveling with the outfitters that follow. If, however, you are planning the trip on your own, please refer to our general resources listed at the beginning of this chapter, as well as the managing agency for each river.

American Creek

Regional location Katmai National Park, The Bush. **Distance** 50 miles. **Difficulty** Class I–III. **Experience level** Intermediate. **Time to paddle** 4–9 days. **Suitable for kids?** Yes. **Best time of year to go** June–September. **Traffic level** Light. **Facilities** None; wilderness float.

PADDLING SUMMARY This river is tucked amid the **Aleutian Range** and makes a good float from two lakes, starting at tiny **Murray Lake** and then continuing to **Lake Colville.** There is some flat-water paddling on the lakes, but there also comes excitement when at one point a narrow gorge creates a technical Class III run-through to more-open water.

American Creek Outfitters

- **Alaska Trophy Adventures:** ☎ 877-801-2289; **www.alaskatrophyadventures.com;** King Salmon. This outfit combines superb fishing guiding with a weeklong float down American Creek for $2,950 per person.

This is a hunter's and fisherman's paradise, with meat-and-potato-style meals and as much leopard rainbow, arctic char, and grayling fishing as you can squeeze in while floating the water.

- **Alaska Wilderness Guides:** ☎ 907-345-4470; **www.akwild.com,** Anchorage. Alaska Wilderness offers four multiday rafting trips throughout Alaska's remote wilderness, including its American Creek float in Katmai National Park. Trips are a mix of white-water rafting and scenic floating, and guides will take you past the famous bears of Katmai. The trip is $3,300 and includes a week of travel and fishing. Custom trips may be available upon request. (For more information on Katmai National Park, contact Field Headquarters, P.O. Box 7, 1 King Salmon Mall, King Salmon 99613; or Administrative Headquarters, 4230 University Drive, Suite 311, Anchorage 99508-4626; ☎ 907-246-3305; **www.nps.gov/katm.**)

unofficial **TIP**
Expedition trips to Alaska rivers require careful planning and the ability to survive in extreme outdoor conditions. It can snow any time of the year in Alaska, and it rains often. At certain times in the summer, the mosquitoes can be horrendous and the winds fierce. This is not to dissuade the outdoor traveler who wants to experience a truly remote expedition—it's simply a fact.

Canning River

Regional location The Bush, Arctic National Wildlife Refuge. **Distance** 125 miles. **Difficulty** Class II–III. **Experience level** Intermediate–advanced. **Time to paddle** 7–12 days. **Suitable for kids?** No. **Best time of year to go** June–September. **Traffic level** Light. **Facilities** None; a wilderness area.

PADDLING SUMMARY The Canning River skirts the western boundary of the **Arctic National Wildlife Refuge,** weaving between the mountains as it makes its way to the Arctic Ocean. The Canning's unusual beauty and gentle water make it an often-overlooked but special place to experience. The water runs clear, and from your boat you can look for musk ox, wolves, bears, and nesting falcons, hawks, and eagles. Also, be sure to get out and explore for fossils on the nearby gravel bars.

Canning River Outfitters

- **Arctic Treks:** ☎ 907-455-6502; **www.arctictreksadventures.com;** Fairbanks–Brooks Range. In business for more than 25 years, Arctic Treks provides visitors with a once-in-a-lifetime adventure through Alaska's great Arctic. Leading more than seven different trips through the Arctic's parks and wildlife refuges, the company also includes the Canning River on its itinerary. The trip is $4,150 and includes ten days of river rafting. Other rivers include the Kongakut, Nigu, Hulahula, and Sheenjek. Arctic Treks also offers other guided activities along the way, and there are options for special trips each year.
- **Wilderness Birding Adventures:** ☎ 907-694-7442; **www.wildernessbirding.com.** This outfit is one of the best in the state, and the only one offering rafting-birding combination tours. The price is $3,500 for 12 days on the Canning River–Marsh Fork. The Canning River delta

features variety in its upriver species, with more chances to see more birds. Wilderness Birding also explores unique birding options on the Kongakut, in the Pribilofs, and in Nome and Gambell.

Copper River

Regional location Southcentral Inland to Southcentral Coastal Alaska. **Distance** 100 miles. **Difficulty** Class I. **Experience level** Beginner (with guide). **Time to paddle** 6 days. **Suitable for kids?** Yes. **Best time of year to go** July–August. **Traffic level** Light. **Facilities** Established put-ins and takeouts, camping on beaches.

PADDLING SUMMARY The river is wide, flat, and swift, but there are no huge rapids to worry about. Calved pieces of glacier in some spots punctuate the gray, silty water. Stay away from the glaciers when they are calving—the waves produced by their weight are surprisingly powerful.

Copper River Outfitters

- **Alaska Wilderness Guides:** ☎ 907-345-4470; **www.akwild.com;** Anchorage. Offers a six-night tour on the Copper River for $1,200 per person. You'll enjoy wilderness camping, wildlife viewing, hiking, and other activities along the way.
- **Copper Oar Alaska Adventure Travel:** ☎ 800-523-4453 or 907-554-4453; **www.copperoar.com;** McCarthy. Copper Oar offers a six-day Copper River floating and camping expedition that takes in wildlife, cascading waterfalls, glaciers that often calve right into the river, and mild white water. The voyage ends in Cordova, in Prince William Sound, where you can fly out to Anchorage or take the Alaska Marine Highway ferry for an added water-based trip back to the mainland. The price is $2,350 to $2,600 for adults, depending on group size.
- **Cordova Coastal Outfitters:** ☎ 800-357-5145 or 907-424-7424; **www.cdvcoastal.com;** Cordova, at the harbor in the brightly colored boathouse. For those planning to do the trip on their own, this outfit can arrange a shuttle. They also rent kayaks, which are suitable for travel on Copper River. Kayaks are $35 per day for singles, $50 for doubles. Guided day trips start at $75, but no overnight trips are operated through the company.

unofficial **TIP**
Native corporations own much of the land along the right-hand bank of the Copper River, and you'll need a permit to camp there. Traveling with an outfitter eliminates the need to obtain permission on your own.

Nizina River

Regional location Southcentral Inland, McCarthy. **Distance** 45 miles. **Difficulty** Class II–III. **Experience level** Beginner–intermediate. **Time to paddle** 2–3 days. **Suitable for kids?** Yes. **Best time of year to go** June–September. **Traffic level** Light. **Facilities** Established put-ins and takeouts.

PADDLING SUMMARY A float along the Nizina combines fast water with glacial runoff and the chance to see much wildlife. The river has several difficult sections on the upper portion. Side trips include the **Kennicott**

River, which can be launched from the end of McCarthy Road and accompanied by a side trip to the historic town. In low water, the Kennicott can become braided and shallow.

Nizina River Outfitters

- **Alaska Outdoors:** ☎ 800-320-2494; **www.alaskaoutdoorstours.com,** Wasilla. Offers a custom rafting adventure in Wrangell–St. Elias National Park. This six-day excursion starts with a guided tour of the park, including a pick-your-own-adventure day that may take you glacier hiking, flightseeing, touring, or rafting. The rest of the trip is spent rafting and camping on the Kennicott, Nizina, and Chitina rivers. The price is $1,700 per person.

Tatshenshini and Alsek Rivers

Regional location Southeast, Haines. **Distance** 129 miles. **Difficulty** Class I–IV. **Experience level** Advanced paddlers only. **Time to paddle** 9–12 days. **Suitable for kids?** Some parts. **Best time of year to go** June–August. **Traffic level** Light. **Facilities** None; very remote.

PADDLING SUMMARY These rivers, which merge into one along the way, make for a challenging route that attracts paddlers from around the world. The heat and bugs in the upper reaches of the river usually contrast with the fog and glacial chill of the lower half, so be prepared for a variety of weather conditions. The **Tatshenshini** starts in Canada and the **Alsek** dumps into the United States; thus, many people fly into Alaska, shuttle to Canada for the put-in at **Dalton Post,** and float the 129 miles to **Dry Bay,** back in Alaska. The Tatshenshini and Alsek are completely protected from headwater to source, creating the only large river drainage in North America that is completely safeguarded. The white water on the Tatshenshini is impressive, but when it joins with the Alsek River 77 miles into the trip, the river makes a dramatic jump in size and power.

Tatshenshini-Alsek Outfitters

- **Alaska Discovery:** ☎ 800-586-1911; **www.akdiscovery.com;** based in Juneau and California. Offers an Alsek River trip and a Tatshenshini adventure. The former is 12 days and costs $3,550 to $3,850, depending upon group size; the latter costs $3,050 to $3,350 for nine days. This outfit does a great job but takes larger groups than most outfitters.
- **Wilderness River Outfitters:** ☎ 800-252-6581; **www.wildernessriver.com;** based in Lemhi, Idaho. Offers an awesome 11-day trip on the Tatshenshini for $2,800. Bring your own gear and get a $75 discount.

PART EIGHTEEN

SKIING

IN ALASKA, YOU CAN SKI YEAR-ROUND. You can ski on a glacier. You can jump out of a helicopter and ski down a mountain. You can ski on a groomed trail. You can ski at a resort. Simply put, there is no shortage of skiing in Alaska.

However, skiing in Alaska is not the resort-packed winter wonderland you might think, but rather an outdoor adventure that usually requires climbing mountains on your own and gliding back down in fluid motion. In the entire state, there is only one ski area that qualifies as a resort (that is, with a fancy hotel, multiple lifts, and an array of fine-dining and entertainment options), not to mention less than a half-dozen local downhill-skiing areas. Considering that Alaska is so vast and covered in snow for so much of the year, this may come as a surprise.

unofficial **TIP**
Late winter and early spring are the best times to visit Alaska for a skiing vacation. The first part of March brings with it warmer temperatures and longer days. It is not uncommon to see sunny, clear afternoons with temperatures in the high 30s, a far cry from the 15-degree days most common during January and February. (In the Interior and the Bush, the average winter temperatures are even lower, often in the negative digits.)

Actually, it's not that surprising at all. The very thing that draws so many visitors to Alaska each year—its remote wilderness—is the thing that makes skiing here such a treat. Here you can slip on a pair of skis and kick and glide your way from one region of the state to another—hundreds of miles—without encountering so much as a road crossing. You can board a helicopter and get dropped off on a steep peak that sees perhaps two dozen humans a year, skiing fresh powder, with not a ski track in sight. Skiing here doesn't offer the glam and glitz of those upscale resorts you see in the Lower 48 and abroad, but it does offer some great snow and fine conditions.

In the lower 48 states, downhill skiing catches most of the spotlight. Resorts from Utah to Colorado to Vermont cater to the thrill of flying down mountains at high speeds. And it is great fun. But the truth is, Nordic skiing reigns supreme in Alaska. And while there are many downhill skiers and some excellent places at which to Alpine-ski here, in Alaska you can access cross-country ski trails from just about anywhere.

First, a short primer on skiing. There are many variations on the activity, but we generally group them in three categories: downhill (or Alpine), cross-country (or Nordic), and backcountry (telemarking, for example). There also is snowboarding, which can be accomplished in the backcountry and on established ski slopes.

This chapter outlines a few of the prime skiing spots in Alaska, and the specialties offered there. We also have included a list of resources for planning your own trip, as well as a few suggested outfitters in the state who can provide the best of whatever skiing you desire. Most skiing outfitters in Alaska offer such adventures as heli-skiing and backcountry skiing. The companies we have listed are all located in prime backcountry and high-mountain country.

Those who prefer downhill skiing, cross-country skiing, and snowboarding should refer to the resources section that follows for a list of popular downhill ski areas and regions.

SKIING RESOURCES

Anchorage

Regional location Southcentral Inland Alaska. **Types of skiing** Downhill, cross-country, randonnée, telemarking. **Difficulty** ★–★★★★★. **Road access?** Yes. **Suitable for kids?** Yes. **Traffic** Moderate–heavy. **Contact** Anchorage Convention and Visitors Bureau, 524 West Fourth Avenue, Anchorage 99501-2212; ☎ 907-276-4118 or 800-478-1255; **www.anchorage.net.** Look for the sod-roofed Log Cabin and Downtown Visitor Information Center at the corner of F Street and Fourth Avenue.

DESTINATION SUMMARY Anchorage has three ski areas close by and offers several options for Alpine skiing. However, cross-country skiing on groomed municipal trails and in **Chugach State Park** are the main attractions. Anchorage has hundreds of miles of trails, many of them groomed and lighted, or at least well established, during the winter months. It is one of the best urban trail systems in the country, and winter travelers will be surprised by how much is available. The most popular areas for Nordic skiing are **Kincaid Park,** the local greenbelt trails, and **Russian Jack Springs Park.** Check with the **Anchorage Parks and Recreation** office (☎ 907-343-4355; **www.muni.org/parks/index.cfm**) and the **Alaska Public Lands Information Center** (605 West Fourth Avenue, Suite 105, Anchorage 99501; ☎ 907-271-2737; **www.nps.gov/aplic**) for more information about trails and skiing options.

Alaska Skiing at a Glance

	Anchorage	Fairbanks and Beyond	Haines
REGIONAL LOCATION	SOUTHCENTRAL INLAND	THE INTERIOR	SOUTHEAST
SKIING TYPES	ALL	ALL	HELI-SKIING, DOWNHILL, X-COUNTRY, TELEMARK
TRAFFIC	MODERATE–HEAVY	LIGHT–MODERATE	LIGHT
DIFFICULTY	🫎–🫎🫎🫎🫎🫎	🫎–🫎🫎🫎	🫎🫎🫎🫎🫎
ROAD ACCESS?	YES	YES	NO
SUITABLE FOR KIDS?	YES	YES	NO
GUIDE SUGGESTED?	RECOMMENDED	NO	YES

	Hatcher Pass–Mat-Su	Juneau	Valdez
REGIONAL LOCATION	SOUTHCENTRAL INLAND	SOUTHEAST	SOUTHCENTRAL COASTAL
SKIING TYPES	ALL	DOWNHILL, CROSS-COUNTRY	ALL
TRAFFIC	LIGHT–MODERATE	MODERATE	LIGHT
DIFFICULTY	🫎🫎–🫎🫎🫎🫎	🫎🫎🫎	🫎🫎🫎🫎🫎
ROAD ACCESS?	YES	YES	NO
SUITABLE FOR KIDS?	YES	YES	NO
GUIDE SUGGESTED?	RECOMMENDED	NO	YES

Fairbanks and Beyond

Regional location The Interior. **Types of skiing** Downhill, cross-country, randonnée, telemarking. **Difficulty** 🫎–🫎🫎🫎. **Road access?** Yes. **Suitable for kids?** Yes. **Traffic** Light–moderate. **Contact** Fairbanks Convention and Visitors Bureau, 550 First Avenue, Fairbanks 99701; ☎ 800-327-5774; **www.explorefairbanks.com.**

DESTINATION SUMMARY Cross-country-skiing opportunities abound in the Interior. Winter trails maintained by the U.S. Bureau of Land Management and other public agencies provide excellent access to open valleys and high traverses. There are also established trails around some communities, as well as at most high schools and the University of Alaska. These trails are multiple-use, however, so beware of snowmobiles and dog teams. Some Alpine skiing is also available. Two ski areas in Fairbanks provide some good local downhill action for Alpine skiers and snowboarders, and are affordable for just about anyone (see "Ski Resorts," page 278).

Haines

Regional location Southeast Alaska. **Types of skiing** Heli-skiing, downhill, cross-country, telemarking. **Difficulty** 🫎🫎🫎🫎🫎. **Road access?** No. **Suitable for kids?** No. **Traffic** Light. **Contact** Haines Convention and Visitors Bureau, P.O. Box 530, Haines 99827; ☎ 907-766-2234; **www.haines.ak.us**.

DESTINATION SUMMARY Haines offers plenty of opportunities for Alpine and cross-country skiing, telemarking and snowboarding. Spring skiing in the area in March and April is unsurpassed. **Haines Summit** and **Chilkat Pass** are the most popular skiing areas, and there are also numerous

Skiing Outfitters at a Glance

Alaska Alpine Adventures
☎ 877-525-2577
www.alaskaalpineadventures.com

REGIONAL LOCATION	THE BUSH
COST	$$$
SUITABLE FOR KIDS?	NO
ACTIVITY LEVEL	HIGH
TRIP LENGTH	7–14 DAYS

Alaska Heliskiing
☎ 907-767-5745
www.alaskaheliskiing.com

REGIONAL LOCATION	SOUTHEAST
COST	$$$$
SUITABLE FOR KIDS?	NO
ACTIVITY LEVEL	HIGH
TRIP LENGTH	1–6 DAYS

Alpine Guides Alaska
☎ 907-373-3051
www.alaska.net/~alpineak

REGIONAL LOCATION	SOUTHCENTRAL INLAND
COST	$$
SUITABLE FOR KIDS?	TEENS
ACTIVITY LEVEL	MODERATE–HIGH
TRIP LENGTH	4–5 DAYS

Chugach Powder Guides
☎ 907-783-4354
www.chugachpowderguides.com

REGIONAL LOCATION	SOUTHCENTRAL INLAND
COST	$$$
SUITABLE FOR KIDS?	TEENS
ACTIVITY LEVEL	HIGH
TRIP LENGTH	1–7 DAYS

Points North Heli-Adventures
☎ 877-787-6784
www.alaskaheliski.com

REGIONAL LOCATION	SOUTHCENTRAL COASTAL
COST	$$$
SUITABLE FOR KIDS?	NO
ACTIVITY LEVEL	HIGH
TRIP LENGTH	6 DAYS

St. Elias Alpine Guides
☎ 888-933-5427 or 907-554-4445
www.steliasguides.com

REGIONAL LOCATION	SOUTHCENTRAL INLAND
COST	$$$
SUITABLE FOR KIDS?	TEENS
ACTIVITY LEVEL	HIGH
TRIP LENGTH	1–6 DAYS

Valdez Heli-Camps
☎ 907-783-3513 or 907-783-3243
www.valdezhelicamps.com

REGIONAL LOCATION	SOUTHCENTRAL COASTAL
COST	$$$$
SUITABLE FOR KIDS?	TEENS
ACTIVITY LEVEL	HIGH
TRIP LENGTH	1–6 DAYS

Valdez Heli-Ski Guides
☎ 907-835-4528
www.valdezheliskiguides.com

REGIONAL LOCATION	SOUTHCENTRAL COASTAL/INLAND
COST	$$$$
SUITABLE FOR KIDS?	NO
ACTIVITY LEVEL	HIGH
TRIP LENGTH	6 DAYS

maintained cross-country trails near town. Lodging is available at hotels and bed-and-breakfasts in and around Haines.

Hatcher Pass–Mat-Su Borough

Regional location Southcentral Inland Alaska. **Types of skiing** Downhill, cross-country, randonnée, telemarking. **Difficulty** –. **Road access?** Yes. **Suitable for kids?** Yes. **Traffic** Light–moderate. **Contact** Mat-Su Convention and Visitors Bureau 7744 E. Visitors View Court, Palmer 99645; ☎ 907-746-5000; **www.alaskavisit.com.** The visitor center is at Mile 35.5 Parks Highway (take the Trunk Road Exit).

DESTINATION SUMMARY This immense area offers Alpine and cross-country skiing and snowboarding. There are no established ski areas here currently, and hike-in and backcountry skiing are most common. The wide glacial valleys and scenic landscapes make for great touring, and the surrounding mountains provide some opportunities for Alpine and telemark skiing and randonnée as well.

One of the best and most popular areas for skiing and other winter recreation is **Hatcher Pass,** about 15 miles outside of Palmer. This area includes **Independence Mine State Historical Park** and gets an abundance of snow during winter months. Hike-in skiing and snowboarding are popular here, and there are also established Nordic trails. Some of the most-used trails include those near Independence Mine and multiuse trails such as the **Gold Mint Glacier** trail. The **Hatcher Pass Recreation Area** is relatively easy to reach, and visitors can drive up, park in an established lot, and hike a short distance for untracked Alaska powder. Lodging and services in the area include the **Hatcher Pass Lodge** and **Motherlode Lodge.** There is also a small ski area and a groomed and lighted Nordic trail system planned for the area.

Juneau

Regional location Southeast Alaska. **Types of skiing** Downhill, cross-country. **Difficulty** . **Road access?** Yes. **Suitable for kids?** Yes. **Traffic** Moderate. **Contact** Juneau Convention and Visitors Bureau, 1 Sealaska Plaza, Suite 305, Juneau 99801-1245; ☎ 907-586-1737; **www.traveljuneau.com.**

DESTINATION SUMMARY The expansive valleys of the Juneau area offer great cross-country skiing. The most popular sites are the **Juneau Ice Field** and **Mendenhall Glacier.** The area offers mainly Nordic skiing, but there are some opportunities for Alpine skiing and snowboarding as well as backcountry touring. Juneau also has an established ski area.

Valdez

Regional location Southcentral Coastal Alaska. **Types of skiing** Heli-skiing, downhill, cross-country, telemarking, randonnée. **Difficulty** . **Road access?** No. **Suitable for kids?** No. **Traffic** Light. **Contact** Valdez Convention and Visitors Bureau, 200 Fairbanks Drive, Valdez 99686; ☎ 800-770-5954; **www.valdezalaska.org.**

DESTINATION SUMMARY With the **Chugach Range** and the mountains in Thompson Pass and around Valdez being some of the most snow-rich areas in the state, Valdez is a popular destination for all skiers. The area offers endless backcountry and front-country opportunities for Alpine skiing, snowboarding, telemarking, randonnée, and cross-country touring. Heli-skiing and Snowcat skiing atop some of the highest peaks in the Chugach are ideal. There are several guides in the area and from out of state. Lodging is at wilderness lodges, hotels, and bed-and-breakfasts in and around Valdez.

SKI RESORTS

OK, WE'RE USING THE TERM *resort* loosely. In Alaska, any ski area that has a chairlift or towrope is close enough, because such things are luxuries. Alaskans generally are hardy folk who won't scoff at climbing a mountain to get in their ski or snowboard run. But when they want a little pampering, they can visit one of these ski areas for a lift.

Alyeska Resort

Regional location Girdwood, Southcentral Inland Alaska. **Types of skiing** Mostly downhill, terrain park, some cross-country, telemarking. **Contact** ☎ 800-880-3880 or 907-754-2111; **www.alyeskaresort.com.**

DESTINATION SUMMARY The only true resort in the state, with a luxury hotel, nearby shops and restaurants, and a lively nightlife. *Tickets:* $50; *terrain:* 2,500 vertical feet; *lifts:* one high-speed detachable quad, two fixed quads, three double chairs, two pony lifts, a magic carpet, one 60-passenger tram; *level:* 52% intermediate, 37% advanced, 11% beginner; *location:* about three miles up the Alyeska Highway off the Seward Highway, 40 miles south of Anchorage.

Alpenglow at Arctic Valley

Regional location Anchorage, Southcentral Inland Alaska. **Types of skiing** Mostly downhill, some cross-country, telemarking. **Contact** ☎ 907-428-1208; **www.skialpenglow.com.**

DESTINATION SUMMARY Longtime Anchorage facilities run completely by volunteers. *Tickets:* $15–$28 (children under 7 and guests over 70 ski free); *terrain:* 1,214 vertical feet; *lifts:* one T-bar/platter, two double chairs, one rope tow; *level:* easiest to more difficult; *location:* just outside Anchorage, Mile 7, Arctic Valley Road.

Eaglecrest

Regional location Juneau, Southeast Alaska. **Types of skiing** Downhill, cross-country, telemarking. **Contact** ☎ 907-790-2000; **www.juneau.org/ecrestftp.**

DESTINATION SUMMARY *Tickets:* $35, Nordic trails $5–$10; *terrain:* 1,400 vertical feet; *lifts:* two double, one surface; *level:* 40% intermediate, 40% expert, 20% novice; *location:* 18 miles from Juneau off Juneau-Douglas Memorial Highway.

Hillberg Ski Area

Regional location Elmendorf Air Force Base, Anchorage, Southcentral Inland Alaska. **Types of skiing** Mostly downhill, some cross-country, telemarking, and snow tubing. **Contact** ☎ 907-552-4838 or 907-552-3472; **www.elmendorfservices.com/content/index.php,** and click on "Travel & Recreation."

DESTINATION SUMMARY You must have military privileges to get to this recreational ski area. *Tickets:* $14 to ski, $19 for skiing and tubing; *terrain:* 236 vertical feet; *lifts:* one chair lift, two surface lifts; *location:* four miles off the main road on Elmendorf Air Force Base just outside of Anchorage.

Hilltop Ski Area

Regional location Anchorage, Southcentral Inland Alaska. **Types of skiing** Downhill (popular for snowboarding), cross-country. **Contact** ☎ 907-346-1407; **www.hilltopskiarea.org.**

DESTINATION SUMMARY *Tickets:* $26, Nordic trails free (maintained by municipality); *terrain:* 294 vertical feet, 2,090 feet in all; *lifts:* one triple chair, one rope tow, one platter lift; *level:* 80% easiest, 10% more difficult, 10% most difficult; *location:* about 15 minutes southeast of downtown Anchorage off Abbott Loop.

Kincaid Park Outdoor Center

Regional location Anchorage, Southcentral Inland Alaska. **Type of skiing** Cross-country. **Contact** ☎ 907-343-6397; **www.muni.org/parks/parkdistrictsw.cfm.**

DESTINATION SUMMARY The best cross-country trails in Southcentral Alaska are in this 1,400-acre park. Skiing is free. Open seven days a week. The sledding hill in front of the chalet is popular with kids. Because this is cross-country skiing, there are no lifts or terrain parks, just a spiderweb maze of beautiful wooded trails.

Moose Mountain Ski Resort

Regional location Fairbanks, the Interior. **Types of skiing** Downhill, telemarking. **Contact** ☎ 907-479-4732; **www.shredthemoose.com.**

DESTINATION SUMMARY *Tickets:* $35; *terrain:* more than 1,250 vertical feet; *lifts:* buses with ski racks; *level:* all levels, all ages; *location:* ten miles west of Fairbanks off Sheep Creek Road.

Mount Aurora Skiland

Regional location Fairbanks, the Interior. **Types of skiing** Downhill, cross-country, telemarking. **Contact** ☎ 907-389-2314; **home.att.net/~skiland.**

DESTINATION SUMMARY *Tickets:* $32; *lifts:* one double chair (farthest north ski lift); *level:* mostly beginner to intermediate with some advanced slopes; *location:* off Steese Highway north of Fairbanks.

Mount Eyak

Regional location Cordova, Southcentral Coastal Alaska. **Types of skiing** Mostly downhill, some cross-country, telemarking. **Contact** ☎ 907-424-7766; **www.cordovaalaska.com/winter/mounteyak.htm.**

DESTINATION SUMMARY *Tickets:* $25 and up; *terrain:* 800 vertical feet; *lifts:* one single chair; *level:* 60% more difficult, 20% most difficult, 20% easiest; *location:* Cordova (take Sixth Avenue off of Council Road).

SKIING OUTFITTERS

IN ALASKA THERE ARE SKIING ADVENTURES for every budget. As the prices at the ski areas listed previously demonstrate, a day of fun on the slopes can come pretty cheap, even free. The outfitters here provide adventures that are considerably pricier, but the excitement they deliver is worth every penny. Many specialize in heli-skiing, the extreme sport of which many a high-decibel action movie is made, and a popular pastime in Alaska.

- **Alaska Alpine Adventures:** ☎ 877-525-2577; **www.alaskaalpineadventures.com;** Port Alsworth, the Bush. In conjunction with All-Mountain Ski Pros, Alaska Alpine offers one- and two-week ski-plane trips to the jagged peaks of the Neacolas in Lake Clark National Park and Preserve. You'll camp at the glacier terminus and practice backcountry and glacier-climbing techniques on this ski-mountaineering trip dedicated to first ascents and descents. Trips are $3,600 to $4,150 per person.
- **Alaska Heliskiing:** ☎ 907-767-5745; **www.alaskaheliskiing.com;** Haines, Southeast Alaska. Offers heli-skiing, ski-plane trips, and guiding school. Ski trips are from one to six days; guiding school is ten days. Helicopter skiing is $600 per person per day (six runs). Packages start at $3,950 and include lodging, five days of skiing, and gear. Private trips and charters are also available.

unofficial **TIP**
The most popular time of year for heli-skiing is February to May; if you'd like to try it, plan your trip for spring. You won't be disappointed.

- **Alpine Guides Alaska:** ☎ 907-373-3051; **www.alaska.net/~alpineak;** Wasilla/Wrangell–St. Elias, Southcentral Inland Alaska. Alpine Guides Alaska offers three spectacular backcountry touring trips, perfect for the Nordic, telemark, or randonnée skier. The company's premier trip is a four- or five-day tour across the superb snow of Snowbird Glacier to the Snowbird Glacier Hut. Other traverses to mountain huts are possible from here. Four- and five-day trips to Mint Glacier and across the Bomber Ski Traverse are also offered. Rates start at $880 and go up to $1,100.
- **Chugach Powder Guides:** ☎ 907-783-4354; **www.chugachpowderguides.com;** Girdwood, Southcentral Inland Alaska. Combines luxury with unsurpassed backcountry skiing and snowboarding on its guided heli-skiing and Snowcat trips. Chugach Powder Guides holds a permit from the Chugach National Forest and has access to terrain inaccessible to any other company and the majority of travelers. The company offers day trips ($870 per person) and weeklong packages (starting at $3,975 per person and as high as $8,900 per week). Other adventures are also available, including the wildly popular spring Kings and Corn fishing and skiing package ($7,900).
- **Points North Heli-Adventures:** ☎ 877-787-6784; **www.alaskaheliski.com;** Cordova, Southcentral Coastal Alaska. This company offers six-day trips in the Chugach. They provide custom trips as needed, but those fill up fast. An average day of skiing or snowboarding consists of 20,000 to 25,000 feet of vertical per day. The price averages about $850 to $950 per day, with about six to ten helicopter runs in a given area.
- **St. Elias Alpine Guides:** ☎ 888-933-5427 or 907-554-4445; **www.steliasguides.com;** Anchorage/Wrangell–St. Elias, Southcentral

Inland Alaska. Takes guests on ski-mountaineering excursions in the Chugach Mountains during the spring and summer seasons. The guides also give ski-mountaineering and avalanche instruction. Unique to St. Elias Alpine Guides is the kite-skiing trip to Bagley Icefield. An awe-inspiring flight through Wrangell–St. Elias starts off the adventure, and an experience like no other follows. The mountaineering classes range from $1,250 for a five-day glacier travel course to $3,750 for a weeklong First Ascents course; the kite-skiing trip starts at $5,250.

- **Valdez Heli-Camps:** ☎ 907-783-3513 or 907-783-3243; **www.valdezhelicamps.com;** Valdez, Southcentral Coastal Alaska. This company's Web site dubs its trips "skiing that will change your life." And they may very well do so, as you spend one to six days floating through virgin powder on some of the Chugach's tallest peaks. Alpine heli-skiing and Snowcat skiing and boarding are offered. The company's most popular trips are all-inclusive, with deluxe accommodations and gourmet food. Valdez Heli-Camps also offers a Sound to Summit adventure that includes some of the world's best fishing coupled with some of the world's best skiing. One day of Snowcat skiing costs $299, and heli-trips start at $999 per day.
- **Valdez Heli-Ski Guides:** ☎ 907-835-4528; **www.valdezheliskiguides.com;** Girdwood, Southcentral Inland Alaska. Valdez Heli-Ski is synonymous with endless powder and phenomenal adventure. Individual and private ski packages are available out of Valdez and renowned Thompson Pass, billed as one of the snowiest places in Alaska. On no-fly days, the company offers alternate activities—ice climbing, sea kayaking, snow machining, and fishing. Rates start at $6,930 per person for six days of skiing (30 to 36 runs), including lodging and meals; private trips are $63,945 per party.

PART NINETEEN

SOUTHCENTRAL INLAND ALASKA

An Oasis of Activity

An OVERVIEW *of the* STATE'S LIVELIEST REGION

TAKE ALASKA AS A WHOLE, AND it can be quite overwhelming, with all there is to do and see. From the windblown tundra of Barrow to the rain-forest lushness of Southeast Alaska, this is a land of diversity and unparalleled natural beauty. But there is one corner of Alaska, flanked by snowy mountain ranges along the northern end and rimmed by sandy, sea-lapped beaches along the southern end, where all of Alaska's best features can be found in one condensed package.

This section of the state, known simply as Southcentral (which Alaskans typically spell as one word), encompasses the state's largest city, its most famed river, its most striking glaciers, and some of its finest and most accessible wildlife-viewing options. Touring the Southcentral region is an affordable and convenient way to glimpse the best of Alaska.

We at *The Unofficial Guide to Adventure Travel in Alaska* realize that so much is happening in Southcentral Alaska, we can't cram it all into one chapter. So you will notice we have two Southcentral chapters: this one focuses on inland outdoor adventure, and the other (page 332) concentrates on coastal activities. The rationale behind this division is that many of the outdoor adventures that travelers seek can be found more predominantly in one region over the other. Southcentral Inland Alaska, for example, is a paradise for backpackers and mountaineers. It features mountains and valleys perfect for exploration. Southcentral Coastal Alaska, on the other hand, is the place to go if you are a kayaker or an angler.

Think of Southcentral Inland Alaska as a giant triangle. Starting north of Valdez on the Richardson Highway, the first communities of the Inland area are **McCarthy** and **Kennicott,** on the edge of the

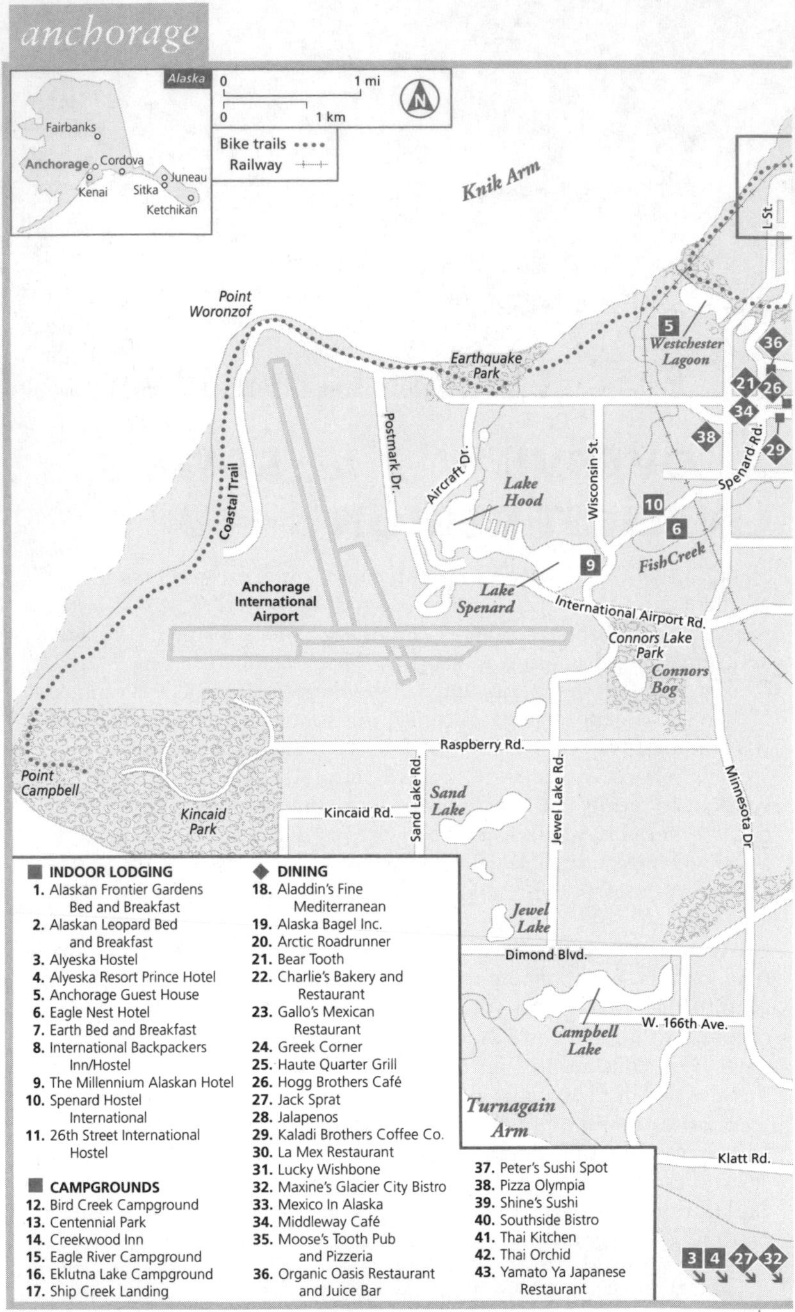
anchorage
Alaska
Fairbanks
Anchorage
Cordova
Juneau
Kenai
Sitka
Ketchikan
0
1 mi
0
1 km
N
Bike trails
Railway
Knik Arm
L St.
Point Woronzof
5
Westchester Lagoon
36
Earthquake Park
21
26
34
38
29
Postmark Dr.
Aircraft Dr.
Wisconsin St.
Spenard Rd.
Coastal Trail
Lake Hood
10
6
9
Fish Creek
Anchorage International Airport
Lake Spenard
International Airport Rd.
Connors Lake Park
Connors Bog
Raspberry Rd.
Point Campbell
Kincaid Park
Kincaid Rd.
Sand Lake Rd.
Sand Lake
Jewel Lake Rd.
Minnesota Dr.
Jewel Lake
Dimond Blvd.
Campbell Lake
W. 166th Ave.
Turnagain Arm
Klatt Rd.
3
4
27
32
INDOOR LODGING
1. Alaskan Frontier Gardens Bed and Breakfast
2. Alaskan Leopard Bed and Breakfast
3. Alyeska Hostel
4. Alyeska Resort Prince Hotel
5. Anchorage Guest House
6. Eagle Nest Hotel
7. Earth Bed and Breakfast
8. International Backpackers Inn/Hostel
9. The Millennium Alaskan Hotel
10. Spenard Hostel International
11. 26th Street International Hostel
CAMPGROUNDS
12. Bird Creek Campground
13. Centennial Park
14. Creekwood Inn
15. Eagle River Campground
16. Eklutna Lake Campground
17. Ship Creek Landing
DINING
18. Aladdin's Fine Mediterranean
19. Alaska Bagel Inc.
20. Arctic Roadrunner
21. Bear Tooth
22. Charlie's Bakery and Restaurant
23. Gallo's Mexican Restaurant
24. Greek Corner
25. Haute Quarter Grill
26. Hogg Brothers Café
27. Jack Sprat
28. Jalapenos
29. Kaladi Brothers Coffee Co.
30. La Mex Restaurant
31. Lucky Wishbone
32. Maxine's Glacier City Bistro
33. Mexico In Alaska
34. Middleway Café
35. Moose's Tooth Pub and Pizzeria
36. Organic Oasis Restaurant and Juice Bar
37. Peter's Sushi Spot
38. Pizza Olympia
39. Shine's Sushi
40. Southside Bistro
41. Thai Kitchen
42. Thai Orchid
43. Yamato Ya Japanese Restaurant

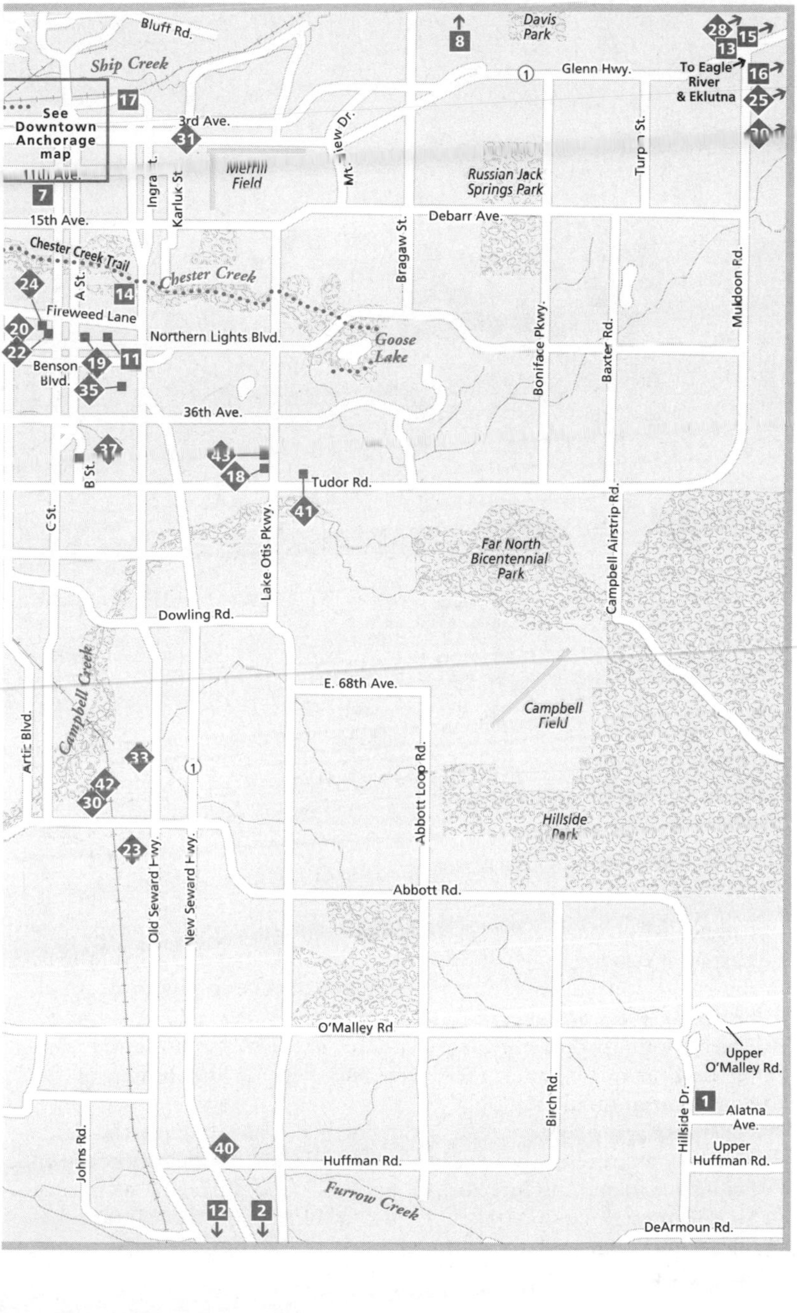
Bluff Rd.
Ship Creek
Davis Park
8
28
15
13
Glenn Hwy.
To Eagle River & Eklutna
16
25
17
See Downtown Anchorage map
3rd Ave.
31
Merrill Field
Russian Jack Springs Park
7
15th Ave.
Karluk St.
Debarr Ave.
Chester Creek Trail
Chester Creek
Bragaw St.
24
A St.
14
Fireweed Lane
Muldoon Rd.
20
22
Northern Lights Blvd.
Goose Lake
Boniface Pkwy.
Baxter Rd.
19
11
Benson Blvd.
35
36th Ave.
37
43
18
B St.
Tudor Rd.
41
C St.
Lake Otis Pkwy.
Far North Bicentennial Park
Campbell Airstrip Rd.
Dowling Rd.
Campbell Creek
E. 68th Ave.
Campbell Field
Abbott Loop Rd.
33
42
30
Hillside Park
23
Old Seward Hwy.
New Seward Hwy.
Abbott Rd.
O'Malley Rd
Upper O'Malley Rd.
Birch Rd.
1
Alatna Ave.
Hillside Dr.
Johns Rd.
40
Huffman Rd.
Upper Huffman Rd.
Furrow Creek
12
2
DeArmoun Rd.

downtown anchorage

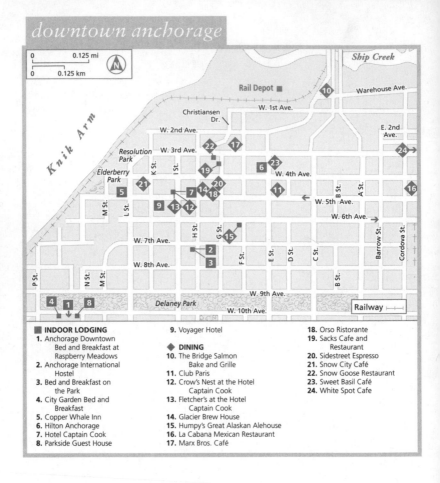

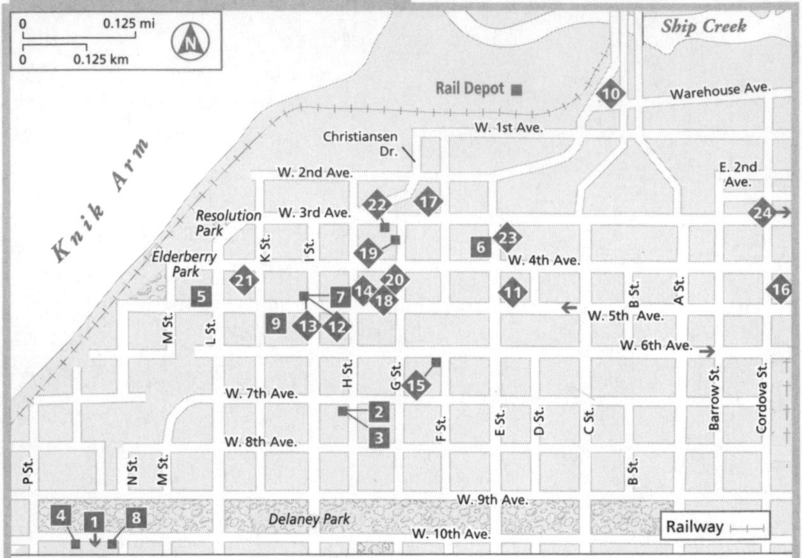

■ **INDOOR LODGING**

1. Anchorage Downtown Bed and Breakfast at Raspberry Meadows
2. Anchorage International Hostel
3. Bed and Breakfast on the Park
4. City Garden Bed and Breakfast
5. Copper Whale Inn
6. Hilton Anchorage
7. Hotel Captain Cook
8. Parkside Guest House
9. Voyager Hotel

◆ **DINING**

10. The Bridge Salmon Bake and Grille
11. Club Paris
12. Crow's Nest at the Hotel Captain Cook
13. Fletcher's at the Hotel Captain Cook
14. Glacier Brew House
15. Humpy's Great Alaskan Alehouse
16. La Cabana Mexican Restaurant
17. Marx Bros. Café
18. Orso Ristorante
19. Sacks Cafe and Restaurant
20. Sidestreet Espresso
21. Snow City Café
22. Snow Goose Restaurant
23. Sweet Basil Café
24. White Spot Cafe

Copper River Basin (the coastal communities of the Copper River Basin are covered in the Southcentral Coastal chapter, which follows this one). Continue north until you reach the Glenn Highway, which heads west toward the Matanuska-Susitna Valley and Anchorage. The community of **Glennallen** is situated at the crossroads and is thus included in this chapter. (See Part One, page 10, for a map of the Southcentral Inland region.)

This chapter covers areas as far north as **Talkeetna,** off the Parks Highway as travelers head north to the Interior. While it borders on being considered the Interior, we have included Talkeetna as part of Southcentral Inland Alaska because it is part of the Matanuska-Susitna Borough and a common day-trip destination for those basing their vacations out of Anchorage.

parks highway

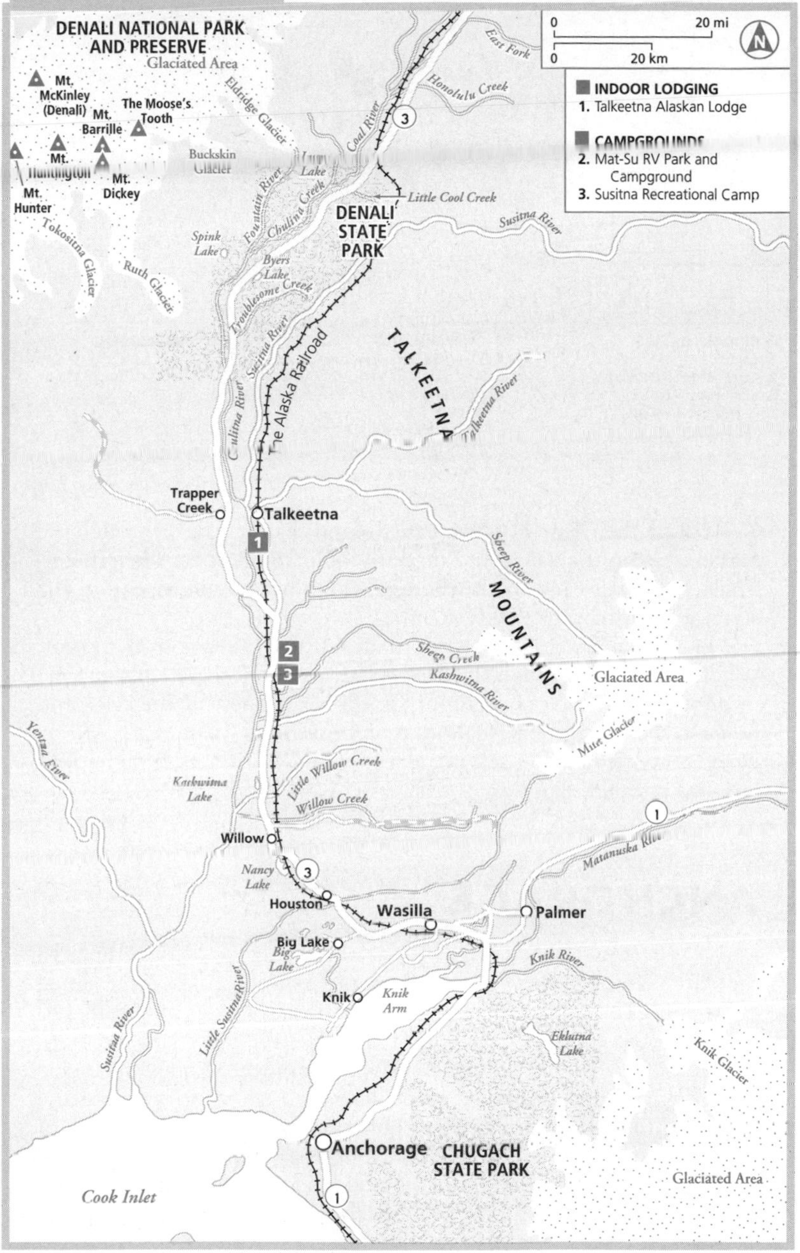

DENALI NATIONAL PARK AND PRESERVE
Glaciated Area
Mt. McKinley (Denali)
Mt. Barrille
The Moose's Tooth
Mt. Huntington
Mt. Dickey
Mt. Hunter
Eldridge Glacier
Buckskin Glacier
Tokositna Glacier
Ruth Glacier
Spink Lake
Byers Lake
Troublesome Creek
Fountain River
Chulitna Creek
Chulitna River
Susitna River
Coal River
East Fork
Honolulu Creek
Little Cool Creek
DENALI STATE PARK
The Alaska Railroad
TALKEETNA MOUNTAINS
Talkeetna River
Sheep River
Sheep Creek
Kashwitna River
Glaciated Area
Mute Glacier
Trapper Creek
Talkeetna
Yentna River
Kashwitna Lake
Little Willow Creek
Willow Creek
Willow
Nancy Lake
Houston
Wasilla
Palmer
Matanuska River
Big Lake
Knik
Knik Arm
Knik River
Knik Glacier
Eklutna Lake
Little Susitna River
Susitna River
Anchorage
CHUGACH STATE PARK
Glaciated Area
Cook Inlet
0 20 mi
0 20 km
N
INDOOR LODGING
1. Talkeetna Alaskan Lodge
CAMPGROUNDS
2. Mat-Su RV Park and Campground
3. Susitna Recreational Camp

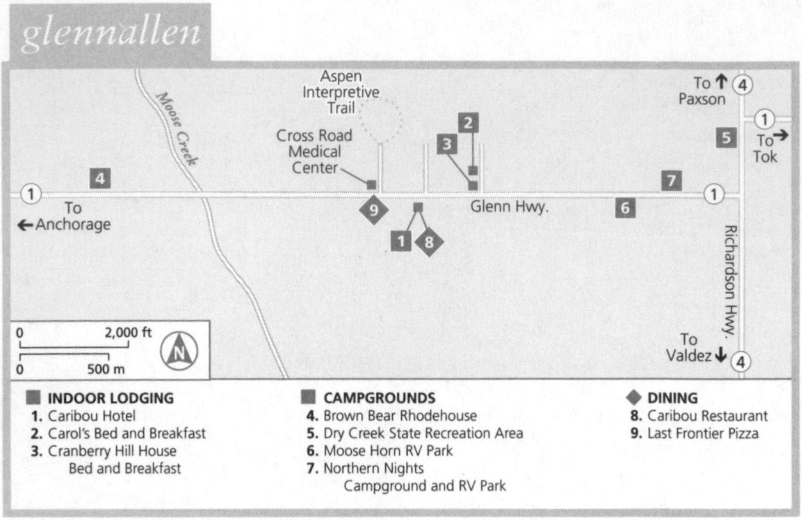

Back on the Glenn Highway, the Inland region travels through the **Matanuska-Susitna Valley** and its outlying communities. Then it continues southward toward **Anchorage,** the most populous city in the state, with nearly 300,000 residents.

No matter where your outdoor adventure takes you in Alaska, you'll likely pass through the Southcentral Inland region at one time or another. It is the major supply point for the rest of the state and home to the Ted Stevens Anchorage International Airport, a bustling, newly renovated facility serving all of the major airlines, both nationally and internationally.

So start here, and let your planning begin.

ANCHORAGE

ALASKANS WHO DON'T LIVE IN ANCHORAGE sometimes refer to the state's largest city as "Los Anchorage," as if it were some booming metropolis. They prefer their small towns and isolated communities to the hustle and bustle of city life.

But as cities go, Anchorage is welcoming indeed. And while it may seem big to those in tiny, remote villages, in reality it is one of the friendliest midsize cities in the country, with the added benefit of having the wilderness right at its back door. Consider this: where can you jump in a dogsled and mush along a snow-covered trail, hop on a plane and fly over a glacier, then still have time to change into fancy clothes and enjoy a night of fine dining and theater? In Anchorage, of course. This city of nearly 300,000 is a modern gem in the roughs glenn highway–glennallen area

CAMPGROUNDS
1. Dry Creek State Recreation Area
2. Tolsona Wilderness Campground and RV Park

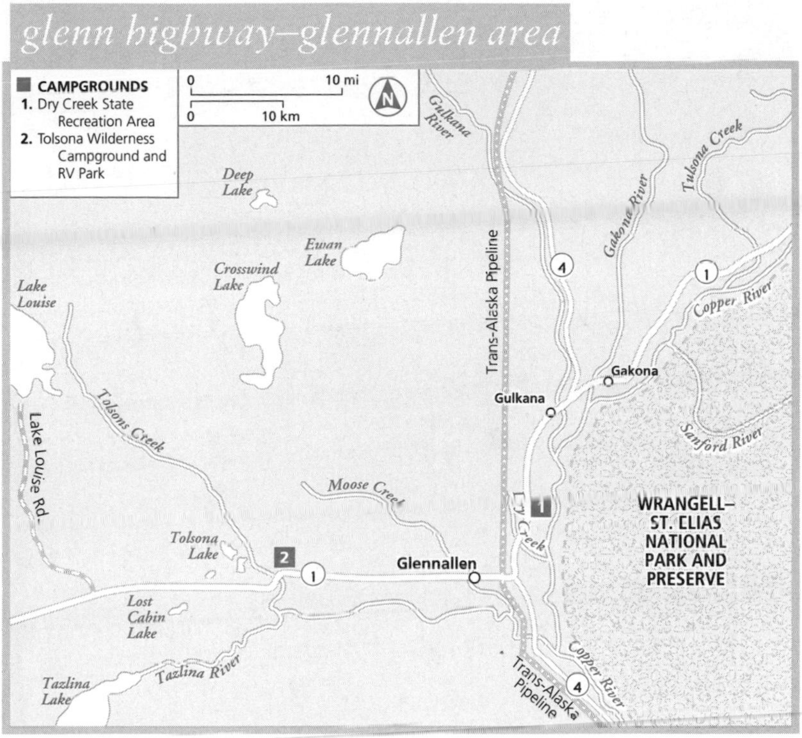

of Alaska, surrounded partly by the **Chugach Mountains** and partly by the waters of **Cook Inlet.** It encompasses some 1,955 square miles. Its boundaries extend from the **Eklutna** region, about 25 miles to the north, to the laid-back ski town of **Girdwood,** 37 miles to the south.

In the late 1700s, when Captain James Cook arrived in this spruce-tree-covered region, he saw little more than boggy areas with no inhabitants, despite the presence of many native settlements nearby. But soon after, Anchorage developed a small port for incoming ships, and the city grew. A railroad was built, and it grew even more. By the 1930s, Anchorage was well on its way to becoming a thriving city.

Today, Anchorage has all the amenities of Lower 48 cities. It boasts a community opera, a civic orchestra, a concert association, and several theater companies. Movie theaters are scattered throughout town, and major musicians, bands, and sports teams play at the city's

Anchorage Convention and Visitors Bureau
524 West Fourth Avenue
Anchorage 99501-2212
☎ 907-276-4118 or 800-478-1255
www.anchorage.net
Look for the sod-roofed Log Cabin and Downtown Visitor Information Center at the corner of F Street and Fourth Avenue.

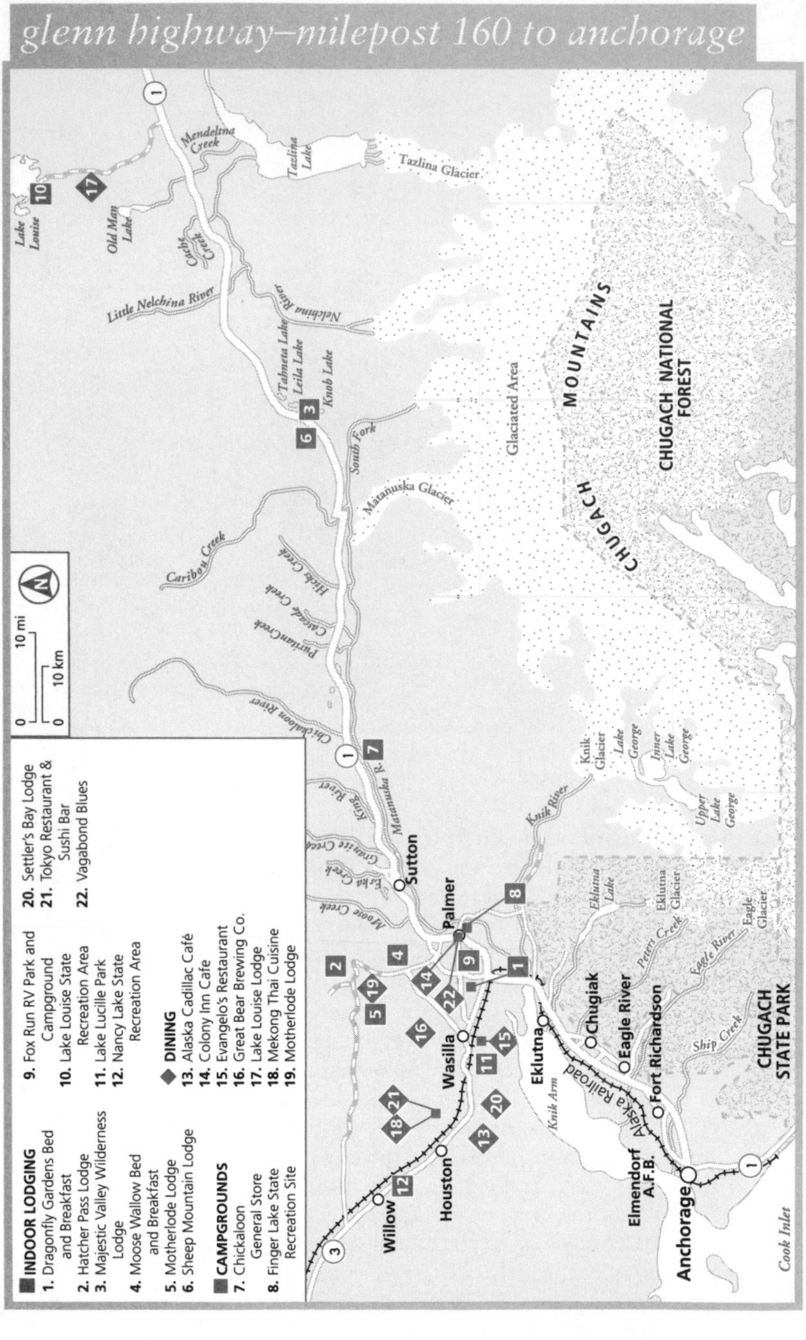
glenn highway–milepost 160 to anchorage
INDOOR LODGING
1. Dragonfly Gardens Bed and Breakfast
2. Hatcher Pass Lodge
3. Majestic Valley Wilderness Lodge
4. Moose Wallow Bed and Breakfast
5. Motherlode Lodge
6. Sheep Mountain Lodge
CAMPGROUNDS
7. Chickaloon General Store
8. Finger Lake State Recreation Site
9. Fox Run RV Park and Campground
10. Lake Louise State Recreation Area
11. Lake Lucille Park
12. Nancy Lake State Recreation Area
DINING
13. Alaska Cadillac Café
14. Colony Inn Cafe
15. Evangelo's Restaurant
16. Great Bear Brewing Co.
17. Lake Louise Lodge
18. Mekong Thai Cuisine
19. Motherlode Lodge
20. Settler's Bay Lodge
21. Tokyo Restaurant & Sushi Bar
22. Vagabond Blues
0 10 mi
0 10 km
N
Lake Louise
Old Man Lake
Mendeltna Creek
Tazlina Lake
Tazlina Glacier
Cache Creek
Little Nelchina River
Nelchina River
Tahneta Lake
Leila Lake
Knob Lake
South Fork
Matanuska Glacier
Glaciated Area
CHUGACH MOUNTAINS
CHUGACH NATIONAL FOREST
Caribou Creek
Hicks Creek
Cascade Creek
Purinton Creek
Chickaloon River
King River
Matanuska R.
Granite Creek
Eska Creek
Moose Creek
Knik River
Knik Glacier
Lake George
Inner Lake George
Upper Lake George
Eklutna Lake
Eklutna Glacier
Peters Creek
Eagle River
Eagle Glacier
Ship Creek
CHUGACH STATE PARK
Sutton
Palmer
Wasilla
Houston
Willow
Eklutna
Chugiak
Eagle River
Fort Richardson
Elmendorf A.F.B.
Anchorage
Knik Arm
Alaska Railroad
Cook Inlet

talkeetna

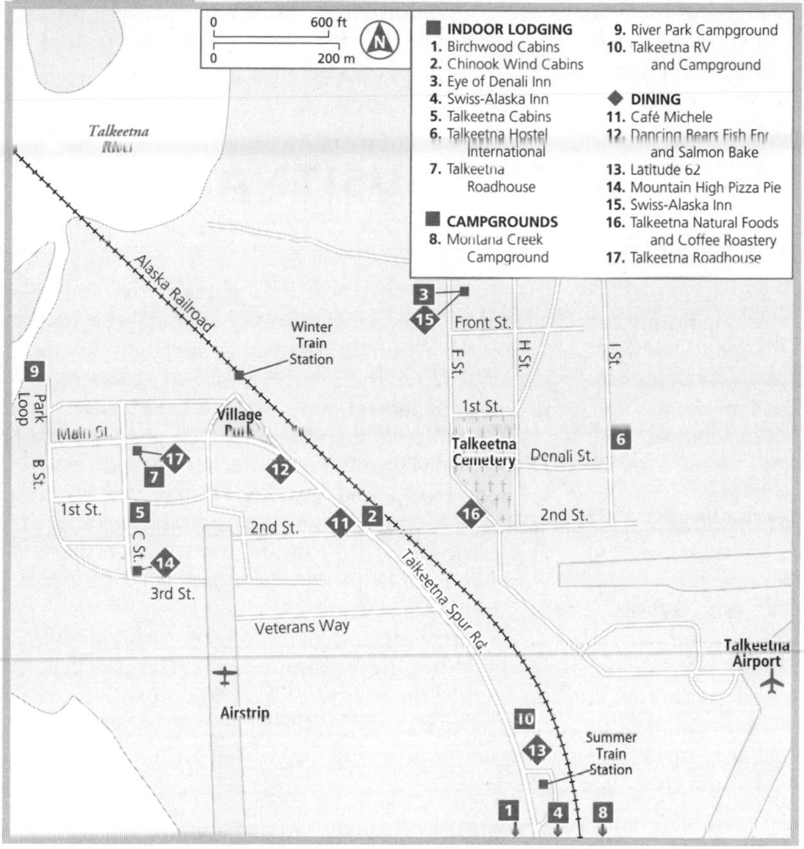

civic center and performing arts center throughout the year. It has a bustling international airport that services passengers and cargo from all over the world. The **Alaska Railroad** still travels to points north and south. And two main highways access the Interior and Kenai Peninsula.

There are places to eat, too. From a simple meal of Chinese stir-fry to elegant French cuisine with an Alaskan twist, the city has it all. Choose your pleasure: Thai, Korean, Mexican, or Greek. Italian, Vietnamese, Japanese, or Cajun. Chefs from around the globe, lured by Alaska's beauty, have established their own niches in Anchorage, surprising even the savviest traveler with their culinary skills out here on the Last Frontier.

Lodging in Anchorage runs from a simple bed in a hostel to the lavish multiroom suites for rent in some of Anchorage's finest hotels. Bed-and-breakfasts, too, run a thriving business in the summer, attracting visitors who prefer a more intimate view of the city as seen in area neighborhoods. Even campers can find a place to sleep in Anchorage.

MATANUSKA-SUSITNA VALLEY

ABOUT 35 MILES NORTH OF ANCHORAGE is a place that most locals simply call "The Valley." In fact, they are talking about a vast expanse of land, part of the Matanuska-Susitna Borough, which stretches from the northern end of **Eklutna** to just beyond **Talkeetna** and east to **Lake Louise.**

Mat-Su Convention and Visitors Bureau
7744 East Visitors View
Palmer 99645
☎ 907-746-5000
www.alaskavisit.com
Visitor center is at Mile 35.5 Parks Highway (Trunk Road Exit).

The Valley is a sportsman's paradise. Easily accessible lakes and rivers offer several species of salmon, trout, and grayling. There are great trails for hiking and mountain biking, and several rafting and ice-climbing options for those who like their outdoor adventures with a bit of an adrenaline rush.

The Hatcher Pass area is one of the highlights of the Valley. In the summer, it offers excellent biking, hiking, and birding. In the winter, skiers, dog mushers, and snowmobilers flock there since it is one of the first areas to get snow. For more on Hatcher Pass, see our listing in this chapter under "Wild Lands" (page 295).

If Alaska has a breadbasket, the Valley is it. This was no-man's-land until 1935 when, at the height of the Great Depression, the Federal Relief Administration sent struggling Midwesterners to Palmer to build new lives. The land was theirs, the government said, as long as they could make a living off of it. Today, some of those same farms still thrive, and the Palmer-Wasilla area bears some of the richest produce in the state.

Driving into the town of **Palmer** may remind you of Small Town U.S.A.—and it is. This close-knit community is home to the annual **Alaska State Fair**, which attracts thousands of carnival-goers at summer's end. Giant vegetables that grow fast under Alaska's constant summertime sun are heaved out of area gardens, weighed, and then judged. Hundred-pound cabbages, zucchinis, and squash are among the contestants. Agriculture exhibits, including milking cows, nursing sow pigs, and dog-handling competitions, keep the youngsters thrilled. And adults can join in the fun by entering any number of pie-baking, model-car-building, or quilt-making contests.

Neighboring **Wasilla** is a community gone to the dogs. Billing itself as "Home of the Iditarod," it is the official restarting point of the **Iditarod Trail Sled Dog Race** (the ceremonial start is in downtown Anchorage). Although the original Iditarod Trail started down in Seward, Congress has officially recognized the current route as a Millennium Trail. Race headquarters, just down Knik–Goose Bay Road, proudly displays videos and photographs of this 1,000-mile dogsled route to Nome, as well as a mount of beloved lead dog Togo. While Balto may be the lead dog who claimed most of the fame of the lifesaving diphtheria-medication run to Nome in 1925, it was faithful Togo whom musher Leonard Seppala loved most.

TALKEETNA

WHILE STILL PART OF THE MATANUSKA-SUSITNA BOROUGH, this independent community of about 850 considers itself its own destination. Talkeetna serves as the starting point for the hundreds of mountaineers who attempt to climb **Mount McKinley** (called **Denali** locally) each year. Come late spring, Talkeetna changes from a sleepy little outpost of locals to a melting pot of international guests from all over the world, and their accents and languages can be heard from the local saloon to the community mercantile.

Talkeetna Chamber of Commerce
P.O. Box 334
Talkeetna 99676
☎ 907-733-2330
www.talkeetnachamber.org

The town is at the junction of the Talkeetna and Susitna rivers, 99 miles north of Anchorage via the Parks Highway (the 14-mile Talkeetna Spur Road gets you to the center of town). It is also accessible by Alaska Railroad from Fairbanks or Anchorage, or by small aircraft. Within its 43 square miles are rivers, mountains, valleys, and lakes. Its location at the base of Denali (and other surrounding and equally impressive mountains) means Talkeetna gets a lot of snow, too, attracting skiers and dog mushers in the winter with its average 70-inch snowfall each year.

In the summer, it can get as warm as 83°F, but it also can get buggy. The lakes and rivers attract pests by the millions, and they can drive one to distraction.

Talkeetna (pronounced Tall-**KEET**-nah) is a Dena'ina Indian word meaning "river of plenty." The area was settled as a mining town and Alaska Commercial company trading post in 1896. Gold prospectors came to the area, and by 1910, Talkeetna was a riverboat-steamer station. In 1915, Talkeetna was chosen as the headquarters for the Alaska Engineering Commission, who built the Alaska Railroad, and the community population peaked near 1,000. When World War I began and the railroad was completed, however, many people left. The community has maintained many of its historic buildings, though, and today Talkeetna is listed on the National Register of Historic Places.

One of Talkeetna's largest economic mainstays is the local fleet of air-taxi operators that help climbers reach their destinations. Local businesses also provide helicopters, guiding, and related services.

GLENNALLEN

Greater Copper Valley Chamber of Commerce
P.O. Box 469
Glennallen 99588
☎ 907-822-5558
www.traveltoalaska.com

GLENNALLEN IS THE SUPPLY HUB for the surrounding Copper River Basin region, with a centralized location and most agencies that serve the people of this part of the state. Police, government, and federal land offices are in Glennallen, as well as transportation-department facilities.

The 550-person community is not so spectacular to look at as you drive along the Glenn Highway, but if you get out and beyond the road system, you can truly appreciate its outdoor beauty. Most people come to Glennallen as they are passing through to other destinations, but some people choose to stop and explore. Off-road adventures, dog mushing, and fishing are some of the more popular pastimes.

Glennallen is located along the Glenn Highway at its junction with the Richardson Highway, 189 road miles east of Anchorage. It is just outside the western boundary of **Wrangell–St. Elias National Park and Preserve,** the country's largest national park. It is bordered by four mountain ranges, which attract climbers during the season. There are dozens of rivers from which to fish.

The area gets long, cold winters and relatively warm summers. The mean temperature in January is –10°F; in July, it is 56°F. It's a relatively dry area, though, with snowfall averaging 39 inches, with total precipitation (including melted snow and rain) of 9 inches per year.

Glennallen's name derived from Major Edwin Glenn and Lieutenant Henry Allen, both leaders in the early explorations of the Copper River region. It is one of the few communities in the region that was not built on the site of a native village.

COPPER VALLEY

STRETCHING ALONG EITHER SIDE of the Copper River and spreading for 3.5 million acres in either direction is the Copper Valley, a region of the state that offers just about any outdoor adventure you can imagine, whether on a river, glacier, or mountain. The Copper Valley, which includes **Wrangell–St. Elias National Park and Preserve,** is located 189 miles northwest of Anchorage, 250 miles south of Fairbanks, and 115 miles north of Valdez. It is only 200 miles from

Canada and is accessed by two main roads, the Richardson and Glenn highways.

Summer recreational activities in the Copper Valley include rafting, hiking, and excellent fishing for king and red salmon in the rivers, as well as trout and grayling in the lakes and streams. The **Copper, Klutina, and Gulkana rivers** are major fishing destinations that offer excellent angling without the crowds of some of the state's other rivers.

Greater Copper Valley Chamber of Commerce
P.O. Box 469
Glennallen 99588
☎ 907-822-5558
www.traveltoalaska.com

In the winter, Copper River visitors can enjoy snowmobiling, skiing, ice fishing, snowboarding, and the **Copper Basin 300** sled-dog race, which has become a qualifying race for the Iditarod.

The largest Southcentral Inland community in the Copper Valley is **Glennallen**, outlined in the previous section. But other smaller communities that fall within the Southcentral Inland–Copper Valley region include **Copper Center, Kenny Lake,** and **McCarthy.**

The 61-mile **McCarthy Road** offers access directly into Wrangell–St. Elias National Park and Preserve. Driving this road is an adventure, with its gravel-and-dirt surface making for slow travel. It can take as long as three hours to cover the 60 miles, and flat tires are not uncommon. At the end of the road, you will find parking areas and two footbridges that cross the Kennicott River and lead to the historic communities of **McCarthy** and **Kennicott.** Access to McCarthy is by foot, bike, or shuttle. Traveling the McCarthy Road provides access to some incredible hiking, fishing, and camping.

WILD LANDS

CHUGACH STATE PARK

(Primary activities: backpacking, hiking, mountain biking, birding, mountaineering, off-road travel, kayaking, fishing, skiing, rafting)

THERE'S REALLY NOT MUCH YOU *can't* do in the great outdoor playground that is Chugach State Park. The park's 500,000 acres of glaciers, mountains, and valleys are right in Anchorage's backyard, surrounding the city like a comfortable blanket. Grizzly bears, wolves, moose, and even the occasional lynx will sometimes wander into town, reminding Alaskans of just how close the wilderness is to our civilization.

Chugach State Park is the third-largest state park in America—a half-million acres of some of the most accessible outdoor activity on the

Chugach State Park
Potter Section House
Mile 115 Seward Highway
HC 52, Box 8999
Indian 99540
☎ 907-345-5014
www.dnr.state.ak.us/parks/units/chugach

Division of Natural Resources Public Information Center
Robert Atwood Building
550 West Seventh Avenue
Suite 1260
Anchorage 99501-3557
☎ 907-269-8400
www.dnr.state.ak.us/pic/index.htm

planet. For many people who live in Anchorage, reaching the park is simply a matter of slipping on their skis and heading out their front doors, or lacing up their boots and climbing the mountain directly behind their homes.

Access to the park is amazingly simple—you can even take a taxi to local trailheads. But first you must get to Anchorage, which is accessible by daily jet service from most major airlines, or the Glenn Highway, which is the sole feeder highway from all points north.

Several highlights of Chugach State Park include the **Flattop Trail,** which overlooks the city and is perhaps the most-hiked trail in all of Alaska; the **Eagle River Nature Center,** run by a nonprofit park-supporter and offering dozens of interpretive programs year-round; and **Eklutna Lake,** an aquamarine lake at the northern edge of Alaska with everything from kayaking to mountaineering to fishing.

WRANGELL–ST. ELIAS NATIONAL PARK AND PRESERVE

(Primary activities: backpacking, hiking, mountaineering, skiing, dog mushing, kayaking, fishing, rafting)

MANY SUPERLATIVES ARE ASSOCIATED with Wrangell–St. Elias National Park and Preserve. At 13 million acres, it is the nation's largest national park. It includes the continent's largest assemblage of glaciers and the greatest collection of peaks above 16,000 feet—**Mount Sanford** (16,237 feet), and **Mount Blackburn** (16,390 feet), to name just a few. **Mount St. Elias,** at 18,008 feet, is the second-highest peak in the United States, after Denali, a few hundred miles to the northeast.

Wrangell–St. Elias National Park and Preserve
106.8 Richardson Highway
P.O. Box 439
Copper Center 99573
☎ 907-822-5234
www.nps.gov/wrst

Here's another way to think about it, as National Park Service rangers often do when trying to convey the region's vastness: Wrangell–St. Elias is as big as six Yellowstones!

Wrangell–St. Elias became a national park and preserve in 1980, and ever since has maintained its rugged remoteness. Most people access the area by the Richardson Highway, to the Edgerton Highway, which goes to the in-park community of **McCarthy.** You can also take the less-traveled Nabesna Road, north of Glennallen, in what we consider to be part of the Interior. Or you can fly in. There are several charter operators that can fly guests into areas of the park ranging from glacier landings to river drop-offs.

Wildlife is abundant in the area. The park has the largest concentration of Dall sheep in North America. Other large-animal species include goats, caribou, moose, grizzly bears, black bears, and bison. The more elusive lynx, wolverine, marten, fox, and wolf also prowl the landscape.

Most travelers into Wrangell–St. Elias choose to tent-camp, but this park is unique in that it also has 13 public-use cabins, most of which were old mining, trapping, or hunting cabins. The National Park Service has restored them all, and all but two of them are free and available on a first-come, first-served basis. They have a woodstove and bunks, but you have to supply the rest. Replenish any firewood stored in the cabins for the next user.

Anchorage Parks and Recreation
☎ 907-343-4474

Eagle River–Chugiak Parks and Recreation
☎ 907-601-2011
www.muni.org/parks/parks.cfm

To get an Anchorage Parks and Trails Map:
Anchorage Parks and Recreation
P.O. Box 196650
120 South Bragaw Street
Anchorage 99519

MUNICIPALITY OF ANCHORAGE

(Primary activities: hiking, mountain biking, skiing, dog mushing)

THE ANCHORAGE PARKS AND RECREATION DEPARTMENT maintains a surprising number of parks from Eagle River to Girdwood and points between. Of the 120-plus locations, a select few are perennial favorites among outdoors-lovers. These locations are perfect day-outings for those based in Anchorage.

Dog mushers go to the **Beach Lake Trails** in **Chugiak,** about 20 miles north of Anchorage and considered the center of dog mushing for Anchorage-area residents. The extensive trail system there is managed by the Chugiak Dog Mushers Association, an involved group of folks dedicated to providing access for dog mushing in their community.

In **Anchorage,** skiers like **Hillside Park** and **Hilltop Ski Area** off Abbott Loop Road (from the Seward Highway, turn east toward the mountains at the Abbott Lake–Dimond exit) or 1,400-acre **Kincaid Park** (take Minnesota Boulevard to Raspberry Road and follow it to its end). **Russian Jack Springs** is another favorite for those just getting started in cross-country skiing, with beginner trails (take DeBarr Road east to the turnoff on the right).

Mountain bikers are drawn to Hillside, Kincaid, and Russian Jack Springs for its extensive trail system, as well. Beach Lake Trails are mushing-only trails, however, and too wet to ride in the summer.

A number of other leisure areas are maintained by Anchorage Parks and Recreation, ranging from covered picnic spots to playgrounds to athletic and sports fields. Purchasing a park map is a great idea for anyone spending time in Anchorage. It's amazing how far out you can feel when just minutes from the highway.

U.S. BUREAU OF LAND MANAGEMENT

(Primary activities: hiking, mountain biking, skiing, dog mushing)

THE BUREAU OF LAND MANAGEMENT IN ALASKA manages 85.5 million acres of land across the state, and the **Anchorage Field Office,** including 700 acres right in the city, manages 16 million acres. A popular jumping-off point for day-trip adventures within the park is at the **Campbell Creek Science Center,** which is run by BLM employees

BLM–Alaska State Office
222 West Seventh Avenue
Number 13
Anchorage 99513
☎ 907-271-5960
www.blm.gov/ak/st/en.html

Campbell Creek Science Center
6865 Abbott Loop Road
Anchorage, Alaska
99507-2599
☎ 907-267-1247

and serves as an education and interpretive center for Anchorage residents and visitors.

The **Campbell Tract** area surrounding the Science Center has a series of trails used by dog mushers, skijorers (skiers who are pulled by sled dogs), hikers, mountain bikers, and horsemen. The BLM office works with different user groups to provide multiuse trails and offer other programs for those who want to explore nature within the city limits.

HATCHER PASS–SUMMIT LAKE STATE RECREATION SITE

(Primary activities: hiking, skiing, dog mushing, mountain biking)

Mat-Su Area Park Office
Mile 0.7 Bogard Road
HC 32 Box 6706
Wasilla 99654
☎ 907-745-3975
www.dnr.state.ak.us/parks/units/summit.htm

AS YOU CLIMB THE HATCHER PASS ROAD that winds up, up, and up toward Summit Lake, it feels as if you are in Switzerland. The rugged peaks get taller and closer, and the small A-frame chalets near the pass add a winter-resort feel to this gem in the Matanuska-Susitna Borough.

The Hatcher Pass area is managed by **Alaska State Parks,** but the Summit Lake State Recreation Site, located at Mile 19 of Hatcher Pass Road, and about two miles past the historic and recently renovated Independence Mine State Historic Park, is the highlight. Hatcher Pass Summit is in the park at an elevation of 3,886 feet, and it is here that the first snows of the season usually arrive.

There is road access to the Summit Lake area, but it is closed as soon as the snow conditions make it undrivable. You can, however, reach as far as Hatcher Pass Lodge and Independence Mine, 17 miles in, year-round.

The Summit Lake recreation site encompasses **Summit Lake,** a small, steep-banked lake, or tarn, that is about 20 feet deep at its deepest point. It is the remains of an old glacier, and it is easy to imagine that it was once a snow-covered area year-round.

Above Summit Lake is **April Bowl,** a favorite among skiers and snowboarders who flock to the area as soon as there is enough snow to cover the rocks. On weekend days, it is not uncommon to see these winter alpinists climbing up and boarding or skiing down the bowl over and over.

unofficial **TIP**
A trail around Summit Lake is great for family hiking, and the views are incredible. Sometimes paragliders launch from here, which is fun to watch on nice days.

However, avalanches occur regularly on the steep slopes in the area. Use extreme caution when doing any wintertime activities in the park, and know how to read the snow.

NANCY LAKE STATE RECREATION AREA
(Primary activities: canoeing, camping, fishing, dog mushing, skiing)

JUST OUTSIDE OF WASILLA AND 67 MILES NORTH of Anchorage is one of Valley residents' favorite places to play, the Nancy Lake State Recreation Area. This 22,685-acre park has canoe trails, ski trails, cabins, and more.

Nancy Lake Ranger Station
Mile 1.3 Nancy Lake Parkway
P.O. Box 10
Willow 99688
☎ 907-495-6273
www.dnr.state.ak.us/parks/units/nancylk/nancylk.htm

To get there, turn west onto Nancy Lake Parkway at Mile 67.3 of the Parks Highway. In the summer, the road is open to Mile 6.5, at the South Rolly Lake Campground. In the winter it is not plowed, as is closed from Mile 2.2 at the Winter Trailhead.

Through the years, most of the Nancy Lake area has remained wild and natural. The area is too wet for ideal cultivation and is not mineral-rich, so it has escaped large-scale human settlement. The weather in the summer stays in the 70°F range, but in the winter it can fall to –40°F and seldom rises above freezing until mid-March. The first snow usually arrives by late October, about the same time the lakes freeze over. Snow depth in late winter averages three to four feet. Lakes are usually free of ice by late May.

Among the great things about this recreation area are the public-use cabins located on **Red Shirt, Lynx, Nancy, James, and Bald lakes.** They're insulated and equipped with wooden bunks, counters, and wood-burning stoves. Each cabin has an outhouse and an outdoor fire ring. The cabins rent for $25 to $60 per night depending upon which one is reserved.

Birding in the area is another favorite pastime, and canoeists can enjoy hearing the call of the common loon and, occasionally, their smaller, grey-headed relative, the Pacific loon.

Other wildlife in the area include moose, which love to munch on the sludge from shallow ponds or the brushy areas surrounding the lakes. Black bears also are common, and grizzlies are spotted now and then.

GETTING *around* SOUTHCENTRAL INLAND ALASKA

ANCHORAGE

ACCESS BY AIR IS THROUGH **Alaska Airlines** (☎ 800-252-7522; **www.alaskaair.com**). You can also drive to Fairbanks from the Richardson or Parks highways.

unofficial **TIP**
Loons sitting on the shore should always be given a wide berth. They come ashore only to nest and will often desert their nests when disturbed.

More than a dozen car-rental options are available in the Anchorage area, but we have found **Budget** (☎ 800-527-0700; **www.budgetrentacar.com**), **Enterprise** (☎ 800-261-7331; **www.enterprise.com**), **Hertz** (☎ 800-654-3131; **www.hertz.com**), and **Denali Car Rental** (☎ 907-276-1230; **www.denalicarrentalak.com**) to be the best.

Anchorage has fair bus service, called the **People Mover** (700 West Sixth Avenue, at the transit center; ☎ 907-343-6543; **www.peoplemover.org).** The system has 15 regular routes that travel to specified areas as reserved. Fares are $1.75 for adults, one-way. Day passes are available for $4, and you can travel all routes. The bus runs from 5:45 a.m. to 11:55 p.m. weekdays and from 7:45 a.m. to 9:15 p.m. Saturdays. On Sundays it operates from 9:30 a.m. to 7 p.m.

The **Ship Creek Shuttle,** also affiliated with People Mover, offers free transportation in the downtown and Ship Creek areas.

- **ABC Motorhome and Car Rentals** ☎ 800-421-7456, **www.abcmotorhome.com**
  This company has a range of RVs, as well as a luxury van for large groups and camper rentals for smaller parties. No smoking vehicles. No pets allowed. Rates in the $220-to-$250 range.
- **Alaska Affordable Motor Home Rental** ☎ 907-349-4878 or 360-624-6507; **www.alaska-rv-rental.com**
  Much less expensive than its competitors, with rates at $165 per day with free, unlimited miles in Alaska. Vehicles are not as fancy, but quite functional. No smoking or pets allowed.
- **Alaska Best RV Rentals** ☎ 866-544-4981 or 907-344-4981; **www.alaskabestrvrentals.com**
  With rates lower than the large-company averages—$160 to $175. No smoking or pets allowed.
- **Alaska Railroad** 327 West Ship Creek Avenue; ☎ 907-265-2494 or 800-544-0552; **www.alaskarailroad.com**
  The railroad has daily routes serving Anchorage, the Valley, and Talkeetna, among other regions. One-way rates from Anchorage are $50 to the Valley, $82 to Talkeetna.
- **Magic Bus** ☎ 907-268-6311; **www.themagicbus.com**
  If you have a group and want to travel anywhere within the Southcentral Coastal Alaska to the southern edge of the Interior and all points between, you can rent these private motorcoaches and vans, complete with a driver.
- **Park Connection** ☎ 800-266-8625; **www.alaskacoach.com**
  This driver-supplied option offers twice-daily coach service between Anchorage and Seward, including connecting service between Denali Park, Talkeetna, Anchorage, and Seward.

MATANUSKA-SUSITNA VALLEY

- **Classy Cars Sales and Rentals** 2970 Cottle Loop off the Palmer-Wasilla Highway; ☎ 888-323-3023 or 907-373-3023; **www.classycarrentals.com**
  Rentals start at $53 per day with unlimited miles.

- **Valley Car Rentals** 435 South Knik Street, Wasilla; ☎ 888-719-2880 or 907-775-2880; **www.valleycarrental.com**
  Cars, RVs, and SUVs, free miles, and delivery/pickup. Also offers an airport shuttle to and from Anchorage.

TALKEETNA/GLENNALLEN/COPPER VALLEY

- **Alaska Railroad** 327 West Ship Creek Avenue; ☎ 907-265-2494 or 800-544-0552; **www.alaskarailroad.com**
  The railroad has daily routes serving Anchorage and Talkeetna. The cost is $82.
- **Backcountry Connection** ☎ 907-822-5292; **www.alaska-backcountry-tours.com**
  Backcountry Connection offers one-way and round-trip transportation to and from most locations within the Interior. They sometimes have Web specials if you plan ahead.
- **Sparks General Store and Automotive** Mile 188.5 Glenn Highway; ☎ 907-822-5990 or 907-822-5991; **www.sparksgeneralstore.com**
  They carry everything from groceries to auto supply parts and cell phones, and they also rent vehicles. We're not making this up, we promise.
- **Talkeetna Shuttle Service** ☎ 888-288-6008 or 907-733-1725; **www.denalicentral.com**
  The shuttle caters mostly to climbers, running from Anchorage to Talkeetna at regularly scheduled times during the season. Rates are $65 and $125 for one-way or round-trip.
- **Wrangell Mountain Air** ☎ 800-478-1160 or 907-554-4411; **www.wrangellmountainair.com**
  This company is the one to use if you want to be dropped off in the wilderness. They know Wrangell–St. Elias National Park and Preserve intimately and can land safely. Additional companies that provide air service into the park and other locations throughout the Copper Valley include **Copper Valley Air Service** (☎ 866-570-4200 or 907-822-4200; **www.coppervalleyair.com**), **Ellis Air Taxi** (☎ 800-478-3368 or 907-822-3368; **www.ellisair.com**), and **Lee's Air Taxi** (☎ 907-822-5030; **www.leesairtaxi.com**).
- **Wrangell–St. Elias Lodging and Tours** Mile 7.5 Edgerton Highway, between Kenny Lake and Copper Center; ☎ 907-822-5978; **www.alaskayukontravel.com**
  The company does tours but also offers shuttle service for backpackers and anglers traveling in the area.

GEARING UP

SOUTHCENTRAL INLAND ALASKA is the place to gear up to go anywhere in the state. This region boasts more stores, more selection, and in most cases better prices than anywhere else in the state.

The majority of choices are in the Anchorage area, with a few good retailers in the Matanuska-Susitna Valley. The nice thing about buying

unofficial **TIP**
As you would when traveling elsewhere in the state, check with the air carriers on which you will be flying for regulations on carrying items such as knives, guns, camp stoves, and camp fuel. You may need to purchase certain items at your final destination and leave them behind when you fly home.

some of your supplies in these communities instead of purchasing them ahead of time is that most shops have experience in the places to which you will be traveling, and they can recommend the most appropriate gear. Stores such as **REI** and **Alaska Mountaineering and Hiking,** both in Anchorage, offer prices that are just as good as what you will find in Lower 48 cities, although not always as low as discounts you may be able to find online. We still think shopping locally is the way to go, though, because unless you know exactly which product you want, online discounts won't help much if the gear you've selected turns out to be wrong for Alaska conditions.

This section of the book is broken down by the main communities in Southcentral Inland Alaska with shops that will help you find what you are looking for. We list sporting goods/camping supplies and groceries separately, but many stores in the communities along the Copper River Basin carry a little of everything in one stop.

SPORTING GOODS AND CAMPING SUPPLIES

Anchorage

- **Alaska Mountaineering and Hiking** 2633 Spenard Road; ☎ 907-272-1811; **www.alaskamountaineering.com**
  An Anchorage favorite, featuring skiing, mountaineering, and other outdoor clothing and gear. Locally owned.
- **Barney's Sports Chalet** 906 West Northern Lights Boulevard; ☎ 907-561-5242
  A longtime Anchorage business that offers high-quality camping and skiing gear at competitive prices.
- **The Bicycle Shop** 1035 West Northern Lights Boulevard; ☎ 907-272-5219
  These guys carry Cannondale, Rocky Mountain, Specialized, Trek, and other popular brands; they no longer rent bikes, though.
- **McAfee's Fly Shop** 750 West Dimond Boulevard; ☎ 907-344-1617
  Not an easy shop to find, tucked away in a strip mall, but it carries the best fly tackle around.
- **Mountain View Sports** 3838 Old Seward Highway; ☎ 907-563-8600
  This longtime sporting-goods store has everything for outdoor adventures, especially fishing and other water sports.
- **Paramount Cycles** 1320 Huffman Park Drive, South Anchorage; ☎ 907-336-2453
  They carry Raleigh, Gary Fisher, Giant, LeMond, and a few other brands.
- **Chain Reaction Cycles** 12201 Industry Way, Unit 2, South Anchorage; ☎ 907-336-0383; **www.chainreactioncycles.us**
  They carry Litespeed, Orbea, Cervelo, Klein, Ellsworth and other high-end brands, and are the bike shop of choice for elite riders and triathletes.

- **Peter Glenn Ski and Sport** 1520 O'Malley Road; ☎ 907-349-2929
  The shop is located in a faux castle, but it has great selection and quick service for snowboards and skis.
- **Recreational Equipment Inc. (REI)** 1200 West Northern Lights Boulevard; ☎ 907-272-4565; **www.rei.com/stores/anchorage**
  The newly renovated store is massive, with just about any type of outdoor gear you will ever need. Doing (brisk) business in Anchorage since 1980.
- **Skinny Raven Sports** 800 H Street, downtown; ☎ 907-274-7222
  This is a local favorite among runners and triathletes. Plenty of outdoor gear, including the hottest in local sports such as Frisbee golf and handball.
- **The Sport Shop** 570 East Benson Boulevard; ☎ 907-272-7755
  A great choice for women's outdoor apparel. Not too much in the way of technical outdoors gear, though.

Matanuska-Susitna Valley

- **Windy Corner** 1551 East Parks Highway, Wasilla; ☎ 907-373-6117
  For climbing supplies and gear.

Glennallen–Copper River Basin

- **The Hub of Alaska** Mile 114 Richardson Highway; ☎ 907-822-3555
  They carry limited sporting goods and sell hunting and fishing licenses.
- **Tolsona Lake Resort** Mile 173 Glenn Highway; ☎ 907-822-3433
  They offer boat and canoe rentals and sell hunting and fishing licenses.

GROCERY

Anchorage

- **Carrs/Safeway** Locations at Abbott Road, Dimond Boulevard, Huffman Road, Northern Lights Boulevard, and Eagle River
  This full-service grocery store has a very limited supply of sporting goods, mostly fishing tackle. They all sell fishing and hunting licenses.
- **Fred Meyer** Locations at Abbott Road, Dimond Boulevard, Muldoon Road, Northern Lights Boulevard, and Eagle River
  There are locations spread across town, and this is the best choice for one-stop shopping, including sporting goods, fishing licenses, and full-service groceries.
- **The Natural Pantry** 3901 Old Seward Highway; ☎ 907-770-1444 and 601 East Dimond Boulevard; ☎ 907-522-4330
  Both locations offer all-organic and health foods, as well as a tasty cafe for lunches. We like the Old Seward Highway location best.
- **New Sagaya** 900 West 13th Avenue; ☎ 907-274-6173 and 3700 Old Seward Highway; ☎ 907-561-5173
  Organic and hard-to-find foods with cafes in both locations.

Matanuska-Susitna Valley

- **Carrs** 595 East Parks Highway, Wasilla; ☎ 907-352-1100 and at Palmer Square Mall, Palmer; ☎ 907-761-1400
  Both locations offer a full line of groceries. Fishing licenses available.

- **Chickaloon General Store** Mile 76.3 Glenn Highway; ☎ 907-746-4520
  If you forgot something in Palmer, here's another chance to find it. Groceries, gas, and liquor are available, as well as fishing licenses. Camping also is allowed by the river.
- **Fred Meyer** 1601 East Parks Highway, Wasilla; ☎ 907-352-5000 and at intersection of Palmer-Wasilla Highway, 650 South Cobb Street, Palmer; ☎ 907-761-4200
  Both locations offer a full line of groceries and sporting goods. Fishing licenses available.

Talkeetna

- **Nagley's General Store** ☎ 907-733-3663
  General groceries, household supplies, and ice cream, plus a gift shop upstairs. *Note:* The shop is for sale, so it could be under a different name at press time.
- **Talkeetna Natural Foods and Coffee Roastery** 2137 Talkeetna Townsite, downtown (across from the airport); ☎ 907-733-3882
  Organic coffee, Internet access, and organic groceries and dry goods.

Glennallen–Copper River Basin

- **Glennallen Chiropractic Organic Garden** Mile 187.5 Glenn Highway; ☎ 907-822-3353
  Get your back adjusted while enjoying fresh smoothies and stocking up on health-food supplies.
- **Park's Place** Mile 188 Glenn Highway; ☎ 907-822-3334
  Full-service grocery and hand-packed meats. Also serves espresso and deli sandwiches to order.
- **Sparks General Store and Automotive** Mile 188.5 Glenn Highway, Glennallen; ☎ 907-822-5990 or 907-822-5970
  They carry everything from groceries to auto-supply parts, and they also rent vehicles.

WHERE *to* STAY

WHERE THERE ARE MORE PEOPLE, there also are more lodging opportunities. In Southcentral Inland Alaska, the offerings range from fine hotels housing restaurants that serve foie gras to one-room cabins with no running water or electricity. Each option has a charm all its own—it just depends on what kind of adventure you envision.

In this section, we offer our favorite choices, places that we have tried ourselves and found to be memorable.

ANCHORAGE

Indoor Lodging

- **Alaskan Frontier Gardens Bed and Breakfast** 7440 Alatna Avenue, on the Anchorage Hillside; ☎ 907-345-6556; **www.alaskafrontiergardens.com**

QUALITY ★★★★ VALUE ★★★ $125–$225

This award-winning bed-and-breakfast is beautiful inside and out. The breakfasts are elegant, and on-site spa services are available.

- **Alaskan Leopard Bed and Breakfast** 16136 Sandpiper Drive; ☎ 907-868-1594 or 877-454-3046; **www.alaskanleopard.com**

QUALITY ★★★★★ VALUE ★★★★★ $119–$159

With outstanding views from its Upper Hillside location, this little-known but excellent bed-and-breakfast is a true treat. The chefs' food rivals that of the fine restaurants in town.

- **Alyeska Hostel** Alpina Way, Girdwood, 35 miles south of Anchorage; ☎ 907-783-2222; **www.alyeskahostel.com**

QUALITY ★★★ VALUE ★★★★★ $20–$80

Accommodations consist of bunks and private rooms, and also a new cabin, great for families.

- **Alyeska Resort Prince Hotel** In Girdwood, 35 miles south of Anchorage on the Seward Highway; ☎ 907-754-2111 or 800-880-3880; **www.alyeskaresort.com**

QUALITY ★★★★★ VALUE ★★★★ $199–$2,200

This luxurious year-round hotel in the ski town of Girdwood is at the base of the ski resort of the same name, and it is a favorite getaway for South-central Alaskans. Enjoy the fine dining at the top of the mountain via the scenic tram, or indulge in the giant hot tub with a view of the mountains. Lodging/ski packages are available. New ownership in 2007 has pointed to serious posh upgrades.

- **Anchorage Downtown Bed and Breakfast at Raspberry Meadows** 1401 West 13th Avenue; ☎ 907-278-9275; **www.anchoragedowntown.com**

QUALITY ★★★★ VALUE ★★★★★ $89–$139

This historic downtown bed-and-breakfast is within walking distance of all downtown shops, hotels, tourist attractions, and outdoor activities. It's a favorite lodging choice among active travelers, with two private suites and one room in the house. A guesthouse is available for extended stays.

- **Anchorage Guest House** 2001 Hillcrest Drive off L Street; ☎ 907-274-0408; **www.alaska.net/~house/index.html**

QUALITY ★★★★★ VALUE ★★★★★ $30–$140

This is probably the nicest hostel in Anchorage, in a good section of town. The guesthouse is located right off the Tony Knowles Coastal Trail, which is a great link to the rest of the city. Private rooms and bunks are available.

- **Anchorage International Hostel** Seventh Avenue and H Street; ☎ 907-276-3635; **www.anchorageinternationalhostel.org**

QUALITY ★★★ VALUE ★★★★ $25–$65

Practically downtown, this convenient hostel has 95 beds that fill up fast. There's a 1 a.m. curfew, and no parking is available other than metered parking on the street. A $3 discount is available for Hostelling International members. Private rooms are available at a higher rate, but they must be reserved in advance by phone.

- **Bed and Breakfast on the Park** 602 West Tenth Avenue; ☎ 907-277-0878 or 800-353-0878; **www.bedandbreakfastonthepark.net**

  QUALITY ★★★★ VALUE ★★★ $125+

  You can't miss this bed-and-breakfast, which is a refurbished log church first built in 1946.

- **City Garden Bed and Breakfast** 1352 West Tenth Avenue; ☎ 907-276-8686; **www.citygarden.biz**

  QUALITY ★★★★ VALUE ★★★★ $100–$150

  The rooms are bright and sunny, with beautiful artwork.

- **Copper Whale Inn** 440 L Street; ☎ 907-258-7999; **www.copperwhale.com**

  QUALITY ★★★★★ VALUE ★★★★ $185–$210

  The excellent location is reason enough to stay here, with great views of the inlet, and easy access to downtown or the Tony Knowles Coastal Trail.

- **Eagle Nest Hotel** 4110 Spenard Road; ☎ 907-243-3433 or 866-344-6835; **www.alaskabestinn.com**

  QUALITY ★★★ VALUE ★★★ $150–$198

  A basic hotel that looks better inside than out. But it is close to the airport—and cheap if you book online and take advantage of the often-found discounts.

- **Earth Bed and Breakfast** 1001 West 12th Avenue; ☎ 907-279-9907; **www.alaskaone.com/earthbb**

  QUALITY ★★★ VALUE ★★★★★ $99–$119

  This wonderful B&B has gained a reputation among mountaineers who choose it as their lodging while in Anchorage. Rates are based on shared versus private baths.

- **Hilton Anchorage** ☎ 907-272-7411 or 800-445-8667; **www.hilton.com**

  QUALITY ★★★★★ VALUE ★★★ $270–$975

  If you prefer the swankiness of major chain hotels, we suggest the Hilton over the Sheraton. While the latter is quite nice, it's not as centrally located as the Hilton, and it overlooks a cemetery instead of Cook Inlet. In the summer, rates are outrageously expensive, but you will notice this at all the larger hotels.

- **Hotel Captain Cook** Fourth Avenue and K Street; ☎ 907-276-6000 or 800-843-1950; **www.captaincook.com**

  QUALITY ★★★★★ VALUE ★★★ $250–$1,500

  Perhaps Anchorage's finest hotel, with valet parking, an outstanding athletic club, and some of the best food in the city. The rooms are nice, too, and expensive. But the hotel's Web site often offers specials that drastically cut the rate, so check online while planning your trip to see if you can get a deal.

- **International Backpackers Inn/Hostel** 3601 Peterkin Avenue; ☎ 907-274-3870

  QUALITY ★★ VALUE ★★★ $15

  The hostel itself is OK, but the section of town is a bit rough. And we say that kindly. But it's literally the cheapest alternative you'll find to sleeping in the streets.

- **The Millennium Alaskan Hotel** 4800 Spenard Road; ☎ 907-243-2300 or 800-544-0553; **www.millenniumhotels.com**

  QUALITY ★★★★ VALUE ★★★ $200–$350

  A very Alaska-looking hotel that serves as headquarters during the Iditarod each March. In the summer, its adjoining restaurant is a great place to sit outside on the patio and watch floatplanes land on nearby Lakes Hood and Spenard. The rooms, compared with those at such places as the Captain Cook, are overpriced.

- **Parkside Guest House** downtown off the Delaney Park Strip; ☎ 907-683-2290; **www.campdenali.com/parkside.htm**

  QUALITY ★★★★★ VALUE ★★★ $150–$175

  Those who appreciate fine architecture and decorating will immediately notice the quality that infuses this Arts and Crafts–inspired home. Mission-style furniture complements the decor and design. Rates are based on shared baths versus private baths.

- **Spenard Hostel International** 2845 West 42nd Avenue; ☎ 907-248-5036; **www.alaskahostel.org**

  QUALITY ★★★★ VALUE ★★★★★ $21

  This one fills up fast, so it helps to make reservations in advance. There is no curfew, and some coed rooms are available. Potluck dinners every Wednesday night. Our hostel of choice because of the friendly staff, but note that they are in the process of trying to sell.

- **26th Street International Hostel** 1037 26th Street, Spenard; ☎ 907-274-1252; **www.26streethostel.com**

  QUALITY ★★ VALUE ★★★★ $25–$65

  Basic hostel in a quiet neighborhood that has upgraded under new management. Bunks and private rooms are available.

- **Voyager Hotel** 501 K Street, at Fifth Avenue; ☎ 907-277-9501 or 800-247-9070; **www.voyagerhotel.com**

  QUALITY ★★★★ VALUE ★★★★ $189–$220

  Step into this small hotel and you might feel as if you're in Europe. The decor and feel of the building are unique to Anchorage, and a wonderfully different place to stay. Unlike many European hotels, this one has spacious rooms.

Southcentral Inland Alaska Indoor Lodging

NAME	TYPE(S) OF LODGING	QUALITY RATING	VALUE RATING	COST
ANCHORAGE				
Alaskan Frontier Gardens B&B	B&B	★★★★	★★★	$125–$225
Alaskan Leopard B&B	B&B	★★★★★	★★★★★	$119–$159
Alyeska Hostel	hostel	★★★	★★★★★	$20–$80
Alyeska Resort Prince Hotel	hotel	★★★★★	★★★★	$199–$2,200
Anchorage Downtown B&B at Raspberry Meadows	B&B	★★★★	★★★★★	$89–$139
Anchorage Guest House	hostel	★★★★★	★★★★★	$30–$140
Anchorage International Hostel	hostel	★★★	★★★★	$25–$65
Bed and Breakfast on the Park	B&B	★★★★	★★★	$125+
City Garden Bed and Breakfast	B&B	★★★★	★★★★	$100–$150
Copper Whale Inn	B&B	★★★★★	★★★★	$185–$210
Eagle Nest Hotel	hotel	★★★	★★★	$150–$198
Earth Bed and Breakfast	B&B	★★★	★★★★★	$99–$119
Hilton Anchorage	hotel	★★★★★	★★★	$270–$975
Hotel Captain Cook	hotel	★★★★★	★★★★	$250–$1,500
International Backpackers Inn/Hostel	hostel	★★	★★★	$15
The Millennium Alaskan Hotel	hotel	★★★★	★★★	$200–$350
Parkside Guest House	B&B	★★★★★	★★★	$150–$175
Spenard Hostel International	hostel	★★★★	★★★★★	$21
26th Street International Hostel	hostel	★★	★★★★	$25–$65
Voyager Hotel	hotel	★★★★	★★★★	$189–$220
MATANUSKA-SUSITNA VALLEY				
Dragonfly Gardens B&B	B&B	★★★★	★★★★	$109
Hatcher Pass Lodge	cabins/lodge	★★★★	★★★★★	$95–$165
Majestic Valley Wilderness Lodge	lodge	★★★★	★★★★★	$115–$140
Moose Wallow Bed and Breakfast	cabins	★★★	★★★★	$110–$145
Motherlode Lodge	lodge	★★★	★★★	$135–$150

NAME	TYPE(S) OF LODGING	QUALITY RATING	VALUE RATING	COST
MATANUSKA-SUSITNA VALLEY (CONTINUED)				
Sheep Mountain Lodge	cabins/ hostel	★★★★	★★★★	$60–$189
TALKEETNA				
Birchwood Cabins	cabins	★★★★★	★★★★	$125–$175
Chinook Wind Cabins	B&B/ cabins	★★★	★★	$95–$160
Eye of Denali Inn	B&B	★★★★	★★★★★	$89–$129
Swiss-Alaska Inn	hotel	★★★	★★★	$138+
Talkeetna Alaskan Lodge	lodge/ hotel	★★★★★	★★★	$145–$555
Talkeetna Cabins	cabins	★★★★	★★	$165
Talkeetna Hostel International	hostel	★★	★★★★	$21–$65
Talkeetna Roadhouse	hotel/ hostel	★★★	★★★	$21–$126
GLENNALLEN				
Caribou Hotel	hotel	★★★	★★★★	$85–$115
Carol's Bed and Breakfast	B&B	★★★	★★★	$100
Cranberry Hill House Bed and Breakfast	B&B/ cabins	★★★★	★★★	$110–$139
COPPER RIVER BASIN				
Copper Center Lodge	inn	★★★	★★★	$120–$165
Copper Moose B&B	B&B	★★★★	★★★★	$125
Copper River Princess Wilderness Lodge	hotel	★★★★★	★★★★	$179–$240
Kennicott Glacier Lodge	motel	★★★★★	★★★★	$165–$305
Kennicott River Lodge and Hostel	cabins/ hostel	★★★	★★★★	$28–$150
Kenny Lake Hotel	motel-style	★★	★★★	$80
McCarthy Lodge–Lancaster Hotel	lodge/ hotel	★★★	★★★	$68–$159
Pippin Lake Bed and Breakfast	cabin	★★★★	★★★★	$200+

Southcentral Inland Alaska Camping

NAME	TYPE(S) OF LODGING	QUALITY RATING	VALUE RATING	COST
ANCHORAGE				
Bird Creek Campground	RV/tent	★★★★	★★★★	$15
Centennial Park	RV/tent	★★★	★★★	$20
Creekwood Inn	RV only	★★★	★★★★	$22–$28
Eagle River Campground	RV/tent	★★★★	★★★★★	$15
Eklutna Lake Campground	RV/tent	★★★★★	★★★★★	$10
Ship Creek Landing	RV	★★	★★★	$15–$30
MATANUSKA-SUSITNA VALLEY				
Chickaloon General Store	tent	★★★	★★★	$15
Finger Lake State Recreation Site	RV/tent	★★★★	★★★★	$15
Fox Run RV Park and Campground	RV/tent	★★★	★★★★	$15–$22
Lake Louise State Recreation Area	RV/tent	★★★	★★★★	$5–$15
Lake Lucille Park	tent	★★★	★★★★★	$10
Mat-Su RV Park and Campground	RV/tent	★★★	★★★	$17–$30
Nancy Lake State Recreation Area	RV/tent	★★★★	★★★★	$10
Montana Creek Campground	RV/tent	★★★★	★★★	$18–$23

Camping

Within the city limits are three Alaska State Parks campgrounds—**Bird Creek, Eklutna Lake,** and **Eagle River**—where nature can be enjoyed just a short drive from town. For more information, visit **www.dnr.state.ak.us/parks/units/chugach** or **www.lifetimeadventures.net,** the company that manages two of the campgrounds.

- **Bird Creek Campground** 20 miles south of Anchorage at Mile 101 on the Seward Highway; ☎ 907-345-5014

  QUALITY ★★★★ VALUE ★★★★ $15

  Twenty-eight sites, some overlooking the inlet. Overflow camping area. Fishing, walking, birding, and cycling are among the recreational options.

- **Centennial Park** Off the Muldoon Road exit, Anchorage; ☎ 907-343-6986, **www.muni.org/parks/camping.cfm**

  QUALITY ★★★ VALUE ★★★ $20

  Nice enough, but theft can be a problem. Showers are available for $3.

- **Creekwood Inn** Off Gambell Street, Anchorage; ☎ 907-258-6006; **www.creekwoodinn-alaska.com**

NAME	TYPE(S) OF LODGING	QUALITY RATING	VALUE RATING	COST
TALKEETNA				
River Park Campground	tent	★★★	★★★	$13+
Talkeetna RV and Campground	RV/tent	★★★★	★★★★	$13+
GLENNALLEN				
Brown Bear Rhodehouse	tent	★★★	★★★	$8
Dry Creek State Recreation Area	RV/tent	★★★★	★★★★	$10
Moose Horn RV Park	RV/tent	★★★★	★★★★★	$12–$18
Northern Nights Campground and RV Park	RV/tent	★★★★	★★★★★	$12–$22
Tolsona Wilderness Campground and RV Park	RV/tent	★★★	★★★★	$14–$21
COPPER RIVER BASIN				
End of the Road Camping	tent	★★★★	★★★★	$10–$15
Glacier View Campground	tent	★★★	★★★★	$18
Kenny Lake Mercantile/RV Park	RV/tent	★★★	★★★★	$12–$20

QUALITY ★★★ VALUE ★★★★ $22–$28

It's off the Chester Creek Greenbelt and bike trail, and it's more secure than Centennial Park and Ship Creek Landing. But it's also right off a busy road. No tent camping is available.

- **Eagle River Campground** 12 miles north of Anchorage, off the Hiland Road exit; ☎ 907-694-7982

QUALITY ★★★★ VALUE ★★★★★ $15

Fifty-seven sites, some right on the river. Overflow camping area of ten sites. Fishing, white-water rafting or kayaking, and hiking are popular. Right off the highway, so expect the associated noise. *Note:* Half of the sites are available by reservation.

- **Eklutna Lake Campground** 45 minutes north of Anchorage; ☎ 907-345-5014

QUALITY ★★★★★ VALUE ★★★★★ $10

Offering 50 sites, some of which are walk-in tent sites. Overflow camping area of 15 sites. Fishing, hiking, mountain biking, mountaineering, and off-roading are popular. Best during weekdays when the local crowd has not shown up.

- **Ship Creek Landing** In the downtown industrial area, Anchorage; ☎ 907-277-0877 or 888-778-7700

  QUALITY ★★ VALUE ★★★ $15–$30

  Adequate facilities, but theft can be a problem, and homeless people hang out nearby.

MATANUSKA-SUSITNA VALLEY

Indoor Lodging

- **Dragonfly Gardens Bed and Breakfast** On the west shoreline of Cottonwood Lake in Wasilla; ☎ 907-357-8498 or 877-357-8498; **www.dragonflygardensbnb.com**

  QUALITY ★★★★ VALUE ★★★★ $109

  We especially like this place because it welcomes dogs but still manages to be clean and friendly. Rooms have a private entry and kitchen for making your own meals.

- **Hatcher Pass Lodge** Mile 17 Hatcher Pass Road; ☎ 907-745-1200; **www.hatcherpasslodge.com**

  QUALITY ★★★★ VALUE ★★★★★ $95–$165

  Our favorite destination in the Valley, with Swiss-looking A-frame chalets and cabins for wintertime and summertime fun. Pets are allowed for an extra $15.

- **Majestic Valley Wilderness Lodge** Mile 115 Glenn Highway, north of Palmer; ☎ 907-746-2930; **www.majesticvalleylodge.com**

  QUALITY ★★★★ VALUE ★★★★★ $115–$140

  This beautiful log lodge on ten acres offers comfortable lodging, with meals provided when you reserve ahead of time. Access to skiing, hiking, and other activities is right outside the door.

- **Moose Wallow Bed and Breakfast** Off Mile 53 Glenn Highway, near Sutton; ☎ 907-745-7777; **www.moosewallow.com**

  QUALITY ★★★ VALUE ★★★★ $110–$125

  An off-the-beaten path location for private lodging; walking trails are nearby.

- **Motherlode Lodge** Mile 14 Fishhook Road, Hatcher Pass; ☎ 907-688-4055 or 866-369-4050; **www.motherlodelodge.com**

  QUALITY ★★★ VALUE ★★★ $135–$150

  After you've spent a day hiking or skiing at Hatcher Pass, it won't matter what you eat—it will taste delicious. Motherlode does a great job with both meals and presentation, but the view is its greatest asset.

- **Sheep Mountain Lodge** Mile 113.5 Glenn Highway, north of Palmer; ☎ 877-645-5121; **www.sheepmountain.com**

  QUALITY ★★★★ VALUE ★★★★ $60–$189

This lodge in the shadow of Sheep Mountain is popular among skiers and dog mushers. There are 14 cabins, plus a bunkhouse in the summer. One of our favorite destinations.

Camping

- **Chickaloon General Store** Mile 76.3 Glenn Highway; ☎ 907-746-1801

  QUALITY ★★★ VALUE ★★★ $15

  Camping is allowed by the river. Showers and laundry facilities on site.

- **Finger Lake State Recreation Site** Mile 0.7 Bogard Road; ☎ 907-745-2827

  QUALITY ★★★★ VALUE ★★★★ $15

  Thirty-six campsites.

- **Fox Run RV Park and Campground** Mile 36.3 Glenn Highway; ☎ 877-745-6120 or 907-745-6120; **foxrun.freeservers.com**

  QUALITY ★★★ VALUE ★★★★ $15–$22

  Right off the highway near Kepler-Bradley State Recreation Area, which is great for fishing and hiking but can get pretty buggy in the summer. Camping fees include your shower. You can also rent a boat and explore the lake.

- **Lake Louise State Recreation Area** At Lake Louise, off Mile 159.8 Glenn Highway; ☎ 907-441-7575 or 907-278-7575; **www.dnr.state.ak.us/parks/aspbro/charts/matglenn.htm**

  QUALITY ★★★ VALUE ★★★★ $5–$15

  Primitive RV and tent sites; offers some of the best lake fishing in the state.

- **Lake Lucille Park** Mile 2.4 Knik Road; ☎ 907-745-9690; **www.matsugov.us/RecServices/parks.cfm**

  QUALITY ★★★ VALUE ★★★★★ $10

  This park is about the closest place to town that you can camp. There are some nice trails in the area, as well as good fishing in the lake.

- **Mat-Su RV Park and Campground** Outside of Willow, Mile 90.8 Parks Highway; ☎ 907-495-6300; **www.matsurvpark.com**

  QUALITY ★★★ VALUE ★★★ $17–$30

  The park is right off the road, but convenient, with a small store for grabbing snacks.

- **Nancy Lake State Recreation Area** Off Nancy Lake Parkway; ☎ 907-745-3975; **www.dnr.state.ak.us/parks/units/nancylk/nancylk.htm**

  QUALITY ★★★★ VALUE ★★★★ $10

  The South Rolly Campground and Nancy Lake Campground are both available for summer camping.

- **Montana Creek Campground** On Montana Creek, between Willow and Talkeetna; ☎ 907-733-5267 or 877-475-2267; **www.montanacreekcampground.com**

  QUALITY ★★★★ VALUE ★★★ $20–$40

This is a great spot for anglers. Tent and RV camping are in a pretty, tree-shaded area just by the creek. The campground is spotless but can get crowded.

TALKEETNA

Indoor Lodging

- **Birchwood Cabins** Three miles from downtown area; ☎ 907-733-8431 or 866-247-2496; **www.birchwoodcabins.com**

  QUALITY ★★★★★ VALUE ★★★★ $125–$175

  Small wood cabins for your own temporary private home.

- **Chinook Wind Cabins** Within walking distance of downtown; ☎ 907-733-1899 or 800-643-1899; **www.chinookwindcabins.com**

  QUALITY ★★★ VALUE ★★ $95–$160

  The six well-built cabins are side by side but still very private. Rates are higher than average in the area, but for those without a vehicle, the convenience of being in town is worth it.

- **Eye of Denali Inn** Within walking distance of town; ☎ 907-733-8728; **www.eyeofdenali.com**

  QUALITY ★★★★ VALUE ★★★★★ $89–$129

  This place bills itself as a no-host bed-and-breakfast, which we find delightful because we get the perk of a hot breakfast but the privacy to do what we want at our own pace.

- **Swiss-Alaska Inn** F Street, off Talkeetna Spur Road (visit Web site for full directions and PDF map); ☎ 907-733-2424; **www.swissalaska.com**

  QUALITY ★★★ VALUE ★★★ $138+

  This longtime inn features a casual dining room with a full menu. It's an aging but well-kept facility.

- **Talkeetna Alaskan Lodge** ☎ 907-733-9500 or 877-777-4067; **www.talkeetnalodge.com**

  QUALITY ★★★★★ VALUE ★★★★ $145–$555

  A very nice native-owned lodge that tends to attract tour and cruise-ship travelers. Rooms are elegant but still maintain an Alaska feel. The restaurant is a fine-dining experience, and the wine list is extensive. Easily the fanciest place in town.

- **Talkeetna Cabins** Another option close to downtown; ☎ 907-733-2227 or 888-733-9933; **www.talkeetnacabins.org**

  QUALITY ★★★★ VALUE ★★ $165

  These small log cabins, just a five-minute walk from town, are well built and comfortable.

- **Talkeetna Hostel International** On I Street, just east of the town site; ☎ 907-733-4678; **www.talkeetnahostel.com**

  QUALITY ★★ VALUE ★★★★ $21–$65

No lockouts or curfews, and they have a book exchange and bike rentals for getting around town. We love the VW minibus you can sleep in.

- **Talkeetna Roadhouse** ☎ 907-733-1351; **www.talkeetnaroadhouse.com**

  QUALITY ★★★ VALUE ★★★ $21–$126

  This locally famous roadhouse is in the middle of downtown—another favorite among climbers for lodging. All the rooms come with shared baths. The rates are affordable, but this is definitely for the traveler who does not mind mingling with strangers. Free Internet access is a plus. Cabins also are available.

Camping

- **River Park Campground** At the end of Main Street; ☎ 907-745-9690 or 907-745-2856

  QUALITY ★★★ VALUE ★★★ $13+

  Informal camping close to the activity of downtown.

- **Talkeetna RV and Campground** ☎ 907-733-2604

  QUALITY ★★★★ VALUE ★★★★ $13+

  The campground has 60 wooded sites right off the boat launch, with showers and bathrooms. Talkeetna River Guides manages it (☎ 800-353-2677; **www.talkeetnariverguides.com).**

GLENNALLEN

Indoor Lodging

- **Caribou Hotel** In Glennallen; ☎ 907-822-3302; **www.caribouhotel.com**

  QUALITY ★★★ VALUE ★★★★ $85–$115

  This modern hotel offers two-room suites with kitchens available. An adjoining annex has less-expensive rooms.

- **Carol's Bed and Breakfast** Mile 187 Glenn Highway, Glennallen; ☎ 907-822-3594; **www.alaska.net/~neeley**

  QUALITY ★★★ VALUE ★★★ $100

  Carol's breakfast includes homemade wild-berry jams and jellies, sourdough hotcakes, and reindeer sausage.

- **Cranberry Hill House Bed and Breakfast** Mile 187 Glenn Highway, Glennallen; ☎ 907-822-3711; **www.caribouhotel.com**

  QUALITY ★★★★ VALUE ★★★ $110–$139

  The house is perched atop a hill and features interesting architecture and very nicely appointed rooms. The owners also run the nearby Caribou Hotel, but their bed-and-breakfast is for those who prefer a more intimate experience.

Camping

- **Brown Bear Rhodehouse** Mile 183.5 Glenn Highway; ☎ 907-822-3663

  QUALITY ★★★ VALUE ★★★ $8

  A restaurant and cocktail lounge that also offers camping. Inquire within.

- **Dry Creek Recreation Site** Mile 117 Richardson Highway; ☎ 907-259-5558 or 907-822-5208

QUALITY ★★★★ VALUE ★★★★ $10

This site has 50 campsites and 4 walk-in wilderness sites; the latter are our favorites.

- **Moose Horn RV Park** Mile 187.5 Glenn Highway; ☎ 907-822-3953; **www.mhrvp.com**

QUALITY ★★★★ VALUE ★★★★★ $12–$18

The park has RV and tent sites and doesn't allow generators, so it stays quieter than other campgrounds.

- **Northern Nights Campground and RV Park** Mile 188.7 Glenn Highway; ☎ 907-822-3199; **www.northern-nights-rv.com**

QUALITY ★★★★ VALUE ★★★★★ $12–$22

Tent-camping sites are shaded and have tent platforms, but this place mostly attracts the RV crowd. Showers cost extra.

- **Tolsona Wilderness Campground and RV Park** Mile 173 Glenn Highway, about 14 miles west of Glennallen; ☎ 907-822-3865; **www.tolsona.com**

QUALITY ★★★ VALUE ★★★★ $14–$21

This full-service campground features tent sites, restrooms, a dump station, showers, laundry facilities, free Wi-Fi, and a mini-store. There are some fine hiking trails and fishing nearby as well.

COPPER RIVER BASIN

Indoor Lodging

- **Copper Center Lodge** Mile 101 Old Richardson Highway Loop; ☎ 866-330-3245 or 907-822-3245; **www.coppercenterlodge.com**

QUALITY ★★★ VALUE ★★★ $120–$165

This aging but historic lodge has private or shared baths. The rooms are small to accommodate the plumbing that was added years after the lodge was built, but they are cozy and comfortable.

- **Copper Moose Bed and Breakfast** Mile 5.8 Edgerton Highway, toward McCarthy; ☎ 907-822-4244 or 866-922-4244; **www.coppermoosebb.com**

QUALITY ★★★★ VALUE ★★★★ $125

This gorgeous log home, built by the owner himself, makes a splendid home away from home when you're staying in the area. The friendly owners are a real treat. Guests are invited to eat with the family at all meals due to the scarcity of restaurants in the area.

- **Copper River Princess Wilderness Lodge** Mile 102 Richardson Highway; ☎ 907-822-4000; **www.princesslodges.com**

QUALITY ★★★★★ VALUE ★★★★ $179–$240

This is a newer and more luxurious alternative to the Copper Center Lodge, but the price is higher and the atmosphere more corporate.

- **Kennicott Glacier Lodge** On Main Street, Kennicott, Wrangell–St. Elias National Park; ☎ 800-582-5128; **www.kennicottlodge.com**

  QUALITY ★★★★★ VALUE ★★★★ $165–$305

  This is a rustic, historic renovated lodge in the heart of the nation's largest national park. The rooms are simple, but that's part of the charm—no TVs or phones to interrupt the tranquility. The restaurant, by the way, serves outstanding gourmet meals and shows flair even with its sandwiches. The package prices, which include all meals, are the best deals.

- **Kennicott River Lodge and Hostel** ☎ 907-554-4441; **www.kennicottriverlodge.com**

  QUALITY ★★★ VALUE ★★★★ $28–$150

  Private cabins, hostel bunks, and a six-person suite available. Within walking distance to McCarthy and the Kennicott River.

- **Kenny Lake Hotel** Mile 7.2 Edgerton Highway, toward McCarthy; ☎ 907-822-3313; **www.kennylake.com**

  QUALITY ★★ VALUE ★★★ $80

  Large rooms, all with gorgeous views of the surrounding mountains.

- **McCarthy Lodge–Lancaster Hotel** In downtown McCarthy; ☎ 907-554-4402; **www.mccarthylodge.com**

  QUALITY ★★★ VALUE ★★★ $68–$159

  This historic hotel includes Ma Johnson's Hotel, with great food and drinks. Lodging options include traditional rooms and economical accommodations in the very simple Lancaster Hotel, designed for backpackers.

- **Pippin Lake Bed and Breakfast** Mile 82.2 Richardson Highway; ☎ 907-822-3046 or 907-320-0435; **www.pippinlakebnb.com**

  QUALITY ★★★★ VALUE ★★★★ $200+

  The closest community to this quaint B&B in the woods is Copper Center, 20 miles away. The cabins sleep up to five comfortably; rates include breakfast fixings. Located right on the lake, where you can use the paddleboat or canoe and explore or go fishing.

Camping

- **End of the Road Camping** Right at the end of McCarthy Road, near the footbridge

  QUALITY ★★★★ VALUE ★★★★ $10–$15

  The river breeze keeps bugs to a minimum, but the sites are not as nice as those at Glacier View Campground. There's no phone, so you can just show up. Spaces are always available.

- **Glacier View Campground** Less than a mile from the Kennicott River footbridge, near the end of McCarthy Road; ☎ 907-243-6677; **www.glacierviewcampground.com**

  QUALITY ★★★ VALUE ★★★★ $18

  There are always spaces open.

- **Kenny Lake Mercantile/RV Park** Mile 7.2 Edgerton Highway, toward McCarthy; ☎ 907-822-3313; **www.kennylake.com**

  QUALITY ★★★ VALUE ★★★★ $12–$20

  Camping for RVs and tents, as well as showers, laundry facilities, and assistance planning tours.

WHERE *to* EAT

ANCHORAGE

BECAUSE THERE ARE SO MANY PLACES in Anchorage from which to choose, we've arranged the food into categories, giving you simple listings and locations. We've eaten at every one of these restaurants and recommend any of them.

Burgers

- **Arctic Roadrunner** 5300 Old Seward Highway; ☎ 907-561-1245; 2477 Arctic Boulevard; ☎ 907-279-7311

  BURGERS QUALITY ★★★★ $5–$9 SUITABLE FOR KIDS? Y

  Consistently voted Anchorage's best burger joint.

Cafes

- **Alaska Bagel Inc.** 113 West Northern Lights Boulevard; ☎ 907-276-3900

  SANDWICHES QUALITY ★★★★ $5–$9 SUITABLE FOR KIDS? Y

  Bagel sandwiches in just about any variety you can imagine. Cream cheeses and other toppings make a filling meal.

- **Kaladi Brothers Coffee Co.** 6921 Brayton Drive; ☎ 907-344-5483

  NEIGHBORHOOD QUALITY ★★★ $2–$5 SUITABLE FOR KIDS? Y

  The "it" cafe in town, whether it's this one or the one on Tudor Road or downtown.

- **Middleway Café** 1200 West Northern Lights Boulevard; ☎ 907-272-6433

  NEIGHBORHOOD QUALITY ★★★★ $5–$9 SUITABLE FOR KIDS? Y

  A trendy coffee shop that gets slammed at lunchtime because of its excellent organic and vegetarian selections.

- **Organic Oasis Restaurant and Juice Bar** 2610 Spenard Road; ☎ 907-277-7882

  VEGETARIAN QUALITY ★★★ $5–$9 SUITABLE FOR KIDS? Y

  A good choice for those on strict vegetarian diets. Espresso and teas available, too.

- **Sidestreet Espresso** 412 G Street; ☎ 907-258-9055

  BAKED GOODS QUALITY ★★★★ $2–$5 SUITABLE FOR KIDS? Y

  Yummy sweets and other snacks in a very casual atmosphere.

- **Snow City Café** 1034 West Fourth Avenue; ☎ 907-272-2489

AMERICAN QUALITY ★★★★ $6–$10 SUITABLE FOR KIDS? Y

Breakfast is their strong suit. The eggs dishes are imaginative, and there are plenty of options for vegetarians.

- **Sweet Basil Café** 335 E Street; ☎ 907-274-0070

NEIGHBORHOOD QUALITY ★★★★ $6–$12 SUITABLE FOR KIDS? Y

Has inexpensive, healthy meals, espresso, and a bountiful juice bar. Delicious desserts, too.

Casual and Innovative (our favorite category after sushi)

- **Bear Tooth** 1230 West 27th Avenue; ☎ 907-276-4200

FUSION QUALITY ★★★★ $9–$25 SUITABLE FOR KIDS? Y

The same folks who own Moose's Tooth Pub (page 324) own and operate this eatery, which is next to a second-run-movie theater. You can dine in or have your order delivered to you in the theater.

- **The Bridge Salmon Bake and Grille** 221 West Ship Creek Avenue; ☎ 907-677-6771

FUSION QUALITY ★★★★ $7–$29 SUITABLE FOR KIDS? N

One of the newest additions to the Anchorage dining scene, perched over Ship Creek in downtown. The menu is ambitious, with roasted duck, lamb, and, of course, salmon.

- **Fletcher's at the Hotel Captain Cook** Fourth Avenue at K Street; ☎ 907-276-6000

FUSION QUALITY ★★★★★ $7–$21 SUITABLE FOR KIDS? N

The food is just as good as what you'll find up in the Crow's Nest, only at half the price and in a swank mahogany-colored bar. Located on the floor level of the hotel.

- **Glacier Brew House** 737 West Fifth Avenue, Suite 110; ☎ 907-274-2739

FUSION QUALITY ★★★★ $9–$30 SUITABLE FOR KIDS? Y

We've always enjoyed the food, but the prices are kind of high. Ask for a table near the fireplace.

- **Jack Sprat** Olympic Circle in Girdwood, 35 miles south of Anchorage; ☎ 907-783-5225

FUSION QUALITY ★★★★★ $8–$17 SUITABLE FOR KIDS? N

Some of the most creative food in all of Anchorage, but without the large prices. The granola atmosphere fits in well with the entire laid-back-town attitude in Girdwood. Our favorite restaurant here.

- **Humpy's Great Alaskan Alehouse** 610 West Sixth Avenue; ☎ 907-276-2337

CASUAL/BAR QUALITY ★★★ $5–$12 SUITABLE FOR KIDS? N

Great bar, great food. The halibut tacos are a local favorite.

- **Maxine's Glacier City Bistro** On Crow Creek Road in Girdwood; ☎ 907-783-1234

FUSION QUALITY ★★★★ $8–$24 SUITABLE FOR KIDS? Y

Another Girdwood favorite, with an exceptionally creative menu. The downside: sometimes you have to wait a long, long time for your food. It's good, don't get us wrong, but don't go if you're in a hurry.

- **Sacks Cafe & Restaurant** 328 G Street; ☎ 907-276-3546

FUSION QUALITY ★★★★★ $10–$34 SUITABLE FOR KIDS? N

On the upper end of casual, serving tasty seafood dishes and pastas, among other selections. Known for its outstanding wine list.

- **Snow Goose Restaurant** 17 West Third Avenue; ☎ 907-277-7727

FUSION QUALITY ★★★ $8–$28 SUITABLE FOR KIDS? Y

The food is imaginative and ranges from basic burgers to flavorful salmon and halibut dishes. We like this place, though, for its picturesque deck dining, with prime views of the Inlet.

Chinese

- **Charlie's Bakery and Restaurant** 2729 C Street; ☎ 907-677-7777

CHINESE QUALITY ★★★★ $5–$15 SUITABLE FOR KIDS? Y

This tucked-away strip-mall spot is the only one in town that serves dim sum. It's our only choice for Chinese in a city that seems packed with Chinese restaurants.

Diners

- **Hogg Brothers Café** 1049 West Northern Lights Boulevard; ☎ 907-276-9649

AMERICAN QUALITY ★★ $5–$9 SUITABLE FOR KIDS? Y

If you like your food fried, Hogg Brothers will not disappoint.

- **Lucky Wishbone** 1033 East Fifth Avenue; ☎ 907-272-3454

AMERICAN QUALITY ★★ $6–$12 SUITABLE FOR KIDS? Y

They've been in business forever; you'll feel like you're stepping back in time when you enter the place. Gets crowded with locals at lunchtime. The French fries are excellent.

- **White Spot Cafe** 109 West Fourth Avenue; ☎ 907-279-3954

AMERICAN QUALITY ★★★ $4–$8 SUITABLE FOR KIDS? Y

A true corner diner with lots of plastic, lots of burgers being flipped, and lots of baskets o' fries. Has a following among locals and downtown workers.

Fine Dining

- **Club Paris** 417 West Fifth Avenue; ☎ 907-277-6332

STEAKS QUALITY ★★★★ $9–$40 SUITABLE FOR KIDS? N

An Anchorage institution specializing in tender steaks and gourmet hamburgers; the salads are a disappointment, though.

- **Crow's Nest at the Hotel Captain Cook** Fourth Avenue at K Street; ☎ 907-276-6000

  FUSION QUALITY ★★★★★ $12–$40 SUITABLE FOR KIDS? N

  Where Anchorage couples go to celebrate very special occasions; one of the best, and most romantic places, in town.

- **Haute Quarter Grill** 11221 Old Glenn Highway; ☎ 907-622-4745

  FUSION QUALITY ★★★★ $11–$28 SUITABLE FOR KIDS? N

  This will require a drive to Eagle River, but the food is excellent, and chef-owner Alex Perez has experience at some of the finest restaurants in the state. The ahi tuna is wonderful. They only serve beer and wine, though. No cocktails.

- **Marx Bros. Café** 627 West Third Avenue; ☎ 907-278-2133

  FUSION QUALITY ★★★★★ $12–$39 SUITABLE FOR KIDS? N

  A true dinner house, open only at night and serving top-notch meals in an elegant atmosphere.

- **Southside Bistro** 1320 Huffman Park Drive; ☎ 907-348-0088

  FUSION QUALITY ★★★★★ $12–$36 SUITABLE FOR KIDS? N

  The food looks as good as it tastes, with artful presentation and interesting taste combinations. Our favorite special-occasion restaurant, after Crow's Nest.

International

- **Aladdin's Fine Mediterranean** 4240 Old Seward Highway, Suite 20; ☎ 907-561-2373

  MEDITERRANEAN QUALITY ★★★★ $8–$25 SUITABLE FOR KIDS? N

  A wide range of Mediterranean favorites at reasonable prices.

- **Greek Corner** 302 West Fireweed; ☎ 907-276-2820

  GREEK QUALITY ★★★ $5–$12 SUITABLE FOR KIDS? Y

  Aging restaurant that still serves great Greek food, including moussaka and baklava.

- **Orso Ristorante** 737 West Fifth Avenue; ☎ 907-222-3232

  GREEK QUALITY ★★★★★ $7–$35 SUITABLE FOR KIDS? N

  This Italian restaurant has taken over the fine-dining scene for those who like Tuscan-influenced meals. They also have some fine fusion items on the menu, and an extensive wine list.

Mexican

- **La Mex Restaurant** 8330 King Street; ☎ 907-344-6399

  MEXICAN QUALITY ★★★ $5–$12 SUITABLE FOR KIDS? Y

  With several locations throughout town, this is the widely accepted Mexican restaurant among locals.

- **Gallo's Mexican Restaurant** 8311 Arctic Boulevard; ☎ 907-344-6735

  MEXICAN QUALITY ★★★ $6–$16 SUITABLE FOR KIDS? Y

  The building is older and more authentic than the other locations in town.

Southcentral Inland Alaska Dining

NAME	CUISINE	FOOD QUALITY	COST
ANCHORAGE			
Aladdin's Fine Mediterranean	Mediterranean	★★★★	$8–$25
Alaska Bagel Inc.	sandwiches	★★★★	$5–$9
Arctic Roadrunner	burgers	★★★★	$5–$8
Bear Tooth	fusion	★★★★	$9–$25
The Bridge Salmon Bake and Grille	fusion	★★★★	$7–$29
Charlie's Bakery and Restaurant	Chinese	★★★★	$5–$15
Club Paris	steaks	★★★★	$9–$40
Crow's Nest at the Hotel Captain Cook	fusion	★★★★★	$12–$40
Fletcher's at the Hotel Captain Cook	fusion	★★★★★	$7–$21
Gallo's Mexican Restaurant	Mexican	★★★	$6–$16
Glacier Brew House	Fusion	★★★★	$9–$30
Greek Corner	Greek	★★★	$5–$12
Haute Quarter Grill	fusion	★★★★	$11–$28
Humpy's Great Alaskan Alehouse	casual/bar	★★★	$5–$12
Hogg Brothers Café	American	★★	$5–$9
Jack Sprat	fusion	★★★★★	$8–$17
Jalapenos	Mexican	★★★★	$8–$15
Kaladi Brothers Coffee Co.	neighborhood	★★★	$2–$5
La Cabana Mexican Restaurant	Mexican	★★★★	$6–$14
La Mex Restaurant	Mexican	★★★	$5–$12
Lucky Wishbone	American	★★	$6–$12
Marx Bros. Café	fusion	★★★★★	$12–$39
Maxine's Glacier City Bistro	fusion	★★★★	$8–$24
Mexico in Alaska	Mexican	★★★★	$9–$18
Middleway Café	neighborhood	★★★★	$5–$9
Moose's Tooth Pub and Pizzeria	Pizza	★★★★★	$8–$26
Organic Oasis Restaurant and Juice Bar	vegetarian	★★★	$5–$9
Orso Ristorante	Italian	★★★★★	$7–$35
Peter's Sushi Spot	Japanese	★★★★★	$7–$34
Pizza Olympia	Pizza	★★★	$5–$21
Sacks Cafe & Restaurant	fusion	★★★★★	$10–$34
Shine's Sushi	Japanese	★★★★★	$6–$24

NAME	CUISINE	FOOD QUALITY	COST
ANCHORAGE (CONTINUED)			
Sidestreet Espresso	baked goods	★★★★	$1–[illegible]
Snow City Café	American	★★★★	$6–$10
Snow Goose Restaurant	fusion	★★★	$8–$28
Southside Bistro	fusion	★★★★★	$12–$36
Sweet Basil Café	neighborhood	★★★★	$6–$12
Thai Orchid Restaurant	Thai	★★★	$6–$12
Thai Kitchen	Thai	★★★★	$6–$14
White Spot Cafe	American	★★★	$4–$8
Yamato Ya Japanese Restaurant	Japanese	★★★★	$6–$26
MATANUSKA-SUSITNA VALLEY			
Alaska Cadillac Café	American	★★★	$5–$12
Colony Inn Café	American	★★★	$8–$20
Evangelo's Restaurant	Italian/Pizza	★★★	$8–$21
Great Bear Brewing Co.	American	★★★	$6–$16
Mekong Thai Cuisine	Thai	★★★★	$7–$14
Motherlode Lodge	American	★★★	$7–$27
Settler's Bay Lodge	American	★★★★	$9–$25
Tokyo Restaurant & Sushi Bar	Japanese	★★★	$6–$24
Vagabond Blues	neighborhood	★★★★★	$3–$7
TALKEETNA			
Café Michele	fusion	★★★★★	$8–$29
Dancing Bears Fish Fry and Salmon Bake	outdoors	★★★	$9–$18
Latitude 62	American	★★★	$8–$25
Mountain High Pizza Pie	Pizza	★★★★	$7–$19
Swiss-Alaska Inn	American	★★	$8–$15
Talkeetna Natural Foods and Coffee Roastery	neighborhood	★★★★	$4–$9
Talkeetna Roadhouse	American	★★★	$6–$16
GLENNALLEN			
Caribou Restaurant	American	★★★	$7–$19

Southcentral Inland Alaska Dining (cont'd)

NAME	CUISINE	FOOD QUALITY	COST
GLENNALLEN (CONTINUED)			
Lake Louise Lodge	American	★★★	$8–$24
Last Frontier Pizza	Pizza	★★★	$9–$17
COPPER RIVER BASIN			
Copper Center Lodge	American	★★★	$7–$27
Copper River Princess Wilderness Lodge	upscale regional	★★★★★	$9–$29
Kennicott Glacier Lodge	fusion	★★★★★	$9–$25
Kenny Lake Diner	American	★★	$8–$20
McCarthy Lodge	American	★★★	$8–$25

- **La Cabana Mexican Restaurant** 312 East Fifth Avenue; ☎ 907-272-0135

  MEXICAN QUALITY ★★★★ $6–$14 SUITABLE FOR KIDS? Y

  The location leaves a bit to be desired, but the food is truly authentic.

- **Jalapenos** 11823 Old Glenn Highway, Eagle River, 15 miles north of Anchorage; ☎ 907-694-1888

  MEXICAN QUALITY ★★★★ $8–$15 SUITABLE FOR KIDS? Y

  This Eagle River restaurant does a good job with its Mexican seafood dishes, and the homemade salsa is just right. Try the sopapillas if you have room left for dessert.

- **Mexico in Alaska** 7305 Old Seward Highway; ☎ 907-349-1528

  MEXICAN QUALITY ★★★★★ $9–$18 SUITABLE FOR KIDS? Y

  Nobody makes mole like the folks at this longtime Anchorage restaurant.

Pizza

- **Moose's Tooth Pub and Pizzeria** 3300 Old Seward Highway; ☎ 907-258-2537

  PIZZA QUALITY ★★★★★ $8–$26 SUITABLE FOR KIDS? Y

  Very popular hangout. They make more than 15 of their own microbrews, and the 39-plus topping choices on the pizza menu range from halibut to pepperoni to eggplant. *Warning:* It's busy all the time, so try to go at non-peak hours.

- **Pizza Olympia** 2809 Spenard Road; ☎ 907-561-5464

  PIZZA QUALITY ★★★ $5–$21 SUITABLE FOR KIDS? Y

  A longtime pizza shop that also has some good salads and Italian and Greek dishes. It's never as busy as Moose's Tooth.

Sushi

- **Peter's Sushi Spot** 4140 B Street, Midtown; ☎ 907-276-5188

  JAPANESE QUALITY ★★★★★ $7–$34 SUITABLE FOR KIDS? N

  Another local favorite. It gets crowded, and there are so many choices on the menu, you may have trouble making a decision.

- **Shine's Sushi** 11401 Old Glenn Highway in Eagle River; ☎ 907-622-8889

  JAPANESE QUALITY ★★★★★ $6–$24 SUITABLE FOR KIDS? Y

  You have to drive all the way to Eagle River, but when it comes to sushi, Shine's is the best of the best.

- **Yamato Ya Japanese Restaurant** 3700 Old Seward Highway; ☎ 907-561-2128

  JAPANESE QUALITY ★★★★ $6–$26 SUITABLE FOR KIDS? Y

  In the City Market building; not fancy but plenty authentic.

Thai

- **Thai Orchid Restaurant** 219 East Dimond Blvd.; ☎ 907-868-5226

  THAI QUALITY ★★★ $6–$12 SUITABLE FOR KIDS? Y

  A local favorite with very reasonable prices.

- **Thai Kitchen** 3405 East Tudor Road; ☎ 907-561-0082

  THAI QUALITY ★★★★ $6–$14 SUITABLE FOR KIDS? Y

  The wraps and fresh rolls are fabulous. Good choices for vegetarians, too. Service can be slow, so don't go if you're in a hurry.

MATANUSKA-SUSITNA VALLEY

- **Alaska Cadillac Café** Mile 49 Parks Highway just outside of Wasilla; ☎ 907-376-5833

  AMERICAN QUALITY ★★★ $5–$12 SUITABLE FOR KIDS? Y

  It's a gas station on one side and an impressively well-managed restaurant on the other. The service and ambience are good, though the pizzas have gotten mixed reviews. We go for their sandwiches and burgers.

- **Colony Inn Café** 325 East Elmwood, Palmer; ☎ 907-745-3330

  AMERICAN QUALITY ★★★ $8–$20 SUITABLE FOR KIDS? Y

  The dining room is cozy and comfortable, and the meals are some of the nicer ones you'll find in town.

- **Evangelo's Restaurant** At 301 Parks Highway, Wasilla; ☎ 907-376-1249

  ITALIAN/PIZZA QUALITY ★★★ $8–$21 SUITABLE FOR KIDS? N

  This very large restaurant can serve many people at a time and is a favorite among Valley folks for banquets and special events. They have Italian food and pizza, both of which are popular.

- **Great Bear Brewing Co.** 238 North Boundary Street, Wasilla; ☎ 907-373-4782

  AMERICAN QUALITY ★★★ $6–$16 SUITABLE FOR KIDS? Y

They make their own microbrew here and have begun packaging "backpacker's beer," sold in pouches to go along on your travels.

- **Mekong Thai Cuisine** 473 West Parks Highway, Wasilla; ☎ 907-373-7690

  THAI QUALITY ★★★★ $7–$14 SUITABLE FOR KIDS? Y

  Very reasonable prices, and they know how to prepare tofu just right.

- **Motherlode Lodge** Mile 14 Fishhook Road, Hatcher Pass; ☎ 907-746-1464

  AMERICAN QUALITY ★★★ $7–$27 SUITABLE FOR KIDS? Y

  After you've spent a day hiking or skiing at Hatcher Pass, it won't matter what you eat—it will taste delicious. The Motherlode scores high on both food and presentation.

- **Settler's Bay Lodge** Mile 8 Knik–Goose Bay Road, outside of Wasilla

  AMERICAN QUALITY ★★★★ $9–$25 SUITABLE FOR KIDS? N

  Experience fine dining in a rural setting. Lovely views and lots of warm wood and stonework throughout.

- **Tokyo Restaurant & Sushi Bar** 735 West Parks Highway, Wasilla; ☎ 907-357-8888

  JAPANESE QUALITY ★★★ $6–$24 SUITABLE FOR KIDS? Y

  The tempura is a local favorite, but we like the fish bait. It's fresh, and the chefs create edible art.

- **Vagabond Blues** 642 South Alaska Street, Palmer; ☎ 907-745-2233

  NEIGHBORHOOD QUALITY ★★★★★ $3–$7 SUITABLE FOR KIDS? Y

  The soups are delicious, and the atmosphere is hip and relaxed. Mellow live entertainment some nights. This is our favorite hangout in Palmer.

TALKEETNA

- **Café Michele** Talkeetna Spur Road and Second Street; ☎ 907-733-5300; **www.cafemichele.com**

  FUSION QUALITY ★★★★★ $8–$29 SUITABLE FOR KIDS? N

  The best eatery in town, period. The food is inventive, healthful, and filling. Whenever possible the restaurant uses locally grown organic produce and free-range meats and poultry.

- **Dancing Bears Fish Fry and Salmon Bake** Under the burled-wood deck in Talkeetna; ☎ 907-733-4425

  OUTDOORS QUALITY ★★★ $9–$18 SUITABLE FOR KIDS? Y

  They make hot doughnuts from scratch and serve grilled king salmon, halibut nuggets, fiddlehead ferns, reindeer dogs, and other all-things-Alaskan food.

- **Latitude 62** Just before the Main Street area on your right; ☎ 907-733-2262

  AMERICAN QUALITY ★★★ $8–$25 SUITABLE FOR KIDS? Y

  Locals love the tasty burgers and steaks.

- **Mountain High Pizza Pie** ☎ 907-733-1234

  PIZZA QUALITY ★★★★ $7–$19 SUITABLE FOR KIDS? Y

  A favorite among locals and guests, with outdoor picnic-table seating in the summer. They serve salads, sandwiches, beer, and wine as well.

- **Swiss-Alaska Inn** ☎ 907-733-2424; **www.swissalaska.com**

  AMERICAN QUALITY ★★ $8–$15 SUITABLE FOR KIDS? Y

  Casual dining with breakfast, lunch, and dinner menu.

- **Talkeetna Natural Foods and Coffee Roastery** Downtown, across from the airport; ☎ 907-733-3882

  NEIGHBORHOOD QUALITY ★★★★ $4–$9 SUITABLE FOR KIDS? Y

  Organic coffee; Internet access; and wraps, salads, soups, and other organic foods made to order.

- **Talkeetna Roadhouse** On Main Street; ☎ 907-733-1351; **www.talkeetnaroadhouse.com**

  AMERICAN QUALITY ★★★ $6–$16 SUITABLE FOR KIDS? N

  Their breakfasts, especially the huge cinnamon rolls, are delicious.

GLENNALLEN

- **Caribou Restaurant** In Glennallen; ☎ 907-822-3149; **www.caribouhotel.com**

  AMERICAN QUALITY ★★★ $7–$19 SUITABLE FOR KIDS? Y

  Basic food and filling breakfasts in a family-style atmosphere.

- **Lake Louise Lodge** Mile 16 Lake Louise Road, outside of Glennallen; ☎ 907-822-3311

  AMERICAN QUALITY ★★★ $8–$24 SUITABLE FOR KIDS? Y

  Full restaurant and bar. They make their bread from scratch.

- **Last Frontier Pizza** ☎ 907-822-3030

  PIZZA QUALITY ★★★ $9–$17 SUITABLE FOR KIDS? Y

  All-you-can-eat pizza that the locals favor.

COPPER RIVER BASIN

- **Copper Center Lodge** Mile 101 Old Richardson Highway loop; ☎ 866-330-3245 or 907-822-3245; **www.coppercenterlodge.com**

  FUSION QUALITY ★★★ $7–$27 SUITABLE FOR KIDS? Y

  This aging but historic lodge has a nice dining room with full meals available.

- **Copper River Princess Wilderness Lodge** Mile 102 Richardson Highway; ☎ 800-426-0500 or 907-822-4000; **www.princesslodges.com**

  UPSCALE REGIONAL QUALITY ★★★★★ $9–$29 SUITABLE FOR KIDS? N

  This is a new and luxurious hotel with excellent food in a beautiful dining room.

- **Kennicott Glacier Lodge** On Main Street, Kennicott, Wrangell–St. Elias National Park; ☎ 800-582-5128; **www.kennicottlodge.com**

  FUSION QUALITY ★★★★★ $9–$25 SUITABLE FOR KIDS? Y

  This first-class, historic renovated lodge serves outstanding gourmet meals and shows flair even with its sandwiches.
- **Kenny Lake Diner** Mile 7.2 Edgerton Highway, toward McCarthy; ☎ 907-822-3313; **www.kennylake.com**

  AMERICAN QUALITY ★★ $8–$20 SUITABLE FOR KIDS? Y

  Home-style cooking with chicken, shrimp, pies, and sandwiches. Those staying in the nearby RV park or hotel get a 10% discount.
- **McCarthy Lodge** In downtown McCarthy; ☎ 907-554-4402; **www.mccarthylodge.com**

  AMERICAN QUALITY ★★★ $8–$25 SUITABLE FOR KIDS? Y

  Also called Ma Johnson's Hotel, this renovated lodge offers nice dining.

ON THE TOWN: *What to Do after the Outdoor Adventure*

ANCHORAGE HAS NO SHORTAGE OF PLACES to hang out in the evenings, as well as many daytime activities that will keep you busy. The pickings get a bit slim in outlying communities, though.

This section offers our suggestions for museums, nightclubs, and other points of interest in each region of Southcentral Inland Alaska.

ANCHORAGE

Attractions

- **Alaska Botanical Garden** Tudor and Campbell Airstrip roads; ☎ 907-770-3692; **www.alaskaabg.org**
  Wander through 110 acres of immaculate grounds, featuring an herb garden, a wildflower trail, perennial gardens, and a rock garden dotted with dozens of fabulous plants. Admission is free, but donations are encouraged.
- **Alaska Native Heritage Center** 8800 Heritage Center Drive. ☎ 907-333-8000 or 800-315-6608; **www.alaskanative.net**
  Learn about Alaska's indigenous peoples at this comprehensive living museum dedicated to preserving native history and culture. Admission is a little steep—$23.50 for adults, but it can be an all-day experience, and if there are dance performances scheduled, it is well worth it.
- **The Alaska Zoo** 4731 O'Malley Road; ☎ 907-346-1285; **www.alaskazoo.org**
  For the size of Alaska, the zoo here is pretty impressive. It somehow manages to maintain a natural feel, with trails meandering through the woods and cages scattered throughout. Most of the residents are animals who are accustomed to cold climates such as Alaska's; many have also been rehabilitated

after being brought in orphaned or injured. The grizzly bears, Jake and Oreo, and the polar bear, Aphun, are the highlights, but we like the two snow leopards the best. Admission is $9 for adults, $5 for children 12 to 17, and $4 for those 3 to 11. The zoo is open daily except Christmas and Thanksgiving.

- **Anchorage Market and Festival** Third Avenue and E Street; ☎ 907-272-5634; **www.anchoragemarkets.com**
  Arts, crafts, fresh Valley produce, and an assortment of food and entertainment are available at this open-air market, held weekends during the summer. More than 300 vendors and a chance to meet talented local artists in person.
- **Anchorage Museum of History and Art at Rasmuson Center** 121 West Seventh Avenue; ☎ 907-343-4326; **www.anchoragemuseum.org**
  This is the state's largest museum, and a place you could spend an entire day browsing. We like the special native-dance performances that are scheduled during the summer, as well as the gallery featuring works by some of the state's most renowned artists. Admission is $6.50 for adults and free for children younger than 17.
- **Title Wave Book Co.** 1360 West Northern Lights Boulevard, ☎ 907-278-9283, and 15 West Fifth Avenue, ☎ 907-258-7323; **www.wavebooks.com**
  Entering this bookstore is like getting a history lesson in Alaska. All things and subjects Alaskan can be found in this great downtown bookstore. Its other location, at 1360 West Northern Lights Boulevard (☎ 907-278-9283), is even bigger and better, although not as convenient for downtown visitors. The ever-popular Kaladi Bros. Coffeehouse adjacent to the store is a good place to unwind and check e-mail.
- **Heritage Library Museum** 301 West Northern Lights Boulevard, in the Wells Fargo bank building; ☎ 907-265-2834
  This is an easily overlooked destination, but stop by the bank and take a look. There are native artifacts and baskets that date back hundreds of years, and artwork by such famous Alaska artists as Sydney Laurence and Fred Machetanz. Free admission.

Entertainment

- **Bear Tooth Theatrepub** 1230 West 27th Avenue; ☎ 907-276-4200; **www.beartooththeatre.net**
  This awesome movie and lunch/dinner house shows alternative, second-run, and independent films, and serves delicious Tex-Mex food and pizza from the locally famous Moose's Tooth Pub. They also serve a fine selection of microbrews, all of which you can enjoy while watching the movie.
- **Cyrano's Off-Center Playhouse** 413 D Street; ☎ 907-274-2599; **www.cyranos.org**
  Hours vary, but plays are 7 p.m. Thursday to Saturday and 3 p.m. Sundays. The theater-cafe-bookstore has goodies, and the monthly performances range from Alaska favorites to contemporary offbeat productions. Other attractions include a house jazz band, a comedy improv troupe, poetry readings, and special events. $15 for adults (not suitable for children most of the time).
- **Fourth Avenue Dinner Theatre** 630 West Fourth Avenue; ☎ 907-257-5609; **www.4thavenuetheater.com**

This Art Deco building opened in 1947 and somehow survived the devastating 1964 earthquake that brought down much of Anchorage. It has a beautiful historic interior with wide, sweeping steps. The dinner theater serves up Alaska-themed musical comedy, along with a buffet. Admission is $17 for adults, $12 for children.

- **The Great Alaskan Bush Co.** 631 East International Airport Road; ☎ 907-561-2609; **www.akbushcompany.com**
  Want to see Alaskan women without all their clothes on? This is the perennial favorite among the guys (and gals) who like strip joints. No cover charge.
- **Live After Five** Peratrovich Park, Fourth Avenue and E Street, downtown; ☎ 907-279-5650; **www.ancdp.com**
  These 5 p.m. to 7 p.m. Friday evening outdoor concerts feature some of the area's most popular bands and performers, ranging from bagpipes to top 40. Also featured in the same location is Music in the Park, noon to 1 p.m. Wednesdays and Fridays. Both events are free.

Bars

- **Bernie's Bungalow** 626 D Street; ☎ 907-276-8808
  This house-in-the-city bar features primo martinis and outside patio partying for some of Anchorage's hippest. Definitely the happening spot of the past few years.
- **Chilkoot Charlie's** 2435 Spenard Road; ☎ 907-272-1010; **www.koots.com**
  The rambling log-facade building, perennially voted a favorite by Anchorage folks, has four dance floors and ten bars. Even national magazines have rated it a number-one bar. Live entertainment and plenty of hook-up opportunities.
- **Club Millennium** 420 West Third Avenue; ☎ 907-277-1428
  An 18-and-over dance club that gets freakin' packed on the weekends. Stamps separate drinkers from nondrinkers.
- **Club Soraya** 333 West Fourth Avenue; ☎ 907-563-6940
  A very popular place for Latin dance; watching the experts on the floor will blow you away. The Latin gentlemen are not shy, either: they will ask you to dance, so be prepared. If you don't know how, they *will* show you.
- **Darwin's Theory** 426 G Street; ☎ 907-277-5322; **www.alaska.net/~thndrths**
  Very small and smoky—despite the citywide smoking ban—this bar is an Anchorage institution. It's the kind of place where everyone feels truly welcome, no matter their age, size, color, or sexual orientation.
- **F Street Station** 325 F Street; ☎ 907-272-5196
  Well loved by locals and visitors alike, including regular visitors such as traveling pilots and flight attendants. The "cheese wheel" story is so old we refuse to tell it, but if you happen into the bar and see it sitting there, ask anyone and they'll be glad to regale you.
- **Humpy's Great Alaskan Alehouse** 610 Sixth Avenue; ☎ 907-276-2337
  Live music is featured just about every night, and paired with the excellent bar food (probably the best bar food in Anchorage) and the great beer selection, Humpy's is a home run.

- **The Peanut Farm** Old Seward Highway and International Airport Road; ☎ 907-563-3283; **www.peanutfarmsportsgrill.com**
  Favored by sports fanatics because of its multiple TV screens—even little ones at many of the tables, so you can watch what you want while you imbibe.

MATANUSKA-SUSITNA VALLEY

- **Alaska State Fair** Palmer State Fairgrounds off the Glenn Highway; ☎ 907-745-4827; **www.alaskastatefair.org**
  If you happen to be in Southcentral during the week before Labor Day, you should stop by this huge fair, which features everything from a rodeo to arts-and-crafts booths to monster trucks and the famed lumberjack show.
- **Iditarod Trail Headquarters** Mile 2.2 Knik–Goose Bay Road; ☎ 907-376-5155
  Learn more about the most famous dog-mushing race in history, as well as the story behind this great battle of canine athletes. For more musher and dog history, keep traveling to Mile 13.9 Knik–Goose Bay Road to the **Knik Museum and Mushers Hall of Fame** (☎ 907-376-7755).
- **Independence Mine State Historical Park Visitor Center** ☎ 907-745-2827; **www.dnr.state.ak.us/parks/units/summit.htm**
  This old abandoned gold mine is spectacular to visit on a clear day. Recently refurbished, it tells the tale of Southcentral Alaska's gold-rush past. Daily tours take place during the summer. For more information, contact the Mat-Su Area Park Office, Mile 0.7 Bogard Road, HC 32 Box 6706, Wasilla 99654; ☎ 907-745-3975.
- **Musk Ox Farm** Mile 50.1 Glenn Highway, past the Palmer–Wasilla Highway stop light on the left; ☎ 907-745-4151; **www.muskoxfarm.org**
  See these ancient creatures up close and learn about their excellent wool, called *quviut,* used in hats and mittens.
- **Reindeer Farm** Off Bodenburg Loop Road in Butte; ☎ 907-745-4000
  Take tours of this reindeer farm and learn about the differences between the domesticated version of caribou and Rudolph.

TALKEETNA

- **Fairview Inn** On Main Street
  Features music sometimes, alcohol all the time. Or wander in and out while exploring the historic buildings along Main Street. Walking the street takes all of five minutes, even if your faculties aren't at their sharpest.
- **Latitude 62** Just before the downtown area; ☎ 907-733-2262
  The lodge offers a wide range of food and cocktails, and is a favorite for socializing and listening to music.
- **Museum of Northern Adventure** Downtown; ☎ 907-733-3999
  This gift shop–museum highlights Alaska's history in 24 dioramas, including homesteading, prospecting, wildlife, mushing, Bush pilots, and more.
- **Talkeetna Historical Society Museum** On the village airstrip, just before the heart of town; ☎ 907-733-2487
  Contains displays and information from its gold-mining past as well as items commemorating the life of Bush pilot Don Sheldon, a longtime Talkeetnan who died in 1975. Admission is $3.

PART TWENTY

SOUTHCENTRAL COASTAL ALASKA

Where Mountains and Sea Meet

An **OVERVIEW** *of the* **STATE'S PLAYGROUND**

EVERY SUMMER, TRAFFIC ON THE SEWARD HIGHWAY heading south to the Kenai Peninsula gets unbelievably busy. On the weekends, it is not uncommon to slow down to 50 miles per hour on a highway that's easily traveled at faster speeds under normal conditions.

That's because the secret is out: Southcentral Coastal Alaska is the place to be. Folks from Southcentral Inland communities such as Anchorage and the Matanuska-Susitna Valley head south almost every weekend to have fun and unwind. With the region's fish-rich rivers and bays, protected paddling locations, and world-class hiking trails, it's no wonder. It is a given that this region in Alaska is beautiful—to be honest, that adjective can be applied to most of the state. The advantage of the Southcentral Coastal region, however, is that it is easily accessible. While reaching paradise in the Bush may require two, three, sometimes even four airplane flights, getting to most of Southcentral Coastal Alaska requires only a few hours in a car.

This section of the state is part of what most Alaskans collectively call Southcentral—with the exception of **Kodiak Island,** which is part of Southwest Alaska in many guidebooks. But we at *The Unofficial Guide to Adventure Travel in Alaska* are thinking as an outdoors person would. Many of the same outdoor activities popular in Southcentral communities on the **Kenai Peninsula** and **Prince William Sound** are also popular on Kodiak Island. Kodiak Island has much more in common with these places than some of the farther-flung communities of the Bush. Like the Bush, though, it is remote, accessible only by plane or ferry. Still, flights leaving for Kodiak are easily arranged and most take off from Anchorage. Those taking the Alaska Marine Highway ferry system to Kodiak must first drive clear through the Kenai Peninsula to board at the ferry dock in Homer, thus getting a tour of this region anyway.

True to its name, Southcentral Coastal Alaska is made up of the southernmost lands in the central part of Alaska that are bordered by or close to, coastal waters (see Part One, page 11, for a map of the region). For our purposes, that area begins at **Turnagain Arm,** just south of Girdwood, and continues along the Seward Highway through the small community of **Moose Pass** and then into the coastal fishing town of **Seward.** It also extends from the Seward Highway–Sterling Highway cutoff as it heads west through **Cooper Landing** and **Sterling** and then reaches **Soldotna.** Keep going south on the Sterling Highway, through the communities of **Kasilof, Clam Gulch, Ninilchik,** and **Anchor Point,** and the road eventually will end at a tiny spit of land in the picturesque town of **Homer.** Other communities that can be reached by turning left here or right there (it's amazing how easy it is to get around in such a vast land!) include **Hope,** off the Seward Highway on the Hope Highway, and **Kenai** and **Nikiski,** accessed at the Y in Soldotna, where the Kenai Spur Highway heads northwest, then north.

Southcentral Coastal Alaska also includes Prince William Sound, which can be reached by road by turning onto the Portage Glacier Road, which leads to **Whittier,** on the west side of the Sound. An exciting drive through the longest tunnel in North America will get you to Whittier, where you can then embark on a ferry or boat trip across the entire Prince William Sound to reach **Valdez** or **Cordova.** Both communities are beautiful waterfront fishing villages that offer endless outdoor recreation opportunities. Cordova is one of the best birding spots in the state. Valdez is where you want to go for sea kayaking. Both areas offer excellent fishing, especially from the deck of a charter boat, while jigging for giant halibut deep in the ocean.

Prince William Sound is a spectacular maritime habitat and one of the highlights of any Alaska vacation. It also is the site of the nation's most devastating oil spill in history, which occurred in 1989 when the *Exxon Valdez* oil tanker ran aground on Bligh Reef and dumped 11.3 million gallons of North Slope crude oil into the sound. More than 1,500 miles of coastline were affected, killing plants by the millions, and birds and sea mammals by the thousands. Fisheries were devastated. Fishermen went broke. Today, after more than 15 years of rehabilitation, the recovery process is still under way.

Prince William Sound is the ideal recreation destination. It offers fishing, kayaking, hiking, backpacking, ice climbing, and mountain biking. There are cabins tucked in the woods for camping, or you can choose an open beach and pitch a tent. The people in the communities are friendly and will help you plan the perfect trip to suit your needs—in fact, that's an advantage of working with the smaller, family-owned businesses: they tend to cater each trip to the clients they are serving.

Lastly, there is Kodiak Island, one of our favorite destinations. Dubbed the Emerald Isle (though we beg to differ, Kodiak is beautiful,

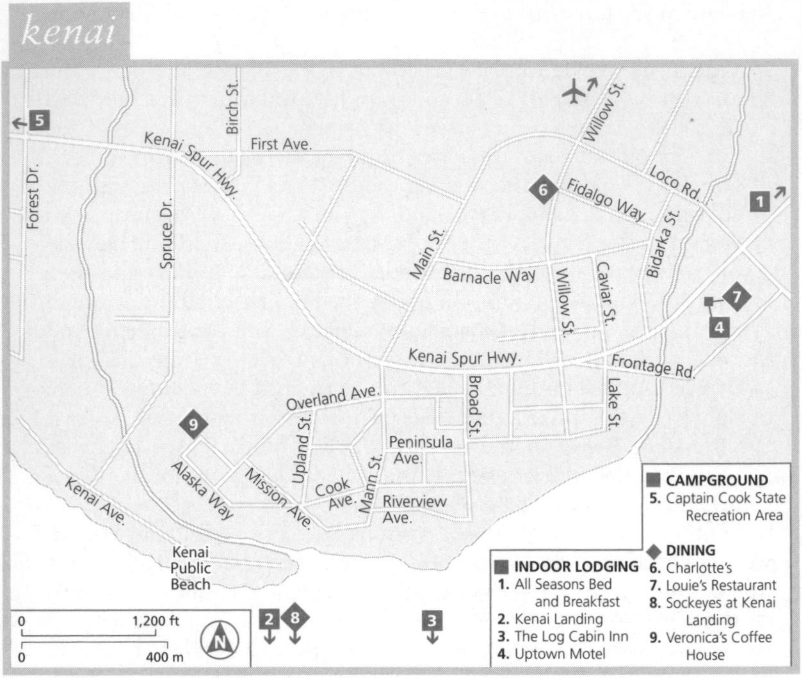

but the term "Emerald Isle" rightly belongs to Ireland), Kodiak Island is home to more than 14,000 people, stretching from **Akhiok** to the south to **Ouzinkie** to the north. It is popular among fishermen, birders, and wildlife watchers.

KENAI PENINSULA

LOOK AT THE WORD *Kenai* and you might be tempted to pronounce it "Keh-NIGH." Don't feel bad: a lot of people do it. In fact, it is "KEY-nigh," a peninsula that offers open valleys, high mountain passes, glaciers, oceans, and a even a little bit of sophistication amid all that wilderness. It truly is one of the most diverse areas of the state.

About 51,300 people live in the Kenai Peninsula Borough, and the area continues to grow. The Kenai Peninsula Borough is composed of the Kenai Peninsula, Cook Inlet, and a large, unpopulated area northeast of the Alaska Peninsula. The Borough includes portions of the **Chugach National Forest, Kenai National Wildlife Refuge, Kenai Fjords National Park,** and portions of **Lake Clark** and **Katmai national parks** (although those last two parks are more associated with Southwest Alaska, and thus discussed in the Bush chapter [page 453]). The

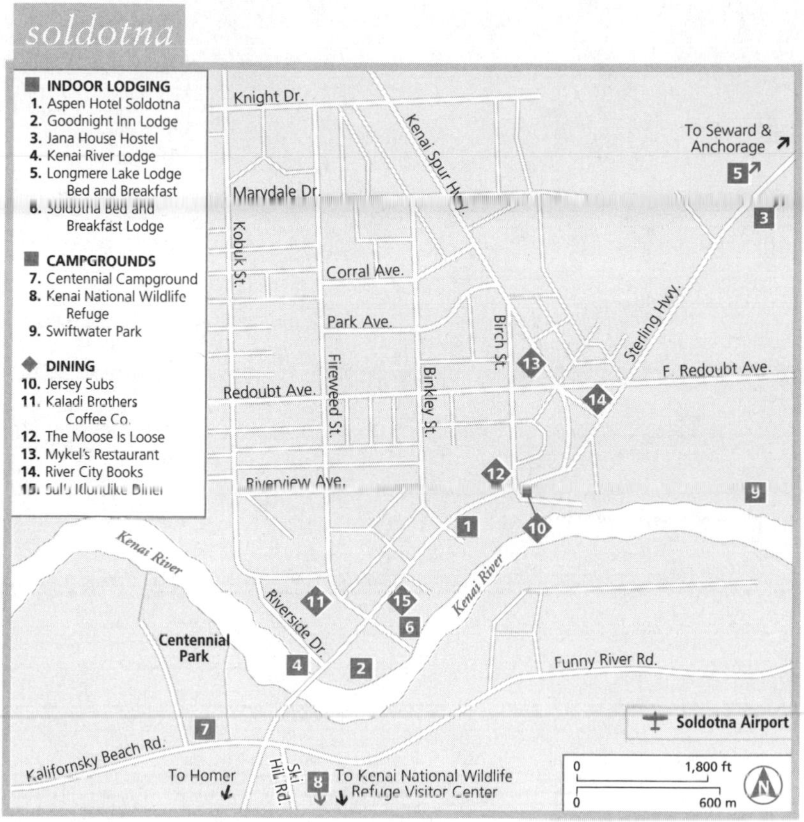

most populated areas of the Kenai Peninsula are **Soldotna** and **Kenai,** known as the Twin Cities because they are side by side.

The Kenai is a region of varied weather, with temperature ranges from 4°F in January to as warm as 65°F in July. Often it will get much colder or warmer, depending upon the weather patterns, so it's not uncommon to get winter lows of –20°F and summer highs in the 70s. It is dominated by the Kenai Mountains, Harding Ice Field, four active volcanoes, and the protected lands of Kachemak Bay State Park, Kenai Fjords National Park, and the Kenai National Wildlife Refuge.

The larger communities that make up the Kenai Peninsula include Seward, Homer, Soldotna, and Kenai. We have discussed each community in depth on the following pages. Several outlying communities include **Hope, Moose Pass, Cooper Landing, Sterling, Ninilchik,** and **Anchor Point.** We provide limited information on these towns under "Surrounding Areas" (page 344).

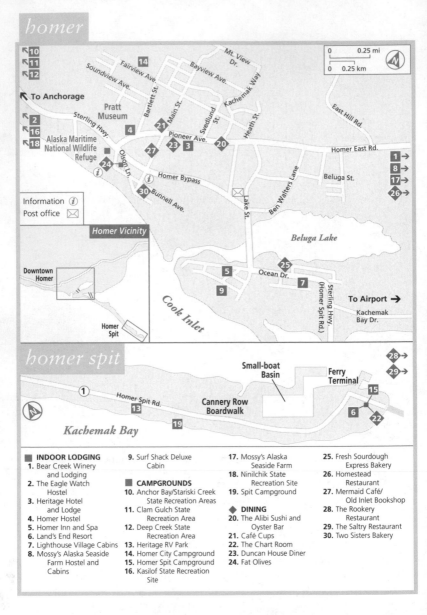

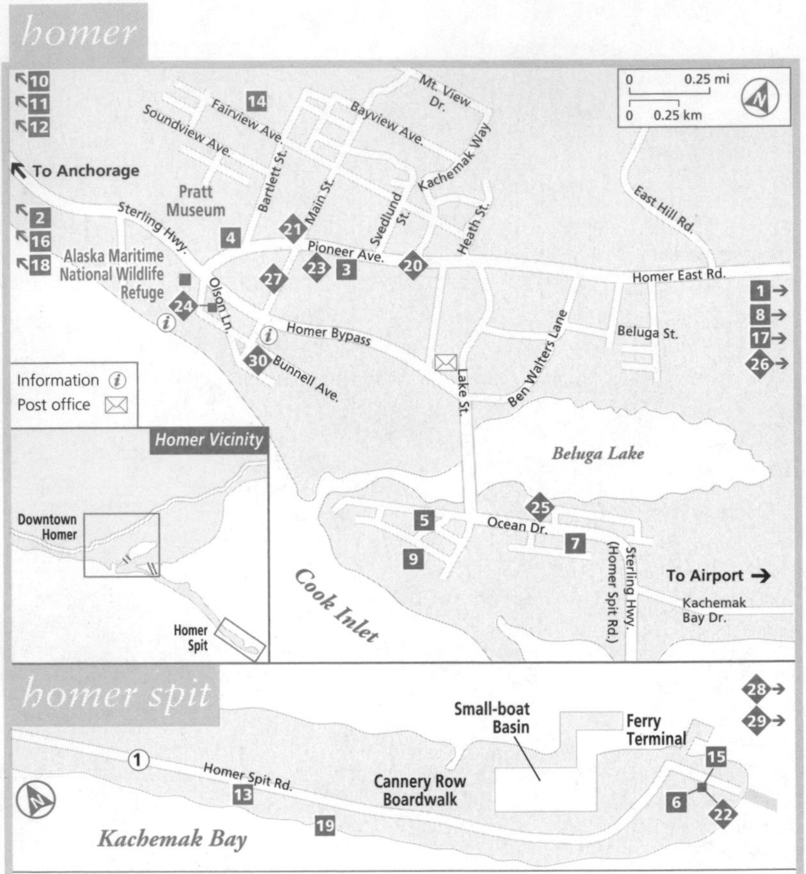

INDOOR LODGING

1. Bear Creek Winery and Lodging
2. The Eagle Watch Hostel
3. Heritage Hotel and Lodge
4. Homer Hostel
5. Homer Inn and Spa
6. Land's End Resort
7. Lighthouse Village Cabins
8. Mossy's Alaska Seaside Farm Hostel and Cabins
9. Surf Shack Deluxe Cabin

CAMPGROUNDS

10. Anchor Bay/Stariski Creek State Recreation Areas
11. Clam Gulch State Recreation Area
12. Deep Creek State Recreation Area
13. Heritage RV Park
14. Homer City Campground
15. Homer Spit Campground
16. Kasilof State Recreation Site
17. Mossy's Alaska Seaside Farm
18. Ninilchik State Recreation Site
19. Spit Campground

DINING

20. The Alibi Sushi and Oyster Bar
21. Café Cups
22. The Chart Room
23. Duncan House Diner
24. Fat Olives
25. Fresh Sourdough Express Bakery
26. Homestead Restaurant
27. Mermaid Café/ Old Inlet Bookshop
28. The Rookery Restaurant
29. The Saltry Restaurant
30. Two Sisters Bakery

While most people think of the North Slope when they think of Alaska's oil reserves, it actually was on the Kenai Peninsula that the first oil was discovered, in 1957. It has been a center for exploration and production ever since.

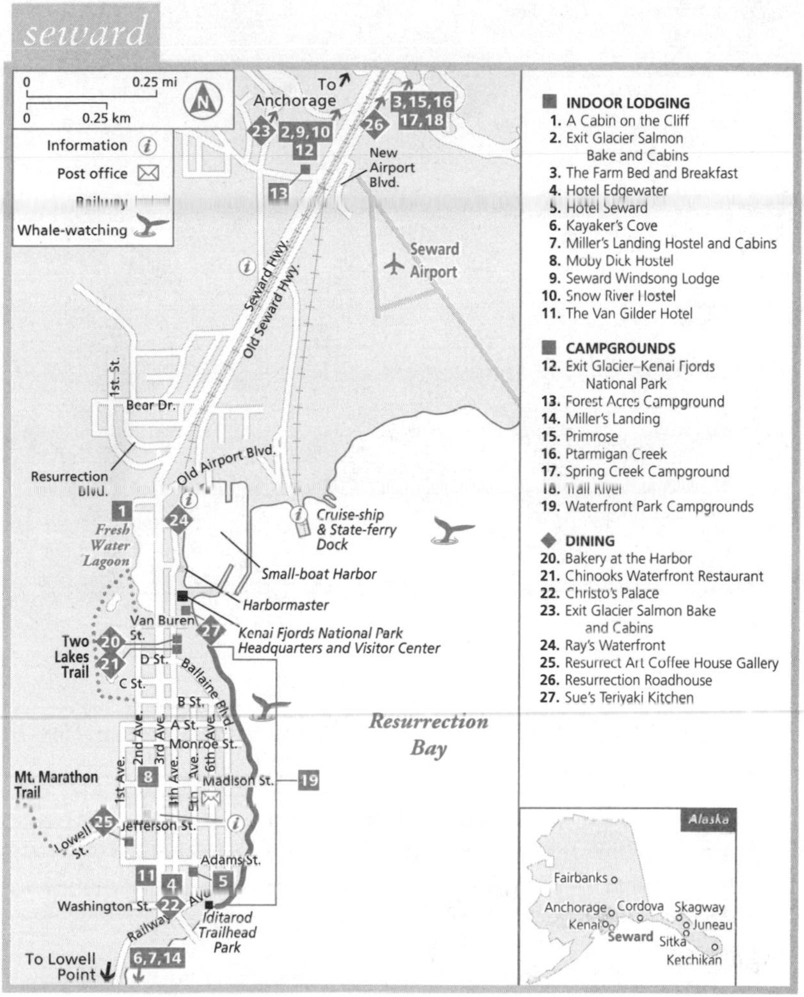

One of the Kenai Peninsula's most famed attributes is the **Kenai River,** a major sportfishing location for Anchorage residents and tourists alike. The river is world-renowned for trophy king, silver, and red salmon, so it attracts visitors whose sole purpose is to land a giant fish.

The community has grown to accommodate these visitors, and there is a small (albeit busy) airport, along with roads, plenty of guides, and tackle shops to outfit even the newest of anglers. Still, the economy of the Borough consists of industries such as commercial fishing, mining, and timber, as well as petroleum-industry activities. While the natural beauty and recreational activities have led to a growing tourism industry, the

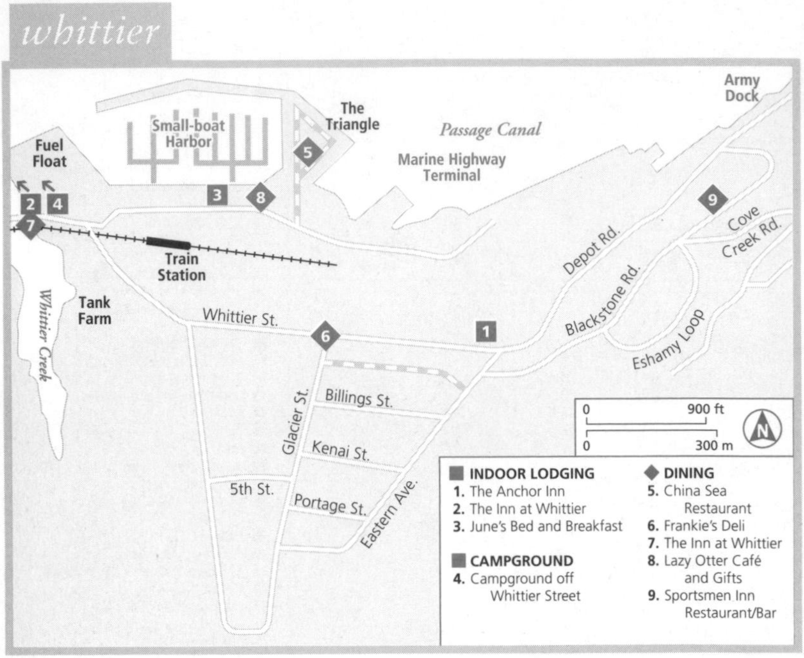

area maintains a certain remoteness that still allows the visitor to feel like he or she is getting away from it all.

Access to the Kenai Peninsula is by the Sterling and Seward highways from the north, the Alaska Marine ferry from the south, and by scheduled flights from varying directions, mostly Anchorage. When driving from Anchorage, allow at least three hours to reach Soldotna, more if you want to stop often and take photos. The drive is stunning.

KENAI

THE CITY OF KENAI was founded in 1791 as a Russian fur-trading post, and in the early 1900s cannery operations started to crop up, providing jobs and allowing the community to grow. Today, nearly 6,800 people live in the area for which the peninsula was named, specifically on the western coast of the Kenai Peninsula, fronting **Cook Inlet.** Kenai is approximately 65 air miles and 155 highway miles southwest of Anchorage via the Sterling Highway. The central airport for the peninsula is located in Kenai, and this is where many an adventure begins.

Kenai Visitors and Cultural Center
11471 Kenai Spur Highway
Kenai 99611
☎ 907-283-1991
www.visitkenai.com

As you walk through the original Kenai town site, it is easy to imagine its historic past. The log buildings tell of a simpler time, and the onion-domed church is evidence of the Russian Orthodox

valdez

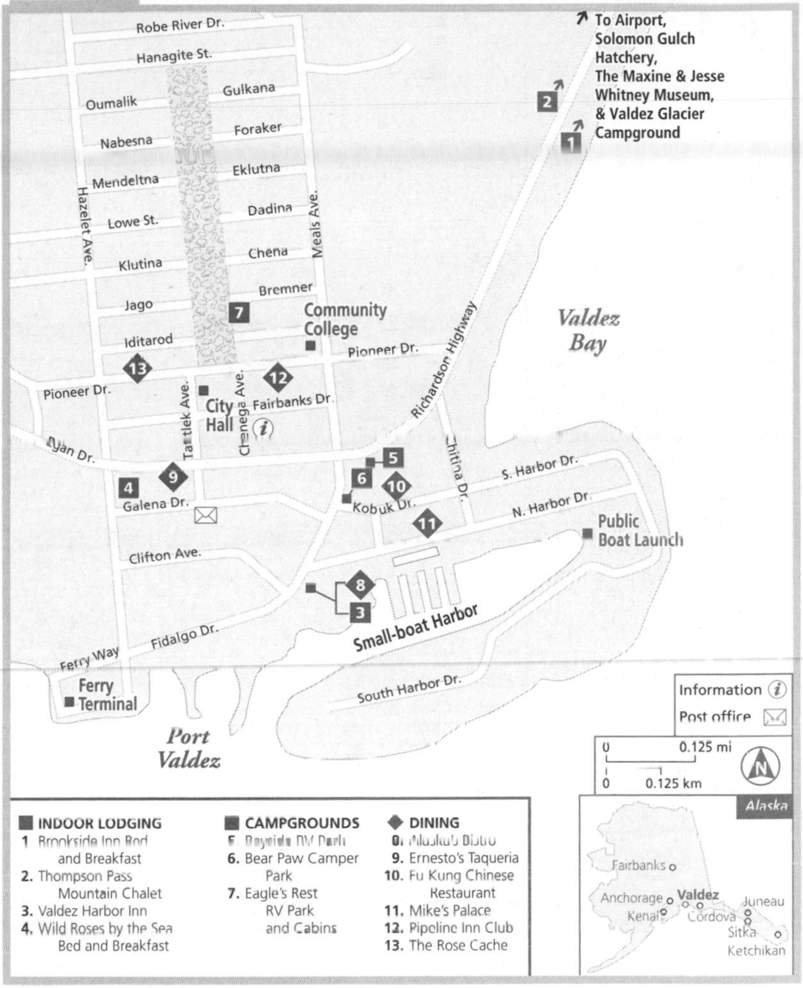

influence, which remains in many Kenai Peninsula communities today. When Russians settled the area in 1791, they first named it Fort St. Nicholas. It was the second permanent Russian settlement in Alaska (the first was in Kodiak). In 1849, the Holy Assumption Russian Orthodox Church was established, and in 1869 the U.S. military established a post for the Dena'ina Indians in the area, called Fort Kenay. The area was abandoned in 1870 after the United States purchased Alaska. Still, residents continued to live there, developing commercial fishing and settling the wild lands first by clearing the spruce trees away and planting

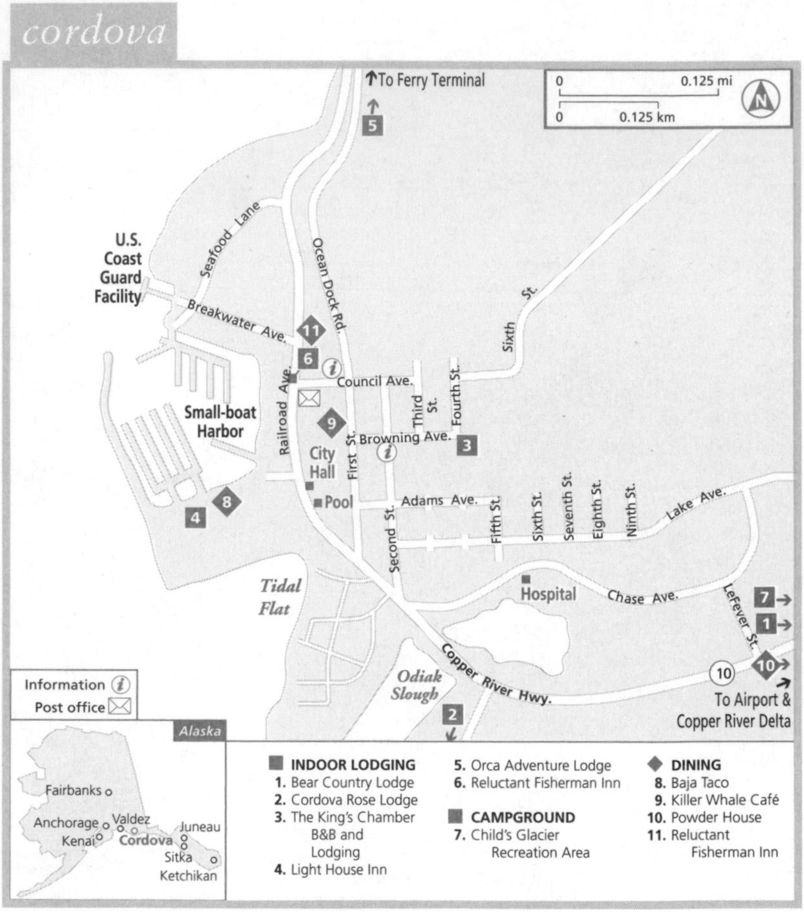

crops and farms. The first dirt road from Anchorage was constructed in 1951, and the discovery of oil in 1957 along the Swanson River, 20 miles northeast of Kenai, prompted a flurry of activity and rapid development. Kenai has been a growing center for oil exploration, production, and services ever since.

The Kenaitze (Tanaina Athabascans) are the primary indigenous population in the area, although the city is predominantly nonnative.

Greater Soldotna Chamber of Commerce
44790 Sterling Highway
Soldotna 99669
☎ 907-262-9814
www.soldotnachamber.com

SOLDOTNA

KENAI'S SISTER CITY IS SOLDOTNA, population about 3,800—although locals seem to have an unspoken rivalry more than a sisterhood. The famed **Kenai River** flows through Soldotna, which

kodiak area

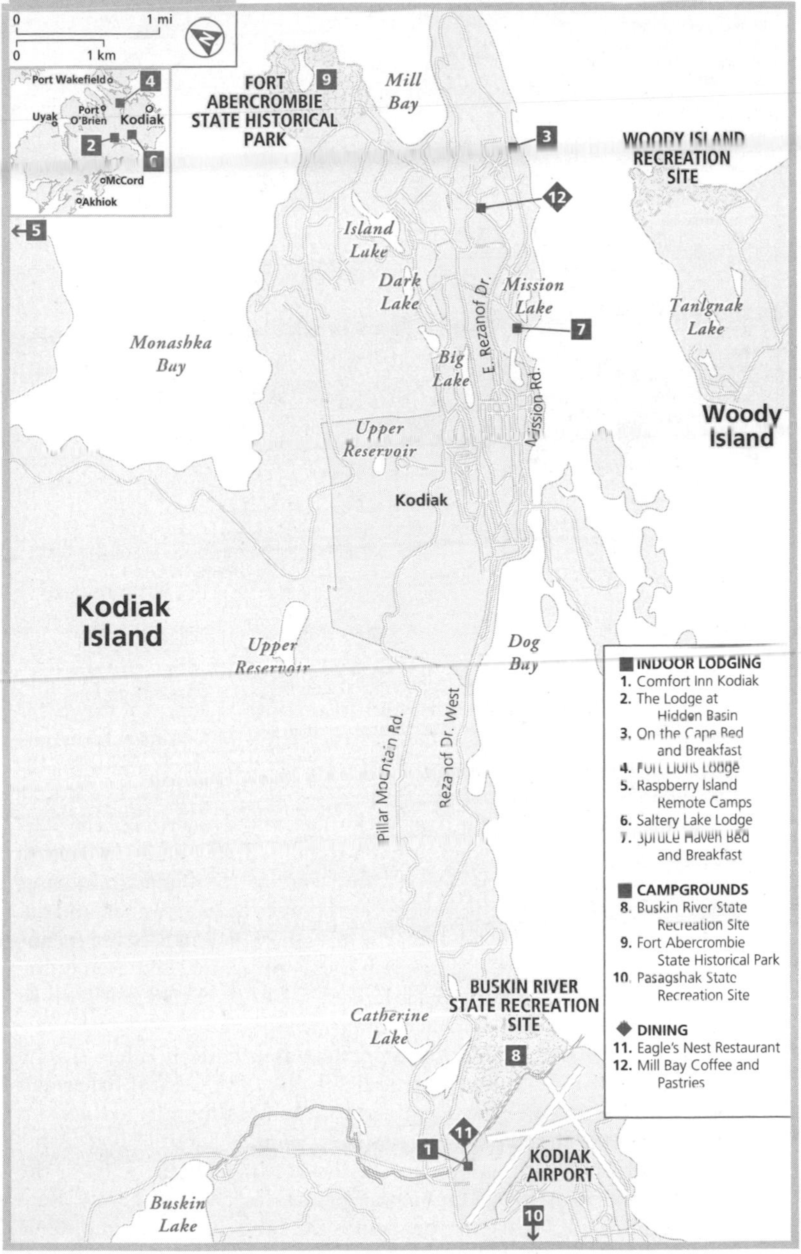

0 ____ 1 mi
0 ____ 1 km

Port Wakefield **4**
Uyak Port **2** Kodiak
O'Brien
McCord **6**
Akhiok

5

FORT
ABERCROMBIE **9**
STATE HISTORICAL
PARK

*Mill
Bay*

3

WOODY ISLAND
RECREATION
SITE

12

*Island
Lake*

*Dark
Lake*

E. Rezanof Dr.

*Mission
Lake*

7

*Tanignak
Lake*

*Monashka
Bay*

Mission Rd.

*Big
Lake*

**Woody
Island**

*Upper
Reservoir*

Kodiak

**Kodiak
Island**

*Upper
Reservoir*

*Dog
Bay*

Pillar Mountain Rd.

Rezanof Dr. West

■ **INDOOR LODGING**
1. Comfort Inn Kodiak
2. The Lodge at
 Hidden Basin
3. On the Cape Bed
 and Breakfast
4. Port Lions Lodge
5. Raspberry Island
 Remote Camps
6. Saltery Lake Lodge
7. Spruce Haven Bed
 and Breakfast

■ **CAMPGROUNDS**
8. Buskin River State
 Recreation Site
9. Fort Abercrombie
 State Historical Park
10. Pasagshak State
 Recreation Site

◆ **DINING**
11. Eagle's Nest Restaurant
12. Mill Bay Coffee and
 Pastries

*Catherine
Lake*

**BUSKIN RIVER
STATE RECREATION
SITE**

8

11

1

**KODIAK
AIRPORT**

10
↓

*Buskin
Lake*

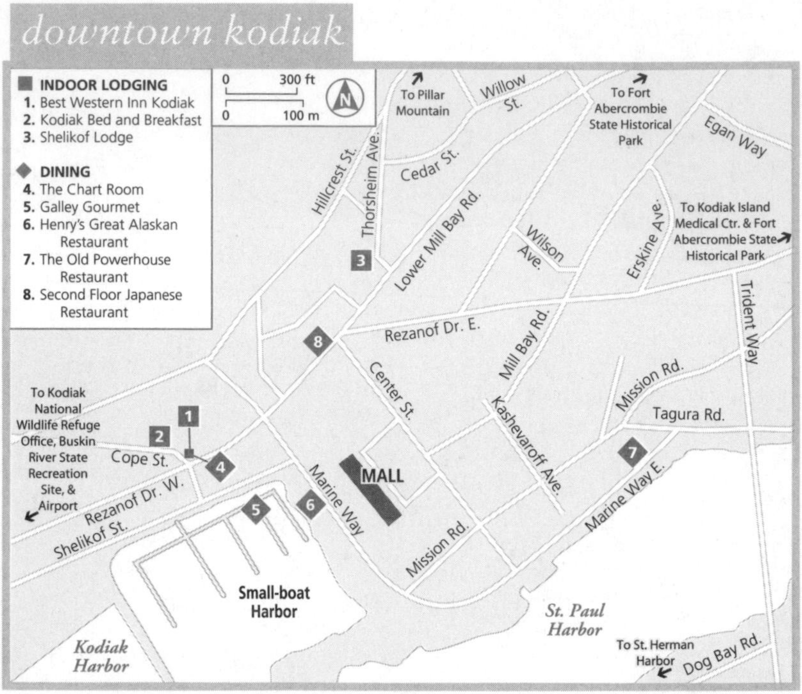

is on the main road system as you drive south. Kenai, the town for which the peninsula got its name, however, is off on a spur road, offering governmental and air support for travelers who fly in and immediately head for Soldotna.

Soldotna is 150 miles south of Anchorage, at the junction of the Sterling and Kenai Spur highways. It has a similar climate and temperature range to Kenai's, and was historically home to the Kenaitze Indians, then developed by nonnatives for such resources as fish, timber, and oil.

The city got its name for a nearby stream, which in Russian means "soldier"—at least that's what some locals proclaim. Like Kenai, the area grew quickly with the discovery of oil in the Swanson River in 1957. By 1960, the area was named a city.

The Kenai River is Soldotna's greatest asset, and it offers trophy king salmon fishing during June and July. In 1985, a local fisherman hoisted a 97-pound, 4-ounce world-record king salmon from the river. Catching a king that tops the scales at 65 pounds is not uncommon.

Access to Soldotna is mostly via the Sterling Highway from the north, although there is a municipal airport for charter service. Regularly scheduled flights to the peninsula land at the larger **Kenai Municipal Airport,** ten miles away.

HOMER

Homer Chamber of Commerce
P.O. Box 541
Homer 99603
☎ 907-235-7740
www.homeralaska.org

THIS COMMUNITY OF 5,400 FRIENDLY, sometimes funky, and always interesting people is our favorite location in Alaska. Unfortunately, it has grown tremendously in the past decade, and we hope it will not lose its small-town charm over the next ten years. Still, it is a beautiful place, located on the north shore of **Kachemak Bay** on the southwestern edge of the Kenai Peninsula, where the mountains meet the ocean in stark and beautiful contrast. **Homer Spit,** a 4.5-mile-long bar of gravel, extends out from the Homer shoreline.

Homer is 227 road miles south of Anchorage, at the southernmost point of the Sterling Highway, so it's more than a day trip for travelers based in the big city. And it should be. There is so much to do in Homer, from kayaking to fishing to hiking, that it is hard to limit your stay to just a day.

The community is in a maritime climate zone, which means winter temperatures are slightly higher (14°F to 27°F is the average range), and summer temperatures tend to be cooler than inland towns (45°F to 65°F in the summer).

The name came from Homer Pennock, a gold-mining company promoter, who arrived in 1896 and built living quarters for his crew of 50 on the spit. But today, the name most associated with Homer is Jewel, the pop-singer-turned-poet who grew up there, riding horses on the Kilcher family homestead.

While commercial and sportfishing are the center of the economic activity, Homer has a large community of artists. The **Homer Jackpot Halibut Derby** runs from May 1 through Labor Day each year, and brings in halibut anglers from all over the country. The visitor industry also is growing as people discover Homer's beauty. About ten cruise ships dock each summer, and during the summer, the population swells with students and others seeking cannery or fishery employment.

Homer is accessible by the Sterling Highway, which links to Anchorage and the rest of the Lower 48. It is often referred to as "The End of the Road," because it lies at the terminus of the Sterling Highway. The **Homer Airport** also provides daily air service to Anchorage and connecting communities. The **Alaska Marine Highway** and local ferry services provide water transportation.

SEWARD

Seward Chamber of Commerce
P.O. Box 749
Seward 99664
☎ 907-224-8051
www.seward.com

ON THE EASTERN TIP OF THE KENAI PENINSULA is another water-meets-mountains community called Seward, population 2,500. This small city is only a two-and-a-half-hour drive from Anchorage and makes a pleasant day trip, although it, too, is worth exploring more in-depth.

Looming over the city is **Mount Marathon,** a peak that attracts mountain runners worldwide every July 4 for the annual Mount Marathon race. Spreading out on the other end of town are **Kenai Fjords National Park** and **Resurrection Bay,** an oceanfront playground that affords wonderful sea kayaking, fishing, and exploring. **Bear Creek** and **Lowell Point** are adjacent to Seward and offer wilderness access as well.

Like Homer, Seward has a maritime climate that brings lots of rain and temperatures that are a bit milder in the winter. It does, however, tend to get more snow than Homer, about 80 inches per year versus 50 in Homer.

The name Seward is heard often in Alaska. From 1861 to 1869, the then–U.S. Secretary of State William Seward was responsible for the U.S. purchase of Alaska from the Russians during the Lincoln administration. Naysayers thought it was a huge mistake to buy a frozen wasteland, and they called the deal "Seward's Folly" or "Seward's Icebox."

Turns out Seward was a very wise man, because Alaska's natural resources have brought trillions of dollars to the United States. The last Monday in March, Alaskans celebrate Seward's Day to celebrate the man's accomplishment. The town of Seward is especially proud of the name for that reason.

As the southern terminus for the **Alaska Railroad** and a road link to Anchorage and the Interior, Seward has long been a transportation center. The economy has diversified with tourism, commercial fishing and processing, ship services, and other natural resource endeavors. As an ice-free harbor, Seward has become an important supply center for Interior Alaska.

Cuise ships flock to Seward in the summer, justifying such state-of-the-art visitor attractions as the **Alaska SeaLife Center,** a marine-animal research and education facility. More than 320,000 cruise-ship passengers visit Seward annually, spending hundreds of thousands of dollars as they come.

Besides the railroad and driving your own vehicle, there is also bus service to and from Anchorage daily. Air service and charters are available at the state-owned airport. The Alaska Marine Highway ferry also brings passengers from the Lower 48 and other Alaska communities.

SURROUNDING AREAS

THERE ARE MANY, MANY SMALL COMMUNITIES along the roads and even off the road system that comprise the whole of the Kenai Peninsula. There are so many, in fact, that each one, with its own unique characteristics, could be a visitor destination.

In this section, we share just a few of the larger ones. If you have time, stop by these tiny villages. They could be the most interesting. Check out the gift shop in Ninilchik. Eat lunch at the local diner in Hope. Take a hike in Cooper Landing. Sometimes, it is the small things you do in an epic adventure-based vacation that have the most impact. These communities can provide such moments.

HOPE (population 140) lies on the northern end of Kenai Peninsula, on the south shore of the Turnagain Arm of Cook Inlet. Access it by driving south on the Seward Highway, and turning right on 17-mile-long Hope Highway, near the mouth of Resurrection Creek. "Hope City" was a mining camp for Resurrection Creek, established in 1896. Portions of the town were destroyed in the 1964 earthquake, but several old and historic buildings remain. Hiking, backpacking, mountain biking, and rafting are popular sports here.

MOOSE PASS (population 200) is 26 miles north of Seward on the Kenai Peninsula. It is on the southwest shore of Upper Trail Lake, off the Seward Highway. The community was first named in 1912 as a station on the Alaska Railroad. The name is reportedly derived from a mail carrier's team of dogs that in 1903 had a moose–dog misunderstanding: the moose would not move out of the way, and the dogs would not take no for an answer. Kayaking, fishing, and canoeing are popular sports here.

COOPER LANDING (population 350) is at the west end of Kenai Lake on a stretch of the Sterling Highway, 30 miles northwest of Seward in the Chugach Mountains. Cooper Landing was named for Joseph Cooper, a miner who discovered gold here in 1884. In 1948, a road to Kenai provided vehicle access to Cooper Landing. By 1951, a road to Anchorage completed the link. The population of the area nearly doubles each summer to support tourism businesses and activities. Fishing, backpacking, canoeing, kayaking, skiing, hiking, rafting, and mountain biking are popular sports here.

STERLING (population 5,000) is located on the Sterling Highway at the junction of the Moose and Kenai rivers, just north of Soldotna. Sterling became the name of this collection of homes when in 1954, the first post office was established. The community caters to the sportfishing industry and summer influx of recreational enthusiasts. Fishing, canoeing, skiing, kayaking, and rafting are popular sports here.

KASILOF (population 550) is on the east shore of Cook Inlet on the Kenai Peninsula. It is accessed via the Sterling Highway, just south of Soldotna. Unlike many fishing-based communities, Kasilof was an agricultural settlement of Kenaitze Indians. Today, however, fishing is an integral part of the community. More than 155 Kasilof residents hold commercial fishing permits, and sportfishing is also very popular in the Kasilof River. Fishing, canoeing, skiing, hiking, and dog mushing are popular sports here.

NINILCHIK (population 780) lies on the western coast of the Kenai Peninsula along the Sterling Highway, 188 road miles from Anchorage. The **Ninilchik River, Deep Creek,** and **Cook Inlet** are the

Ninilchik Chamber of Commerce
P.O. Box 39164
Ninilchik 99636
☎ 907-567-3670
www.alaskan.com/bells/ninilchik.html

reasons the community exists, and sportfishing is one of the most popular summertime endeavors pursued here today. The community's history is steeped in Dena'ina Indian tradition. The Dena'ina word *niqnilchint* means "lodge by the river," which is how the name Ninilchik came to be. The Russian influence also is found here, and the Russian Orthodox Church, constructed in 1901, is still a stunning sight to see when you drive into town. Fishing, retail businesses, tourism, and logging comprise the majority of private-sector activities in Ninilchik. Fishing, hiking, camping, and dog mushing are popular sports here.

Anchor Point Chamber of Commerce
P.O. Box 610
Anchor Point 99556
☎ 907-235-2600
www.anchorpointalaska.info

ANCHOR POINT (population 1,800) is on the Kenai Peninsula at the junction of the Anchor River and its north fork, 14 miles northwest of Homer. It lies at Mile 156 of the Sterling Highway. The community got its name when, in the summer of 1778, Captain James Cook and his crews sailed into the inlet looking for a northwest passage, and lost an anchor to the strong tides there. Many residents work in nearby Homer or work in town catering to the sportfishing industry. Fishing is the primary pastime here.

Seldovia Chamber of Commerce
P.O. Drawer F
Seldovia 99663
☎ 907-234-7803
www.xyz.net/~seldovia

SELDOVIA (population 280) is on the Kenai Peninsula across from Homer, on the south shore of Kachemak Bay. It is a 15-minute flight from Homer, or 45 minutes from Anchorage. Many people take a water taxi to get there, and the Alaska Marine Highway ferry also stops there. The name Seldovia comes from *seldevoy,* a Russian word meaning "herring bay." In the mid- to late 1800s, a trading post was established, and commercial fishing and fish processing were the major industries. Today, Seldovia remains a commercial fishing center. It is a quaint town to visit while in Homer, and a fun place to be for its annual Fourth of July parade.

PRINCE WILLIAM SOUND

THE 70-MILE-WIDE PRINCE WILLIAM SOUND is a kayaker's dream, and as you ply the waters of this protected coastal region in Southcentral Alaska, you'll notice the small boats everywhere, usually close to shoreline exploring the nooks and crannies that make this area so interesting.

The sound is at the northern end of the Gulf of Alaska and is dominated by high cliffs, protected inlets, and many glaciers and mountains to be enjoyed at a distance or up close. Dall sheep, mountain goats, sea lions, seals, and otters can be found in this area, as well as thousands of shorebird and seabird species, and plenty of salmon and halibut.

One of the large sightseeing destinations in Prince William Sound is **Columbia Glacier,** one of the largest tidewater glaciers on the Alaska coast. It got its name in 1899, during the Harriman expedition to Alaska, and is named for the university of the same name in New York City. In fact, several of the surrounding glaciers are named for colleges, including Bryn Mawr, Harvard, and Princeton, to name a few.

The sound has 3,000 miles of shoreline and is surrounded by the **Chugach Mountains** to the east, west, and north. Fifty-mile-long **Montague Island** and several smaller islands form natural breakwaters between the sound and the Gulf of Alaska, calming the swells and providing protected boating.

Fewer than 10,000 people live in all of Prince William Sound's three main and several outlying communities. In fact, more visitors come to the area each year than there are year-round residents.

This section tells you a little more about the three largest communities—**Valdez, Cordova,** and **Whittier.** Even though the best of Prince William Sound is out in the wild, you'll likely embark on your trip from one of these town centers.

WHITTIER

Greater Whittier Chamber of Commerce
P.O. Box 607
Whittier 99693
www.whittieralaskachamber.org

OF THE THREE MAIN COMMUNITIES in Prince William Sound, Whittier has the fewest people—only about 150 live here year-round—but it is in a geographically significant location. Accessible by road from Anchorage, the community is a launching point for many an outdoor adventure. Located on the northeast shore of the Kenai Peninsula, at the head of Passage Canal, it is also on the west side of Prince William Sound, 75 miles southeast of Anchorage.

Whittier is, to say the least, a funky community, featured once in *Outside* magazine as the ugliest town on the planet. Of course, that isn't true: the natural beauty surrounding Whittier is astounding, and it literally takes five minutes to reach it.

But the town itself? There's not much to be said for the collection of boxy, run-down-looking high-rises that scar the landscape. But there is a reason. Let us explain.

The town started as an entrance point for U.S. troops during World War II, and the buildings were constructed as purely functional living quarters for troops. The 14-story **Hodge Building** (now called **Begich Towers**) had 198 apartments and housed families and bachelors. The nearby **Buckner Building,** completed in 1953, had 1,000 apartments and was once the largest building in Alaska. It was called the "city under one roof," and boasted a bowling alley, theater, swimming pool, and shops for Army personnel. The hospital also was housed there. **Whittier Manor** was built in the early 1950s as rental units for civilians. During this time, there were more than 1,000 people living there, while the facility remained active. But once the Army closed the port in 1960, the population quickly dived, leaving the behemoth buildings behind. Whittier Manor was converted to condominiums in 1964, and Begich Towers now is home to the majority of the residents. The Buckner building is no longer occupied, although there has been talk of refurbishing it.

The weather in Whittier is blustery and often wet. Winter temperatures range from 17°F to 28°F; summer temperatures average 49°F to 63°F. Average annual precipitation includes 66 inches of rain and 80 inches of snow. Summer tourism is the primary economic driver in Whittier, and the summer stays busy with boaters and fishermen loading up and heading out to the sound. There are charter tours, glacier sightseeing tours, and other activities available in the area.

Whittier has become even more attractive to travelers now that it is more easily accessible. A $70 million road connection was completed in the summer of 2000, creating the **Anton Anderson Memorial Tunnel.** The tunnel allows access to Whittier via Anchorage, and can accommodate vehicles and trains. The railway carries passengers, vehicles, and cargo 12 miles from the **Portage Station,** east of Girdwood.

VALDEZ

HERE IS A COMMUNITY that can be downright intimidating when the weather socks in and the rain goes on for days. But come the first sunshiny day, the views open up and the mountains surrounding this seaside community make one understand what is so great about Valdez: it's gorgeous.

Valdez Convention and Visitors Bureau
200 Fairbanks Drive
Valdez 99686
☎ 800-770-5954
www.valdezalaska.org

About 4,400 people live in Valdez (pronounced Val-**DEEZ,** even though it is a Spanish word that is supposed to be pronounced Val-**DEHZ**) promoting their area through tourism, fishing, or oil development. Valdez is the southern terminus to the **Trans-Alaska Pipeline System,** which feeds crude oil from the North Slope clear to the port for passage south.

Port Valdez is a deep-water fjord located 305 miles east of Anchorage and 364 miles south of Fairbanks. Even though it is right on the water and many coastal communities do not get much snow, Valdez is different. January temperatures range from 21°F to 30°F, and July temperatures are in the 46°F-to-61°F range. Annual precipitation is 62 inches, but average snowfall—and this is not a typo—is 325 inches, or 27 feet!

Naturally, snow sports are popular here. Valdez is the heli-skiing capital of the state, and any skiing extremist will be floored by the skiing and snowboarding possibilities. Valdez is where those insane scenes from extreme-ski movies are shot: skiers flipping upside down and landing backward skiing down sheer cliffs—that sort of thing.

Ice climbers and mountaineers are drawn by the great ice and numerous glaciers. On the Richardson Highway, there is one scenic spot along the road that is a rushing waterfall during the summer—**Bridal Veil Falls.** But come winter, you'll see hardy ice climbers making their way up the steep pitch of ice, and it will give you chills.

Farther north is Valdez's famed **Thompson Pass,** almost 2,800 feet above sea level and owning the coveted superlative of being the location in Alaska that gets more snow than anywhere else in the state. The record 24-hour snowfall there is five feet.

Valdez got its beginnings as yet another point of entry for goldseekers in 1898 (although it had been discovered and named by Spanish explorers back in 1790). It became incorporated as a city in 1901, and in the 1920s the Alaska Road Commission further developed a road for travel to Fairbanks. The original waterfront community was destroyed by the 1964 Good Friday earthquake, which also killed several residents. Today, the community is rebuilt on a more stable bedrock foundation four miles to the west.

In March 1989, Valdez was the center for the massive oil-spill cleanup after the *Exxon Valdez* catastrophe. In a few short days following the spill, the population of the town tripled. Today, the town is recovering, but effects of the spill are long-lasting, and watchdog groups constantly monitor the safety of fuel transportation in the area.

For those looking for summer activities in Valdez, there also are some great hiking trails (see our Day Hiking chapter, page 186, for details), excellent road and mountain biking, fishing, kayaking, rafting, and birding.

CORDOVA

CORDOVA IS LOCATED AT THE SOUTHEASTERN end of Prince William Sound in the Gulf of Alaska, and is home to about 2,200 Alaskans. The community was built on **Orca Inlet,** at the base of **Eyak Mountain,** 52 air miles southeast of Valdez and 150 miles southeast of Anchorage.

Cordova Chamber of Commerce and Visitors Center
P.O. Box 99
Cordova 99574
☎ 907-424-7260
www.cordovachamber.com

Cordova has many beautiful aspects, but one of its biggest outdoor draws is the excellent birding. The area is home to one of the largest shorebird migrations in the world, and each spring bird enthusiasts congregate to watch it all happen.

The area has average winters, with temperatures in the 17°F-to-28°F range. Summer temperatures average 49°F to 63°F. Annual precipitation is 167 inches, and average snowfall is 80 inches.

Cordova originally was named Puerto Cordova, by the same Spanish explorers who named Valdez, but the *Puerto* was dropped (no one really knows when) and the city was formed in 1909. Cordova became the railroad terminus and ocean-shipping port for copper ore from the Kennicott Mine up the Copper River.

Today, Cordova supports a large fishing fleet for Prince William Sound and several fish-processing plants. Copper River red salmon, pink salmon, herring, halibut, bottom fish, and other fisheries are harvested and sent to fancy restaurants in the Lower 48 to be consumed within 48 hours. Copper River reds have gained a reputation worldwide, and their journey to outside markets often begins in Cordova.

Other outdoor activities popular in Cordova include mountain biking, hiking, fishing, and rafting.

KODIAK ISLAND

Kodiak Island Convention and Visitors Bureau
100 Marine Way, Suite 200
Kodiak 99615
☎ 800-789-4782 or 907-486-4782
www.kodiak.org

AT 3,588 SQUARE MILES, KODIAK ISLAND is the second-largest island in the United States, following the Big Island of Hawaii (the archipelago—all the islands that make up the entire Kodiak Island Borough—is 6,559 square miles). It is located on the eastern side of the Gulf of Alaska, 252 air miles south of Anchorage, which is about a 50-minute flight, and three hours from Seattle. It takes nine and a half hours to travel to Kodiak from Homer via the Alaska Marine Highway ferry system. About 13,000 people populate the island, about 5,900 of them living in the small city of Kodiak.

Kodiak's climate is dominated by a strong marine influence, which means it rains or is foggy much of the time. But the temperature rarely dips below freezing, even in the winter, and summer days, when they are sunny, can be glorious. Annual precipitation is 60 inches on the windward side of the island, and 40 inches on the leeward side.

Kodiak has maintained its working-man feel while still offering plenty of amenities to the visitor. It's not uncommon to see commercial fishermen swabbing the decks of their fishing vessels or repairing their nets, but it's also not difficult to find a hotel or bed-and-breakfast that can meet your every need. Hardware stores are next to gift shops, and the visitor center can accommodate cannery workers or cruise-ship passengers. It's a place without pretensions, comfortable the moment you step off the plane or boat.

unofficial **TIP**
Seeing a Kodiak brown bear up close is probably something you don't want to do, but there are plenty of air-taxi operators and guides who can get you closer to these behemoths safely.

The halibut and silver-salmon fishing here are spectacular, and that's what most people come for. There is no shortage of charter-boat operators, remote lodge owners, and air taxis eager to take you to uncharted territory to not only catch a big fish but catch it in a gorgeous setting.

But it's not all about fishing. The wildlife is worth seeing, too. The island is home to the largest of the three brown-bear subspecies, ***Ursus arctos middendorffi,*** aka the Kodiak brown bear. In general, Alaska brown bears live along the coast, grizzlies live in the Interior, and Kodiaks live only on the island for which they are named.

Other recreation opportunities include kayaking (**Shuyak Island State Park** is a particular favorite place to do it), mountain biking, hiking, and birding.

The area has a rich history, too, having been inhabited since 8,000 BC, according to archeological evidence. Russian fur trappers settled in the area in 1792, and Kodiak was actually the capital of Russian Alaska before it was moved to Sitka in 1867. Several branches of the military have maintained a presence in Kodiak since World War II, and today the U.S. Coast Guard has the largest facility in the world based there. "Coasties," as they are called, add great cultural diversity to Kodiak, coming from all over the country and sharing their experiences.

Commercial and subsistence fishing is still prevalent in Kodiak, as close to 20% of its residents are Alaska native or part native. Their culture is still strong in the community, and is celebrated through several museums and presentations offered to the public on a regular basis. (See the Kodiak section of "On the Town," pages 396–397, for more.)

WILD LANDS

CHUGACH NATIONAL FOREST

(Primary activities: fishing, hiking, backpacking, mountaineering, mountain biking, kayaking, rafting)

Chugach National Forest
3301 C Street, Suite 300
Anchorage 99503
☎ 907-743-9500
www.fs.fed.us/r10/chugach

CHUGACH NATIONAL FOREST SURROUNDS Southcentral Coastal, beckoning outdoor travelers with all of its recreation opportunities. The forest consists of three ranger districts—**Glacier, Cordova,** and **Seward**—and 5 million acres of federal land. That's about the size of Maryland.

There are more than 40 public-use cabins available for rent, ranging from $25 to $45 per night, depending on the location. There also are public campgrounds available with reasonable $10-per-night camping fees.

For Southcentral Coastal residents, the Chugach is the place to play. It's where most of the maintained trails can be found, and it has easy road access from just about anywhere along the Seward and Sterling highways, and all along Prince William Sound.

The best place for information on the Chugach National Forest is at the informative **Begich, Boggs Visitor Center,** at the end of Portage Valley Road, about 50 miles south of Anchorage on the Seward Highway.

The center is located at what used to be the face of **Portage Glacier.** Today, that glacier has retreated, and an iceberg-studded lake greets visitors. There are several interpretive programs showcasing the special qualities of the Chugach. Call ☎ 907-783-3242 or 907-783-2326 for hours of operation.

KENAI NATIONAL WILDLIFE REFUGE

(Primary activities: backpacking, hiking, skiing, dog mushing, canoeing, fishing)

Kenai National Wildlife Refuge
Ski Hill Road
P.O. Box 2139
Soldotna 99669-2139
☎ 907-262-7021
kenai.fws.gov

THE KENAI NATIONAL WILDLIFE REFUGE is Alaska's most-visited refuge, partly because it is one of two Alaska refuges (out of 16) that are accessible by road. But this place is also special, and outdoors travelers can easily recognize the appeal in its numerous possibilities. Canoe the "Mini–Boundary Waters" system on the **Kenai Canoe Trails.** Run a dog team across frozen **Tustumena Lake.** Hike into the backcountry, and set up a remote camp from which to explore. The possibilities are endless.

Today, the Kenai National Wildlife Refuge is a good sampling of all of Alaska's habitats, and often is referred to as a mini-Alaska. You can see glaciers, valleys, mountains, and everything in between.

Sportfishing is the top activity in the refuge, and hundreds of thousands of visitors come here each year, searching for king, red, and silver salmon, as well as Dolly Varden, rainbow trout, and arctic grayling.

The refuge was established in 1941 to protect the many moose you'll see there today. The lanky ungulates share the refuge with brown and black bears, caribou, Dall sheep, mountain goats, wolves, wolverines, and countless bird species.

Accessing the refuge is easy. From Anchorage, take the Seward Highway south to the Sterling Highway. The eastern refuge boundary is at Mile 55 of the Sterling Highway. The west entrance to the Skilak Wildlife Recreation Area is five miles farther down the road. The refuge visitor center is based in Soldotna.

KENAI FJORDS NATIONAL PARK

(Primary activities: hiking, kayaking, birding, mountaineering)

Seward Information Center
1212 Fourth Avenue
Seward 99664
☎ 907-224-2132 or
907-224-7500
www.nps.gov/kefj

BY ALASKA STANDARDS, Kenai Fjords National Park is not all that big—607,805 acres. That's a laughable thought, actually, because that much land is huge. The vastness of the area strikes you, though, as soon as you take a gander at a calving glacier or snow-covered mountain.

The park is located on the southeast coast of Alaska's Kenai Peninsula, capped by the **Harding Ice Field,** the largest ice field in U.S. borders. Otters, puffins, bear, moose, and mountain goats are just a few of the creatures that can be spotted here. Glaciers are everywhere, and whales breach often.

Access to this park is relatively easy compared with other national parks in Alaska. Take the Seward Highway south to its terminus in Seward (or the train or bus). Board a day cruise for as little as $59, and watch for whales and other wildlife for an entire afternoon. Or go with a guide. Commercial outfitters provide camping, fishing, and kayaking services. Air charters fly over the coast for access to the fjords.

unofficial **TIP**
Kenai Fjords National Park is one of the best places to spot the gray whale on its annual migration from Baja California.

The climate of the park is maritime, meaning it rains often and is windy most of the time. Dress in layers in gear that can get ultra-wet without getting you wet. Camping is allowed in most areas of the park, and there are four public-use cabins available on a reservation basis. They are at **Aialik, Holgate,** and **Northarm,** along the Kenai Fjords coast, and are accessible by boat or floatplane. For reservations, contact the **Alaska Public Lands Information Center** in Anchorage at ☎ 907-271-2737. **Willow Cabin** at Exit Glacier is available for winter use from mid- to late fall through early April. Contact the Park at ☎ 907-224-7500 for reservations.

ALASKA MARITIME NATIONAL WILDLIFE REFUGE

(Primary activities: birding, kayaking, fishing)

Alaska Maritime National Wildlife Refuge
95 Sterling Highway, Suite 1
Homer 99603
☎ 907-235-6546
alaskamaritime.fws.gov

THE ALASKA MARITIME NATIONAL WILDLIFE REFUGE encompasses a tremendous 4.9 million acres and stretches along Alaska's coast from the Southeast panhandle west to the tip of the **Aleutian Chain,** then heads north all the way to the Bering Sea and above the Arctic Circle. It is the most extensive public land in all of the National Wildlife Refuge System and exists to protect marine mammals and birds throughout Alaska.

More than 2,500 islands, spires, rocks, and coastal headlands provide a habitat for the 40 million marine birds and mammals that live in the refuge. Seabirds, sea lions, fur seals, and whales are just part of the overall diversity found here. In fact, new species of marine life are yet to be found here, researchers speculate.

Getting to the refuge can be expensive, since so much of it is so remote. Even though we have listed the refuge in this chapter, its territory extends into the Bush and Southeast as well, and it is not accessible by road. You'll need a boat to get to most areas, a plane to get to others.

There are no campgrounds, although camping is allowed on most of the refuge. Recreational facilities on the refuge are limited to a few first-come, first-served public-use cabins on Adak.

KACHEMAK BAY STATE PARK AND STATE WILDERNESS PARK

(Primary activities: hiking, birding, mountaineering, skiing, kayaking, fishing)

Kachemak Bay State Park and State Wilderness Park
Kenai Area Office
P.O. Box 1247
Soldotna 99669
☎ 907-262-5581
www.dnr.state.ak.us/parks/units/ kbay/kbay.htm

THERE ARE NINE ALASKA STATE PARKS on the Kenai Peninsula, each of which offers great outdoor opportunities. But our very favorite is Kachemak Bay State Park (and Wilderness Park, which technically makes the total number of parks ten).

Kachemak Bay is Alaska's first state park and its only wilderness park, composed of roughly 400,000 acres of mountains, glaciers, forests, and ocean. There are roughly 80 miles of developed trails and unlimited kayaking opportunities in the park. The wildlife in the park is both fun and fascinating to watch. Sea otters bob on the water, seals haul out on the beaches, and porpoises and whales surface occasionally, as if to say hello. Even the less-noticeable marine life is noticeable: the tide pools are home to an amazing array of sea stars, anemones, and other intertidal species. Land mammals include moose, black bear, mountain goats, coyotes, and wolves, although even the moose seem to avoid humans.

Hiking and camping along the shoreline and in the surrounding forests and mountains is excellent. Above tree line, skiers and hikers will find glaciers and snowfields stretching for miles. Access to the park is by boat or airplane only—no roads lead to this special place. There are several camping areas that have been developed that may include fireplaces, picnic tables, tent platforms, outhouses, or food caches. There are five public-use cabins available, too, at **Halibut Cove Lagoon, Leisure Lake, Moose Valley,** and **Tutka Bay.** The $65-per-night getaways can be reserved up to six months in advance (seven months for Alaskans), and should be. They fill up fast, so start planning early.

The **Halibut Cove Ranger Station** (☎ 907-235-6999) can answer questions in the summer.

SHUYAK ISLAND STATE PARK

(Primary activities: kayaking, birding, hiking, fishing)

Alaska State Parks
Kodiak District Office
1400 Abercrombie Drive
Kodiak 99615
☎ 907-486-6339
www.dnr.state.ak.us/parks/units/kodiak/shuyak.htm

SHUYAK ISLAND STATE PARK IS ONE of six state parks managed by the Kodiak area and, in our opinion, the most beautiful and diverse for outdoor recreation. Shuyak Island is the northernmost of the islands that make up the Kodiak Archipelago, and the state park comprises most of the island's 47,000 acres. The park encompasses part of a coastal forest system unique to the archipelago: it has only one tree species, the

Sitka spruce. Shuyak Island provides access to an intricate maze of sheltered bays, channels, and inlets, making it a paddler's paradise.

The park is 54 air miles north of Kodiak and accessible by boat or plane. It is a relatively small place, only 12 miles long and 11 miles wide, but it contains miles of coastal waterway for kayaking, a limited but impressive trail system for hiking, and fishing opportunities in just about every lake, stream, or saltwater location (especially in August and September when the silver salmon are spawning). There is an infinite variety of seabirds, otters, whales, harbor seals, sea lions, and Dall porpoises. Even some of Kodiak's famed brown bears wander the island.

Visitors to Shuyak can choose from tent camping just about anywhere on the island, or renting one of four $65-per-night public-use cabins, which are wonderful retreats when it is raining—and it rains often. There is a ranger station at one end of the park, but other than that, there are no facilities, and groceries and other supplies must be purchased in Kodiak (or Homer, as some people fly in from that direction).

KODIAK NATIONAL WILDLIFE REFUGE

(Primary activities: fishing, kayaking, birding, hiking, camping)

FAMOUS FOR ITS KODIAK BROWN BEARS, the Kodiak National Wildlife Refuge is also home to a diverse ecosystem of other plants, animals, and fish that make it a wonderful outdoor destination. Bears, bald eagles, salmon, and a host of other wildlife are numerous on the 1.9 million acres of upland and waters. The terrain is not easily traveled, and is dotted with fjords and soggy in many places. It is the perfect habitat for the Kodiak brownies—about 2,300 of them live on the refuge and can be found wandering the land or feeding on fish in the rivers and streams.

Kodiak National Wildlife Refuge
1390 Buskin River Road
Kodiak 99615
☎ 888-408-3514 or
907-487-2600
kodiak.fws.gov

The refuge boundary is about 20 miles from the city of Kodiak, and can be accessed only by floatplane or boat. A rarity in the refuge system, the Kodiak National Wildlife Refuge offers seven public-use cabins to make camping in the more remote areas more enjoyable.

The plentiful salmon streams on the refuge—117 of them, to be exact—offer food for other species besides just the brown bear. Bald eagles thrive on the refuge thanks to all the fish, and 600 breeding pairs of eagles live there.

Despite its rugged beauty and recreation opportunities, the Kodiak refuge does not get too many visitors, only 8,000 to 10,000 a year. This is good for the ecosystem, and good for travelers who want the place to themselves. Reserving the public-use cabins is generally not difficult and can be done in advance. Be prepared for a maritime climate, with wet conditions and lots of fog. Generally, the west side of the refuge receives less rain due to weather patterns.

GETTING *around* SOUTH-CENTRAL COASTAL ALASKA

KENAI PENINSULA

From Anchorage

Access to Anchorage, in Southcentral Inland Alaska, by air is through **Alaska Airlines** (☎ 800-252-7522; **www.alaskaair.com**). We suggest that anyone arriving in Anchorage but headed to the Kenai Peninsula rent transportation in the city. The rates are lower, the limits fewer, and the selection larger. Plus, the drive to the Kenai Peninsula is worth seeing on your own. Most of our rental suggestions originate in Anchorage, but we have listed a few options at the end that are available on the Kenai.

More than a dozen rental options are available in the Anchorage area, but we've found **Budget** (☎ 800-527-0700; **www.budgetrentacar.com**), **Enterprise** (☎ 800-261-7331; **www.enterprise.com**), **Hertz** (☎ 800-654-3131; **www.hertz.com**), and **Denali Car Rental** (☎ 907-276-1230) to be the best.

- **ABC Motorhome and Car Rentals** ☎ 800-421-7456; **www.abcmotorhome.com**
  This company has a range of RVs, as well as a luxury van for large groups and camper rentals for smaller parties. No smoking vehicles. No pets allowed.
- **Alaska Affordable Motor Home Rental** ☎ 907-349-4878 or 907-227-6463; **www.alaska-rv-rental.com**
  Much less expensive than its competitors, with rates at $165 per day with free, unlimited miles in Alaska. Vehicles are not as fancy, but quite functional. No smoking or pets allowed.
- **Alaska Best RV Rentals** ☎ 866-544-4981 or 907-344-4981; **www.alaskabestrvrentals.com**
  With rates lower than the large-company averages—$165 to $190. No smoking or pets allowed.
- **Alaska Railroad** 327 West Ship Creek Avenue; ☎ 800-544-0552 or 907-265-2494; **www.alaskarailroad.com**
  The railroad has daily routes serving Anchorage to Seward. The round-trip fare is $69 for adults.
- **Magic Bus** ☎ 907-268-5311; **www.themagicbus.com**
  If you have a group and want to travel anywhere within Southcentral Coastal Alaska to southern edge of the Interior and all points in between, you can rent these private motorcoaches and vans, complete with a driver.

Options on the Kenai

The **Alaska Marine Highway ferry** system serves Homer and Seward on the Kenai Peninsula, with service from southern and southwestern ports. The ferry, the **M/V *Tustumena*,** has a regular schedule, and reservations can be made online (☎ 800-526-6731 or 800-642-0066; **www.ferryalaska.com**).

Era Aviation (☎ 800-866-8394; **www.eraaviation.com**) and **Alaska Airlines** (☎ 800-252-7522; **www.alaskaair.com**) travel to the Kenai Peninsula on regularly scheduled flights.

Car rentals are available at **Hertz** in Kenai (352 Airport Way; ☎ 907-283-8080; **www.hertz.com**) and **Wheels 4 Rent** in Soldotna (224 Karen Street; ☎ 907-262-6102; **wheels4rent@acsalaska.net**). Rates begin at about $65 per day.

The **Hertz** in Homer, located at the Homer Airport (☎ 907-235-0734), rents vehicles starting at $83 per day. Other Homer rental-car companies include **Adventure Alaska Car Rentals** (1368 Ocean Drive; ☎ 800-882-2808 or 907-235-4022), and **Polar Car Rental** (☎ 800-876-6417 or 907-235-5998, at the airport).

Seward car rentals also are available through **Hertz.** Rates begin at $83 (600 Port Avenue; ☎ 800-654-3131 or 907-224-4378).

Taxis in Homer include **Chux Cab** (☎ 907-235-2489), **Kachecab** (☎ 907-235-1950), and **Kosta's Taxi Service** (☎ 907-399-8008 or 907-399-8115).

Taxi service is available in Kenai-Soldotna through **Alaska Cab** (in Soldotna; ☎ 907-262-5050 or 907-262-1555; and in Kenai; ☎ 907-283-6000) and **Yellow Cab of the Kenai** (in Soldotna; ☎ 907-260-1900; or 907-283-1900 in Kenai).

Seward taxis include **PJ's Taxi** (☎ 907-224-5555), and **Seward Independent Cab Co.** (☎ 907-224-8463).

Homer Stage Line provides motorcoach connection between Homer and Seward or Homer and Anchorage (☎ 907-235-2252; **www.homerstageline.com**).

Recreational vehicles are available through **Kenai Riverfront RV Rentals** in Soldotna (☎ 907-262-1717; **www.kenairiverfront.com**) or **Wilson's RV Rentals,** near the Kenai Airport (☎ 907-283-4370; **www.wilsonsrvrentals.com**). **Wheels 4 Rent** in Soldotna also rents RVs (224 Kenai Avenue; ☎ 907-262-6102; **wheels4rent@acsalaska.net**).

Seward bus-and-trolley service allows you to get around town on a day pass. Contact **Seward Trolley Company** (☎ 907-224-4378; **www.sewardtrolley.com**).

PRINCE WILLIAM SOUND

THE ALASKA MARINE HIGHWAY ferry system serves all the communities of Prince William Sound. The ferry **M/V *Kennicott*** has a regular schedule, and reservations can be made online. The newer fast ferry, the **M/V *Chenega*,** also serves the Sound. The one-way adult fare is $89 for passage from Whittier to Valdez (☎ 800-526-6731 or 800-642-0066; **www.ferryalaska.com**).

Whittier

For road access to Whittier, use the **Anton Anderson Memorial Tunnel** (**tunnel.alaska.gov**). The price is $12 for a round-trip.

Avis Alaska (4900 Aircraft Drive, Anchorage; ☎ 907-243-4300 or 907-472-2277; **www.avisalaska.com**) rents cars in Anchorage and now in Whittier. This is a good option if you are on a cruise ship and want to explore inland for the day.

The **Magic Bus** is a better deal if you can get a seat. The rate is $54 for adults, one-way (☎ 907-268-6311; **www.themagicbus.com**). If you are coming from Seward, **Two Dogs Truckin' and Transportation** can get you to Whittier for $225 with a four-person minimum, which includes the $12 tunnel fare (☎ 907-224-2746 or 907-362-2209; **home.gci.net/~twodogs**).

Cordova

Access to Cordova by air is available from **Alaska Airlines** (☎ 800-252-7522; **www.alaskaair.com**) via Seattle and Anchorage, and **Era Aviation** (☎ 800-866-8394; **www.eraaviation.com**) via Anchorage.

The **Cordova Shuttle Van** meets most flights and runs into town for $12 (☎ 907-424-3272).

Auto rentals are available at **Cordova Auto Rentals** (☎ 907-424-5982) and **Wild Hare Taxi Service** (☎ 907-424-3939). Prices start at $70 per day for an auto rental.

Valdez

Rental cars are available at **Valdez U-Drive,** at the Valdez airport (☎ 800-478-4402 or 907-835-4402; **www.valdezudrive.com**).

You can fly into Valdez on **Era Aviation** (6160 Carl Brady Drive; ☎ 800-478-1947 or 907-248-4422; **www.eraaviation.com**); or **Alaska Airlines** (☎ 800-252-7522; **www.alaskaair.com**) via Seattle and Anchorage.

Valdez Yellow Cab is four miles east of Valdez. A one-way fare to town from the airport is approximately $10 (☎ 907-835-2500).

KODIAK ISLAND

CAR RENTALS ARE AVAILABLE AT **Avis Rent a Car** (☎ 800-331-1212 or 907-487-2264; **www.avis.com**), **Budget Rent A Car** (☎ 907-487-2220), and **Rent-a-Heap** (☎ 907-487-4001).

Taxi service is available through **Bay Shuttle** (☎ 907-486-2345), **Garrett's Taxi Service** (☎ 907-654-3535), **Alaska Cab Co.** (☎ 907-481-3400), and A and B Taxicab (☎ 907-486-4343).

The **Alaska Marine Highway** offers ferry passage to Kodiak. The one-way adult fare is $72 (100 Marine Way; ☎ 800-526-6731 or 907-486-3800; **www.ferryalaska.com**).

Alaska Airlines provides daily jet service to Kodiak (1200 Airport Way; ☎ 800-252-7522 or 907-487-4000; **www.alaskaair.com**).

Era Aviation also provides service from Anchorage and other locations (☎ 800-866-8394 or 907-487-4000).

GEARING UP

SOUTHCENTRAL COASTAL ALASKA has some surprisingly well-stocked sporting-goods and camping-supply stores, even in some of the smaller communities. You may pay higher prices than in Southcentral Inland. (A bonus to buying in Anchorage is that there is no sales tax. In most of Alaska's smaller communities, there is a sales tax.)

As with any travel in the state, check with the air carriers on which you will be traveling for regulations on carrying items such as knives, guns, camp stoves, and camp fuel. Some items, such as fuel, you may need to purchase at your final destination and leave behind when flying home.

This section of the book is broken down by the main communities in Southcentral Coastal Alaska with shops that will help you find what you are looking for. We generally list sporting goods/camping supplies and groceries separately, but many stores in smaller communities such as Whittier and Cordova are one-stop shopping destinations.

SPORTING GOODS AND CAMPING SUPPLIES

Kenai Peninsula

- **Alaska Canoe and Campground** 35292 Sterling Highway, Soldotna; ☎ 907-262-2331; **www.alaskacanoetrips.com**
  Canoes start at $25 for a half day, sea kayaks start at $40 per day. Unique to this company is its gear rental—everything from hip waders to tents and fishing poles.
- **Kenai Riverfront Bed and Breakfast and RV Park** 36193 Douglas Drive, Soldotna; ☎ 907-262-1717; **www.kenairiverfront.com**
  The company also rents powerboats for fishing on the Kenai River; $50 per hour, with an eight-hour minimum.
- **Sweeney's Clothing** 35081 Kenai Spur Highway, Soldotna; ☎ 907-262-5916
  This longtime outfitter (look for the green shamrock sign) carries Alaska Wear, a favorite local alternative to Carhartt, as well as other must-have gear.
- **Weigner's Backcountry Guiding** Sterling; ☎ 907-262-7840; **www.alaska.net/~weigner**
- **Wilderness Way** 41735 Sterling Highway, north of Soldotna; ☎ 907-262-3880; **www.wildernessway.com**
  A great place to find quality outdoor gear, skis, kayaks, and camping equipment. Our favorite outdoor shop on the peninsula.

Homer

- **Eagle Enterprises** 1067 Ocean Drive; ☎ 907-235-7907
  Mostly a marine safety shop, but it also sells clothing and outdoor wear.

- **Homer's Jeans Inc.** 564 East Pioneer Avenue, Homer; ☎ 907-235-6234
- **Kachemak Gear Shed** 3625 East End Road, Homer; ☎ 800-478-8612 or 907-235-8612
  More functional gear available here.
- **Main Street Mercantile** 104 East Pioneer Avenue; ☎ 907-235-9102
  Offering basic sporting-good supplies and fishing licenses.
- **NOMAR** 104 East Pioneer Avenue, Homer; ☎ 907-235-8363
  The fleece clothing and travel bags are Alaska-made and developed from technology in the fishing industry.

Seward

- **Bay Traders True Value** 1301 Fourth Avenue; ☎ 800-257-7760 or 907-224-3674
  This hardware store is where the locals get their waders and duct tape.
- **Helly Hansen** 1304 Fourth Avenue, at the small-boat harbor; ☎ 888-414-3559 or 907-224-3041; **www.hellyalaska.com**
  Offering the best in wet-weather gear in a town where you'll need it often.
- **Miller's Landing** At Lowell Point, 3.5 miles south of Seward; ☎ 866-541-5739 or 907-224-5739; **www.millerslandingak.com**
  Boat and motor rentals are available for $100 for four hours. Rod and reel rentals are $15 for a half day, $25 for 8 to 16 hours. Kayak rentals are $40 for singles, $50 for doubles, per day.
- **Seward Bike Shop** 411 Port Avenue; ☎ 907-224-2448
  Offering bike rentals starting at $13. This is also are the place to visit if you want updated information on mountain-bike-trail conditions.

Whittier

- **The Anchor Inn** Off the waterfront, near the residential area, Whittier; ☎ 907-472-2354 or 877-870-8787; **www.anchorinnwhittier.com**
  It has an attached store with everything from clothing to camping gear to groceries. It's a limited supply, but could be a lifesaver if you left the big city without some important item.
- **The Outpost/RC's Dock & Harbor Store** In Whittier; ☎ 907-529-5635
  They sell everything from liquor to hardware to dock services and some groceries; mostly fishing tackle and bait.

Valdez

- **Acres Kwik Trip** At Richardson Highway and Airport Way, Valdez; ☎ 907-835-3278
  A good place to get a fishing license and a few supplies fast. No lines.
- **Anadyr Adventures** 225 North Harbor Drive, Valdez; ☎ 800-865-2925 or 907-835-2814; **www.anadyradventures.com**
  Offering kayak rentals to experienced kayakers only. They can provide water taxis to more-remote destinations, too. Rentals are $45 per day for singles, $65 for doubles, with discounts for multiple days.

- **Fish Central** In Valdez; ☎ 888-835-5002 or 907-835-5090; **www.fishcentral.net** For bait and tackle supplies, fish licenses, kayak and boat rentals starting at $250 per day for an 18-foot skiff.
- **Hook, Line and Sinker** 200 Chitina Street, Valdez; ☎ 907-835-4410 Sells fishing tackle, licenses, and other accessories, as well as sporting goods.
- **The Prospector** 141 Galena Street, Valdez; ☎ 907-835-3858 Sporting goods, camping gear, and a wide selection of outdoor clothing.

Cordova

- **Cordova Coastal Outfitters** At the harbor in the brightly colored boathouse; ☎ 907-424-7424; **www.cdvcoastal.com** The company rents kayaks, canoes, small boats with outboards, bikes, and fishing and camping gear. They also offer guided boat and bike tours. Kayaks are $35 per day for singles, $50 for doubles. Canoes are $30 per day. Bikes are $18 a day. Camping gear ranges from $5 to $15 per day for everything you can think of.
- **Whiskey Ridge Trading Co.** 201 Whiskey Ridge Road, Cordova; ☎ 907-424-3354 Sporting-goods supplier of high-quality outdoor gear.

Kodiak Island

- **Cy's Sporting Goods** 117 Lower Mill Bay Road; ☎ 907-486-3900; **www.kodiak-outfitters.com** Fishing licenses available here. Locals go here often; not as tourist-oriented.
- **58 Degrees North** 1231 Mill Bay Road; ☎ 907-486-6249 They can rent bikes by the hour or day or week, and repair your bike if you end up crashing; $25 per day.
- **Mack's Sport Shop & Alaskan Gifts** 212 Lower Mill Bay Road; ☎ 907-486-4276; **www.mackssportshop.com** Everyone who works here, down to the teenager with the nose piercing, knows their stuff and can suggest just the right lure for the fish you are trying to catch or just the right jacket for the conditions you will be in. Our favorite sporting-goods shop in Kodiak. Plus, the local T-shirts are cool. Fishing licenses are available.
- **Mythos Expeditions** Kodiak; ☎ 907-486 5536; **www.thewildcoast.com** This outfitter is the only company with a permit to lease kayaks out of Shuyak Island State Park. If you don't have your own kayak or don't want to pay to have it shipped to Shuyak, this is the only other option. The rate is $175 for three days, which is the minimum, for a double; $141 for singles.
- **Orion's Sports** 1247 Mill Bay Road; ☎ 907-486-8380 Carrying kayaking and climbing/backing supplies; the best in outdoor gear.
- **Sutliff's Hardware** 210 Shelikof Avenue; ☎ 888-848-5579 or 907-486-5797 This hardware store carries outdoor gear for any situation, including U.S. Geological Survey maps, which are essential for any travel in Kodiak. The employees are really friendly, too.

GROCERIES

Kenai Peninsula

- **Carrs** 10480 Kenai Spur Highway, Kenai; ☎ 907-283-6300
- **Central Kenai Peninsula Farmers' Market** At the intersection of East Corral Avenue and the Kenai Spur Highway; Soldotna; ☎ 907-262-5463 or 907-262-7502
  Held 10 a.m. to 2 p.m. Saturdays in summer. Features locally grown produce, herbs, flowers, and plants.
- **Country Foods IGA** 140 South Willow Street, Kenai; ☎ 907-283-4834
- **Fred Meyer** 43843 Sterling Highway, Soldotna; ☎ 907-260-2200
  Also sells sporting goods and camping equipment.
- **Safeway** 44428 Sterling Highway, Soldotna; ☎ 907-714-5400
- **Three Bears** 10575 Kenai Spur Highway, Kenai; ☎ 907-283-6577

Homer

- **The Grog Shop** 369 East Pioneer Avenue; ☎ 907-235-5601
  We just love the name. The shop stays busy and has a great selection of spirits.
- **Safeway** 90 Sterling Highway; ☎ 907-235-2408
  The largest selection of foods; limited outdoor and sporting-goods items.
- **Save-U-More** 3611 Greatland Street; ☎ 907-235-8661
  If you're on a budget, this is the place to pinch pennies.
- **Smoky Bay Natural Foods** 248 West Pioneer Avenue; ☎ 907-235-7252
  This is a natural-food lover's paradise, with more products and gourmet food items than you can find in some big-city stores. Bulk foods are available, as well as fresh veggies and household items–all good for you and all nice to the environment.

Seward

- **Safeway** Mile 1.5 Seward Highway; ☎ 907-224-3698
  Full-service grocery store, newly remodeled with espresso stand, outdoor/sporting-goods section, and of course, lots of groceries.
- **Three Bears** 1711 Seward Highway; ☎ 907-224-2081; **www.threebearsalaska.com**
  Larger than a convenience store but smaller than a full-service store. Usually it's not as crowded as Safeway.

Valdez

- **Carrs/Eagle** 185 Meals Avenue, Valdez; ☎ 907-835-2100
  This is a full-service grocery store with some sporting goods, mostly fishing tackle. The salad bar is cheap and fresh.
- **Three Bears** 103 Egan Street, Valdez; ☎ 907-835-5480; **www.threebearsalaska.com**
  Larger than a convenience store but smaller than a full-service store.

Cordova

- **Alaska Commercial Co.** 106 Nicholoff Way, Cordova; ☎ 907-424-7141
  Close to the small-boat harbor. Featuring groceries, spirits, fishing licenses, and some camping and sporting-goods supplies.
- **Laura's Liquor Shoppe** Downtown Cordova; ☎ 907-424-3144
  The shop sells delicious espresso from Kaladi Brothers (an Alaskan-grown company that is well loved statewide) as well as liquor, limited groceries, and other goodies.
- **Serendipi Tea** 412 First Street, Cordova; ☎ 907-424-8327 or 907-424-8328 This is an offbeat option featuring organic vegetables, meat, and other foods. The tea selection is wonderful.

Kodiak Island

- **Alaska Commercial Co.** In downtown Kodiak at 111 West Rezanof Drive, but don't pay attention to the address because it gets confusing at the intersection; ☎ 907-486-5761
  Full-service grocery store, with a clothing/household/sporting-goods section in the back. You can get just about anything there, although you're still better off going to the sporting-goods store for specific gear.
- **Safeway** 2685 Mill Bay Road; ☎ 907-486-6811
  Full-service grocery store with the best prices and produce. Not within walking distance of town, though.

WHERE *to* STAY

BECAUSE THIS IS SUCH A POPULAR PLACE to play, Southcentral Coastal Alaska's residents and business owners have learned that there's rarely a shortage of customers. On the weekends, especially, people unwind, pull out their fishing poles, and enjoy the beauty of the area. There is a multitude of bed-and-breakfasts, small motels and inns, and even a few large, fancy hotels. Camping options are abundant, too. Most federal and state land agencies have at least one campground in every town—some of them have several places at which to pitch a tent.

In this section, we offer you our favorite choices, places that we have tried ourselves and found to be memorable.

KENAI

Indoor Lodging

- **All Seasons Bed and Breakfast** ☎ 907-283-7050; **www.allseasonsbnb.com**

  QUALITY ★★★★ VALUE ★★★★ $85

  From the outside, this place doesn't have the charm you might expect in a bed-and-breakfast, but the inside is meticulously clean and spacious

(2,000 square feet), and the price is absolutely right. You get two bedrooms, a fully equipped kitchen, and all the other amenities you need. Plus, it's on a quiet street, away from tourists.

- **Kenai Landing** 2101 Bowpicker Lane; ☎ 907-335-2500; **www.kenailanding.com**

  QUALITY ★★★★ VALUE ★★★ $70–$200

  This newly renovated cannery houses a restaurant, a museum (coming soon), arts and entertainment, and a variety of lodging options. Prices depend on size and bathroom configuration.

- **The Log Cabin Inn** Off Kalifornsky Beach Road; ☎ 907-283-3653; **www.acsalaska.net/~ted.titus**

  QUALITY ★★★★ VALUE ★★★ $110–$130

  Even the locals love looking at this beautiful home, with an active beaver pond right in front. The rooms are comfortable, and the view toward the river flats is beautiful though it's across the road. There are cabins for rent, too.

- **Uptown Motel** 47 Spur View Drive; ☎ 800-777-3650 or 907-283-3660; **www.uptownmotel.com**

  QUALITY ★★★ VALUE ★★★ $135–$185

  It's not much to look at from the outside, but the rooms are actually quite clean and comfortable, and the downstairs restaurant and bar give a good sampling of what life is like for Kenai locals. Nonsmoking rooms available.

Camping

- **Captain Cook State Recreation Area** End of North Road, Nikiski; ☎ 907-262-5581; **www.dnr.state.ak.us/parks/units/captcook.htm**

  QUALITY ★★★★ VALUE ★★★★ $10

  This beautiful campground is out of the way but quite worth the 25-minute drive into north Kenai. Named after the British explorer Captain James Cook, who discovered the inlet in 1778, this area offers great fishing, canoeing, and skiing in the winter, and has excellent water views. Two campgrounds are within the area—Bishop Creek and Discovery.

SOLDOTNA

Indoor Lodging

- **Aspen Hotel Soldotna** 326 Binkley Circle; ☎ 866-483-7848; **www.aspenhotelsak.com**

  QUALITY ★★★★ VALUE ★★★★ $130–$170

  This is where you stay if you like creature comforts such as a pool, in-room hair dryers, and such. It's fairly new, and the rooms are very nice, although not very "Alaska" at all.

- **Goodnight Inn Lodge** 44715 Sterling Highway; ☎ 907-262-4584

  QUALITY ★★★ VALUE ★★★★ $89–$119

A longtime lodge right in town offering small but affordable, very nice, and clean rooms.

- **Jana House Hostel** Swanson River Road, Sterling, off Mile 83.6 of the Sterling Highway; ☎ 907-260-4151

QUALITY ★★★ VALUE ★★★★ $25–$50

This hostel just north of Sterling offers dorm-style bunks, tent and RV camping, and private rooms on 19 acres. The 8,900-square-foot building looks more like a hotel than a hostel, but the rates are right.

- **Kenai River Lodge** ☎ 800-977-4292 or 907-262-4292; www.kenairiverlodge.com

QUALITY ★★★★ VALUE ★★★ $150–$190

On the banks of the Kenai River in Soldotna, the lodge has river-view rooms and barbecuing right on site, so you can cook what you catch. Rates include breakfast in the summer.

- **Longmere Lake Lodge Bed and Breakfast** 35955 Ryan Lane; ☎ 907-262-9799; www.longmerelakelodge.com

QUALITY ★★★★ VALUE ★★★ $105–$150

It's about six miles out of Soldotna but worth the drive just for the peace and quiet you will enjoy. The rooms are spacious, with lots of windows overlooking the lake. A great location for birders.

- **Soldotna Bed and Breakfast Lodge** 399 Lovers Lane; ☎ 877-262-4779 or 907-262-4779; www.soldotnalodge.com

QUALITY ★★★★ VALUE ★★★ $99–$380

People love the owners of this bed-and-breakfast, which also offers guided fishing, canoeing, and other activities. Rooms start at $99, but your best bet is to go with one of the package deals that include fishing.

Camping

- **Centennial Campground** Right by the river off Kalifornsky Beach Road; ☎ 907-262-3151; www.ci.soldotna.ak.us/parks_rec.html

QUALITY ★★★ VALUE ★★★ $14.70

Run by the city of Soldotna; the sites are first-come, first-served.

- **Kenai National Wildlife Refuge** ☎ 907-262-7021; kenai.fws.gov

QUALITY ★★★ VALUE ★★★★ FREE–$10

The refuge maintains 13 campgrounds, located along Skilak Lake Wildlife Recreation Area and Swanson River Road. Hidden Lake Campground is the largest and most developed site ($10 fee). Lower Skilak Lake Campground has a boat launch for Skilak Lake and Kenai River fishing activities ($10 fee). All of the others, with the exception of the $10 Kenai–Russian River campground, are free. All sites are first-come, first-served. No reservations.

Southcentral Coastal Alaska Indoor Lodging

NAME	TYPE(S) OF LODGING	QUALITY RATING	VALUE RATING	COST
KENAI				
All Seasons B&B	B&B	★★★★	★★★★	$85
Kenai Landing	hotel/lodge	★★★★	★★★	$70–$200
The Log Cabin Inn	B&B/cabins	★★★★	★★★	$110–$130
Uptown Motel	motel	★★★	★★★	$135–$185
SOLDOTNA				
Aspen Hotel Soldotna	hotel	★★★★	★★★★	$130–$170
Goodnight Inn Lodge	hotel	★★★	★★★★	$89–$119
Jana House Hostel	hostel	★★★	★★★★	$25–$50
Kenai River Lodge	hotel	★★★★	★★★	$150–$190
Longmere Lake Lodge	B&B	★★★★	★★★	$105–$150
Soldotna B&B Lodge	B&B	★★★★	★★★★	$99–$380
HOMER				
Bear Creek Winery and Lodging	suites/B&B	★★★★★	★★★	$225–$260
The Eagle Watch Hostel	hostel	★★★	★★★★	$13–$35
Heritage Hotel and Lodge	hotel	★★★	★★★	$119–$165
Homer Hostel	hostel	★★★	★★★	$23–$70
Homer Inn and Spa	spa	★★★★★	★★★★	$159–$259
Land's End Resort	hotel	★★★★	★★★	$135–$275
Lighthouse Village Cabins	cabins	★★★★	★★★	$100–$165
Mossy's Alaska Seaside Farm Hostel and Cabins	hostel/cabins	★★★	★★★★	$10–$55
Surf Shack Deluxe Cabin	cabin	★★★★	★★★	$155
SEWARD				
A Cabin on the Cliff	cabin	★★★★★	★★★	$369–$469
Exit Glacier Salmon Bake and Cabins	cabins	★★★	★★★★	$110
The Farm B&B	B&B	★★★	★★★★★	$82–$113
Hotel Edgewater	hotel	★★★★	★★★	$155–$275
Hotel Seward	hotel	★★★★	★★★	$155–$224

NAME	TYPE(S) OF LODGING	QUALITY RATING	VALUE RATING	COST
SEWARD (CONTINUED)				
Kayaker's Cove	hostel/cabins	★★★	★★★★★	$20–$60
Miller's Landing Hostel and Cabins	hostel/cabins	★★	★★★	$45–$250
Moby Dick Hostel	hostel	★★	★★	$19–$70
Seward Windsong Lodge	hotel	★★★★★	★★★	$139–$289
Snow River Hostel	hostel	★★★★	★★★★	$15–$40
The Van Gilder Hotel	hotel	★★★★	★★★	$135–$175
SURROUNDING AREAS				
Kenai Backcountry Lodge	wilderness lodge	★★★★★	★★★★	$1,073/ 2 nights
Kenai Princess Lodge	hotel/lodge	★★★★★	★★★	$239–$329
Trail Lake Lodge	motel	★★	★★★	$99–$115
WHITTIER				
The Anchor Inn	inn	★★	★★★	$80–$100
The Inn at Whittier	hotel	★★★★	★★★	$149–$229
June's Bed and Breakfast	B&B	★★★★	★★★★	$115–$375
VALDEZ				
Brookside Inn B&B	B&B/cabins	★★★	★★★	$125–$160
Thompson Pass Mountain Chalet	cabins	★★★★★	★★★★★	$140
Valdez Harbor Inn	hotel	★★★★	★★★	$139–$175
Wild Roses by the Sea B&B	B&B	★★★★	★★★	$130–$170
CORDOVA				
Bear Country Lodge	cabins	★★★	★★★	$125
Cordova Rose Lodge	lodge	★★★	★★★	$95–$125
The King's Chamber B&B and Lodging	B&B/ apartments	★★★	★★★	$75–$145
Light House Inn	inn	★★★★	★★★	$175–$310
Orca Adventure Lodge	lodge	★★★	★★★	$110–$150
Reluctant Fisherman Inn	inn	★★★	★★★	$130–$160

Southcentral Coastal Alaska Indoor Lodging (cont'd.)

NAME	TYPE(S) OF LODGING	QUALITY RATING	VALUE RATING	COST
KODIAK ISLAND				
Best Western Inn Kodiak	hotel	★★★	★★★	$149–$209
Comfort Inn Kodiak	hotel	★★★★	★★★	$145–$175
Kodiak Bed and Breakfast	B&B	★★★★	★★★★	$128
The Lodge at Hidden Basin	wilderness lodge	★★★	★★★	$3,995/ 6 days
On the Cape B&B	B&B	★★★★	★★★★	$135–$160
Port Lions Lodge	wilderness lodge	★★★	★★★	$3,095/ 5 days
Raspberry Island Remote Camps	wilderness lodge	★★★★	★★★★	$3,000/ 5 days
Saltery Lake Lodge	wilderness lodge	★★★★	★★★★	$2,400/ 6 days
Shelikof Lodge	motel	★★	★★★★	$75–$95
Spruce Haven B&B	B&B	★★★	★★★	$100–$125

- **Swiftwater Park** On the river; ☎ 907-262-3151; **www.ci.soldotna.ak.us/parks_rec.html**

  QUALITY ★★★ VALUE ★★★ $14.70

  Small campground run by the city of Soldotna; sites are first-come, first-served.

HOMER

Indoor Lodging

- **Bear Creek Winery and Lodging** Bear Creek Drive, out East End Road; ☎ 907-235-8484; **www.bearcreekwinery.com**

  QUALITY ★★★★★ VALUE ★★★ $225–$260

  This newly opened winery also features wonderful suites for rent. Everything is first-class, down to the bath towels and bedding. A splurge for sure. The winery also offers daily tastings in the summer.

- **The Eagle Watch Hostel** Mile 3 Oilwell Road in Ninilchik; ☎ 907-567-3905; **home.gci.net/~theeaglewatch**

  QUALITY ★★★ VALUE ★★★★ $13–$35

  Offers dorm-style bunks and private rooms.

- **Heritage Hotel and Lodge** 147 East Pioneer Avenue; ☎ 800-380-7787 or 907-235-7787; **www.alaskaheritagehotel.com**

  QUALITY ★★★ VALUE ★★★ $119–$165

A log hotel right in the center of the business part of town. The rooms are nice and clean, but some are better than others when it comes to location. Pet-friendly.

- **Homer Hostel** 304 West Pioneer Avenue; ☎ 907-235-1463; **www.homerhostel.com**

QUALITY ★★★ VALUE ★★★ $23–$70

Located conveniently at the business end of town, with access to local museums and shops.

- **Homer Inn and Spa** 895 Ocean Drive; ☎ 800-294-7823 or 907-235-2501; **www.homerinn.com**

QUALITY ★★★★★ VALUE ★★★★ $159–$259

This luxurious getaway is a great reward after a long kayaking or backpacking trip. Complete massage services are available, and there's an outdoor hot tub overlooking the water. Rates are surprisingly competitive with the cheaper places. Of course, the full-body massage will cost extra.

- **Land's End Resort** At the end of Homer Spit Road; ☎ 000 470 0400 or 907-235-0400; **www.lands-end-resort.com**

QUALITY ★★★★ VALUE ★★★ $135–$275

This is the getaway of choice for many an Alaskan who wants to go to Homer for a weekend. The food in the restaurants is delicious, the lodging is beautiful albeit a bit generic, and the view of the bay is unsurpassed.

- **Lighthouse Village Cabins** 1477 Bay Avenue; ☎ 907-235-7007; **www.lighthousecabins.com**

QUALITY ★★★★ VALUE ★★★ $100–$165

They may look sort of cheesy, but the convenient location is great if the Homer Spit is your destination. Easy access to Homer Brewing Co., local eateries, and the Homer Spit and bike path. Birders like these cabins for their close proximity to the shorebirds. The Tidewater is our favorite.

- **Mossy's Alaska Seaside Farm Hostel and Cabins** 40904 Seaside Farm Road, just outside of town; ☎ 907-235-7850; **www.xyz.net/~seaside/home.htm**

QUALITY ★★★ VALUE ★★★★ $10–$55

A nontouristy option on a sprawling all-organic farm with animals wandering all over; very hippielike atmosphere. Tent camping, hostel, and cabins available.

- **Surf Shack Deluxe Cabin** Ocean Drive Loop; ☎ 907-235-7873; **www.surfshackhomeralaska.com/theshack**

QUALITY ★★★★ VALUE ★★★ $155

It's not actually a shack, but rather an awesome little cabin with a log bed and spiral staircase sitting on the bluff above the bay. It's a killer deal that's also a romantic getaway. The outside fire ring is a plus, but the road on which the cabin is perched is sort of shabby. Just look toward the bay, and all will be wonderful.

Southcentral Coastal Alaska Camping

NAME	TYPE(S) OF LODGING	QUALITY RATING	VALUE RATING	COST
KENAI				
Captain Cook State Recreation Area	tent/RV	★★★★	★★★★	$10
SOLDOTNA				
Centennial Campground	tent/RV	★★★	★★★	$14.70
Kenai National Wildlife Refuge	tent/RV	★★★	★★★★	free–$10
Swiftwater Park	tent/RV	★★★	★★★	$14.70
HOMER				
Anchor River/Stariski Creek State Recreation Areas	tent/RV	★★★★	★★★★	$10
Clam Gulch State Recreation Area	tent/RV	★★★★	★★★	$10
Deep Creek State Recreation Area	tent/RV	★★★★	★★★	$10
Heritage RV Park	RV	★★★	★★	$55
Homer City Campground	tent	★★★	★★★★	$8
Homer Spit Campground	tent/RV	★★★	★★★	$22–$32
Kasilof State Recreation Site	tent/RV	★★★	★★★	$10
Mossy's Alaska Seaside Farm	tent	★★★	★★★★	$10
Ninilchik State Recreation Site	tent	★★★	★★★	$10
Spit Campground	tent	★★★★	★★★★★	$8
SEWARD				
Exit Glacier–Kenai Fjords National Park	tent	★★★★	★★★★★	free
Forest Acres Campground	tent	★★★★	★★★★	$8
Miller's Landing	tent/RV	★★★★	★★★	$25–$35
Spring Creek Campground	tent	★★★	★★★	$8
USDA Forest Service–Trail River, Ptarmigan Creek, Primrose	tent/RV	★★★★	★★★★	$10
Waterfront Park Campgrounds	tent/RV	★★★	★★★★	$2–$25

Camping

There are several good camping choices in and around Homer:

- **Anchor River State Recreation Area/Stariski State Recreation Site**
  About 15 miles from Homer; ☎ 907-262-5581;
  www.dnr.state.ak.us/parks/units/anchoriv.htm

  QUALITY ★★★★ VALUE ★★★★ $10

NAME	TYPE(S) OF LODGING	QUALITY RATING	VALUE RATING	COST
SURROUNDING AREAS				
USDA Forest Service Glacier Ranger District Campgrounds	tent/RV	★★★★	★★★★	$10
USDA Forest Service Seward Ranger District Campgrounds	tent/RV	★★–★★★★	★★–★★★	$10
WHITTIER				
Campground off Whittier Street	tent	★★	★★★★	$5
USDA Forest Service Chugach Glacier Ranger District Campgrounds	cabins	★★★	★★★★	$35
VALDEZ				
Bayside RV Park	RV/tent	★★	★★★	$18–$31
Bear Paw Camper Park	RV/tent	★★★	★★★	$17–$40
Eagle's Rest RV Park and Cabins	RV/tent/cabins	★★	★★★	$17–$55
CORDOVA				
Alaska State Parks Campgrounds	tent	★★★★	★★	free
Child's Glacier Recreation Area	tent	★★★★★	★★★★	$5
KODIAK ISLAND				
Buskin River State Recreation Site	tent	★★★	★★★★	$15
Fort Abercrombie State Historical Park	tent	★★★	★★★	$15
Pasagshak State Recreation Site	tent	★★★★	★★★★★	free

A nice and private place to camp, located on a high bluff tucked in the woods overlooking the water. Geography buffs will appreciate that the campground also happens to be at the most westerly point on the U.S. highway system.

- **Clam Gulch State Recreation Area** Mile 117.5 Sterling Highway; ☎ 907-262-5581; **www.dnr.state.ak.us/parks/units/clamglch.htm**

QUALITY ★★★★ VALUE ★★★ $10

Offers some of the best clam digging in the state, at a campground high on the bluff overlooking Cook Inlet.

- **Deep Creek State Recreation Area** Mile 137 Sterling Highway; ☎ 907-262-5581; **www.dnr.state.ak.us/parks/units/deepck.htm**

  QUALITY ★★★★ VALUE ★★★ $10

  There are three campgrounds from which to choose.

- **Heritage RV Park** On Homer Spit Road, across from Spit Campground; ☎ 800-380-7787 or 907-226-4500; **www.alaskaheritagervpark.com**

  QUALITY ★★★ VALUE ★★ $55

  This park catering to RV-ers shares an incredible view with Spit Campground. It can get rowdy on weekends, but no one seems to mind.

- **Homer City Campground** At the top of Bartlett Street (follow the signs); ☎ 907-235-3170

  QUALITY ★★★ VALUE ★★★★ $8

  Facilities at this peaceful, family-oriented campground include restrooms, picnic area, and playground equipment. It's a little out of the way, but quiet.

- **Homer Spit Campground** At the end of Homer Spit Road; ☎ 907-235-8206; **www.alaskacampgrounds.net/members/HomerSpitCampground/HomerSpitCampground.htm**

  QUALITY ★★★ VALUE ★★★ $22–$32

  This privately run campground is locally—and nationally—famous, and the resident "Eagle Lady" has been featured in numerous news articles. She feeds the eagles fish scraps daily; thus, they congregate here. Ten tent sites and plenty of RV sites.

- **Kasilof State Recreation Site** About 15 miles south of Soldotna on the way toward Homer; ☎ 907-262-5581; **www.dnr.state.ak.us/parks/units/kasilof.htm**

  QUALITY ★★★ VALUE ★★★ $10

  Three campground options at Crooked Creek, Johnson Lake, and Kasilof River state recreation areas. *Note:* The Kasilof River site fills up fast.

- **Mossy's Alaska Seaside Farm** 40904 Seaside Farm Road, just outside of town; ☎ 907-235-7850; **www.xyz.net/~seaside/home.htm**

  QUALITY ★★★ VALUE ★★★★ $10

  No reservations are needed, but a limited number of campsites are available. Kids under 12 stay free.

- **Ninilchik State Recreation Site** Mile 135 Sterling Highway

  QUALITY ★★★ VALUE ★★★ $10

  Three camping areas, one right on the beach.

- **Spit Campground** On Homer Spit Road, Homer; ☎ 907-235-3170

  QUALITY ★★★★ VALUE ★★★★★ $8

  If you're going to be in a tent, we suggest enjoying the ocean sounds at this informal city-run site with camping on the right-hand side of the road.

SEWARD

Indoor Lodging

- **A Cabin on the Cliff** 309 Third Avenue; ☎ 888-227-2424 or 907-224-2411; **www.acabinonthecliff.com**

  QUALITY ★★★★★ VALUE ★★★ $369–$469

  One of the most notable lodging options in town, perched at the base of Mount Marathon with a commanding view across the road and toward the harbor. The hot tub alone is worth it.

- **Exit Glacier Salmon Bake and Cabins** ¼ Mile Exit Glacier Road; ☎ 907-224-4752; **www.sewardalaskacabins.com**

  QUALITY ★★★ VALUE ★★★★ $110

  We haven't stayed here ourselves, but we can tell you that these newer cabins come highly recommended from several local outdoors outfitters, who say the salmon bake is delicious, too. The cabins—tucked into the woods, tiny but cozy—sleep four, and pets are welcome. Sounds like our kind of place.

- **The Farm Bed and Breakfast** Three miles from Seward on Salmon Creek Road; ☎ 907-224-5691; **www.thefarmbedandbreakfast.com**

  QUALITY ★★★ VALUE ★★★★★ $82–$113

  This old but remodeled farm is in a nice, quiet area. We like this spot because the longtime owners are superfriendly, and the grassy field on their ten-acre spread is a great place to wander.

- **Hotel Edgewater** 200 Fifth Avenue; ☎ 888-793-6800 or 907-224-2700; **www.hoteledgewater.com**

  QUALITY ★★★★ VALUE ★★★ $155–$275

  It's got a bit of a corporate feel, but you have to admit the rooms are nice, and the view is superb. One of the better hotels in town if you don't like surprises; underwent renovations in the winter of 2007.

- **Hotel Seward** 221 Fifth Avenue; ☎ 800-440-2444 or 907-224-8001; **www.hotelsewardalaska.com**

  QUALITY ★★★★ VALUE ★★★ $155–$224

  Popular downtown hotel specializing in rooms with a view. Rates are steep, but oh, what a view it is!

- **Kayaker's Cove** On Resurrection Bay; ☎ 907-224-8662; **www.geocities.com/kayakerscove_99664**

  QUALITY ★★★ VALUE ★★★★★ $20–$60

  This is one of our favorite places to stay in Seward: a rustic wilderness lodge across the bay, with kayaks for the paddling (for a small fee, of course). The main lodge is a hostel setup; private cabins are available for up to three people. A kayak rental will you $20 per day, and a water taxi to get there (contact Miller's Landing to arrange that) is $55 round-trip. All in all, it's an affordable wilderness getaway that you'd pay a guide twice as much to arrange.

- **Miller's Landing Hostel and Cabins** Located at Lowell Point, a nice wooded campground that also has a hostel and private cabins for rent; ☎ 866-541-5739 or 907-224-5739; **www.millerslandingak.com**

  QUALITY ★★ VALUE ★★★ $45–$250

  Lodging options range from two-person hostel rooms to a fancy six-person cabin.

- **Moby Dick Hostel** 432 Third Avenue; ☎ 907-224-7072; **www.mobydickhostel.com**

  QUALITY ★★ VALUE ★★ $19–$70

  Offers dorm-style rooms right in town, albeit a good walk from the harbor. The owners are friendly, which makes up for the very used beds. The convenient location makes this a place worth staying at.

- **Seward Windsong Lodge** Exit Glacier Road; ☎ 877-777-4079 or 907-224-7116; **www.sewardwindsong.com**

  QUALITY ★★★★★ VALUE ★★★ $139–$289

  A true lodge feel but only minutes to town. It's owned by Alaska Heritage Tours, an Alaska native–run company that has begun building high-quality lodges throughout the state, including Kenai Fjords Wilderness Lodge on Fox Island and Talkeetna Alaskan Lodge in Southcentral Inland.

- **Snow River Hostel** Mile 16 Seward Highway; ☎ 907-440-1907; **www.snowriverhostel.org**

  QUALITY ★★★★ VALUE ★★★★ $15–$40

  A stone building off the highway offering very clean hostel facilities. Separate men's and women's bunks; a private room is also available.

- **The Van Gilder Hotel** 308 Adams Street; ☎ 800-204-6835 or 907-224-3079; **www.vangilderhotel.com**

  QUALITY ★★★★ VALUE ★★★ $135–$175

  A time-honored alternative to today's hotels, with a lovely antiques collection and historic displays to boot. Built in 1916, the renovated Van Gilder offers several small rooms, each of them unique.

Camping

- **Exit Glacier–Kenai Fjords National Park** ☎ 907-224-2132 or 907-224-7500; **www.nps.gov/kefj**

  QUALITY ★★★★ VALUE ★★★★★ FREE

  This drive-to site, off Exit Glacier Road, has a 12-site walk-in tent campground. Sites are available on a first-come, first-served basis. There are no reservations or camping fees; stays are limited to 14 days. *Warning:* It fills fast in July and August. Pets are not allowed.

- **Forest Acres Campground** Off Hemlock Street, away from the harbor area; **www.cityofseward.net/parksRec/parks.htm**

  QUALITY ★★★★ VALUE ★★★★ $8

One of our favorite city-run tenting options. You're on the honor system—you self-register on-site.

- **Miller's Landing** At Lowell Point; ☎ 866-541-5739 or 907-224-5739; **www.millerslandingak.com**

QUALITY ★★★★ VALUE ★★★ $25–$35

A nice wooded campground three miles outside of Seward, on the water. If you're kayaking, this is a great launching point.

- **Spring Creek Campground** Off Nash Road, at the edge of town (go five miles and turn right, toward the water and the primitive campground); **www.cityofseward.net/parksRec/parks.htm**

QUALITY ★★★ VALUE ★★★ $8

Another good city-run camping choice. Again, you're on the honor system, self-registering on-site.

- **USDA Forest Service Seward Ranger District Campgrounds** Seward Ranger District, 334 Fourth Avenue; ☎ 907-224-3374; reserve spots at ☎ 877-444-6777 or **www.recreation.gov**

QUALITY ★★★★ VALUE ★★★★ $10

Three campgrounds are available along the Seward Highway. Within 25 miles of Seward is **Trail River,** at Mile 24.2 (63 sites, no hookups); **Ptarmigan Creek,** at Mile 23.1 (16 sites, no hookups); and **Primrose,** at Mile 17 (10 sites, no hookups).

- **Waterfront Park Campgrounds** Near the water at Ballaine Boulevard, from Railway Avenue to D Street; **www.cityofseward.net/parksRec/campgrounds.htm**

QUALITY ★★★ VALUE ★★★★ $2–$25

The Seward Parks and Recreation Department runs five campgrounds within Waterfront Park. Here again, the honor system is the rule, with self-registration on-site. Not the quietest choice, but the view is to die for.

SURROUNDING AREAS

Indoor Lodging

- **Kenai Backcountry Lodge** In Cooper Landing; ☎ 800-334-8730 or 907-783-2928; **www.alaskawildland.com/kenaibackcountrylodge.htm**

QUALITY ★★★★★ VALUE ★★★★ $1,075/2 NIGHTS

To stay here you have to purchase a package trip, with a minimum two-night stay, and the prices are high. But the lodge's owner, Alaska Wildland Adventures, was voted one of the best eco-tour businesses in the world by *Condé Nast Traveler* in 2005, and their environmentally aware way of doing business is noticeable. We're talking high quality. All meals and activities are covered.

- **Kenai Princess Lodge** In Cooper Landing; ☎ 800-426-0500; **www.princesslodges.com/kenai_lodge.cfm**

QUALITY ★★★★★ VALUE ★★★ $239–$329

This beautiful log lodge, off a back road in Cooper Landing, combines comfort with ruggedness. The rooms are like mini-cabins, although they are attached to each other. The communal hot tub is nice when you can get it to yourself. Dinner at the Eagle's Crest Restaurant is memorable.

- **Trail Lake Lodge** Mile 29.5 Seward Highway, Moose Pass; ☎ 888-395-3624; **www.traillakelodge.com**

  QUALITY ★★ VALUE ★★★ $99–$115

  Nice enough, right on the water, and an alternative to staying in Seward. If you're craving complete isolation, however, you won't find it here: the lodge is right off the two-lane highway.

Camping

- **USDA Forest Service Glacier Ranger District Campgrounds** Glacier Ranger District; ☎ 907-783-3242; reserve spots through ☎ 877-444-6777 or **www.recreation.gov**

  QUALITY ★★★★ VALUE ★★★★ $10

  Camping on the Seward Highway from Girdwood to Hope at Bertha Creek, Black Bear, Granite Creek, and Williwaw campgrounds.

- **USDA Forest Service Seward Ranger District Campgrounds** Seward Ranger District; 334 Fourth Avenue; ☎ 907-224-3374; reserve spots through ☎ 877-444-6777 or **www.recreation.gov**

  QUALITY ★★–★★★★ VALUE ★★–★★★ $10

  Camping in Hope, Cooper Landing, and all along the Seward and Sterling highways within Seward Ranger District boundaries.

WHITTIER

Indoor Lodging

- **The Anchor Inn** Off the waterfront, near the residential area in Whittier; ☎ 877-870-8787 or 907-472-2354; **www.anchorinnwhittier.com**

  QUALITY ★★ VALUE ★★★ $80–$100

  The building isn't much to look at, but each room is different. A restaurant-bar and store are attached to the inn.

- **The Inn at Whittier** ☎ 866-472-5757 or 907-472-7000; **www.innatwhittier.com**

  QUALITY ★★★★ VALUE ★★★★ $149–$229

  The newest and really the only fine-lodging option in this tiny community. The rooms range from mountain view (least costly) to town-house suites with fireplace, Jacuzzi, and two floors of luxury and views.

- **June's Bed and Breakfast** In Historic Begich Towers (you have to see it to believe it), Whittier; ☎ 888-472-2396; **www.breadnbuttercharters.com**

  QUALITY ★★★★ VALUE ★★★★ $115–$375

  Like most of Whittier's population, this longtime bed-and-breakfast inhabits former military housing. The suites are surprisingly luxurious; you will not be disappointed, especially for this end of town. The owners also offer great fishing charters out of Whittier.

Camping

- **Campground off Whittier Street** Near the public-parking area

QUALITY ★★ VALUE ★★★★ $5

The campground is little more than a parking lot itself, but it's the cheapest way to sleep in Whittier.

- **USDA Forest Service Chugach Glacier Ranger District Campgrounds** Reserve ahead of time at ☎ 877-444-6777 or **www.recreation.gov**

QUALITY ★★★ VALUE ★★★★ $35

Public-use cabins are available throughout the sound outside of Whittier-Pigot Bay, Paulsen Bay, Shrode Lake, Coghill Lake, Harrison Lagoon, and South Culross Passage. You'll need a boat—or someone with a boat who can take you—to get to them, but they offer some affordable lodging in a gorgeous setting.

VALDEZ

Indoor Lodging

- **Brookside Inn Bed and Breakfast** 1465 Richardson Highway; ☎ 866-316-9130 or 907-835-9130; **www.brooksideinnbb.com**

QUALITY ★★★ VALUE ★★★ $125–$160

The owners have a friendly dog, and the breakfast area is a lovely covered and heated patio. The rooms are spacious, especially the suite. You're right off the road, though, and some might not like the occasional highway noise.

- **Thompson Pass Mountain Chalet** Mile 19 Richardson Highway; ☎ 907-835-4817; **www.thompsonpass.com**

QUALITY ★★★★★ VALUE ★★★★★ $140

This is the choice for those who want the mountains out their back door, especially in the winter. This custom cabin is gorgeous, and guided skiing or hiking is available if you want to explore with an expert.

- **Valdez Harbor Inn** 100 Harbor Drive; ☎ 888-222-3440 or 907-835-2308; **www.valdezharborinn.com**

QUALITY ★★★★ VALUE ★★★ $139–$175

One of the nicest hotels in town, this inn also boasts one of the best views. Plus, the bar is a nice place to hang out after a day of hiking.

- **Wild Roses by the Sea Bed and Breakfast** 629 Fiddlehead Lane; ☎ 907-835-2930; **www.alaskabytheseabnb.com**

QUALITY ★★★★ VALUE ★★★ $130–$170

Close to the beach and town. Private Jacuzzi is a plus.

Camping

- **Bayside RV Park** ☎ 888-835-4425; **www.baysiderv.com**

QUALITY ★★ VALUE ★★★ $18–$31

It's basically a cleared parking lot, but you can't get much better than a Valdez view on a clear day, so it doesn't seem to matter.

- **Bear Paw Camper Park** On the small-boat harbor; ☎ 907-835-2530; **www.bearpawrvpark.com**

QUALITY ★★★ VALUE ★★★ $17–$40

The in-town location makes this convenient, although not necessarily wilderness-like. The owners have two parks—one for families and an adults-only establishment for those who don't want to deal with crying or rambunctious children. The tent camping is in a wooded area, which is nice.

- **Eagle's Rest RV Park and Cabins** 139 East Pioneer Drive; ☎ 800-553-7275 or 907-835-2373; **www.eaglesrestrv.com**

QUALITY ★★ VALUE ★★★ $25–$125

If you only are interested in a convenient location, this is the place for you: a big cleared area for RV-ers, tenters, and cabin dwellers right in town; the cabins are $125.

CORDOVA

Indoor Lodging

- **Bear Country Lodge** On the shore of Lake Eyak; ☎ 907-424-5901; **www.bearcountrylodge.net**

QUALITY ★★★ VALUE ★★★ $125

This quiet lakefront lodge is perfect for families or small groups seeking solitude. Two cabins to choose from.

- **Cordova Rose Lodge** 1315 Whitshed, on the waterfront; ☎ 907-424-7673; **www.cordovarose.com**

QUALITY ★★★ VALUE ★★★ $95–$125

Birders like this scenic little lodge and stay here often; the owners can fill you in on the rich birdlife in the area. Choose from rooms with shared or private baths; breakfast is included in the rate for the latter.

- **The King's Chamber B&B and Lodging** 511 Fourth Street; ☎ 907-424-3373; **www.thekingschamber.com**

QUALITY ★★★ VALUE ★★★ $75–$145

This historic building was moved into town close to a decade ago and now can house guests in bed-and-breakfast rooms, efficiency apartments, or three- and four-bedroom apartments for extended stays.

- **Light House Inn** Located right at the Cordova Boat Harbor; ☎ 907-424-7080 or 907-424-7673; **www.cordovalighthouseinn.com**

QUALITY ★★★★ VALUE ★★★ $175–$310

A good lodging choice because of its convenient location and wonderful bakery just downstairs. The owners grind their own whole-wheat flour and make their own granola—yummy! The comfy rooms have Internet access.

- **Orca Adventure Lodge** ☎ 866-424-6722 or 907-424-7249; **www.orcaadventurelodge.com**

QUALITY ★★★ VALUE ★★★ $110–$150

This lodge is out of town and housed in a refurbished cannery. The rooms are basic, as is the food (meat or fish and potatoes), but the owner knows the area well and can accommodate just about anyone's needs.

- **Reluctant Fisherman Inn** 407 Railroad Avenue; ☎ 877-770-3272 or 907-424-3272

QUALITY ★★★ VALUE ★★★ $130–$160

The starting rate gets you a room by the bay.

Camping

- **Alaska State Parks Campgrounds** ☎ 907-262-5581

QUALITY ★★★★ VALUE ★★ FREE

Convenient in-town or nearby camping is hard to find in Cordova (the only RV/tent park is basically a gravel lot in town), but the rest of the surrounding city is wide-open wilderness. Alaska State Parks has three beautiful recreation areas that allow camping: Boswell Bay, Canoe Passage, and Kayak Island state marine parks. There are no fees, but the campgrounds are only accessible by water taxi or floatplane—which gets expensive (thus our relatively low value rating).

- **Child's Glacier Recreation Area** 48 miles out the Copper River Highway

QUALITY ★★★★★ VALUE ★★★★ $5

There are 15 wooded tent sites here.

KODIAK ISLAND

KODIAK ISLAND HAS SOME of the best remote lodges in the state. If you're staying in town, we have several hotel/B&B recommendations. But if you have a chance, hit one of the lodges we suggest, where you can fish, hike, or relax to your heart's content.

Indoor Lodging

- **Best Western Inn Kodiak** 236 West Rezanof Drive; ☎ 888-563-4254 or 907-486-5712; **www.kodiakinn.com**

QUALITY ★★★ VALUE ★★★ $149–$209

Right downtown; some rooms are small, but all are clean and comfortable.

- **Comfort Inn Kodiak** 1395 Airport Way; ☎ 800-544-2202 or 907-487-2700; **www.choicehotels.com**

QUALITY ★★★★ VALUE ★★★ $145–$175

Now part of the Choice chain, the popular hotel formerly known as the Buskin River Inn still seems to be drawing clients. The Comfort Inn has excellent rooms and dining. The drawback is that it's a few miles out of town by the airport, so getting downtown is kind of inconvenient if you're without wheels.

- **Kodiak Bed and Breakfast** 308 Cope Street; ☎ 907-486-5367; **home.gci.net/~mmonroe**

QUALITY ★★★★ VALUE ★★★★ $128

Located one block back from the harbor and within walking distance of most downtown attractions, this is our top pick among the bed-and-breakfasts in Kodial. There are two comfortable rooms plus your own private living room.

- **The Lodge at Hidden Basin** ☎ 907-345-7017; **www.hiddenbasinalaska.com**

  QUALITY ★★★ VALUE ★★★ $3,995/6 DAYS

  This intimate lodge hosts a maximum of six people at a time in a rough-cut-spruce building that is simple and comfortable. We like the homey feel of the place, complete with mismatched furniture.

- **On the Cape Bed and Breakfast** 3476 Spruce Cape Road, three minutes from downtown; ☎ 907-486-4185; **www.onthecape.net**

  QUALITY ★★★★ VALUE ★★★★ $135–$160

  This new home features beautiful rooms with their own bathrooms and ocean views. One of the nicest places in town.

- **Port Lions Lodge** In the village of Port Lions, on the northwest end of Kodiak Island, accessible by ferry or small plane; ☎ 800-808-8447 or 907-454-2264; **www.portlionslodge.com**

  QUALITY ★★★ VALUE ★★★ $3,095/5 DAYS

  This remote, beautiful lodge offers weeklong packages that include air transport from Kodiak, five days of guided fishing, lodging, and all meals. They even clean, package, and ship all your fish home. The price may seem steep, but all the details are taken care of, so you can simply relax.

- **Raspberry Island Remote Camps** Raspberry Island; ☎ 907-486-1781; **www.raspberryisland.com**

  QUALITY ★★★★ VALUE ★★★★ $2,500/5 DAYS

  A truly secluded lodge that concentrates equally on activities other than fishing. While most lodges can accommodate just about any interest, Raspberry owners encourage it all—hiking, kayaking, and canoeing pack trips, as well opportunities for relaxing back at the lodge.

- **Saltery Lake Lodge** Near Ugak Bay, on the eastern side of Kodiak Island; ☎ 800-770-5037 or 907-486-7083; **www.salterylake.com**

  QUALITY ★★★★ VALUE ★★★★ $2,400/6 DAYS

  Another fishing destination; packages include six days of fishing, lodging, meals, and transportation from Kodiak. Not as nice as Port Lions, but the fishing is excellent.

- **Shelikof Lodge** 211 Thorsheim Avenue; ☎ 907-486-4141; **www.ptialaska.net/~kyle**

  QUALITY ★★ VALUE ★★★★ $75–$95

  The rooms are surprisingly nice considering the exterior of the building, and the convenient location makes it easy to stroll down to the city center. Smoking and nonsmoking rooms available.

- **Spruce Haven Bed and Breakfast** 2109-C Mission Road; ☎ 907-486-5171

  QUALITY ★★★ VALUE ★★★ $100–$125

  Located out on a spruce-covered spit of land with a lake on one side and the ocean on the other. Nice and secluded for being just a few miles from downtown. The owners, longtime Kodiak residents, can share much of the area's history with guests.

Camping

You won't see many recreational vehicles in Kodiak, thus the lack of campgrounds on every corner. This is a good thing, though: as a result, most camping areas maintain a very natural feel. The three best camping areas are all managed by the Alaska State Parks system, Division of Parks and Outdoor Recreation. For more information, contact Alaska State Parks, Kodiak District Office, 1400 Abercrombie Drive, Kodiak 99615; ☎ 907-486-6339; **www.dnr.state.ak.us/parks/units/kodiak/index.htm.**

- **Buskin River State Recreation Site** Mile 4.1 West Rezanof Drive

  QUALITY ★★★ VALUE ★★★★ $15

  This 15-site camping area is conveniently located only 4.1 miles from downtown and is close to one of the most productive salmon-fishing rivers on Kodiak island. The Alaska Department of Fish and Game operates a weir just outside the park. From downtown, follow Rezanof Drive west for 4.1 miles, and then turn left at the park sign at Mile 4.5 West Rezanof Drive. *Warning:* The campground is right by the airport, thus airplane noise is right overhead.

- **Fort Abercrombie State Historical Park** Mile 3.7 East Rezanof Drive

  QUALITY ★★★ VALUE ★★★ $15

  This is a hiker's campground, with 13 sites and great hiking trails leading to a rugged coastline, in addition to a lake stocked with rainbow trout and arctic grayling. This is our favorite location because the sites are also designed with tent campers in mind, although RV-ers can use the overflow area. Remnants of a World War II military installation are scattered all over, giving the area a sort of deserted feel. From downtown, head east on Rezanof Drive and drive 3.7 miles; turn right onto Abercrombie Drive, which goes into the park.

- **Pasagshak State Recreation Site** 40 Pasagshak River Road

  QUALITY ★★★★ VALUE ★★★★★ FREE

  This small riverside park on the mouth of the Pasagshak River is a popular fishing area; the species found here include silver and king salmon and Dolly Varden. Take Rezanof Drive west out of town and drive 30 miles; then turn right onto Pasagshak Road just past the Kalsin River, and continue nine miles.

WHERE *to* EAT

KENAI PENINSULA

DINING ON THE KENAI PENINSULA is an interesting experience. Figuratively speaking, if you attached weights to the best restaurants on the peninsula, the southern tip, near Homer and Kachemak Bay, would sink right into the ocean there. Seward, on the east side, might sag a bit, but Kenai and Soldotna, to the west, would barely move.

The truth is, the best dining options exist in the smaller Alaska communities, in Seward or Homer; Kenai and Soldotna tend to cater to the McDonald's-and-Subway crowd. We like dining options that say something about the communities in which they are located, that either step it up a notch with fine ingredients and creative presentation, or offer casual confidence and a $1 cookie that will melt in your mouth. It's not about how much you spend, just how well you spend it.

Because Kenai and Soldotna are so close to each other, we've opted to combine their dining listings. Seward and Homer have separate listings; we also have a couple of suggestions for the drive there, in the outlying communities.

Kenai and Soldotna

- **Charlotte's** 115 South Willow Street, Kenai; ☎ 907-283-2777

  CASUAL QUALITY ★★★★ $8–$18 SUITABLE FOR KIDS? N

  Homemade bread, salad from their garden, and wonderful desserts make this one of the most charming eateries in Kenai.

- **Jersey Subs** At the North Cohoe turnoff, Kasilof; ☎ 907-260-3343

  SUBS QUALITY ★★★ $4–$9 SUITABLE FOR KIDS? N/A

  It's just a shack set up by the side of the road, but the subs satisfy.

- **Kaladi Brothers Coffee Co.** 315 South Kobuk Suite C, Soldotna; ☎ 907-262-5980

  ESPRESSO QUALITY ★★★★ $2–$7 SUITABLE FOR KIDS? N

  Kaladi Brothers sells the best coffee in Alaska, in our opinion. The Soldotna location, one of the original stores, isn't as spacious as others elsewhere in the state–it's about the size of a large living room–so it's probably not the best place to bring rowdy kids unless you're just making a quick stop.

- **Louie's Restaurant** In the Uptown Motel, 47 Spur View Drive; ☎ 800-777-3650 or 907-283-3660

  SEAFOOD QUALITY ★★★ $8–$29 SUITABLE FOR KIDS? Y

  A family-friendly restaurant that has a long and varied seafood menu. Plenty of red-meat options, very few vegetarian-friendly items.

- **The Moose Is Loose** On the Sterling Highway, just past the Y in Soldotna; ☎ 907-260-3036

  BAKERY QUALITY ★★★ $3–$8 SUITABLE FOR KIDS? Y

This is a good place to pick up some fresh baked goods on your way to wherever.

- **Mykel's Restaurant** In the Soldotna Inn, 35041 Kenai Spur Highway; ☎ 866-262-9169 or 907-262-4305; **www.mykels.com**

  AMERICAN QUALITY ★★★ $6–$27 SUITABLE FOR KIDS? Y

  Family-style meals and something to please everyone. We like Mykel's because it's so clean, but it's a bit overpriced for what it offers.

- **River City Books** 43977 Sterling Highway, Suite A, Soldotna; ☎ 907-260-7722

  ESPRESSO QUALITY ★★★★ $2–$6 SUITABLE FOR KIDS? N

  Enjoy some espresso and a muffin, then spend hours browsing the great book selection in this much-needed bookstore.

- **Sal's Klondike Diner** 44619 Sterling Highway, Soldotna; ☎ 907-262-2220

  BURGERS QUALITY ★★★★ $4–$19 SUITABLE FOR KIDS? Y

  It is what it says: a diner. And it's fast, friendly, and affordable. A family of four can eat for $30. Featuring burgers, fish and chips, and sandwiches. Open 24 hours for those on weird schedules or with hangovers to feed.

- **Sockeyes at Kenai Landing** 2101 Bowpicker Lane, Kenai; ☎ 907-335-2500; **www.kenailanding.com**

  AMERICAN QUALITY ★★★ $7–$24 SUITABLE FOR KIDS? Y

  This newly renovated cannery houses a restaurant with a sit-down dining area for those who want to enjoy a bottle of wine or beer with their meal, along with an express-order area at which food is delivered as your number is called.

- **Veronica's Coffee House** In Historic Old Town Kenai, across from the Russian Church; ☎ 907-283-2725

  CASUAL QUALITY ★★★★ $4–$14 SUITABLE FOR KIDS? Y

  This funky cafe serves breakfast, lunch, and dinner; features homemade soups, sandwiches, quiches, desserts, and daily specials.

Homer

- **The Alibi, Sushi and Oyster Bar** 453 East Pioneer Avenue; ☎ 907-235-9199

  SUSHI QUALITY ★★★★ $8–$25 SUITABLE FOR KIDS? N

  Well, what can we say? You're right on the ocean, and the fish couldn't get any fresher. This is the place for fish bait, and the restaurant does it well.

- **Café Cups** 162 West Pioneer Avenue; ☎ 907-235-8330; **www.cafecupshomer.com**

  FUSION QUALITY ★★★★ $8–$24 SUITABLE FOR KIDS? N

  With its funky giant teacups hanging off the eaves, you can't really miss the place. The food is excellent, creative, and on the healthful side. The Caesar salad is delicious, and the dressings are made in-house.

Southcentral Coastal Alaska Dining

NAME	CUISINE	FOOD QUALITY	COST
KENAI AND SOLDOTNA			
Charlotte's	casual	★★★★	$8–$18
Jersey Subs	subs	★★★	$4–$9
Kaladi Brothers Coffee Co	espresso	★★★★	$2–$7
Louie's Restaurant	seafood	★★★	$8–$29
The Moose Is Loose	bakery	★★★	$3–$8
Mykel's Restaurant	American	★★★	$6–$27
River City Books	espresso	★★★★	$2–$6
Sal's Klondike Diner	burgers	★★★★	$4–$10
Sockeyes at Kenai Landing	American	★★★	$7–$24
Veronica's Coffee House	casual	★★★★	$4–$14
HOMER			
The Alibi, Sushi and Oyster Bar	sushi	★★★★	$8–$25
Café Cups	fusion	★★★★	$8–$24
The Chart Room	fusion	★★★★	$9–$35
Duncan House Diner	diner	★★★	$4–$9
Fat Olives	casual	★★★★	$8–$18
Fresh Sourdough Express Bakery	casual	★★★★	$8–$15
Homestead Restaurant	fusion	★★★★	$13–39
Mermaid Café/Old Inlet Bookshop	casual	★★★	$4–$10
The Rookery Restaurant	fusion/seafood	★★★★	$9–$29
The Saltry Restaurant	fusion	★★★★★	$8–$24
Two Sisters Bakery	bakery	★★★	$4–$12
SEWARD			
Bakery at the Harbor	bakery	★★★	$2–$7
Chinooks Waterfront Restaurant	fusion/seafood	★★★	$7–$32
Christo's Palace	Greek/pizza	★★★	$8–$25
Exit Glacier Salmon Bake	seafood	★★★	$9–$19
Ray's Waterfront	fusion/seafood	★★★★	$9–$34
Resurrect Art Coffee House Gallery	espresso	★★★	$2–$6
Resurrection Roadhouse	fusion/pizza	★★★★	$6–$19
Sue's Teriyaki Kitchen	Asian	★★★	$5–$16

NAME	CUISINE	FOOD QUALITY	COST
SURROUNDING AREAS			
Eagle's Crest/Kenai Princess Lodge	fusion	★★★★	$9–$31
Tito's Discovery Cafe	American	★★★	$6–$15
WHITTIER			
China Sea Restaurant	Chinese/Korean	★★	$5–$14
Frankie's Deli	sandwiches	★★	$5–$10
The Inn at Whittier	fusion	★★★★	$8–$29
Lazy Otter Café and Gifts	American	★★★	$5–$9
Sportsmen Inn Restaurant/Bar	American/diner	★★	$4–$21
VALDEZ			
Alaska's Bistro	Mediterranean	★★★★	$7–$34
Ernesto's Taqueria	Mexican	★★★	$5–$17
Fu Kung Chinese Restaurant	Chinese	★★	$7–$15
Mike's Palace	Greek/Italian/ Tex-Mex	★★	$6–$24
Pipeline Inn Club	surf 'n' turf	★★★	$8–$28
The Rose Cache	fancy lunch	★★★★	$9–$16
CORDOVA			
Baja Taco	Tex-Mex	★★★	$5–$12
Killer Whale Café	casual	★★★	$5–$10
Powder House	American/ sushi	★★★★	$6–$19
Reluctant Fisherman Inn	casual	★★★★	$6–$18
KODIAK ISLAND			
The Chart Room	fusion	★★★★	$9–$29
Eagle's Nest Restaurant	fusion	★★★★	$9–$29
Galley Gourmet	cruise	★★★★	$75–$105
Henry's Great Alaskan Restaurant	American/seafood	★★★	$5–$19
Mill Bay Coffee and Pastries	bakery	★★★★	$2–$9
The Old Powerhouse Restaurant	Japanese	★★★★	$7–$29
Second Floor Japanese Restaurant	Japanese	★★★	$7–$26

- **The Chart Room** At the end of Homer Spit Road, at Land's End Resort; ☎ 907-235-0400 or 800-478-0400; **www.lands-end-resort.com**

  FUSION QUALITY ★★★★ $9–$35 SUITABLE FOR KIDS? Y

  The Land's End resort is a top destination for Alaskans who want to get away to Homer for the weekend. The food at the Chart Room is delicious (the Sunday brunch will fill you up for the entire day), and an extensive wine list accompanies the dinner menu.

- **Duncan House Diner** 125 East Pioneer Avenue; ☎ 907-235-5344

  DINER QUALITY ★★★ $4–$9 SUITABLE FOR KIDS? Y

  The best place to go for diner food or a filling breakfast. The service is fast, the food is good, and the place is packed with locals.

- **Fat Olives** 276 Ohlson Lane; ☎ 907-235-8488

  CASUAL QUALITY ★★★★ $8–$18 SUITABLE FOR KIDS? Y

  The place has awesome wines and beers, and although the pizzas are popular, don't overlook the other offerings, including pasta.

- **Fresh Sourdough Express Bakery** 1316 Ocean Drive; ☎ 907-235-7571

  CASUAL QUALITY ★★★★ $8–$15 SUITABLE FOR KIDS? Y

  The place attracts tourists, but even locals will admit the food is incredible, balancing healthful, delicious, and affordable perfectly. The salad and soup selections are diverse, and the spinach-and-cheese croissant is something to return for over and over. The prices are outstanding, considering what other restaurants charge for similar meals.

- **Homestead Restaurant** Mile 8.2 East End Road; ☎ 907-235-8723; **www.homesteadrestaurant.net**

  FUSION QUALITY ★★★★ $13–$39 SUITABLE FOR KIDS? N

  This restaurant has withstood the test of time, which shows that quality works. It has been a mainstay in Homer for more than ten years and has a faithful following of folks who appreciate fine food and are willing to drive out East End Road to get it. Everything in Homer is casual, and if you walk in after a week of backpacking in most places, no one would bat an eye. Here, though, we'd suggest you at least shower first. Nationally recognized for its wine selection.

- **Mermaid Café** At the Old Inlet Bookshop, 3487 Main Street; ☎ 907-235-7984

  CASUAL QUALITY ★★★ $4–$10 SUITABLE FOR KIDS? Y

  Offering used, rare, and out-of-print books, this is a place that you can get lost in. The cafe is attached, and there is a bed-and-breakfast upstairs for those who can't pull themselves away from the books or food.

- **The Rookery Restaurant** At the Resort at Otter Cove, across Kachemak Bay, Homer; ☎ 800-426-6212 or 907-235-7770

  FUSION/SEAFOOD QUALITY ★★★★ $9–$29 SUITABLE FOR KIDS? N

  Here's a newer option for across-the-bay dining, with the same special-event feel offered by The Saltry and the *Danny J* Dinner Cruise (see next listing).

Leave from Homer aboard the resort's boat for a tour across the water. Eat lunch or dinner at The Rookery, selecting from such items as seafood étouffée or salmon shark or smoked-clam chowder; $55 for the lunch cruise (including meal). The dinner cruise is $20 per person, not counting the meal, which is about $25 per person. We recommend the Sunday-night sushi specials.

- **The Saltry Restaurant** On the boardwalk in Halibut Cove, across Kachemak Bay, Homer; ☎ 907-296-2223 or 907-235-7487

  FUSION QUALITY ★★★★★ $8–$24 SUITABLE FOR KIDS? N

  The food is as fresh as possible, the fish is pulled from local waters, and the vegetables come from the garden patch behind the restaurant. Take the *Danny J* Dinner Cruise across the bay and make a night of it (the rate is cheaper than the day cruise). Central Charters does the booking (☎ 800-478-7847 or 907-235-7847; **www.centralcharter.com**). The round-trip boat ride is $25. Meals are extra; about $60 for a couple is average.

- **Two Sisters Bakery** 106 West Bunnell Street; ☎ 907-235-2280

  BAKERY QUALITY ★★★ $4–$12 SUITABLE FOR KIDS? N

  A very hip, very small cafe and bakery offering creative meals for a lot less than the more touristy spots on the spit.

Seward

- **Bakery at the Harbor** 1210 Fourth Avenue; ☎ 907-224-6091

  BAKERY QUALITY ★★★ $2–$7 SUITABLE FOR KIDS? Y

  Featuring basic but tasty baked goods. Caters to tourists.

- **Chinooks Waterfront Restaurant** 1404 Fourth Avenue, on the waterfront; ☎ 907-224-2207; **www.chinookswaterfront.com**

  FUSION/SEAFOOD QUALITY ★★★ $7–$32 SUITABLE FOR KIDS? Y

  A new and direct competitor to longtime favorite Ray's Waterfront (bottom). Menu features seafood, steaks, and pastas, all innovatively prepared.

- **Christo's Palace** 133 Fourth Avenue, across the Sealife Center; ☎ 907-224-5255

  GREEK/PIZZA QUALITY ★★★ $9–$25 SUITABLE FOR KIDS? N

  This is one we haven't been to but have heard only good things about. The dining room is quite beautiful and richly decorated, and the antique bar is a local conversation piece. The pizzas are a favorite.

- **Exit Glacier Salmon Bake and Cabins** ¼ Mile Exit Glacier Road; ☎ 907-224-2204; **www.sewardalaskacabins.com**

  SEAFOOD QUALITY ★★★ $9–$19 SUITABLE FOR KIDS? Y

  A local outfitter turned us on to this eatery, featuring delicious halibut, snapper, and salmon, as well as other meats and veggies. The microbrew selection from Alaska's best breweries is much appreciated.

- **Ray's Waterfront** 1316 Fourth Avenue, on the waterfront; ☎ 907-224-5606

  FUSION/SEAFOOD QUALITY ★★★★ $9–$34 SUITABLE FOR KIDS? Y

A perennial favorite featuring seafood, steaks, and a nice wine-and-beer list. It gets packed in the summer, and for good reason.

- **Resurrect Art Coffee House Gallery** 320 Third Avenue; ☎ 907-224-7161

ESPRESSO QUALITY ★★★ $2–$6 SUITABLE FOR KIDS? Y

The name is a mouthful, but the coffee and snacks in this renovated church are wonderful, and the antique tables are fun for just sitting and relaxing. Local artwork is on display here, and local performances are often held (call ahead to find out their schedule).

- **Resurrection Roadhouse** ⅔ Mile Exit Glacier Road; ☎ 907-224-7116

FUSION/PIZZA QUALITY ★★★★ $6–$19 SUITABLE FOR KIDS? Y

The hand-tossed gourmet pizzas are the locals' favorite here, but the restaurant is only open seasonally. The view out the windows and the big, chunky tables and chairs make for a nice dining experience. They also carry a good selection of Alaskan microbrewed beer.

- **Sue's Teriyaki Kitchen** 303 South Harbor; ☎ 907-224-4593

ASIAN QUALITY ★★★ $5–$16 SUITABLE FOR KIDS? Y

From the outside the place doesn't look all that remarkable, but Sue's does a good job with basic Asian food, and the limited sushi menu is surprisingly yummy.

Surrounding Areas

- **Eagle's Crest/Kenai Princess Lodge** In Cooper Landing; ☎ 800-426-0500; **www.princesslodges.com/kenai_lodge.cfm**

FUSION QUALITY ★★★★ $9–$31 SUITABLE FOR KIDS? N

This beautiful log lodge also features Eagle's Crest Restaurant, which offers fine dining in a setting of wooded trees and the Kenai River. There's also an espresso bar in the hotel for those needing a midday pick-me-up.

- **Tito's Discovery Café** In Hope at the end of the Hope Highway; ☎ 907-782-3274

AMERICAN QUALITY ★★★ $6–$15 SUITABLE FOR KIDS? N

The new rebuilt Tito's features the same great food that Alaskans loved at the old, historic Tito's that burned down in 1999. Featuring pies, soups, and chili—all homemade, of course.

PRINCE WILLIAM SOUND

Whittier

- **China Sea Restaurant** ☎ 907-472-2222

CHINESE/KOREAN QUALITY ★★ $5–$14 SUITABLE FOR KIDS? Y

Basic Chinese and Korean food, served in plain but clean surroundings on the water.

- **Frankie's Deli** ☎ 907-472-2477

SANDWICHES QUALITY ★★ $5–$10 SUITABLE FOR KIDS? Y

A good place to stop for a quick lunch. Serves sandwiches and other fast fare.

- **The Inn at Whittier** ☎ 907-472-7000; www.innatwhittier.com

FUSION QUALITY ★★★★ $8–$29 SUITABLE FOR KIDS? N

The newest and really the only fine-dining option in this tiny community. The menu ranges from stuffed halibut to sesame-crusted salmon to filet mignon.

- **Lazy Otter Cafe and Gifts** ☎ 800-587-6887, 907-472-6887, or 907-694-6887; www.lazyotter.com

AMERICAN QUALITY ★★★ $5–$9 SUITABLE FOR KIDS? Y

Our fave snack place in Whittier, serving espresso and baked goods.

- **Sportsmen Inn Restaurant/Bar** In the Anchor Inn, off the waterfront, near the residential area; ☎ 877-870-8787 or 907-472-2354; www.anchorinnwhittier.com

AMERICAN/DINER QUALITY ★★ $4–$21 SUITABLE FOR KIDS? Y

The building's not much to look at, and the inside isn't that fancy either, with Formica tables and vinyl-covered chairs. But it's a local hangout where you can learn more about this tiny community. They serve breakfast, lunch, and dinner, with a diner-style menu ranging from eggs to halibut fish-and-chips to burgers to steaks.

Valdez

- **Alaska's Bistro** At the Valdez Harbor Inn, 100 Fidalgo Drive; ☎ 907-835-5688; www.alaskasbistro.com

MEDITERRANEAN QUALITY ★★★★ $7–$34 SUITABLE FOR KIDS? N

A fine-dining experience overlooking the water. A blend of Mediterranean and American dishes and an impressive wine list. Meals range from seafood paella to shrimp and scallops livornese.

- **Ernesto's Taqueria** 328 Egan Drive; ☎ 877-835-2800 or 907-835-2519

MEXICAN QUALITY ★★★ $5–$17 SUITABLE FOR KIDS? Y

Delicious fresh guacamole and even Mexican-inspired breakfasts. The prices are reasonable, too.

- **Fu Kung Chinese Restaurant** 207 Kobuk Avenue; ☎ 907-835-5255

CHINESE QUALITY ★★ $7–$15 SUITABLE FOR KIDS? Y

This Chinese restaurant also dabbles in sushi and other Asian dishes. Apparently, they do it successfully, because the restaurant is large and always bustling.

- **Mike's Palace** 201 North Harbor Drive; ☎ 907-835-2365

GREEK/ITALIAN/TEX-MEX QUALITY ★★ $6–$24 SUITABLE FOR KIDS? Y

Restaurants that serve wildly different types of ethnic food on the same menu are something you'll see a lot of in small-town Alaska. Take Mike's Palace, which offers an interesting combo of Greek, Italian, and south-of-the-border fare. The menu offers basic burgers, calzones, and pizza. You also can get quesadillas, burritos, or a full steak dinner. There's a wide selection of Italian pasta dishes on the dinner menu.

- **Pipeline Inn Club** 112 Egan Drive; ☎ 907-835-4444

  SURF 'N' TURF QUALITY ★★★ $8–$28 SUITABLE FOR KIDS? N

  An exclusive and dimly lit restaurant that specializes in steak and seafood. You feel like you should be in the Mafia when you enter the place, but the service and food are excellent.

- **The Rose Cache** 321 Egan Drive, in the Main Street Plaza; ☎ 907-835-8383

  FANCY LUNCH QUALITY ★★★★ $9–$16 SUITABLE FOR KIDS? N

  Another fine-dining option in town, although this one is open for lunch only. The ornately decorated restaurant serves such specialties as spicy chicken salad, quiche, a soup of the day, and baked macaroni and cheese the way your mother made it. Seatings between 11 a.m. and 1:30 p.m. only, and reservations are recommended.

Cordova

- **Baja Taco** At New Harbor, downtown; ☎ 907-424-5599 or 907-424-7141

  TEX-MEX QUALITY ★★★ $5–$12 SUITABLE FOR KIDS? Y

  Offering local seafood with Mexican style served out of a red bus, with the menu scrawled on a surfboard. Because it's so close to the harbor and ocean and you can eat outside, the fish tacos seem to taste even better!

- **Killer Whale Café** 507 First Avenue, in the back of Orca Book and Sound Co.; ☎ 907-424-7733

  CASUAL QUALITY ★★★ $5–$10 SUITABLE FOR KIDS? N

  This bookstore-cafe features organic foods, lots of vegetarian choices, and wonderful espresso. It can get busy, and the prices are higher than other choices in town. But you get what you pay for, right?

- **Powder House** Mile 2.1 Copper River Highway; ☎ 907-424-3529

  AMERICAN/SUSHI QUALITY ★★★★ $6–$19 SUITABLE FOR KIDS? Y

  The restaurant features homemade soups, sandwiches, and sushi, as well as fresh fish in season. Dining on the deck is delicious.

- **Reluctant Fisherman Inn** 407 Railroad Avenue; ☎ 907-424-3272; **www.cordovalighthouseinn.com**

  CASUAL QUALITY ★★★★ $6–$18 SUITABLE FOR KIDS? Y

  Our favorite choice for eating because the atmosphere is nice and the prawns and fish and chips are made spot-on every time.

Kodiak Island

Kodiak has several wonderful eating options, including fresh, organic food, island-roasted coffee, sushi, fine-dining, and local favorites such as beer-battered halibut and pizza. Here are our favorites.

- **The Chart Room** In the Best Western Kodiak Inn; ☎ 888-563-4254 or 907-486-5712

  FUSION QUALITY ★★★★ $9–$29 SUITABLE FOR KIDS? Y

  The food is well prepared, with a wide selection of modern, innovative seafood and meat dishes, as well as several vegetarian options. The downtown location is a plus.

- **Eagle's Nest Restaurant** In the former Buskin River Inn, now the Comfort Inn Kodiak; ☎ 800-544-2202 or 907-487-2700

  FUSION QUALITY ★★★★ $9–$29 SUITABLE FOR KIDS? Y

  A local favorite for fine dining, despite owner changes. Features an extensive wine-and-spirits list.

- **Galley Gourmet** ☎ 800-253-6331 or 907-486-5079; **www.kodiak-alaska-dinner-cruises.com**

  CRUISE QUALITY ★★★★ $95–$120 SUITABLE FOR KIDS? N

  Now *here's* a way to enjoy dinner. Kodiak residents Marty and Marion Owen offer wonderful onboard dinner cruises that explore the island while enjoying exquisite meals provided by Mill Bay Coffee and Pastries' award-winning French chef Joel Chenet (go two listings down for more on Chenet's wonderful cafe). This outing gets our number-one vote.

- **Henry's Great Alaskan Restaurant** 512 Marine Way; ☎ 907-486-8844

  AMERICAN/SEAFOOD QUALITY ★★★ $5–$19 SUITABLE FOR KIDS? Y

  The beer-battered halibut at this downtown institution is a favorite, and the bar is a hopping place on weekends.

- **Mill Bay Coffee and Pastries** 3833 Rezanof Drive; ☎ 907-486-4411; **www.millbaycoffee.com**

  BAKERY QUALITY ★★★★ $2–$9 SUITABLE FOR KIDS? Y

  French-born Martine and Joel Chenet own this superb pastry shop. They roast their own coffee, and Joel creates works of art with pastries and other sweets. Trained in Paris, he is an award-winning spinner of sugar. Not to be missed—we mean it!

- **The Old Powerhouse Restaurant** 516 East Marine Way, down by the water, near the bridge; ☎ 907-481-1088

  JAPANESE QUALITY ★★★★ $7–$29 SUITABLE FOR KIDS? N

  "The Old Powerhouse" might not be the most appropriate name for a restaurant that specializes in Japanese and wonderful sushi, but we love this place just the same. It is indeed housed in a renovated powerhouse, yet it's so much more. The view over the water is wonderful, too—sit at the tables and watch sea lions swim by.

- **Second Floor Japanese Restaurant** 116 West Rezanof Drive, right downtown, across from Alaska Commercial Co.; ☎ 907-486-8555

  JAPANESE QUALITY ★★★ $7–$26 SUITABLE FOR KIDS? Y

  While the atmosphere is not as nice as the Old Powerhouse's, the sushi and sashimi selections are more diverse and less expensive.

ON *the* TOWN: *What to Do after the Outdoor Adventure*

SOUTHCENTRAL COASTAL ALASKA IS A FUNNY PLACE. There's so much happening in the great outdoors that in some of the smaller communities you might not be able to find much to do that doesn't involve hiking, biking, or paddling somewhere. In some of the larger communities, such as Soldotna and Homer, there is enough to keep one busy day and night, whether it's fishing for halibut or fishing for a hot date at the next bar stool.

We've included some of our favorite by-day or by-night things to do in these towns. The pickings get slim in the more remote communities, but don't worry: there's enough outdoors to keep anyone busy.

KENAI PENINSULA

Kenai

- **The Backdoor Lounge** In the Uptown Motel, 47 Spur View Drive; ☎ 800-777-3650 or 907-283-3660
  The pub is a popular spot among locals, with a nice ornate wood bar and an old-timey cash register that looks too fancy to actually use. Features lots of TVs for watching sports; pool tables; and complimentary hors d'oeuvres.
- **Challenger Learning Center of Alaska** 9711 Kenai Spur Highway; ☎ 907-283-2000; **www.akchallenger.org**
  It may seem oddly out of place among all the Alaskan-themed visitor attractions, but the Challenger Learning Center of Alaska is the 39th in a worldwide network of Challenger Centers. These are basically living laboratories for youngsters to learn more about space exploration and the value of math and science, but adults will be mesmerized, too. You can even get a ride in a spaceship simulator.
- **Kenai Fine Arts Center** In Old Town, 810 Cook Avenue; ☎ 907-283-7040
  This aging building provides studio space for members of the Peninsula Art Guild and the Kenai Potters Guild. There are monthly art exhibitions, and an artist sales gallery.
- **Kenai Landing** 2101 Bowpicker Lane, Kenai; ☎ 907-335-2500; **www.kenailanding.com**
  This newly renovated cannery houses a restaurant, lodging, a museum (in the works), arts, and entertainment.
- **Kenai Visitors and Cultural Center** 11471 Kenai Spur Highway; ☎ 907-283-1991
  The center was built to celebrate Kenai's 200th anniversary and houses museum displays and exhibits, original and traveling art exhibitions, and all sorts of cultural and natural-history programs. Learn more about the Athabascan, Aleut, and Russian cultures, homesteading, mining, commercial fishing, and the oil industry. The natural-history displays are particularly interesting for children. Admission is $3.

- **Old Town Kenai Tour**
  This is an easy self-guided endeavor; check at the cultural center for details. The city's Russian heritage can be seen here as you walk by the Holy Assumption of the Virgin Mary Russian Orthodox Church, behind the cultural center. The nearby St. Nicholas Chapel is equally as pretty but in a more rustic manner. Fort Kenay is the log structure built during the 1967 Alaska Purchase centennial to commemorate the original Army fort that was there in the late 1800s. Beluga Lookout, at the end of Main Street, is also worth seeing, if only for the commanding view.
- **Peninsula Oilers Baseball** ☎ 907-283-7133; **www.oilersbaseball.com**
  Take in a baseball game if the team happens to be playing while you're in town. The Peninsula Oilers are three-time national champions in their minor-league division.
- **Veronica's Coffee House** 1506 Tyoyn Way, Historic Old Town Kenai, across from the Russian Church; ☎ 907-283-2725
  This funky cafe features live entertainment Thursdays, Fridays, and Saturdays in a laid-back atmosphere. It's also a teen magnet.

Soldotna

- **BJ's** ☎ 907-262-1882
  BJ's is the bar of choice in Soldotna and fills with locals and visitors, young and old. Come as you are; it'll be a blast. Pool, darts, sports on the TV. Local entertainer Hobo Jim plays there almost every weekend.
- **Decanter Inn** ☎ 907-262-5917
  A Kasilof favorite with dim lighting and you-never-know-what playing on the jukebox. Lodging is available if you end up needing it; $85 for singles.
- **Go Kart Race Track** Off Funny River Road; ☎ 907-262-1562
  Have a go at outmaneuvering your friends.
- **Homestead Museum** In Centennial Park; ☎ 907-262-3832
  Wander through the six-acre park and take a look at some of these historic homesteaders' cabins that have been relocated. No fee, but donations are encouraged.

Homer

Homer is a happening place, and for those who enjoy nightlife, we have a few must-visits for you to check off your list:

- **Alaska Islands and Ocean Visitor Center** 95 Sterling Highway; ☎ 907-235-6961 or 907-226-4624; **www.islandsandocean.org**
  Learn more about the Alaska Maritime National Wildlife Refuge, Kachemak Bay, and other protected waters in Alaska at this very comprehensive and nicely designed visitor center.
- **Alice's Champagne Palace** 195 Pioneer Avenue; ☎ 907-235-0630
  This is for the rock 'n' roll crowd, with lots of movement going on; open until 5 a.m. for insomniacs.
- **Bayside Lounge** On Pioneer Avenue
  This joint offers up country music for those who like a twang in their nightlife.

- **Bear Creek Winery** On Bear Creek Drive, off East End Road; ☎ 907-235-8484; **www.bearcreekwineryalaska.com**
  Take a drive out to this gorgeous winery if only to see how beautiful it is. Wine tastings are held daily in the summer.
- **Beluga Lake Lodge** 204 Ocean Drive; ☎ 907-235-5995
  Features live entertainment on the weekends.
- **Bunnell Street Gallery** 106 West Bunnell Street; ☎ 907-235-2662; **www.bunnellstreetgallery.org**
  A cross-section of Homer and Alaska artwork is on display here, with shows being held regularly. Concerts, readings, and workshops are also featured.
- **Carl E. Wynn Nature Center** East Hill to East Skyline, drive 1.5 miles; ☎ 907-235-6667; **www.akcoastalstudies.org**
  This tucked-away nature center is a great place to explore the meadows above Homer. Wildflower walks are held in the summer.
- **Center for Alaskan Coastal Studies** ☎ 907-235-6667; **www.akcoastalstudies.org**
  The organization offers natural-history tours across the bay. They are fully guided and a good way to learn more about the flora and fauna of Homer.
- **Duggan's Waterfront Irish Pub** 120 West Bunnell Street; ☎ 907-235-9949
  This is fast becoming the place to be on the weekends.
- **Homer Brewing Company** 1411 Lake Shore Drive; ☎ 907-235-3626
  Stop by this out-of-the-way microbrewery for a sampling of some of Alaska's finest microbrew. Buy a growler of your favorite flavor, and take it to the beach for a bonfire—that's the best nightlife of all.
- **Homer Family Theatre** On Pioneer Avenue; ☎ 907-235-6728
  The small theater shows movies, sometimes double features, in a fun environment. A perk: they sell snacks that are a cut above the bulk junk food you find at most movie houses.
- **Kenai Peninsula Orchestra** 315 West Pioneer Avenue; ☎ 907-235-4899; **www.kpoalaska.org** The group often performs publicly. Check ahead of time to see if you can catch a performance.
- **Pier One Theatre** On the Homer Spit; ☎ 907-235-7333; **www.pieronetheatre.org**
  Local live theater during the summer on weekends. General admission is $17. Families pay $50.
- **Pratt Museum** 3779 Bartlett Street; ☎ 907-235-8635; **www.prattmuseum.org**
  This is an excellent museum of natural history with permanent native Alaskan displays and lots of remnants from the early Homer pioneers. Look for the ship-model display, too, which the kids love. Admission is $6 for adults (and worth it).
- **Salty Dawg Saloon** On the Homer Spit; ☎ 907-235-6718
  A historic monument with wood shavings on the floor. You'll see rugged types ranging from outdoors preps to grizzled fishermen. It would be a crime to visit Homer and not at least set foot into the place.

Seward

- **Seward Museum** 336 Third Avenue; ☎ 907-224-3902
  The museum has an interesting mix of Iditarod memorabilia, state and U.S. flag tidbits, and all sorts of military information. Admission is $4.
- **Alaska SeaLife Center** 301 Railway Avenue; ☎ 800-224-2525 or 907-224-6300; **www.alaskasealife.org**
  This state-of-the-art research and education facility takes care of injured or orphaned sea animals with the goal of releasing them back into the wild. Meanwhile, we as visitors get to see them up close. Woody the sea lion is an unbelievably playful creature, for instance, and seems to enjoy it when children walk up to his giant see-through water world. Admission is $15 adults, $12 for youth. It's an excellent destination for children.
- **Explore Exit Glacier** Reached by Exit Glacier Road just outside of town; information is available at Kenai Fjords National Park Service visitor center; ☎ 907-224-2131; **www.nps.gov/kefj**
  This is one of the few places where you can actually approach the glacier on foot. Beware, though: the glaciers do calve and can injure or even kill you if the ice lands on you. Stay on marked trails and use common sense.
- **Godwin Glacier Dog Sled Tour** ☎ 888-989-8239 or 907-224-8239; **www.alaskadogsled.com**
  Because the Iditarod Trail originally started in Seward, you may get the urge to hop on a dogsled and go for a ride. For this tour, you fly on a helicopter to Godwin Glacier and ride in a real sled. Or you could go to Iditarod Sled Dog race winner Mitch Seavey's kennel and do an IdidaRide (Mile 1.1 Old Exit Glacier Road; ☎ 800-478-3139 or 907-224-8607; **www.ididaride.com**), a dog-lot tour and cart ride. Godwin Glacier is $430; IdidaRide is $59.
- **Local Watering Holes** Yukon Bar (Fourth Avenue and Washington Street; ☎ 907-224-3063) and the seedier Pioneer Bar (406 Washington; ☎ 907-224-3161)
- **New Seward Hotel and Saloon** 209 Fifth Avenue; ☎ 907-224-3095
  This bar is popular not only among the younger folks but among those who love oysters. The oyster bar is a great place to enjoy fresh shellfish while washing it down with a cold one.

PRINCE WILLIAM SOUND

Whittier

- **The Anchor Inn** Off the waterfront, near the residential area; ☎ 877-870-8787 or 907-472-2354; **www.anchorinnwhittier.com**
  The inn has an attached restaurant-bar that also features nightly entertainment in the summers. It's not New York City (or even Fargo, North Dakota), but people seem to have a great time.

Valdez

In Valdez, there are a couple of options for day cruising for wildlife and glacier viewing. We like **Stan Stephens Wildlife and Glacier Cruises**

(☎ 866-867-1297; **www.stanstephenscruises.com**) because Stephens has been in the business long enough to know the sound intimately. Children are welcome, and the food onboard is delicious. The other companies seem a bit stuffy by comparison.

- **Local Watering Holes** (Contact information below)
  There is no shortage of bars in Valdez, but a few of the ones we like include the **Pipeline Club** (112 Egan Drive; ☎ 907-835-4332), which is a bit on the upscale end but has a friendly crowd; the **Egan Street Pub** (210 Egan Drive; ☎ 907-835-3545); and the **Wheelhouse Lounge** at the Valdez Harbor Inn (100 Fidalgo Street; ☎ 907-835-5688).
- **Maxine and Jesse Whitney Museum** At the Valdez airport; ☎ 907-834-1690
  Featuring an impressive—and completely donated—collection of Eskimo artifacts, animal mounts, a native kayak, and more. Prince William Sound Community College is the official curator, but the location at the airport makes it convenient for everyone. Admission is $5.
- **Valdez Museum and Historical Archive** 217 Egan Drive; ☎ 907-835-2764; **www.valdezmuseum.org**
  Featuring local history exhibits, with information on native culture, the gold rush, Richardson Highway, and the oil spill. Admission is $5 for adults.

Cordova

- **Alaskan Hotel and Bar** On First Street downtown; ☎ 907-424-3299
  The bar is your typical place until its Wednesday wine tastings take place in the early-evening hours. Belly up to the bar in your Carhartts and make way for some fine vino.
- **Cordova Arts Walks**
  These community events take place the first Wednesday of the month during the summer. Area businesses featuring Alaska artwork host salmon samples, and street musicians play fun music.
- **Cordova Historical Museum** At the south end of First Street; ☎ 907-424-6665
  The cultural heritage of the Chugach, Eyak, and Tlingit peoples is highlighted at the museum. It also has coverage of the *Exxon Valdez* oil spill, which decimated much of the sea life in Prince William Sound in 1989 and still is affecting the ecosystem today. The museum is open daily in the summer.
- **Powder House** Mile 2.1 Copper River Highway; ☎ 907-424-3529
  The bar is a nice place to grab a bite and enjoy some drinks with friends. They feature bluegrass, country, folk, and even karaoke, to be enjoyed on the deck overlooking Eyak Lake.

KODIAK ISLAND

- **Alutiiq Museum & Archaeological Repository** 215 Mission Road, Suite 101; ☎ 907-486-7004; **www.alutiiqmuseum.com**
  Explore 7,500 years of Kodiak native history at this interesting museum. Usually closed on Sundays. Admission is $3 for adults.

- **Baranov Museum–Kodiak Historical Society** 101 Marine Way; ☎ 907-486-5920; **www.baranov.us**
  This museum, located in the renovated Erskine House, focuses on the Russian influence of Kodiak Island but also has plenty of cultural and natural artifacts from the Alutiiq peoples. Admission is $3 for adults.
- **Kodiak Alutiiq Dancers** 713 Rezanof Street; ☎ 907-486-4449
  This talented group performs daily in the summer, telling stories through music and drumming. Performances are at 2:30 p.m. in a *barabara*, the traditional Alutiiq dwelling.
- **Kodiak Island Winery** 38057 Chiniak Highway; ☎ 907-486-4848; **www.kodiakwinery.com**
  Wine tours are from 1 p.m. to 5 p.m. daily. Take a cab. The price is steep to get there, but worth it if you want to enjoy lots of wine. Or just sip and spit, like the connoisseurs do.
- **Kodiak Launch Complex** Mile 15.2 Pasagshak Bay Road; take the Chiniak Highway to its intersection with the Pasagshak Bay Road; the complex is on the left side
  A $38 million low-Earth-orbit launch facility on 27 acres was recently completed at Cape Narrow. It is operated by the Alaska Aerospace Development Corporation, and is the only commercial launch range in the United States that is not colocated with a federal facility. You can't go inside the center, and security is pretty tight, but you can drive by just to say you've seen it. Occasionally there will be public events; check at the visitor center for possibilities.
- **The Mecca Bar** 302 West Marine Way; ☎ 907-486-3364
  The dancing, drinking, and meeting place in Kodiak—the local saying is that you haven't experienced Kodiak until you've been "Mecca-nized." But don't expect anything fancy—this is a fishing town, after all. There are two bars, a dance floor, and live music on the weekends. Clientele runs the gamut.
- **Village Bar** On the mall in downtown Kodiak; ☎ 907-486-3412
  A cowboy's hangout, although there are wine nights and other special events, as well as big screen TVs for sports lovers.

PART TWENTY-ONE

SOUTHEAST ALASKA

Home of Glaciers and Whales

An **OVERVIEW** *of the* **INSIDE PASSAGE**

ON A MAP, SOUTHEAST ALASKA looks like an afterthought, following the spine of British Columbia like a long, skinny snake. It's easy to wonder why it's even part of Alaska. The narrow, island-studded strip of land seems almost inconsequential. (See Part One, page 12, for a map of the region.)

Of course, that is the furthest thing from the truth. The fact is, Southeast Alaska—or the Panhandle as it is often called—has some of the most stunning scenery in the state. It has more than 1,000 islands, all of them surrounded by or filled with waterfalls, streams, rivers, and oceans that create lush old-growth forests. The snow-covered mountains and seemingly infinite number of glaciers is the backdrop to it all.

Southeast is a land of culture and history, too. It is home to the Tlingit, Haida, and Tsimshian native peoples who made Southeast Alaska their home before the United States even existed. Their artwork is incredible, with totem poles and carvings that depict a way of life that is centered on their connections with the land and animals of the area.

The Panhandle's turn-of-the-century gold-rush history lives on as well. In communities such as Skagway and Juneau, there are many ways to learn more about the stampede for gold that turned this sleepy sliver of land into a boomtown almost overnight. Museums, businesses, even entire national parks are devoted to preserving that history, and today's visitor has easy access to it.

About three-fourths of the 500-mile-long Southeast region is part of **Tongass National Forest,** so there is no shortage of land to explore. Southeast is one of the premier spots for water sports such as kayaking and rafting. Backpackers will like some of its historic trails, as well as the trailless adventures that can be had from just about any mountaintop location.

And then there is the **Inside Passage,** the destination of most Alaska adventure cruises available to today's traveler. The Inside Passage is the sheltered seawater that surrounds the Panhandle, providing excellent protected-water adventures for cruise ships, kayaks, and even the occasional rowboat.

The communities that make up the Panhandle are as varied as the scenery, but one thing you will notice immediately is how friendly everyone is. Southeastern Alaskans long ago discovered that one of their greatest assets is their land—the glaciers and whales and mountains that lure so many visitors this far north in the first place. Tourism has become one of the primary industries for the area, and the people know that visitors are their livelihood.

Southeast Alaska's climate is a bit rainier than the rest of the state's, and it often is fogged in or experiences days on end of drizzle and dampness. The temperatures are warmer, too, and when the rest of the state is getting snow, Southeast Alaska often just gets more rain. Take one look at a cascading waterfall or behemoth Sitka spruce and you'll see it is this rainy climate that gives the area such beauty.

This chapter focuses on the largest communities through which you may travel while headed for your ultimate outdoor destination. These are the places where you can gear up and move out, but surprisingly, many of them have amenities that rival anything found in cities with millions of people. We have created subchapters for **Haines, Skagway, Juneau** (Alaska's capital), **Sitka,** and **Ketchikan.**

HAINES

Haines Convention and Visitors Bureau
P.O. Box 530
Haines 99827
☎ 907-766-2234
www.haines.ak.us

HAINES IS ONE OF ONLY TWO SOUTHEAST communities accessible by road. From the Alaska Highway, the northbound traveler can turn onto the Haines Highway and reach a community that has a reputation as one of the driest in the region. At the northern end of America's longest fjord, Haines shares a border with 20 million acres of protected wilderness. It is located on the western shore of **Lynn Canal,** between the **Chilkoot and Chilkat rivers.**

Haines is 80 air miles northwest of Juneau, and 600 air miles southeast of Anchorage and Fairbanks. By road, it is 775 miles from Anchorage. It also can be reached by marine ferry. It has cool maritime summers, with temperatures in the 60°F range, and mild winters. Total precipitation averages 52 inches a year, with 133 inches of snowfall.

The community is home to about 1,500 year-round residents and more wildlife than you can count. Whales are common, and bald eagles flock here by the thousands. In fact, Haines is home to one of

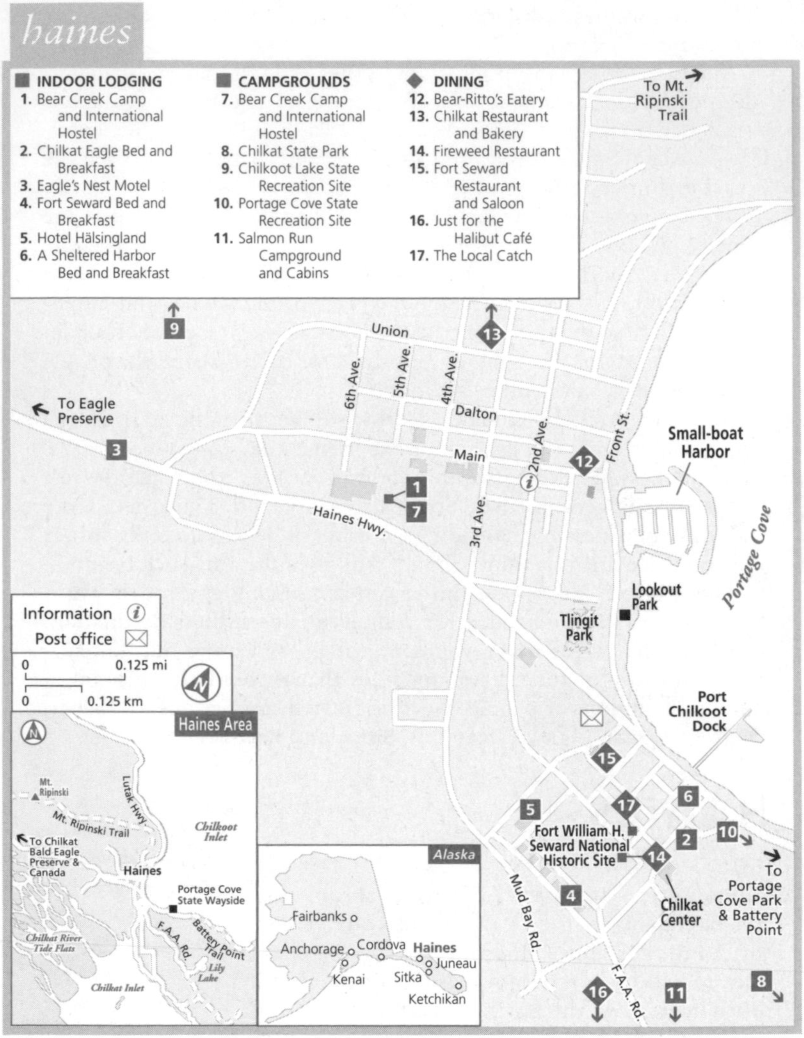

the largest bald-eagle congregations in the world, and each fall the entire town turns out to celebrate the arrival of the birds there to follow the late salmon runs of November.

Haines was at one time called *Dei Shu* ("end of the trail") by the Tlingit. The first nonnative to settle here was trader George Dickinson, who came to the area in 1880. In 1881, a Presbyterian minister

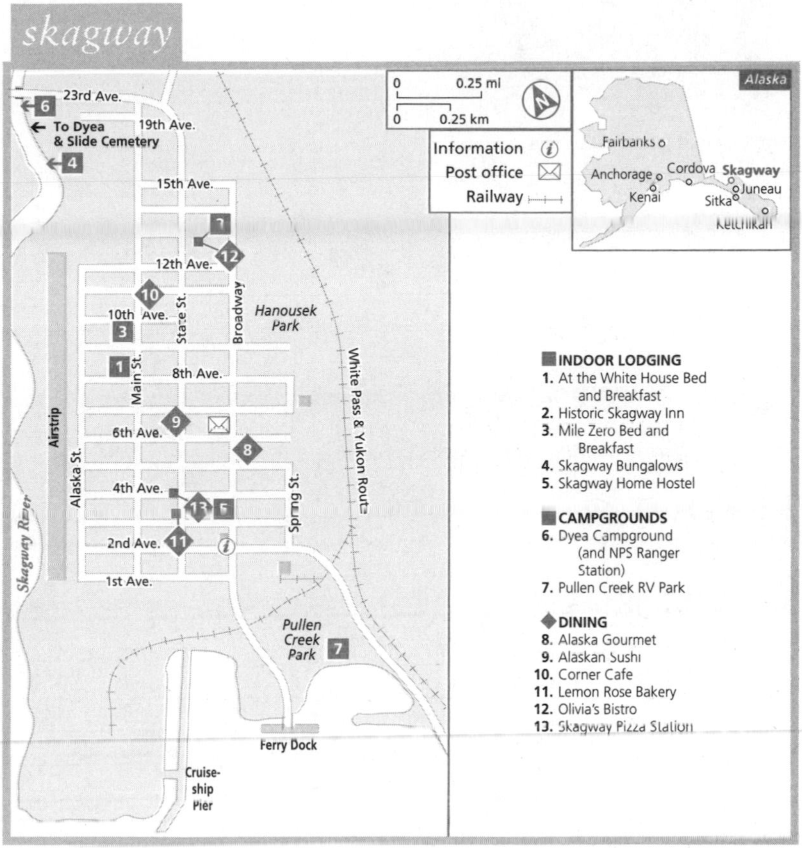

received permission from the Chilkat Tlingits to build a mission and school, which eventually was named Haines in honor of Francina Electra Haines, a woman active in the Presbyterian Women's Executive Society of Home Missions. As the area became more and more developed with nonnative people, the name Haines stuck.

Haines has a military background, too. The first permanent U.S. military installation, Fort William H. Seward, was constructed in 1904, and in 1910 the city was incorporated. Until World War II, it was the only U.S. Army post in Alaska.

Commercial fishing, timber, government, and tourism are the primary employers. Around 45,000 cruise-ship passengers visit every year. The **Chilkat Bald Eagle Preserve** also draws visitors from around the world.

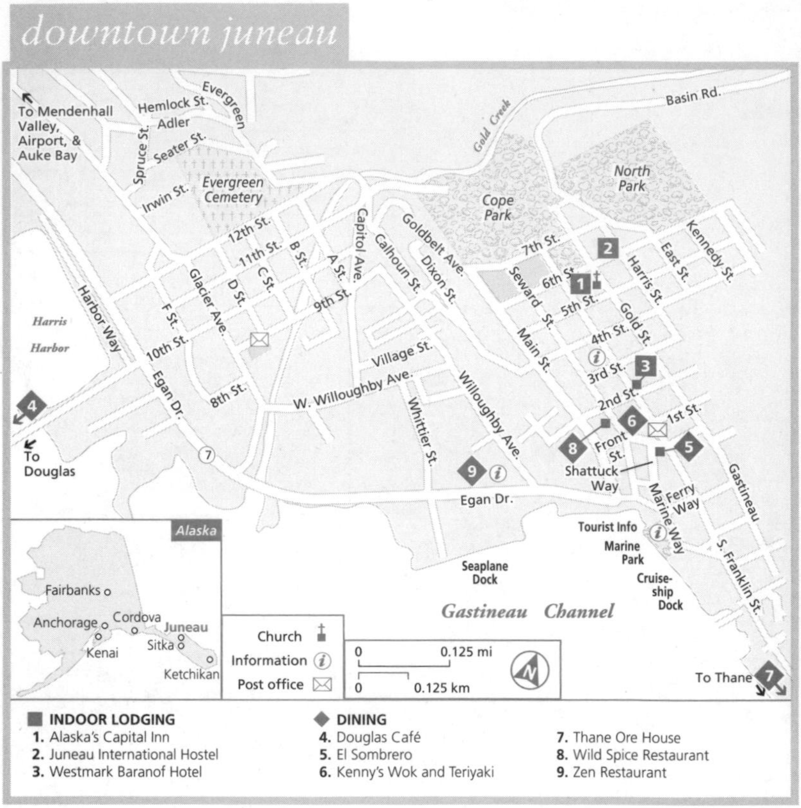

SKAGWAY

SKAGWAY IS 90 MILES NORTHEAST of Juneau at the northernmost end of **Lynn Canal,** and the only other Southeast Alaska community that is accessible by road. Take the Klondike Highway from the Alaska Highway, and you will land in this tiny town whose identity is entirely consumed with its rich gold-rush past. You can also reach Skagway by air or marine ferry and cruise ship.

Skagway Convention & Visitors Bureau
P.O. Box 1029
Skagway 99840
☎ 907-983-2854
www.skagway.com

The climate is pleasant in Skagway, with cool summers and mild winters. The average temperature in the summer rarely rises above 65°F, and in the winter there are many days above freezing. With the surrounding mountains as a shroud, the area is also protected from the frequent Southeast rains, so Skagway, like Haines, gets below-average rainfall—averaging 26 inches of precipitation per year, along with 39 inches of snow.

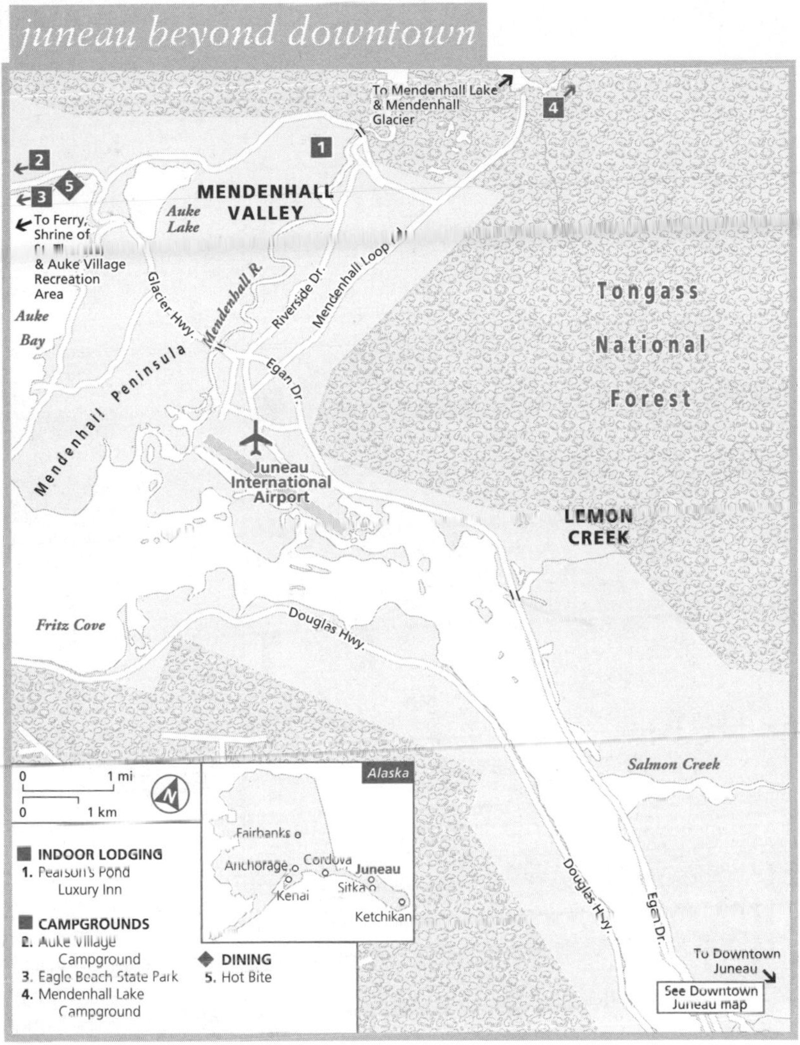

The town is small, with only 850 year-round residents, most of whom make their living through tourism. In fact, much of the town today makes up what is part of **Klondike Gold Rush National Historical Park.** In 1898, when gold was first discovered in the area, the town ballooned with nearly 20,000 would-be prospectors. Many of them were earnest, working hard and finding their gold. Others were up to no good, wreaking havoc wherever they went and turning Skagway into a lawless place.

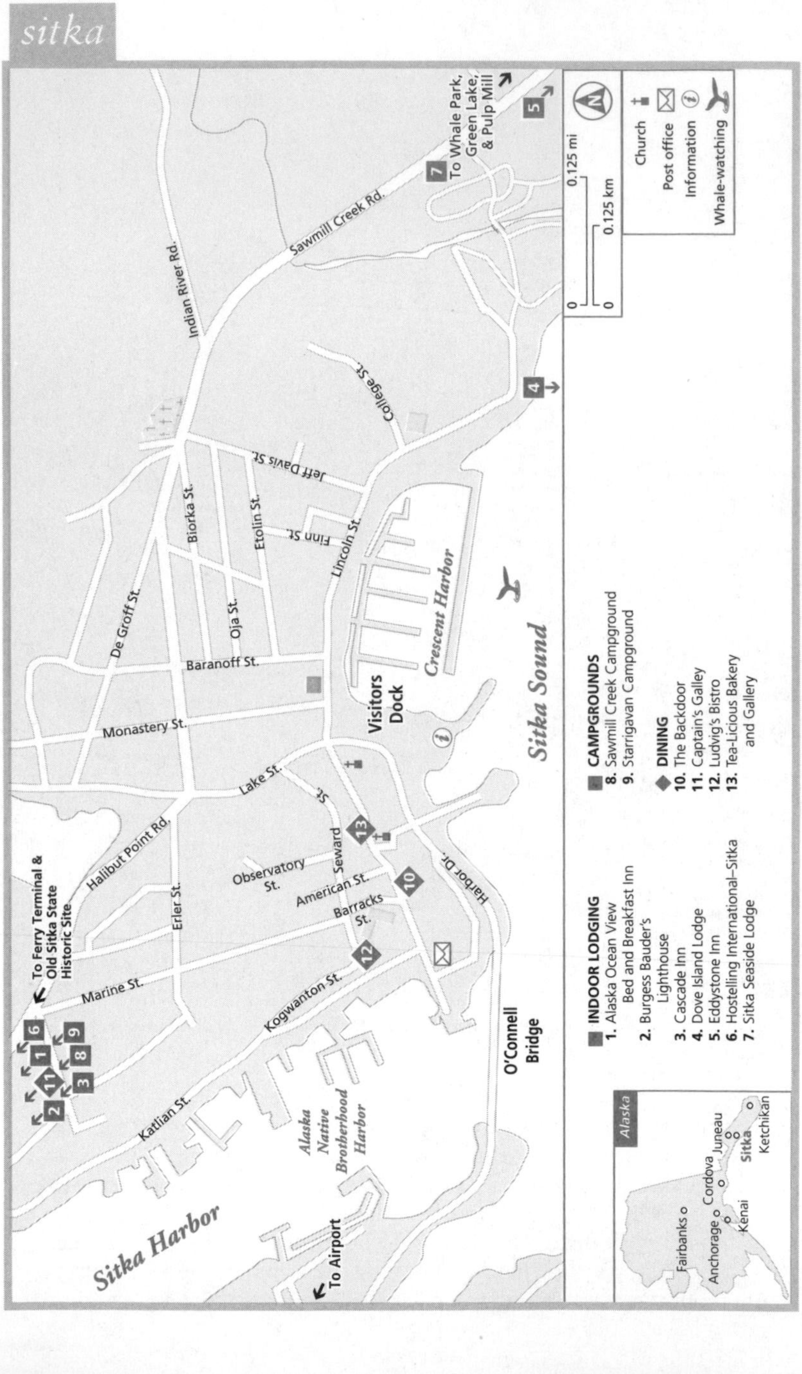
sitka
INDOOR LODGING
1. Alaska Ocean View Bed and Breakfast Inn
2. Burgess Bauder's Lighthouse
3. Cascade Inn
4. Dove Island Lodge
5. Eddystone Inn
6. Hostelling International–Sitka
7. Sitka Seaside Lodge
CAMPGROUNDS
8. Sawmill Creek Campground
9. Starrigavan Campground
DINING
10. The Backdoor
11. Captain's Galley
12. Ludvig's Bistro
13. Tea-Licious Bakery and Gallery
Church
Post office
Information
Whale-watching
0.125 mi
0.125 km
To Whale Park, Green Lake, & Pulp Mill
To Ferry Terminal & Old Sitka State Historic Site
To Airport
Sitka Harbor
Sitka Sound
Crescent Harbor
Alaska Native Brotherhood Harbor
Visitors Dock
O'Connell Bridge
Sawmill Creek Rd.
Indian River Rd.
College St.
Jeff Davis St.
Biorka St.
Etolin St.
Finn St.
Lincoln St.
De Groff St.
Oja St.
Baranoff St.
Monastery St.
Lake St.
Seward St.
Halibut Point Rd.
Observatory St.
American St.
Barracks St.
Harbor Dr.
Erler St.
Marine St.
Kogwanton St.
Katlian St.
Alaska
Fairbanks
Anchorage
Cordova
Kenai
Juneau
Sitka
Ketchikan

ketchikan

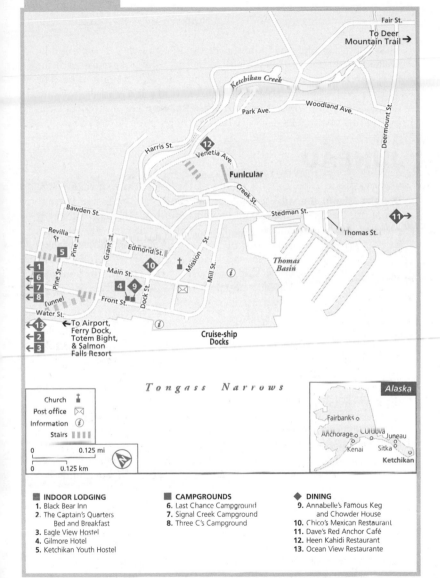

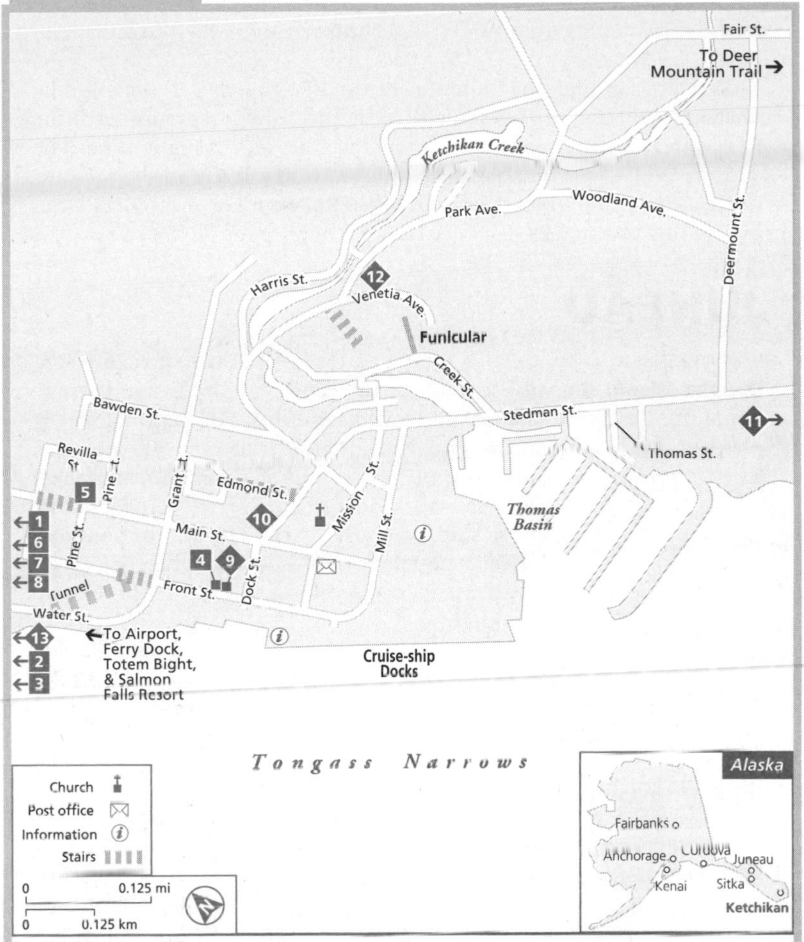

■ INDOOR LODGING

1. Black Bear Inn
2. The Captain's Quarters Bed and Breakfast
3. Eagle View Hostel
4. Gilmore Hotel
5. Ketchikan Youth Hostel

■ CAMPGROUNDS

6. Last Chance Campground
7. Signal Creek Campground
8. Three C's Campground

◆ DINING

9. Annabelle's Famous Keg and Chowder House
10. Chico's Mexican Restaurant
11. Dave's Red Anchor Café
12. Heen Kahidi Restaurant
13. Ocean View Restaurante

Those days were short-lived. After the gold disappeared, the town shrunk to its original, smaller size, and that's what visitors get to appreciate today. The smaller population is much more conducive to the surrounding area, and a perfect place from which to launch an outdoor adventure.

Primary among the outdoor lures of Skagway is the 33-mile **Chilkoot Trail,** one of two trails used by the gold seekers to reach the headwaters of the **Yukon River,** where the gold was thought to be. The 40-mile **White Pass Trail** began at Skagway and paralleled the present-day route of the **White Pass** and **Yukon Railway.** For more details on hiking this trail, go to Part Six, Backpacking (page 82).

JUNEAU

LOCATED ON THE MAINLAND OF SOUTHEAST ALASKA, opposite **Douglas Island,** Juneau was built at the center of the Inside Passage along the **Gastineau Channel** and is the capital of Alaska (many people mistakenly assume that it is Anchorage). Juneau is 900 air miles northwest of Seattle and 577 air miles southeast of Anchorage. Most people arrive here by plane, cruise ship, or marine ferry. During the summer, Juneau's population of 31,000 doubles as cruise-ship passengers disembark to explore this city by the water.

Juneau Convention and Visitors Bureau
1 Sealaska Plaza, Suite 305
Juneau 99801-1245
☎ 907-586-1737
www.traveljuneau.com

And it is a beautiful city. **Mendenhall Glacier, Juneau Ice Field, Tracy Arm Fjord Glacier,** the **Alaska State Museum,** and the **Mount Roberts Tramway** are among the local attractions. There are plenty of hiking and birding opportunities to be found. The fishing is incredible. Outdoor travelers will especially like the kayaking options.

Juneau has mild but often wet weather, which is the norm for most of this region. The average summer temperature ranges from 45°F to 65°F, although most days it is closer to 60°F. In the winter, the mercury stays around 25°F to 35°F. Annual precipitation is 92 inches in downtown Juneau, and 54 inches ten miles north at the airport. Snowfall averages 101 inches.

Tlingit Indians were the first known inhabitants of Juneau, and the area was a good source of harvesting salmon. By the late 1800s, as fortune seekers discovered Alaska's wealth of gold, Juneau became yet another gold-rush town. In 1900, the city of Juneau was formed, named for one of those prospectors. At the time, Sitka was the capital of the territory of Alaska, but by 1906, officials moved it to the more bustling Juneau, where active mining was going on.

Today, government is the heart of Juneau, and when the legislature is in session between January and May, the population increases. Tourism also is a major employer, adding about 2,000 seasonal jobs to the area. Nearly 700,000 visitors arrive by cruise ship, and another 100,000 independent travelers visit Juneau each year.

SITKA

SITKA IS ON THE WEST COAST of Baranof Island along the Pacific Ocean on **Sitka Sound.** Its most noticeable natural feature is **Mount Edgecumbe**, an extinct volcano rising some 3,200 feet above the community. It is 95 air miles southwest of Juneau, and 185 miles northwest of Ketchikan. Seattle is 862 air miles to the south. Visitors to Alaska often comment that Sitka is the prettiest town of all, and we tend to agree that it is indeed beautiful. Of all the towns in Southeast Alaska, we think Sitka is the most picturesque, although outdoor opportunities are more abundant in such places as Skagway and Haines.

Sitka Convention and Visitors Bureau
P.O. Box 1226, Sitka 99835
☎ 907-747-5940
www.sitka.org

Sitka temperatures are a bit cooler than the rest of Southeast Alaska, with winter temperatures dipping into the teens sometimes. In the summer, the temperature range is 48°F to 61°F. Average annual precipitation is 96 inches, including 39 inches of snowfall.

About 8,800 people call Sitka home year-round. This historic community originally was inhabited by a major tribe of Tlingits, who called the village "Shee Atika." It was discovered by the Russian Vitus Bering's expedition in 1741, and the site became New Archangel in 1799. A tumultuous few years followed as the Russians fought for power and the Tlingits fought to keep their land. By 1808, Sitka was the capital of Russian Alaska, and it remained the center of trade and commerce for years. After the United States purchased Alaska in 1867, Sitka remained the capital of the territory until 1906, when the seat of government was moved to Juneau.

Sitka's economy centers on fishing, fish processing, and tourism. Cruise ships bring more than 200,000 visitors annually. Access to the area is by cruise ship, marine ferry, or airlines. The local airport offers daily jet service from the lower 48 states and the rest of Alaska.

KETCHIKAN

KETCHIKAN IS ON THE SOUTHWESTERN COAST of **Revillagigedo Island,** opposite Gravina Island, near the southern boundary of Alaska. It is 679 miles north of Seattle and 235 miles south of Juneau. Many call Ketchikan the "Gateway to Alaska" because it often is the first port of call for cruise ships coming from the south.

Ketchikan Convention and Visitors Bureau
131 Front Street
Ketchikan 99901
☎ 907-225-6166
www.visit-ketchikan.com

The 2.2-million-acre **Misty Fjords National Monument** is the highlight of the Ketchikan area, and it attracts kayakers by the hundreds. But there also are numerous other outdoor activities to pursue, including hiking, fishing, birding, and canoeing.

The area lies in the maritime climate zone and enjoys warmer-than-average winters than its neighbors, with temperatures above freezing for much of the winter. Summer temperatures are in the 50°F-to-65°F range. The area gets lots of rain, though, with an average of 162 inches of precipitation annually, including 32 inches of snowfall.

unofficial **TIP**
Backpacking in Glacier Bay requires a backcountry permit and orientation. This park, like Denali National Park and Preserve, limits its backcountry visitors to maintain the wild feel of the area. The best way to see the park, however, is by kayak or boat.

Ketchikan's population is about 7,600. The town's name comes from the Tlingit word *kitschk-hin,* meaning "thundering wings of an eagle." Fishing and fish processing is indeed one of the mainstays of the local economy, as is timber harvesting, which peaked in the late 1980s and 1990s before declining sharply. Ketchikan's pulp mill closed in 1997, after its 50-year contract with the U.S. Forest Service for timber was canceled.

Tourism is important to Ketchikan, with more than 650,000 cruise-ship passengers visiting the area each summer. Another half-million independent travelers come to the town, as well. It is the ideal jumping-off point for such trips as mountain biking on **Prince of Wales Island,** backpacking in Misty Fjords, or kayaking in the Inside Passage.

Regular jet service comes and goes from Ketchikan daily. Access also is via **Alaska Marine Highway** ferry and cruise ship.

WILD LANDS

GLACIER BAY NATIONAL PARK AND PRESERVE

(Primary activities: cruising, kayaking, rafting, mountaineering)

GLACIER BAY NATIONAL PARK AND PRESERVE has snow-covered mountain ranges rising to more than 15,000 feet, coastal beaches with protected coves, deep fjords, tidewater glaciers, coastal waters, and freshwater lakes. It is the ideal place to visit for paddlers. **Alaska Airlines** provides daily jet service from Seattle via Juneau during the summer, and a more limited schedule in the winter. Air taxis in the outlying communities also can take you to the park. There is a passenger ferry to the town of **Gustavus,** but there's no way to bring your own vehicle to the

Glacier Bay National Park and Preserve
P.O. Box 140
Gustavus 99826-0140
☎ 907-697-2230
www.nps.gov/glba

area. A private car-rental operation in Gustavus and a few taxis can get you where you need to go (visit **www.nps.gov/glba** for details). Otherwise, most lodge and B&B owners provide transportation from the airport to your lodging.

TONGASS NATIONAL FOREST

(Primary activities: bear viewing, fishing)

Tongass National Forest
Federal Building
648 Mission Street
Ketchikan 99901
☎ 907-225-3101
www.fs.fed.us/r10/tongass

TONGASS NATIONAL FOREST, at nearly 17 million acres, is the largest unit in the national-forest system, and recreation opportunities abound here. Mountain biking, backpacking, hiking, fishing, and birding are all popular activities within the forest.

Access to the forest is available from just about every community in Southeast Alaska, but as with most areas here, you'll probably need to fly in to get where you want to go. The Tongass is one of only two national forests in the country you can't drive to. You can, however, take your vehicle to **Haines** or **Skagway,** get on the **Alaska Marine Highway** ferry, and head to **Ketchikan** or **Juneau. Alaska Airlines** provides daily jet service into the major towns of the Panhandle—Ketchikan, Sitka, and Juneau. From there, charter flights on smaller planes are available to the other towns as well as to remote cabins and lakes.

About 150 cabins are scattered throughout Tongass National Forest. They cost $25 to $45 a night and make a great base camp for any outdoor adventure within the area. For specific details on reserving the cabins, go to the special-interest chapters to explore each activity individually.

MISTY FJORDS NATIONAL MONUMENT

(Primary activities: hiking, kayaking, fishing)

Misty Fjords National Monument
3031 Tongass Avenue
Ketchikan 99901
☎ 907-225-2148
www.fs.fed.us/r10/tongass

THE REMOTE MISTY FJORDS National Monument covers about 3,570 square miles of land and coastal habitat, including several major rivers and hundreds of streams. The monument is part of Tongass National Forest and managed as such. It is located in the southernmost part of the region, from **Dixon Entrance** to beyond the **Unuk River.** The closest community is Ketchikan.

CHILKAT BALD EAGLE PRESERVE–ALASKA STATE PARKS

(Primary activities: birding, fishing, kayaking, rafting)

Alaska State Parks
Haines Ranger Station
P.O. Box 430
Haines 99827
☎ 907-766-2292
www.dnr.state.ak.us/parks/units/eagleprv.htm

THE CHILKAT BALD EAGLE PRESERVE was created in 1982 to protect the world's largest concentration of bald eagles and their habitat. It also protects the natural salmon runs that pass through each year. The preserve consists of 48,000 acres of river bottom land of the **Chilkat, Kleheni, and Tsirku rivers** and is an excellent place for water sports. Birders by the thousands flock to the area in the fall to watch the eagles during spawning season.

The preserve is accessible by road along the Haines Highway, or travelers can reach the area by flying directly into Haines and driving the road from town. Birding must be done from a distance.

Klondike Gold Rush National Historical Park
Second Avenue and Broadway Street
P.O. Box 517
Skagway 99840
☎ 907-983-2921 or 907-983-2921
www.nps.gov/klgo

KLONDIKE GOLD RUSH NATIONAL HISTORICAL PARK

(Primary activities: backpacking, camping, hiking)

Klondike Gold Rush National Historical Park exists to celebrate the Klondike gold rush of 1897 to 1898. It has 15 restored buildings within the Skagway Historic District and also manages the well-known **Chilkoot Trail,** which prospectors followed to reach the gold fields. The park also administers a small portion of the **White Pass Trail.**

unofficial **TIP**
Hiking the Chilkoot Trail, which travels through Klondike Gold Rush National Historic Park into Canada, requires permits and fees. Have your passport ready too.

About 843,000 visitors came to the 13,000-acre national park last year, mostly by means of cruise ships that offload thousands of passengers at a time into the tiny community of Skagway. You can also fly into Skagway from Juneau or take the South Klondike Highway from Whitehorse, Yukon Territory, into town.

GETTING *around* SOUTHEAST ALASKA

HAINES

ACCESS IS THROUGH **Alaska Airlines** (☎ 800-252-7522; **www.alaskaair.com**) by air and **Alaska Marine Highway** ferry (☎ 800-642-0066; **www.ferryalaska.com**) by water. You can also drive to Haines from Canada by taking the Haines Highway off the Alaska Highway.

AFFORDABLE CARS Located in the Captain's Choice Motel, Second Avenue and Dalton Street. Cars are $75 a day, with unlimited mileage. ☎ 800-478-2345 or 907-766-3111; **www.capchoice.com.**

EAGLE'S NEST CAR RENTAL Located at Eagle's Nest Motel, Mile 1 Haines Highway. Cars start at $49 a day, with 100 free miles (40 cents a mile after that). ☎ 800-354-6009 or 907-766-2891; **www.alaskaeagletours.com/carrental.htm.**

SKAGWAY

ACCESS IS THROUGH **Alaska Airlines** (☎ 800-252-7522; **www.alaska air.com**) by air or **Alaska Marine Highway** ferry (☎ 800-642-0066; **www.ferryalaska.com**) by water. You can also get to Skagway by taking the Klondike Highway off the Alaska Highway.

MUNICIPAL BUS SERVICE Skagway Municipal and Regional Transit, 1325 State Street; ☎ 907-983-2743 or 907-723-3536; **www.skagway transit.com;** $1.50 to get around town.

DYEA DAVE'S SHUTTLE AND TOURS Open seasonally, this outfit can deliver you where you need to go; ☎ 907-209-5031.

AVIS RENT A CAR Third Avenue, in the Westmark Hotel. Rates start at $65. ☎ 800-331-1212 or 907-983-2247; **www.avis.com.**

SOURDOUGH VEHICLE & BICYCLE RENTALS 351 Sixth Avenue. This is our choice because they are family-owned and rent vehicles that can handle the roads; rates are $60 to $114 a day. ☎ 907-983-2523 or 907-209-5026; **www.geocities.com/sourdoughcarrentals.**

JUNEAU

ACCESS IS THROUGH **Alaska Airlines** (☎ 800-252-7522; **www.alaska air.com**) by air or **Alaska Marine Highway** ferry (☎ 800-642-0066; **www.ferryalaska.com**) by water.

KIPCO AUTO RENTAL Located at the Juneau airport. This is a good choice for travelers needing vans or larger-capacity vehicles; ☎ 907-796-2880.

BUDGET RENT-A-CAR Located at the Juneau Airport. An affordable choice for vehicles with unlimited miles; ☎ 800-796-1086.

HERTZ RENT A CAR Located at the Juneau Airport; ☎ 907-789-9494; **www.hertz.com.**

EVERGREEN TAXI For around-town destinations; ☎ 907-586-2121.

SITKA

ACCESS IS THROUGH **Alaska Airlines** (☎ 800-252-7522; **www.alaska air.com**) by air or **Alaska Marine Highway** ferry (☎ 800-642-0066; **www.ferryalaska.com**) by water.

NORTH STAR RENT-A-CAR Located at the Sitka airport; ☎ 800-722-6927 or 907-966-2552.

AIRPORT SHUTTLE Provides transportation to the downtown area or to any accommodations during the summer only. Rate is $6 one-way, $8 round-trip; ☎ 907-747-8443.

FERRY SHUTTLE Available at the terminal upon all ferry arrivals. Rate is $5 one-way, $7 round-trip; ☎ 907-747-8443.

HANK'S TAXI & TOUR SERVICE We like Hank because he's smoke-free! ☎ 907-747-8888; **www.hankstours.com.**

TRANSIT SHUTTLE The shuttle makes regular passes through town, stopping at all the highlights. Get on and drop off as often as you wish. $10 for an all-day pass or $5 for a round-trip; ☎ 907-747-7290.

YELLOW JERSEY CYCLE SHOP Located at 805 Halibut Point Road. If you want to get around by bike, try this shop, which rents by the day or week. ☎ 907-747-6317; **yellowj@ptialaska.net.**

KETCHIKAN

ACCESS IS THROUGH **Alaska Airlines** (☎ 800-252-7522; **www.alaskaair.com**) by air or **Alaska Marine Highway** ferry (☎ 800-642-0066; **www.ferryalaska.com**) by water.

KETCHIKAN GATEWAY BOROUGH TRANSIT (☎ 907-225-8726) operates seven days a week. Fares start at $1; buses run hourly.

GEARING UP

MOST OF THE LARGER COMMUNITIES of Southeast Alaska have places to resupply or buy gear that you may have forgotten.

Grocery stores in the area are surprisingly well stocked, and fresh food is readily available. Note, however, that you may not have such luck if you travel beyond the major towns covered in this chapter.

Check with the air carriers on which you will be traveling for regulations on carrying items such as knives, guns, camp stoves, and camp fuel. Many airlines no longer even allow lighters on board, so these are items you may need to purchase at your destination and leave behind when flying home.

unofficial **TIP**
When shopping for food in Southeast Alaska, be prepared to pay higher-than-average prices, especially on perishable items such as milk, vegetables, and fruits.

This section of the book is broken down by the main communities in Southeast with shops that will help you find what you're looking for. We list sporting goods/camping supplies and groceries separately, but many stores carry a little of everything—a characteristic of Alaska stores that you will soon notice is commonplace.

SPORTING GOODS AND CAMPING SUPPLIES

Haines

- **Alaska Backcountry Outfitter Store** Main Street; ☎ 907-766-2876
  Offers skiing, snowboard, camping, and climbing gear.
- **Outfitter Sporting Goods** Mile 0, Haines Highway; ☎ 907-767-3221
  Hiking, camping, and climbing gear; hunting and fishing supplies, too.

Skagway

- **The Mountain Shop** 355 Fourth Avenue, ☎ 907-983-2544; **www.packerexpeditions.com**

Gear shop operated by adventure-travel outfitter Packer Adventures; sells apparel, camping supplies, and sporting goods.

- **Sockeye Cycle Co.** 381 Fifth Avenue, ☎ 907-983-2851; **www.cyclealaska.com**
  Offers bike repairs and supplies.

Juneau

- **Alaska Paddle Sports** 800 Sixth Street; ☎ 907-463-5678
  For paddling gear and accessories.
- **Foggy Mountain Shop** 800 Sixth Street; ☎ 907-586-6780
  For backpacking, mountaineering, and skiing.
- **Fred Meyer** 8181 Old Glacier Highway; ☎ 800-478-9944 or 907-789-6500
  Sells camping equipment, sporting goods, fishing licenses, and full-service groceries.
- **Juneau Flyfishing Goods** 175 South Franklin Street, Floor 2; ☎ 907-586-3754
  Fishing gear and licenses are available here.
- **Mountain Gears** 126 Front Street; ☎ 907-586-4327
  Outdoor gear and bike supplies.
- **Nugget Alaskan Outfitter** 8745 Glacier Highway; ☎ 907-789-0956; **www.nuggetoutfitter.com**
  Outdoor clothing, footwear, and rain gear.

Sitka

- **Baidarka Boats** 201 Lincoln Street, Suite 201; ☎ 907-747-8996
- **Mac's Sporting Goods** 213 Harbor Drive; ☎ 907-747-6970
- **Murray Pacific Supply** 475 Katlian Street; ☎ 907-747-3171
- **Work & Rugged Gear Store** 407 Lincoln Street, Suite F; ☎ 907-747-6238
  Outerwear and footwear for those often rainy days.
- **Yellow Jersey Cycle Shop** 805 Halibut Point Road; ☎ 907-747-6317; **yellowj@ptialaska.net**

Ketchikan

- **Alaska Wilderness Outfitting** 3857 Fairview Avenue; ☎ 907-225-7335
- **Bob's Guns and Sporting Goods** 685 Pond Reef Road North; ☎ 907-247-8139
- **Murray Pacific Supply** 1050 Water Street; ☎ 907-225-3135
- **The Outfitter** 201 Dock Street; ☎ 907-225-5101
- **Plaza Sports** 2415 Hemlock Avenue; Suite 1110; ☎ 907-225-1587

GROCERY

Haines

- **Alaska Meat & Grocery** 420 Main Street; ☎ 907-766-2441
  Full-service grocery store.

- **Howsers IGA** 335 Main Street; ☎ 907-766-2040
  Full-service grocery store.
- **Mountain Market & Mountain Spirits** 289 Third Avenue and Haines Highway; ☎ 907-766-3340
  Specializing in natural foods, beer, wine, and spirits.

Skagway

- **Fairway Market** 377 State Street; ☎ 907-983-2220
  Full-service groceries.
- **You Say Tomato** 872 State Street; ☎ 907-983-2784
  Open year-round; more-specialized and organic groceries.

Juneau

- **Carrs Quality Center** 3033 Vintage Boulevard; ☎ 907-790-5500
  Offering full-service groceries; fishing licenses, and some camping and fishing gear.
- **Costco Wholesale** 5225 Commercial Boulevard; ☎ 888-556-4333 or 907-780-6740
  Offering bulk groceries, some camping and sporting goods, depending upon supplies. Entrance requires membership.
- **Fred Meyer** 8181 Old Glacier Highway; ☎ 800-478-9944 or 907-789-6500
  Offering camping equipment, sporting goods, fishing licenses, and full-service groceries.

Sitka

- **Cascade Convenience Center** 2035 Halibut Point Road; ☎ 907-747-8313
  Small selection of groceries.
- **Lakeside Grocery** 705 Halibut Point Road; ☎ 907-747-3317
  Full-service groceries.
- **Sea Mart** 210 Baranof Street; ☎ 907-747-6686
  Full-service groceries.
- **Sea Mart** 1867 Halibut Point Road; ☎ 907-747-6266
  Full-service groceries.

Ketchikan

- **Carrs Quality Center** 2417 Tongass Avenue; ☎ 907-225-9880
- **JR's Grocery** 407 Dock Street; ☎ 907-225-7489
- **Lighthouse Grocery & Liquor** 10750 North Tongass Highway; ☎ 907-247-2626
- **Sea Mart Supermarket** 2417 Tongass Avenue; ☎ 907-225-9880
- **Tatsuda IGA** 633 Stedman Street; ☎ 907-225-4125
- **Ward Cove Market & Liquor** 7196 North Tongass Highway; ☎ 907-247-8200
- **Woodenwheel Cove Trading Post** 29 Port Protection; ☎ 907-489-2222

WHERE *to* STAY

SOUTHEAST ALASKANS KNOW WHAT the discriminating traveler likes, and you should not have a problem finding adequate lodging in most of the larger communities. Alaska as a whole seems to have many family-run operations such as bed-and-breakfasts and lodges, so don't be discouraged if the hotels are sold out. There is likely a place to stay if you look hard enough.

If you're opting for the more outdoorsy options, there also are plenty of choices. Most communities have several campgrounds, some run by the government and others privately owned. We recommend taking advantage of the **Tongass National Forest Service** cabins, which are a steal at $25 to $45 a night. However, if you need lodging close to town, you won't have that option.

In this section, we've given you our favorites—places we have tried ourselves and found to be memorable.

HAINES

Indoor Lodging

- **Bear Creek Camp and International Hostel** ☎ 907-766-2259; **www.bearcreekcabinsalaska.com**

  QUALITY ★★★★ VALUE ★★★★★ $18–$48

  This place is about a mile out of town and a good place for backpackers or those traveling on a budget. It's our top pick for the area. Plus, they treat you like an adult, with no lockouts or curfews. Choose from cabins or bunk spaces in the hostel.

- **Chilkat Eagle Bed and Breakfast** ☎ 907-766-2763; **www.eagle-bb.com**

  QUALITY ★★★★ VALUE ★★★★ $80

  Next to the Chilkat Center for the Arts and a favorite among international travelers. The owners speak six languages! Our choice for B&B lovers.

- **Eagle's Nest Motel** ☎ 800-354-6009 or 907-766-3779; **www.alaskaeagletours.com**

  QUALITY ★★ VALUE ★★★ $85–$95

  Near the center of town; not fancy but definitely affordable.

- **Fort Seward Bed and Breakfast** House Number 1 on Officer's Row; ☎ 800-615-6676 or 907-766-2856; **www.fortsewardalaska.com**

  QUALITY ★★★★ VALUE ★★★ $95–$259

  We really like this spot because of its excellent views and elegant rooms.

- **Hotel Hälsingland** ☎ 800-542-6363 or 907-766-2000; **www.hotelhalsingland.com**

  QUALITY ★★★★ VALUE ★★★★ $69–$109

  This is the tourist-oriented place to stay, but we admit it is pretty nice, and the prices are competitive with those of the less-polished places.

Southeast Alaska Indoor Lodging

NAME	TYPE(S) OF LODGING	QUALITY RATING	VALUE RATING	COST
HAINES				
Bear Creek Camp and International Hostel	hostel/ cabins	★★★★	★★★★★	$18–$48
Chilkat Eagle Bed and Breakfast	B&B	★★★★	★★★★	$80
Eagle's Nest Motel	motel	★★	★★★	$85–$95
Fort Seward Bed and Breakfast	B&B	★★★★	★★★	$95–$259
Hotel Hälsingland	hotel	★★★★	★★★	$69–$109
A Sheltered Harbor Bed and Breakfast	B&B	★★★	★★★★	$85
SKAGWAY				
At the White House Bed and Breakfast	B&B	★★★★	★★★	$120–$145
Historic Skagway Inn	inn	★★★★	★★★	$119–$189
Mile Zero Bed & Breakfast	B&B	★★★	★★★	$135
Skagway Bungalows	cabins	★★★	★★★	$99
Skagway Home Hostel	hostel	★★★	★★★★★	$15–$50
JUNEAU				
Alaska's Capital Inn	B&B	★★★★★	★★★★	$149–$279
Juneau International Hostel	hostel	★★★★	★★★★	$10

- **A Sheltered Harbor Bed and Breakfast** ☎ 907-766-2741; **www.geocities.com/asheltered**

  QUALITY ★★★ VALUE ★★★★ $85

  This one is nice because it's on the waterfront. Plus, the owners are superfriendly, and the breakfasts are hearty and filling.

Camping

- **Bear Creek Camp and International Hostel** ☎ 907-766-2259; **www.bearcreekcabinsalaska.com**

  QUALITY ★★★★ VALUE ★★★★ $12

  Good for backpackers or travelers on a budget. Our top pick in the area.

NAME	TYPE(S) OF LODGING	QUALITY RATING	VALUE RATING	COST
JUNEAU (CONTINUED)				
Pearson's Pond Luxury Inn	inn	★★★★★	★★★	$249
Westmark Baranof Hotel	hotel	★★★★	★★★	$129–$219
SITKA				
Alaska Ocean View Bed & Breakfast Inn	inn	★★★★	★★★	$89–$249
Burgess Bauder's Lighthouse	cabins	★★★	★★★★	$125
Cascade Inn	inn	★★★	★★★★	$115
Dove Island Lodge	lodge	★★★★	★★★	$85–$200
Eddystone Inn	inn	★★★	★★★★	$85–$150
Hostelling International–Sitka	hostel	★	★★★★	$19
Sitka Seaside Lodge	lodge	★★★	★★★	$1,800/ 4 nights
KETCHIKAN				
Black Bear Inn	Inn	★★★★★	★★★★	$180–$220
The Captain's Quarters Bed & Breakfast	B&B	★★★	★★★★	$100–$110
Eagle View Hostel	hostel	★★	★★	$28
Gilmore Hotel	hotel	★★★★	★★★★	$95–$145
The Ketchikan Youth Hostel	hostel	★★	★★★	$15

- **Chilkat State Park** ☎ 907-766-2292

  QUALITY ★★★★ VALUE ★★★★ $10

  Located eight miles south of Haines on Mud Bay Road. Tent and RV camping are available, and the tent sites are right on the beach. A summer host is usually on duty. Run by Alaska State Parks.

- **Chilkoot Lake State Recreation Site** Ten miles north of Haines off Lutak Road; ☎ 907-766-2292

  QUALITY ★★★ VALUE ★★★★ $10

  A decent place to pitch a tent, but we like the campgrounds at Chilkat State Park and Portage Cove better (see listings above and following). A summer host is usually on duty. This campground is also run by Alaska State Parks.

Southeast Alaska Camping

NAME	TYPE(S) OF CAMPING	QUALITY RATING	VALUE RATING	COST
HAINES				
Bear Creek Camp and International Hostel	tent	★★★★	★★★★	$12
Chilkat State Park	tent/RV	★★★★	★★★★	$10
Chilkoot Lake State Recreation Site	tent/RV	★★★	★★★★	$10
Portage Cove State Recreation Site	tent	★★★★	★★★★★	$5
Salmon Run Campground and Cabins	tent/RV	★★★★	★★★	$14–$26
SKAGWAY				
Dyea Campground	tent	★★★★	★★★★★	$6
Pullen Creek RV Park	tent/RV	★★★	★★★★	$14–$25
JUNEAU				
Auke Village Campground	tent	★★★	★★★★	$10
Eagle Beach State Park	tent/RV	★★★	★★★★★	$10
Mendenhall Lake Campground	tent/RV	★★★★	★★★	$10–$28
SITKA				
Sawmill Creek Campground	tent	★★★★	★★★★★	free
Starrigavan Campground	tent/RV	★★★	★★★	$12–$16
KETCHIKAN				
Last Chance Campground	tent/RV	★★★	★★★	$10
Signal Creek Campground	tent/RV	★★★	★★★	$10
Three C's Campground	tent/RV	★★	★★★	$10

- **Portage Cove State Recreation Site** 1 mile south of Haines on Beach Road; ☎ 907-766-2292

  QUALITY ★★★★ VALUE ★★★★★ $5

  For backpackers and cyclists only, which means you won't hear the generator buzz of recreational vehicles. Also run by Alaska State Parks.

- **Salmon Run Campground and Cabins** ☎ 907-766-3240; **www.salmonrunadventures.com**

  QUALITY ★★★★ VALUE ★★★ $14–$26

This private campground is about a mile and a half from Haines and tucked into the woods, which gives it a very private feeling.

SKAGWAY

Indoor Lodging

- **At the White House Bed and Breakfast** ☎ 907-983-9000; **www.atthewhitehouse.com**

  QUALITY ★★★★ VALUE ★★★ $120–$145

  Yes, the name might seem a little out of place in Alaska, but we like this scenic home in historic Skagway.

- **Historic Skagway Inn** At Seventh Avenue and Broadway; ☎ 888-752-4929 or 907-983-2289; **www.skagwayinn.com**

  QUALITY ★★★★ VALUE ★★★★ $119–$189

  You may not be able to resist this inn, which once was a brothel but today offers very respectable rooms. Olivia's Restaurant is inside.

- **Mile Zero Bed & Breakfast** At Ninth and Main streets; ☎ 907-983-3045; **www.mile-zero.com**

  QUALITY ★★★ VALUE ★★★ $135

  Convenient central location; great views from the deck.

- **Skagway Bungalows** Mile 1 Dyea Road; ☎ 907-983-2986; **www.aptalaska.net/~saldi**

  QUALITY ★★★ VALUE ★★★ $125

  The one-room log cabins are a bit out of town but feel secluded and rustic (although there is indoor plumbing).

- **Skagway Home Hostel** Third Avenue and Main Street; ☎ 907-983-2131; **www.skagwayhostel.com**

  QUALITY ★★★ VALUE ★★★★★ $15–$50

  The hostel is in a historic building about ten minutes from the ferry dock. It's a great gathering point for Chilkoot Trail hikers. Offers clean rooms and bunks.

Camping

- **Dyea Campground** (and NPS Ranger Station) ☎ 907-983-2921; **www.nps.gov/archive/klgo/dyea_campground.htm**

  QUALITY ★★★★ VALUE ★★★★★ $6

  We like this remote spot because the RV-ers don't come here often. Spaces are first-come, first-served.

- **Pullen Creek RV Park** ☎ 800-936-3731 or 907-983-2768; **www.pullencreekrv.com**

  QUALITY ★★★ VALUE ★★★★ $14–$25

  It's not the most remote site, but the convenient location next to the state ferry dock and right on the water makes this place the choice for the traveler in need of convenient camping.

JUNEAU

Indoor Lodging

- **Alaska's Capital Inn** ☎ 888-588-6507; **www.alaskacapitalinn.com**

  QUALITY ★★★★★ VALUE ★★★★ $149–$279

  This home, located in the historic section of Juneau, is a restored three-level mansion with rooms finely decorated in the Arts and Crafts style.

- **Juneau International Hostel** ☎ 907-586-9559; **www.juneauhostel.org**

  QUALITY ★★★★ VALUE ★★★★ $10

  We like this place in downtown Juneau for its rambling, old-time feel. It has plenty of rooms, but they fill up fast, so don't count on staying here unless you've made reservations in advance.

- **Pearson's Pond Luxury Inn** ☎ 888-658-6328 or 907-789-3772; **www.pearsonspond.com**

  QUALITY ★★★★★ VALUE ★★★ $249

  This outfit is truly luxurious, about 12 miles from downtown Juneau, close to Mendenhall Glacier. Rates are steep but include use of the spas, bikes, and rowboats. Think of these as honeymoon-level accommodations.

- **Westmark Baranof Hotel** ☎ 800-544-0970 or 907-586-2660; **www.westmarkhotels.com**

  QUALITY ★★★★ VALUE ★★★ $129–$219

  This upscale hotel attracts throngs of tourists, but it is conveniently located and usually has openings.

Camping

There are three nice public campgrounds from which to choose in the Juneau area (you won't find much in the way of private camping facilities here).

- **Auke Village Campground** Juneau Ranger District of the Tongass National Forest; ☎ 907-586-8800; **www.fs.fed.us/r10/tongass/recreation/rec_facilities/jnurec.shtml**

  QUALITY ★★★ VALUE ★★★★ $10

  Located near a scenic beach, with 12 camping sites, picnic tables, and fireplaces. A vault toilet and water faucets are available. First-come, first-served; no reservations taken. Only 1.5 miles from the ferry terminal or 15 miles on the Glacier Highway from downtown Juneau.

- **Eagle Beach State Park** A quarter-mile south of the Eagle Beach Picnic Area, at about Mile 28 of the Glacier Highway; ☎ 907-465-4563; **www.dnr.state.ak.us/parks**

  QUALITY ★★★ VALUE ★★★★ $10

  The park provides overnight parking for vehicles and tents on a gravel surface in a large open area. A park host is usually on site. Portable toilets are the only services provided.

- **Mendenhall Lake Campground** Juneau Ranger District of the Tongass National Forest; ☎ 907-586-8800; **www.fs.fed.us/r10/tongass/recreation/rec_facilities/jnurec.shtml**

  QUALITY ★★★★ VALUE ★★★ $10–$28

  On Mendenhall Lake, in view of the Mendenhall Glacier, about 13 miles from downtown Juneau. There are 68 camping sites and a separate walk-in backpacker section. Water and vault toilets throughout the campground.

SITKA

Indoor Lodging

- **Alaska Ocean View Bed & Breakfast Inn** ☎ 888-811-6870 or 907-747-8310; **www.sitka-alaska-lodging.com**

  QUALITY ★★★★ VALUE ★★★ $89–$249

  Three rooms are available in this sunny home overlooking the water. We like the owners' friendly attitude and the B&B's quick access to the rest of town.

- **Burgess Bauder's Lighthouse** ☎ 907-747-3056

  QUALITY ★★★ VALUE ★★★★ $125

  This is a different option for those handy enough to take a skiff to the island where the lighthouse is built. There are small wooden hot tubs for enjoying the night sky, a kitchen, and room enough to sleep eight. Great for families or small groups.

- **Cascade Inn** ☎ 800-532-0908 or ☎ 907-747-6804; **www.cascadeinnsitka.com**

  QUALITY ★★★ VALUE ★★★★ $115

  The inn is nothing fancy to look at, but the location is gorgeous and convenient, with private balconies and kitchenettes.

- **Dove Island Lodge** ☎ 888-318-3474, 907-747-5660, or 907-738-0856; **www.aksitkasportfishing.com**

  QUALITY ★★★★ VALUE ★★★ $85–$200

  This lodge feels like it's in the middle of nowhere even though you're really only five minutes from the Sitka harbor. Fishing and boating packages are available, and guests can rent kayaks as well. The hot tub overlooking the water looks like something out of a movie set.

- **Eddystone Inn** ☎ 907-747-3313; **www.eddystoneinn.com**

  QUALITY ★★★ VALUE ★★★★ $85–$150

  Only ten minutes from downtown, this rambling, window-filled house is on its own private peninsula perched right over the water. The owners also have a beach cottage and vacation rentals if you choose to launch a vacation straight from Sitka.

- **Hostelling International–Sitka** ☎ 907-747-8661

  QUALITY ★ VALUE ★★★★ $19

This well-known organization runs a clean hostel with dorm-style rooms in the basement of the United Methodist Church. Sleeping is on Army cots or in your own sleeping bag, which can get slightly uncomfortable.

- **Sitka Seaside Lodge** ☎ 866-747-8113; **www.sitkaseaside.com**

  QUALITY ★★★ VALUE ★★★ $1,800/4 NIGHTS

  This fairly modern lodge won't feel like the rustic log lodges that you may envision in Alaska, but its location and the stunning views of the water make you salivate to get out there and enjoy. Fishing packages are incorporated into each room rate if you wish.

Camping

The Sitka Ranger District of the Tongass National Forest operates two nice public campgrounds in the Sitka area.

- **Sawmill Creek Campground** Sitka Ranger District of the Tongass National Forest; ☎ 907-747-4216; **www.fs.fed.us/r10/tongass**

  QUALITY ★★★★ VALUE ★★★★★ FREE

  This is a rustic campground suited to backpackers and located up a steep and windy gravel road. There is no fee to camp at any of the 11 campsites.

- **Starrigavan Campground** Sitka Ranger District of the Tongass National Forest; ☎ 907-747-4216; **www.fs.fed.us/r10/tongass;** National Recreation Reservation System, ☎ 877-444-6777 or **www.recreation.gov**

  QUALITY ★★★ VALUE ★★★ $12–$16

  Located seven miles from Sitka, this campground has three loops with 35 sites. Some are better for backpackers and cyclists, while others are suited to RV drivers. Rates depend on which loop you stay in. Advance registration is accepted for a limited number of campsites, which fill up early.

KETCHIKAN

Indoor Lodging

- **Black Bear Inn** ☎ 877-225-4343; **www.stayinlalaska.com**

  QUALITY ★★★★★ VALUE ★★★★ $180–$220

  This newly constructed inn offers some great privacy and amenities such as gas fireplaces, outdoor lounging area, and soaking tubs.

- **The Captain's Quarters Bed & Breakfast** ☎ 907-225-4912; **www.ptialaska.net/~captbnb**

  QUALITY ★★★ VALUE ★★★★ $100–$110

  This custom-built home overlooks the water and has a relaxed atmosphere that makes it one of our favorite places to stay in Ketchikan. Kids aren't allowed here, however.

- **Eagle View Hostel** ☎ 907-225-5461; **www.eagleviewhostel.com**

  QUALITY ★★ VALUE ★★ $28

  Clean rooms, but the rates are a bit steep as hostels go.

- **Gilmore Hotel** ☎ 800-275-9423 or 907-225-9423; **www.gilmorehotel.com**

  QUALITY ★★★★ VALUE ★★★★ $95–$145

  Right in town but often overlooked in favor of the larger chain hotels. On the National Register of Historic Places, it shows its age, but also its charm.

- **Ketchikan Youth Hostel** ☎ 907-225-3319

  QUALITY ★★ VALUE ★★★ $15

  Your typical no-frills hostel.

Camping

The Ketchikan District of the Tongass National Forest has three nice campgrounds from which to choose.

- **Last Chance Campground** Ketchikan District of the Tongass National Forest; ☎ 907-225-3101; **www.fs.fed.us/r10/tongass;** National Recreation Reservation System, ☎ 877-444-6777 or **www.recreation.gov**

  QUALITY ★★★ VALUE ★★★ $10

  This 19-site campground is ten miles north of Ketchikan on Revilla Road. Advance reservations can be made for a limited number of sites by calling the National Recreation Reservation System. The rest of the sites are available on a first-come, first-served basis.

- **Signal Creek Campground** Ketchikan District of the Tongass National Forest; ☎ 907-225-3101; **www.fs.fed.us/r10/tongass;** National Recreation Reservation System, ☎ 877-444-6777 or **www.recreation.gov**

  QUALITY ★★★ VALUE ★★★ $10

  There are 24 units in this campground, which is part of the Ward Lake Recreation Area. Advance reservations can be made for a limited number of sites by calling the National Recreation Reservation System. The rest of the sites are available on a first-come, first-served basis.

- **Three C's Campground** Ketchikan District of the Tongass National Forest; ☎ 907-225-3101; **www.fs.fed.us/r10/tongass**

  QUALITY ★★ VALUE ★★★ $10

  This overflow campground is opened only when Signal Creek fills up. No advance reservations.

WHERE *to* EAT

HAINES

- **Bear-Ritto's Eatery** In the Bear Den Mall; ☎ 907-766-2117

  HEALTHY QUALITY ★★★★ $5–$13 SUITABLE FOR KIDS? Y

  A fine choice for those who prefer healthful eating; serves seafood with a Mexican twist.

Southeast Alaska Dining

NAME	CUISINE	FOOD QUALITY	COST
HAINES			
Bear-Ritto's Eatery	healthy	★★★★	$5–$13
Chilkat Restaurant & Bakery	cafe/bakery	★★★	$5–$11
Fort Seward Restaurant & Saloon	steak/seafood	★★★	$8–$24
Fireweed Restaurant	pizza/organic	★★★★	$8–$21
Just for the Halibut Café	seafood	★★★★	$9–$27
The Local Catch	seafood/Thai	★★★	$7–$19
SKAGWAY			
Alaska Gourmet	soups/sandwiches	★★★	$5–$9
Alaskan Sushi	sushi	★★★★	$9–$25
Corner Café	burgers/soups	★★★	$6–$12
Lemon Rose Bakery	cafe/bakery	★★★★	$4–$11
Olivia's Bistro	fusion	★★★★	$9–$30
Skagway Pizza Station	pizza	★★★	$7–$23
JUNEAU			
Douglas Café	soups/sandwiches	★★★	$5–$9
El Sombrero	Mexican	★★★	$6–$19
Hot Bite	burgers	★★★	$5–$8

- **Chilkat Restaurant & Bakery** Fifth Avenue and Dalton Street; ☎ 907-766-3653

  CAFE/BAKERY QUALITY ★★★ $5–$11 SUITABLE FOR KIDS? Y

  Open year-round for breakfast and lunch only; dinner on Fridays and Saturdays during the summer.

- **Fort Seward Restaurant & Saloon** Mile 0 Haines Highway, Fort Seward; ☎ 800-478-7772 or 907-766-2009

  STEAK/SEAFOOD QUALITY ★★★ $8–$24 SUITABLE FOR KIDS? N

  Great steak and seafood. Closed part of the winter.

- **Fireweed Restaurant** In Fort Seward off Portage Street; ☎ 907-766-3838

  PIZZA/ORGANIC QUALITY ★★★★ $8–$21 SUITABLE FOR KIDS? Y

  They use local and organic food and create some imaginative pizzas.

NAME	CUISINE	FOOD QUALITY	COST
JUNEAU (CONTINUED)			
Kenny's Wok and Teriyaki	sushi/Chinese	★★★	$6–$18
Thane Ore House and Salmon Bake	salmon	★★★★	$25
Wild Spice Restaurant	Mongolian	★★★	$8–$25
Zen Restaurant	fusion/Asian	★★★★	$9–$29
SITKA			
The Backdoor	cafe/soups	★★★	$4–$7
Captain's Galley	American	★★★	$4–$24
Ludvig's Bistro	Mediterranean	★★★★	$9–$29
Tea-Licious Bakery and Gallery	cafe	★★★	$4–$9
KETCHIKAN			
Annabelle's Famous Keg and Chowder House	American	★★★	$7–$26
Chico's Mexican Restaurant	Mexican	★★	$4–$17
Dave's Red Anchor Café	American	★★★	$5–$14
Heen Kahidi Restaurant	fusion	★★★★	$9–$31
Ocean View Restaurante	Italian	★★★	$7–$25

- **Just for the Halibut Café** At the Chilkat Cruises Dock; ☎ 907-766-3800 or 888-766-2103

  SEAFOOD QUALITY ★★★★ $9–$27 SUITABLE FOR KIDS? Y

  Superb seafood in a waterfront atmosphere.
- **The Local Catch** On Portage Street, Fort Seward; ☎ 907-766-3557.

  SEAFOOD/THAI QUALITY ★★★ $7–$19 SUITABLE FOR KIDS? Y

  Their fish tacos and Thai food are marvelous, but they're open in the summer only.

SKAGWAY

- **Alaska Gourmet** 361 Fifth Avenue; ☎ 907-983-2448; www.akgourmet.com

  SOUPS/SANDWICHES QUALITY ★★★ $5–$9 SUITABLE FOR KIDS? Y

The small shop offers breakfast sweets, soups, and sandwiches in an informal atmosphere. The espresso is delicious.

- **Alaskan Sushi** Sixth Avenue; ☎ 907-983-2644

  SUSHI QUALITY ★★★★ $9–$25 SUITABLE FOR KIDS? Y

  Opens in summer to serve raw-fish lovers on the go or in-house.

- **Corner Café** 421 State Street; ☎ 907-983-2155

  BURGERS/SOUPS QUALITY ★★★ $6–$12 SUITABLE FOR KIDS? Y

  Hamburgers and hearty soups make this a local favorite.

- **Lemon Rose Bakery** 330 Third Avenue; ☎ 907-983-3558

  BAKERY/CAFE QUALITY ★★★★ $4–$11 SUITABLE FOR KIDS? Y

  This year-round cafe is another of our favorites. The calzones are big enough to split among three people.

- **Olivia's Bistro** Seventh Avenue and Broadway Street; ☎ 907-983-2289

  FUSION QUALITY ★★★★ $9–$30 SUITABLE FOR KIDS? Y

  A true fine-dining experience where backpackers in Carhartts are welcome. Casual meets refined.

- **Skagway Pizza Station** 444 Fourth Avenue; ☎ 907-983-2200

  PIZZA QUALITY ★★★ $7–$23 SUITABLE FOR KIDS? Y

  Open year-round, this pizza shop is another local favorite.

JUNEAU

- **Douglas Café** 916 Third Street, across the bridge from Juneau; ☎ 907-364-3307

  SOUPS/SANDWICHES QUALITY ★★★ $5–$9 SUITABLE FOR KIDS? Y

  Serves some of the best chowder in the city.

- **El Sombrero** 157 South Franklin Street; ☎ 907-586-6770

  MEXICAN QUALITY ★★★ $6–$19 SUITABLE FOR KIDS? Y

  Locals' top choice for Mexican food among the several options in town.

- **Hot Bite** Outside of town at the Auke Bay dock, 13 miles from Juneau; ☎ 907-790-2483

  BURGERS QUALITY ★★★ $5–$8 SUITABLE FOR KIDS? Y

  Worth stopping at for its burgers. It's only open during the summer, however.

- **Kenny's Wok and Teriyaki** 126 Front Street; ☎ 907-586-3575

  SUSHI/CHINESE QUALITY ★★★ $6–$18 SUITABLE FOR KIDS? N

  This casual eatery can cook from either country—Japanese sushi or Chinese rice and meat dishes. Quick and friendly service right downtown.

- **Thane Ore House and Salmon Bake** 4400 Thane Road; ☎ 907-586-3442

  SALMON QUALITY ★★★ $25 SUITABLE FOR KIDS? Y

It's a bit touristy, and a few miles out of town, but on a good day, it is beautiful to sit outside and enjoy salmon fresh-caught in Alaska. Free transportation is provided with reservations.

- **Wild Spice Restaurant** 140 Seward Street; ☎ 907-523-0344

MONGOLIAN QUALITY ★★★ $8–$25 SUITABLE FOR KIDS? N

This newly opened restaurant offers fresh, fast foods cooked Mongolian-style on an open grill.

- **Zen Restaurant** 51 Egan Drive; ☎ 907-586-5075

FUSION QUALITY ★★★★ $9–$29 SUITABLE FOR KIDS? N

This place, in the Goldbelt Hotel, specializes in Asian-inspired creations of coconut shrimp, crispy duck, and lemongrass-infused fishes. The adjacent lounge features jazz music on weekends.

SITKA

- **The Backdoor** 104 Barracks Street, behind Old Harbor Bookstore; ☎ 907-747-8856

CAFE/SOUPS QUALITY ★★★ $4–$7 SUITABLE FOR KIDS? Y

A cozy, downtown coffeehouse that serves espresso, handmade bagels, pastries, pies, soups, and fresh-squeezed orange juice. It's a favorite among locals. Closed Sundays.

- **Captain's Galley** 1867 Halibut Point Road; ☎ 907-747-6266

AMERICAN QUALITY ★★★ $4–$24 SUITABLE FOR KIDS? Y

Known for its fried chicken, sold by the bucket if you like, with mashed potatoes, country gravy, and biscuits. They also make deli sandwiches, soups, salads, and pizzas, and there's limited seating with great ocean views.

- **Ludvig's Bistro** 256 Katlian Avenue; ☎ 907-966-3663

MEDITERRANEAN QUALITY ★★★★ $9–$29 SUITABLE FOR KIDS? N

Food with a Mediterranean flair, specializing in Alaska seafood and fresh-baked bread. They also operate the soup cart Ludvig's on Lincoln next to Harry Race Pharmacy. Ludvig's is a bit upscale, so reservations are recommended.

- **Tea-Licious Bakery and Gallery** 315 Lincoln Street; ☎ 907-747-4535

CAFE QUALITY ★★★ $4–$9 SUITABLE FOR KIDS? Y

A new addition to the Sitka dining scene, offering freshly baked scones, bread, cakes, imaginative salads, soups, and sandwiches.

KETCHIKAN

- **Annabelle's Famous Keg and Chowder House** 326 Front Street, off the lobby of the Gilmore Hotel; ☎ 907-225-6009

AMERICAN QUALITY ★★★ $7–$26 SUITABLE FOR KIDS? Y

A somewhat pricey menu but very good food, with lots of healthful choices.

- **Chico's Mexican Restaurant** 435 Dock Street; ☎ 907-225-2833

  MEXICAN QUALITY ★★ $4–$17 SUITABLE FOR KIDS? Y

  Basic Mexican fare at affordable prices.

- **Dave's Red Anchor Café** 1935 Tongass Avenue; ☎ 907-247-5287

  AMERICAN QUALITY ★★★ $5–$14 SUITABLE FOR KIDS? Y

  A local favorite with a friendly staff and an easygoing atmosphere.

- **Heen Kahidi Restaurant** 800 Venetia Way; ☎ 907-225-8001

  FUSION QUALITY ★★★★ $9–$31 SUITABLE FOR KIDS? N

  The name means "tree house on the creek." Has lovely views out to the Tongass Narrows. This is where locals go for a special night out or to celebrate anniversaries. Prices are a bit high, but it's nice for special occasions.

- **Ocean View Restaurante** 3159 Tongass Avenue; ☎ 907-225-7566

  ITALIAN/MEXICAN QUALITY ★★★ $7–$25 SUITABLE FOR KIDS? Y

  An Italian menu with lots of variety, and we do mean variety. Can you say pizza, Mexican, seafood, *and* croissants?

ON *the* TOWN: *What to Do after the Outdoor Adventure*

SOUTHEAST ALASKA HAS NO SHORTAGE of things to do after you've exhausted your outdoor-recreation reserves. Each town has its own character—take Skagway's over-the-top gold-rush theme, for example.

This section will give you a sampling of what you can do when you're relaxing in town before or after your outdoor adventure.

HAINES

- **Alaska Indian Arts** 13 Fort Seward Drive; ☎ 907-766-2160; **www.alaskaindianarts.com**

  See artists at work creating totems, masks, and ceremonial baskets.

- **American Bald Eagle Foundation** ☎ 907-766-3094; **www.baldeagles.org**

  This nonprofit educational and research foundation features a natural-history museum containing more than 100 full-size specimens.

- **Chilkat Dancers Storytelling Theater** ☎ 907-766-2540; **www.tresham.com/show**

  Performances are held in the Totem Village Tribal House at the Fort Seward Parade Field throughout the summer. Adults $12; children $6.

SKAGWAY

- **Corrington Museum of Alaskan History** 525 Broadway; ☎ 907-983-2579

  With local history and lots of gold-rush history.

- **The Days of '98 Show with Soapy Smith** 590 Broadway; ☎ 907-983-2545

  It's a lot of fun if you like this kind of entertainment. Gives you a glimpse of what the gold rush was all about.

JUNEAU

- **Alaskan Brewing Co.** 5429 Shaune Drive; ☎ 907-780-5866; **www.alaskanbeer.com**
  Try the company's award-winning beers on tap during its daily tours, 11 a.m. to 5 p.m. in the summer (last tour is at 4:30 p.m.).
- **Alaska State Museum** 395 Whittier Street; ☎ 907-465-2901
  The Alaska State Museum is home to more than 23,000 artifacts, works of fine art, and natural history. There's a kids' room that simulates Captain James Cook's 18th-century vessel, the *Discovery.*
- **Juneau/Douglas City Museum** Located at Fourth Avenue and Main Street; ☎ 907-586-3572
  With more than 6,000 historical and fine-art objects, the City Museum offers year-round exhibits and fall and winter community programming.

SITKA

- **Alaska Raptor Center** ☎ 907-747-8662; **www.alaskaraptor.org**
  The Raptor Center's goal is to release all rehabilitated birds, but some stay behind for visitors to learn from. Admission is $12 for adults, $6 for children.
- **Castle Hill** On Harbor Road, on your way to the airport
  Also known as the Baranof Castle site, this area is an early stronghold of the Kiksadi clan. The site is on the National Register of Historic Places.
- **Russian Bishop's House** ☎ 907-747-6281; **www.nps.gov/sitk**
  The oldest intact Russian building in Sitka was built in 1842. The area is registered as a National Historic Landmark. Admission is $4.
- **Sheet'ka Kwaan Naa Kahidi Native Dancers** ☎ 888-270-8687 or 907-747-7290; **www.sitkatribe.org**
  The Tlingit Dancers perform in connection with Sitka Tribal Tours at the Sheet'ka Kwaan Naa Kahidi Community House. $7 per person.
- **Southeast Alaska Indian Cultural Center** ☎ 907-747-8061; **seaicc@gci.net**
  The Cultural Center provides a place for local Sitka Tlingits to teach themselves about their own culture. It also helps visitors understand the native people of the area. Admission is $3 per person or $15 for families.

KETCHIKAN

- **Creek Street District**
  This area off Stedman Street includes a former brothel, called Dolly's House, which has been made into a museum.
- **Saxman Native Village** Mile 2.5 South Tongass Highway
  Totem poles can be viewed at this 2.5-acre park that has preserved these works of art. Cape Fox Tours (☎ 907-225-4846; **www.capefoxtours.com**) conducts tours as well.
- **Tongass Historical Society Museum** 629 Dock Street; ☎ 907-225-5600
  Houses artifacts from Ketchikan's native past and mining, fishing, and timber history. Admission is $2.

PART TWENTY-TWO

INTERIOR ALASKA

The Heart of the State

An **OVERVIEW** *of the* **INTERIOR**

WHEN YOU HEAR THE TERM "Land of the Midnight Sun," think of Interior Alaska. Here, more than anywhere else, is where a visitor can truly appreciate what that means. In the summer, the sun really *is* still out at midnight. Because of their more southerly locations, the Southcentral and Southeast regions of the state don't experience the same lightness.

It's warmer, too. Summers in the Interior can reach 90°F for days on end, literally giving summer vacationers endless sunshine. In the winter, it can get inversely cold—down to –40°F is common. But Alaskans dress appropriately and simply continue to go about their business.

Interior Alaska is a land of vast proportions, too. From **Anaktuvuk Pass** to **Denali State Park,** the Interior seems to go on forever. You can drive and drive and drive and see nothing but wildness. It is the ideal place to gain perspective on just how large Alaska really is. (See Part One, page 13, for a map of the region.)

Interior Alaska is home to some incredible natural wonders. **Mount McKinley,** or **Denali,** as most Alaskans prefer to call it, is in the Interior, looming 20,320 feet above the rest of North America. The mighty **Yukon River,** too, flows through the region, a river rich in history and overflowing with flora and fauna to be discovered.

Gold mining brought Interior Alaska into the forefront of the collective imagination, and during the late 1800s and early 1900s, it dominated the thoughts of hopeful prospectors there to find the big vein and become rich overnight.

But once the gold rush ebbed, Interior was still the same great mass of land filled with rivers and valleys and mountains. Sure, the gold may have seemed like the region's biggest asset, but in fact, as visitors to this area see on a daily basis, it is the natural beauty. It's a magical place, Interior Alaska, sure to astound you.

Interior Alaska is a culturally diverse region, too, with Alaska natives making up a large percentage of its residents. The region's rich Athabascan heritage is on display in museums, stores, villages, and art galleries.

This chapter focuses on the largest communities through which you may travel while headed for your ultimate outdoor destination in Interior Alaska. These are the places where you can gear up and move out. Specifically, we have created subchapters for **Fairbanks,** the communities north of Fairbanks, and the area around **Denali National Park.**

FAIRBANKS

Fairbanks Convention and Visitors Bureau
(plus information about Circle, Manley Hot Springs, and Coldfoot)
550 First Avenue
Fairbanks 99701
☎ 800-327-5774
www.explorefairbanks.com

WHEN YOU THINK *Interior,* Fairbanks may be the first place that comes to mind. On a map, the city seems smack-dab in the middle of the state—and it is, sort of. About 30,000 people live in Fairbanks, which is a large and sprawling place with its own university, hospital, government, schools, and all the amenities of a large community. There is even a military presence, with **Eielson Air Force** and **Fort Wainwright Army bases** nearby.

Physically, the city is located on the banks of the **Chena River,** in the Tanana Valley. It takes only 45 minutes to fly there from Anchorage, but a road trip will take upwards of six hours. The average winter temperatures range from −19°F to −2°F; in the summer the mercury can rise to 72°F on an average day (although days in the 80s and even 90s are not uncommon).

Athabascans have lived in the Fairbanks area for thousands of years, but it was the nonnative Capt. E. T. Barnette who first established a trading post on the Chena River in 1901, marking the beginnings of what would one day be Fairbanks. A year later, gold was discovered 16 miles north of the post, and like every other place affected by the gold, the outpost turned into an overnight city. The town continued to grow and in 1902 was named Fairbanks after Indiana Senator Charles Fairbanks, who eventually became vice president. A year later, the third judicial court was moved from Eagle to Fairbanks, followed by more and more government. A jail, post office, and several supply stores opened, and before long, Fairbanks was a thriving city of 3,500, although thousands more were in surrounding areas actively mining.

Today, Fairbanks continues to thrive. Government, transportation, manufacturing, and tourism are its main economic driving factors. Gold mining still goes on, but on a much smaller scale than those earlier gold rushes. The **University of Alaska Fairbanks** is also a major employer. Approximately 325,000 tourists visit Fairbanks each summer.

greater fairbanks

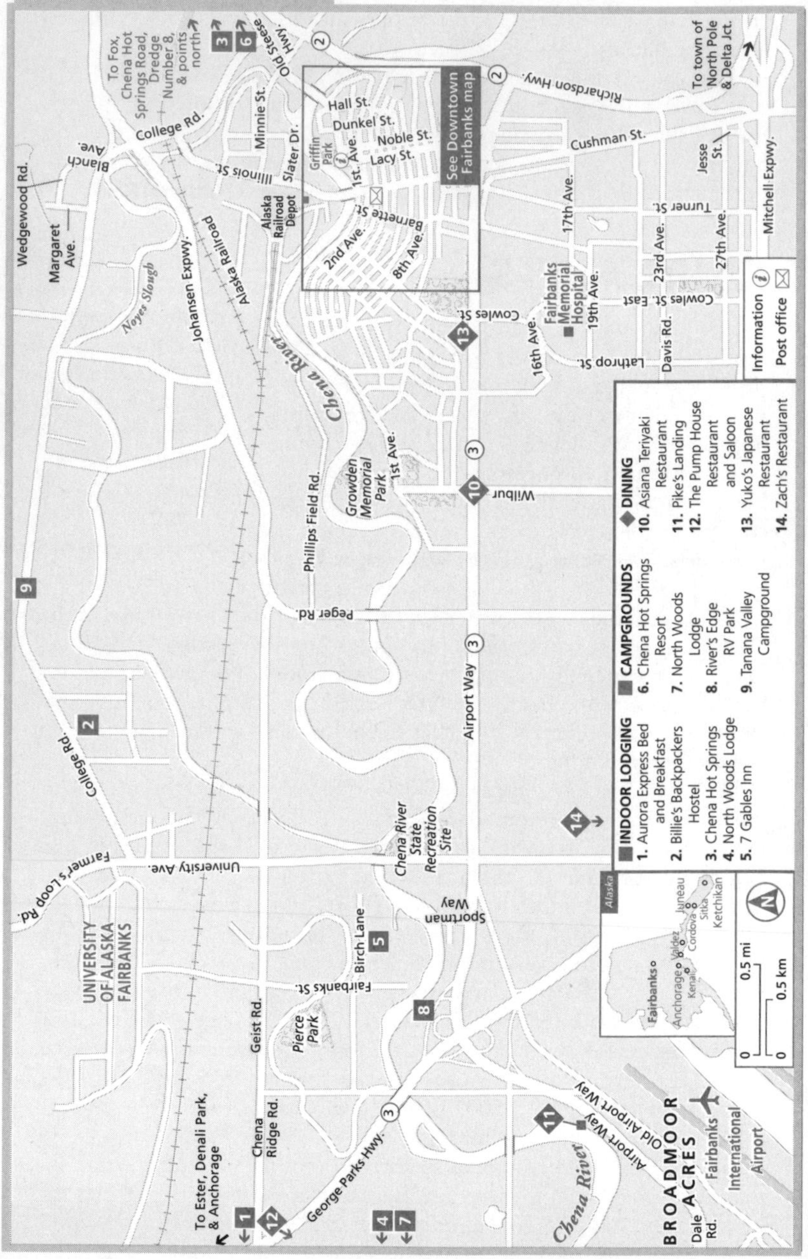

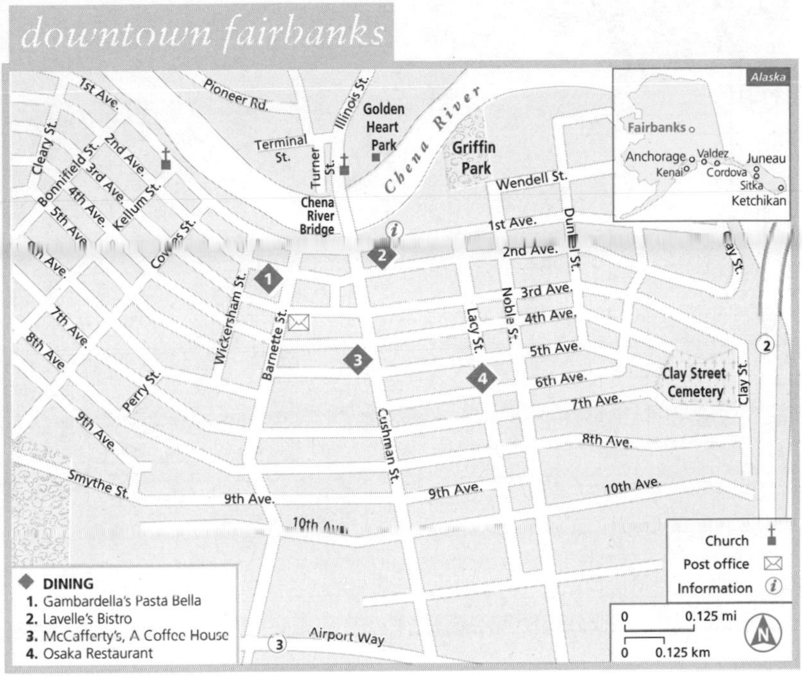

Access to Fairbanks is via the Richardson or Parks highways from the south and the Steese and Elliott highways from the north. There is regularly scheduled jet service from the lower 48 states, Canada, and Anchorage. The **Alaska Railroad** also provides access, although only from within the state (Anchorage, Seward, and Talkeetna).

NORTH *of* FAIRBANKS

CIRCLE

CIRCLE IS LOCATED ON THE SOUTH BANK of the Yukon River at the edge of the **Yukon Flats,** 160 miles northeast of Fairbanks, at the eastern end of the Steese Highway. Because of its subarctic climate, it gets very hot in the summers and very cold in the winters. The temperature range can go from 72°F in the summer to –72°F in the winter. This is a popular spot from which to launch a Yukon River trip, and most people who come this far usually spend some time on the water.

The community was established in 1893 as a supply point for goods shipped up the Yukon River and hauled overland to the gold-mining camps. It got its original name, Circle City, by miners who thought its location was on the Arctic Circle. They were off a bit, but

denali national park

INDOOR LODGING

1. Blue Home Bed and Breakfast
2. Camp Denali–North Face Lodge
3. Denali Dome Home Bed and Breakfast
4. Denali Mountain Morning Hostel and Lodge
5. Denali Touch of Wilderness Bed and Breakfast Inn
6. Denali's Earthsong Lodge

CAMPGROUNDS

7. Carlo Creek Campground
8. Denali Grizzly Bear Cabins and Campground
9. Riley Creek Campground
10. Sanctuary River Campground
11. Savage River Campground
12. Teklanika Campground
13. Wonder Lake Campground

DINING

14. Denali Perch Lodge
15. The Lunch Box
16. Lynx Creek Pizza Parlor
17. McKinley Creekside Café
18. Rabideau's Clear Sky Lodge
19. 229

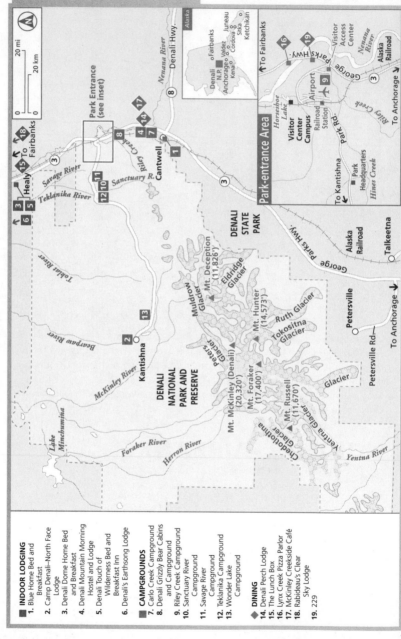

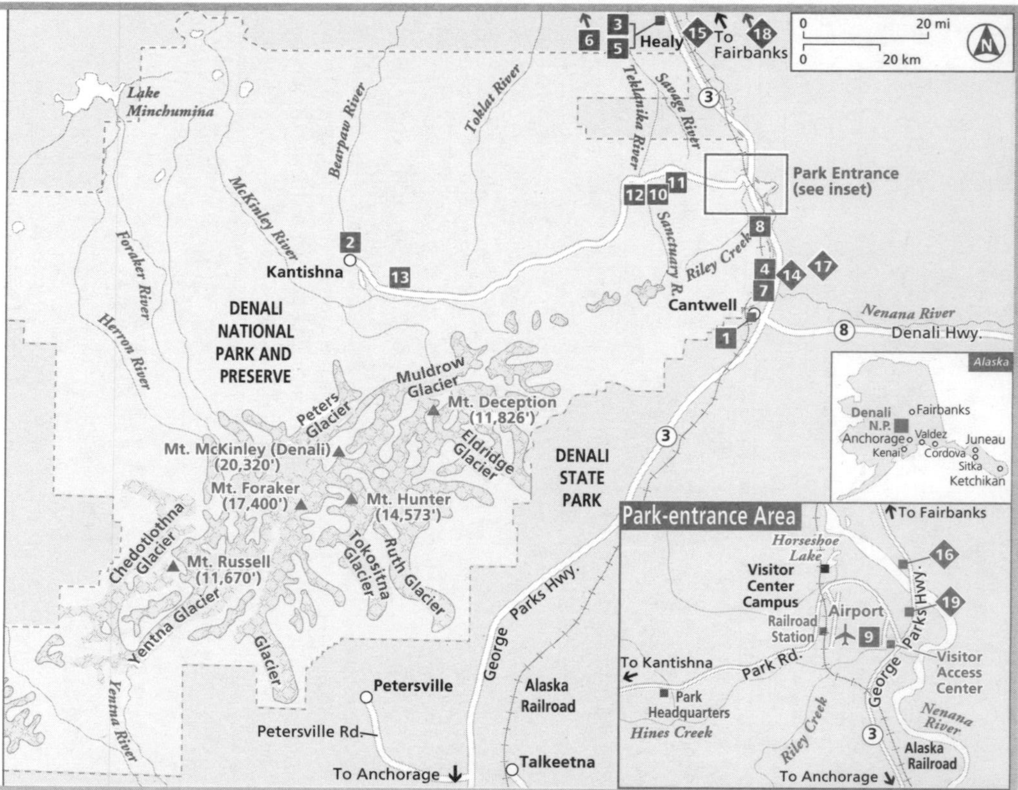

the name remained. During the height of the gold rush, the town bustled with dance halls, mercantiles, lodges, and other businesses. Today the place is home to only 99 people, based on the latest U.S. Census information. Recreation is the largest draw there now, with freshwater fishing and boating a large part of that.

You can get to Circle from Fairbanks by taking the Steese Highway. Barges deliver goods by the Yukon River during summer. A new state-owned gravel airstrip is available, too.

MANLEY HOT SPRINGS

AT THE END OF THE ELLIOTT HIGHWAY, 160 miles west of Fairbanks, you'll come to Manley Hot Springs, a community of about 75 people living along the **Tanana River.** It, too, is a community that got its start as a base of operations for gold miners, in early 1902. The first resident began farming and raising livestock in the area, quite a feat considering the environmental challenges. The area is cool in the summer, around 55 degrees, and can dip way below zero in the winter.

The hot springs were a natural draw, though, and as early as 1907, a resort centered around the hot waters was erected and bringing passengers via steamers off the Tanana River. At one time the population in the area climbed to nearly 500. Eventually the resort burned, mining declined, and the community almost disappeared. But in 1959, after the completion of the Elliott Highway, Manley Hot Springs had a road link to the rest of Alaska, and the town began to grow again.

COLDFOOT

A WHOPPING 13 PEOPLE CALL THIS SPOT in the road home. It is located at Mile 175 of the Dalton Highway at the mouth of **Slate Creek,** on the east bank of the **Middle Fork Koyukuk River.** Its temperature swings are not as noticeable as its more northerly neighbors, with averages in the 50°F range in the summer and going as low as –20°F in the winter.

Coldfoot originally was named Slate Creek but was renamed after gold seekers at the turn of the century went up the Koyukuk to start searching for their riches and chickened out. When they got cold feet, it is reported, the town became known as such. At the time, Coldfoot really was a town, with two roadhouses, a couple of stores, and seven saloons. Eventually, like so many other gold-rush towns, the gold disappeared and so did the town. There's not much there now except for a motel, a restaurant, a gas station, and an RV park. There are a few other small businesses that serve those traveling the Dalton Highway, but it is a quiet place otherwise.

ANAKTUVUK PASS

THIS 300-PERSON COMMUNITY is at 2,200 feet on the divide between the Anaktuvuk and John

City of Anaktuvuk Pass
P.O. Box 21030,
Anaktuvuk Pass
99721-0030
☎ 907-661-3612
cityoakp@astacalaska.net

rivers in the central **Brooks Range,** and is the last remaining settlement of the Nunamiut (inland northern Inupiat Eskimo). Because of its high elevation, summers are cool and winters are cold—often –20°F and colder.

Nunamiut bands left the Brooks Range and scattered because of the collapse of caribou populations in 1926–27, and also because of cultural changes brought by the influx of Western civilization. In the late 1930s, however, a group of Nunamiut families returned to the mountains and settled. Others eventually followed, and thus the community formed.

Job opportunities are limited in Anaktuvuk Pass because it is so isolated. Hunting and trapping for the sale of skins, guiding hunters, or making traditional caribou-skin masks or clothing provides income for the residents there. Some residents have seasonal employment outside the community. Caribou is the primary source of meat; other subsistence foods include trout, grayling, moose, sheep, brown bear, ptarmigan, and waterfowl.

Access to the area is by small aircraft, several of which fly there regularly. In the winter, a snow road can create access to the village by way of the Dalton Highway, but it is only for bringing supplies.

DENALI AREA

THERE IS MORE TO THE DENALI AREA than just the fact that it is home to the most-visited national park in Alaska. The Denali area includes the communities of Anderson, Cantwell, Clear, Ferry, Healy, and Mount McKinley Village, which among them all have fewer than 2,000 year-round residents. Most of these people live off the beaten track, and their homes are not easily seen from the road.

Denali Visitors Center
Mile 240, Parks Highway
☎ 907-683-2294
www.nps.gov/dena

Denali Chamber of Commerce
☎ 907-683-4636
www.denalichamber.com

Tourism is the mainstay for the folks living in the Denali area, and during the summer residents stay busy showing folks from the outside world their special corner of the earth. In the winter, however, things slow down. While some winter visitors come to Denali to experience such sports as snowmobiling, dog mushing, and skiing, for the most part, Denali becomes a ghost town.

The town of **Cantwell** is at the crossroads of the Parks and Denali highways, 27 miles south of the entrance to **Denali National Park.** The **Alaska Railroad** passes through town. **Ferry** is the smallest of the communities, at just 27 residents at last count, and is adjacent to the Alaska Railroad. Twelve miles north of Ferry is **Healy,** the largest community in the Denali area, with about 1,000 permanent residents. This is where most supplies for the region can be purchased, although there are no true big-box stores until you get to Fairbanks. **Mount McKinley Village,** just outside the park entrance, and **Anderson** round out the region. For more information on the park, see the listing under "Wild Lands" below.

WILD LANDS

DENALI NATIONAL PARK AND PRESERVE

(Primary activities: birding, backpacking, mountain biking, mountaineering, dog mushing)

THIS 6-MILLION-ACRE SPREAD of wild land includes **Mount McKinley,** North America's highest mountain at 20,320 feet tall, as well as countless other mountains and glaciers that seem to go on forever. The park encompasses a complete subarctic ecosystem teeming with such wildlife as moose, grizzly bears, Dall sheep, and wolves.

The park was established as Mount McKinley National Park in 1917, but in 1980 the name was changed to honor the Athabascan word for the mountain: **Denali,** or "high one." Today the park gets the most visitors of any in the state—about 400,000 each year.

Access to the park is via the Alaska Railroad from Fairbanks or Anchorage, the Parks Highway, or small charter plane.

Denali National Park
P.O. Box 9
Denali Park 99755-0009
☎ 907-683-2294
www.nps.gov/dena

unofficial **TIP**
Most people choose to drive to Denali National Park, as it is the least expensive option. However, the **Alaska Railroad** offers a scenic view of parts of the state not seen from the road.

DENALI STATE PARK

(Primary activities: backpacking, fishing, hiking, skiing, mountain biking)

DENALI STATE PARK COMPRISES 325,240 acres and often is overlooked as people rush to get to the national park of the same name. It's about 100 air miles north of Anchorage and lies roughly on either side of the Parks Highway. Sandwiched between the **Talkeetna Mountains** to the east and the **Alaska Range** to the west, Denali State Park offers wonderful ridge walks for backpackers, as well as shorter trails for mountain bikers seeking technical single track.

Fishing is excellent in the area as well. All five species of Pacific salmon spawn within the waters of the park and share the streams with rainbow trout, arctic grayling, and Dolly Varden. Small numbers of lake trout inhabit **Byers, Spink, and Lucy lakes.** Burbot and whitefish can also be found in Byers Lake. The large rivers are clouded with glacial silt, though, and make for poor sportfishing.

Visitor Center (at Alaska Veterans Memorial)
Mile 147.1 Parks Highway
Denali Ranger Station
Alaska State Parks/Mat-Su Area Headquarters
HC 32, Box 6706
Wasilla 99654-9719
☎ 907-745-3975
www.dnr.state.ak.us/parks/units/denali1.htm

Moose, as well as grizzly and black bears, are found throughout the park, and occasionally a wolf or wayward caribou is spotted. Smaller, elusive residents include lynx, coyote, red fox, snowshoe hare, land otter, and flying and red squirrel.

There are two campgrounds, accessible by the Parks Highway: **Denali View North Campground,** at Mile 162.7, and **Byers Lake Campground,** at Mile 147.

WHITE MOUNTAINS NATIONAL RECREATION AREA

(Primary activities: backpacking, fishing, rafting, skiing, dog mushing)

White Mountains National Recreation Area
www.blm.gov/ak/st/en/prog/sa/white_mtns.html
(for general White Mountains information, mileage between cabins, and a detailed map of the area)

THAT FAIRBANKS RESIDENTS HAVE SUCH a huge playground in their backyard, only 30 miles to the north of town, is remarkable. Outdoor recreationists flock to the more than 200 miles of maintained trails in the White Mountains National Recreation Area.

The seeds of the White Mountains National Recreation Area were planted nearly 20 years ago, with the passage of the Alaska National Interest Land Conservation Act, which aimed to set aside valuable acreage for multiple purposes. Unlike most federal land in Alaska, this recreation area is managed by the U.S. Bureau of Land Management. Not only does the BLM maintain a wealth of trails and cabins for winter use, but it has also established two campgrounds and created hiking areas for those visiting the land in the summer. Today, White Mountains is the largest national recreation area in the United States, the only national recreation area in Alaska, and the only one in the nation managed by the BLM.

Accessing the White Mountain National Recreation Area is easy. From Fairbanks, drive north on the Elliott or Steese highways, depending upon where in the recreation area your trip will begin. Four pull-offs, two along each highway, allow for long-term parking. Cross-country skiing and dog mushing are the most popular activities in the winter, although you do share the trail with snowmobiles, so be prepared for some occasional noise. Hiking near **Wickersham Dome** and **Mount Prindle** (the highest point in the White Mountains at 5,286 feet) is popular in the dry summer months. Floating the **Beaver Creek National Wild River** is fast becoming popular, too. BLM cabins are available up to 30 days in advance for $20 Sundays through Thursdays and $25 on Fridays and Saturdays. Reservations can be made in person at the BLM Public Room, 1150 University Avenue, Fairbanks 99709, or by

unofficial **TIP**
Because its many wet, boggy areas freeze over and get covered in snow, White Mountains National Recreation Area is a better winter destination than a summer one, but backpackers and boaters still come here in the summer.

calling ☎ 907-474-2000 or 800-437-7021. Trail maps can also be ordered by calling this number.

ARCTIC NATIONAL WILDLIFE REFUGE

(Primary activities: backpacking, camping, rafting)

THE 9.6-MILLION-ACRE ARCTIC NATIONAL WILDLIFE REFUGE supports the greatest variety of plant and animal life of any park or refuge above the Arctic Circle in the entire world. That's an impressive superlative, and one that you may not immediately notice when entering this place. The land is so vast that one often feels all alone, but the fact is, the area teems with wildlife, whether it be the pygmy shrew or the giant grizzly bear.

Arctic National Wildlife Refuge
101 12th Avenue
Box 20, Room 236
Fairbanks 99701
☎ 800-362-4546 or 907-456-0250
arctic.fws.gov
Go to **arctic.fws.gov/airtaxi.htm** for air-taxi information.

The land is inhabited by 45 species of land and marine mammals, and 36 species of fish occur in the refuge's waters. More than 180 species of birds have been spotted there as well.

Most people recognize the Arctic National Wildlife Refuge as the land at the center of the ongoing oil-drilling debate in Congress. Some want to open up the land to oil exploration, while others say the land was set aside for a reason: to stay wild. Outdoor travelers can appreciate this wildness while traveling down one of the many rivers or backpacking across the open tundra. It's a vast and intimidating place, but awe-inspiring at the same time.

The refuge remains roadless, with the exception of the limited access provided by the Dalton Highway, which passes through the western tip of the refuge. Most visitors choose to take a private charter plane into their location of choice and arrange pickup at a later time. Many visitors take a commercial flight to **Fort Yukon, Arctic Village, Deadhorse,** or **Kaktovik,** and charter a smaller plane into the refuge from there.

YUKON FLATS NATIONAL WILDLIFE REFUGE

(Primary activities: birding, rafting, canoeing, kayaking, fishing)

YUKON FLATS NATIONAL WILDLIFE REFUGE is just slightly smaller than Arctic National Wildlife Refuge, with 9 million acres of wild land in eastern Interior Alaska. It includes the **Yukon Flats,** a vast wetland basin bisected by the Yukon River and dotted with a network of lakes, streams, and rivers.

Yukon Flats National Wildlife Refuge
101 12th Avenue
Room 264, Box 264
Fairbanks 99701
☎ 907-456-0440
yukonflats.fws.gov

The refuge is home to the largest density of breeding ducks in Alaska and takes in one of the greatest waterfowl-breeding areas in North America, so it is a

unofficial **TIP**
Because of its subarctic climate, Yukon Flats National Wildlife Refuge experiences great seasonal extremes in temperature and daylight. It can get as hot as 100°F in the summer and as cold as –70°F in the winter.

bird lover's paradise. Migrating birds pass through the flats by the thousands, but a hardy few species—only about 12—live in the refuge year-round.

Wildlife ranges from grizzly bears to moose to wolves, although none of these creatures are seen as frequently as in other regions of the state. Black bears are more common in the refuge than grizzlies.

Access to the refuge is primarily by boat or aircraft. The refuge is about 100 miles north of Fairbanks, by taking the Steese Highway from Fairbanks to the Yukon River at Circle. From Circle, you travel down the river via watercraft into the refuge. Charter service to remote lakes and gravel bars along rivers is also available from Fairbanks and Fort Yukon. Visitors may also drive up the Dalton Highway to the Yukon River Bridge and travel upriver about five miles to reach the refuge.

GETTING AROUND *the* INTERIOR

FAIRBANKS

ACCESS BY AIR IS THROUGH **Alaska Airlines** (☎ 800-252-7522; **www.alaskaair.com**). You can also drive to Fairbanks from the Richardson or Parks highways.

- **Airport Car Rentals** Avis Rent-A-Car (☎ 800-331-1212 or 907-474-0900; **www.avis.com**); Budget Rent-A-Car (☎ 800-474-0855 or 907-474-0855; **www.budget.com**); and Dollar Rent-A-Car (☎ 907-451-4360)
  All the rates are comparable, at $50 and up per day.
- **Go North Alaska Travel Center** ☎ 866-236-7272 or 907-479-7272; **www.paratours.net**
  They offer camper vans and trucks beginning at $165.
- **National-Alamo Car and Truck Rental** 4960 Dale Road; ☎ 800-227-7368 or 907-451-7368; **www.nationalcar.com**
  Cars, trucks, and vans available and two locations, one at the airport and one downtown.

NORTH OF FAIRBANKS

- **Arctic Outfitters** ☎ 907-474-3530; **www.arctic-outfitters.com** or **www.daltonhighway.com**
  This outfit rents vehicles for driving the Dalton Highway. The vehicles are gravel-road ready and come with emergency gear in case of breakdowns. Based in Fairbanks, but it is the only outfit that rents vehicles for the areas north of Fairbanks.

- **Dalton Highway Express** ☎ 907-474-3555; **www.daltonhighwayexpress.com**
  Offers transportation along the Dalton Highway and Fairbanks.

DENALI AREA

- **Teresa's Denali Car Rental** In Healy; ☎ 907-683-1377; **www.alaskanchateau.com**
  This company can offer you wheels for your local travels. They pick you up at the railroad depot, and can arrange drops in Anchorage and Fairbanks; $85 per day and up.

GEARING UP

FAIRBANKS IS YOUR BEST OPPORTUNITY to get your gear and supplies in order, although there are other opportunities in the region. As is the rule everywhere in Alaska, the more remote the area, the more you will pay. Despite advances in transportation and the higher efficiency of moving goods, it is still difficult to get the freshest or best of anything in outlying communities.

This section of the book is broken down by the main communities in the Interior with shops that will help you find what you are looking for. We list sporting goods and camping supplies and groceries separately, but many stores carry a little of everything—a characteristic of Alaska stores that you will soon notice is commonplace.

SPORTING GOODS AND CAMPING SUPPLIES

Fairbanks

- **Alaska Outdoor Rentals and Guides** ☎ 907-457-2453; **www.2paddle1.com**
  Outfitting adventurers with kayaks, canoes, and mountain bikes, as well as accessories. They're also a good source for finding out where to go.
- **Alaska Tent & Tarp Inc.** 529 Front Street; ☎ 907-456-6328
  This outfit sells some of the best cold-weather camping tents on the market today. Locally owned and a local favorite.
- **All Weather Sports** 4001 Geist Road; ☎ 907-474-8184; **www.allweathersports.com**
  For all your cycling needs in the area, especially for those brave enough to try snow-biking or riding during winter.
- **Beaver Sports** 3480 College Road; ☎ 907-479-2494; **www.beaversports.com**
  The largest sporting-goods store in the area, carrying names such as The North Face, Marmot, Dana Designs, etc. Skis, camping gear, kayaks, and more.
- **Big Ray's Store** 507 Second Avenue; ☎ 907-452-3458; **www.bigrays.com**
  An excellent source for heavy-duty winter clothing, boots, hats, mittens, Carhartts, and such. A longtime local favorite, Big Ray's serves Bush communities as well.

- **Fred Meyer** 3755 Airport Way; ☎ 907-474-1400
  This full-service grocery store has everything you would need, from camping supplies to fresh vegetables. They sell fishing licenses, as well, and have a wide selection of fishing tackle.

Denali Area

- **Denali Mountain Morning Hostel and Lodge** Just outside Denali National Park; ☎ 907-683-7503; **www.hostelalaska.com**
  Proprietor Bill Madsen offers an entire backpacking-gear rental kit, which includes pack, tent, stove, pad, sleeping bag, and other accessories for just $40 per day. This is a great deal, not to mentiuon very convenient for the spontaneous outdoor traveler who may not have intended to do any backpacking.
- **Denali Mountain Works** Across from the McKinley Chalets; ☎ 907-683-1542; **www.akrivers.com**
  They sell everything from outdoor clothing to backpacks, stoves, Carhartts, and fuel, as well as guide some awesome raft and river trips.

GROCERY

Fairbanks

- **Asian Food Market** 1616 South Cushman Street, ☎ 907-455-7814
  A good place to shop for alternative ingredients that may not be readily available at the typical full-service grocery stores. A great resource for vegetarian eaters.
- **Carrs/Safeway** 30 College Road; ☎ 907-456-8501 and 3627 Airport Way; ☎ 907-479-4231
  Full-service groceries and limited camping/fishing supplies.
- **Fred Meyer** 3755 Airport Way; ☎ 907-474-1400
  This full-service grocery store has everything you would need, from camping supplies to fresh vegetables.

North of Fairbanks

- **Fox General Store** 2226 Old Steese Highway North; ☎ 907-457-8903
  Known locally for their delicious pies, and it's worth the drive to get them.

Denali Area

- **McKinley RV & Campground** Mile 248 Parks Highway; ☎ 800-478-2562
  Limited groceries available.

WHERE *to* STAY

WE THINK OF THE LODGING SITUATION in Interior Alaska as feast or famine. In the populated areas your choices are vast. The Denali area has dozens of bed-and-breakfasts, hotels, and hostels from which to choose. Fairbanks has more than we can count.

But head out into the fringe areas, such as the Dalton Highway, north of Fairbanks, or south along the Richardson Highway, and the selections become few and far between. Still, there are a few gems out there that we'd like to share with you.

FAIRBANKS

Indoor Lodging

- **Aurora Express Bed and Breakfast** 1540 Chena Ridge Road; ☎ 800-221-0073; **www.fairbanksalaskabedandbreakfast.com**

  QUALITY ★★★★ VALUE ★★★ $135–$200

  Choose from a whole lineup of refurbished rail cars in the side yard of this home. It sounds crazy, but it's not—they're actually pretty neat.

- **Billie's Backpackers Hostel** 2895 Mack Boulevard; ☎ 907-479-2034; **www.alaskahostel.com**

  QUALITY ★★★ VALUE ★★★ $28

  This one gets the highest ratings among independent travelers, although we also like the North Woods Lodge (two listings down). Billie's Backpackers is off College Road, near the university. Everyone loves Billie, too. Look for the house with all the international flags hanging out front.

- **Chena Hot Springs Resort** ☎ 907-452-7867; **www.chenahotsprings.com**

  QUALITY ★★★★★ VALUE ★★★★ $65–$220

  This special place is on Chena Hot Springs Road, outside of town but worth the drive. The hot springs are incredible, especially in the winter when paired with northern lights viewing in subzero temperatures.

- **North Woods Lodge** Chena Hills Drive; ☎ 800-478-5305 or 907-479-5300

  QUALITY ★★★★ VALUE ★★★★★ $15

  Lodging is available in the main cabin, as well as loft hostel space. Owner Tom Ridner has added a few one-room log cabins for rent in addition to tent space. The 12-person hot tub is a bonus.

- **7 Gables Inn** 4312 Birch Lane; ☎ 907-479-0751; **www.7gablesinn.com**

  QUALITY ★★★★ VALUE ★★★★ $150–$200

  Centrally located near major attractions, with affordable rooms, private Jacuzzi baths, and a full gourmet breakfast.

Camping

- **Chena Hot Springs Resort** At the end of Chena Hot Springs Road, Mile 56; ☎ 907-452-7867; **www.chenahotsprings.com**

  QUALITY ★★★★★ VALUE ★★★★ $20

  Get the most out of the hot springs, but stay in an economical camp spot instead of a pricey room. The hot springs are incredible.

- **North Woods Lodge** Chena Hills Drive; ☎ 800-478-5305 or 907-479-5300

  QUALITY ★★★★ VALUE ★★★★ $12–$15

Interior Alaska Indoor Lodging

NAME	TYPE(S) OF LODGING	QUALITY RATING	VALUE RATING	COST
FAIRBANKS				
Aurora Express Bed and Breakfast	B&B	★★★★	★★★	$135–$200
Billie's Backpackers Hostel	hostel	★★★	★★★	$28
Chena Hot Springs Resort	bunks/cabins/resort	★★★★★	★★★★	$65–$220
North Woods Lodge	hostel/cabins/lodge	★★★★	★★★★★	$15
7 Gables Inn	inn	★★★★	★★★★★	$150–$200
NORTH OF FAIRBANKS				
Arctic Circle Hot Springs	hostel/cabins	★★★	★★★	$95
Coldfoot Camp	motel style	★★	★	$169
DENALI				
Blue Home Bed and Breakfast	B&B	★★★	★★★	$135+
Camp Denali–North Face Lodge	wilderness lodge	★★★★★	★★★★	$3,045/week
Denali Dome Home Bed and Breakfast	B& B	★★★★	★★	$165
Denali Mountain Morning Hostel and Lodge	hostel/cabins	★★★★★	★★★★★	$25–$75
Denali Touch of Wilderness Bed and Breakfast Inn	B&B	★★★★	★★★★	$135–$180
Denali's Earthsong Lodge	B&B/cabins/lodge	★★★★★	★★★★	$155–$195

Tent campers are welcome at this Interior lodge, which also caters to hostellers.

- **River's Edge RV Park** 4140 Boat Street; ☎ 800-770-3343 or 907-474-0286; **www.riversedge.net**

QUALITY ★★★★ VALUE ★★★ $19–$30

Offers great views, free showers, and a close-to-the-airport location.

- **Tanana Valley Campground** 1800 College Road; ☎ 907-451-5557; **www.tananavalleyfair.org**

QUALITY ★★★ VALUE ★★★★★ $14–$18

Interior Alaska Camping

NAME	TYPE(S) OF CAMPING	QUALITY RATING	VALUE RATING	COST
FAIRBANKS				
Chena Hot Springs Resort	tent/RV	★★★★★	★★★★	$20
North Woods Lodge	hostel/ cabins/lodge	★★★★	★★★★	$12–$15
River's Edge RV Park	tent/RV	★★★★	★★★	$19–$30
Tanana Valley Campground	tent sites	★★★	★★★★★	$14–$18
NORTH OF FAIRBANKS				
Campgrounds along the Dalton Highway	tent sites/ RV space	★★★	★★★★★	free
Coldfoot Camp	motel style	★★	★★★	$15–$35
DENALI AREA				
Carlo Creek Campground	tent/ RV/cabins	★★★	★★★	$12–$77
Denali Grizzly Bear Cabins and Campground	tent/ RV/cabins	★★★	★★★	$22–$61
Riley Creek Campground	tent/RV	★★★★	★★★★	$12–$20
Sanctuary River Campground	tent sites	★★★★	★★★★	$9
Savage River Campground	tent/RV	★★★★	★★★★	$20–$40
Teklanika Campground	tent/RV	★★★★	★★★★	$16
Wonder Lake Campground	tent sites	★★★★★	★★★★★	$16

This campground is a find for the budget-conscious camper. Tent sites are cheap, showers free.

NORTH OF FAIRBANKS

Indoor Lodging

- **Arctic Circle Hot Springs** Mile 8 Arctic Circle Hot Springs Road in the town of Central; ☎ 907-520-5113

  QUALITY ★★★ VALUE ★★★ $95

  Featuring a hot mineral pool, cabins, bar, and restaurant. Choose from cabins or hostel rooms (bring your own sleeping bag).

- **Coldfoot Camp** Mile 175 Dalton Highway, in Coldfoot; ☎ 866-474-3400 or 907-474-3500; **www.coldfootcamp.com**

  QUALITY ★★ VALUE ★ $169

Rooms are simple and clean, albeit expensive for what you get, as this is the only place around for miles.

Camping

- **Campgrounds along the Dalton Highway** U.S. Bureau of Land Management (BLM) camps, various locations; ☎ 907-474-2200; **www.blm.gov/ak/dalton**

  QUALITY ★★★ VALUE ★★★★★ FREE

  The BLM manages much of the land along the road and has ten campgrounds, three of which are primitive camping areas. The locations are **Finger Mountain** (Mile 98), **Arctic Circle** (Mile 115), **Gobblers Knob** (Mile 131), **Grayling Lake** (Mile 150), **South Koyukuk River** (Mile 156), **Marion Creek** (Mile 179), **Middle Fork Koyukuk River** (Mile 204), **Last Spruce Tree** (Mile 235), **Galbraith Camp** (Mile 274), and **Last Chance** (Mile 355). Some sites have pit toilets and other amenities; none have fees.

- **Coldfoot Camp** Mile 175 Dalton Highway, in Coldfoot; ☎ 866-474-3400 or 907-474-3500; **www.coldfootcamp.com**

  QUALITY ★★ VALUE ★★★ $15–$35

  Outside the camp are places for tent and RV camping.

DENALI AREA

Indoor Lodging

- **Blue Home Bed and Breakfast** In Cantwell, 40 minutes south of Denali; ☎ 907-768-2020; **www.cantwell-bluehome.de**

  QUALITY ★★★ VALUE ★★★ $135+

  Two guest rooms with lovely mountain views. The owners speak Dutch and make fine leather artwork. It's the nicest place to stay in Cantwell.

- **Camp Denali–North Face Lodge** ☎ 907-683-2290; **www.campdenali.com**

  QUALITY ★★★★★ VALUE ★★★★ $3,045/WEEK

  Our choice for end-of-the-road fine wilderness lodging. The owners are longtime Alaskans who've operated the lodge since 1952, and they offer some of the best food, friendship, and stories you will enjoy your entire trip. Daily outings, special naturalist programs, and just about any other outdoor adventure you want is possible. Highly recommended, although admittedly expensive.

- **Denali Dome Home Bed and Breakfast** In Healy; ☎ 800-683-1239 or 907-683-1239; **www.denalidomehome.com**

  QUALITY ★★★★ VALUE ★★ $135–$165

  This family-run bed-and-breakfast is hosted by the gracious Miller family, whose friendliness is why we recommend it. Plus, it's open year-round.

- **Denali Mountain Morning Hostel and Lodge** 13 miles south of Denali National Park; ☎ 907-683-7503; **www.hostelalaska.com**

  QUALITY ★★★★★ VALUE ★★★★★ $25–$75

This is our lodging choice for those wanting to explore the park but not lodge in the bustling McKinley Village chaos. The hostel has rooms, bunks, and cabins for rent, and welcomes guests of all ages. The creekside bonfire is always nice, too.

- **Denali Touch of Wilderness Bed and Breakfast Inn** In Denali Park; ☎ 800-683-2459 or 907-683-2459; **www.touchofwildernessbb.com**

  QUALITY ★★★★ VALUE ★★★★ $135–$180

  This longtime bed and breakfast has many rooms from which to choose and a soothing outdoor hot tub for stargazing or wildlife-watching. Rates drop in the winter.

- **Denali's Earthsong Lodge** In Healy; ☎ 907-683-2863 or 907-460-1451; **www.earthsonglodge.com**

  QUALITY ★★★★★ VALUE ★★★★ $155–$195

  Ten charming log cabins with private baths and amenities. Longtime Denali residents Jon and Karin Nierenberg offer meals and slide-show programs. These naturalists can share their knowledge of the area as well as or better than most people in Denali. This is our number-one choice for lodging in the Healy area. The Nierenbergs also offer sled-dog kennel tours. Rates start at $155 for a cabin.

National Park Service Campgrounds

The National Park Service operates five campgrounds, the first three of which are accessible by vehicle. For more information, call ☎ 907-683-2294 or visit **www.nps.gov/dena.** Sites can be reserved online at **www.reservedenali.com** or by calling ☎ 800-622-7275 or 907-272-7275. The campgrounds are listed below.

- **Riley Creek Campground** A quarter-mile west of the Parks Highway

  QUALITY ★★★★ VALUE ★★★★ $12–$20

  Has 150 sites for RVs and tents. Open year-round.

- **Sanctuary River Campground** Mile 22 Park Road

  QUALITY ★★★★ VALUE ★★★★ $9

  Has seven sites for tents only. Open seasonally. A one-time reservation fee of $4 is required in addition to the standard nightly fee. Accessible only by camper bus.

- **Savage River Campground** Mile 13 Park Road

  QUALITY ★★★★ VALUE ★★★★ $20

  Has 33 sites for RVs and tents. Open seasonally. (The nearby Savage River Group Camp sites are $40.)

- **Teklanika Campground** Mile 29 Park Road

  QUALITY ★★★★ VALUE ★★★★ $16

  Three-day passes are now required. Check with Denali officials before registering.

- **Wonder Lake Campground** Mile 85 Park Road

  QUALITY ★★★★★ VALUE ★★★★★ $16

  Has 28 sites for tents only. Open seasonally. A one-time reservation fee of $4 is required in addition to the standard nightly fee. Accessible only by camper bus.

Other Denali Campgrounds

- **Carlo Creek Campground** South of Denali Park; ☎ 907-683-2576; **www.carlocreek.com**

  QUALITY ★★★ VALUE ★★★ $12–$77

  They have nice log cabins, but we prefer the camping. Children stay free.

- **Denali Grizzly Bear Cabins and Campground** In Denali Park; ☎ 866-583-2696 or 907-683-2696; **www.denaligrizzlybear.com**

  QUALITY ★★★ VALUE ★★★ $22–$61

  Camping right on the Nenana River (and close to the road, but you probably won't notice it over the river noise). Options range from tents to small cabins.

WHERE *to* EAT

FAIRBANKS

- **Asiana Teriyaki Restaurant** 2001 Airport Way; ☎ 907-457-3333

  ASIAN QUALITY ★★★ $8–$18 SUITABLE FOR KIDS? Y

  Offers an affordable and interesting mix of Korean and Japanese .

- **Gambardella's Pasta Bella** 706 Second Avenue; ☎ 907-456-3417

  ITALIAN QUALITY ★★★★ $9–$29 SUITABLE FOR KIDS? N

  Italian cuisine in a hidden-away section of downtown Fairbanks. Fine wines accompany large portions.

- **Lavelle's Bistro** 575 First Avenue; ☎ 907-450-0555; **www.lavellesbistro.com**

  FUSION QUALITY ★★★★★ $11–$32 SUITABLE FOR KIDS? N

  The wine experts here can help pick the perfect accompaniment to your meal.

- **McCafferty's, A Coffee House** 408 Cushman Street; ☎ 907-456-6853

  CAFÉ QUALITY ★★★★ $2–$6 SUITABLE FOR KIDS? Y

  Their soups are delicious. Live entertainment on weekends.

- **Osaka Restaurant** 402 Fifth Avenue; ☎ 907-452-5560

  JAPANESE QUALITY ★★★★★ $7–$29 SUITABLE FOR KIDS? N

  The best Japanese fare in town.

- **Pike's Landing** 4438 Airport Road; ☎ 907-479-7113; **www.pikeslodge.com**

  BAR/AMERICAN QUALITY ★★★ $6–$18 SUITABLE FOR KIDS? Y

Interior Alaska Dining

NAME	CUISINE	FOOD QUALITY	COST
FAIRBANKS			
Asiana Teriyaki Restaurant	Asian	★★★	$8–$18
Gambardella's Pasta Bella	Italian	★★★★	$9–$29
Lavelle's Bistro	fusion	★★★★★	$11–$32
McCafferty's, A Coffee House	cafe	★★★★	$2–$6
Osaka Restaurant	Japanese	★★★★★	$7–$29
Pike's Landing	bar/American	★★★	$6–$18
The Pump House Restaurant and Saloon	fusion	★★★★★	$9–$34
Yuko Japanese Restaurant	Japanese	★★★	$6–$19
Zach's Restaurant	fusion	★★★★	$8–$20
NORTH OF FAIRBANKS			
The Inn at Coldfoot Camp	American	★★★	$8–$26
Manley Roadhouse	American	★★	$9–$25
DENALI AREA			
Denali Perch Lodge	American	★★★★	$10–$30
The Lunch Box	Asian, Mexican	★★★	$4–$9
Lynx Creek Pizza Parlor	Pizza	★★★★★	$7–$24
McKinley Creekside Café	American	★★★★	$7–$28
Rabideau's Clear Sky Lodge	American	★★	$8–$28
229	fusion	★★★★★	$11–$34

This restaurant draws the tourists, but the food is very good. We still go here every time we visit Fairbanks.

- **The Pump House Restaurant and Saloon** Chena Pump Road; ☎ 907-479-8452; **www.pumphouse.com**

FUSION QUALITY ★★★★★ $9–$34 SUITABLE FOR KIDS? N

The Pump House serves one of the best Sunday brunches in town. The dining area overlooks the Chena River and is an absolutely gorgeous place to eat on a sunny day.

- **Yuko Japanese Restaurant** 1900 Airport Way; ☎ 907-459-2211

JAPANESE QUALITY ★★★ $6–$19 SUITABLE FOR KIDS? Y

This place serves up fresh, fast offerings.

- **Zach's Restaurant** 1501 Queens Way; ☎ 800-528-4916 or 907-479-3650; **www.fountainheadhotels.com**

FUSION QUALITY ★★★★ $8–$20 SUITABLE FOR KIDS? N

For a hotel restaurant, this one seems to go above and beyond the norm. We've always had good dining experiences here. The dinner menu is dominated by steaks and Alaska seafood.

NORTH OF FAIRBANKS

- **The Inn at Coldfoot Camp** Mile 175 Dalton Highway, in Coldfoot; ☎ 907-474-3500 or 866-474-3400; **www.coldfootcamp.com**

AMERICAN QUALITY ★★★ $8–$26 SUITABLE FOR KIDS? Y

Homestyle cooking, and prime rib almost anytime. There's also an accompanying bar, the Frozen Foot Saloon, if you want to kick up your heels.

- **Manley Roadhouse** Mile 152 Elliott Highway; ☎ 907-672-3161

AMERICAN QUALITY ★★ $9–$25 SUITABLE FOR KIDS? N

This historic roadhouse offers food, rooms, and cabins for those who drive this far. The roadhouse also features lots of historic artifacts from the area's rich mining past. The food is basic, but the pies and cinnamon rolls are fresh-baked and delicious.

DENALI AREA

- **Denali Perch Lodge** ☎ 888-322-2523 or 907-683-2523; **www.denaliperchresort.com**

AMERICAN QUALITY ★★★★ $10–$30 SUITABLE FOR KIDS? N

The locals eat here, and the owners know everyone. The food is great, and the wine selection is surprisingly good for being so far out in the middle of nowhere. They've also recently added cabins starting at $85 per night.

- **The Lunch Box** In Healy; ☎ 907-683-6833 or 907-322-5256

ASIAN, MEXICAN QUALITY ★★★ $4–$9 SUITABLE FOR KIDS? Y

Offers food that ranges from Asian-American to Mexican—they do it all out here in the middle of nowhere! The prices are right, though, and the service is extra-friendly. The Lunch Box also prepares sack lunches to take into the park with you for your all-day adventures.

- **Lynx Creek Pizza Parlor** Mile 238.4 Parks Highway, Denali Park; ☎ 907-683-2547

PIZZA QUALITY ★★★★★ $7–$24 SUITABLE FOR KIDS? Y

It's filled to bursting all the time, but the pizza really earns its reputation. Pizza can be eaten in-house or delivered to your hotel, lodge, or camp.

- **McKinley Creekside Café** ☎ 888-533-6254 or 907-683-2277; **www.mckinleycabins.com**

AMERICAN QUALITY ★★★★ $7–$28 SUITABLE FOR KIDS? Y

Near Carlo Creek, 13 miles south of the Denali National Park entrance; offers delicious food and great cabin lodging.

- **Rabideau's Clear Sky Lodge** In Anderson; ☎ 907-582-2251

  AMERICAN QUALITY ★★ $8–$28 SUITABLE FOR KIDS? Y

  This couple has been in business for more than 40 years, and it's easy to see why. The food isn't fancy, but it is fairly priced, fresh, and filling. The perfect backpacker's meal, we say, including steaks, chicken, and burgers. They also have beer, wine, and spirits for sale.

- **229** In Denali National Park; ☎ 907-683-2567; **www.campdenali.com**

  FUSION QUALITY ★★★★★ $11–$34 SUITABLE FOR KIDS? N

  This newer restaurant, at the park entrance, takes fine food to new levels, and so far we love what we've tasted. Owners Laura and Land Cole know what they're doing. Land was raised in Denali and built the timber-frame restaurant himself. The Coles also run Camp Denali, one of our choices for lodging in the area.

ON *the* TOWN: *What to Do after the Outdoor Adventure*

WHETHER YOU'RE NURSING BLISTERS from your multiday hike or recovering from a week of paddling on some remote river, you shouldn't have trouble finding ways to unwind once you're back in town: Fairbanks has numerous attractions and entertainment venues to choose from, and even outlying areas such as Denali offer some fun things to do.

FAIRBANKS

- **Alaska Salmon Bake & Palace Theatre** 3175 College Road; ☎ 800-354-7274 or 907-452-7274; **www.akvisit.com**

  Performed by a professional cast, "The Golden Heart Revue" features music and lyrics by Fairbanks composer Jim Bell. It's a lighthearted, comic look at the characters from early and present-day Fairbanks. Rates are $10 for adults.

- **Ester Gold Camp** In Ester, just outside of Fairbanks; ☎ 800-676-6925, 907-479-2500, or 888-452-1737

  Special guest attractions at Ester Gold Camp include the Ester Gold Camp Dining Hall Buffet Dinner, as well as the locally famous Malemute Saloon Show, featuring a professional cast performing songs, hilarious sketches, and the poetry of Robert Service. Rates start at $55.

- **Georgeson Botanical Garden** On the University of Alaska Fairbanks campus, 117 West Tanana Drive; ☎ 907-474-6921; **www.uaf.edu**

  While away an afternoon enjoying the flowers that grow under the power of the 24-hour midnight sun.

- **Large Animal Research Station** ☎ 907-474-7207; **www.uaf.edu**

  See the large animals of Alaska, thanks to the research efforts of professors at University of Alaska Fairbanks. There are daily guided tours of musk oxen, caribou, and reindeer.

- **University of Alaska Museum of the North** On the University of Alaska Fairbanks campus; ☎ 907-474-7505; **www.uaf.edu/museum**
  This museum is jam-packed with artifacts, natural and historical exhibits, and other interesting tidbits. One of the highlights is Blue Babe, a 36,000-year-old Steppe bison that was recovered from a mining site nearby. Admission is $10.

NORTH OF FAIRBANKS

- **Arctic Circle Trading Post** Mile 49.5 Elliott Highway; ☎ 907-474-4565
  At this shop you can get your official certificate stating that you have passed the Arctic Circle. It's slightly touristy, but a milestone nonetheless.
- **Circle District Historical Society** Mile 128 Steese Highway, in Central; ☎ 907-520-1893
  Learn about the area's mining history, see mammoth tusk and bones, and check out local beadwork, wildflowers, and gold displays.
- **Old F. E. Gold Camp** Mile 27.5 Steese Highway, in the tiny community of Chatanika; ☎ 907-389-2414; **www.fegoldcamp.com**
  The site is on the National Register of Historic Places, and you can see old mining equipment from decades ago. The camp also has rooms if you want to stop for the night.
- **Simon Paneak Memorial Museum** 341 Mekiana Road, in Anaktuvuk Pass; ☎ 907-661-3413
  Visit America's farthest-north museum to learn about the Nunamiut people.

DENALI AREA

- **Alaska Cabin Nite** Performances at the McKinley Chalet Resort; ☎ 800-276-7234 or 907-264-4600; **www.denaliparkresorts.com/activities/detail.cfm**
  These evening events offer a gold-rush tale of adventure in the early 1900s. Heroine Fanny Quigley was a real-life pioneer in the Kantishna area, deep in Denali National Park. Performers tell her story with humor, music, and colorful acting, all while doubling as your servers for the all-you-can-eat buffet. It's a blast, even for those who don't think much of theater. The cost is $50. Suitable for all ages.
- **Goose Lake Kennels** ☎ 907-683-2904; **www.huskyhomestead.com**
  Take a tour of an Iditarod Sled Dog Race champion's kennel. Jeff King has a hand-built log cabin in the mountains surrounding the park; daily tours of his kennels introduce the neophyte to the state sport of dog mushing. Cuddle puppies, hear trail stories, and get a feel for what it's like to have the job of dog musher. Tours are $45 and last an hour and a half.

PART TWENTY-THREE

BUSH ALASKA

Solitude at Its Best

AN OVERVIEW *of the* ROADLESS REGIONS

FANNING OUT FROM THE INTERIOR is land so remote, it is simply called the Bush. The majority of Alaska's native people choose to reside here, often living off the land by fishing, hunting, and gathering as their ancestors did before them. The largest communities are **Barrow, Nome,** and **Kotzebue,** augmented by dozens of villages scattered across the region. We have also included Southwest Alaska as part of our Bush chapter because of its remote, sparsely populated environment. Its larger communities are **Unalaska–Dutch Harbor, Dillingham,** and **Bethel,** as well as **King Salmon,** a smaller community that serves as a hub for many outdoor adventures. (See Part One, pages 14–17, for maps of the Bush Southwest and Bush Far North regions.)

The Bush's Inupiat, Yup'ik, and Aleut natives depend on boats, snowmobiles, and dog teams to get around mostly roadless communities. During the winter the rivers freeze, creating ribbon highways for snowmobile and dog-team travel. In summer, boats provide transportation. Today, most communities also have air service, connecting the world to these once-inaccessible places. The Bush is where some of the most adventurous of the adventurous roam, rafting rivers that perhaps see fewer than a dozen people in any given year, or fishing lakes that don't know the feel of human footprints.

To be honest, the communities of the Bush are a bit drab at first glance, with the exception of Unalaska, which has some fabulous scenery right off the bat. Barrow, for instance, is flat, treeless, and cold year-round. It seems desolate and lifeless, which is to be expected considering the extreme climate. Bethel and Dillingham are much the same: flat, expansive, and void.

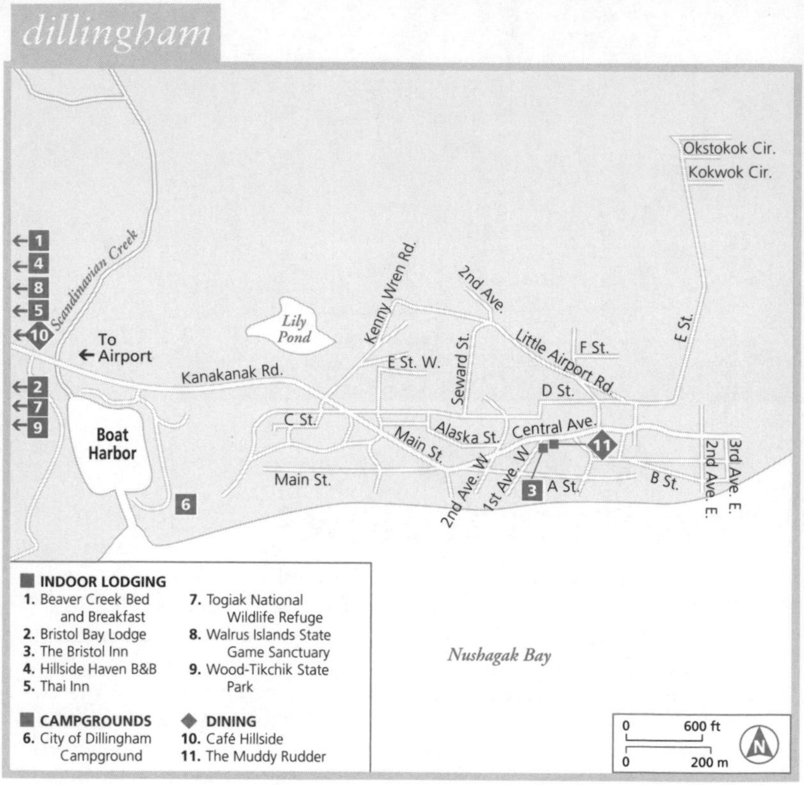

In the summer, though, the tundra of these places comes alive with colorful wildflowers and varying degrees of green with the other plants that cling to life there. The rivers are great for rafting and fishing. The wilderness beckons to backpackers who want to see new places.

The real appeal of Bush Alaska is that, for the outdoors traveler, there are millions of acres of public—and sometimes private—land upon which to explore. Some of Alaska's most remote and rugged national parks, preserves, and other protected lands are located here, and are well worth checking out. It's an adventurous feeling, exploring such uncharted territory. For that reason, most of this chapter focuses on the national parks and preserves, wild rivers, and monuments worth seeing when in this region.

unofficial **TIP**
The Bush is worth exploring if for no other reason than its remoteness, the fact that your adventure is taking place so far off the beaten path that often no one's even bothered to give the places a name.

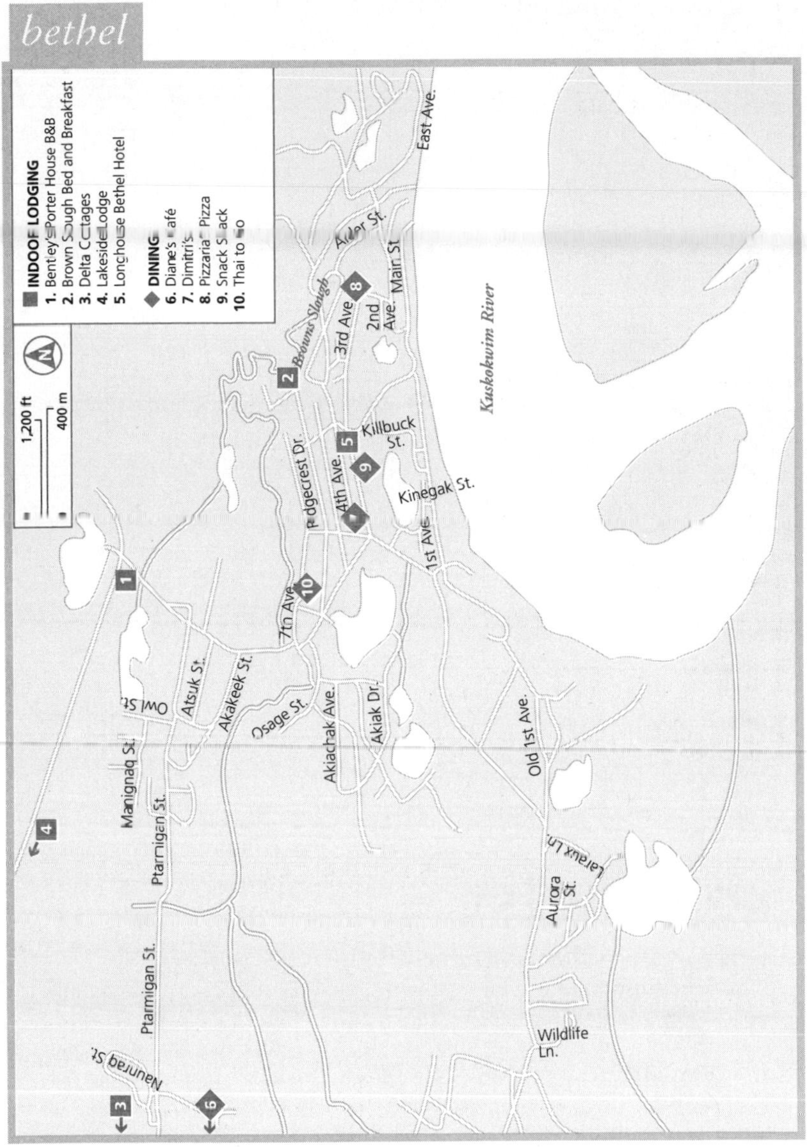

Lodging and eateries are few and far between in the main communities, but we have offered a few suggestions of places we think are suitable while in towns or resupplying for your backcountry trips.

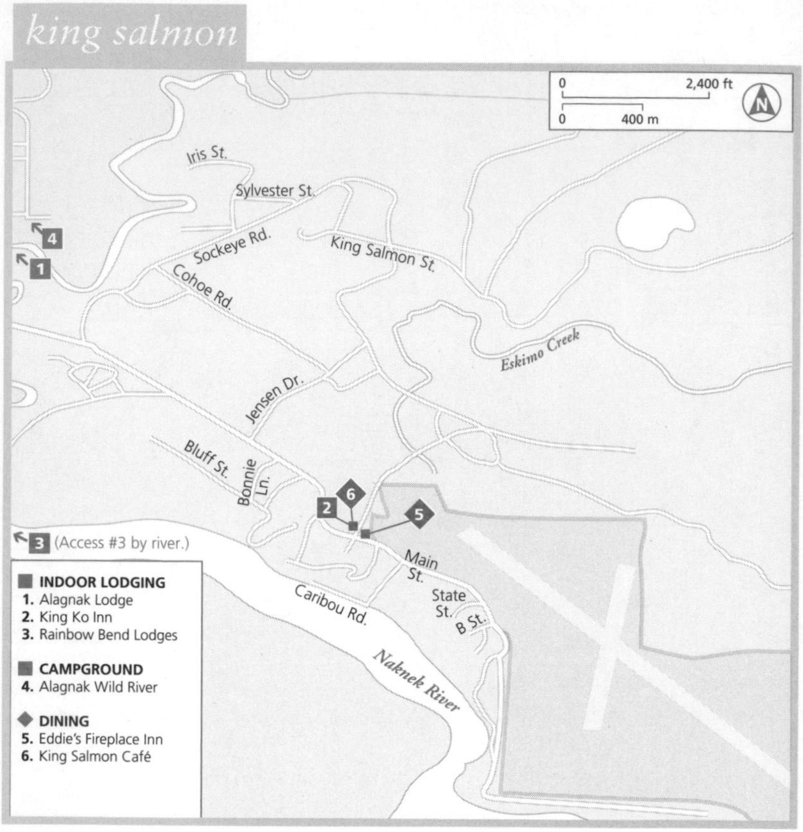

SOUTHWEST

THIS PART OF ALASKA is often overlooked when travelers come here, in part because what it offers—unparalleled fishing, backpacking, and boating opportunities—can be found in more-accessible areas of the state. Southwest Alaska is composed of the **Aleutian Islands,** which stretch from the end of the Alaska Peninsula almost to Japan; the **Pribilof Islands,** which include **St. George and St. Paul islands; Bethel,** the largest "city" in the region; and the **Iliamna–Lake Clark** region. Some guidebooks include Kodiak Island as part of Southwest Alaska, but we have opted to group it with the Southcentral Coastal region because it shares many of the same outdoor recreation opportunities found in Southcentral Alaska, and is easily accessed from that region.

Southwest Alaska, geographically, is a diverse place, with active volcanoes, wild rivers—the **Yukon** and **Kuskokwim** are two of the better-known ones—and plenty of open wild land in the form of

unalaska–dutch harbor

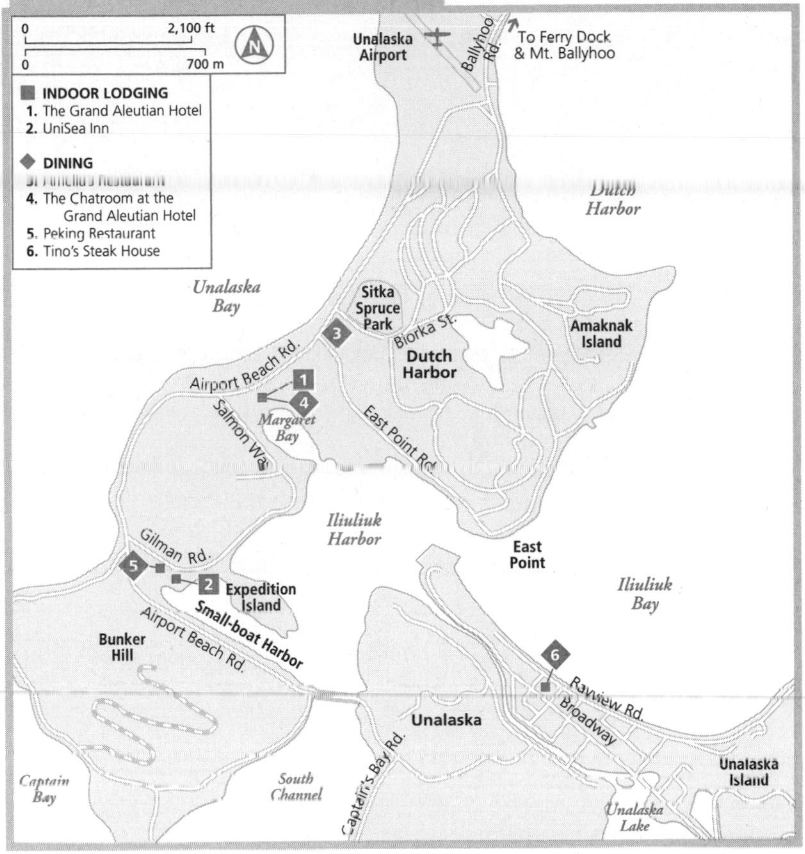

national parks and preserves in which to explore. Among native residents in this region are the Yu'pik Eskimos on the western mainland and the Aleuts on the Aleutian and Pribilof islands.

Our favorite places to visit in this region of the state include the **Lake Clark–Iliamna Lake** area and **Katmai National Park,** both of which have some of the best bear viewing and fishing in the entire state.

Brief descriptions of the major towns that serve as jumping-off points for adventures are provided below and following.

Dillingham Chamber of Commerce and Visitor Center
P.O. Box 348
Dillingham 99576
☎ 907-842-5115
www.dillinghamak.com

DILLINGHAM

WITH A POPULATION OF AROUND 2,400, Dillingham is a hub community for surrounding

nome

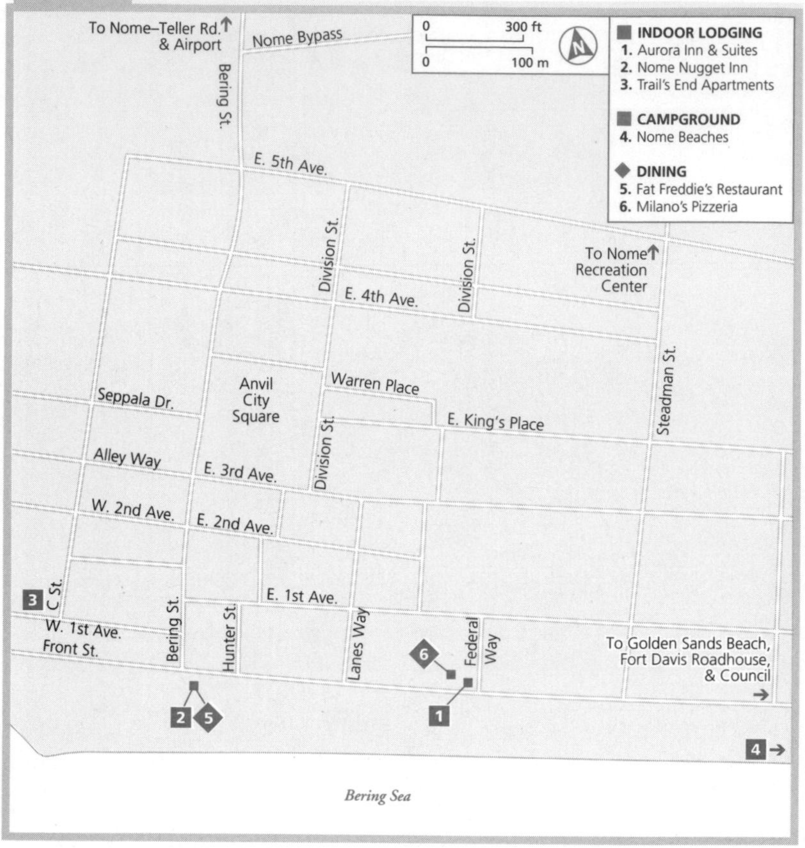

villages in **Bristol Bay.** The city is located on the north shore of **Nushagak Bay** at the confluence of the **Nushagak and Wood rivers.**

BETHEL

Bethel Chamber of Commerce
P.O. Box 329
Bethel 99559
☎ 907-543-2911

LOCATED ON THE BANKS OF THE **Kuskokwim River,** the village of Bethel is home to about 5,800 year-round residents, many of whom fish for a living in the **Bering Sea.** The primary native population consists of Yup'ik Eskimo, and many of them still live a subsistence lifestyle.

KING SALMON

WITH ONLY 400 OR SO RESIDENTS, King Salmon is a small village, but serves as one of the primary starting points for many Southwest

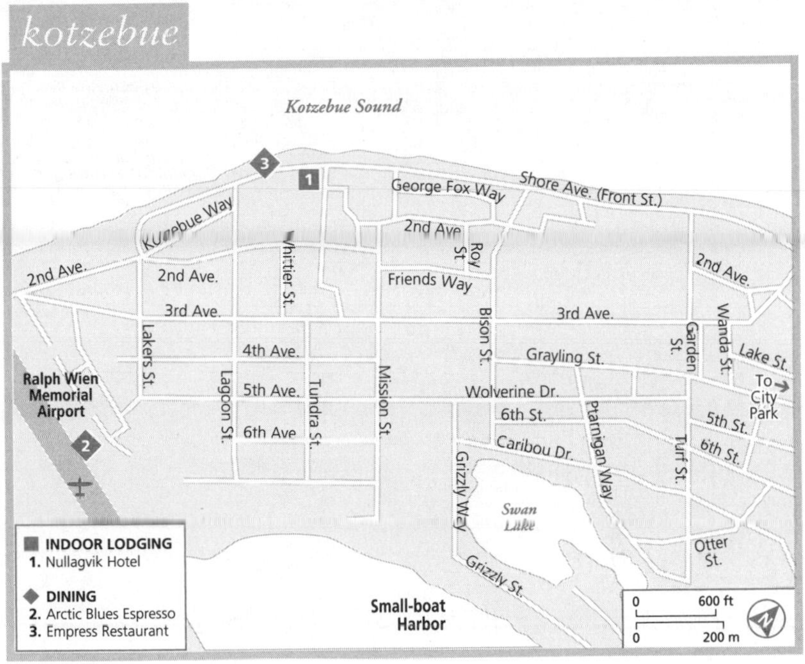

Alaska adventures. It is located on the north bank of the **Naknek River** on the Alaska Peninsula, about 15 miles upriver from the village of **Naknek.** The native population is a mixture of Aleuts, Indians, and Eskimos. King Salmon is a transportation hub for Bristol Bay, and fishermen launch from there regularly.

King Salmon Visitors Center
P.O. Box 298
King Salmon 99613
☎ 907-246-4250

UNALASKA

UNALASKA OVERLOOKS **Iliuliuk Bay** and **Dutch Harbor** on Unalaska Island in the Aleutian Chain. It lies 800 air miles from Anchorage and 1,700 miles northwest of Seattle. It is a rapidly growing and diverse community, focused on fishing and fish processing.

Unalaska/Port of Dutch Harbor Convention and Visitors Bureau
☎ 877-581-2612
www.unalaska.info

LAKE CLARK NATIONAL PARK AND PRESERVE

(Primary activities: backpacking, rafting, fishing)

LAKE CLARK IS ONE OF THE LEAST-VISITED but most spectacular of the national parks in Alaska, and a great starting point for any unique outdoor adventure. Its 4 million acres attract less than 5,000

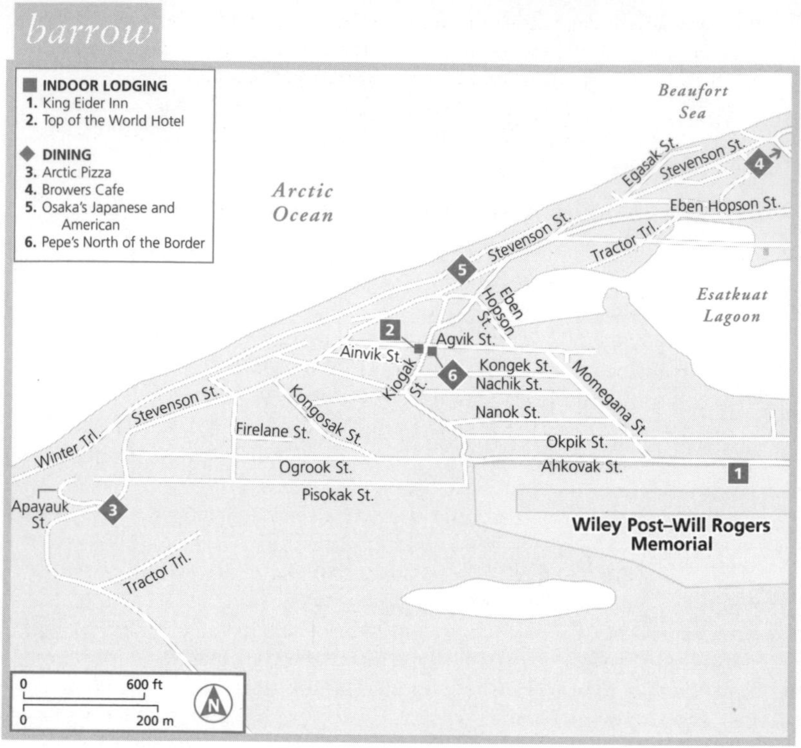

Field Headquarters
1 Park Place
Port Alsworth 99653
☎ 907-781-2218

Administrative Headquarters
240 W. Fifth Ave.
Anchorage 99501
www.nps.gov/lacl

visitors a year, making it the type of place where you can have an adventure in which you cross paths with no one.

Lake Clark National Park and Preserve stretches from the shores of **Cook Inlet,** across the **Chigmit Mountains,** to the open hills of the western Interior. The Chigmits, where the Alaska and Aleutian ranges meet, comprise rugged and jagged-looking mountains and glaciers, which include two active volcanoes, **Mounts Redoubt** and **Iliamna.** The 40-mile-long **Lake Clark** is critical salmon habitat to the Bristol Bay salmon fishery, one of the largest sockeye-salmon fishing grounds in the world. The park is open year-round, although most of its visitors come between June and September.

Access to the Lake Clark region is by small aircraft from Anchorage, Kenai, or Homer. Floatplanes can land on the many lakes throughout the area, or wheeled planes can land on beaches or the few private airstrips in the region. Scheduled commercial flights between Anchorage and Iliamna, 30 miles outside the boundary, provide another means of access. There are no roads in the park. A 2.5-mile trail to **Tanalian Falls** and **Kontrashibuna Lake** is accessible from the town of Port Alsworth. The 50-mile Telaquana Trail, depicted on maps, is an undeveloped historic route from Lake Clark to Telaquana Lake.

KATMAI NATIONAL PARK AND PRESERVE

(Primary activities: bear viewing, fishing)

Field Headquarters
P.O. Box 7
1 King Salmon Mall
King Salmon 99613
☎ 907-246-3305

Administrative Headquarters
240 West Fifth Avenue
Anchorage 99501
www.nps.gov/katm

KATMAI IS A 4.7-MILLION-ACRE national park and preserve located on the Alaska Peninsula, across from Kodiak Island, which also includes the mystical area known as the **Valley of 10,000 Smokes.** The area was named so in the early 1900s, when explorers discovered huge smoldering volcanoes, one of which, Novarupta, had deposited hundreds of feet of volcanic ash across the valley floor. This 40-square-mile area is still stark today, although lush vegetation surrounds it. The National Park Service reports that there are at least 14 volcanoes in Katmai considered active, although none of them are currently erupting. Brown bears and salmon are very active in Katmai, which is why it receives so many more visitors than Lake Clark. In 2004, there were about 57,000 visitors, most of them there to see and photograph bears, go fishing, or both. The number of brown bears in the region has grown to more than 2,000, and during the peak of the sockeye-salmon run in July, as many as 60 bears at a time congregate in **Brooks Camp** along the **Brooks River** and the **Naknek Lake** and **Brooks Lake** shorelines. However, the bears' range goes beyond this region, and they can be found all along the 480-mile Katmai Coast feeding on clams, crabs, and an occasional whale carcass.

Katmai National Park is open year-round, though most visitors travel there between June and September. Prime bear-viewing months are July and September, although a few bears may be in the area at any time between late May and December.

Access is via small plane. Park headquarters are in King Salmon, about 290 air miles southwest of Anchorage. Several commercial airlines provide daily flights into King Salmon as there is no road access. Brooks Camp, along the Brooks River approximately 30 air miles from King Salmon, is a common destination for visitors to the park. Brooks Camp can be reached only via small floatplane or boat.

unofficial **TIP**
Be prepared for anything when traveling to Katmai National Park. Weather and bears are always a factor here, so plan extra time to work around delays. There are occasions, especially in July, when visitors are unable to get to the Falls Platform due to time constraints and flight schedules.

ANIAKCHAK NATIONAL MONUMENT AND PRESERVE

(Primary activities: rafting, fishing, backpacking)

ANIAKCHAK NATIONAL MONUMENT AND PRESERVE is for those who seek a destination like no other. This area is best suited for rafting, fly-fishing, and hiking, and a trip to the **Aniakchak Caldera** is unparalleled. The caldera is a giant dry crater that is the result of a series of eruptions, the latest dating to 1931 and the earliest as long ago as 3,500 years. It's nearly six miles in diameter and covers more than ten miles, making it a great destination hike. The 2,000-foot caldera was thought to once be a 7,000-foot mountain that collapsed after the eruptions. While exploring the area, you'll see many outstanding examples of volcanic features, such lava flows, cinder cones, and explosion pits. **Surprise Lake,** located within the caldera, is the source of the **Aniakchak River,** which flows through a giant crack in the caldera wall. The site also contains the **Aniakchak Wild River.**

Aniakchak National Monument and Preserve
P.O. Box 7
King Salmon 99613
☎ 907-246-3305

Administrative Headquarters
240 W. Fifth Ave.
Anchorage 99501
www.nps.gov/ania

Access to the park is by plane or floatplane from King Salmon, or by powerboat from any one of the numerous villages along the Pacific Ocean coastline. There are no formal trails within the preserve, although open ash fields make the backpacking and hiking options easier than bushwhacking. Conditions are usually windy within the caldera, and the coastal region is often cloudy and foggy. There are plenty of bears in the area, too, so be sure to pack food well away from camp and be on the lookout. While exploring, also look for great birding and wildlife-watching options. The waterfowl and migratory bird habitat of Bristol Bay's coastal plain is west of the caldera. To the east, the Pacific Coast and offshore islands provide habitat for sea mammals and seabirds.

ALAGNAK WILD RIVER

(Primary activities: rafting, fishing)

ALAGNAK WILD RIVER WINDS THROUGH THE **Aleutian Range** on the Alaska Peninsula and is a great destination for scenic and white-water rafting, as well as fishing for rainbow, sockeye, king salmon, northern pike, arctic char, and grayling. The area was designated as a wild river in 1980, preserving the upper 56 miles of water and protecting the river and its immediate environments for future generations. It's the most popular fly-in fishery in Southwest Alaska and is inaccessible by road.

Alagnak Wild River
P.O. Box 7
King Salmon 99611
☎ 907-246-3305
www.nps.gov/alag

Access to the Alagnak is by charter flights from Anchorage and King Salmon or by powerboat from one of the villages along the river. The area is great not only for fishing but also for viewing wildlife such as caribou, beaver, lynx, mink, otter, fox, wolverine, and occasionally wolf.

ALEUTIAN WORLD WAR II NATIONAL HISTORIC AREA

(Primary activities: birding, hiking, interpretive programs, wildlife viewing)

Aleutian World War II Visitor Center
☎ 907-581-9944
www.ounalashka.com
Open all year

WHILE THIS AREA IS MORE DEDICATED to preserving history, the Aleutian World War II National Historic Area is also a remarkable place in which to explore. Located just outside of the Aleutian Island community of Unalaska, it follows the history of the U.S. Army **Fort Schwatka,** at Ulakta Head on Mount Ballyhoo. The fort is one of four coastal-defense posts built in the early 1940s to protect the **Dutch Harbor Naval Operating Base.** The fort overlooks Dutch Harbor and was key to its protection. Although today many of the bunkers and wooden structures of Fort Schwatka have collapsed, the gun mounts and lookouts are among the most intact in the country. There also is a visitor center, in the renovated Naval Air **Transport Services Aerology Building at the Unalaska Airport.** It's a good place to explore in town.

WOOD-TIKCHIK STATE PARK

(Primary activities: kayaking, rafting, fishing)

UNDEVELOPED AND QUITE WILD, Wood-Tikchik State Park holds the distinction of being the largest state park in the nation, covering 1.6 million acres of wilderness land that managers have worked hard to keep unspoiled. The park embraces a low-impact-camping mentality, so it is the perfect destination for outdoor travelers who appreciate land that remains untouched by vehicles, trails, and other amenities.

Wood-Tikchik State Park
550 West Seventh Avenue
Suite 1390
Anchorage 99501-3561
☎ 907-269-8698

Wood-Tikchik Ranger Station
P.O. Box 3022
Dillingham 99576
☎ 907-842-2375
www.dnr.state.ak.us/parks/units/woodtik
Open seasonally, late May through late September

The park was created in 1978 to protect fish- and wildlife-breeding habitats and allow an uninterrupted place for native subsistence practices and recreation. Its name is derived from the two lakes that dominate the region, but there are many others, as the park comprises a water-based ecosystem that is perfect for sea kayaking and river running.

Bordered by the **Nushagak Lowlands** on the east and the **Wood River Mountains** to the west, the lake system spans a variety of terrain and vegetative zones that are known for their rugged beauty. Pointed peaks, alpine valleys, and steep V-shaped arms make the western edge of the lakes look almost like a fjord. The lakes, which vary from 15 to 45 miles long, are deep and relatively temperate

unofficial **TIP**
Although the weather in Wood-Tikchik State Park between late May and early October permits outdoor recreational activities almost daily, flying, boating, and alpine activities are occasionally hampered or unsafe. Prepare for such changes in your schedule should bad weather appear.

for this part of the state, with water temperatures ranging from 40°F to 60°F during the summer.

Access to Wood-Tikchik State Park begins from Dillingham, in Southwest Alaska. Daily commercial-airline service is available from Anchorage, and air charter by floatplane is the most common mode of reaching the park; plus, the entire park is open to private-aircraft landings. You can also get to the Wood River Lakes via Aleknagik, 24 miles north of Dillingham by road, although you won't save a lot of money this way.

The weather is generally cool and moist, with average daily July temperatures in the low 60s. Precipitation is most prevalent in the summer, especially August.

Freshwater sportfish are generally prolific throughout the area and include rainbow trout, grayling, lake trout, arctic char, Dolly Varden, and northern pike. In addition, whitefish are an important subsistence species in the Tikchik Lakes, and all five species of salmon can be found. Wildlife includes such species as brown bears and occasionally black bears, ungulates such as moose and caribou, and small animals such as rabbits, otters, beavers, and wolverines. The shrill calls of ground squirrels and marmots are heard frequently.

TOGIAK NATIONAL WILDLIFE REFUGE

(Primary activities: fishing, wildlife viewing, backpacking, rafting, kayaking, birding)

Togiak National Wildlife Refuge
6 Main Street
Kangiiqutaq Building
P.O. Box 270
Dillingham 99576
☎ 907-842-1063
togiak.fws.gov

MANAGED BY THE U.S. FISH AND WILDLIFE SERVICE in Alaska, this 4.7-million-acre area was designated to conserve fish and wildlife populations. It's located in Southwest Alaska between **Kuskokwim Bay** and **Bristol Bay,** about 350 air miles southwest of Anchorage. It is bordered on the north by **Yukon Delta National Wildlife Refuge** and on the east by **Wood-Tikchik State Park.**

unofficial **TIP**
There are no roads connecting Togiak National Wildlife Refuge to anyplace else, nor are there any trails, campgrounds, or facilities for those looking for a comfortable camping experience. Access is by air or water during ice-free months.

Togiak is a challenging place to reach. Its sea cliffs, fast-flowing rivers, and coastal lagoons are beautiful in the lowlands, and the surrounding **Ahklun Mountains** add grandeur in the form of craggy peaks.

One of the primary draws to the refuge is **Cape Peirce,** on the western edge of Bristol Bay and composed of rocky cliffs, ledges, and inaccessible beaches. It is a spectacular place to see such wildlife as Pacific walrus, spotted and harbor seals, puffins, and other rare and common seabirds. Access to the area, however, is limited due to the sensitive nature of the habitat, so visitors must obtain a permit ahead of time.

Access to the refuge is primarily by air taxis based in Dillingham, although there are a couple in King Salmon and Bethel.

U.S. Geological Survey topographic maps of the area may be purchased online at **topomaps.usgs.gov/ordering_maps.html.**

WALRUS ISLANDS STATE GAME SANCTUARY—ROUND ISLAND

(Primary activities: wildlife viewing, backpacking, birding)

VISITS TO THIS SANCTUARY, particularly the rugged **Round Island,** are limited because it is a critical habitat to the walrus. Each year in spring and summer, thousands of male walrus gather on this group of seven islands in Bristol Bay. The islands have enjoyed protected status since 1960, and visitors must obtain permits to travel here.

Walrus Islands State Game Sanctuary
Alaska Department of Fish and Game, Division of Wildlife Conservation
P.O. Box 1030
Dillingham 99576-1030
☎ 907-842-2334
www.wildlife.alaska.gov
(go to "Walrus Island" link)

FAR NORTH

ANY REGION IN THE FAR NORTH that is not accessible by road is included in this chapter on the Bush. That includes such far-flung communities as Nome, Barrow, and Kotzebue, but also encompasses some vast territories of land owned by the federal government and protected for centuries to come for outdoors travelers to enjoy.

The Far North is quintessential Alaska, the stereotype one often envisions when thinking of Alaska: long, cold winters; lots of dark nights; and plenty of wild animals roaming freely.

It is a land of extremes. At its northernmost reaches, the region enjoys the country's longest period of daylight, with 84 continuous days of constant daylight from May 10 to August 2. In contrast, during the dark days of winter, it is a cold, lonely place, and the sun remains set for 67 days. This is where polar bears roam—nowhere else in Alaska will you find them, despite what the movies portray. Grizzly bears, caribou, and moose are common, as well as tundra creatures such as arctic foxes and hares.

Among the native people living in the Far North, there are two groups of Eskimos: Inupiat on the mainland and Yu'piks, who reside in **Savoonga** and **Gambell,** on **St. Lawrence Island.**

Like Southwest Alaska, the Far North is home to some of the best national parks and preserves in the state, most of which are a result of the Alaska National Interest Lands Conservation Act, which in the late 1970s set aside millions of acres of land for public protection and use.

These areas are the places we recommend visiting, although stopping at some of the predominantly native communities along the way can remind one of being in a different country altogether, adding a cultural aspect to your trip that really can't be matched elsewhere in the state. Our favorites are **Kobuk Valley National Park,** where you can experience miles of sand dunes, and **Bering Land Bridge National Preserve,** where the Serpentine Hot Springs beckon year-round. We have included a few other options, as well, that are worth exploring.

Brief descriptions of the major towns that serve as jumping-off points for adventures are provided below.

NOME

Nome Convention and Visitors Bureau
☎ 907-443-6624
www.nomealaska.org

THIS BERING SEA–COAST COMMUNITY boomed at the turn of the century, when gold was discovered on its beaches, prompting one of the biggest gold rushes in history. Today, gold and other mineral mining still is the major economic force in Nome, home to about 3,500 residents, more than half of them Alaska natives. Nome is on the Seward Peninsula, some 540 miles from Anchorage, and off the road system. Nome's other claim to fame is the **Iditarod Trail Sled Dog Race,** the annual dog-mushing race from Anchorage to Nome.

KOTZEBUE

Kotzebue Visitor Information Center
154 Second Street
Kotzebue 99752
☎ 907-442-3890
(Open during summer months; in the off-season, call and leave a message to arrange a visit.)

THE MOSTLY NATIVE COMMUNITY of Kotzebue lies 26 miles north of the Arctic Circle and 550 air miles northwest of Anchorage. There is not a lot in the way of visitor amenities here, but Kotzebue is one of the main starting points for forays farther into the wilderness. This is where you will arrange flights into the public lands and get to remote lodges scattered across the land.

BARROW

City of Barrow
P.O. Box 629
Barrow 99723
☎ 907-852-5211

North Slope Barrow Public Information Division
P.O. Box 69
Barrow 99723
☎ 907-852-0215

BARROW IS ABOUT AS FAR NORTH as you can go in Alaska, and once there you will truly feel that you are on the edge of the earth. The land is vast, open, and flat, and seems to go on forever. Located 330 air miles north of the Arctic Circle, Barrow is in fact the farthest-north community in the Western Hemisphere. It is easily accessed via daily jet service from Anchorage or Fairbanks.

Barrow is another one of those Alaska communities that doesn't have much for the visitor looking for entertainment. But outdoor travelers are not necessarily seeking that sort of experience. Instead, the remoteness alone is the draw. If that is what you seek, then by all means visit this community—we've eaten at and stayed at a few places there that we recommend. Otherwise, your Far North adventure is likely going to be more outdoors adventurous if embarking from Nome or Kotzebue.

BERING LAND BRIDGE NATIONAL PRESERVE

(Primary activities: birding, hiking, backpacking, fishing, dog mushing, skiing)

Bering Land Bridge National Preserve
P.O. Box 220
Nome 99762
☎ 907-443-2522
www.nps.gov/bela

THE BERING LAND BRIDGE NATIONAL PRESERVE is one of the most remote national-park areas, on the Seward Peninsula in northwest Alaska, with its headquarters based in Nome. It is a remnant of the land bridge that connected Asia with North America more than 13,000 years ago. Archaeologists believe it was across the Bering Land Bridge, also called "Beringia," that humans first passed from Asia to populate the Americas.

Camping, hiking, backpacking, and other exploration of the surrounding area are possible with charter flights that can be arranged from Nome. Access to the preserve, in fact, is via Bush plane or small boat in the summer, and skis, snowmobile, or dog team in the winters. There are no roads that lead directly into it, but that's part of the appeal. The park is open year-round, although most people visit in the summer months.

unofficial **TIP**
As is typical in the Bush, Serpentine Hot Springs has always had a casual, relaxed, and sharing atmosphere. Be sure to care for the facilities as you would if you were a guest in someone's home.

One of the best-kept secrets of this rarely visited preserve is **Serpentine Hot Springs,** a natural hot spring that offers year-round relaxation and a bunkhouse-style cabin for those who don't mind sharing with others in exchange for a truly unique experience. The cabin sleeps 15 to 20 people in two sections and includes a wooden tub for bathing in a small bathhouse, which is fed by the waters of the hot spring. You can't reserve the cabin, and you may have to share it with other visitors who show up at the same time—it's considered Bush etiquette, so please resist the urge to claim "first-come, first-served." There is unlimited camping, too, for those who want more privacy if others show up. There is no developed water or power, and there are no sanitation facilities.

CAPE KRUSENSTERN NATIONAL MONUMENT

(Primary activities: backpacking, kayaking, dog mushing)

Cape Krusenstern National Monument
P.O. Box 1029
Kotzebue 99752
☎ 907-442-3890 or 907-442-3760

CAPE KRUSENSTERN NATIONAL MONUMENT is an interesting study in Alaska beach life, and a place not visited often by outdoor travelers. While you can go backpacking and kayaking in this area, it often is windy and chilly, even in the middle of summer. Winter travel by dogsled is often the best means of travel, although it gets bone-chillingly cold, often –20°F or lower for days on end.

The area is beautiful, though. It is a coastal plain dotted with lagoons and pothole lakes, and surrounded by gently rolling limestone hills. Cape Krusenstern's bluffs and beach ridges are a great place for those curious about archaeology or geology, and the presence of prehistoric inhabitation goes back some 9,000 years.

In summer, wildflowers dot the landscape and huge numbers of migratory birds come from all over the world to nest. They use the lagoons as feeding and staging areas.

Alaska natives still hunt marine mammals along the beaches, and local rural residents are allowed to hunt in the monument. A local zinc mine operates along the northern boundary, so travelers are best suited to choose the southern side for more solitude.

Access to the monument is by private charter plane out of Kotzebue or Nome. Commercial airlines provide service from Anchorage or Fairbanks to Nome or Kotzebue. There are scheduled flights to villages and chartered flights to specific park areas. Summer access may include motorized or nonmotorized watercraft, aircraft, or walking. Winter access may include snowmobiles, aircraft, or walking.

The monument is open year-round, and the headquarters are in Kotzebue. There are no developed facilities such as camping or hiking trails, so be prepared for true wilderness travel. Summer hikes are possible, but there also is a lot of private land surrounding the monument, so be sure of where you are traveling. Kayaking is possible on several of the larger lagoons, but constant windy conditions can make it feel quite cold, even in the summer.

KOBUK VALLEY NATIONAL PARK

(Primary activities: backpacking, wildlife viewing, dog mushing, boating)

Kobuk Valley National Park
P.O. Box 1029
Kotzebue 99752
☎ 907-442-3890 or 907-442-3760
www.nps.gov/kova

THE BAIRD AND WARING MOUNTAIN ranges make up Kobuk Valley National Park, a park that is incredible in many ways but a must-see for those outdoor travelers who want a truly unique adventure. Located within the park is the 25-square-mile **Great Kobuk Sand Dunes,** as well as the **Little Kobuk and Hunt River dunes.** The unusual sand dunes look oddly out of place in Alaska but are there nonetheless, the result of ancient glaciers grinding together with the wind and rain. The dunes now cover much of the southern portion of the Kobuk Valley, where they are stabilized by vegetation. River bluffs, composed of sand and standing as high as 150 feet, hold permafrost ice wedges and the fossils of Ice Age mammals.

The closest towns to Kobuk Valley National Park are Kotzebue and Nome, both of which have daily jet service from Anchorage and

Fairbanks. Access to the park is by air taxi, which can take you to most places within the park that you'd like to see. You can also travel the Kobuk River by boat to access the area, as well as backpack in, although there are no trails. In the winter, access is via snowmobile, dog team, or skis if you're brave enough. Tundra and river bars are often used for primitive camping. Do not camp in archaeological areas or on private property.

unofficial **TIP**
Use river bars with caution. Rapid changes in the river level can occur without warning. Camp only where escape routes are available to safe higher ground. Keep gear above river level and secure boats and other floatable items.

The park is open year-round, although winter conditions are typical of the Arctic, with temperatures routinely plummeting to as low as −50°F. Throughout the year, educational and interpretive programs are offered at the **Kotzebue Public Lands Information Center** (☎ 907-442-3760).

NOATAK NATIONAL PRESERVE

Noatak National Preserve
P.O. Box 1029
Kotzebue 99752
☎ 907-442-3890 or 907-442-3760
www.nps.gov/noat

(Primary activities: backpacking, wildlife viewing, boating, dog mushing, skiing)

AS ONE OF NORTH AMERICA'S LARGEST MOUNTAIN-RINGED river basins with an intact ecosystem, the **Noatak River** environs feature some of the Arctic's finest arrays of plants and animals. The river is classified as a National Wild and Scenic River, and offers superlative wilderness float-trip opportunities—from deep in the **Brooks Range** to the tidewater of the **Chukchi Sea.**

There are no trails or roads in the park.

Throughout the year programs are offered at the Kotzebue Public Lands Information Center. Activities include occasional guided hikes and slide-show lectures on various features of the preserve.

Noatak National Preserve is open year-round. The headquarters office, located in Kotzebue, is open from 8 a.m. to 5 p.m. Monday through Friday. The visitor center, also located in Kotzebue, is open for the summer, Tuesday through Friday from noon to 8 p.m. and Saturday from noon to 4 p.m.

unofficial **TIP**
Arctic winter conditions—snow, ice, wind, and below-freezing temperatures—exist in Noatak National Preserve from October through April. Snow or freezing temperatures may occur any time, even in summer.

Commercial airlines provide service from Anchorage or Fairbanks to Nome or Kotzebue. From Kotzebue to the parklands, fly with various air-taxi operators. There are scheduled flights to villages and chartered flights to specific park areas. Summer access may include motorized or nonmotorized watercraft, aircraft, or walking. Winter access may include snowmobiles, aircraft, or walking.

GETTING *around the* BUSH

SOUTHWEST

Dillingham

Access by air is through **Alaska Airlines** (☎ 800-252-7522; **www.alaskaair.com**); **Frontier Flying** (☎ 800-478-6779 or 907-543-5863; **www.frontierflying.com**); and **Peninsula Airways** (☎ 800-448-4226; **www.penair.com**).

Cabs are available through **Nushagak Cab Co.** (☎ 907-842-4403) or **Issama Cab** (☎907-842-4881).

Bethel

Access by air is through the following air companies, although there are smaller charter-flight operators in town for forays into the wilderness: **Alaska Airlines** (☎ 800-252-7522; **www.alaskaair.com**); **Era Aviation** (☎ 907-543-3905; **www.era-aviation.com**); and **Frontier Flying** (☎ 800-478-6779 or 907-543-5863; **www.frontierflying.com**).

Cab fares within Bethel are set by city ordinance, which makes getting around affordable. A few choices include **Alaska/Checker Cab** (☎ 907-543-2111; fares are $4 within the city); **Camai** (☎ 907-543-5800); **City Cab** (☎ 907-543-4141); and **Kusko** (☎ 907-543-2169).

King Salmon

Access by air is through **Alaska Airlines** (☎ 800-252-7522; **www.alaskaair.com**) and **Peninsula Airways** (☎ 800-448-4226; **www.penair.com**).

There are no car rentals or cab companies, but you can pretty much get where you need to on foot.

Unalaska

Access by air is through **Alaska Airlines** (☎ 800-252-7522; **www.alaskaair.com**) and **Peninsula Airways** (☎ 800-448-4226; **www.penair.com**), with connecting service also to the Pribilof Islands).

Access by sea is on the **Alaska State Ferry M/V *Tustumena,*** which travels to Unalaska monthly (☎ 800-642-0066; **www.ferryalaska.com**).

Cars can be rented from **B. C. Vehicle Rental** (☎ 907-581-6777), inside the Unalaska Airport; a range of vehicles are available.

FAR NORTH

Nome

Access by air is through **Alaska Airlines** (☎ 800-252-7522; **www.alaskaair.com**); **Frontier Flying** (☎ 800-478-6779 or 907-543-5863; **www.frontierflying.com**); and **Bering Air** (☎ 907-442-3943; **www.beringair.com**).

Cars can be rented from **Stampede Ventures** (☎ 800-354-4606 or 907-443-3838; **www.aurorainnome.com/stampede.htm**).

For cab service, call **Checker Cab** at ☎ 907-443-5136.

Kotzebue

Access by air is through **Alaska Airlines** (☎ 800-252-7522; **www.alaska air.com**); **Frontier Flying** (☎ 800-478-6779 or 907-543-5863; **www .frontierflying.com**); **Baker Aviation** (☎ 907-442-3108); and **Bering Air** (☎ 907-442-3943; **www.beringair.com**).

Cars can be rented from **Kikiktagruk Inupiat Corporation** at ☎ 907-442-3165.

Cab companies include **B&D Cab Co.** (☎ 907-442-2244) and **Kobuk Cab** (☎ 907-442-3651).

Barrow

Access by air is through **Alaska Airlines** (☎ 800-252-7522; **www.alaska air.com**) and **Frontier Flying** (☎ 800-478-6779 or 907-543-5863; **www .frontierflying.com**).

Cars can be rented from **UIC Auto Rentals** (☎ 907-852-2700; prices are on the high side, about $75 per day) or **King Eider Inn** (☎ 888-303-4337 or 907-852-4700; **www.kingeider.net**) for those who are lodging there. The other option is to call a taxi: **Alaska Taxi** (☎ 907-852-3000); **Arcticab** (☎ 907-852-2227); **Barrow Taxi** (☎ 907-852-2222); or **City Cab** (☎ 907-852-5050).

GEARING UP

YOU'LL SAVE MONEY WHEN TRAVELING to the Bush if you buy most or all of your supplies ahead of time. Some of the larger towns, such as Bethel and Nome, will have supply stores and even grocery stores, but prices are high, especially for perishable items such as milk, vegetables, and fruits. These supplies are also often at less than their peak, and it can be disappointing, say, to buy a bag of overpriced apples and discover that half of them are soft and mushy.

In most chapters of this book, we have broken down the "Gearing Up" sections into sporting goods, camping supplies, and groceries. However, because the communities of the Far North and Southwest Alaska are so small, you won't likely find such diversity. In the Bush, it's not uncommon to see baked beans next to hip waders in the local grocery store, or to buy your fishing license in the same place you'll purchase postage stamps.

unofficial **TIP**
In the Bush, do not count on local grocery, sporting-goods, and camping stores to have what you will need, because many of these shops are sparsely supplied and carry only the basics such as batteries, candles, and other necessities.

Out of necessity, shop owners in the Bush have learned to diversify their stores to meet the needs of their customers. This attitude can make shopping in the Bush convenient; still, your choices will be limited to whatever the local shop owner has on hand. Therefore, we've broken the sections of this chapter into town names and listed the few choices available in each town, and what you can find at each store or shop.

SOUTHWEST

Dillingham

- **AC Value Center–Alaska Commercial Company** First and Main streets; ☎ 907-842-5444
  The best place in town for groceries. Also a good source for sporting goods, fishing licenses, and some camping supplies.
- **Alaska Department of Fish and Game Office** ☎ 907-842-2427
  Sporting goods, fishing licenses, and permits.
- **N&N Market** 10 Main Street; ☎ 907-842-5283
  Groceries, sporting goods, and fishing licenses.

Bethel

- **AC Value Center–Alaska Commercial Company** ☎ 907-543-2661 or 907-543-3463
  Groceries, some camping supplies, and sporting goods.
- **Kwethluk Sport Store** 12 miles from Bethel in the village of Kwethluk; ☎ 907-757-6412
  Sporting goods, fishing licenses.
- **Swanson's** 830 River Street; ☎ 907-543-3221
  Hardware, sporting goods, fishing licenses, tackle, and camping gear.

King Salmon

- **Alaska Commercial Company** ☎ 907-246-6109
  Groceries, sporting goods, camping supplies, fishing licenses.
- **City Market** 1 Peninsula Avenue; ☎ 907-246-6109
  Groceries and other limited supplies.

Unalaska

- **AC Value Center–Alaska Commercial Company** 100 Salmon Way; ☎ 907-581-1245
  Sporting goods and fishing licenses.
- **Aleutian Commercial Company and Alaska Ship Supply** ☎ 907-581-1284; **www.westernpioneer.com**
  These two companies, owned by the same outfit, Western Pioneer, provide marine hardware, fishing gear, bait, groceries, clothing, tools, and many other goods and services.
- **Eagle Food Center** 2029 Airport Beach Road; ☎ 907-581-4040
  Groceries, fishing licenses.

FAR NORTH

Nome

- **AC Value Center–Alaska Commercial Company** ☎ 907-443-2243
  Groceries, sporting goods, camping supplies, fishing licenses.

- **Hanson's Safeway** ☎ 907-443-5454
  Groceries and some sporting goods and camping supplies, along with fishing licenses.
- **Nome Outfitters** ☎ 907-443-2880
  Fishing licenses, sporting goods, camping supplies.

Kotzebue

- **Country Store** Off Front Street; ☎ 907-443-5666
  Groceries, fishing licenses, limited camping supplies, and sporting goods.
- **Alaska Commercial Co.** ☎ 907-442-3285
  The largest grocer, with fishing licenses, limited camping supplies, and sporting goods.
- **Rotman Stores** 500 Shore Avenue; ☎ 907-442-3123

Barrow

- **AC Value Center–Alaska Commercial Company** 4725 Ahakvoak Street; ☎ 907-852-6711
  Groceries, fishing licenses, camping supplies, and some sporting goods.

WHERE *to* STAY

THE BUSH IS A VAST LAND DOMINATED by wilderness and dotted by only a handful of lodging options. You may have difficulty finding a place to sleep in some of the smaller villages and towns in this region. Many of the options are basic at best, so with a few exceptions, do not expect luxury.

In this section, we've given you a few options, places that we have tried ourselves and found to be acceptable.

SOUTHWEST INDOOR LODGING

Dillingham

- **Beaver Creek Bed and Breakfast** ☎ 866-252-7335 or 907-842-7335; **www.dillinghamalaska.com**

  QUALITY ★★★ VALUE ★★★★ $95 $155

  We like this place because you have your choice of a room in the main house or your own house or log cabin just a mile down the road. Hosts Susan and Gorden Isaacs couldn't be more gracious.
- **Bristol Bay Lodge** ☎ 907-842-2500; **www.bristolbaylodge.com**

  QUALITY ★★★★★ VALUE ★★★★ $6,850/WEEK

  For the visitor with plenty of cash to spend, a week or two at the Bristol Bay Lodge is luxurious, with great food, lodging, and some of the best fishing in the state, tucked away within Wood-Tikchik State Park. You'll fly out by small plane each day to some of the remotest fishing spots in the world, then come home to meals and fine lodging. Rate does not include gratuities, fishing

Bush Southwest Indoor Lodging

NAME	TYPE(S) OF LODGING	QUALITY RATING	VALUE RATING	COST
DILLINGHAM				
Beaver Creek Bed and Breakfast	B&B/cabins	★★★	★★★★	$95–$155
Bristol Bay Lodge	wilderness lodge	★★★★★	★★★★	$6,850/ week
The Bristol Inn	hotel	★★★	★★	$160–$190
Hillside Haven B&B	B&B	★★★	★★★	$140–$210
Thai Inn	B&B	★★★	★★★★	$120
BETHEL				
Bentley's Porter House B & B	hotel/B&B	★★★★	★★★★	$110–$160
Brown Slough Bed & Breakfast	cabins	★★★★	★★★	$100–$150
Delta Cottages	B&B	★★	★★	$100–$120
Lakeside Lodge	B&B	★★★	★★★★	$105
Longhouse Bethel Hotel	hotel	★★★	★★★	$149–$189
KING SALMON				
Alagnak Lodge	wilderness lodge	★★★	★★★	$2,450/ 3 nights
King Ko Inn	duplex	★★	★★★★	$210
Rainbow Bend Lodges	cabins	★★★★	★★★★	$800/ 2 nights
UNALASKA				
The Grand Aleutian Hotel	hotel	★★★★★	★★★★	$179–$320
UniSea Inn	inn	★★★	★★★	$110–$130

license, or fishing tackle. You also have the option of staying at small out-camps run by the lodge. Fly out to the small camps for some true solitude, then return to the main lodge a day or two later.

- **The Bristol Inn** 104 Main Street; ☎ 800-764-9704 or 907-842-2240; **www.alaskaoutdoors.com/bristolinn**

QUALITY ★★★ VALUE ★★ $160–$190

Bush Southwest Camping

NAME	TYPE(S) OF CAMPING	QUALITY RATING	VALUE RATING	COST
DILLINGHAM				
City of Dillingham Campground	tent	★★	★★★★	free
Goodnews, North Fork or Middle Fork rivers	tent	★★★★★	★★★★	free
Kanektok or Arolik rivers	tent	★★★★	★★★★	free
Nushagak River	tent	★★★	★★★★	free
Picnic Beach and Cape Constantine	tent	★★★★★	★★	free
Round Island	tent	★★★★★	★★★★★	free
Togiak River	tent	★★★★	★★★★	free
Wood-Tikchik State Park and Togiak National Wildlife Refuge	tent	★★★★★	★★★★★	free
KING SALMON				
Alagnak Wild River	tent	★★★★	★★★★★	free
Unalaska Lands	tent	★★★★	★★★★	free

This small hotel is downtown and pretty basic, but it's clean and has a free shuttle to the airport; nonsmoking rooms are available.

- **Hillside Haven B&B** ☎ 907-842-3523

  QUALITY ★★★ VALUE ★★★ $140–$210

  Donna and Henry Shade make your stay here enjoyable. One of the more popular B&Bs in the area, and one of the best places to eat good food. Their Café Hillside features gourmet fare.

- **Thai Inn** ☎ 907-842-7378; **www.thai-inn.com**

  QUALITY ★★★ VALUE ★★★★ $120

  The inn features rooms completely separate from the residence, offering privacy, but the amenities of a B&B. As the name implies, the lodging has an Asian-inspired theme.

Bethel

- **Bentley's Porter House B & B** 624 First Avenue; ☎ 907-543-5923 or 907-543-3552

  QUALITY ★★★★ VALUE ★★★★ $110–$160

  Of the hotels in town, this one is the most highly recommended. There are 26 rooms; rates include breakfast.

Bush Far North Indoor Lodging

NAME	TYPE(S) OF LODGING	QUALITY RATING	VALUE RATING	COST
NOME				
Aurora Inn & Suites	hotel	★★★★	★★★	$130–$220
Nome Nugget Inn	hotel	★★★	★★	$120–$160
Trail's End Apartments	apartments	★★★	★★★	$110
KOTZEBUE				
Nullagvik Hotel	hotel	★★★	★★★	$170–$190
BARROW				
King Eider Inn	hotel	★★★★	★★★★	$140–$210
Top of the World Hotel	hotel	★★★	★★★	$145–$200

- **Brown Slough Bed & Breakfast** 923 Sixth Avenue; ☎ 888-543-4334 or 907-543-4334; **www.bethelhotel.com**

  QUALITY ★★★★ VALUE ★★★ $100–$150

  We really like the Alaska log-and-timber-frame houses, and the owners, Grant and Debbie Fairbanks, are friendly and accommodating. Wireless Internet is available.

- **Delta Cottages** 124 Gunderson Court; ☎ 907-543-3610

  QUALITY ★★ VALUE ★★ $100–$120

  Rooms are basic but clean.

- **Lakeside Lodge** H-Marker Lake; ☎ 907-543-5275; **www.lakesidelodgebnb.com**

  QUALITY ★★★ VALUE ★★★★ $105

  There are only three rooms, with two beds per room. The owners are friendly and the atmosphere relaxed. Amenities include free airport pickup and wireless Internet.

- **Longhouse Bethel Hotel** 751 Third Avenue; ☎ 866-543-4613 or 907-543-4612; **www.longhousebethelinn.com**

  QUALITY ★★★ VALUE ★★★ $149–$189

  Offers the amenities of larger lodgings with a smaller, more intimate feel. High-speed Internet access is available, and all rooms are nonsmoking.

King Salmon

- **Alagnak Lodge** ☎ 800-877-9903; **www.alagnaklodge.com**

  QUALITY ★★★ VALUE ★★★ $2,450/3 NIGHTS

Bush Far North Camping

NAME	TYPE(S) OF CAMPING	QUALITY RATING	VALUE RATING	COST
NOME				
Nome Beaches	tent	★★★★★	★★★★★	free

Yet another great fishing destination, this is on the more affordable end of the remote-lodging options. The lodge is on a bluff over the Alagnak River, affording great views. All meals are provided, and the food is excellent.

- **King Ko Inn** ☎ 866-234-3474 or 907-246-3377; www.kingko.com

 QUALITY ★★ VALUE ★★★★ $210

This is the place to stay for those who enjoy socializing and meeting fun people. The King Ko Inn features tidy duplexes nestled in the woods, complete with small kitchenettes that are functional but not fancy. The accompanying King Ko Bar is a great nightspot, although it does not interfere with the peace and quiet of the duplexes. Our personal choice.

- **Rainbow Bend Lodges** ☎ 888-575-4249 or 907-246-1500; www.bristolbayfishing.com

 QUALITY ★★★★ VALUE ★★★★ $800/2 NIGHTS

Rainbow Bend offers small, fully equipped cabins right on the Naknek River, which is a prime spot for fishing. A bit spendy at $800 for two nights and two days, but it's scenic and comes with its own boat rental so you can get out and fish. Plus, the cabins have their own kitchenettes.

Unalaska

- **The Grand Aleutian Hotel** 498 Salmon Way; ☎ 866-581-3844; www.grandaleutian.com

 QUALITY ★★★★★ VALUE ★★★★ $179–$320

The Grand Aleutian offers luxury in the middle of nowhere. Rooms have expansive views of the surrounding mountains and waterways, and the local artwork on the walls makes you feel as if you're visiting an exclusive museum.

- **UniSea Inn** 188 Gilman Way; ☎ 866-581-3844; www.grandaleutian.com

 QUALITY ★★★ VALUE ★★★ $110–$130

Offers simple, clean, and comfortable rooms at economical rates.

SOUTHWEST CAMPING

Dillingham

- **City of Dillingham Campground** ☎ 907-842-5211

 QUALITY ★★ VALUE ★★★★ FREE

The city has designated seasonal camping sites at the boat harbor.

- **Goodnews, North Fork, or Middle Fork rivers** ☎ 907-967-8520

 QUALITY ★★★★★ VALUE ★★★★ FREE

 For land-use permits, contact the land manager of Mumtram Pikkai, Inc. at the number above.

- **Kanektok or Arolik rivers** ☎ 907-556-8289

 QUALITY ★★★★ VALUE ★★★★ FREE

 For land-use permits, contact the land manager at Kanektok, Inc. at the number above.

- **Nushagak River** ☎ 907-842-5218

 QUALITY ★★★ VALUE ★★★★ FREE

 Camping can be found on state lands along the Nushagak and Mulchatna drainages. There is a three-day limit on stays here. If you're camping above the high-water mark, a use permit from a local native corporation may be necessary. Contact the land manager of Choggiung Ltd. at the number above.

- **Picnic Beach and Cape Constantine**

 QUALITY ★★★★★ VALUE ★★ FREE

 There are several camping possibilities along the coast; these spots are most readily accessible by air (thus the relatively low value rating).

- **Round Island** In the Walrus Islands State Game Sanctuary

 QUALITY ★★★★★ VALUE ★★★★★ FREE

 Permit camping is allowed.

- **Togiak River** ☎ 907-493-5520

 QUALITY ★★★★ VALUE ★★★★ FREE

 For land-use permits, contact the land manager of Togiak Natives Ltd. at the number above.

- **Wood-Tikchik State Park and Togiak National Wildlife Refuge**

 QUALITY ★★★★★ VALUE ★★★★★ FREE

 Wilderness camping can be found in these nearby public lands.

Bethel

There are no designated camping areas in Bethel, but most people who prefer to camp seek out riverbank areas along the Kuskokwim River. Practice low-impact camping methods, and be aware that you may be sharing space with subsistence fishermen in the area.

King Salmon

- **Alagnak Wild River** ☎ 907-246-4250

 QUALITY ★★★★ VALUE ★★★★★ FREE

 This area is available for primitive camping only, and permits are recommended for users. They are available at no charge at the **King Salmon Visitor Center** (P.O. Box 298, King Salmon 99613; see phone number above).

Unalaska

- **Unalaska Lands** ☎ 907-581-1276; **www.ounalashka.com**

QUALITY ★★★★ VALUE ★★★★ FREE

The Ounalashka Corporation privately owns much of the land of Unalaska, Amaknak, and Sedanka islands. To camp—or hike, ski, camp, bike, or snowmobile—you must obtain a permit from the corporation's offices at 400 Salmon Way, in Margaret Bay (see contact information above). Camping is free and popular along local creeks and at the beach.

FAR NORTH INDOOR LODGING

Nome

- **Aurora Inn & Suites** ☎ 907-443-3838 or 800-354-4606; **www.aurorainnome.com**

QUALITY ★★★★ VALUE ★★★ $130–$220

The Aurora was new in 1999. The 68 units, some with kitchenettes, are sort of plain but are the best equipped of any of the hotels in Nome.

- **Nome Nugget Inn** Downtown; ☎ 877-443-2323

QUALITY ★★★ VALUE ★★ $120–$160

Convenient downtown location gives access to the many attractions and areas of interest in this frontier town; the 47 rooms aren't as nice as the Aurora's, but they offer impressive views of the Bering Sea.

- **Trail's End Apartments** 308 West First Street; ☎ 907-443-3600

QUALITY ★★★ VALUE ★★★ $110

This modest lodging option is for those staying in town for more than a few days. Not fancy, but the apartment gives you cooking options.

Kotzebue

- **Nullagvik Hotel** 300 Shore Avenue; ☎ 907-442-3331; **www.nullagvik.com**

QUALITY ★★★ VALUE ★★★ $170–$190

The hotel isn't fancy from the outside, but the rooms actually are quite nice.

Barrow

- **King Eider Inn** ☎ 888-303-4337 or 907-852-4700; **www.kingeider.net**.

QUALITY ★★★★ VALUE ★★★★ $140–$210

Our favorite lodging option by far in Barrow is the King Eider Inn, which opened in 1998 and has nice log-decor furniture and fully modern rooms. It's also within easy walking distance of the airport.

- **Top of the World Hotel** ☎ 907-852-3900; **www.alaskaone.com/topworld**

QUALITY ★★★ VALUE ★★★ $145–$200

This is one of the more popular lodging options because the hotel is hooked up with tour operators, but the King Eider's rooms are nicer.

FAR NORTH CAMPING

Nome

- **Nome Beaches** ☎ 907-443-6624; **www.nomealaska.org**

QUALITY ★★★★★ VALUE ★★★★★ FREE

The best camping in Nome is on the beaches, where many people still search for gold much like the prospectors who came here in the early 1900s. The camping is free, but there are limitations on locations. Call for details.

WHERE *to* EAT

SOUTHWEST EATERIES

Dillingham

- **The Muddy Rudder** 100 Main Street; ☎ 907-842-2634

AMERICAN QUALITY ★★★ $7–$20 SUITABLE FOR KIDS? Y

This centrally located eatery has a diverse menu for breakfast, lunch, and dinner, and a family-friendly atmosphere. Only open seasonally, though.

- **Café Hillside** ☎ 907-842-3523

GOURMET QUALITY ★★★ $9–$17 SUITABLE FOR KIDS? Y

For eat-in or to-go orders, all meals are made from scratch with healthful ingredients. The Portuguese ham-and-bean soup, turkey and veggie wraps, and strawberry-spinach salads are favorites. Menu changes often.

Bethel

- **Diane's Café** 1220 Hoffman Highway; ☎ 907-543-4305

AMERICAN QUALITY ★★★★ $12–$29 SUITABLE FOR KIDS? N

Diane's has some of the best food in town, especially because the owners keep the menu fresh by changing it seasonally. The prices are a little steep, but if you're staying at the adjoining Pacifica Hotel, they're often lowered.

- **Dimitri's** 281 Fourth Avenue; ☎ 907-543-3434

GREEK/AMERICAN QUALITY ★★★★ $7–$29 SUITABLE FOR KIDS? N

The prices are a bit high, but the soups are worth it.

- **Pizzaria's Pizza** 942 Third Avenue; ☎ 907-543-1400.

PIZZA QUALITY ★★★ $4–$20 SUITABLE FOR KIDS? Y

Local pizzeria with dine-in or eat-out options.

- **Snack Shack** 520 Third Avenue; ☎ 907-543-2218

AMERICAN QUALITY ★★★ $6–$12 SUITABLE FOR KIDS? Y

Basic burger-and-sandwich place.

- **Thai to Go** 270 Sixth Avenue; ☎ 907-543-4449

THAI QUALITY ★★★★ $6–$24 SUITABLE FOR KIDS? Y

A local standby for quick and authentic Thai food.

Bush Southwest Dining

NAME	CUISINE	FOOD QUALITY	COST
DILLINGHAM			
The Muddy Rudder	American	★★★	$7–$20
Café Hillside	gourmet	★★★★	$9–$17
BETHEL			
Snack Shack	American	★★★	$6–$12
Thai to Go	Thai	★★★★	$6–$24
Pizzaria's Pizza	pizza	★★★★	$4–$20
Diane's Café	American	★★★★	$12–$29
Dimitri's	Greek/American	★★★★	$7–$29
KING SALMON			
Eddie's Fireplace Inn	American	★★★★	$6–$28
King Salmon Café	neighborhood	★★★	$7–$12
UNALASKA			
Amelia's Restaurant	American	★★★★	$12–$27
The Chartroom at the Grand Aleutian Hotel	fusion	★★★★★	$13–$32
Peking Restaurant	Chinese/Sushi	★★★★	$10–$29
Tino's Steak House	Mexican/Steaks	★★★	$10–$30

King Salmon

- **Eddie's Fireplace Inn** ☎ 907-246-3435

  AMERICAN QUALITY ★★★★ $6–$28 SUITABLE FOR KIDS? N

  Full-service restaurant and bar that also offers video rentals.

- **King Salmon Café** ☎ 907-246-2233

  NEIGHBORHOOD QUALITY ★★★ $7–$12 SUITABLE FOR KIDS? Y

  Standard cafe food; one of the only choices in town.

Unalaska

- **Amelia's Restaurant** ☎ 907-581-2800

  AMERICAN QUALITY ★★★★ $12–$27 SUITABLE FOR KIDS? Y

  It looks rather like a shack, but the food is fresh and affordable.

Bush Far North Dining

NAME	CUISINE	FOOD QUALITY	COST
NOME			
Fat Freddie's Restaurant	Diner	★★★	$9–$19
Milano's Pizzeria	Pizza/Chinese	★★★	$9–$24
KOTZEBUE			
Arctic Blues Espresso	Espresso	★★★	$2–$6
Empress Restaurant	Chinese	★★★	$10–$20
BARROW			
Arctic Pizza	Chinese/steak/pizza	★★★	$9–$29
Browers Cafe	Diner	★★	$7–$16
Osaka's Japanese and American	Japanese/American	★★★	$11–$20
Pepe's North of the Border	Mexican	★★★★	$11–$22

- **The Chartroom at the Grand Aleutian Hotel** 498 Salmon Way; ☎ 866-581-3844; **www.grandaleutian.com**

  FUSION QUALITY ★★★★★ $13–$32 SUITABLE FOR KIDS? N

  The Chartroom does great things with seafood plucked right from the sea. Prices are steep but the food is excellent.

- **Peking Restaurant** Gilmore Road; ☎ 907-581-2303

  CHINESE/SUSHI QUALITY ★★★★ $10–$29 SUITABLE FOR KIDS? Y

  Chinese food and dim sum, plus fabulously fresh sushi here.

- **Tino's Steak House** 11 North Second Street; ☎ 907-581-4288

  MEXICAN/STEAKS QUALITY ★★★ $10–$30 SUITABLE FOR KIDS? N

  We have friends who will walk across town to get to this excellent eatery, which offers delicious Mexican food and steaks.

FAR NORTH EATERIES

Nome

- **Fat Freddie's Restaurant** Front Street; ☎ 907-443-5899

  DINER QUALITY ★★★ $9–$19

  Honest diner food with a view of the Bering Sea.

- **Milano's Pizzeria** 110 West Front Street; ☎ 907-443-2924

  PIZZA/CHINESE QUALITY ★★★ $9–$24 SUITABLE FOR KIDS? Y

Craving pizza but your traveling companion is in the mood for Chinese? Not to worry—you can get both here.

Kotzebue

- **Arctic Blues Espresso** At the Kotzebue airport; ☎ 907-442-2554

ESPRESSO QUALITY ★★★ $2–$6 SUITABLE FOR KIDS? Y

Fresh-brewed coffee and snacks, with friendly employees.

- **Empress Restaurant** In downtown Kotzebue; ☎ 907-442-4304 or 907-442-4305

CHINESE QUALITY ★★★ $10–$20 SUITABLE FOR KIDS? Y

The restaurant is family-owned, and the Mongolian beef is top-notch.

Barrow

- **Arctic Pizza** 125 Upper Apayauk Street; ☎ 907-852-4222

CHINESE/STEAK/PIZZA QUALITY ★★★ $9–$29 SUITABLE FOR KIDS? Y

As you will notice in Alaska, there are restaurants that claim to specialize in everything under the sun—a Chinese, pizza, and steak place is not all that unusual, and we salute this can-do attitude. Stick with the pizza, though.

- **Browers Cafe** ☎ 907-852-3663

DINER QUALITY ★★ $7–$16 SUITABLE FOR KIDS? Y

We were a little disappointed when we first saw this cafe—it's weatherbeaten and sort of shabby-looking, but it is really the best place in Barrow to get a home-cooked burger and decent French fries.

- **Osaka's Japanese and American** 980 Stevenson Street; ☎ 907-852-4200

JAPANESE/AMERICAN QUALITY ★★★ $11–$20 SUITABLE FOR KIDS? Y

The American is all right, but go with what the owners know—their great sushi and Japanese dishes.

- **Pepe's North of the Border** ☎ 907-852-8200 or 852-6199

MEXICAN QUALITY ★★★★ $11–$22 SUITABLE FOR KIDS? Y

The dining pickings in Barrow are slim, and Pepe's North of the Border is one of the best. Over the years, longtime owner Fran Tate has remodeled the place from a slight two-room affair to a brightly decorated restaurant that can now serve more than 200 guests at a time. Probably the farthest-north Mexican restaurant in which you could ever eat.

ON *the* TOWN: *What to Do after the Outdoor Adventure*

TRUTH IS, THESE SMALL TOWNS DON'T have much in the way of attractions; still, a few places are interesting to visit if you have time.

SOUTHWEST

Dillingham

- **Samuel K. Fox Museum** D and Seward streets; ☎ 907-842-5610
  Features carvings, baskets, and other works by local native artists. Artifacts on display include the Shaman's Hands, old Yup'ik masks, and photos from the area. Open noon to 4 p.m. Monday through Friday.

Bethel

- **Bethel Museum and Cultural Center** ☎ 907-543-1819; 420 Chief Eddie Hoffman Highway
  Showcases traditional and contemporary works by some of the region's most talented artists. Closed Sundays and Mondays.

Unalaska

- **Russian Orthodox Church of the Holy Ascension** ☎ 907-581-6404
  This church is more than 200 years old and is a great subject for photos (no cameras are allowed inside the building, though). Tours take place Saturdays at 6 p.m. and Sundays at 9 a.m.

FAR NORTH

Nome

- **Old St. Joseph's Church** Anvil City Square; ☎ 907-443-6624
  Newly restored, this is one of the few structures that survived Nome's 1934 fire, which destroyed most of the town.

Kotzebue

- **Museum of the Arctic** ☎ 800-468-2248 or 907-442-3747; **www.tour-arctic.com**
  Run by the Northwest Alaska Native Association, it features a two-hour show that highlights some fine Eskimo dancing, a slide show, traditional sewing and leather craft, and ivory carving. Tours are $29.

Barrow

- **Inupiat Heritage Center** P.O. Box 69, Barrow 99723 or National Park Service/INUP, 240 West Fifth Avenue, Anchorage 99501; ☎ 907-852-0422 or 907-852-4594
  Dedicated in 1999, the center features exhibits, artifacts, a library, a gift shop, and an impressive display of mounted birds and other small animals. Learn about commercial whaling and the influence of the Far North's native peoples in its growth. Open weekdays year-round. Free admission.

INDEX

Unofficial Guide Reader Survey

If you would like to express your opinion in writing about Alaska or this guidebook, complete the following survey and mail it to:

> *Unofficial Guide* Reader Survey
> P.O. Box 43673
> Birmingham, AL 35243

Inclusive dates of your visit: ________________

Members of your party (circle M or F):

	Person 1	Person 2	Person 3	Person 4	Person 5
Gender:	M F	M F	M F	M F	M F
Age:					

How many times have you been to Alaska? ________________

On your most recent trip, where did you stay? ________________

Concerning your accommodations, on a scale of 100 as best and 0 as worst, how would you rate:

The quality of your room?______ The value of your room?______

The quietness of your room?______ Check-in/check-out efficiency?______

List the outdoor adventure(s) you took part in (guided or unguided):

____

____

____

For those adventures, on a scale of 100 as best and 0 as worst, how would you rate:

The value of guided trips?______ The ease of planning unguided trips?______

The quality of guided and/or unguided trips?______

Concerning your dining experiences:

Estimate your meals in restaurants per day: ________________

Favorite restaurants in Alaska: ________________

____

Which, if any, maps would you like to see added to future editions?

____

Did you buy this guide before leaving? While on your trip?

How did you hear about this guide? Check all that apply:

Loaned or recommended by a friend ☐
Newspaper or magazine ☐
Just picked it out on my own ☐
Internet ☐
Radio or TV ☐
Bookstore salesperson ☐
Library ☐

Unofficial Guide Reader Survey (continued)

What other guidebooks did you use on this trip? ______________

____

____

____

On a scale of 100 as best and 0 as worst, how would you rate them?

____

____

____

Using the same scale, how would you rate the *Unofficial Guide*(s)?

____

Are *Unofficial Guides* readily available at bookstores in your area? ______

Have you used other *Unofficial Guides*? ______________

Which one(s)? ______________

____

____

Comments about your Alaska trip or the *Unofficial Guide*(s):

____

____

____

____

____

____

____

____

____

____

____

____

____

____

____

____

____

____

____

____